lonely planet

W9-AQJ-000

FRANCE'S BEST TRIPS

39 AMAZING ROAD TRIPS

This edition written and researched by

Oliver Berry
Stuart Butler, Jean-Bernard Carillet, Gregor Clark,
Donna Wheeler, Nicola Williams

SYMBOLS IN THIS BOOK

Top Tips	History & Culture	Essential Photo
Link Your Trips	Family	Walking Tour
Tips from Locals	Food & Drink	Eating
Trip Detour	Outdoors	Sleeping

📞 Telephone Number	@ Internet Access	📖 English-Language Menu
⊘ Opening Hours	📶 Wi-Fi Access	👪 Family-Friendly
P Parking	🥗 Vegetarian Selection	🐾 Pet-Friendly
⊖ Nonsmoking	🏊 Swimming Pool	
❄ Air-Conditioning		

MAP LEGEND

Routes
- Trip Route
- Trip Detour
- Linked Trip
- Walk Route
- Tollway
- Freeway
- Primary
- Secondary
- Tertiary
- Lane
- Unsealed Road
- Plaza/Mall
- Steps
-)= = Tunnel
- Pedestrian Overpass
- Walk Track/Path

Boundaries
- International
- State/Province
- Cliff
- Wall

Population
- 🟢 Capital (National)
- ◉ Capital (State/Province)
- ● City/Large Town
- ● Town/Village

Transport
- ✈ Airport
- Cable Car/Funicular
- P Parking
- Train/Railway
- Tram
- Ⓜ Underground Train Station

Trips
- 1 Trip Numbers
- 9 Trip Stop
- Walking tour
- Trip Detour

Route Markers
- E44 E-road network
- M100 National network

Hydrography
- River/Creek
- Intermittent River
- Swamp/Mangrove
- Canal
- Water
- Dry/Salt/Intermittent Lake
- Glacier

Areas
- Beach
- Cemetery (Christian)
- Cemetery (Other)
- Park
- Forest
- Urban Area
- Sportsground

CONTENTS

Paris &
Northern France
p35

Loire Valley &
Central France
p133

Atlantic Coast &
Western France
p353

Alps &
Eastern
France
p183

Pyrenees &
Southwest France
p313

Provence &
Southeast
France p231

Contents cont.

ROAD TRIP
ESSENTIALS

Classic Trips

Look out for the Classic Trips stamp on our favourite routes in this book.

Provence Rolling fields of lavender (Trip 22)

WELCOME TO
FRANCE

Iconic monuments, island abbeys, fabulous food, world-class wines – there are so many reasons to plan your very own French *voyage*.

Whether you're planning on cruising the corniches of the French Riviera, getting lost among the snowcapped Alps or tasting your way around Champagne's hallowed vineyards, this is a nation that's made for road trips. In this book, we've put together 39 unforgettable routes that will plunge you straight into France's heart and soul.

There's a trip for everyone here: family travellers, history buffs, culinary connoisseurs and outdoors adventurers. And if you've only got time for one trip, why not make it one of our 10 Classic Trips, which take you to the very best France has to offer. Turn the page for more.

Buckle up, and bon voyage – you're in for quite a ride.

→

FRANCE
Classic Trips

9

What Is a Classic Trip?

All the trips in this book show you the best of France, but we've chosen 10 as our all-time favourites. These are our Classic Trips – the ones that lead you to the best of the iconic sights, the top activities and the unique French experiences. Turn the page to see the map, and look out for the Classic Trip stamp throughout the book.

17 Alpine Adventure
Wander the town of Annecy alongside geranium-strewn houses and romantic canals

9 D-Day's Beaches
Caen's Mémorial – Un Musée pour la Paix remembers those who died in WWII

7 Unesco Treasures
Sunset over Avignon and its Unesco-listed Palais des Papes

7

9

FRANCE
Classic Trips

1 Essential France
Tick off the mustn't-misses on this epic cross-country adventure. **2 WEEKS**

11 Châteaux of the Loire
France's greatest châteaux, from medieval towers to royal palaces. **5 DAYS**

9 D-Day's Beaches
Follow the course of the WWII invasion on Normandy's beaches. **3 DAYS**

5 Champagne Taster
Taste your way around the cellars of Champagne on this fizz-fuelled trip. **3 DAYS**

7 Unesco Treasures
From Gothic cathedrals to papal palaces, tour France's World Heritage Sites. **10 DAYS**

17 Alpine Adventure
Mountain grandeur, from lakeside Annecy to lofty Chamonix. **6 DAYS**

23 The Corniches
Not one but three thrilling coastal roads – the ultimate French drive. **3 DAYS**

24 Riviera Cruising
The best beaches, cities, villages and nature along the legendary Med coast. **7 DAYS**

32 Pyrenees
Explore this majestic mountain landscape, easily the equal of the Alps. **2 DAYS**

39 Atlantic to Med
The ultimate south-of-France trip, linking two very different seas. **10 DAYS**

France's best sights and experiences, and the road trips that will take you there.

FRANCE
HIGHLIGHTS

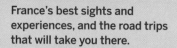

Paris

What is there to say about the City of Light that hasn't been said a thousand times before? Quite simply, this is one of the world's essential cities: sexy, suave, sophisticated and more than a little snooty. There's a lifetime of experiences here, from the treasures of the Louvre to the cafes of Montmartre – but you'll need nerves of steel to brave the traffic.

TRIPS 7

Paris The Eiffel Tower and Seine River

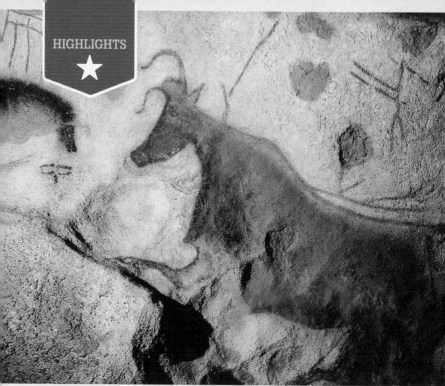

Vézère Valley Prehistoric cave art in the Grotte de Lascaux

Vézère Valley

Prehistoric people left an astonishing legacy of paintings and sculptures in the caves of the Vézère Valley. These artworks provide a glimpse into the lives of our ancient ancestors – but opinion is divided on what purpose they served. Were they sacred works imbued with magical significance, or simply prehistoric posters? The truth is, no one knows. Decide for yourself on **Trip 36: Cave Art of the Vézère Valley**.

TRIP 36

Mont St-Michel

Perched on an island and connected to the Norman coast by a causeway, this 11th-century abbey is one of France's most recognisable sights. Crowned by spires, ringed by ramparts and thronged by crowds, it looks like it's fallen from the pages of a fairy tale. It's a long climb to the top, but the views are worth every step. We've linked it with other unmissable sights in **Trip 1: Essential France**.

TRIP 1

D-Day Beaches

On 6 June 1944 the largest invasion the world has ever seen stormed ashore on the beaches of Normandy. Now known as D-Day, this audacious assault marked the turning point of WWII, and on **Trip 9: D-Day's Beaches**, you'll see many reminders of the fateful campaign – from the forbidding guns of Longues-sur-Mer to the moving cemetery above Omaha Beach.

TRIP 9

Pyrenees Hairpin-bend along a country road

BEST ROADS FOR DRIVING

The Three Corniches Cliff roads, sparkling seas, the drive of a lifetime. **Trip** 23

Gorges du Tarn Drive through a dramatic ravine in the Cévennes hills. **Trip** 29

Route des Vins d'Alsace Meander among vines with views of the Vosges. **Trip** 6

Col de l'Iseran Brave the Alps' highest road pass. **Trip** 17

The Lot Valley Cruise limestone cliffs beside the Lot River. **Trip** 38

Pyrenees

With their lofty passes and wide-open skies, the Pyrenees have the wow factor. Running along the Franco–Spanish border, they're home to some of the nation's wildest landscapes, and some of its hairiest roads – although the closest you'll get to a traffic jam here is getting stuck behind a herd of cows. Take **Trip 32: Pyrenees** through quiet valleys, traditional villages and mountain-top observatories.

TRIP 32

15

French Riviera The port and old town at Cannes (Trip 24)

French Riviera

If it's a top-down, open-road, wind-in-your-hair drive you're after, there's only one corner of France that hits the mark, and that's the flashy Riviera. Synonymous with glitz and glamour since the 19th century, it's still one of Europe's most fashionable spots. **Trip 24: Riviera Cruising** twists through hilltop towns and hairpin-bend roads – just remember to pack a camera and a pair of shades.

TRIPS 23 24

BEST TOWNS FOR WINE-LOVERS

Beaune The heart and soul of Burgundy wine. **Trip** 15

St-Émilion Winemakers outnumber residents in this honey-stoned town. **Trip** 39

Bergerac Lesser-known vintages on the edge of the Dordogne. **Trip** 35

Épernay Tour the cellars of Champagne's classic brands. **Trip** 5

Colmar Sip Alsatian wines with a view of the canals. **Trip** 6

17

Hilltop villages Dusk over Gordes (Trip 22)

Châteaux of the Loire Lavish Château de Chambord (Trip 11)

Hilltop Villages

From red-roofed hamlets to hillside hideaways, France's *villages perchés* will be a highlight of your trip. Most are medieval, and replete with flower-filled lanes, hidden courtyards and quiet squares. Life ticks along at a snail's pace, and there's nowhere better to settle in for a leisurely lunch. **Trip 22: Lavender Route** travels through some of Provence's prettiest.

TRIPS 6 19 22 37

Châteaux of the Loire

For sky's-the-limit extravagance, don't miss **Trip 11: Châteaux of the Loire**. Constructed by France's aristocratic elite between the 15th and 17th centuries, these lavish mansions were designed to show off their owners' wealth – something they manage to achieve in spectacular fashion. Chambord's the jewel in the crown, but there are many more to visit.

TRIPS 7 11

Champagne Vineyards

Let's face it – celebrations wouldn't be the same without a bottle of bubbly. The world's most exclusive tipple is produced on a handful of Champagne vineyards, many of which offer tours and the chance to taste the fruits of their labour. **Trip 5: Champagne Taster** takes in tiny family producers as well as big-name châteaux around Épernay and Reims.

TRIP 5

The Camargue

Sprawling across the western edge of
Provence, this huge natural wetland
is a paradise for nature-lovers, with
its population of seabirds, wild horses
and pink flamingos. **Trip 28: The
Camargue** takes a leisurely wander
along the back roads, with plenty
of time factored in along the way to
immerse yourself in the unique cowboy
culture.

TRIP 28

Brittany's Coastline

Golden beaches, surf-battered cliffs,
quiet creeks, lonely lighthouses – **Trip
10: Breton Coast** is one long parade
of postcard views. Some stretches
of the coastline are busy, others feel
wonderfully wild and empty – so plan
your route, pack a decent map and just
hit the Breton road.

TRIP 10

(left) **The Camargue** Pink flamingoes in the wetlands

(below) **Pont du Gard** Traversing the Roman aqueduct

Pont du Gard

The scale of this Roman aqueduct is astonishing: 35 arches straddle the 275m upper tier, and it once carried 20,000 cu metres of water per day. View it from beside the Gard River, clamber along the top deck, or arrive after dark to see it lit up in impressive fashion. It marks the start of **Trip 29: Pont du Gard to Viaduc du Millau**, which travels through the Cévennes to another amazing bridge.

TRIP 29

BEST HILLTOP VILLAGES

Gordes The quintessential Provençal village. **Trip** 22

Vézelay Get spiritual in this ancient pilgrim village. **Trips** 7 14

St-Paul de Vence Dreamy Med vistas drew countless artists. **Trip** 24

St-Jean Pied de Port Fortified town overlooking the Spanish border. **Trip** 33

21

IF YOU LIKE

Camembert World-famous cheese (Trip 3)

Art

Impressionist masterpieces, modernist marvels, landmark museums – France's astonishing artistic legacy is guaranteed to be one of the most memorable parts of your trip.

2 A Toast to Art Inspiring architecture meets cutting-edge art on this trip via the new Louvre-Lens museum, the Centre Pompidou-Metz and Nancy's art nouveau architecture.

8 Monet's Normandy Cruise through the countryside that inspired the impressionists, finishing with a walk around Monet's own lily garden.

25 Modern Art Meander Chagall, Cézanne, Picasso and Van Gogh were just a few of the artists who were inspired by the Provençal landscape.

French Cuisine

French food might be synonymous with sophistication, but there's more to this foodie nation than fine dining – there's a whole culinary culture to experience, whether that's guzzling oysters, hunting for truffles, savouring cheeses or buying fresh baguettes from a village *boulangerie* (bakery).

3 Tour des Fromages Taste your way around Normandy's world-famous cheeses – Camembert, Pont L'Évêque, Livarot and more.

35 Gourmet Dordogne For rich French food, there's nowhere like the Dordogne, the spiritual home of foie gras and the black truffle.

20 Rhône Valley Fill up on Lyonnaise cuisine in a cosy *bouchon* (small bistro), then head for Montélimar to indulge in nougat treats.

Nature

With seven national parks and a host of other protected areas, France's natural landscapes are ripe for outdoor adventure.

17 Alpine Adventure Hike trails and spot wildlife among the peaks and ski resorts of France's highest mountain chain.

27 Corsican Coast Cruiser Escape the French mainland for a cruise around the wild landscapes and coastline of Corsica, aptly named the *île de beauté*.

13 Volcanoes of the Auvergne Discover this chain of extinct volcanoes that stretches across much of central France.

28 The Camargue Keep your eyes peeled for pink flamingos and wild horses in France's largest wetlands.

Burgundy Wine maturing in an underground cellar (Trip 15)

Wine Tasting

If there's one thing France knows about, it's wine. Viticulture has been a cornerstone of French culture for hundreds of years, and the merest mention of the nation's top vineyards makes even hardened sommeliers go weak at the knees.

5 Champagne Taster
Cellars echo to the sound of popping corks on this effervescent adventure through Champagne's hallowed brands.

15 Route des Grands Crus Few regions command more cachet in the wine world than Burgundy. Follow the trail along the Côte de Nuits and Côte d'Or.

6 Alsace Accents
Glossy vines and traditional villages form the backdrop to this meander along the Route des Vins d'Alsace.

Architecture

France has never been shy about showing off its taste for extravagant architecture. Castles and palaces, abbeys and cathedrals – France offers them all, and more.

11 Châteaux of the Loire
Resplendent châteaux line the banks of the Loire, each one more extravagant than the last.

1 Essential France
From Mont St-Michel to the palace of Versailles, this route explores France's unmissable sites.

31 Cheat's Compostela
Tick off churches and cathedrals along the old pilgrim route from Le Puy-en-Velay to St-Jean Pied de Port.

30 The Cathar Trail
Trek across the parched Languedoc plains, which feature crumbling fortresses and hilltop strongholds.

Historic Sites

With a history stretching back several millennia, it's little wonder that France is littered with reminders of its past – both ancient and recent.

21 Roman Provence
Travel back to the heyday of Gaul with an expedition around southern France's Roman ruins.

14 Medieval Burgundy
Once an independent duchy, Burgundy is home to marvellous medieval buildings and timeless villages.

4 In Flanders Fields
Take an emotional tour around the battlegrounds and cemeteries of the Great War.

9 D-Day's Beaches
The events of D-Day still resonate along the beaches of Normandy, while museums and memorials provide historical context.

NEED ^{TO} KNOW

CURRENCY
Euro (€)

LANGUAGE
French

VISAS
Generally not required for stays of up to 90 days (or at all for EU nationals); some nationalities need a Schengen visa.

FUEL
Petrol stations are common around main roads and larger towns. Unleaded costs from around €1.60 per litre; *gazole* (diesel) is usually at least €0.15 cheaper.

RENTAL CARS
ADA (www.ada.fr)

Auto Europe (www.autoeurope.com)

Avis (www.avis.com)

Europcar (www.europcar.com)

Hertz (www.hertz.com)

IMPORTANT NUMBERS
Ambulance (🗗15)

Police (🗗17)

Fire brigade (🗗18)

Europe-wide emergency (🗗112)

Climate

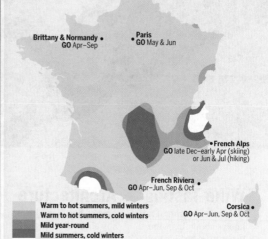

Brittany & Normandy ●
GO Apr–Sep

● Paris
GO May & Jun

● French Alps
GO late Dec–early Apr (skiing) or Jun & Jul (hiking)

French Riviera ●
GO Apr–Jun, Sep & Oct

Corsica ●
GO Apr–Jun, Sep & Oct

Warm to hot summers, mild winters
Warm to hot summers, cold winters
Mild year-round
Mild summers, cold winters
Alpine climate

When to Go

High Season (Jul & Aug)
》 The main holiday season in France – expect traffic jams and big queues, especially in August.

》 Christmas, New Year and Easter are also busy times to travel.

》 Late December to March is high season in French ski resorts.

Shoulder Season (Apr–Jun & Sep)
》 Balmy temperatures, settled weather and light crowds make this an ideal time to travel.

》 Hotel rates drop in busy areas such as southern France and the Atlantic coast.

》 The *vendange* (grape harvest) happens in early autumn.

Low Season (Oct–Mar)
》 Expect heavy discounts on accommodation (sometimes as much as 50%).

》 Snow covers the Alps and Pyrenees, as well as much of central France.

》 Many sights and hotels close down for winter.

Daily Costs

Budget: Less than €100

» Double room in a budget hotel: €50–70

» Set lunchtime menus: €10–15

Midrange: €100–€200

» Double room in a midrange hotel: €70–120

» À la carte mains: €15–20

Top End: Over €200

» Luxury hotel room: €150–200

» Top-end restaurant meal: menus from €50, à la carte from €80

Eating

Cafes Coffee, drinks and bar snacks.

Bistros Serve anything from light meals to sit-down dinners.

Restaurants Range from simple *auberges* (country inns) to Michelin-starred wonders.

Vegetarians Limited choice on most menus; look out for *restaurants bios* in cities.

In this book, price symbols indicate the cost of a two-course set menu:

€	under €20
€€	€20–40
€€€	more than €40

Sleeping

Hotels France has a wide range of hotels, from budget to luxury. Unless indicated otherwise, breakfast is extra.

Chambres d'hôte The French equivalent of a B&B; prices nearly always include breakfast.

Hostels Most large towns have a hostel operated by the FUAJ (Fédération Unie des Auberges de Jeunesse).

Price symbols indicate the cost of a double room with private bathroom in high season unless otherwise noted:

€	under €80
€€	€80–180
€€€	more than €180

Arriving in France

Aéroport Roissy Charles de Gaulle (Paris)

Rental cars Major car-rental agencies have concessions at arrival terminals.

Trains, buses and RER To Paris centre every 15 to 30 minutes, 5am to 11pm.

Taxis €50 to €60; 30 minutes to Paris centre.

Aéroport d'Orly (Paris)

Rental cars Desks beside the arrivals area.

Orlyval rail, RER and buses At least every 15 minutes, 5am to 11pm.

Taxis €45 to €60; 25 minutes to Paris centre.

Mobile Phones

Most European and Australian phones work, but turn off roaming to avoid heavy data charges. Buying a French SIM card provides much cheaper call rates.

Internet Access

Wi-fi is available in most hotels and B&Bs (usually free, but sometimes for a small charge). Many cafes and restaurants also offer free wi-fi to customers.

Money

ATMs are available everywhere. Most major credit cards are accepted (with the exception of American Express). Larger cities have *bureaux de change*.

Tipping

By law, restaurant and bar prices are *service compris* (include a 15% service charge). Taxis expect around 10%; round up bar bills to the nearest euro.

Useful Websites

France Guide (www.franceguide.com) Official website run by the French tourist office.

Lonely Planet (www.lonelyplanet.com/france) Travel tips, accommodation, forum and more.

Mappy (www.mappy.fr) Online tools for mapping and journey planning.

France Meteo (www.meteo.fr) The lowdown on the French weather.

About France (www.about-france.com/travel.htm) Tips for driving in France.

For more, see Road Trip Essentials (p418).

CITY GUIDE

PARIS

If ever a city needed no introduction, it's Paris – a trend setter, fashion former and style icon for centuries, and still very much at the cutting edge. Whether you're here to tick off the landmarks or seek out the secret corners, Paris fulfils all your expectations, and still leaves you wanting more.

Paris The city at sunset, viewed from Cathédrale de Notre-Dame

Getting Around

Driving in Paris is a nightmare. Happily, there's no need for a car. The metro is fast, frequent and efficient; tickets cost €1.70 (day passes €6.70) and are valid on the city's buses. Bikes can be hired from 1800 Vélib (www.velib.paris.fr) stations; insert a credit card, authorise a €150 deposit and pedal away. Day passes cost €1; first 30 minutes free, subsequent 30 minutes from €2

Parking

Meters don't take coins; use a chip-enabled credit card. Municipal car parks cost €2 to €3.50 an hour, or €20 to €25 per 24 hours.

Discover the Taste of Paris

Le Marais is one of the best areas for eating out, with its small restaurants and trendy bistros. Don't miss Paris' street markets: the Marché Bastille, rue Montorgueil and rue Mouffetard are full of atmosphere.

Live Like a Local

Base yourself in Montmartre for its Parisian charm, if you don't mind crowds. Le Marais and Bastille provide style on a budget, while St-Germain is good for a splurge.

Useful Websites

Paris Info (http://en.parisinfo.com) Official visitor site.

Lonely Planet (www.lonelyplanet.com/paris) Lonely Planet's city guide.

Secrets of Paris (www.secretsofparis.com) Local's blog full of insider tips.

Paris by Mouth (www.parisbymouth.com) Eat and drink your way round the capital.

Trips Through Paris:

For more, check out our city and country guides. www.lonelyplanet.com

TOP EXPERIENCES

➡ Eiffel Tower at Twilight
Any time is a good time to take in the panorama from the top of the 'Metal Asparagus' (as Parisians snidely call it) – but the twilight view is extra special (www.toureiffel.fr).

➡ Musée du Louvre
France's greatest repository of art, sculpture and artefacts, the Louvre is a must-visit – but don't expect to see it all in a day (www.louvre.fr).

➡ Basilique du Sacré-Coeur
Climb inside the cupola of this Montmartre landmark for one of the best cross-city vistas (www.sacre-coeur-montmartre.com).

➡ Musée d'Orsay
Paris' second-most-essential museum, with a fabulous collection encompassing originals by Cézanne, Degas, Monet, Van Gogh and more (www.musee-orsay.fr).

➡ Cathédrale de Notre-Dame
Peer over Paris from the north tower of this Gothic landmark, surrounded by gargoyles and flying buttresses (www.cathedraledeparis.com).

➡ Les Catacombes
Explore more than 2km of tunnels beneath the streets of Montparnasse, lined with the bones and skulls of millions of Parisians (www.catacombes.paris.fr).

➡ Cimetière Père-Lachaise
Oscar Wilde, Edith Piaf, Marcel Proust and Jim Morrison are just a few of the famous names buried in this wildly overgrown cemetery (www.perelachaise.com).

➡ Canal St-Martin
Join the locals for a walk or bike ride along the tow-paths of this 4.5km canal, once derelict but now reborn as a haven from the city hustle.

Lyon The Saône River at nightfall

LYON

For centuries, Lyon has served as a crossroads between France's south and north, as well as a gateway to the nearby Alps. A commercial and industrial powerhouse for over 500 years, it's now a cosmopolitan and sophisticated city, with some outstanding museums and a notoriously lively nightlife.

Getting Around

Cars aren't much use for getting around Lyon itself. The same €1.60 tickets are valid on all the city's public transport, including buses, trams, the four-line metro and the two funiculars linking Vieux Lyon to Fourvière and St-Just. Day passes cost €4.90.

Parking

As always, parking is expensive, so pick a hotel with a private car park if you're planning on arriving with wheels.

Discover the Taste of Lyon

The classic place to eat in Lyon is a *bouchon* (literally, 'bottle stopper'), a small, cosy bistro that cooks up regional cuisine such as *boudin blanc* (veal sausage) and *quenelles de brochet* (pike dumplings in a creamy crayfish sauce). Afterwards, browse the stalls of the city's wonderful covered market, Les Halles de Lyon.

Live Like a Local

Vieux Lyon and Presqu'Île both have a fantastic range of hotels and guesthouses that combine old Lyonnaise architecture with modern style. Croix Rousse is the handiest area for visiting the Roman remains around Fourvière.

Useful Websites

Lyon (www.lyon.fr) Official city website.

My Little Lyon (www.mylittle.fr/mylittlelyon, in French) Catch up with the cultural trends.

Petit Paume (www.petitpaume.com, in French) Savvy city guide written by students.

Trips Through Lyon

LILLE

Lille may be France's most underrated major city. This once-tired industrial metropolis has transformed itself into a stylish, self-confident city with a strong Flemish accent. Three art museums, lots of stylish shops and a lovely old town make it well worthy of investigation.

Getting Around

Driving into Lille is incredibly confusing, even with a good map; just suspend your sense of direction and blindly follow the 'Centre Ville' signs. Lille's buses and two speedy metro lines run until about 12.30am. Tickets cost €1.40; a Pass' Journée (all-day pass) costs €4.10.

Parking

If you're driving, the best idea is to leave your vehicle at the park-and-ride at Champ de Mars on bd de la Liberté (open from 10am to 6pm or 7pm, closed Saturdays & Sundays, September to March), 1.2km northwest of the centre. It costs €3.25 a day and includes return travel for five people to central Lille on bus 12.

Discover the Taste of Lille

Lille's proximity to Alsace and Belgium has influenced its cuisine. Cosy *estaminets* (Flemish eateries) serve Lillois specialities such as *carbonade* (braised beef stewed with beer, spiced bread and brown sugar) and *potjevleesch* (jellied chicken, pork, veal and rabbit).

Live Like a Local

Most hotels are within striking distance of the city centre, but Lille's business focus means many are short on charm. On the plus side, rates drop at weekends.

Useful Websites

Lille Tourisme (www. lilletourism.com) Comprehensive city site.

Trips Through Lille

NICE

The classic metropolis of the French Riviera, Nice has something to suit all moods: exceptional museums, atmospheric street markets, glittering Mediterranean beaches and a rabbit-warren old town, all bathed in radiant year-round sunshine. With its blend of city grit and old-world opulence, it deserves as much time as you can spare.

Getting Around

The complicated one-way system and heavy traffic can make driving in Nice stressful, especially in the heat of summer. Walking is the easiest way to get around. There's a handy tram line from the train station all the way to Vieux Nice and place Garibaldi; tickets cost €1 and are valid on buses.

Parking

Nearly all parking in Nice is *payant* (chargeable) – assuming you manage to find a space. Car parks are usually cheapest (around €2 to €3 per hour, or €17 to €30 per day). All parking meters take coins; car-park pay stations also accept credit cards.

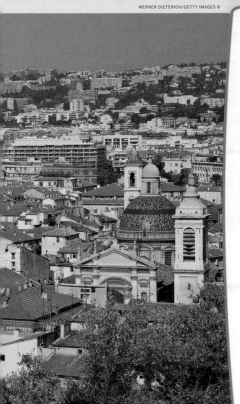

Nice View across the city

TOP EXPERIENCES

➡ Strolling the Promenade des Anglais
Join sun worshippers, inline skaters and dog walkers on this magnificent boulevard, which runs right along Nice's shimmering seafront.

➡ Musée Matisse
Just 2km north of the centre, this excellent art museum documents the life and work of Henri Matisse in painstaking detail. You'll need good French to get the most out of your visit (www.musee-matisse-nice.org).

➡ Shopping on Cours Saleya
This massive market captures the essence of Niçois life. A chaotic assortment of stalls sells everything from fresh-cut flowers to fresh fish.

➡ Parc du Château
Pack a picnic and head to this hilltop park for a panorama across Nice's red-tiled rooftops.

Discover the Taste of Nice
Head for the alleyways of Vieux Nice (Old Nice) for the most authentic neighbourhood restaurants. Don't miss the local specialities of *socca* (chickpea-flour pancake), *petits farcis* (stuffed vegetables) and *pissaladière* (onion tart topped with black olives and anchovies).

Live Like a Local
Old town equals atmosphere, but for the best views and classiest rooms you'll want to base yourself near the seafront – the Promenade des Anglais has several landmark hotels. The city's cheapest hotels are clustered around the train station.

Useful Websites
Nice Tourisme (http://en.nicetourisme. com) Informative city website with info on accommodation and attractions.

Trips Through Nice 23 24

FRANCE
BY REGION

From rugged mountain roads to quiet country lanes, France is a driver's dream. Here's your guide to what each region has to offer, along with suggestions for our top road trips.

Paris & Northern France (p35)

No French trip would be complete without Paris, still one of the world's most vital cities. Beyond the capital, you could explore artistic connections in Giverny, tour Alsatian vineyards, or delve into the region's war-ravaged past along the beaches of Normandy and in the fields of Flanders.

Check off Unesco-listed treasures on Trip 7

Atlantic Coast & Western France (p353)

France's west coast is wonderfully varied, stretching from the vineyards of Bordeaux down to the busy beach towns of Arcachon and Biarritz. The southwest is a stronghold of French Basque culture, while the Dordogne and the Lot Valley offer a dreamy vision of the French countryside.

Gorge on foie gras and hunt for truffles on Trip 35

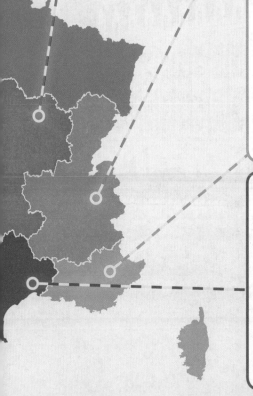

Loire Valley & Central France (p133)

The Loire is rightly famous for its châteaux, but there's more here than over-the-top architecture. A world of wine awaits in Burgundy, and the region's medieval heritage is a must for history buffs. Meanwhile, volcanic vistas unfold in the Auvergne, perhaps France's most undiscovered corner.

Taste Grand Cru wine on Trip 15

Alps & Eastern France (p183)

Mountains spiral skywards and the roads get ever higher as you drive through the Alps and the Jura, both alive with outdoor possibilities. Brave the slopes and hike the trails, then head into the Rhône Valley for hearty food and postcard-pretty villages.

Enjoy sky-high views on Trip 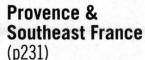 17

Eat in bouchons on Trip 20

Provence & Southeast France (p231)

Sparkling beaches, glitzy towns, hilltop hamlets, lavender fields: Provence is the stuff of French-themed dreams. Cruise the corniches, head inland for Roman ruins and Provençal markets, and if you're feeling adventurous, the wild island of Corsica is only a boat ride away.

Follow the Riviera on Trip 24

Pyrenees & Southwest France (p313)

Straddling the Franco–Spanish border, the valleys and passes of the Pyrenees make for fantastic driving, but you'll need to keep your eyes on the road. Switch to the slow lane in the Languedoc, with its laid-back pace of life, Cathar castles and pilgrims' churches.

Head to the hills on Trip 29

Paris & Northern France

FROM THE BOULEVARDS OF PARIS TO THE CLIFFS OF BRITTANY, northern France is primed with possibilities – whether that means touring Champagne's vineyards, sampling Norman cheeses, admiring art in Metz or simply moseying around Rouen's old town. And with its abundance of coast and countryside, it's a pleasure to drive, too.

It's a region whose long (and turbulent) history is plain to see. Two thousand years of royalty, renaissance and revolution have left their mark on the streets of Paris, while the scars of war can still be traced on the fields of Flanders and the beaches of Normandy. Elsewhere, cathedrals and châteaux hint at the splendour of a bygone age, and experimental art museums point to an equally flashy future.

Paris Conciergerie and the Seine River
SYLVAIN SONNET/GETTY IMAGES ©

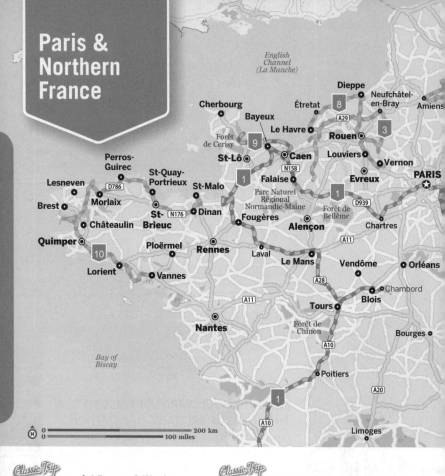

Paris & Northern France

English Channel
(La Manche)

Dieppe
Neufchâtel-
en-Bray
Amiens
Cherbourg
Étretat
8
Bayeux
Le Havre
N158
A29
3
Rouen
Forêt
de Cerisy
9
Caen
Louviers
Vernon
PARIS
Perros-
Guirec
St-Lô
1
Falaise
Evreux
St-Quay-
Portrieux
St-Malo
Parc Naturel
Régional
Normandie-Maine
1
D939
Lesneven
D786
St-
Brieuc
N176
Dinan
Fougères
Forêt de
Bellême
Chartres
Brest
Morlaix
Châteaulin
Alençon
A11
Quimper
Ploërmel
Rennes
Laval
Le Mans
Vendôme
Orléans
10
Lorient
Vannes
A28
A11
Tours
Chambord
Nantes
Forêt de
Chinon
Blois
A10
Bourges
Bay of
Biscay
Poitiers
A20
1
A10
Limoges

Ⓝ 0 ——— 200 km
0 ——— 100 miles

Classic Trip
1 Essential France 2 Weeks
Tick off the mustn't-misses on this epic cross-country adventure. (p39)

2 A Toast to Art 7 Days
Visit art galleries in Lens and Metz, then get lost in old Strasbourg. (p51)

3 Tour des Fromages 5 Days
Fatten yourself up on this tour of Normandy's creamy cheeses. (p59)

4 In Flanders Fields 3 Days
The ghosts of the Great War still linger on the battlefields of northern France. (p67)

Classic Trip
5 Champagne Taster 3 Days
Taste your way around the cellars of Champagne on this fizz-fuelled trip. (p75)

6 Alsace Accents 3 Days
Alsace's rich cuisine and crisp wines combine on this eastern road trip. (p85)

Classic Trip
7 Unesco Treasures 10 Days
From Gothic cathedrals to papal palaces, take a tour through France's World Heritage Sites. (p93)

Centre Pompidou-Metz

It's hard to know here which is more avant-garde – the architecture or the art. Take in this groundbreaking gallery on Trip 2

Vimy Ridge

Walk through one of the only surviving trench systems from WWI on Trip 4

Musée Bartholdi

Visit the Colmar home of the man who made Lady Liberty – and see a life-sized model of the statue's earlobe – on Trip 6

Distillerie Christian Drouin

Taste two of Normandy's top tipples – Calvados and cider – at this traditional distillery. Refresh yourself on Trip 3

Musée d'Art Moderne André Malraux

This museum in Le Havre contains the best impressionist collection outside Paris. Soak it all in on Trip 8

---

8 Monet's Normandy 4 Days
Investigate the origins of impressionism, from Étretat's cliffs to Monet's lily garden. (p105)

Classic Trip
9 D-Day's Beaches 3 Days
Follow the course of the WWII invasion on Normandy's beaches. (p113)

10 Breton Coast 8 Days
Brittany's coastline is all about big beaches and wild views. (p123)

Mont St-Michel *A stunning 11th-century abbey set in a golden bay*

Classic Trip

Essential France

1

City to city, coast to coast, this grand tour follows a route around some of France's most unmissable sights. There's some epic driving involved, but this is one trip you won't forget in a hurry.

TRIP HIGHLIGHTS

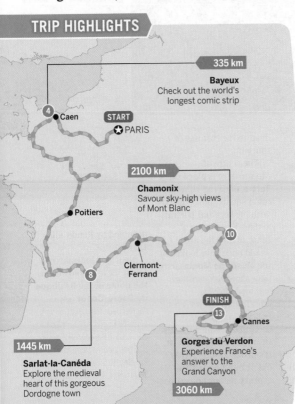

335 km

Bayeux
Check out the world's longest comic strip

4 ● Caen

START
✪ PARIS

2100 km

Chamonix
Savour sky-high views of Mont Blanc

● Poitiers

10

8

Clermont-Ferrand

FINISH
13
● Cannes

1445 km

Sarlat-la-Canéda
Explore the medieval heart of this gorgeous Dordogne town

Gorges du Verdon
Experience France's answer to the Grand Canyon

3060 km

**2 WEEKS
3060KM / 1902 MILES**

GREAT FOR...

BEST TIME TO GO
April to June.

 ESSENTIAL PHOTO

Overlooking the Parisian panorama from the Basilique du Sacré-Coeur.

 BEST FOR FAMILIES

Brave the space-age rides and roller-coaster thrills of Futuroscope.

1 Essential France

This is the big one – an epic trek that travels all the way from the chilly waters of the English Channel to the gleaming blue Mediterranean. Along the way, you'll stop off at some of France's most iconic sights: the château of Versailles, the abbey of Mont St-Michel, the summit of Mont Blanc and the beaches of the French Riviera. *Allez-y!*

Bayeux 4
St-Lô
St-Brieuc
A84 Falaise
Mont St-Michel 5
Fougères
Rennes
A81
A1
Angers
Nantes
A83
Parc Naturel Interrégional du Marais Poitevin
La Rochelle
A10
ATLANTIC OCEAN
Saintes
A89
Bordeaux 7
Parc Naturel Régional des Landes de Cascogne
A62
Bay of Biscay
A70
A65
San Sebastián
Pau

1 Paris

For that essentially Parisian experience, it's hard to beat Montmartre – the neighbourhood of cobbled lanes and cafe-lined squares beloved by writers and painters since the 19th century. This was once a notoriously ramshackle part of Paris, full of bordellos, brothels, dance halls and bars, as well as the city's first can-can clubs. Though its hedonistic heyday has long since passed, Montmartre still retains a villagey charm, despite the throngs of tourists.

The centre of Montmartre is **place du Tertre**, once the village's main square, now packed with buskers and portrait artists. You can get a sense of how the area would once have looked at the **Musée de Montmartre** (www.museedemontmartre. fr; 12 rue Cortot, 18e; adult/18-25yr/10-17yr €8/6/4; ☺10am-6pm; ⓜLamarck-Caulaincourt), which details the area's bohemian past. It's inside Montmartre's oldest building, a 17th-century manor house once occupied by Renoir and Utrillo.

Nearby, Montmartre's finest view unfolds from the dome of the **Basilique du Sacré-Coeur** (www. sacre-coeur-montmartre.com; place du Parvis du Sacré Coeur; dome €5, cash only; ☺6am-10.30pm, dome 9am-7pm Apr-Sep, to 5.30pm Oct-Mar; ⓜAnvers). On a clear day,

you can see for up to 30km.

To see more Parisian sights, check out our walking tour on p130.

✗ 🛏 p48

The Drive » From the centre of Paris, follow the A13 west from Porte d'Auteuil and take the exit marked 'Versailles Château'. Versailles is 28km southwest of the city.

LINK YOUR TRIP

17 Alpine Adventure

Chamonix features on our Alps trip, so it's easy to launch a cross-mountain adventure from there.

24 Riviera Cruising

Combine this journey with our jaunt down the French Riviera, which begins in Cannes.

Classic Trip

② Versailles

Louis XIV transformed his father's hunting lodge into the **Château de Versailles** (www. chateauversailles.fr; estate-wide admission €18, palace only €15; ⏰8am-6pm Tue-Sat, 9am-6pm Sun Apr-Oct, 8.30am-5.30pm Tue-Sat, 9am-5.30pm Sun Nov-Mar) in the mid-17th century, and it remains France's most majestic palace. The royal court was based here from 1682 until 1789, when revolutionaries massacred the palace guard and dragged Louis XVI and Marie Antoinette back to Paris, where they were ingloriously guillotined.

The architecture is truly eye-popping. Highlights include the **Grands Appartements du Roi et de la Reine** (State Apartments) and the famous **Galerie des Glaces** (Hall of Mirrors), a 75m-long ballroom filled with chandeliers and floor-to-ceiling mirrors. Outside, the vast park incorporates terraces, flower beds, paths and fountains, as well as the **Grand and Petit Canals**.

Northwest of the main palace is the **Domaine de Marie-Antoinette** (Marie-Antoinette's Estate; admission €10; ⏰noon-6.30pm Tue-Sat Apr-Oct, to 5.30pm Tue-Sat Nov-Mar), where the royal family would have taken refuge from the intrigue and etiquette of court life.

✗ p48

The Drive » The N10 runs southwest from Versailles through pleasant countryside and forest to Rambouillet. You'll join the D906 to Chartres. All told, it's a journey of 76km.

③ Chartres

You'll know you're nearing Chartres long before you reach it thanks to the twin spires of the **Cathédrale Notre Dame** (www. diocese-chartres.com; place de la Cathédrale; ⏰8.30am-7.30pm, to 10pm Tue, Fri & Sun Jun-Aug), considered to be one of the most important structures in Christendom.

The present cathedral was built during the late 12th century after the original was destroyed by fire. It's survived wars and revolutions remarkably intact, and the brilliant-blue stained-glass windows have even inspired their own shade of paint (Chartres blue). The cathedral also houses the Sainte Voile (Holy Veil), supposedly worn by the Virgin Mary while giving birth to Jesus.

The best views are from the 112m-high **Clocher Neuf** (New Belltower; adult/18-25yr/under 18yr €7/4.50/free).

✗ 🛏 p48

The Drive » Follow the D939 northwest for 58km to Verneuil-sur-Avre, then take the D926 west for 78km to Argentan – both great roads through typical Norman countryside. Just west of Argentan, the D158/N158 heads north to Caen, then turns northwest on the N13 to Bayeux, 94km further.

VISITING VERSAILLES

Versailles is one of the country's most popular destinations, so planning ahead will make your visit more enjoyable. Avoid the busiest days of Tuesday and Sunday, and remember that the château is closed on Monday. Save time by pre-purchasing tickets on the château's website, or arrive early if you're buying at the door – by noon queues spiral out of control.

You can also access off-limits areas (such as the Private Apartments of Louis XV and Louis XVI, the Opera House and the Royal Chapel) by taking a 90-minute **guided tour** (📞01 30 83 77 88; tours €16; ⏰English-language tours 9.30am & 2pm Tue-Sun).

4 Bayeux

The **Tapisserie de Bayeux** (Bayeux Tapestry; www.tapisserie-bayeux.fr; rue de Nesmond; adult/child €7.80/3.80; ⊕9am-6.30pm mid-Mar–mid-Nov, to 7pm May-Aug, 9.30am-12.30pm & 2-6pm mid-Nov–mid-Mar) is without doubt the world's most celebrated (and ambitious) piece of embroidery. Over 58 panels, the tapestry recounts the invasion of England in 1066 by William I, or William the Conqueror, as he's now known.

Commissioned in 1077 by Bishop Odo of Bayeux, William's half-brother, the tapestry retells the battle in fascinating detail: look out for Norman horses getting stuck in the quicksands around Mont St-Michel, and the famous appearance of Halley's Comet in scene 32. The final showdown at the Battle of Hastings is particularly graphic, complete with severed limbs, decapitated heads, and the English King Harold getting an arrow in the eye.

✕ ⨭ p121

The Drive » Mont St-Michel is 125km southwest of Bayeux; the fastest route is along the D6 and then the A84 motorway.

5 Mont St-Michel

You've already seen it on a million postcards, but nothing prepares you for the real **Mont St-Michel** (☎02 33 89 80 00; www.monuments-nationaux.fr; adult/child incl guided tour €9/free; ⊕9am-7pm, last entry 1hr before closing). It's one of France's architectural marvels, an 11th-century island abbey marooned in the middle of a vast golden bay.

When you arrive, you'll be steered into one of the Mont's huge car parks. You then walk along the causeway (or catch a free shuttle bus) to the island itself. Guided tours are included, or you can explore solo with an audioguide.

The **Église Abbatiale** (Abbey Church) is reached via a steep climb along the **Grande Rue**. Around the church, the cluster of buildings known as **La Merveille** (The Marvel) includes the cloister, refectory, guest hall, ambulatory and various chapels.

For a different perspective, take a guided walk across the sands with **Découverte de la Baie du Mont-Saint-Michel** (☎02 33 70 83 49; www.decouvertebaie.com; adult/child from €6/4) and **Chemins de la Baie** (☎02 33 89 80 88; www.cheminsdelabaie.com; adult/child from €6.50/4.50), both based in Genêts. Don't be tempted to do it on your own – the bay's tides are notoriously treacherous.

✕ ⨭ p49

The Drive » Take the A84, N12 and A81 for 190km to Le Mans and the A28 for 102km to Tours, where you can follow our tour through the Loire Valley if you wish (see p137). Chambord is about 75km from Tours via the D952.

6 Chambord

If you only have time to visit one château in the Loire, you might as well make it the grandest – and **Chambord** (www.chambord.org; adult/child €9.50/free, parking €3, ⊕9am-6pm Apr-Sep, 10am-5pm Oct-Mar) is the most lavish of them all. It's a showpiece of Renaissance architecture, from the double-helix staircase up to the turret-covered rooftop. With over 440 rooms, the sheer scale of the place is mindboggling – and in the Loire, that's really saying something.

⨭ p145

The Drive » It's 425km to Bordeaux via Blois and the A10 motorway. You could consider breaking the journey with stop-offs at Futuroscope and Poitiers, roughly halfway between the two.

7 Bordeaux

When Unesco decided to protect Bordeaux's medieval architecture in 2007, it simply listed half

J BOYER/GETTY IMAGES ©

SILVIA OTTE/GETTY IMAGES ©

LOCAL KNOWLEDGE
PATRICK DESGUÉ,
MONT ST-MICHEL
WALKING GUIDE

There's nowhere else like Mont St-Michel in France. Most people only visit the island and the abbey, but it's only once you see it from the sands that you appreciate what a unique place this is. Every day the bay is covered by the sea, creating a new landscape which is completely different to the one of the day before. I have been working here as a guide for many years, but I never seem to get tired of it here. I'm not a spiritual man, but there is something magical about this place.

Top: Women crushing walnuts
Left: Cathédrale St-André, Bordeaux
Right: Market stall, Aix-en-Provence

PETE GODING/4CORNERS ©

the city in one fell swoop. Covering 18 sq km, this is the world's largest urban World Heritage Site, with grand buildings and architectural treasures galore.

Top of the heap is the **Cathédrale St-André**, known for its stone carvings and generously gargoyled belfry, the **Tour Pey-Berland** (adult/child €5.50/free; ⊙10am-1.15pm & 2-6pm Jun-Sep, shorter hr rest of year). But the whole old city rewards wandering, especially around the **Jardin Public** (cours de Verdun), the pretty squares of **esplanade des Quinconces** and **place Gambetta**, and the city's 4km-long **riverfront esplanade**, with its playgrounds, paths and paddling pools.

✗ ⟩ p372

The Drive ⟫ Sarlat-la-Canéda is a drive of 194km via the A89 motorway, or you can take a longer but more enjoyable route via the D936.

- - - - - - - - - - - - -

TRIP HIGHLIGHT

8 Sarlat-la-Canéda

If you're looking for France's heart and soul, you'll find it among the forests and fields of the Dordogne. It's the stuff of French fantasies: riverbank châteaux, medieval villages, wooden-hulled *gabarres* (barges) and market stalls groaning with foie gras, truffles, walnuts and wines. The medieval

Classic Trip

town of Sarlat-la-Canéda makes the perfect base, with a beautiful medieval centre and lots of lively markets.

It's also ideally placed for exploring the Vézère Valley, about 20km to the northwest, home to France's finest cave paintings. Most famous of all are the ones at the **Grotte de Lascaux** (☎05 53 51 95 03; www. semitour.com; adult/child €9.50/6; ☾9am-8pm Jul & Aug, 9.30am-6pm Apr-Jun & Sep–early Nov, 10am-12.30pm & 2-5.30pm rest of year, closed Jan), although to prevent damage to the paintings, you now visit a replica of the cave's main sections in a nearby grotto.

✕ ⊨ p381, p389

The Drive ›› The drive east to Lyon is a long one, covering well over 400km and travelling across the spine of the Massif Central. A good route is to follow the A89 all the way to exit 6, then turn off onto the N89/D89 to Lyon. This route should cover between 420km and 430km.

- - - - - - - - - - - - -

⑨ Lyon

Fired up by French food? Then you'll love Lyon, with its *bouchons* (small bistros), bustling markets and fascinating food culture. Start in **Vieux Lyon** and the picturesque quarter of **Presqu'île**, then catch the funicular to the top of **Fourvière** to explore the city's Roman ruins and enjoy cross-town views.

Film buffs will also want to make time for the **Musée Lumière** (www.institut-lumiere.org; 25 rue du Premier Film, 8e; adult/child €6.50/5.50; ☾10am-6.30pm Tue-Sun; Ⓜ Monplaisir-Lumière), where the Lumière Brothers

(Auguste and Louis) shot the first reels of the world's first motion picture, *La Sortie des Usines Lumières,* on 19 March 1895.

✕ ⊨ p227

The Drive ›› Take the A42 towards Lake Geneva, then the A40 towards St-Gervais-les-Bains. The motorway becomes the N205 as it nears Chamonix. It's a drive of at least 225km.

- - - - - - - - - - - - -

TRIP HIGHLIGHT

⑩ Chamonix

Snuggling among snow-clad mountains – including Europe's highest summit, Mont Blanc – adrenaline-fuelled Chamonix is an ideal springboard for the French Alps. In winter, it's a mecca for skiers and snowboarders, and in summer, once the snows thaw, the high-level trails become a trekkers' paradise.

There are two really essential Chamonix experiences. First, catch the dizzying cable car to the top of the **Aiguille du Midi** (place de l'Aiguille du Midi; adult/child return to Aiguille du Midi €45.60/38.50, Plan de l'Aiguille €26.40/22.30; ☾8.30am-4.30pm) to snap a shot of Mont Blanc.

Then take the combination mountain train and cable car from the **Gare du Montenvers** (35 place de la Mer de Glace; adult/child/family €26.40/22.30/79.20; ☾10am-4.30pm) to the

---

FUTUROSCOPE

Halfway between Chambord and Bordeaux on the A10, 10km north of Poitiers, **Futuroscope** (www. futuroscope.com; adult/child €38/28; ☾9am-11.30pm, closed Jan–mid-Feb) lies one of France's top theme parks. It's a futuristic experience that takes you whizzing through space, diving into the ocean depths, racing around city streets and on a close encounter with creatures of the future. Note that many rides have a minimum height of 120cm.

You'll need at least five hours to check out the major attractions, or two days to see everything. The park is in the suburb of Jaunay-Clan; take exit 28 off the A10.

Mer de Glace (Sea of Ice), France's largest glacier. Wrap up warmly if you want to visit the glacier's sculptures and ice caves.

 p203

The Drive » The drive to the Riviera is full of scenic thrills. An attractive route is via the D1212 to Albertville, and then via the A43, which travels over the Italian border and through the Tunnel de Fréjus. From here, the N94 runs through Briançon, and a combination of the A51, N85 and D6085 carries you south to Nice. You'll cover at least 430km.

---

⑪ French Riviera

If there's one coast road in France you simply have to drive, it's the French Riviera, with its rocky cliffs, maquis-scented air and dazzling Med views. Sun-seekers have been flocking here since the 19th century, and its scenery still never fails to seduce.

Lively **Nice** and cinematic Cannes make natural starts, but for the Riviera's loveliest scenery, you'll want to drive down the gorgeous **Corniche de l'Estérel** to **St-Tropez**, still a watchword for seaside glamour. Summer can be hellish, but come in spring or autumn and you'll have its winding lanes and fragrant hills practically to yourself. For maximum views, stick to the coast roads: the D6098 to Antibes and Cannes, the D559 around the Corniche de l'Estérel, and the D98A to St-Tropez. It's about 120km via this route.

 p271

The Drive » From St-Tropez, take the fast A8 for about 230km west to Aix-en-Provence.

---

⑫ Aix-en-Provence

Sleepy Provence sums up the essence of *la douce vie* (the gentle life). Cloaked in lavender and spotted with hilltop villages, it's a region that sums up everything that's best about France.

Cruising the back roads and browsing the markets are the best ways to get acquainted. **Carpentras** and **Vaison-la-Romaine** are particularly detour-worthy, while artistic **Aix-en-Provence** encapsulates the classic Provençal vibe, with its pastel buildings and Cézanne connections.

 p281

The Drive » The gorges are 230km northeast of Aix-en-Provence via the A51 and D952.

TRIP HIGHLIGHT

⑬ Gorges du Verdon

Complete your cross-France adventure with an unforgettable expedition to the **Gorges du Verdon** – sometimes known as the Grand Canyon of Europe. This deep ravine slashes 25km through the plateaus of Haute-Provence; in places, its walls rise to a dizzying 700m, twice the height of the Eiffel Tower (321m).

The two main jumping-off points are the villages of **Moustiers Ste-Marie**, in the west, and **Castellane**, in the east. Drivers and bikers can take in the canyon panorama from two vertigo-inducing cliffside roads, but the base of the gorge is only accessible on foot or by raft.

 p49

Eating & Sleeping

Paris ❶

🍴 Cul de Poule   Modern French €€

(📞01 53 16 13 07; 53 rue des Martyrs, 9e; 2-/3-course menus lunch €15/18, dinner €23/28; 🕑lunch & dinner Mon-Sat, dinner Sun; Ⓜ Pigalle) Don't be deceived by the plastic chairs outside: this is one of the best kitchens in the Pigalle neighbourhood, with excellent neo-bistro fare. And yes, there is a chicken's *derrière* mounted on the wall.

🍴 Le Miroir   Bistro €€

(📞01 46 06 50 73; 94 rue des Martyrs, 18e; menus lunch €18, dinner €25-40; 🕑lunch Tue-Sun, dinner Tue-Sat; Ⓜ Abbesses) This modern bistro is on the Montmartre tourist trail, yet remains a local favourite. There are pâtés and rillettes to start, followed by well-prepared standards like stuffed veal shoulder. The lunch special includes a glass of wine, coffee and dessert.

🛏 Hôtel Amour   Boutique Hotel €€

(📞01 48 78 31 80; www.hotelamourparis. fr; 8 rue Navarin, 9e; s €105, d €155-215; 📶; Ⓜ St-Georges or Pigalle) One of Paris' trendiest hotels, the black-clad Amour (formerly a love hotel by the hour) features original design and artwork in each of the rooms. There are no TVs, but who needs them when you're in love?

🛏 Hôtel des Arts   Hotel €€

(📞01 46 06 30 52; www.arts-hotel-paris.com; 5 rue Tholozé, 18e; s €105, d €140-165; 📶; Ⓜ Abbesses or Blanche) The Hôtel des Arts is a friendly, attractive 50-room hotel, convenient to both place Pigalle and Montmartre. It has comfortable midrange rooms that are excellent value; consider spending an extra €25 for the superior rooms, which have nicer views.

Versailles ❷

🍴 À la Ferme   Southwest French €€

(📞01 39 53 10 81; www.alaferme-versailles.com; 3 rue du Maréchal Joffre; menus lunch €14-24, dinner €20-24; 🕑lunch & dinner Wed-Sun) Cowhide seats and rustic garlands strung from old wooden beams add a country air 'At the Farm', a temple to grilled meats and cuisine from southwest France.

🍴 Angelina   Tearoom €

(www.angelina-versailles.fr; mains €10-24; 🕑10am-6pm Tue-Sat Apr-Oct, to 5pm Tue-Sat Nov-Mar) This tearoom inside the Versailles estate is famed for its decadent hot chocolate. In addition to the branch by the Petit Trianon, there's another inside the palace.

Chartres ❸

🍴 Le Saint-Hilaire   Regional Cuisine €€

(📞02 37 30 97 57; www.restaurant-saint-hilaire. fr; 11 rue du Pont Saint-Hilaire; 2-/3-course menus from €27/42; 🕑lunch & dinner Tue-Sat) Local products are ingeniously used in to-die-for dishes like stuffed mushrooms with lentils, snails in puff pastry with leek fondue, a seasonal lobster menu, and aromatic cheese platters at this pistachio-painted, wood-beamed charmer.

🍴 Le Serpente   Brasserie, Tearoom €

(📞02 37 21 68 81; www.leserpente.com; 2 Cloître Notre Dame; mains €16-18.50; 🕑11am-11pm) Its location slap-bang opposite the cathedral ensures this traditional brasserie and *salon de thé* (tearoom) – one of the oldest in Chartres – is always full. Specialities span everything from pigs' trotters and veal kidneys to fresh fish and salads.

⨼ Best Western
Le Grand Monarque Hotel €€

(☎02 37 18 15 15; www.bw-grand-monarque.
com; 22 place des Épars; d/tr from €132/195;
❄ @ 🛜) With its teal-blue shutters gracing
its 1779 façade, lovely stained-glass ceiling
and treasure trove of period furnishings, the
refurbished Grand Monarch is a historical gem
and very central. Its restaurant has a Michelin
star.

⨼ Hôtel du Boeuf Couronné Hotel €€

(☎02 37 18 06 06; www.leboeufcouronne.com;
15 place Châtelet; s €65-85, d €75-109; @ 🛜)
The red-curtained entrance lends a vaguely
theatrical air to this two-star Logis guesthouse
in the centre of everything. Its summertime
terrace restaurant cooks up cathedral-view
dining.

Mont St-Michel ❺

⨼ Hôtel Du Guesclin Hotel €€

(☎02 33 60 14 10; www.hotelduguesclin.com;
Grande Rue, Mont St-Michel; d €77-93; ⌚mid-
Mar–mid-Nov) This hotel on the Mont is worth
recommending for its affordable rates, even in
high season – a rarity for the location. Best of all,
five rooms have views of the bay – priceless! –
as does the on-site restaurant.

⨼ La Bourdatière B&B €

(☎02 33 68 11 17; www.la-bourdatiere.com;
8 rue Maurice Desfeux, Beauvoir; d €39-43;
⌚Apr-Sep) This charming stone farmhouse in
Beauvoir is excellent value. The decor of the
four rooms could do with updating, but the rural
setting and blissful gardens are tough to top.

Gorges du Verdon ⓲

✕ Auberge
du Teillon Provençal, Gastronomic €€

(☎04 92 83 60 88; www.auberge-teillon.com;
D4805, direction Grasse, La Garde; menus
€26-38, d €60; ⌚lunch Tue-Sun, dinner Tue-Sat
Apr-Jun, Sep & Oct, lunch Wed-Sun, dinner Tue-
Sat Jul & Aug, closed Nov-Mar) Roadside *auberge*
(country inn) serving the best food this side of
Moustiers – pâtés, tender-roasted pigeon and
unusual *tarte tatin au foie gras*. Reservations
essential; located 5km east of Castellane.

✕ La Bastide
de Moustiers Gastronomic €€€

(☎04 92 70 47 47; www.bastide-moustiers.com;
d from €240, menus €55-75) This splurge-worthy
Provençal nest, domain of legendary chef Alain
Ducasse, is famous for fine cuisine – hence the
helicopter pad in the garden – and provides a
chance to dress for dinner, a rarity in Provence.

✕ La Ferme Ste-Cécile Gastronomic €€

(☎04 92 74 64 18; D952; menus €27-36;
⌚lunch Tue-Sat, dinner Tue-Sun, closed
Nov–mid-Mar) The delicious culinary surprises
served on the terrace of this authentic *ferme
auberge* (farm restaurant) may include the
thinnest slice of Roquefort and pear warmed in
filo pastry, or foie gras wrapped in sweet quince.

⨼ La Ferme Rose Hotel €€

(☎04 92 75 75 75; www.lafermerose.com;
chemin de Quinson; d €80-150; ❄ 🛜) This
inviting converted farmhouse, now a three-star
hotel, contains quirky collectibles – Wurlitzer
jukebox, display case of coffee grinders – but its
dozen rooms are uncluttered, colourful and airy.
Great bathrooms.

E. ANDRÉ
Arch¹ᵗᵉ 1903
A. GENY
Entrepreneur

A Toast to Art

2

One for culture vultures: an artistic expedition across northeastern France, taking in art nouveau in Nancy, glorious glass in Baccarat and avant-garde experimentation in Metz and Strasbourg.

TRIP HIGHLIGHTS

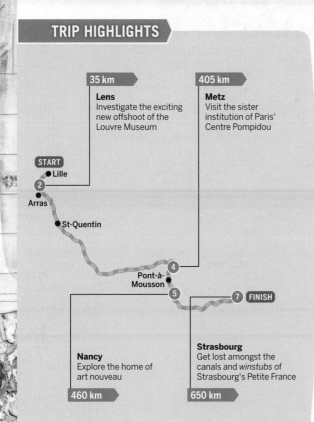

35 km

Lens
Investigate the exciting new offshoot of the Louvre Museum

405 km

Metz
Visit the sister institution of Paris' Centre Pompidou

START
● Lille

2

Arras ●

● St-Quentin

Pont-à-
Mousson

4

5

7 FINISH

Nancy
Explore the home of art nouveau

460 km

Strasbourg
Get lost amongst the canals and *winstubs* of Strasbourg's Petite France

650 km

**7 DAYS
650KM / 404 MILES**

GREAT FOR...

BEST TIME TO GO
April to July (avoid the school-holiday crowds).

 **ESSENTIAL
PHOTO**

Snap yourself sipping a coffee on Nancy's grand central square, place Stanislas.

**BEST FOR
SHOPPING**

Strasbourg's old quarters for chocolate, glassware and other souvenirs.

2 A Toast to Art

France's northeast is rapidly gaining a reputation as one of the country's most artistic corners, especially since the recent high-profile openings of the Louvre-Lens and Metz's Centre Pompidou – but these glitzy new museums are simply the continuation of a long artistic legacy. This high-culture tour takes in Gothic cathedrals, neoclassical squares, chic crystalware and art nouveau mansions – not to mention some of Europe's most experimental art.

① Lille

Once grimy, now groovy, industrial Lille has reinvented itself as a centre of shopping, art and culture. To underline its renaissance, it's now home to not one but three top-class art museums.

Classic works find a home at the **Palais des Beaux Arts** (Fine Arts Museum; www.pba-lille.fr; place de la République; adult/student/child €6.50/4/free; ⊙2-6pm Mon, 10am-6pm Wed-Sun), which owns a first-rate collection of Old

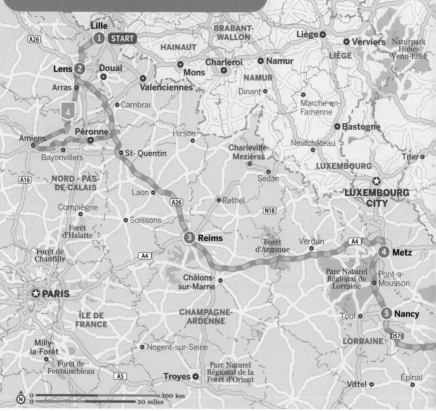

Masters, including works by Rubens, Van Dyck and Manet.

Contrast these with the playful – and sometimes just plain weird – works on show at the **Musée d'Art Moderne Lille-Métropole** (☎03 20 19 68 68; www.musee-lam.fr; 1 allée du Musée; adult/student/child €7/5/free, incl temporary exhibits €10/7/free; ⏱10am-6pm Tue-Sun). Big names including Braque, Calder, Léger, Miró, Modigliani and Picasso are the main draws. It's in Villeneuve-d'Ascq, 9km east of Gare Lille-Europe.

A few miles north at **La Piscine Musée d'Art et d'Industrie** (www.roubaix-lapiscine.com; 23 rue de l'Espérance, Roubaix; adult/child €4.50/free, incl temporary exhibits €7/free; ⏱11am-6pm Tue-Thu, to 8pm Fri, 1-6pm Sat & Sun; Ⓜ Gare Jean Lebas), the building is almost as intriguing as the art: a glorious art deco swimming pool has been beautifully converted into a cutting-edge gallery, showing contemporary paintings and sculptures.

 p73

The Drive » The quickest route to Lens is via the A1, but a less hectic route takes the N41 and N47. It's a 37km drive from the outskirts of Lille.

- - - - - - - - - - - -

TRIP HIGHLIGHT

② Lens

A depressed coal-mining town 37km south of Lille might not seem like the most obvious place to continue investigation of French art, but *au contraire*. As of December 2012,

the run-down industrial town of Lens is home to the country's highest-profile new art museum, the **Louvre-Lens** (www.louvrelens.fr). An offshoot of the Paris original, this impressive new museum aims to broaden access to the Louvre's treasures, and hopefully help kick-start the town's regeneration in the process.

It's early days, so the museum is still very much a work in progress – check the website for the latest news of what's on show.

The Drive » This time it's worth taking the motorway. Follow the N17 south of town and join the A26 for 178km to Reims, about a two- to 2½-hour drive away.

- - - - - - - - - - - -

③ Reims

Along with its towering Gothic cathedral and Champagne connections, Reims is also worth visiting for its splendid **Musée des Beaux-Arts** (8 rue Chanzy; adult/child €3/free; ⏱10am-noon & 2-6pm

🔗 **LINK YOUR TRIP**

4 In Flanders Fields
The main French battlefields of WWII are covered in this emotional tour; loop back at the end to Lille, and it makes an ideal combo with this trip.

6 Alsace Accents
Our drive along the Route des Vins d'Alsace starts in Strasbourg, so it's an ideal way to extend your journey at the end of this trip.

Wed-Mon), located inside an 18th-century abbey. Highlights include 27 works by Camille Corot (only the Louvre has more), 13 portraits by German Renaissance painters Cranach the Elder and the Younger, lots of Barbizon School landscapes and two works each by Monet, Gauguin and Pissarro. But its most celebrated possession is probably Jacques-Louis David's world-famous *The Death of Marat,* depicting the Revolutionary leader's bloody, just-murdered corpse in the bathtub. It's one of only four known versions of the painting in the world, and is worth the admission fee on its own.

✖ 🛏 p83

The Drive » Metz is 192km east of Reims via the A4 motorway, another two-hour drive.

- - - - - - - - - - - -

TRIP HIGHLIGHT

④ Metz

Opened in 2010 to much fanfare, the swoopy, spaceship façade of the **Centre Pompidou-Metz** (www.centrepompidou-metz.

fr; 1 parvis des Droits de l'Homme; adult/child €7/free; ⊘11am-6pm Mon & Wed-Fri, 10am-8pm Sat, 10am-6pm Sun) fronts France's boldest new gallery. Drawing on the Pompidou's fantastic modern art collection, it's gained a reputation for ambitious exhibitions, such as the recent one spotlighting the graphic works of American conceptual artist Sol LeWitt.

While you're in town, don't miss Metz's amazing **Cathédrale St-Étienne** (place St-Étienne; admission free; ⊘8am-6pm), a lacy wonder lit by kaleidoscopic curtains of stained glass. It's known as 'God's lantern' for good reason – look out for the technicolour windows created by the visionary artist Marc Chagall.

✖ 🛏 p57

The Drive » The most scenic option to Nancy is the D657, which tracks the banks of the Moselle River. Head southwest on the A31, then take exit 30a (signed to Jouy les Arches). Follow the road through rolling Alsatian countryside as far as Pont-à-Mousson, then continue through town on the D657 all

the way to Nancy. It's a point-to-point drive of about 65km.

- - - - - - - - - - - -

TRIP HIGHLIGHT

⑤ Nancy

Home of the art nouveau movement, Nancy has an air of grace and refinement that's all its own. Start your art appreciation at the **Musée de l'École de Nancy** (School of Nancy

---

✓ **TOP TIP:**
PASS NANCY TROIS MUSÉES

This good-value pass gets you into the Musée de l'École de Nancy, the Musée Lorrain and the Musée des Beaux-Arts, and is sold at each museum.

Metz Centre Pompidou-Metz

Museum; www.ecole-de-nancy. com; 36-38 rue du Sergent Blandan; adult/child €6/4; ⊙10am-6pm Wed-Sun), an art nouveau showpiece of dreamy interiors and curvy glass, housed in a 19th-century villa 2km southwest of the centre.

Next, head into the city's heart, magnificent **place Stanislas**, a vast neoclassical square that's now a Unesco World Heritage Site. Designed by Emmanuel Héré in the 1750s, it's encircled by glorious buildings, including the **hôtel de ville** and the **Opéra National de Lorraine**, and contains a treasure trove of statues, rococo fountains and wrought-iron gateways.

On one side of the square is the city's **Musée des Beaux-Arts** (3 place Stanislas; adult/child €6/ free; ⊙10am-6pm Wed-Mon), where Caravaggio, Rubens, Picasso and Monet hang alongside works by Lorraine-born artists, including the dreamlike landscapes of Claude Lorrain and the pared-down designs of Nancy-born architect Jean Prouvé (1901–84).

On nearby Grand Rue, the regal Renaissance

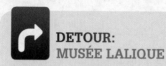

DETOUR:
MUSÉE LALIQUE

Start ❼ Strasbourg

René Lalique was one of the great figures of the art nouveau movement, and the **Musée Lalique** (www.musee-lalique.com; Rue du Hochberg, Wingen-sur-Moder; adult/child €6/3; ⊘10am-7pm daily, closed Mon Oct-Mar) provides a fitting tribute to his talents.

Opened on the site of the old Hochberg glassworks in 2011, the museum investigates Lalique's fascination with naturalistic forms (especially flowers, insects and foliage), not to mention the curvaceous lines of the female body. The collection illustrates his astonishing breadth of work, from gem-encrusted jewellery to perfume bottles and sculpture.

The museum is 60km north of Strasbourg in Wingen-sur-Moder.

Palais Ducal was once home to the Dukes of Lorraine. It's now the **Musée Lorrain** (64 & 66 Grande Rue; adult/child for both sections €5.50/3.50; ⊘10am-12.30pm & 2-6pm Tue-Sun), with a rich fine-art and history collection, including medieval statuary and faience (glazed pottery).

✖ 🛏 p57

The Drive » Head south from Nancy on the main A330 motorway. Take exit 7, signed to Flavigny-sur-Moselle, which will take you onto the rural riverside D570. Stay on this road all the way to Bayon, then cross the river through town, following the D22 east through quiet countryside to Baccarat. It's a drive of 78km.

- - - - - - - - - - - - - -

❻ Baccarat

The glitzy glassware of Baccarat was considered the height of sophistication in 18th-century France, and its exquisite crystal could be found gracing mansions and châteaux all over Europe. The **Musée Baccarat** (www.baccarat.fr, in French; 2 rue des Cristalleries; adult/child €2.50/free; ⊘9am-noon & 2-6pm) displays 1100 pieces, and the boutique out front is almost as dazzling as the museum. Nearby crystal shops sell lesser, and less expensive, brands.

Glass aficionados will also want to stroll across the River Meurthe to the 1950s-built **Église St-Rémy** (⊘8am-5pm), whose austere façade conceals a blindingly bright interior containing 20,000 Baccarat panels.

The Drive » Take the D590 southeast to Raon-l'Étape, then turn northeast on the D392A, a lovely back road that winds up through woodland and mountains, offering great views of the Vosges en route. Eventually you'll link up with the D1420, which will take you on to Strasbourg. It's a good two-hour drive of about 100km.

- - - - - - - - - - - - - -

TRIP HIGHLIGHT

❼ Strasbourg

Finish with a couple of days exploring the architectural splendour of Strasbourg and visiting the **Musée d'Art Moderne et Contemporain** (place Hans Jean Arp; adult/child €7/free; ⊘noon-7pm Tue, Wed & Fri, to 9pm Thu, 10am-6pm Sat & Sun; 🚋Musée d'Art Moderne), a striking glass-and-steel cube showcasing fine art, graphics and photography. The art's defiantly modern: Kandinsky, Picasso, Magritte and Monet canvases can all be found here, alongside curvaceous works by Strasbourg-born abstract artist Hans Jean Arp.

Afterwards, have a good wander around **Grande Île**, Strasbourg's historic and Unesco-listed old quarter, as well as **Petite France**, the canal district.

✖ 🛏 p57

Eating & Sleeping

Metz ➍

✗ Restaurant Thierry — Fusion €€

(☎03 87 74 01 23; www.restaurant-thierry.fr; 5 rue des Piques; menus €20-37; ☺lunch & dinner Mon, Tue & Thu-Sat) Combining Moroccan flair with an attractive setting in a 16th-century town house, this is one of Metz's most coveted tables. An aperitif in the candlelit salon works up an appetite for dishes such as sweet duck *pastilla* (pie) and seafood and dried-fruit tagine. Often full, so call ahead.

⬛ Hôtel de la Cathédrale — Historic Hotel €€

(☎03 87 75 00 02; www.hotelcathedrale-metz.fr; 25 place de Chambre; d €75-110; ☎) Classy and historic hotel opposite the cathedral. Climb the staircase to your classically elegant room, with high ceilings, hardwood floors and antique trappings. Book well ahead for a cathedral view.

⬛ Residhome Metz — Aparthotel €

(☎03 87 57 97 06; www.residhome.com; 10 rue Lafayette; d €58-65; P @) Part of a small French chain, Residhome has an excellent price–quality ratio and is two minutes' walk from the station. Light, roomy and done out in contemporary style, the studios and apartments make a comfy self-catering base, with kitchenettes, flat-screen TVs and free internet access.

Nancy ➎

✗ La Primatiale — International €€

(☎03 83 30 44 03; www.la-primatiale.com, in French; 14 rue de la Primatiale; menus €18-28; ☺lunch & dinner Mon & Wed-Sat, lunch Tue) The food looks as good as it tastes at this upbeat, art-strewn bistro. Clean, bright flavours such as tartar of marinated salmon with dill and star anise and rack of lamb in a herb-olive crust reveal a definite Mediterranean slant.

✗ Le V-Four — Bistro €€

(☎03 83 32 49 48; 10 rue St-Michel; menus €19-50; ☺lunch & dinner Tue-Sat, lunch Sun) With

just a handful of tables, this petit bistro is all about intimacy and understated sophistication. Mulberry chairs and crisp white tablecloths set the scene for original creations like grilled scallops with wasabi cream and tomato confit. Book ahead.

⬛ Hôtel de Guise — Boutique Hotel €€

(☎03 83 32 24 68; www.hoteldeguise.com; 18 rue de Guise; s/d/tr/q €68/80/92/98; ☎) Boutique chic meets 17th-century elegance at this backstreet hotel. A wrought-iron staircase sweeps up to old-fashioned rooms, with antique furnishings, inlaid parquet and heavy drapes.

⬛ Hôtel des Prélats — Historic Hotel €€

(☎03 83 30 20 20; www.hoteldesprelats.com; 56 place Monseigneur Ruch; s €75-95, d €105-115; ✴ ☎) It's not every day you get to sleep in a former 17th-century bishop's palace right next to the cathedral. This elegant hotel plays up the romance in rooms with stained-glass windows, four-poster beds and shimmery drapes. Service is as polished as the surrounds.

Strasbourg ➐

✗ Le Gavroche — Mediterranean €€

(☎03 88 36 82 89; www.restaurant-gavroche.com; 4 rue Klein; menu €38; ☺lunch & dinner Mon-Fri; ⊞; 🚇Porte de l'Hôpital) Bistro food is given a pinch of creativity and southern sunshine at intimate, softly lit Le Gavroche. Mains like veal in a mint crust with crispy polenta and coriander-infused artichoke tagine are followed by zingy desserts like lime tart with lemon-thyme sorbet.

⬛ Cour du Corbeau — Boutique Hotel €€€

(☎03 90 00 26 26; www.cour-corbeau.com; 6-8 rue des Couples; r €190-330; ✴ @ ☎; 🚇Porte de l'Hôpital) A 16th-century inn converted into a boutique hotel, Cour du Corbeau wins you over with its half-timbered charm and near-the-river location. Gathered around a courtyard, rooms blend original touches like oak parquet and Louis XV furnishings with mod cons like flat-screen TVs.

Camembert Renowned worldwide for its delicious soft cheese

Tour des Fromages

3

On this gastronomic drive you'll devour some of the best cheese in France and see where the seaside inspired artists, where Joan of Arc was executed and where Richard the Lionheart prowled.

TRIP HIGHLIGHTS

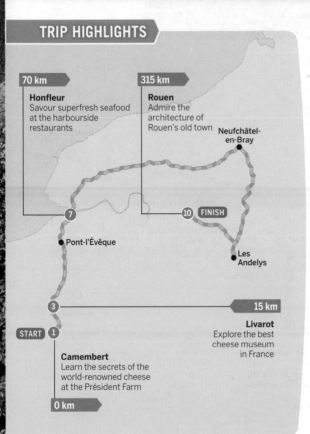

70 km

Honfleur
Savour superfresh seafood at the harbourside restaurants

315 km

Rouen
Admire the architecture of Rouen's old town

Neufchâtel-en-Bray

● Pont-l'Évêque

7

10 FINISH

● Les Andelys

3

15 km

Livarot
Explore the best cheese museum in France

START **1**

Camembert
Learn the secrets of the world-renowned cheese at the Président Farm

0 km

5 DAYS
315KM / 196 MILES

GREAT FOR...

BEST TIME TO GO

In May Pont L'Évêque celebrates all that is cheese during the Fête du Fromage.

 ESSENTIAL PHOTO

Snap a shot of the Seine from the platform near the Château Gaillard.

☑ **BEST FOR HISTORY**

Pay your respects to the memory of Joan of Arc in Rouen.

3 Tour des Fromages

More cheese, please! It's said that in France there is a different variety of cheese for every day of the year. On this driving culinary extravaganza you'll taste, and learn about, some of the very finest of French cheeses. Cheese cravings sated, explore the backstreets of Rouen, build castles made of sand on the seashore and clamber up to castles made of stone in the interior.

TRIP HIGHLIGHT

❶ Camembert

Thanks to a delicious soft cheese, the name Camembert is known the world over. Therefore, it can come as a surprise to learn that Camembert is merely a small, but very picturesque, classic Norman village of half-timbered buildings. The big attraction here is of course the aforementioned cheese and you can learn all about it during a guided tour of the **Président**

p64

Farm (02 33 36 06 60; www.fermepresident.com; adult/child €3/2; 10am-7pm May-Aug, 10am-5pm or 6pm Sep, Oct, Mar & Apr), an early-19th-century farm restored by Président, one of the region's largest Camembert producers.

The Drive » It's a 5km, 10-minute drive along the D246 and then the D16 from Camembert village to the Musée du Camembert in Vimoutiers.

❷ Musée du Camembert

Recently reopened after two years of extensive renovations, the small **Musée du Camembert** (02 33 39 30 29; 10 Av du Général de Gaulle; adult/child €3/2; 2-5.30pm Thu-Mon Apr-Oct), in the village of Vimoutiers, gives you the lowdown on the history and culture of the smelly stuff. It's a privately run affair; you might have to call for them to open up.

The Drive » It's another 10-minute drive north to stop 3, Livarot, along the D579.

TRIP HIGHLIGHT

❸ Livarot

Although not as famous internationally as Camembert, Livarot is a big deal in France. The town where the cheese of the same name originated is home to probably the best cheese tour in Normandy. **Le Village Fromager** (L'Atelier Fromager; 02 31 48 20 10; www.graindorge.fr; 42 rue du Général Leclerc; 9.30am-1pm & 2-5.30pm Mon-Sat, 10.30am-1pm & 3-5.30pm Sun) offers a free tour and tasting at the Graindorge factory. A self-guided tour accompanied by multimedia displays leads through a series of whiffy viewing rooms where you can watch Livarot, Camembert and Pont l'Évêque being made.

After you've expanded your waistline on the cheese tour, work it all off again with a walk around the town. Its wobbly-wiggly half-timbered buildings make it a real charmer.

The Drive » Using the D579 it's only a 15km drive through leafy countryside to Le Domaine Saint Hippolyte, just on the outskirts of the village of St Martin de la Lieue (take the third exit off the roundabout at the entrance to the village).

❹ Le Domaine Saint Hippolyte

There's fun for all the family at **Le Domaine Saint Hippolyte** (02 31 31 30 68; www.domaine-saint-hippolyte.fr; rte de Livarot/D579, St Martin de la Lieue; adult/child €5.90/free;

🄢 LINK YOUR TRIP

4 In Flanders Fields
The war memorials of northern France are a powerful symbol of the wastefulness of war. Amiens, the start of our Flanders Fields drive, is 120km from Rouen.

5 Champagne Taster
From Rouen it's 284km to Reims and the start of another culinary adventure – this one fuelled by the bubbly stuff.

⏱10am-6pm Mon-Tue & Thu-Sat, to 7pm Wed), which is both a cheese producer and a retailer where you can witness the process behind turning milk into cheese. There's also a small museum and, most interestingly for children, a working farm where you can pat cows and stroll through the grounds to the river.

The Drive » A gentle countryside cruise of just over half an hour (31km) up the D45 and D101 will see you easing into Pont l'Évêque.

- - - - - - - - - - - -

⑤ Pont l'Évêque

Since the 13th century this unpretentious little town with rivers meandering through its centre has been known for its eponymous cheese. Although two-thirds of the town was destroyed in WWII, careful reconstruction has brought much of it back to life.

Half-timbered buildings line the main street and 1960s stained glass bathes the 15th-century **Église St-Michel** (place de l'Église) in coloured light.

There's no shortage of **cheese shops** in town.

If you're passing through over the second weekend in May, don't miss the **Fête du Fromage**, when the townsfolk throw a little party for cheese – only in France!

The Drive » To get to the Distillerie Christian Drouin, your next stop, head out of Pont l'Évêque in a northeasterly direction on the D675. At the roundabout on the edge of the town, take the third exit (rue Saint-Mélaine/D677) and continue for about 2.5km until you see the farm on your left.

- - - - - - - - - - - -

⑥ Distillerie Christian Drouin

In case you were starting to wonder if Normandy was merely a one-cheese

pony, pay a visit to the **Distillerie Christian Drouin** (☎02 31 64 30 05; www.calvados-drouin.com; rte de Trouville, Coudray-Rabut; ⏱9am-noon & 2-6pm), which will let you in on the delights of Norman cider and Calvados (that other classic Norman tipple). Entrance is free.

The Drive » It's a simple enough 17km drive along the D579 to Honfleur and your first sea views (yes, the sun will be out by the time you get there...).

- - - - - - - - - - - -

TRIP HIGHLIGHT

⑦ Honfleur

Long a favourite with painters, Honfleur is

NORMAN CUISINE

Normandy may be the largest region of France not to contain a single vineyard, but its culinary wealth more than makes up for what it lacks in the wine department – besides, any self-respecting Norman would far rather partake in a locally produced cider or Calvados. This is a land of soft cheeses, apples, cream and an astonishingly rich range of seafood and fish. You simply shouldn't leave Normandy without trying classics like *coquilles St-Jacques* (scallops) and *sole dieppoise* (Dieppe sole). And whatever you do, don't forget your *trou normand* ('Norman hole') – the traditional break between courses for a glass of Calvados to cleanse the palate and improve the appetite for the next course!

Les Andelys Medieval village along the Seine

arguably Normandy's most charming seaside town.

On the west side of the **Vieux Bassin** (Old Harbour), with its many pleasure boats, **quai Ste-Catherine** is lined with tall, taper-thin houses – many protected from the elements by slate tiles – dating from the 16th to the 18th centuries. The **Lieutenance**, at the mouth of the old harbour, was once the residence of the town's royal governor.

Initially intended as a temporary structure, the **Église Ste-Catherine** (place Ste-Catherine; ⊙9am-6pm) has been standing in the square for over 500 years. The church is particularly notable for its double-vaulted roof and twin naves, which from the inside resemble a couple of overturned ships' hulls.

✗ ⊨ p65

The Drive ⟩⟩ You've had nice, mellow country lanes so far. Time to speed things up for the 111km race (not too fast, please!) down the A29 to Neufchâtel-en-Brey.

- - - - - - - - - - - -

8 Neufchâtel-en-Bray

The small market town of Neufchâtel-en-Brey is renowned for its heart-shaped cheese called, imaginatively, Neufchâtel. To buy it in the most authentic way, try to time your arrival to coincide with the Saturday-morning **market**.

Appetite satisfied, it's now time for some culture. Check out the **Musée Mathon-Durand** (⟩02 35 93 06 55; Grande Rue Saint-Pierre; adult/child €2.35/free; ⊙3-6pm Tue-Sun), inside a gorgeous medieval building that once belonged to a knight. He's long since gone off to fight dragons in the sky, and today the

DETOUR: AMIENS

Start ⑧ Neufchâtel-en-Brey

One of France's most awe-inspiring Gothic cathedrals is reason enough to make a detour to Amiens, the comfy, if reserved, former capital of Picardy. The **Cathédrale Notre Dame** (place Notre Dame; north tower adult/child €5.50/free; ⊙cathedral 8.30am-6.15pm daily, north tower afternoon only Wed-Mon) is the largest Gothic cathedral in France and a Unesco World Heritage Site. Begun in 1220, the magnificent structure was built to house the **skull of St John the Baptist**, shown – framed in gold and jewels – in the northern outer wall of the ambulatory. Connoisseurs rave about the soaring Gothic arches, the unity of style and the immense interior, but for locals the 17th-century statue known as the **Ange Pleureur** (Crying Angel), in the ambulatory directly behind the over-the-top baroque high altar, remains a favourite.

From Neufchâtel-en-Brey head 73km (one hour) down the A29 toll road. In order to rejoin the main part of the trip, take the A16 toll road via Beauvais (129km, one hour and 50 minutes) straight to stop 9, Les Andelys.

house contains a small museum of local culture.

The Drive ≫ The most obvious route between Neufchâtel-en-Brey and stop 9, Les Andelys, is along the A28, but that means skirting around Rouen – time it badly and you'll be sitting in traffic breathing in carbon monoxide. Instead, take the more serene D921 back road. Going this way should take you about 80 minutes to cover the 75km.

- - - - - - - - - - - - - - - -

⑨ Les Andelys

On a hairpin curve in the Seine lies Les Andelys (the 's' is silent), the old part of which is crowned by the ruins of Château Gaillard, the 12th-century hilltop fastness of Richard the Lionheart.

Built from 1196 to 1197, **Château Gaillard** (☏02 32 54 41 93; adult/child €3.15/2.60; ⊙10am-1pm & 2-6pm Wed-Mon mid-Mar–mid-Nov) secured the western border of English territory along the Seine until Henry IV ordered its destruction in 1603. Fantastic views of the Seine's white cliffs can be enjoyed from the platform a few hundred metres up the one-lane road from the castle.

 p65

The Drive ≫ It's a 45km, 50-minute scamper (well, as long as you don't hit rush-hour traffic) down the D6014 to your final stop, Rouen.

- - - - - - - - - - - - - - - -

`TRIP HIGHLIGHT`

⑩ Rouen

With its elegant spires, beautifully restored medieval quarter and soaring Gothic cathedral, the ancient city of Rouen is one of Normandy's highlights. It was here that the young French heroine Joan of Arc (Jeanne d'Arc) was tried for heresy.

Rouen's stunning **Cathédrale Notre Dame** (place de la Cathédrale; ⊙2-6pm Mon, 7.30am-7pm Tue-Sat, 8am-6pm Sun) is the famous subject of a series of paintings by Monet.

Rue du Gros Horloge runs from the cathedral west to **place du Vieux Marché**, where you'll find the thrillingly bizarre **Église Jeanne d'Arc**, with its fish-scale exterior. It sits on the spot where the 19-year-old Joan was burned at the stake.

 p65

Eating & Sleeping

Honfleur ❼

✕ Le Bréard   Gastronomic €€€

(📞02 31 89 53 40; www.restaurant-lebreard.
com; 7 rue du Puits; menus €29-55; 🕒lunch &
dinner Wed-Sun) *The* place to go in Honfleur for
gastronomique specialties of the highest order,
served in two chic, modern dining rooms. The
cuisine is wonderfully imaginative and gleaned
from every region of France.

✕ Le Gambetta   Modern French €€

(📞02 31 87 05 01; 58 rue Haute; mains €15-20,
menu €23; 🕒lunch Sat-Wed, dinner Fri-Wed)
Honfleur's latest addition to the restaurant
scene, Le Gambetta is well worth seeking out.
The decor is a lovely mix of traditional and
modern touches, and the food is deliberately
eclectic; seafood predominates, but everything
has a creative twist.

🛏 La Maison
de Lucie   Boutique Hotel €€€

(📞02 31 14 40 40; www.lamaisondelucie.com;
44 rue des Capucins; d €150-200, ste €250-
315; P🛜) This marvellous little hideaway
has just 10 rooms and two suites, which
ensures intimacy. Some of the bedrooms have
Moroccan-tile bathrooms and boast fantastic
views across the harbour to the Pont de
Normandie.

Les Andelys ❾

🛏 Hôtel & Restaurant
de la Chaîne d'Or   Hotel €€

(📞02 32 54 00 31; www.hotel-lachainedor.com;
27 rue Grande, Petit Andely; r €94-149, lunch
menus €20-65; 🕒closed Jan, restaurant closed

Wed mid-Apr–mid-Oct, dinner Sun & all day Mon
& Tue mid-Oct–mid-Apr; P🛜) Right on the
Seine, this little rural hideaway, packed with
character, is rustically stylish without being
twee. The classy restaurant is one of the best
for miles around.

Rouen ❿

✕ Les Nymphéas   Traditional French €€

(📞02 35 89 26 69; www.lesnympheas-rouen.
com; 7-9 rue de la Pie; mains €29-37, menus €34-
52; 🕒lunch & dinner Tue-Sat) Its formal table
settings arrayed under 16th-century beams,
this fine restaurant serves cuisine based on
fresh ingredients. Let chef Patrick Kukurudz and
his team seduce you with meat and fish dishes
accompanied by divinely inspired sauces.

✕ Minute et Mijoté   Bistro €

(58 rue de Fontenelle; mains €20, menus €13-30;
🕒lunch & dinner Mon-Sat) This smart bistro
is one of our favourite finds in Rouen. The
trademark here is freshness and great value for
money, hence its fast-growing reputation.

🛏 Hôtel de Bourgtheroulde   Hotel €€€

(📞02 35 14 50 50; www.hotelsparouen.com; 15
place de la Pucelle; r €240-380; P✳🛜⌨)
This stunning conversion of an old private
mansion brings a dash of glamour and luxury
to Rouen's hotel scene. Rooms are large and
gorgeously designed, with beautiful bathrooms.

🛏 La Boulangerie   B&B €€

(📞06 12 94 53 15; www.laboulangerie.fr; 59
rue St-Nicaise; d €77-92, q €150; P🛜) Tucked
into a quiet side street slightly off the historic
quarter, this adorable B&B occupying a former
bakery offers three pleasingly decorated rooms.

Poppy fields *The red poppy symbolises those who fell in WWI*

In Flanders Fields

4

WWI history comes to life in this tour of the battlefields where Allied and German troops endured three years of trench warfare. Stopovers in Lille, Arras and Amiens offer an urban counterpoint.

TRIP HIGHLIGHTS

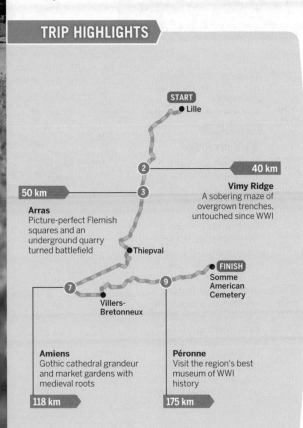

START
● Lille

2

40 km

Vimy Ridge
A sobering maze of overgrown trenches, untouched since WWI

50 km

3

Arras
Picture-perfect Flemish squares and an underground quarry turned battlefield

● Thiepval

 FINISH
Somme American Cemetery

7

9

Villers-Bretonneux

Amiens
Gothic cathedral grandeur and market gardens with medieval roots

118 km

Péronne
Visit the region's best museum of WWI history

175 km

3 DAYS
225KM / 140 MILES

GREAT FOR...

BEST TIME TO GO
March to November; some sites close in winter.

 ESSENTIAL PHOTO
The staggering list of missing soldiers' names at Thiepval.

BEST FOR HISTORY
Carrière Wellington, Arras' riveting quarry turned battlefield.

4 In Flanders Fields

Shortly after WWI broke out in 1914, Allied troops established a line of resistance against further German advances in the northern French countryside near Arras, resulting in one of the longest and bloodiest standoffs in modern military history. This tour of Flanders and Picardy takes in France's most important WWI battle memorials, along with the great cities of Lille, Arras and Amiens.

① Lille

A convenient gateway to northern France's WWI battlefields, cosmopolitan Lille offers an engaging mix of grand architecture and Flemish culture. Stop in for dinner at an *estaminet* (traditional Flemish restaurant) and stroll around the gorgeous pedestrianised centre, whose highlights include the **Vieille Bourse**, a 17th-century Flemish Renaissance extravaganza decorated with caryatids and cornucopia, and the neo-Flemish **Chambre de Commerce**, crowned by a gilded clock atop a 76m-high spire.

 p73

The Drive » Take the N41, N47 and D55 45km southwest to Vimy Ridge.

TRIP HIGHLIGHT

② Vimy Ridge

More than any other site in northern France, the vast crater-pocked battlefield at Vimy allows visitors to imagine the horrors of trench warfare. A long tree-lined drive ushers you into the surreally serene landscape of grass-covered century-old bunkers where 3598 Canadian soldiers lost their lives in April 1917 while taking 14km-long Vimy Ridge from the Germans. Climb to the ridgeline to see the striking allegorical **WWI**

memorial, then visit the **welcome centre** (www.veterans.gc.ca/eng/memorials; ⊙10am–6pm, closed mid-Dec–mid-Jan) for a **guided tour** (⊙ hourly 10am-5pm Tue-Sun Feb-Nov) of the tunnels and trenches, preserved exactly as they were when the guns fell silent.

The Drive ≫ Follow the D55, N17 and D917 12km into Arras.

TRIP HIGHLIGHT

❸ Arras

Contemplating the picture-perfect, reconstructed Flemish-style façades of Arras' two gorgeous market squares (**Grand' Place** and **Petite Place**) today, it's hard to believe that the city centre was largely reduced to rubble in WWI. For a more palpable sense of Arras' wartime realities, head 1km southeast of town to **Carrière Wellington** (www.carriere-wellington.com; rue Delétoille; adult/child

LINK YOUR TRIP

2 **A Toast to Art**
From Vimy, detour 9km to Lens for this tour of northern France's arts scene.

9 **D-Day's Beaches**
Relive Europe's other great war on this tour of Normandy's D-Day sites.

€6.80/3.10; ⊘tours
10am-12.30pm & 1.30-5pm,
closed Christmas–mid-Jan),
a remarkable quarry
turned museum that
served as the staging
area for an ambitious
Allied surprise attack on
the Germans on 9 April
1917. Prior to the attack,
a corps of 500 New
Zealand miners worked
round the clock for five
months expanding Arras'
medieval quarries to
accommodate kitchens,
a hospital and several
thousand Commonwealth
troops. Reminders of
this chapter in history
are everywhere, from
Maori-language graffiti
to candle burn marks
from the Easter Mass
celebrated underground
the day before the
troops surged from their
subterranean hideout
into the German front
lines.

 p73

The Drive » Take the
D919, D174 and D73 31km
southwest to the Newfoundland
Memorial, detouring briefly
at kilometre 15 to the Ayette
Indian and Chinese Cemetery,
where Chinese and Hindi
inscriptions mark the graves
of Indian soldiers and Chinese
noncombat labourers.

- - - - - - - - - - - -

➍ Newfoundland Memorial

On 1 July 1916 the
volunteer Royal
Newfoundland Regiment
stormed entrenched
German positions and

was nearly wiped out.
Like Vimy, the evocative
**Mémorial Terre-Neuvien
de Beaumont-Hamel**
preserves the battlefield
much as it was at
fighting's end. Climb
to the bronze caribou
statue, on a hillside
surrounded by native
Newfoundland plants, for
views of the shell craters,
barbed-wire barriers and
zigzag trenches that still
fill with mud in winter.
The on-site **welcome
centre** (www.veterans.gc.ca/
eng/memorials; ⊘10am-6pm)
offers guided tours.

The Drive » Head 5km east-
southeast on the D73 through
tiny Beaumont-Hamel, across
a pretty stream valley, past
Ulster Tower Memorial (site of a
Northern Irish war monument
and a homey tearoom) and on
to the easy-to-spot Thiepval
memorial.

- - - - - - - - - - - -

➎ Thiepval

On a lonely, windswept
hilltop, the towering
Thiepval memorial
to 'the Missing of the
Somme' marks the site
of a German stronghold
that was stormed
on 1 July 1916 with
unimaginable casualties.
Thiepval catches visitors
off guard both with its
monumentality and its
staggering simplicity.
Inscribed below the
enormous arch, visible
from miles around, are
the names of 73,367
Commonwealth soldiers
whose remains were
never recovered or

identified. A seemingly
endless roll call of
regiments runs down
each column, with the
alphabetised names
of individual soldiers
emphasising the
relentless and arbitrary
nature of war. The glass-
walled **visitors centre**
(⊘10am-6pm) has excellent
displays describing the
battle and its context.

The Drive » A 7km ride
through rolling hills along
the D151 and D20 brings you
through La Boisselle to La
Grande Mine.

- - - - - - - - - - - -

➏ La Boisselle

Just outside this hamlet,
the 100m-wide, 30m-deep
Lochnagar Crater looks
like the site of a meteor
impact. Colloquially
known as **La Grande
Mine**, it was created
on 1 July 1916 by about
25 tonnes of ammonal
laid by British sappers
attempting to breach the
German lines.

🍴 p73

The Drive » Backtrack along
the D20 to the D929, then
turn left (southwest) 35km to
Amiens.

- - - - - - - - - - - -

➐ Amiens

Amiens' pedestrianised
city centre offers a
delightful break from
the battlefields. Climb
the north tower of the
13th-century **Cathédrale
Notre Dame** (place Notre
Dame; north tower adult/child

Newfoundland Memorial

€5.50/free; ⊘cathedral 8.30am-6.15pm daily, north tower afternoons Wed-Mon) for stupendous views of town, and don't miss the free 45-minute **light show** that bathes the façade in vivid medieval colours nightly in summer. (See p64 for more on the cathedral.)

Across the Somme River, gondola-like boats offer tours of Amiens' vast market gardens, the **Hortillonnages** (54 bd Beauvillé; adult/child €5.90/5.20; ⊘1.30-4.30pm), which have supplied the city with vegetables and flowers since the Middle Ages.

Literature buffs will love the **Maison de Jules Verne** (www.jules-verne.net; 2 rue Charles Dubois; adult/child €7/3.50; ⊘10am-12.30pm & 2-6.30pm Mon & Wed-Fri, 2-6.30pm Tue, 11am-6.30pm Sat & Sun), the turreted home where Jules Verne wrote many of his best-known works.

✕ ⊨ p73

The Drive » Take the D1029 19km east to Villers-Bretonneux.

- - - - - - - - - -

❽ Villers-Bretonneux

During WWI, 46,000 of Australia's 313,000 volunteer soldiers

met their deaths on the Western Front (14,000 others perished elsewhere). In the village of Villers-Bretonneux, the **Musée Franco-Australien** (Franco-Australian Museum; www.museeaustralien.com; 9 rue Victoria; adult/child €5/3; ⊘9.30am-5.30pm Mon-Sat) displays a collection of highly personal WWI Australiana, including letters and photographs that evoke life on the front. The names of 10,982 Australian soldiers whose remains were never found are engraved on the 32m-high **Australian**

DETOUR: THE RAILROAD CAR WHERE THE WAR ENDED

Start ⑩ Somme American Cemetery

On the 11th hour of the 11th day of the 11th month in 1918, WWI officially ended at **Clairière de l'Armistice** (Armistice Clearing), 7km northeast of the city of Compiègne, with the signing of an armistice inside the railway carriage of Allied supreme commander Maréchal Ferdinand Foch. In the same forest clearing, in a railroad car of similar vintage, the **Musée de l'Armistice** (www.musee-armistice-14-18. fr; adult/child €5/3; ⊙10am-5.30pm, closed Tue Oct-Mar) commemorates these events with memorabilia, newspaper clippings and stereoscopic photos that capture all the mud, muck and misery of WWI; some of the furnishings, hidden away during WWII, were the ones actually used in 1918.

From the Somme American Cemetery, take the D1044, D1 and D1032 86km southwest towards Compiègne, then follow signs 8km east along the N1031 and D546 to Clairière de l'Armistice.

National War Memorial, 2km north of town.

The Drive » From the Australian memorial, take the D23 briefly north, then meander east through pretty rolling country, roughly paralleling the Somme River along the D71, D1 and D1017 into Péronne.

- - - - - - - -

⑨ Péronne

Housed in a massively fortified château, Péronne's award-winning museum, **Historial de la Grande Guerre** (www.historial. org; Château de Péronne; adult/child €7.50/3.80;

⊙10am-6pm, closed mid-Dec–mid-Jan) provides a superb overview of WWI's historical and cultural context, telling the story of the war chronologically, with equal space given to the French, British and German perspectives. Visually engaging exhibits, including period films and bone-chilling engravings by Otto Dix, capture the aesthetic sensibilities, enthusiasm, patriotism and un-imaginable violence of the time.

For excellent English-language brochures

about the battlefields, visit Péronne's **tourist office** (☎03 22 84 42 38; www.hautesomme-tourisme. com; 16 place André Audinot; ⊙10am-noon & 2-6pm Mon-Sat), opposite the museum.

The Drive » The American cemetery is 24km east-northeast of Péronne via the D6, D406 and D57.

- - - - - - - - -

⑩ Somme American Cemetery

In September 1918, just six weeks before WWI ended, American units, flanked by their Commonwealth allies, launched an assault on the Germans' heavily fortified Hindenburg Line. Some of the fiercest fighting took place near the village of Bony. At the nearby **Somme American Cemetery** (www.abmc.gov; ⊙9am-5pm), criss-crossing diagonals of crosses and stars of David mark the graves of 1844 American soldiers who fell here; the names of 333 other men whose remains were never recovered are inscribed on the walls of the adjacent **Memorial Chapel**.

The Drive » From here, it's an easy drive back to Arras (69km via the A26), Lille (96km via the A26 and A1) or Amiens (98km via the A29).

Eating & Sleeping

Lille ❶

🍴 Au Vieux de la Vieille   Flemish €

(www.estaminetlille.fr; 2-4 rue des Vieux Murs; mains €10-14; ⏲ lunch & dinner) Old-time prints, antiques and fresh hops hanging from the rafters create the cosy ambience of a late 19th-century Flemish village at this beloved *estaminet* (traditional Flemish eatery). On sunny days, sit outdoors on picturesque cobblestoned place de l'Oignon. Specialties include *carbonade* (braised beef stewed with Flemish beer, spice bread and brown sugar) and *potjevleesch* (jellied chicken, pork, veal and rabbit).

🏨 L'Hermitage Gantois   Design Hotel €€€

(☎03 20 85 30 30; www.hotelhermitagegantois. com; 224 rue de Paris; d €219-455; @ 🛜) This five-star hotel creates enchanting, harmonious spaces by complementing its rich architectural heritage with refined ultramodernism. Behind a Flemish-Gothic façade, the 67 rooms are huge and sumptuous, with Starck accessories next to Louis XV–style chairs and bathrooms that sparkle with Carrara marble. One of the four courtyards is home to a 220-year-old wisteria that's been declared a historic monument. The still-consecrated chapel was built in 1637.

Arras ❸

🍴 Carpe Diem   Bistro €

(☎03 21 51 70 08; 8 bis rue des Petits Viéziers; mains €14-16, lunch menus €12; ⏲ lunch & dinner Tue-Sat, lunch Mon) This cosy, beamed-ceilinged eatery serves delicious grilled meats, accompanied by your choice of eight sauces and side dishes such as green beans, basmati rice and beer-braised endives.

🏨 Hôtel Diamant   Hotel €€

(☎03 21 71 23 23; www.arras-hotel-diamant. com; 5 place des Héros; r €75-86, apt for 2/4/6 people €125/145/165; 🛜) Snag a room overlooking the Petite Place and the belfry at this small, ultracentral hotel, or opt for the fully equipped apartment next door with kitchen and laundry facilities. Regular serenades from the chiming bells and the bustle of the Saturday market outside your window may be pluses or minuses, depending on your perspective!

La Boisselle ❻

🍴 Old Blighty Tea Room   Tearoom €

(www.oldblightysomme.com; 1 rue Georges Cuvillier; sandwiches & snacks from €5; ⏲10.30am-5pm Thu-Mon, noon-4pm Tue) Two minutes from the mine crater, this British-run tearoom makes for a convivial midday break.

Amiens ❼

🍴 Le T'chiot Zinc   Bistro €€

(18 rue de Noyon; menus €13-27; ⏲ lunch & dinner Mon-Sat) Bistro-style decor reminiscent of the belle époque provides an inviting backdrop for tasty Picard specialties such as *caqhuse* (pork in a cream, wine vinegar and onion sauce).

🏨 Grand Hôtel de l'Univers   Hotel €€

(☎03 22 91 52 51; www.hotel-univers-amiens. com; 2 rue de Noyon; s €67-89, d €88-156; @ 🛜) This venerable hotel has an enviable park-side location in the city's pedestrianised heart. The immaculate, comfortable rooms surround a four-storey atrium; some on the 4th floor enjoy cathedral views.

Champagne *Sip your way through the region's famed vineyards*

Classic Trip

Champagne Taster

5

From musty cellars to vine-covered hillsides, this oenological adventure explores the world's favourite celebratory tipple. Cleanse your palate and ready your taste buds: it's time to quaff.

TRIP HIGHLIGHTS

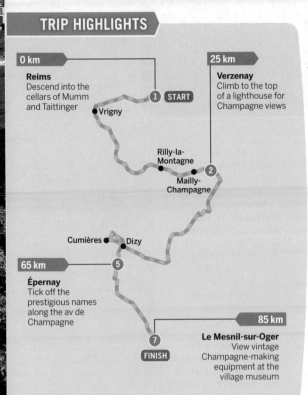

0 km

Reims
Descend into the cellars of Mumm and Taittinger

● Vrigny

1 START

25 km

Verzenay
Climb to the top of a lighthouse for Champagne views

Rilly-la-Montagne ●

Mailly-Champagne ●

2

Cumières ● ● Dizy

5

65 km

Épernay
Tick off the prestigious names along the av de Champagne

85 km

Le Mesnil-sur-Oger
View vintage Champagne-making equipment at the village museum

7

FINISH

3 DAYS
85KM / 53 MILES

GREAT FOR...

BEST TIME TO GO

April to June for spring sunshine or September and October to see the Champagne harvest.

ESSENTIAL PHOTO

Overlooking glossy vineyards from the Phare de Verzenay.

BEST FOR CULTURE

Sip Champagne in the cellars of Moët et Chandon.

Classic Trip

5 Champagne Taster

'My only regret in life is that I didn't drink enough Champagne,' wrote the economist John Maynard Keynes, but by the end of this tour, you'll have drunk enough bubbly to last several lifetimes. Starting and ending at the prestigious Champagne centres of Reims and Épernay, this fizz-fuelled trip includes stops at some of the world's most famous producers – with ample time for tasting en route.

TRIP HIGHLIGHT

1 Reims

There's nowhere better to start your Champagne tour than the regal city of **Reims**. Several big names have their *caves* (wine cellars) nearby. **Mumm** (☎03 26 49 59 70; www.ghmumm.com; 34 rue du Champ de Mars; tours €11; ⊙ tours 9am-11am & 2-5pm daily, closed Sun Nov-Feb), pronounced 'moom', is the only *maison* in central Reims. Founded in 1827, it's the world's third-largest Champagne producer. One-hour tours

explore its enormous cellars, filled with 25 million bottles of bubbly, and include tastings of several vintages.

North of town, **Taittinger** (☎03 26 85 84 33; www.taittinger.com; 9 place St-Niçaise; tours €16; ⊙ tours 9.30-11.50am & 2-4.20pm, closed Sat & Sun Dec–mid-Mar) provides an informative overview of how Champagne is actually made – you'll leave with a good understanding of the production process, from grape to bottle. Parts of the cellars occupy Roman

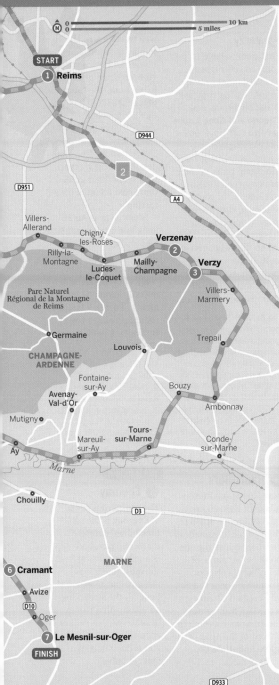

stone quarries dug in the 4th century.

Before you leave town, don't forget to drop by **Waïda** (5 place Drouet d'Erlon; ⊘Tue-Sun), an old-fashioned confectioner which sells Reims' famous *biscuits roses* (pink biscuits), a sweet treat traditionally nibbled with a glass of Champagne.

✕ ⊨ p83

The Drive » The countryside between Reims and Épernay is carpeted with vineyards, fields and back roads that are a dream to drive through. From Reims, head south along the D951 for 13km. Near Mont Chenot, turn onto the D26, signposted to Rilly and the 'Route Touristique du Champagne'. The next 12km takes you through the pretty villages of Rilly-la-Montagne and Mailly-Champagne en route to Verzenay.

- - - - - - - - - - - -

TRIP HIGHLIGHT

2 Verzenay

Reims marks the start of the 70km **Montagne**

§ **LINK YOUR TRIP**

1 **Essential France**
Lying 150km west of Épernay, Paris marks the beginning of our epic journey around France's most essential sights.

2 **A Toast to Art**
Pick up our art-themed tour in Reims, where it takes in the city's renowned Musée des Beaux Arts.

Classic Trip

de Reims Champagne Route, the prettiest (and most prestigious) of the three signposted road routes which wind their way through the Champagne vineyards. Of the 17 Grand Cru villages in Champagne, nine lie on and around the Montagne, a hilly area whose sheltered slopes and chalky soils provide the perfect environment for viticulture (grape growing).

Most of the area's vineyards are devoted to the pinot noir grape. You'll pass plenty of producers offering *dégustation* (tasting) en route. It's up to you how many you visit – but whatever you do, don't miss the panorama of vines from the top of the **Phare de Verzenay** (Verzenay Lighthouse; www.lepharedeverzenay.com; D26; adult/child €3/2, incl museum €7/4; ◐10am-5pm Tue-Fri, to 5.30pm Sat & Sun, closed Jan-Mar), a lighthouse constructed as a publicity gimmick in 1909. Nearby, the **Jardin Panoramique** (admission free) demonstrates the four authorised techniques for tying grapevines to guide wires.

The Drive » Continue south along the D26 for 3km.

3 Verzy

This small village is home to several small vineyards that provide an interesting contrast to the big producers. **Étienne and Anne-Laure Lefevre** (☎03 26 97 96 99; www.champagne-etienne-lefevre.com; 30 rue de Villers) run group tours of their family-owned vineyards and cellars – if you're on your own, ring ahead to see if you can join a pre-arranged tour. There are no flashy videos or multimedia shows – the emphasis is firmly on the nitty-gritty of Champagne production.

The Drive » Stay on the D26 south of Verzy, and enjoy wide-open countryside views as you spin south to Ambonnay. Detour west onto the D19, signed to Bouzy, and bear right onto the D1 along the northern bank of the Marne River. When you reach the village of Dizy, follow signs onto the D386 to Hautvillers. It's a total drive of 32km or 45 minutes.

4 Hautvillers

Next stop is the hilltop village of Hautvillers, a hallowed name among Champagne aficionados: it's where a Benedictine monk by the name of Dom Pierre Pérignon is popularly believed to have created Champagne in the late 16th century. The great man's tomb lies in front of the altar of the **Église Abbatiale** (abbey church; ◐daily).

The village itself is well worth a stroll, with a jumble of lanes, timbered houses and stone-walled vineyards. On place de la République, the **tourist office** (☎03 26 57 06 35; www.tourisme-hautvillers.com; ◐9.30am-1pm & 1.30-5.30pm Mon-Sat, 10am-4pm Sun) hands out free maps detailing local vineyard walks; one-hour guided tours cost €3 (€5 with a tasting).

Steps away is **Au 36** (www.au36.net, in French; 36 rue Dom Pérignon; ◐10.30am-1pm & 3-7pm Thu-Tue), a wine boutique with a 'wall' of Champagne quirkily arranged by aroma. There's a tasting room upstairs; a two-/three-glass session costs €10/15.

The Drive » From the centre of the village, take the rte de Cumières for grand views across the vine-cloaked slopes. Follow the road all the way to the D1, turn left and follow signs to Épernay's *centre-ville*, 6km to the south.

TRIP HIGHLIGHT

5 Épernay

The prosperous town of **Épernay** is the self-proclaimed *capitale du champagne* and is home to many of the most illustrious Champagne houses. Beneath the streets are an astonishing 110km of subterranean cellars, containing an estimated 200 million bottles of vintage bubbly.

Most of the big names are arranged along the grand av de Champagne. **Moët & Chandon** (☏03 26 51 20 20; www.moet.com; 20 av de Champagne; adult incl 1/2 glasses €16.50/23; ☺tours 9.30-11.30am & 2-4.30pm, closed Sat & Sun mid-Nov–mid-Mar) offers frequent and fascinating one-hour tours of its prestigious cellars, while at nearby **Mercier** (☏03 26 51 22 22; www.champagnemercier.fr; 68-70 av de Champagne; adult incl 1/2/3 glasses €11/16/19; ☺tours 9.30-11.30am & 2-4.30pm, closed mid-Dec–mid-Feb) tours take place aboard a laser-guided underground train.

Serious quaffers might prefer the intimate tours at **Comtesse Lafond** (☏03 86 39 18 33; www.deladoucette.net, in French; 79 av de Champagne; 3-glass tasting €9, incl cellar tour €14; ☺10am-noon & 2-5.30pm), owned by wine magnate Baron Patrick de Ladoucette. Tastings of three Champagnes

CHAMPAGNE KNOW-HOW

Champagne Types

» **Blanc de Blancs** Champagne made using only chardonnay grapes. Fresh and elegant, with very small bubbles and a bouquet reminiscent of 'yellow fruits' such as pear and plum.

» **Blanc de Noirs** A full-bodied, deep golden Champagne made solely with black grapes (despite the colour). Often rich and refined, with great complexity and a long finish.

» **Rosé** Pink Champagne (mostly served as an aperitif) with a fresh character and summer-fruit flavours. Made by adding a small percentage of red pinot noir wine to white Champagne.

» **Prestige Cuvée** The crème de la crème of Champagne. Usually made with grapes from Grand Cru vineyards and priced and bottled accordingly.

» **Millésimé** Vintage Champagne produced from a single crop during an exceptional year. Most Champagne is nonvintage.

Champagne Sweetness

» **Brut** Dry; most common style; pairs well with food.

» **Extra Sec** Fairly dry but sweeter than Brut; nice as an aperitif.

» **Demi Sec** Medium sweet; goes well with fruit and dessert.

» **Doux** Very sweet; a dessert Champagne.

Serving & Tasting

» **Chilling** Chill Champagne in a bucket of ice 30 minutes before serving. The ideal serving temperature is 7°C to 9°C.

» **Opening** Grip the bottle securely and tilt it at a 45-degree angle facing away from you. Rotate the bottle slowly to ease out the cork – it should sigh, not pop.

» **Pouring** Hold the flute by the stem at an angle and let the Champagne trickle gently into the glass – less foam, more bubbles.

» **Tasting** Admire the colour and bubbles. Swirl your glass to release the aroma and inhale slowly before tasting the Champagne.

Classic Trip

PLAN DE CRAMANT

MICHEL MASTROJANNI/GETTY IMAGES ©

STEVEN MORRIS PHOTOGRAPHY/GETTY IMAGES ©

LOCAL KNOWLEDGE
DAVID LEVASSEUR, CHAMPAGNE MAKER

We've been making Champagnes at our vineyard for three generations, starting with my grandfather. We're typical of many of the small Champagne producers along the Route du Champagne – a traditional family-run business. If you really want to understand Champagne, visit the winemakers' cellars and see first-hand how they work. Of course, you must also visit the av de Champagne in Épernay, where all the *'grandes maisons'* are based – it's magnificent.

Top: Cramant vineyard
Left: Pinot meunier grapes
Right: Marne River with Épernay in background

YVES TALENSAC/GETTY IMAGES ©

take place in either the house's elegant salon or the manicured gardens.

Finish with a climb up the 237-step tower at **De Castellane** (☎03 26 51 19 11; www.castellane.com, in French; 64 av de Champagne; adult incl 1 glass €10; ⊙ tours 10am-noon & 2-6pm, closed Christmas–mid-Mar), which offers knockout views over the town's rooftops and vine-clad hills.

✕ ⮕ p83

The Drive ›› Head south of town along av Maréchal Foch or av du 8 Mai 1945, following 'Autres Directions' signs across the roundabouts until you see signs for Cramant. The village is 10km southeast of Épernay via the D10.

6 Cramant

You'll find it hard to miss this quaint village, as the northern entrance is heralded by a two-storey-high Champagne bottle. From the ridge above the village, views stretch out in all directions across the Champagne countryside, taking in a patchwork of fields, farmhouses and rows upon rows of endless vines. Pack a picnic and your own bottle of bubbly for the perfect Champagne country lunch.

The Drive ›› Continue southeast along the D10 for 7km, and follow signs to Le-Mesnil-sur-Oger.

PARIS & NORTHERN FRANCE **5** CHAMPAGNE TASTER

THE SCIENCE OF CHAMPAGNE

Champagne is made from the red pinot noir (38%), the black pinot meunier (35%) or the white chardonnay (27%) grape. Each vine is vigorously pruned and trained to produce a small quantity of high-quality grapes. Indeed, to maintain exclusivity (and price), the designated areas where grapes used for Champagne can be grown and the amount of wine produced each year are limited.

Making Champagne according to the *méthode champenoise (*traditional method) is a complex procedure. There are two fermentation processes, the first in casks and the second after the wine has been bottled and had sugar and yeast added. Bottles are then aged in cellars for two to five years, depending on the *cuvée* (vintage).

During the two months in early spring that the bottles are aged in cellars kept at 12°C, the wine turns effervescent. The sediment that forms in the bottle is removed by *remuage,* a painstakingly slow process in which each bottle, stored horizontally, is rotated slightly every day for weeks until the sludge works its way to the cork. Next comes *dégorgement:* the neck of the bottle is frozen, creating a blob of solidified Champagne and sediment, which is then removed.

TRIP HIGHLIGHT

❼ Le Mesnil-sur-Oger

Finish with a visit to the excellent **Musée de la Vigne et du Vin** (☎03 26 57 50 15; www.champagne-launois.fr, in French; 2 av Eugène Guillaume, cnr D10; adult incl 3 flutes Champagne €7.50; ☻tours 10am Mon-Fri, 10.30am Sat & Sun), where a local wine-growing family has assembled a collection of century-old Champagne-making equipment. Among the highlights is a massive 16-tonne oak-beam grape press from 1630. Reservations can be made by phone or online; ask about the availability of English tours when you book.

Round off your trip with a dinner at Le **Mesnil** (☎03 26 57 95 57; www.restaurantlemesnil.com, in French; 2 rue Pasteur; menus €19.50-26; ☻closed Wed, dinner Sun), a quintessentially French restaurant that takes its culinary cue from the seasons – washed down, of course, with a flute or two of vintage Champagne.

Eating & Sleeping

Reims ①

✕ Brasserie Le Boulingrin Brasserie €€

(☎03 26 40 96 22; www.boulingrin.fr; 48 rue de Mars; menus €18.50-29; ⊙lunch & dinner Mon-Sat) A genuine, old-time brasserie – the decor and zinc bar date back to 1925 – whose ambience and cuisine make it an enduring favourite.

✕ Le Foch Gastronomic €€€

(☎03 26 47 48 22; www.lefoch.com, in French; 37 bd Foch; menus lunch €31, dinner €48-80; ⊙lunch & dinner Tue-Fri, dinner Sat, lunch Sun) Described as 'one of France's best fish restaurants' by food critic Michael Edwards, Michelin-starred Le Foch serves up cuisine that is as beautiful as it is delicious.

🛏 Hôtel de la Paix Hotel €€€

(☎03 26 40 04 08; www.bestwestern -lapaix-reims.com; 9 rue Buirette; d €170- 220; ❄@🛜🏊) This contemporary, Best Western–affiliated hotel is just off cafe-lined place Drouet d'Erlon. Relax in your choice of pool, Jacuzzi, hammam or courtyard garden.

🛏 Les Telliers B&B €€

(☎09 53 79 80 74; http://telliers.fr; 18 rue des Telliers; s €76, d €87-110, tr €123, q €142; 🛜🐾) On a quiet alley near the cathedral, this bijou B&B extends one of Reims' warmest bienvenues. The high-ceilinged rooms ooze art deco character, with ornamental fireplaces, polished oak floors and the odd antique.

Épernay ⑤

✕ La Cave à Champagne Regional Cuisine €€

(☎03 26 55 50 70; www.la-cave-a-champagne. com, in French; 16 rue Gambetta; menus €18-34; ⊙lunch & dinner Thu-Mon, lunch Tue) 'The Champagne Cellar' is a local favourite for *champenoise* cuisine such as artichoke hearts with snails in parsley cream, or duck cooked in grape juice. Sample four different Champagnes for €24.

✕ La Grillade Gourmande Regional Cuisine €€

(☎03 26 55 44 22; www.lagrilladegourmande. com, in French; 16 rue de Reims; menus €19-55; ⊙lunch & dinner Tue-Sat) An inviting bistro, ideal for char-grilled meats and rich dishes such as crayfish pan-fried in Champagne and lamb roasted in rosemary and honey. Diners spill onto the covered terrace in the warm months.

✕ La Table Kobus Brasserie €€

(☎03 26 51 53 53; www.latablekobus.com, in French; 3 rue du Docteur Rousseau; menus €19.50-45; ⊙lunch & dinner Tue, Wed, Fri & Sat, lunch Thu & Sun) French cuisine, both traditional and creative, is the speciality at this *fin-de-siècle* brasserie.

🛏 Hôtel Jean Moët Historic Hotel €€

(☎03 26 32 19 22; www.hoteljeanmoet.com; 7 rue Jean Moët; r €125-190; ❄🛜🏊) Housed in an 18th-century mansion, this old-town hotel is big on atmosphere, with its skylit tearoom, antique-meets-boutique-chic rooms and cellar bar, C Comme.

🛏 Le Clos Raymi Historic Hotel €€

(☎03 26 51 00 58; www.closraymi-hotel.com, in French; 3 rue Joseph de Venoge; s €115, d €155- 175; 🛜) Staying here is like being a personal guest of Monsieur Chandon himself, who occupied this luxurious house over a century ago. The seven romantic rooms all have high ceilings, French windows and parquet floors.

Dambach-la-Ville *A pretty medieval village painted in pinks and browns*

Alsace Accents

6

French and German cultures collide in Alsace, renowned for cosy winstubs and centuries-old wine culture. Enjoy castles, vineyards, pastel-shaded towns and the canals of Colmar.

TRIP HIGHLIGHTS

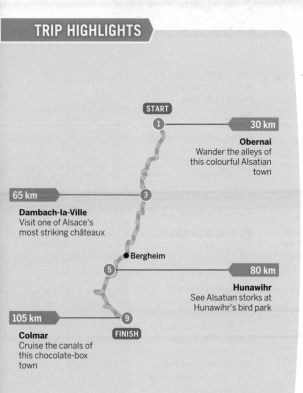

START

1

30 km

Obernai
Wander the alleys of this colourful Alsatian town

65 km

3

Dambach-la-Ville
Visit one of Alsace's most striking châteaux

● Bergheim

5

80 km

Hunawihr
See Alsatian storks at Hunawihr's bird park

105 km

9

FINISH

Colmar
Cruise the canals of this chocolate-box town

3 DAYS
105KM / 66 MILES

GREAT FOR...

BEST TIME TO GO

May to October for the best chance of sunshine.

ESSENTIAL PHOTO

As you're punting along the flower-decked canals of Colmar in a romantic rowboat.

BEST FOR FAMILIES

Watching the storks at the Centre de Réintroduction Cigognes & Loutres.

6 Alsace Accents

Gloriously green and reassuringly rustic, the Route des Vins d'Alsace is one of France's most evocative drives. Vines march up the hillsides to castle-topped crags and the mist-shrouded Vosges, and every mile or so a roadside cellar or half-timbered village invites you to stop and raise a toast. The official route runs between Marlenheim and Thann, but we've factored in a stop at Colmar, too.

TRIP HIGHLIGHT

1 Obernai

Sitting 31km south of Strasbourg (take the A35 and turn off at exit 11) is the typically Alsatian village of **Obernai**. Life still revolves around the market square, where you'll find the 16th-century town hall, the Renaissance **Puits aux Six Seaux** (Six Bucket Well) and the bell-topped **Halle aux Blés** (Corn Exchange). Visit on Thursday mornings for the weekly market.

There are lots of flower-decked alleyways to explore – don't miss **ruelle des Juifs** – and you can access the town's 13th-century ramparts in front of the **Église St-Pierre et St-Paul**.

✕ ⌂ p91

The Drive » Follow the D422 and D1422 for 9km south of Obernai, then turn off onto the D62. Mittelbergheim is another 1.5km west, among dreamy vine-covered countryside.

2 Mittelbergheim

Serene and untouristy, hillside Mittelbergheim sits amid a sea of grapevines and wild tulips, its streets lined with red-roofed houses.

Like most Alsatian towns, it's home to numerous wineries, each marked by a wrought-iron sign. **Domaine Gilg** (www.domaine-gilg.com, in

French; 2 rue Rotland; ⊘8am-noon & 1.30-6pm Mon-Fri, to 5pm Sat, 9.30-11.30am Sun) is a family-run winery that's won many awards for its Grand Cru sylvaners, pinots and rieslings.

From the car park on the D362 next to the cemetery, a vineyard trail winds towards the twin-towered **Château du Haut Andlau** and the forested Vosges.

🛏 p91

The Drive » Follow rue Principale onto the D425, signed to Eichhoffen. The road winds through lush Alsatian countryside and becomes the D35 as it travels to Dambach-la-Ville, 12km south.

- - - - - - - - - - - - - -

TRIP HIGHLIGHT

❸ Dambach-la-Ville

Dambach is another chocolate-box village, with lots of pre-1500 houses painted in

LINK YOUR TRIP

❷ A Toast to Art
Our art tour ends in Strasbourg, so it's a natural addition to this trip along the Route des Vins d'Alsace.

16 The Jura
Travel 170km southwest to Besançon to take a jaunt through the mountains and plateaus of the Jura.

ice-cream shades of pistachio, caramel and raspberry. To the southwest is the **Château du Haut Kœnigsbourg** (www.haut-koenigsbourg.fr; adult/child €8/free; ⊙9.15am-5.15pm), a turreted castle hovering above vineyards and hills. The castle dates back nine centuries, but it was rebuilt (with typical grandiosity) by Kaiser Wilhelm II in 1908. The wraparound panorama from its pink-granite ramparts alone is worth the admission fee.

The Drive ›› Stay on the D35, which becomes the D1B as it nears Ribeauvillé, 22km south. It's a truly lovely drive, travelling through carpets of vines and quiet villages. You'll see the turn-off to the château about halfway to Ribeauvillé.

④ Ribeauvillé

Nestled snugly in a valley and presided over by a castle, medieval Ribeauvillé is a Route des Vins must – so you'll definitely share it with crowds during the busy season. Along the main street, keep an eye out for the 17th-century **Pfifferhüs** (Fifers' House; 14 Grand' Rue), which once housed the town's fife-playing minstrels; the **hôtel de ville** (across from 64 Grand' Rue) and its Renaissance fountain; and the nearby clock-topped **Tour des Bouchers** (Butchers' Bell Tower).

It's also worth stopping in at the **Cave**

de Ribeauvillé (2 rte de Colmar; ⊙8am-noon & 2-6pm Mon-Fri, 10am-12.30pm & 2.30-7pm Sat & Sun), France's oldest winegrowers' cooperative, founded in 1895. It has an interesting viniculture museum and offers free tastings of its excellent wines. It's two roundabouts north from the tourist office.

✕ ⊫ p91

The Drive ›› Hunawihr is 2.5km south of Ribeauvillé.

TRIP HIGHLIGHT

⑤ Hunawihr

Cigognes (white storks) are Alsace's most emblematic birds. They feature in many folk tales and are believed to bring good luck (as well as newborn babies). They've been roosting on rooftops here for centuries, but their numbers fell dramatically during the 20th century as a result of environmental damage and habitat loss.

Thankfully, conservation programs have helped revive the birds' fortunes. The **Centre de Réintroduction Cigognes & Loutres** (Stork & Otter Reintroduction Centre; www.cigogne-loutre.com, in French; adult/child €9/6; ⊙10am-6.30pm, closed mid-Nov–Mar) houses more than 200 storks, plus cormorants, penguins, otters and sea lions.

The Drive ›› Backtrack to the D1B and travel 4km south,

following signs to Riquewihr. Distant hills unfold to the south as you drive.

⑥ Riquewihr

Competition is stiff, but Riquewihr just may be *the* most enchanting town on the Route des Vins. Medieval ramparts enclose a maze of twisting lanes and half-timbered houses, each brighter and lovelier than the next.

On rue du Général de Gaulle, the **Maison de Hansi** (adult/child €2/free; ⊙10am-12.30pm & 1.30-6pm, closed Tue Feb-Jun & Jan) offers a glimpse into the imagination of

FOTOSOL, FOTOSOL/GETTY IMAGES ©

Colmar View along the canal

Colmar-born illustrator Jean-Jacques Waltz (1873–1951), aka Hansi, whose idealised images of Alsace are known around the world.

Meanwhile, the **Tour des Voleurs** (Thieves' Tower; admission €3, incl Dolder €5; ⏰10.30am-1pm & 2-6pm Easter-1 Nov) houses a gruesome torture chamber that's guaranteed to enthral the kids.

 p91

The Drive » A scenic minor road winds 7km south from av Méquillet in Kaysersberg to Kientzheim, then joins the D28 for another 1km to Kaysersberg.

---

⑦ Kaysersberg

Just 10km northwest of Colmar, Kaysersberg is another instant heart-stealer with its backdrop of vines, castle and 16th-century bridge. An old-town saunter brings

TOP TIP: DRIVING THE ROUTE DES VINS

The Route des Vins is signposted, but a copy of Blay's colour-coded map **Alsace Touristique** (€5.50) comes in handy. Tourist offices supply free English-language maps – *The Alsace Wine Route* and *Alsace Grand Cru Wines* – detailing Alsace's prestigious AOC regions, and there's info online at www.alsace-route -des-vins.com.

Parking can be a nightmare in the high season, especially in Ribeauvillé and Riquewihr; your best bet is to park outside the town centre and walk for a few minutes.

you to the Renaissance **hôtel de ville** and the red-sandstone **Église Ste Croix** (⊙9am-4pm), whose altar has 18 painted panels of the Passion and the Resurrection.

Kaysersberg was also the birthplace of Albert Schweitzer (1875–1965), a musicologist, doctor and winner of the Nobel Peace prize. His house is now a **museum** (126 rue du Général de Gaulle; adult/child €2/1; ⊙9am-noon & 2-6pm Easter–early Nov).

The Drive » Take the N415 southeast of Kaysersberg for 7km, passing through Ammerschwihr and then following signs to Katzenthal.

⑧ Katzenthal

A mere 5km south of Kaysersberg, Katzenthal is great for tiptoeing off the tourist trail. Grand

Cru vines ensnare the hillside, topped by the medieval ruins of Château du Wineck, where walks through forest and vineyard begin.

It's also a great place for some wine tasting thanks to **Vignoble Klur** (☎03 89 80 94 29; www.klur. net; 105 rue des Trois Epis; min 3-night stay apt €90-150; 🏠), an organic, family-run winery that also offers cookery classes, vineyard walks and back-to-nature holidays.

The Drive » Rejoin the D415. Colmar is another 8km south and is clearly signed.

TRIP HIGHLIGHT

⑨ Colmar

At times the Route des Vins d'Alsace fools you into thinking it's 1454, but in Colmar the illusion is complete.

It's a town made for wandering. Mosey around the canal quarter of **Petite Venise** (Little Venice), then head along **rue des Tanneurs**, with its rooftop verandahs for drying hides, and **quai de la Poissonnerie**, the former fishermen's quarter. Afterwards, hire a **rowboat** (per 30min €6) beside the rue de Turenne bridge for that Venetian vibe.

The town also has some intriguing museums. The star attraction at the **Musée d'Unterlinden** (www. musee-unterlinden.com; 1 rue d'Unterlinden; adult/ child €8/5; ⊙9am-6pm Mon-Sun) is the Rétable d'Issenheim (Issenheim Altarpiece), a medieval masterpiece that depicts scenes from the New Testament in vivid detail.

Meanwhile, the **Musée Bartholdi** (www.musee -bartholdi.com, in French; 30 rue des Marchands; adult/ child €5/3; ⊙10am-noon & 2-6pm Wed-Mon Mar-Dec) is the birthplace of sculptor Frédéric Auguste Bartholdi, architect of the Statue of Liberty. Highlights include a full-sized model of Lady Liberty's left ear (the lobe is watermelon-sized!) and the family's sparklingly bourgeois apartment.

Look out for the miniature version of the statue on the rte du Strasbourg (N83), erected to mark the centenary of Bartholdi's death.

 p91

🗨 LOCAL KNOWLEDGE: INSIDER'S ALSACE

The Route des Vins is different from France's other wine regions. There are no grand châteaux, but there *is* a real neighbourly feel – our doors are always open. My favourite seasons are autumn, when the scent of new wine is in the air, and spring, when the cherry trees are in bloom.

There's an Alsatian wine for every occasion. Try a light, citrusy sylvaner with *tarte flambée* or foie gras, or a crisp, dry riesling with fish or *choucroute* (sauerkraut). Gewürztraminer is round and full of exotic fruit and spices, making it the ideal partner for Munster cheese, charcuterie and Asian food. Muscat is aromatic and flowery – great with asparagus or as an aperitif. Pick full-bodied pinot noirs for red meat.

Francine Klur of Vignoble Klur, Katzenthal (p90)

Eating & Sleeping

Obernai ❶

✖ La Fourchette des Ducs
Gastronomic €€€

(✆03 88 48 33 38; www.lafourchettedesducs.com; 6 rue de la Gare; menus €95-130; ☻dinner Tue-Sat, lunch Sun) Chef Nicolas Stamm adds imagination to Alsatian ingredients at this two-Michelin-starred restaurant.

✖ Winstub La Dîme
Alsatian €

(✆03 88 95 54 02; 5 rue des Pélerins; menus €12-22; ☻lunch & dinner Thu-Tue; ⊞) Precisely as an Alsatian *winstub* should be: beamed and bustling with diners tucking into earthy dishes like fat pork knuckles and *zweibelkuchen* (onion tart).

⌂ Le Gouverneur
Historic Hotel €€

(✆03 88 95 63 72; www.hotelegouverneur.com; 13 rue de Sélestat; s €55-80, d €60-90, tr €70-100, q €80-110; @ ⊞) The perfect balance between rustic and contemporary, with petite rooms decked out in vivid colours and modern art.

Mittelbergheim ❷

⌂ Hôtel Gilg
Historic Hotel €

(✆03 88 08 91 37; www.hotel-gilg.com; 1 rte du Vin; s €55-65, d €60-90, menus €32-72) This 17th-century half-timbered pile makes a romantic stop. A spiral staircase leads up to spacious pastel rooms, and the rustic restaurant serves classic French-Alsatian cuisine.

Ribeauvillé ❹

✖ Auberge du Parc Carola
International €€

(✆03 89 86 05 75; www.auberge-parc-carola.com, in French; 48 rte de Bergheim; menus lunch €17-20, dinner €27-58; ☻lunch & dinner Thu-Mon) This elegant *auberge* (country inn) is

overseen by much-lauded chef Michaela Peters. Pick a table under the trees and tuck into honey-glazed suckling pig and wild garlic polenta.

⌂ Hôtel de la Tour
Historic Hotel €€

(✆03 89 73 72 73; www.hotel-la-tour.com; 1 rue de la Mairie; s €72-96, d €78-104; ☎) In a converted winery, this half-timbered hotel has quaint, comfy rooms, some with views of the Tour des Bouchers.

Riquewihr ❻

✖ Table du Gourmet
Gastronomic €€€

(✆03 89 49 09 09; www.jlbrendel.com; 5 rue de la Première Armée; menus €38-98; ☻lunch & dinner Fri-Mon, dinner Thu) Jean-Luc Brendel is the culinary force behind this Michelin-starred venture, lodged inside a Zen-meets-medieval house, and known for its natural flavours.

Colmar ❾

✖ L'Atelier du Peintre
Gastronomic €€

(✆03 89 29 51 57; 1 rue Schongauer; menus lunch €20-25, dinner €37-72; ☻lunch & dinnerTue-Sat) With its art-covered walls and exciting cuisine, this Michelin-starred bistro lives up to its 'painter's studio' name. Seasonal dishes like roast lamb with creamed artichokes are served with serious panache.

✖ Le Petit Gourmand
Alsatian €€

(✆03 89 41 09 32; 9 quai de la Poissonnerie; menus €25-27; ☻lunch & dinner Tue-Sat) This cornflower-blue *winstub* sits on a river pontoon and serves regional specialities such as *tarte aux oignons* (onion tart) and *baeckeoffe* (Alsatian stew with riesling).

⌂ Hôtel les Têtes
Historic Hotel €€

(✆03 89 24 43 43; www.maisondestetes.com; 19 rue des Têtes; d €118-152, menus €25-66; ✳☎) Luxurious but never precious, this smart hotel has rooms with wood panelling, marble bathrooms and romantic views.

Palais des Papes *Inside Avignon's immense Gothic cathedral*

Classic Trip

Unesco Treasures

7

This top-to-tail adventure is a must for lovers of French history and architecture. Tour across France to some of its most precious assets, all inscribed on Unesco's list of World Heritage Sites.

TRIP HIGHLIGHTS

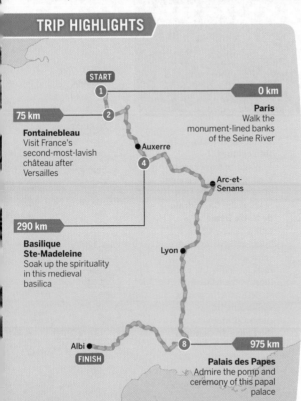

START
1 — 0 km

Paris
Walk the monument-lined banks of the Seine River

75 km
2

Fontainebleau
Visit France's second-most-lavish château after Versailles

● Auxerre
4

● Arc-et-Senans

290 km

Basilique Ste-Madeleine
Soak up the spirituality in this medieval basilica

Lyon ●

Albi ●
FINISH

8 — **975 km**

Palais des Papes
Admire the pomp and ceremony of this papal palace

10 DAYS
1156KM / 718 MILES

GREAT FOR...

BEST TIME TO GO

April to June or September and October to avoid the main French holiday periods.

 ESSENTIAL PHOTO

Standing on the viewing platform of the Eiffel Tower.

 BEST FOR ART

The world-class collection at the Musée Toulouse-Lautrec in Albi.

93

Classic Trip

7 Unesco Treasures

When it comes to World Heritage Sites, France is in the European premier league, with an impressive 35 (topped only by Spain and Italy). This cross-country tour explores some of our favourites – both well known and off the beaten track.

❶ Paris

In 1991, the banks of the River Seine were designated as a World Heritage Site in recognition of the central role the river has played in the city's history.

The site encompasses much of the city centre, from the Pont de Sully (east of the Île de la Cité) to the Pont d'Iéna (west of the Parc du Champ de Mars). Also included are the city's famous boulevards, laid out by Baron Haussmann in the 19th century.

Walking from east to west, you'll pass a string of Parisian landmarks. Start at the **Cathédrale de Notre Dame** (www.cathedraledeparis.com; 6 place du Parvis Notre Dame, 4e; admission free; ☉7.45am-7pm), arguably the world's most precious Gothic structure. Afterwards, walk along bd St-Germain, stopping at the **Église St-Germain des Prés** (www.eglise-sgp.org; 3 place St-Germain des Prés, 6e; ☉8am-7pm Mon-Sat, 9am-8pm Sun), Paris' oldest

standing church, and
Les Deux Magots (www.
lesdeuxmagots.fr; 170 bd
St-Germain, 6e; ⏰7.30am-
1am), a favourite literary
hang-out for many early-
20th-century writers and
philosophers.

Spend the afternoon at
the **Musée d'Orsay** (www.
musee-orsay.fr; 62 rue de Lille,
7e; adult/under 25yr/under 18yr
€9/6.50/free; ⏰9.30am-6pm
Tue, Wed & Fri-Sun, to 9.45pm
Thu), which houses the
country's top collection
of impressionist, post-
impressionist and art
nouveau masterpieces.

Finish with a twilight
climb up the **Eiffel Tower**
(www.tour-eiffel.fr; lift to
3rd fl adult/12-24yr/4-12yr
€14/12.50/9.50, lift to 2nd
fl €8.50/7/4, stairs to 2nd fl
€5/3.50/3; ⏰lifts & stairs
9am-midnight mid-Jun–Aug,
lifts 9.30am-11pm, stairs
9.30am-6pm Sep–mid-Jun) for

LINK YOUR TRIP

14 Medieval Burgundy

Vézelay also features as a
stop on our trip through
Burgundy's rich medieval
heritage.

21 Roman Provence

If Orange's amphitheatre
and the Pont du Gard have
whetted your appetite for
Roman ruins, why not link
up with our longer tour?

a twinkling view across Paris's night-time streets.

If you're still hankering to see more of Paris, try our walking tour on p130.

 p102

The Drive » The most direct route to Fontainebleau from Paris is on the A6 motorway, but there's a more peaceful route on the N104/D606. Head east from Paris on the A4, and look out for signs to the N104, indicated to Troyes. This route covers about 75km.

TRIP HIGHLIGHT

2 Fontainebleau

It might not quite hit the ostentatious heights of Versailles, but in many ways the **Château de Fontainebleau** (www. musee-chateau-fontainebleau. fr; adult/18-25yr/under 18yr €10/8/free, full château tours €21/18/free; ⏱château 9.30am-6pm Wed-Mon Apr-Sep, to 5pm Wed-Mon Oct-Mar, gardens 9am-dusk) is a more rewarding place to visit. The crowds are nothing like as intense as at Versailles, but the history and heritage are just as fascinating. The entire palace complex has been protected by Unesco since 1981.

Built by Louis IX, overhauled during the Renaissance by François I and later enlarged by Henri II, Catherine de Médici and Henri IV, Fontainebleau is a harmonious blend of architectural eras. Highlights include the **Grandes Appartements**, the 30m-long **Salle de Bal** (ballroom), the gilded **Salle de Trône** (Throne Room) and the **Chambre de l'Impératrice** (Empress' Bedroom), designed for Marie-Antoinette but never used. Private tours (in French) explore other areas.

Outside, the château's **gardens** are equally extraordinary, and include the Jardin de Diane, a formal garden created by Catherine de Médici, a 17th-century Jardin Français (French Garden) designed by Le Nôtre and an informal Jardin Anglais (English Garden), laid out in 1812. The Grand Canal was excavated in 1609 and predates the canals at Versailles by more than half a century.

 p102

The Drive » Take the D210 east of Fontainebleau. You'll drive through the Forêt Dominiale de la Champagne and cross under the A5 motorway, then join the D403 to Provins. Plan on 55km.

3 Provins

The walled town of Provins (www.provins. net) is listed by Unesco as the 'Town of Medieval Fairs', and it certainly does a convincing job of transporting you back into the Middle Ages (though, thankfully, minus the stink, plague and squalor). The town is home to over 150 medieval structures including the **Tour César** (adult/child €4.30/2.80; ⏱10am-6pm Mar-Oct, to 5pm Nov-Feb), the church of **Saint Quiriace** (admission free) and the **Grange aux Dîmes** (Tithe Barn; adult/child €4.30/2.80; ⏱10am-6pm Mar-Aug, Sat & Sun only Sep-Feb), where you can watch a live re-enactment of a medieval market. Elsewhere you can explore the town's ramparts, fortified

PROVINS TICKETS

If you're planning on visiting all the museums and shows in Provins, you'll find it cheaper to buy a combination ticket, known as the **Pass Provins**. The most expensive pass (adult/child €29/19, family of four €88) covers all the town's monuments plus the two main shows, and gives you discounts on other spectacles and events. It stays valid for a year; buy online to save time.

gates and over 10km of underground tunnels.

But it's the medieval-themed spectacles that most convincingly bring the period to life. Between April and November there are regular displays of falconry, horsemanship and medieval warfare (complete with trebuchets and jousting), as well as a weekly banquet on Saturday, where you can tuck into medieval food while being entertained by troubadours, acrobats and jugglers.

The Drive » Take the D403 south, then detour south onto the D412 and D976. You'll join up with the D606, a great road that passes through the pleasant towns of Sens and Auxerre and runs south, detouring onto the D951 for the final stretch to Vézelay. You'll cover about 160km.

---

4 Vézelay

France isn't short of churches, but there are few that capture the same sense of spirituality as Vézelay's. Jutting out from a rocky outcrop surrounded by flat fields, it's one of France's most gorgeous holy structures.

The centrepiece of the town is the **Basilique Ste-Madeleine** (www.basiliquedevezelay.org). Founded in the 880s, it's had a chequered history: it was trashed by the Huguenots, desecrated

during the Revolution and, to top off the human ravages, repeatedly struck by lightning. But the basilica was saved by 19th-century architect Viollet-le-Duc, who rebuilt its western façade and preserved its priceless stone carvings, including the famous tympanum (decorative arch) depicting Christ surrounded by the apostles. Viollet-le-Duc's work was rewarded when the basilica was awarded World Heritage status in 1979.

Beyond the basilica itself, Vézelay is an absolute pleasure to wander, with a muddle of cobbled lanes and carefully restored medieval buildings. Don't miss the view from the park behind the church, which affords knockout views across lush Burgundian countryside.

🛏 p102

The Drive » Drive east from Vézelay on the D957, a winding road that runs through Avallon and crosses through delightful Burgundian forests and fields. Just north of the village of Bierry-les-Belles-Fontaines, turn off onto the D957A, signed to Montbard. Follow signs to Montbard, then to the Abbaye de Fontenay. It's a drive of around 63km.

---

5 Fontenay

Many of France's great medieval abbeys were razed to rubble during the Revolution and the

Reign of Terror, which makes the survival of the **Abbaye de Fontenay** (Fontenay Abbey; 📞03 80 92 15 00; www.abbayedefontenay.com; adult/child €9.50/5.50; 🕙10am-6pm Apr-11 Nov, 10am-noon & 2-5pm 12 Nov-Mar) all the more important.

Founded in 1118 and restored a century ago before becoming Unesco listed in 1981, this serene Cistercian abbey gives a unique insight into monastic life during the Middle Ages. You can sit in the refectory where the monks would have eaten their meals, wander the landscaped gardens where they would have raised their crops and livestock, and even peep inside their barrel-vaulted dormitory and metal forge – the earliest surviving example in Europe. There's even a monastic fish pond.

The Drive » Head back towards Montbard and turn onto the D905, following signs to Dijon. Drive through the city, tracking signs to the D905/Dole. Once you reach Dole, you need to find the D7, so following signs to Poligny, then Pontarlier, should get you in the right area. Once you're on the D7, it runs to Arc-et-Senans. All told you'll cover about 165km.

---

6 Arc-et-Senans

Hidden among the verdant plateaus of the Jura mountains, the village of Arc-et-Senans conceals one of France's

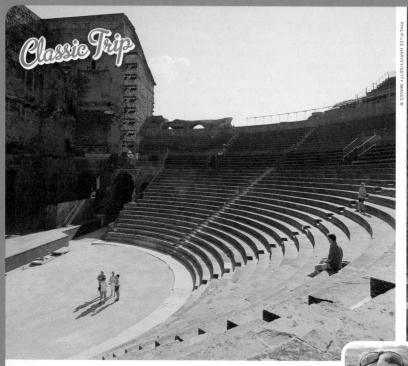

Classic Trip

WHY THIS IS A CLASSIC TRIP
OLIVER BERRY, AUTHOR

Following the Unesco trail across France provides a great introduction to the country's history and landscapes, and also makes sure you'll tick off some of the most important sights along the way. We've picked out a mix of the essential and the esoteric in this trip but, for me, there are two experiences here that sum up everything I love about France: sipping a coffee on the banks of the Seine, and cruising down the Canal du Midi in a river barge. You'll never feel more French.

Top: Théâtre Antique, Orange
Left: Medieval festival, Provins
Right: Cathédrale Ste-Cécile, Albi

more peculiar Unesco-protected sites. This area was once the country's most important centre of salt production – a vital ingredient for preserving food in the days before refrigeration. Lying 35km west of Besançon, the 18th-century **Saline Royale** (Royal Saltworks; www.salineroyale.com, in French; adult/child €7.50/3.50; ☺9am–noon & 2–6pm) was envisaged by its designer, Claude-Nicolas Ledoux, as an 'ideal city', with workers' accommodation and industrial buildings blended into one harmonious whole. Although his urban dream was never fully realised, his semicircular salt works are one of France's finest examples of 18th-century industrial architecture, and have been a Unesco World Heritage Site since 1982.

The Drive ≫ The next stage is a long one – between 390km and 425km – depending on your route. The easiest option is also the fastest. Backtrack to Dole, and pick up the A39, A40 and A42 motorways towards Lyon. South of Lyon, you can follow the more peaceful N7 along the banks of the Rhône as it runs south into Provence and on to Orange.

- - - - - - - - - - - -

TRIP HIGHLIGHT

⑦ Orange

Provence is littered with Roman remains, but to get a sense of the majesty of Roman Gaul, you have to head to Orange's

Théâtre Antique (www. theatre-antique.com; adult/ child €8.50/6.50, 2nd child free; ⊙9am-6pm, to 4.30pm Nov-Feb) – France's answer to the Colosseum. In its heyday, this massive amphitheatre would have staged gladiatorial contests, mock battles and other large-scale spectacles for up to 10,000 spectators. It's in a remarkably good state of repair, considering it's over 2000 years old – the 37m-high stage wall is one of the best preserved anywhere in the world.

Nearby, Orange's 1st-century **Arc de Triomphe** stands on the Via Agrippa, the city's ancient thoroughfare, and commemorates various military victories in stunning stone relief.

✗ ⊫ p103

The Drive » Take the D976 southwest across the Rhône to Roquemaure, then follow signs to Avignon and the D6580. It's a varied drive of 30km that travels through classic Provençal vistas.

TRIP HIGHLIGHT

8 Avignon

When Pope Clement V abandoned Rome in 1309 to settle in Avignon, this southern city became the seat of Catholic power in Europe. Though the popes only remained

here for 70-odd years, they somehow found time to build themselves the immense **Palais des Papes** (www.palais-des-papes.com; place du Palais; adult/child €6/3; ⊙9am-8pm Jul & early–mid-Sep, to 9pm Aug, to 7pm mid-Mar–Jun & mid-Sep–Oct, to 6.30pm early–mid-Mar, to 5.45pm Nov-Feb), France's largest Gothic structure, which has been on the Unesco list since 1995.

The rooms are mostly bare these days, but the gargoyle-covered rooftop view is a wraparound wonder. The immense scale of the palace testifies to the popes' wealth; the 3m-thick walls, portcullises and watchtowers emphasise their insecurity.

Outside, the **place du Palais**, graced with a 4.5-ton golden statue of the Virgin Mary, is also included within the World Heritage Site – as is the **Pont St-Bénezet** (adult/child €4.50/3.50; ⊙9am-8pm, 9.30am-5.45pm Nov-Mar), considered by many to be France's finest medieval bridge. Combination tickets with the Palais des Papes get a €3 discount.

✗ ⊫ p103

The Drive » The Pont du Gard is 26km west via the N100 and D6100.

9 Pont du Gard

Many of Provence's Roman remains have

made it onto Unesco's radar, including this monumental aqueduct over the River Gard. It's a structure that demonstrates ancient Rome's unique combination of art, architecture and engineering, and was built to carry water from Gaul's wet interior to the dry plains of the south, where wine and crops were cultivated. You can walk across the bridge's top tier or, better still, hire a canoe to float under its mighty spans.

The Drive » The most scenic route to Albi is to follow our drive on p317 through the Parc National des Cévennes to Millau, then pick up the D999 west to Albi.

10 Albi

The provincial town of Albi earned its place on the World Heritage list in 2010 thanks to the **Cathédrale Ste-Cécile** (place Ste-Cécile; adult/child €2/free; ⊙9am-6.30pm), which looks closer to some Tolkienesque tower than a place of worship. Its fortified façade is a result of the many religious wars that marked the medieval era, particularly the persecution of the Cathars during the early 13th century. The cathedral was supposed to project the power of the medieval church, and it certainly makes a statement – it's one of the

DETOUR:
CANAL DU MIDI

Start ⑩ Albi

Stretching for 240km between Toulouse and Sète, the Canal du Midi is one of the great waterways of southern France. Completed in 1681 and classified as a World Heritage Site since 1996, the canal was designed to provide a trading route between major French ports: with the Canal de Garonne, it forms part of the 'Canal des Deux Mers' (Canal of the Two Seas), which enables boats to travel all the way from the Atlantic to the Mediterranean.

It's a work of art as much as engineering, lined with stately lime trees, puttering houseboats and gorgeous riverside towns. You can cycle along the tow-paths or, better still, hire a boat and head out onto the canal proper from towns along the canal's route – Toulouse, Agde, Béziers, Narbonne and Sète all make good bases.

It's also worth stopping at the **Musée Canal du Midi** (www.museecanaldumidi.fr; bd Pierre-Paul Riquet; adult/child €4/2; ⏱10am-7pm) in St-Ferréol, which explores the history of the waterway and the life of its chief engineer, Paul Riquet.

largest brick structures on earth.

Apart from its pretty old town, Albi's other selling point is as the birthplace of artist Henri de Toulouse-Lautrec, who depicted the bars and brothels of turn-of-the-20th-century Paris in his own inimitable style. The **Musée Toulouse-Lautrec** (www.museetoulouselautrec.net; place Ste-Cécile; adult/student €5.50/2.50; ⏱9am-6pm Jun-Sep, closed noon-2pm & all day Wed-Mon Tue Oct-Mar) has France's top collection of his works outside the Musée d'Orsay, ranging from portraits to posters.

✕ 🛏 p103

Eating & Sleeping

Paris ❶

✗ Brasserie Lipp · Brasserie €€
(☎01 45 48 53 91; 151 bd St-Germain, 6e; mains €17-24; ⏱11.45am-12.45am; Ⓜ︎St-Germain des Prés) Waiters in black waistcoats, bowties and long white aprons serve brasserie favourites such as *choucroute garnie* and *jarret de porc aux lentilles* (pork knuckle with lentils) at this celebrated wood-panelled establishment.

✗ L'AOC · Regional Cuisine €€
(☎01 43 54 22 52; www.restoaoc.com; 14 rue des Fossés St-Bernard, 5e; 2-/3-course lunch menus €21/29, mains €18-32; ⏱lunch & dinner Tue-Sat; Ⓜ︎Cardinal Lemoine) The concept here revolves around Appellation d'Origine Contrôlée (AOC) status, meaning everything has been produced according to strict guidelines within a tiny geographical area.

⌖ Hôtel Crayon · Boutique Hotel €€€
(☎01 42 36 54 19; www.hotelcrayon.com; 25 rue du Bouloi, 1e; s €129-249, d €149-299; ❄@🖳; Ⓜ︎Les Halles or Sentier) Line drawings by French artist Julie Gauthron adorn walls and doors at this creative boutique hotel. Rooms sport a different shade of each floor's chosen crayon colour.

⌖ L'Hôtel · Boutique Hotel €€€
(☎01 44 41 99 00; www.l-hotel.com; 13 rue des Beaux Arts, 6e; d €285-795; ❄@🖳🛱; Ⓜ︎St-Germain des Prés) This award-winning hotel is the stuff of Parisian legend: rock- and film-star patrons fight to sleep in room 16, where Oscar Wilde died in 1900, or in the art deco room 36 of dancer Mistinguett.

Fontainebleau ❷

✗ Côté Sud · Regional Cuisine €€
(☎01 64 22 00 33; 1 rue Montebello; lunch menu €14.50, mains €16.50-22; ⏱lunch & dinner

daily) Dishes at this welcoming bistro have a southern accent, such as *daube de sanglier* (wild boar stew). Bring your appetite.

✗ Dardonville · Patisserie €
(24 rue des Sablons; ⏱7am-1.30pm & 3.15-7.30pm Tue-Sat, 7am-1.30pm Sun) Join the queues for melt-in-your-mouth macarons and amazing breads at this exceptional patisserie and *boulangerie* (bakery).

⌖ Hôtel de Londres · Hotel €€
(☎01 64 22 20 21; www.hoteldelondres.com; 1 place Général de Gaulle; d €100-180; ❄@🖳) Classy, cosy and beautifully kept, the 16-room 'Hotel London' is charmingly furnished in reds and royal blues. The priciest rooms (eg room 5) have balconies with dreamy château views.

⌖ La Guérinière · B&B €
(☎06 13 50 50 37; balestier.gerard@wanadoo.fr; 10 rue de Montebello; d €70; @) This charming B&B provides some of the best-value accommodation in town. Owner M Balestier speaks English and has five rooms, each named after a different flower.

Vézelay ❹

⌖ Hôtel Le Compostelle · Hotel €
(☎03 86 33 28 63; www.lecompostellevezelay.com; 1 place du Champ-de-Foire; d €50-66; ⏱closed Jan–mid-Feb; 🖳) Eighteen spotless, practical rooms afford romantic views of the valley or the village.

⌖ Les Glycines · Historic Hotel €
(☎03 86 32 35 30; www.glycines-vezelay.com; rue St-Pierre; s €40, d €72-94; 🖳) A 1763 bourgeois town house built and enveloped in ancient wisteria is now a hotel that's overflowing with old-fashioned character. The 11 rooms are all named after famous artists, and solid regional fare is served in the restaurant.

Orange ⑦

✖ À la Maison
Bistro €

(☎04 90 60 98 83; 4 place des Cordeliers; menus lunch €12.50-15, dinner €25-32, mains €10-16; ⊙lunch & dinner Mon-Sat) There's no lovelier spot on a warm night than the leafy fountain courtyard at this simple bistro, which serves consistently good, honest cooking.

🛏 Hôtel Arène
Hotel €€

(☎04 90 11 40 40; www.hotel-arene.fr; place de Langes; d €88-132; P ❄ @ 🛜 🚲 🎏) With the best and biggest bathrooms in Orange, the Arène is the closest you'll get to business class. Kids love the two heated pools (one indoors, one out); parents appreciate the family-sized rooms.

Avignon ⑧

✖ Cuisine du Dimanche
Provençal €€

(☎04 90 82 99 10; www.lacuisinedudimanche. com; 31 rue Bonneterie; mains €15-25; ⊙lunch & dinner daily Jun-Sep, Tue-Sat Oct-May) Spitfire chef Marie shops every morning at Les Halles to find the freshest ingredients for her earthy flavour-packed cooking. Reserve.

✖ L'Epice and Love
Traditional French €

(☎04 90 82 45 96; 30 rue des Lices; mains €11-12; ⊙dinner Mon-Sat) Tables are cheek by jowl at this tiny bohemian restaurant – a favourite for straightforward bistro fare, stews, roasts and other French dishes. Cash only.

🛏 Hôtel Boquier
Hotel €

(☎04 90 82 34 43; www.hotel-boquier.com; 6 rue du Portail Boquier; d €50-70; ❄ 🛜) The owners' infectious enthusiasm informs this upbeat, colourful, small, central hotel; try for themed rooms Morocco or Lavender. Excellent value.

🛏 Le Limas
B&B €€

(☎04 90 14 67 19; www.le-limas-avignon.com; 51 rue du Limas; d/tr from €120/200; ❄ @) Chic B&B in an 18th-century town house straight out of *Vogue Living* – minimalist white decor complements antique fireplaces and 18th-century spiral stairs. Breakfast on the terrace is a treat, as is bubbly owner Marion.

Albi ⑩

✖ L'Epicurien
Modern French €€€

(☎05 63 53 10 70; www.restaurantlepicurien. com; 42 place Jean Jaurès; menus €19-48; ⊙Tue-Sat) The steel-grey and glass façade says it all: this establishment is a temple to contemporary French cuisine, run by Swedish chef Rikard Hult and his wife, Patricia. Presentation takes precedence over portions.

🛏 La Maison
B&B €

(☎05 63 38 17 35; www.chambre-hote-albi. com; 40 bd Andrieu; s €60-75, d €75-90; 🛜) In contrast to Albi's olde-worlde feel, this B&B is a model of modernity. The three rooms are sharp, sexy and swish. It also has a garden and parking.

🛏 La Tour Sainte Cécile
B&B €€

(☎05 81 40 51 52; www.toursaintececile.com; 14bis rue Saint Cécile; d €130-180; 🛜) Built from stout brick with its own tower (hence the name), this attractive *chambre d'hôte* (B&B) has four regal rooms stuffed with period detail. The Toulouse-Lautrec room is reached via its own spiral staircase. Rates include entry to the Toulouse-Lautrec museum.

Normandy *A dramatic view over Étretat's famous white cliffs*

Monet's Normandy

8

This eclectic trip takes art lovers on a fascinating spin around eastern Normandy. En route you'll hit the key landscapes and cities that inspired Monet, the father of impressionism.

TRIP HIGHLIGHTS

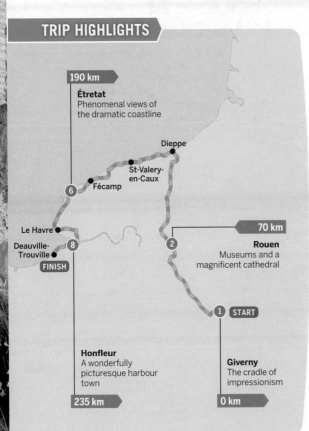

190 km

Étretat
Phenomenal views of the dramatic coastline

Dieppe

St-Valery-en-Caux

6 Fécamp

Le Havre

Deauville-Trouville

8

FINISH

70 km

2

Rouen
Museums and a magnificent cathedral

1 **START**

Honfleur
A wonderfully picturesque harbour town

235 km

Giverny
The cradle of impressionism

0 km

4 DAYS
290KM / 180 MILES

GREAT FOR...

BEST TIME TO GO

Any time from September to June for perfectly nuanced light.

ESSENTIAL PHOTO

Snap the truly extraordinary coastal vista from the cliff top in Étretat.

BEST FOR CULTURE

Rouen has plenty of top-quality museums and historic buildings.

8

Monet's Normandy

Be prepared for a visual feast on this three-day trip around the eastern part of Normandy – the cradle of impressionism. Starting from the village of Giverny, location of the most celebrated garden in France, you'll follow in the footsteps of Monet and other impressionist megastars, taking in medieval Rouen, the dramatic Côte d'Albâtre, Le Havre, Honfleur and Trouville. This is your chance to see first-hand why so many painters were attracted to this place.

TRIP HIGHLIGHT

❶ Giverny

The tiny country village of Giverny is a place of pilgrimage for devotees of impressionism. Monet lived here from 1883 until his death in 1926, in a rambling house – surrounded by flower-filled gardens – that's now the immensely popular **Maison et Jardins de Claude Monet** (☎02 32 51 28 21; www.fondation-monet.com; adult/child €9/5; ☺9.30am-5.30pm Apr-Oct). His pastel-pink

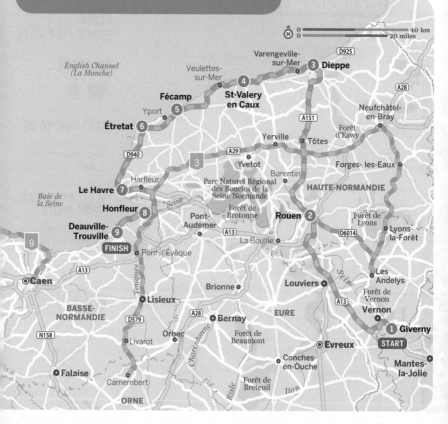

house and Water Lily studio stand on the periphery of the garden (called 'Clos Normand'), with its symmetrically laid out gardens bursting with flowers.

The Drive » It's a 70km trip (one hour) to Rouen. Head to Vernon and follow signs to Rouen along the A13. A more scenic (but longer) route is via Les Andelys, along the east bank of the Seine.

TRIP HIGHLIGHT

② Rouen

With its elegant spires and atmospheric medieval quarter complete with narrow lanes and wonky half-timbered houses, it's no wonder that Rouen has inspired numerous painters,

LINK YOUR TRIP

3 Tour des Fromages

From Honfleur or Rouen you can embark on a gastronomic drive, and taste and learn about some of the best cheese in France at various cheese museums.

9 D-Day's Beaches

From Trouville, it's an easy 50km drive west to Caen, the obvious starting point for the D-Day beaches.

including Monet. Some of his works, including one of his studies of the stunning **Gothic cathedral** (place de la Cathédrale), are displayed at the splendid **Musée des Beaux-Arts** (☎02 35 71 28 40; www.rouen-musees. com; esplanade Marcel Duchamp; adult/child €5/ free; ◷10am-6pm Wed-Mon). Feeling inspired? Sign up for an art class with the **tourist office** (☎02 32 08 32 40; www.rouentourisme. com; 25 place de la Cathédrale; ◷9am-7pm Mon-Sat, 9.30am-12.30pm & 2-6pm Sun & holidays) and create your own Rouen Cathedral canvas from the very room in which Monet painted his series of that building.

If you're at all interested in architectural glories, the 14th-century **Abbatiale St-Ouen** (place du Général de Gaulle), which is a marvellous example of the Rayonnant Gothic style, is a must-see abbey. Also don't miss **Église St-Maclou** (place Barthélémy) and the ornate **Palais de Justice** (Law Courts; rue aux Juifs) – both are typical examples of the Flamboyant Gothic style.

✗ ⛱ p111

The Drive » Follow signs to Dieppe. Count on 45 minutes for the 65km trip.

③ Dieppe

Sandwiched between limestone cliffs, Dieppe

is a small-scale fishing port with a pleasant seafront promenade. Still used by fishing vessels but dominated by pleasure craft, the **port** makes for a bracing sea-air stroll. High above the city on the western cliff, the 15th-century **Château-musée** (☎02 35 06 61 99; www.dieppe.fr; rue de Chastes; adult/child €4/2; ◷10am-noon & 2-6pm, closed Tue Oct-May) is the town's most imposing landmark. Monet immortalised **Pourville**, a seaside village on the western outskirts of Dieppe.

The Drive » Take the scenic coastal roads (D75 and D68), rather than the inland D925, via the resort towns of Pourville, Varengeville-sur-Mer, Quiberville, St-Aubin-sur-Mer, Sotteville-sur-Mer and Veules-les-Roses (35km, 45 minutes).

④ St-Valery en Caux

You're now in the heart of the scenic Côte d'Albâtre (Alabaster Coast), which stretches from Dieppe southwest to Étretat. With its lofty bone-white cliffs, this wedge of coast is a geological wonder world that has charmed a generation of impressionists, including Monet. Once you get a glimpse of sweet little St-Valery en Caux, with its delightful port, lovely stretch of stony beach and majestic cliffs, you'll see why.

⛱ p111

The Drive » Take the coastal road (D79) via Veulettes-sur-Mer. Count on an hour for the 36km trip.

⑤ Fécamp

After all that driving along the Côte d'Albâtre, it's time to stop for a glass of Bénédictine at the **Palais de la Bénédictine** (📞02 35 10 26 10; www.benedictinedom. com; 110 rue Alexandre Le Grand; adult/child €7.50/3.20; ⊙tickets sold 10am-noon & 2-5.30pm, closed Jan). Opened in 1900, this unusually ornate factory is where all the Bénédictine liqueur in the world is made.

Be sure to drive up north to **Cap Fagnet** (110m), which offers gobsmacking views of the town and the coastline.

The Drive » Follow signs to Étretat (17km, along the D940). You could also take the D940 and turn off onto the more scenic D11 (via Yport).

TRIP HIGHLIGHT
⑥ Étretat

Is Étretat the most enticing town in Normandy? It's picture postcard everywhere you look. The dramatic white cliffs that bookend the town, the **Falaise d'Aval** to the southwest and the **Falaise d'Amont** to the northeast, will stick in your memory. Once at the top, you'll pinch yourself to see if it's real – the views are sensational.

Such irresistible scenery made Étretat a favourite of painters, especially Monet, who produced more than 80 canvases of the scenery here.

The Drive » Follow signs to Le Havre (28km, along the D940 and the D147). Count on about half an hour for the journey.

⑦ Le Havre

It was in Le Havre that Monet painted the defining impressionist view. His 1873 canvas of the harbour at dawn was entitled *Impression: Sunrise*. Monet wouldn't recognise present-day Le Havre. All but obliterated in September 1944 by Allied bombing raids, the city centre was totally rebuilt after the war by Belgian architect Auguste Perret. Make sure you visit the fantastic **Musée d'Art Moderne André Malraux** (📞02 35 19 62 62; 2 bd Clemenceau; adult/child €5/free; ⊙11am-6pm Mon-Fri, to 7pm Sat & Sun), which houses a truly fabulous collection of impressionist works – the finest in France outside of Paris, with canvases by Monet, Eugène Boudin, Camille Corot and many more. Then head to the fashionable seaside suburb of **Ste-Adresse**, just north of the centre – another favourite retreat for Monet.

✕ 🛏 p111

GETTY IMAGES ©

Honfleur Harbourside reflection of the town

CLAUDE MONET

The undisputed leader of the impressionists, Claude Monet was born in Paris in 1840 and grew up in Le Havre, where he found an early affinity with the outdoors.

From 1867 Monet's distinctive style began to emerge, focusing on the effects of light and colour and using the quick, undisguised broken brushstrokes that would characterise the impressionist period. His contemporaries were Pissarro, Renoir, Sisley, Cézanne and Degas. The young painters left the studio to work outdoors, experimenting with the shades and hues of nature, and arguing and sharing ideas. Their work was far from welcomed by critics; one of them condemned it as 'impressionism', in reference to Monet's *Impression: Sunrise* when exhibited in 1874.

From the late 1870s Monet concentrated on painting in series, seeking to recreate a landscape by showing its transformation under different conditions of light and atmosphere. In 1883 Monet moved to Giverny, planting his property with a variety of flowers around an artificial pond, the Jardin d'Eau, in order to paint the subtle effects of sunlight on natural forms. It was here that he painted the *Nymphéas* (Water Lilies) series.

For more info on Monet and his work, visit www.giverny.org.

The Drive » Follow signs to Pont de Normandie, which links Le Havre to Honfleur (toll €5.50).

TRIP HIGHLIGHT

8 Honfleur

Honfleur is exquisite to look at. (No, you're not dreaming!) Its heart is the amazingly picturesque **Vieux Bassin** (Old Harbour), from where explorers once set sail for the New World. Marvel at the extraordinary 15th-century wooden **Église Ste-Catherine** (place Ste-Catherine; ⊙9am-6pm), complete with a roof that from the inside resembles an upturned boat, then wander the warren of flower-filled cobbled streets lined with wooden and stone buildings.

Honfleur's graceful beauty has inspired numerous painters, including Eugène Boudin, an early impressionist painter born here in 1824, and Monet. Their works are displayed at the **Musée Eugène Boudin** (☏02 31 89 54 00; www.musees-honfleur.fr; 50 rue de l'Homme de Bois; adult/child €5.80/4.30; ⊙10am-noon & 2-6pm Wed-Mon mid-Mar–Sep, 10am-noon & 2.30-5.30pm Mon & Wed-Fri Oct–mid-Mar).

✕ ⌂ p111

The Drive » From Honfleur it's a 14km trip to Trouville along the D513 (about 20 minutes).

9 Deauville-Trouville

Finish your impressionist road trip in style by heading southwest to the twin seaside resorts of Deauville and Trouville, which are only separated by a bridge but maintain distinctly different personalities. Exclusive, expensive and brash, Deauville is packed with designer boutiques, deluxe hotels and public gardens of impossible neatness, and is home to two racetracks and a high-profile American film festival.

Trouville, another veteran beach resort, is more down to earth. During the 19th century the town was frequented by writers and painters, including Monet, who spent his honeymoon here in 1870. No doubt he was lured by the picturesque port, the 2km-long sandy beach lined with opulent villas and the laid-back seaside ambience.

Eating & Sleeping

Rouen ②

✖ Les Nymphéas Traditional French €€

(☎02 35 89 26 69; www.lesnympheas-rouen.
com; 7-9 rue de la Pie; mains €29-37, menus €34-
52; ⊙lunch & dinner Tue-Sat) Its formal table
settings arrayed under 16th-century beams,
this fine restaurant serves cuisine based on
fresh ingredients. Let chef Patrick Kukurudz and
his team seduce you with meat and fish dishes
accompanied with divinely inspired sauces.

⊨ Hôtel de Bourgtheroulde Hotel €€€

(☎02 35 14 50 50; www.hotelsparouen.com; 15
place de la Pucelle; r €240-380; ⊠ ❄ 🛜 🏊)
This stunning conversion of an old private
mansion is a showstopper. There's a pool (you
can see through the lobby bar's glass floor down
into it), a sauna and a spa in the basement, two
restaurants and a sleek lobby bar.

St-Valery en Caux ④

⊨ La Maison des Galets Hotel €

(☎02 35 97 11 22; www.lamaisondesgalets.com;
22 cours Le Perrey; s €53, d €65-80, restaurant
mains €15-18, menus €19-35; ⊙restaurant
lunch & dinner Fri-Tue; 🛜) This solid two-starrer
on the seafront is an excellent bet. Most of
the rooms have had a modern-day refit and
feature squeaky-clean bathrooms. The on-site
restaurant is well worth considering for its
meaty dishes and seafood.

Le Havre ⑦

✖ La Petite Auberge Traditional French €€

(☎02 35 46 27 32; www.lapetiteauberge-lehavre.
fr; 32 rue de Ste Adresse; mains €13-25, menus
€20-40; ⊙lunch & dinner Tue & Thu-Sat, dinner
Wed, lunch Sun) This gem of a place is possibly
Le Havre's most charming dining option, with
a low-beamed dining room that whispers of
romance. Seafood dominates the inventive yet
traditional menu, but there's plenty of room for
meaty dishes, too.

⊨ Hôtel Vent d'Ouest Boutique Hotel €€

(☎02 35 42 50 69; www.ventdouest.fr; 4 rue
de Caligny; d €110-170, q €184; ⊠ 🛜) This
stylish establishment is decorated in maritime
fashion, with nautical memorabilia downstairs
and a range of posh cream-walled, sisal-floored
rooms upstairs. Facilities include a restaurant, a
tearoom and a sparkling spa.

Honfleur ⑧

✖ Le Bréard Gastronomic €€€

(☎02 31 89 53 40; www.restaurant-lebreard.
com; 7 rue du Puits; menus €29-55; ⊙lunch &
dinner Wed-Sun) Le Bréard is *the* place to go
in Honfleur for *gastronomique* specialities of
the highest order. Served in two chic, modern
dining rooms.

⊨ La Maison de Lucie Boutique Hotel €€€

(☎02 31 14 40 40; www.lamaisondelucie.com;
44 rue des Capucins; d €150-200, ste €250-315;
⊠ 🛜) This marvellous little hideaway has
just 10 rooms and two suites. Some of the
bedrooms, panelled in oak, have Moroccan-tile
bathrooms and boast fantastic views across
the harbour. There's a chic Jacuzzi in the old
brick-vaulted cellar.

Normandy American Cemetery & Memorial *A place to remember*

Classic Trip

D-Day's Beaches

9

Explore the events of D-Day, when Allied troops stormed ashore to liberate Europe from Nazi occupation. From war museums to landing beaches, it's a fascinating and sobering experience.

TRIP HIGHLIGHTS

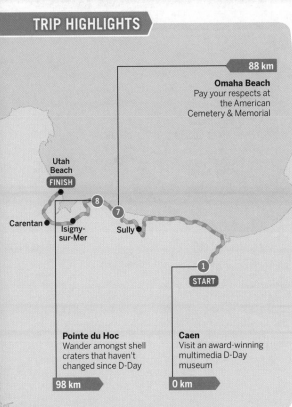

88 km

Omaha Beach
Pay your respects at the American Cemetery & Memorial

Utah Beach
FINISH

8

7

Carentan

Isigny-sur-Mer

Sully

1

START

Pointe du Hoc
Wander amongst shell craters that haven't changed since D-Day

98 km

Caen
Visit an award-winning multimedia D-Day museum

0 km

3 DAYS
142KM / 88 MILES

GREAT FOR...

BEST TIME TO GO
April to July, to avoid summer-holiday traffic around the beaches.

ESSENTIAL PHOTO
Standing next to the German guns at Longues-sur-Mer.

BEST FOR HISTORY
The Caen Mémorial provides you with a comprehensive D-Day overview.

113

9 D-Day's Beaches

The beaches and bluffs are quiet today, but on 6 June 1944 the Normandy shoreline witnessed the arrival of the largest armada the world has ever seen. This patch of the French coast will forever be synonymous with D-Day (known to the French as Jour-J), and the coastline is strewn with memorials, museums and cemeteries – reminders that though victory was won on the Longest Day, it came at a terrible price.

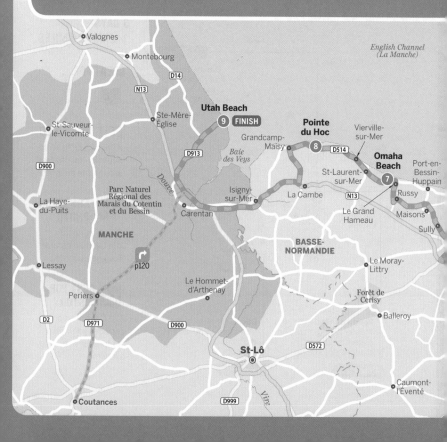

TRIP HIGHLIGHT

❶ Caen

Situated 3km northwest of Caen, the award-winning **Mémorial – Un Musée pour la Paix** (Memorial – A Museum for Peace; ☎02 31 06 06 45; www.memorial-caen.fr; esplanade Général Eisenhower; adult/child €18.80/16.30; ⏰9am-6.30pm, closed Jan & Mon mid-Nov–mid-Dec) is a brilliant place to begin with some background on the historic events of D-Day, and the wider context of WWII. Housed in a purpose-designed building covering 14,000 sq metres, it's an immersive experience, using sound, lighting, film, animation and audio testimony to evoke the grim realities of war, the trials of occupation and the joy of liberation.

The visit begins with a whistle-stop overview of Europe's descent into total war, tracing events from the end of WWI through to the rise of fascism in Europe, the German occupation of France and the Battle of Normandy. A second section focuses on the Cold War. There's also an underground gallery dedicated to winners of the Nobel Peace Prize, located in bunkers used by the Germans in 1944.

On your way round, look out for an original Typhoon fighter plane and a full-size Sherman tank.

✕ 🛏 p121

The Drive » From the museum, head northeast along Esplanade Brillaud de Laujardière, and follow signs to Ouistreham. You'll join the E46 ring road; follow it to exit 3a (Porte d'Angleterre), and merge onto the D515 and D84 to Ouistreham. Park on the seafront on bd Aristide Briand. In all it's a trip of 18km.

❷ Ouistreham

On D-Day, the sandy seafront around Ouistreham was code named **Sword Beach**

LINK YOUR TRIP

1 Essential France
The island abbey of Mont St-Michel is about 140km from the Normandy coastline, about two hours' drive via the A84 motorway.

8 Monet's Normandy
From the end of our Monet-themed trip at Fécamp, drive southwest on the A29 and A13 to Caen, a journey of just under 130km.

Classic Trip

and was the focus of attack for the British 3rd Infantry Division.

There are precious few reminders of the battle now, but on D-Day the scene was very different: most of the surrounding buildings had been levelled by artillery fire, and German bunkers and artillery positions were strung out along the seafront. Sword Beach was the site of some of the most famous images of D-Day – including the infamous ones of British troops landing with bicycles, and bagpiper Bill Millin piping troops ashore while under heavy fire.

The Drive » Follow the seafront west onto rue de Lion, following signs for 'Overlord – L'Assaut' onto the D514 towards Courseulles-sur-Mer, 18km west. Drive through town onto rue de Ver, and follow signs to 'Centre Juno Beach'.

----

❸ Juno & Gold Beaches

On D-Day, Courseulles-sur-Mer was known as **Juno Beach**, and was stormed mainly by Canadian troops. It was here that the exiled French General Charles de Gaulle came ashore after the landings – the first 'official' French soldier

D-DAY DRIVING ROUTES

There are several signposted driving routes around the main battle sites – look for signs for 'D-Day-Le Choc' in the American sectors and 'Overlord – L'Assaut' in the British and Canadian sectors. A free booklet called *The D-Day Landings and the Battle of Normandy,* available from tourist offices, has details on the eight main routes.

Maps of the D-Day beaches are available at *tabacs* (tobacconists), newsagents and bookshops in Bayeux and elsewhere.

to set foot in mainland Europe since 1940. He was followed by Winston Churchill on 12 June and King George VI on 16 June. A Cross of Lorraine marks the historic spot.

The area's only Canadian museum, **Centre Juno Beach** (📞02 31 37 32 17; www.junobeach.org; adult/child €6.50/5; ⏱9.30am-7pm Apr-Sep) has exhibits on Canada's role in the war effort and the landings, and offers guided tours of Juno Beach (€5) from April to October.

A short way west is **Gold Beach**, attacked by the British 50th Infantry on D-Day.

The Drive » Drive west along the D514 for 14km to Arromanches. You'll pass a car-park and viewpoint marked with a statue of the Virgin Mary, which overlooks Port Winston and Gold Beach. Follow the road into town and signs to Musée du Débarquement.

----

❹ Arromanches

This seaside town was the site of one of the great logistical achievements of D-Day. In order to unload the vast quantities of cargo needed by the invasion forces without capturing one of the heavily defended Channel ports, the Allies set up prefabricated marinas off two landing beaches, code named **Mulberry Harbour**. These consisted of 146 massive cement caissons towed over from England and sunk to form a semicircular breakwater in which floating bridge spans were moored. In the three months after D-Day, the Mulberries facilitated the unloading of a mind-boggling 2.5 million men, four million tonnes of equipment and 500,000 vehicles.

At low tide, the stanchions of one of these artificial quays, **Port Winston** (named after Churchill), can still be seen on the sands at Arromanches.

Beside the beach, the **Musée du Débarquement**

(Landing Museum; 📞02 31 22 34 31; www.normandy1944.com; place du 6 Juin; adult/child €7/5; ⏰9am-6pm, closed Jan) explains the logistics and importance of Port Winston.

The Drive ❯❯ Continue west along the D514 for 6km to the village of Longues-sur-Mer. You'll see the sign for the Batterie de Longues on your right.

- - - - - - - - - - - - -

⑤ Longues-sur-Mer

At Longues-sur-Mer you can get a glimpse of the awesome firepower available to the German defenders in the shape of two 150mm artillery guns, still housed in their concrete casements. On D-Day they were capable of hitting targets over 20km away – including Gold Beach (to the east) and Omaha Beach (to the west). Parts of the classic D-Day film, *The Longest Day* (1962), were filmed here.

The Drive ❯❯ Backtrack to the crossroads and head straight over onto the D104, signed to Vaux-sur-Aure/Bayeux for 8km. When you reach town, turn right onto the D613, and follow signs to the 'Musée de la Bataille de Normandie'.

- - - - - - - - - - - - -

⑥ Bayeux

Though best known for its medieval tapestry (see p43), Bayeux has another claim to fame: it was the first town to be liberated after D-Day (on the morning of 7 June 1944).

It's also home to the largest of Normandy's 18 Commonwealth military cemeteries – the **Bayeux War Cemetery**, situated on bd Fabien Ware. It contains 4848 graves of soldiers from the UK and 10 other countries – including

Germany. Across the road is a memorial for 1807 Commonwealth soldiers whose remains were never found. The Latin inscription reads: 'We, whom William once conquered, have now set free the conqueror's native land'.

Nearby, the **Musée Mémorial de la Bataille de Normandie** (Battle of Normandy Memorial Museum; bd Fabien Ware; adult/child €7/3.80; ⏰9.30am-6.30pm May-Sep, 10am-12.30pm & 2-6pm Oct-Apr) explores the battle through photos, personal accounts, dioramas and film.

🍴 🛏 p121

The Drive ❯❯ After overnighting in Bayeux, head northwest of town on the D6 towards Port-en-Bessin-Huppain. You'll reach a Super-U supermarket after about 10km. Go round the roundabout and turn onto the D514 for another 8km. You'll see signs to the

D-DAY IN FIGURES

Code named 'Operation Overlord', the D-Day landings were the largest military operation in history. On the morning of 6 June 1944, swarms of landing craft – part of an armada of over 6000 ships and 13,000 aeroplanes – hit the northern Normandy beaches, and tens of thousands of soldiers from the USA, the UK, Canada and elsewhere began pouring onto French soil. The initial landing force involved some 45,000 troops; 15 more divisions were to follow once successful beachheads had been established.

The majority of the 135,000 Allied troops stormed ashore along 80km of beaches north of Bayeux code named (from west to east) Utah, Omaha, Gold, Juno and Sword. The landings were followed by the 76-day Battle of Normandy, during which the Allies suffered 210,000 casualties, including 37,000 troops killed. German casualties are believed to have been around 200,000; another 200,000 German soldiers were taken prisoner. About 14,000 French civilians also died.

For more background and statistics, see www.normandiememoire.com and www.6juin1944.com.

PAUL THOMPSON/GETTY IMAGES ©

MATTES RENAC/HEMIS.FR/GETTY IMAGES ©

WHY THIS IS A CLASSIC TRIP
OLIVER BERRY, AUTHOR

You'll have heard the D-Day story many times before, but there's nothing quite like standing on the beaches where this epic struggle played out. D-Day marked the turning point of WWII and heralded the end for Nazism in Europe. Paying your respects to the soldiers who laid down their lives in the name of freedom is an experience that'll stay with you forever.

Top: Arromanches and Gold Beach
Left: Normandy American Cemetery & Memorial
Right: Pointe du Hoc

'Cimetière Americain' near the hamlet of Le Bray. Omaha Beach is another 4km further on, near Vierville-sur-Mer.

- - - - - - - - - - - - - - -

TRIP HIGHLIGHT

7 Omaha Beach

If anywhere symbolises the courage and sacrifice of D-Day, it's Omaha – still known as 'Bloody Omaha' to US veterans. It was here, on the 7km stretch of coastline between Vierville-sur-Mer, St-Laurent-sur-Mer and Colleville-sur-Mer, that the most brutal fighting on D-Day took place. US troops had to fight their way across the beach towards the heavily defended cliffs, exposed to underwater obstacles, hidden minefields and withering crossfire. The toll was heavy: of the 2500 casualties at Omaha on D-Day, over 1000 were killed, most within the first hour of the landings.

High on the bluffs above Omaha, the **Normandy American Cemetery & Memorial** (www.abmc.gov; Colleville-sur-Mer; ☺9am-5pm) provides a sobering reminder of the human cost of the battle. Featured in the opening scenes of *Saving Private Ryan,* this is the largest American cemetery in Europe, containing the graves of 9387 American soldiers, and a memorial to 1557 comrades 'known only unto God'.

White marble crosses and stars of David stretch off in seemingly endless rows, surrounded by an immaculately tended expanse of lawn. The cemetery is overlooked by a large colonnaded memorial, centred on a statue dedicated to the spirit of American youth. Nearby is a reflective pond and a small chapel.

The Drive » From the Vierville-sur-Mer seafront, follow the rural D514 through quiet countryside towards Grandcamp-Maisy. After about 10km you'll see signs to 'Pointe du Hoc'.

TRIP HIGHLIGHT

8 Pointe du Hoc

West of Omaha, this craggy promontory was the site of D-Day's most audacious military exploit. At 7.10am, 225 US Army Rangers commanded by Lt Col James Earl Rudder scaled the sheer 30m cliffs, where the Germans had stationed a battery of artillery guns trained onto the beaches of Utah and Omaha. Unfortunately, the guns had already been moved inland, and Rudder and his men spent the next two days repelling

DETOUR: COUTANCES

Start 9 Utah Beach

The lovely old Norman town of **Coutances** makes a good detour when travelling between the D-Day beaches and Mont St-Michel. At the town's heart is its Gothic **Cathédrale de Coutances** (parvis Notre-Dame; admission free; 9am-7pm). Interior highlights include several 13th-century windows, a 14th-century fresco of St Michael skewering the dragon, and an organ and high altar from the mid-1700s. You can climb the lantern tower on a **tour** (adult/child €7/4; in French 11am & 3pm Mon-Fri, 3pm Sun Jul & Aug).

Coutances is about 50km south of Utah Beach by the most direct route.

counterattacks. By the time they were finally relieved on 8 June, 81 of the rangers had been killed and 58 more had been wounded.

Today the **site** (02 31 51 90 70; admission free; 9am-5pm), which France turned over to the US government in 1979, looks much as it did on D-Day, complete with shell craters and crumbling gun emplacements.

The Drive » Stay on the D514 to Grandcamp-Maisy, then continue south onto the D13 dual carriageway. Stay on the road till you reach the turn-off for the D913, signed to St-Marie-du-Mont/Utah Beach. It's a drive of 44km.

9 Utah Beach

The D-Day tour ends at St-Marie-du-Mont, aka

Utah Beach, assaulted by soldiers of the US 4th and 8th Infantry Divisions. The beach was relatively lightly defended, and by midday the landing force had linked with paratroopers from the 101st Airborne. By nightfall, some 20,000 men and 1700 vehicles had arrived on French soil, and the road to European liberation had begun.

Today the site is marked by military memorials and the **Musée du Débarquement** (Landing Museum; 02 33 71 53 35; www.utah-beach. com; Ste-Marie du Mont; adult/child €7.50/3; 9.30am-7pm) inside the former German command post.

Eating & Sleeping

Caen ❶

✕ A Contre Sens — Modern French €€

(📞02 31 97 44 48; www.acontresenscaen.fr;
8 rue Croisiers; mains €28-32, menus €22-48;
🕐lunch Wed-Sat, dinner Tue-Sat) Under the
helm of young chef Anthony Caillot, meals are
thoughtfully crafted and superbly presented.
Given its quality, A Contre Sens is remarkably
good value, especially at lunchtime.

✕ Le Bouchon du Vaugueux — Norman €€

(📞02 31 44 26 26; www.bouchonduvaugueux.
com; 4 rue Graindorge; menus €15-28; 🕐lunch
& dinner Tue-Sat) Caen's most popular and
buzzing restaurant. You may well be the only
foreigner here, so don't expect a translation of
the chalkboard menu – but if your French is up
to it, you'll enjoy modern Norman cooking and
well-priced wines. Book ahead.

🛏 Hôtel des Quatrans — Hotel €€

(📞02 31 86 25 57; www.hotel-des-quatrans.
com; 17 rue Gémare; s €68-81, d €80-95; 📶) The
outside might look like a set of concrete boxes,
but inside this typically modern hotel you'll find
a surprising range of comfy, unfussy rooms,
handy for exploring the city centre.

🛏 La Maison de Famille — B&B €€

(📞06 61 64 88 54; www.maisondefamille.sitew.
com; 4 rue Elie de Beaumont; d €70-90, q €105-
130; 🅿📶) A divine four-room town house B&B.
Each room has personality: Baldaquin has a
romantic four-poster bed, wooden floors and an
old fireplace, while families plump for spacious
Sous Les Toits ('Under the Roof') or garden-side
Suite Jardin. Private parking is a bonus.

Bayeux ❻

✕ La Rapière — Norman €€

(📞02 31 21 05 45; 53 rue St-Jean; menus €15-34;
🕐lunch & dinner Fri-Tue) Housed in a late-1400s
mansion, this beamed restaurant specialises
in Normandy staples such as terrine, duck, and
veal with Camembert. Four fixed-price menus
assure a splendid meal on any budget.

✕ Le Pommier — Norman €€

(📞02 31 21 52 10; www.restaurantlepommier.
com; 38-40 rue des Cuisiniers; menus €15-30;
🕐closed Sun Nov-Mar & mid-Dec–mid-Jan, lunch
& dinner daily Apr-Oct, Mon-Sat Nov–mid-Dec &
mid-Jan–Mar, closed mid-Dec–mid-Jan; 🖋) A
celebration of all things Norman, Le Pommier's
menus include such classics as Caen-style tripe
and steamed pollock. A vegetarian menu – a
rarity in Normandy – is also available.

🛏 Les Logis du Rempart — B&B €

(📞02 31 92 50 40; www.lecornu.fr; 4 rue
Bourbesneur; d €60-80, q €130; 📶) This
three-room maison de famille (guesthouse)
oozes old-fashioned cosiness. Our favourite, the
Bajocasse, has a parquet floor and Toile de Jouy
wallpaper. There's a tasting shop downstairs
that sells homemade Calvados and cider, and
breakfast features organic apple juice and
apple jelly.

🛏 Villa Lara — Boutique Hotel €€€

(📞02 31 92 00 55; www.hotel-villalara.com;
6 place de Québec; d €180-280, ste €290-450;
🅿❄📶) Clean lines, trendy colour schemes
and minimalist motifs distinguish this new
boutique hotel, which also has a bistro and a
gym. The best rooms are blessed with views of
the cathedral.

St-Malo *A genteel walled town hemmed by pretty beaches*

Breton Coast

10

On this maritime-flavoured drive you'll experience serene seaside towns, sparkling beaches, dramatic storm-lashed headlands and the world's greatest concentration of megalithic sites.

TRIP HIGHLIGHTS

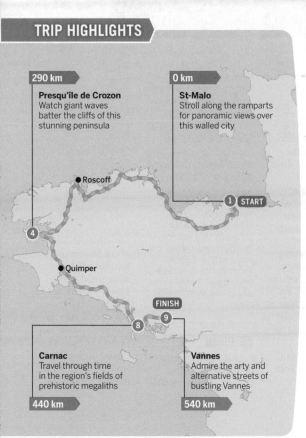

290 km

Presqu'île de Crozon
Watch giant waves batter the cliffs of this stunning peninsula

0 km

St-Malo
Stroll along the ramparts for panoramic views over this walled city

● Roscoff

1 START

4

● Quimper

FINISH

9

8

Carnac
Travel through time in the region's fields of prehistoric megaliths

440 km

Vannes
Admire the arty and alternative streets of bustling Vannes

540 km

---

8 DAYS
540KM / 336 MILES

GREAT FOR...

BEST TIME TO GO

April and May *can* see fine sunny weather and no crowds.

ESSENTIAL PHOTO

Standing on the precipice of the cliffs of Pointe de Pen-Hir.

BEST FOR FAMILIES

Splashing about on the beaches of Concarneau or Carnac.

123

10 | Breton Coast

This is a trip for explorers who want to experience a very different slice of French life. Instead of the Eiffel Tower, fine wine and sun-soaked beaches, you'll take in a drama-filled coastline, medieval towns, prehistoric mysticism and a proud Celtic streak.

Ploudalmezeau •   Lesneven •
Le Folgoët •
Landernea
St-Renan •   Brest •
Camaret-sur-Mer •   Plougastel-Daoulas •
Presqu'île ④   • Le Fao
de Crozon • Morgat
Baie de Douarnenez   Châteaulin •
Douarnenez •
Audierne •
Quimper ⑤
Ploneour-Lanvern •   Benode
Pont-l'Abbé •

ATLANTIC OCEAN

TRIP HIGHLIGHT

❶ St-Malo

Once renowned for being a haven for pirates and adventurers, the enthralling walled town of St-Malo is today a genteel mast-filled port hemmed by pretty beaches and guarded by an array of offshore islands. The walled quarter of **Intra Muros** is arguably the most interesting urban centre in Brittany, but it's not as old as it appears. Most of the town was flattened in WWII and has since been lovingly rebuilt.

Beyond the walls of Intra Muros is the **Fort de la Cité**, which was used as a German base during WWII. One of the bunkers now houses the **Mémorial 39-45** (☎02 99 82 41 74; adult/child €6/3; ⊗ guided visits 10.15am, 11am, 2pm, 3pm, 4pm & 5pm), which depicts St-Malo's violent WWII history.

✕ 🛏 p129

The Drive » The 33km, half-hour drive along the N136 between St-Malo and Dinan is through a largely built-up area and offers little of interest. Be warned that this road, like most others around St-Malo, can be subject to heavy traffic and delays.

---

❷ Dinan

Set high above the fast-flowing River Rance, Dinan's old town is like something straight out of the Middle Ages, with narrow cobblestoned streets and squares lined with crooked half-timbered houses. The appeal isn't lost on summer visitors, but by around 6pm it's as though someone has waved a magic wand: most of the deluge

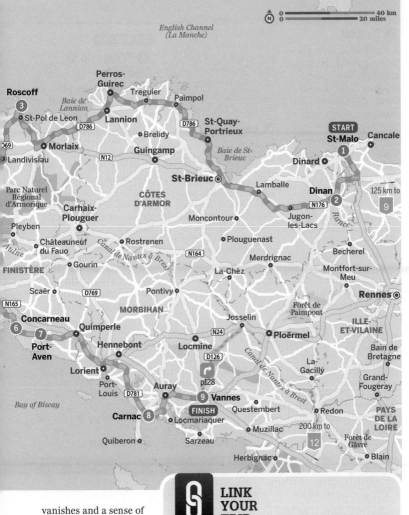

vanishes and a sense of
calm falls over the town.

The Drive » If time allows,
take the wiggly, and very slow
(count on a 3½-hour drive)
coastal D786 between Dinan
and Roscoff. Highlights include
the pretty port of Paimpol and
the breathtaking Côte de Granit
Rose, which extends either side
of the town of Perros-Guirec.
This leg is 209km.

LINK YOUR TRIP

9 D-Day's Beaches

Combining a drive
around the Breton coast
with the war memorials
of Normandy is easy.
Caen is 174km along the
A84 from St-Malo.

12 Caves & Cellars of the Loire

From Vannes it's 264km
to Montsoreau, where
you can pick up our tour
of the Western Loire's
cave dwellings and wine
cellars.

③ Roscoff

Set around an arcing harbour studded with granite cottages and seafront villas, Roscoff is one of the more captivating cross-channel ferry ports.

After you've explored the town, set sail for the peaceful **Île de Batz**, which sits a short way offshore. The mild island climate supports the luxuriant **Jardins Georges Delaselle** (☎02 98 61 75 65; www.jardin -georgesdelaselle.fr; adult/child €5/2.50; ☺1-6.30pm Jul & Aug, 2-6pm Wed-Mon Apr-Oct), with over 1500 plants from all five continents.

Ferries (adult/child return €8/4, bikes €8, 15 minutes each way) between Roscoff and Île de Batz run every 30 minutes in July and August; less frequently the rest of the year.

✕ 🛏 p129

The Drive ≫ Taking the D69, D18 and D791, allow one hour and 40 minutes to drive the 86km between Roscoff and Crozon, the main town on the Presqu'île de Crozon. The route takes you through the western edge of the Parc Naturel Régional d'Armorique, a beautiful region of rocky uplands and myth-shrouded forests that blends into the Presqu'île de Crozon.

TRIP HIGHLIGHT

④ Presqu'île de Crozon

With long sweeps of golden sand, silent loch-like estuaries bordered by dense forest, pretty rocky coves lapped by azure waters, and huge cliffs hammered by slate-grey Atlantic swells, the anchor-shaped Crozon Peninsula is without doubt one of the most scenic spots in Brittany.

At the western extremity of the peninsula, **Camaret-sur-Mer** is a classic fishing village that lures artists. Three kilometres south

---

MIGHTY MEGALITHS

Two perplexing questions arise from the region's Neolithic menhirs, dolmens, cromlechs, tumuli and cairns. Just *how* did the original constructors hew, then haul these blocks (the heaviest weighs 300 tonnes), millennia before the wheel and the mechanical engine reached Brittany? And *why*?

Theories and hypotheses abound, but the vague yet common consensus is that they served some kind of sacred purpose.

Sign up for a one-hour guided visit at the **Maison des Mégalithes** (☎02 97 52 29 81; rte des Alignements; tours adult/child €6/free; ☺10am-8pm Jul & Aug, to 5.15pm Sep-Apr, to 7pm May & Jun). Tour times vary considerably depending on the time of year, but they run regularly in French in summer and at least once or twice a day at other times. English tours are usually held at 3pm Wednesday, Thursday and Friday from early July to late August. Because of severe erosion, the sites are fenced off to allow the vegetation to regenerate. However, between 9am and 5pm from October to March you can wander freely through some parts.

Opposite the Maison des Mégalithes, the largest menhir field – with 1099 stones – is the **Alignements du Ménec**, 1km north of Carnac-Ville; the eastern section is accessible in winter. From here, the D196 heads northeast for about 1.5km to the equally impressive **Alignements de Kermario** (which is open year-round). Climb the stone observation tower midway along the site to see the alignment from above.

For some background, the **Musée de Préhistoire** (☎02 97 52 22 04; www. museedecarnac.fr; 10 place de la Chapelle, Carnac-Ville; adult/child €5/2.50; ☺10am-6pm) will do very nicely.

Roscoff

of the village is the spectacular **Pointe de Pen-Hir** headland.

Nearby **Morgat** is one of the prettier resorts in this part of Brittany, with colourful houses piled up at one end of a long sandy beach.

 p129

The Drive » Using the D63 it's just 55km from Crozon, the main town on the peninsula, to Quimper. Along the way you'll be rewarded with pretty views westward over the sea.

- - - - - - - - - - - -

⑤ Quimper

Small enough to feel like a village, with its slanted half-timbered houses and narrow cobbled streets, and large enough to buzz as the troubadour of Breton culture and arts, Quimper is the Finistère region's thriving capital.

At the centre of the city is the **Cathedral St-Corentin** (☺8.30am-noon & 1.30-6.30pm Mon-Sat, 8.30am-noon & 2-6.30pm Sun), with its distinctive kink, said to symbolise Christ's inclined head as he was dying on the cross. Beside the cathedral, the superb **Musée Départemental Breton** (☎02 98 95 21 60; 1 rue du Roi Gradlon; adult/child €4/free; ☺9am-6pm) showcases Breton history, furniture, costumes, crafts and archaeology.

The Drive » Rather than taking the faster N165 between Quimper and Concarneau, meander along the more scenic D783. Even on this slower road you only need 30 minutes to travel the 22km between the two towns.

- - - - - - - - - - - -

⑥ Concarneau

The sheltered harbour of Concarneau is one of the busiest fishing ports in Brittany and is a hugely popular summer-holiday destination. In the middle of the harbour is the old quarter of the

Ville Close, encircled by medieval walls and crammed with enchanting old stone houses.

Surrounding the town are numerous highly attractive **beaches** and coves, which are sheltered from the anger of the Atlantic and are ideal for families.

The Drive » Cross the scenic River Moros on the D783 and trundle for 16km (30 minutes) through rural scenery to Port-Aven.

❼ Port-Aven

The tiny village of Pont-Aven, nestled in the 'valley of willows', is a delightful place to break your journey eastward. Long ago discovered by artists, it's brimming with galleries. For an

insight into the town's place in art history, stop by the **Musée des Beaux-Arts de Pont-Aven** (📞02 98 06 14 43; www.museepontaven.fr; place de l'Hôtel de Ville; adult/child €4.50/free; ⏱10am-12.30pm & 2-6.30pm, closed Jan).

The Drive » From Port-Aven to Carnac it's a fast but dull one-hour (81km) drive down the N165 dual carriageway past the large industrial city of Lorient.

TRIP HIGHLIGHT

❽ Carnac

With enticing beaches and a pretty town centre, Carnac would be a popular tourist town even without its collection of magnificent **megalithic sites**, which predate Stonehenge by around 100 years. The area surrounding the town has 3000 of these

upright stones – the world's largest concentration – most around thigh-high, erected between 5000 and 3500 BC. For more information on the stones and visiting the sites, see p126.

🛏 p129

The Drive » Rather than taking the N165 to Vannes, opt for the coastal route. From Carnac head down to Carnac Plage and follow the coastal road to attractive La Trinité-sur-Mer. Join the D781 and then the D28 inland to Auray (well worth a poke around). From here join the D101, which swings into Vannes. This 40km route takes just over an hour.

TRIP HIGHLIGHT

❾ Vannes

Street art, sculptures and intriguing galleries pop up unexpectedly through the half-timbered, cobbled city of Vannes, which has a quirky, creative bent. Surrounding the walled old town is a flower-filled moat. Inside, you can weave through the web of narrow alleys ranged around the 13th-century Gothic **Cathédrale St-Pierre**.

The nearby Golfe du Morbihan is one of France's most attractive stretches of coastline. From April to September, **Navix** (📞08 25 13 21 00; www.navix.fr) runs a range of cruises (from €14.90 per person).

🛏 p129

DETOUR: JOSSELIN

Start ❾ Vannes

In the shadow of an enormous, witch's-hat-turreted 14th-century castle, the story-book village of Josselin lies on the banks of the River Oust, 43km northeast of Vannes. Place Notre Dame, a beautiful square of 16th-century half-timbered houses, is the little town's heart, but it's for the magnificent **Château de Josselin** (📞02 97 22 36 45; www.chateaujosselin.com; adult/child €8/5.20; ⏱11am-6pm mid-Jul–Aug, 2-6pm Apr–mid-Jul, 2-5.30pm Sep) that you'd really make this detour. The treasure-filled château can only be visited by guided tour.

From Vannes it's an easy one-hour drive along the D126 through an increasingly green and rural landscape of cows and forests.

Eating & Sleeping

St-Malo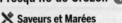

✖ Le Bistro de Jean — Bistro €

(☎ 02 99 40 98 68; 6 rue de la Corne-de-Cerf; mains €15-19, menus from €12; ☺ lunch & dinner Mon, Tue, Thu & Fri, dinner Wed & Sat) Peer through the windows of this lively and highly authentic bistro in Intra Muros and you'll find it packed at lunchtimes with loyal locals all enjoying the best bistro meals in St-Malo.

⌂ La Rance Hotel — Boutique Hotel €

(☎ 02 99 81 78 63; www.larancehotel.com; 15 quai Sébastopol; r €65-84; ☎) This is a fabulous little hotel with searing white rooms decorated with hand-painted wooden ship-communication flags. Chantal and Thierry are warm and helpful hosts, and there's a nice little garden and a charming breakfast room.

Roscoff ③

✖ L'Ecume des Jours — Regional Cuisine €€

(☎ 02 98 61 22 83; quai d'Auxerre; menus €15-55; ☺ lunch & dinner Thu-Mon Sep-Jun, Thu-Tue Jul & Aug) Regarded as the best restaurant in town, this elegant place serves magnificent and inventive local dishes that marry seafood tastes with landlubbers' delights.

⌂ Le Temps de Vivre — Boutique Hotel €€

(☎ 02 98 19 33 19; www.letempsdevivre.net; 19 place Lacaze Duthiers; d from €145; ☎) This glamorous place is hidden away in a lovely stone mansion complete with its own tower just opposite the church. With fantastic sea views from some rooms, decor that's a great blend of modernity and tradition, and friendly staff, this is one of Roscoff's very best options. There's a car park nearby.

Presqu'île de Crozon ④

✖ Saveurs et Marées — Seafood €€

(☎ 02 98 26 23 18; 52 bd Plage, Morgat; menus €14-45; ☺ lunch & dinner daily Mar-Jan) Our pick of Morgat's clutch of restaurants is this lemon-yellow cottage overlooking the sea with its breezy dining room, sunny terrace and consistently good, locally caught seafood.

Carnac ⑧

⌂ Plume au Vent — B&B €€

(☎ 06 16 98 34 79; www.plume-au-vent.com; 4 Venelle Notre Dame; d €90) This two-room *chambre d'hôte* (B&B) in the town centre is all mellow shades of blue and grey, hundreds of neatly bound books, knick-knacks discovered washed up on the high-tide line and polished-cement showers and sinks.

Vannes ⑨

⌂ Hôtel Villa Kerasy — Boutique Hotel €€

(☎ 02 97 68 36 83; www.villakerasy.com; 20 av Favrel-et-Lincy; d €141-198; ☺ closed mid-Nov–mid-Dec; P ☎) On entering this smart hotel you'll discover an exotic world of spices and far-away tropical sea ports. Rooms are individually decorated in Indian and Far Eastern styles, and the garden, crowded with Buddha statues and koi-filled ponds, is a little slice of Japan.

STRETCH YOUR LEGS
PARIS

Start Place de la Concorde

Finish Place du Panthéon

Distance 4.5km

Duration Three hours

Paris is one of the world's most strollable cities, whether that means window-shopping on the boulevards or getting lost among the lanes of Montmartre. This walk starts by the Seine, crosses to the Île de la Cité and finishes in the Latin Quarter, with monuments and museums aplenty en route.

Take this walk on Trips

Place de la Concorde

If it's Parisian vistas you're after, the place de la Concorde makes a fine start. From here you can see the Arc de Triomphe, the Assemblée Nationale (the lower house of parliament), the Jardin des Tuileries and the Seine. Laid out in 1755, the square was where many aristocrats lost their heads during the Revolution, including Louis XVI and Marie Antoinette. The obelisk in the centre originally stood in the Temple of Ramses at Thebes (now Luxor).

The Walk » Walk east through the Jardin des Tuileries.

Jardin des Tuileries

This 28-hectare landscaped **garden** (⊘7am-7.30pm, 9pm or 11pm) was laid out in 1664 by André Le Nôtre, who also created Versailles' gardens. Filled with fountains, ponds and sculptures, the gardens are now part of the Banks of the Seine World Heritage Site, created by Unesco in 1991.

The Walk » Walk across place du Carrousel onto the Cour Napoleon.

Musée du Louvre

Overlooking the Cour Napoleon is the mighty Louvre, with its controversial 21m-high glass **Grande Pyramide**, designed by IM Pei in 1989. Nearby is the **Pyramide Inversée** (Upside-Down Pyramid), which acts as a skylight for the underground Carrousel du Louvre shopping centre.

The Walk » Continue southeast along the riverside Quai du Louvre to the Pont Neuf metro station.

Pont Neuf

As you cross the Seine, you'll walk over Paris' oldest bridge – ironically known as the 'New Bridge', or Pont Neuf. Henri IV inaugurated the bridge in 1607 by crossing it on a white stallion.

The Walk » Cross the Pont Neuf onto the Île de la Cité. Walk southeast along Quai des Horloges, and then turn right onto bd du Palais.

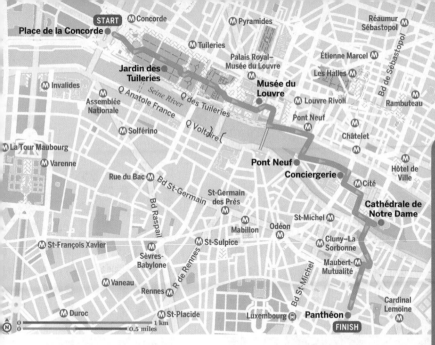

Conciergerie

On bd du Palais, the elegant **Conciergerie**
(www.monuments-nationaux.fr; 2 bd du Palais, Île de
la Cité, 1e; adult/child €8.50/free; ⏰9.30am-6pm;
ⓂCité) is a royal palace that became a
prison and torture chamber for enemies
of the Revolution. The 14th-century Salle
des Gens d'Armes (Cavalrymen's Hall) is
Europe's largest surviving medieval hall.

The nearby church of **Sainte-Chapelle**
(combined ticket with Conciergerie €12.50/free)
has stunning stained glass.

The Walk » Continue east along rue de Lutèce,
then cross place du Parvis Notre Dame and walk
towards the cathedral.

Cathédrale de Notre Dame

At the eastern end of Île de la Cité, showstopper **Notre Dame** (www.cathedraledeparis.
com; 6 place du Parvis Notre Dame, 4e; admission
free; ⏰7.45am-7pm) is the heart of Paris in
more ways than one – it's from here that
all distances in France are measured.

Built in stages between the 11th and
15th centuries, it's on a gargantuan
scale; the interior alone is 130m long,

48m wide and 35m high. Don't miss
the three rose windows, the 7800-pipe
organ and a walk up the gargoyle-
covered Gothic towers.

The Walk » Cross the river on Pont au Double
and follow rue Lagrange to bd St-Germain. Then
take rue des Carmes and rue Valette south to the
place du Panthéon.

Panthéon

Once you reach the left bank you'll be in
the Latin Quarter, the centre of Parisian
higher education since the Middle Ages,
and still home to the city's top university, the Sorbonne.

It's also where you'll find the
Panthéon (www.monum.fr; place du Panthéon;
adult/child €8.50/free; ⏰10am-6.30pm
Apr-Sep, to 6pm Oct-Mar), the neoclassical
mausoleum where some of France's
greatest thinkers are entombed, including Voltaire, Rousseau and Marie Curie.

The Walk » It's a long walk back, so it's easier
to catch the metro. Walk east to place Monge, take
Line 7 to Palais Royal Musée du Louvre, then Line 1
west to Concorde.

Loire Valley & Central France

WORLD-RENOWNED CHÂTEAUX AND FINE WINES may be the two most obvious reasons to visit central France, but they're only the tip of the iceberg. This region was also once the site of Europe's grandest volcanoes, its largest concentration of cave dwellings and some of its finest medieval architecture. When you've had your fill of château gawking and vineyard hopping, make some time for roads less travelled: wind through the Auvergne's magnificent landscape of green pastures and vestigial cinder cones; go underground to discover the Loire's ancient troglodyte culture; or spend a week exploring Burgundy's medieval churches, abbeys and walled towns.

Central France is also prime walking and cycling country; look for paths wherever you go.

Azay-le-Rideau Châteaux and moat (Trip 11)
RICCARDO SPILA/SIME/4CORNERS ©

Loire Valley & Central France

Classic Trip

11 Châteaux of the Loire 5 Days
Tour France's greatest châteaux, from austere medieval towers to exuberant royal palaces. (p137)

12 Caves & Cellars of the Loire 3 Days
Discover the Loire's subterranean world: wine cellars, cave dwellings and mushroom farms. (p147)

13 Volcanoes of the Auvergne 4 Days
Green pastures, volcanic scenery, fabulous hiking and some of France's finest cheeses. (p157)

14 Medieval Burgundy 6 Days
Search for medieval treasures in Burgundy's churches, monasteries and fortified villages. (p165)

15 Route des Grands Crus 2 Days
Sample France's most venerable vintages on this wine lover's tour of Burgundy. (p173)

DON'T MISS

Hôtel Grand St-Michel, Chambord

Wake up to sunrise over Chambord's turrets and stroll the grounds before the tour buses arrive. Stay here on Trip 11

Chapelle Ste-Radegonde, Chinon

Behind a red door in a stone wall is a cave church with 12th-century frescos. Discover it on Trips 11 12

Ancient Green Volcanoes, Auvergne

The Auvergne's three dormant volcanoes are a hiker's paradise. Climb them on Trip 13

Temptation of Eve, Musée Rolin, Autun

This startlingly sensual image is the work of 12th-century stone carver Gislebertus. See it on Trip 14

Caveau de Puligny-Montrachet

Sample some of Burgundy's extraordinary white wines without breaking the bank. Enjoy on Trip 15

Amboise Château Royal d'Amboise (Trip 11)

Villandry Château de Villandry and its glorious ornamental garden

Classic Trip

Châteaux of the Loire

11

For centuries, France's great river has been the backdrop for royal intrigue and extravagant architecture. This trip weaves together nine of the Loire Valley's most classic châteaux.

TRIP HIGHLIGHTS

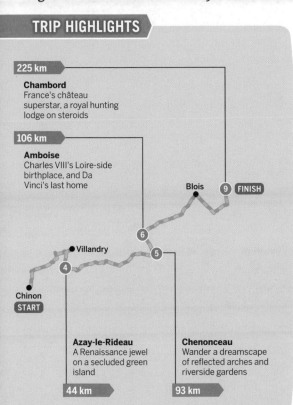

225 km

Chambord
France's château superstar, a royal hunting lodge on steroids

106 km

Amboise
Charles VIII's Loire-side birthplace, and Da Vinci's last home

● Blois **9** **FINISH**

6

● Villandry **5**

4

● Chinon
START

Azay-le-Rideau
A Renaissance jewel on a secluded green island

44 km

Chenonceau
Wander a dreamscape of reflected arches and riverside gardens

93 km

---

5 DAYS
225KM / 140 MILES

GREAT FOR...

BEST TIME TO GO

May and June for good cycling weather; July for gardens and special events.

 ESSENTIAL PHOTO

Chenonceau's graceful arches reflected in the Cher River.

BEST TWO DAYS

The stretch between Chenonceau and Chambord takes in all the classics.

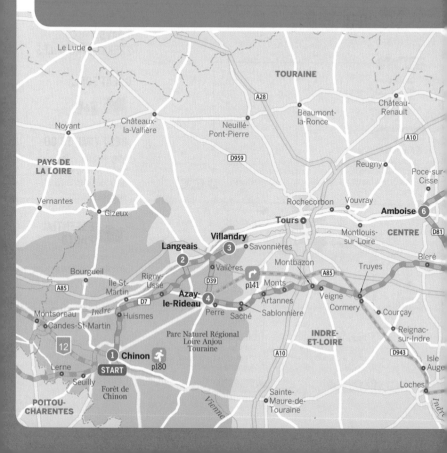

Classic Trip

11 Châteaux of the Loire

From warring medieval counts to the kings and queens of France, countless powerful figures have left their mark on the Loire Valley. The result is France's most diverse and magnificent collection of castle architecture. This itinerary visits nine of the Loire's most iconic châteaux, running the gamut from austere medieval fortresses to ostentatious royal palaces; midway through, a side trip leads off the beaten track to four lesser-known châteaux.

❶ Chinon

Tucked between its medieval fortress and the Vienne River, Chinon is a lovely place to start exploring the magnificent châteaux of central France. The town is forever etched in France's collective memory as the place where Joan of Arc first met future King Charles VII in 1429. Take in all the highlights on our walk (p180), and stay overnight to appreciate the town's relaxed pace.

🛏 p145

The Drive » Follow the D16 north of Chinon for 10km, then head 15km east on the D7 past the fairy-tale Château d'Ussé (the inspiration for *Sleeping Beauty*) to Lignières, where you catch the D57 3km north into Langeais.

❷ Langeais

Built in the 1460s to cut off the likely invasion route from Brittany, **Château de Langeais** (www.chateau-de-langeais.com; adult/child €8.50/5; ⏰9.30am-6.30pm Apr–mid-Nov, 10am-5pm mid-Nov–Mar) was designed first and foremost as

a fortress. Ironically, three decades later this was the very same château where Charles VIII married Anne of Brittany, bringing about the historic union of France and Brittany and effectively ending the threat of Breton invasion.

One of the few châteaux with its original medieval interior, the castle (reached via a creaky drawbridge) is fantastically preserved inside and out, its flag-stoned rooms filled with 15th-century furniture, its crenellated ramparts and defensive towers jutting out from the jumbled rooftops of the surrounding village.

Up top, stroll the castle's **ramparts** for a soldier's-eye view of the town: gaps underfoot enabled boiling oil, rocks and ordure to be dumped on attackers. Across the courtyard,

🔗 LINK YOUR TRIP

12 Caves & Cellars of the Loire

Tour wineries and centuries-old cave dwellings between Chinon and Saumur.

14 Medieval Burgundy

Three hours east of Blois, steep yourself in the world of Burgundy's medieval churches and abbeys.

Langeais' ruined **keep**, constructed in 992 by the granddaddy of medieval power mavens, Foulques Nerra, is the oldest such structure in France.

 p145

The Drive >> Backtrack south across the Loire on the D57, then follow the riverbank east 10km on the D16 to Villandry.

❸ Villandry

Renowned for its glorious landscaped gardens, **Château de Villandry** (www.chateauvillandry.com; château & gardens adult/child €9.50/5.50, gardens only €6.50/4; ☺9am-6pm Apr-Oct, earlier closing Nov-Mar, closed mid-Nov–Dec) was the brainchild of Jean le Breton, François I's finance minister and Italian ambassador. Today visitors can stroll pebbled walkways through 6 hectares of formal **water gardens**, a **maze**, **vineyards** and multiple themed gardens including the fabulous 16th-century **potager** (kitchen garden), where even the vegetables are laid out in regimental colour-coordinated fashion. The gardens bloom between April and October, although they're most spectacular in midsummer.

For bird's-eye views across the gardens and the nearby Loire and Cher Rivers, climb to the top of the **donjon** (keep), the only medieval remnant in this otherwise Renaissance-style château.

The Drive >> Go southwest 4km on the D7, then turn south 7km on the D39 into Azay-le-Rideau.

TRIP HIGHLIGHT

❹ Azay-le-Rideau

Romantic, moat-ringed **Azay-le-Rideau** (azay-le-rideau.monuments-nationaux.fr/en; adult/child €8.50/free; ☺9.30am-6pm Apr-Sep, 10am-5.15pm Oct-Mar) is one of France's absolute gems, wonderfully adorned with slender turrets, geometric windows and decorative stonework, all wrapped up within a shady landscaped park on a natural island in middle of the Indre River. Built in the 1500s, the château's most famous feature is its open **loggia staircase**, in the Italian style, overlooking the central courtyard and decorated with the royal salamanders and ermines of François I and Queen Claude. In summer, one of the region's oldest and best **son et lumière (sound and light) shows** is projected onto the castle walls nightly.

The Drive >> Follow the D84 east 6km through the tranquil Indre valley, then cross the

river south into Saché, home to an attractive château and Balzac museum. From Saché continue 26km east on the D17, 11km northeast on the D45 and 9km east on the D976. Cross north over the Cher River and follow the D40 east 1.5km into Chenonceau.

TRIP HIGHLIGHT

❺ Chenonceau

Spanning the languid Cher River via a series of supremely graceful arches, **Château de Chenonceau** (www.chenonceau.com; adult/child €11/8.50; ☺from 9am year-round, closes 5pm to 8pm depending on month) is a study in elegance, with its remarkable architecture, exquisite landscaping and fabulous furnishings.

Several noteworthy women have left their mark on Chenonceau, hence its alternative name, Le Château des Dames (Ladies' Château). The distinctive arches were added by Diane de Poitiers, mistress of King Henri II. Henri's widow, Catherine de Médici, added the yew-tree **labyrinth** and the western rose garden. In the 18th century, the aristocrat Madame Dupin made Chenonceau a centre of fashionable society and attracted guests including Voltaire and Rousseau. Legend has it that she also single-handedly saved the château from destruction during the

Revolution, thanks to her popularity with local villagers.

The château's *pièce de résistance* is the 60m-long window-lined **Grande Gallerie** spanning the Cher, scene of many a wild party over the centuries. The gallery was legendarily also used as an escape route for refugees fleeing the Nazi occupation during WWII, when the Cher marked the boundary between free and occupied France.

In summer, don't miss the chance to stroll Chenonceau's illuminated grounds at night during the **Promenade Nocturne** (adult/child €5/free).

The Drive » Follow the D81 north 13km into Amboise; 2km south of town, you'll pass the Mini-Châteaux theme park, whose intricate scale models of 44 Loire Valley châteaux are great fun for kids!

- - - - - - - - - - - - -

TRIP HIGHLIGHT

6 Amboise

Elegant Amboise perches on the Loire's southern bank, overlooked by the fortified 15th-century **Château Royal d'Amboise** (www.chateau-amboise.com; adult/child €10/7; ⏱ from 9am year-round, closes

DETOUR:
SLEEPY CHÂTEAUX OF THE SOUTH

Start 4 **Azay-le-Rideau**

Escape the crowds by detouring to four less-visited châteaux between Azay-le-Rideau and Chenonceau.

First stop: **Loches**, where Joan of Arc, fresh from her victory at Orléans in 1429, famously persuaded Charles VII to march to Reims and claim the French crown. The undisputed highlight here is the **Cité Royale** (www.chateau-loches.fr; adult/child €7.50/5.50; ⏱9am-7pm Apr-Sep, 9.30am-5pm Oct-Mar), a royal citadel that spans 500 years of French château architecture in a single site, from Foulques Nerra's austere 10th-century **keep** to the Flamboyant Gothic and Renaissance styles of the **Logis Royal**. To get here from Azay-le-Rideau, head 55km east along the D751, A85 and D943.

Next comes the quirky **Château de Montrésor** (www.chateaudemontresor.fr; adult/child €8/4; ⏱10am-7pm Apr-Oct, to 6pm Sat & Sun Nov-Mar), 19km east of Loches on the D760, still furnished much as it was over a century ago when it belonged to Polish count, financier and railroad magnate Xavier Branicki. The eclectic decor includes a Cuban mahogany spiral staircase, a piano once played by Chopin and a treasury room filled with Turkish hookahs and other spoils from the 17th-century Battle of Vienna.

Next, head 20km north on the D10 and D764 to **Château de Montpoupon** (www.chateau-loire-montpoupon.com; adult/child €8/4.50; ⏱10am-7pm), idyllically situated in rolling countryside. Opposite the castle, grab lunch at the wonderful **Auberge de Montpoupon** (www.aubergedemontpoupon.com; menus €21-67; ⏱lunch & dinner daily).

Continue 12km north on the D764 to **Château de Montrichard**, another ruined 11th-century fortress constructed by Foulques Nerra. After visiting the château, picnic in the park by the Cher River, or go wine tasting at **Caves Monmousseau** (www.monmousseau.com; 71 rte de Vierzon; tours adult/child €3.50/free; ⏱10am-noon & 2.30-5.30pm).

From Montrichard, head 10km west on the D176 and D40 to rejoin the main route at Chenonceau.

Classic Trip

CHRISTOPHE LEHENAFF/GETTY IMAGES ©

MARC DOZIER/GETTY IMAGES ©

LOCAL KNOWLEDGE
ELSA SAUVÉ,
CHÂTEAU DE
CHAMBORD

The double-helix staircase that whisks visitors from Chambord's ground floor to its rooftop keep is the highlight, the magic being that two people can see each other go up and down it without their paths ever crossing. A magnificent view of the estate unfolds from the rooftop terrace, an unforgettable place with its sculpted chimney and turrets, really a place of contemplation and daydream.

Top: St Hubert Chapel, Château Royal d'Amboise
Left: Château de Chambord
Right: Château de Langeais

4.45pm to 7pm depending on month). Thanks to the château's easily defensible position, it saw little military action, serving more often as a weekend getaway from the official royal seat at nearby Blois. Charles VIII, born and bred here, was responsible for the château's Italianate remodelling in 1492.

Just up the street, Amboise's other main sight is **Le Clos Lucé** (www.vinci-closluce.com; adult/child €13.50/8.50; ⊘9am-7pm Feb-Oct, 10am-6pm Nov-Jan), the grand manor house where Leonardo da Vinci took up residence in 1516 and spent the final years of his life at the invitation of François I. Already 64 by the time he arrived, da Vinci spent his time sketching, tinkering and dreaming up new contraptions, scale models of which are now abundantly displayed throughout the home and its expansive gardens.

✕ 🖿 p145

The Drive » Follow the D952 northeast along the Loire's northern bank, enjoying 35km of beautiful river views en route to Blois. The town of Chaumont-sur-Loire makes a pleasant stop for lunch (see p146) or for its imposing château and gardens.

- - - - - - - - - - - - - -

⑦ Blois

Straddling a rocky escarpment on the Loire's northern bank, the **Château Royal de Blois**

Classic Trip

(www.chateaudeblois.fr; place du Château; adult/child €9.50/4; ⏰9am-6.30pm Apr-Sep, to 12.30pm & 1.30-5.30pm Oct-Mar) bears the creative mark of several successive French kings. More a showpiece than a military stronghold, its four grand wings offer a superb overview of Loire Valley architectural styles, with elements of Gothic (13th century), Flamboyant Gothic (1498–1503), early Renaissance (1515–24) and classical (1630s).

Highlights include the **loggia staircase**, decorated with salamanders and curly 'F's (François I's heraldic symbols); the **studiolo**, within whose elaborately panelled walls Catherine de Médici allegedly maintained secret cupboards for stashing poisons; and the 2nd-floor **king's apartments**, which witnessed one of the bloodiest episodes in French royal history. In 1588 Henri III had his arch-rival, Duke Henri I de Guise, murdered here by royal bodyguards (the king himself hid behind a tapestry). Period paintings chronicle the gruesome events.

The Drive » Cross the Loire and continue 16km southeast into Cheverny via the D765 and D102.

⑧ **Cheverny**

A masterpiece of French classical architecture, beautifully proportioned **Château de Cheverny** (www.chateau-cheverny.fr; adult/child €9/6; ⏰9.15am-6.15pm Apr-Sep, 9.45am-5pm Oct-Mar) was built between 1625 and 1634 by Jacques Hurault, an *intendant* (royal administrative official) to Louis XII, and has been continuously inhabited by the same family for four centuries. Highlights of the sumptuously furnished interior include a **formal dining room** decorated with scenes from *Don Quixote* and a **children's playroom** filled with Napoléon III–era toys.

Outside amid sprawling lawns, Cheverny's **kennels** house pedigreed hunting dogs; feeding time, known as the **Soupe des Chiens**, takes place daily at 5pm. Behind the château, the 18th-century **Orangerie**, which sheltered priceless artworks including the *Mona Lisa* during WWII, is now a tearoom.

Tintin fans may recognise the château's façade as the model for Captain Haddock's ancestral home, Marlinspike Hall.

🛏 p145

The Drive » Take the D102 10km northeast into Bracieux, then turn north on the D112 for the final 8km run through the forested Domaine National de Chambord (Europe's largest hunting reserve). Catch your first dramatic glimpse of France's most famous château on the right as you arrive in Chambord.

TRIP HIGHLIGHT

⑨ **Chambord**

For over-the-top splendour, nothing compares to **Château de Chambord** (www.chambord.org; adult/child €9.50/free, parking €3; ⏰9am-6pm Apr-Sep, 10am-5pm Oct-Mar), one of the supreme examples of French Renaissance architecture.

Begun in 1519 as a weekend hunting lodge by François I, it quickly snowballed into France's most ambitious (and expensive) royal architectural project. When construction finally ended 30-odd years later, the castle boasted some 440 rooms, 365 fireplaces and 84 staircases, all built around a rectangular **keep**, crossed by four great hallways and flanked at the corners by circular bastions. Up through the centre of it all winds Chambord's crowning glory, the famous **double-helix staircase** designed by Leonardo da Vinci, with two intertwining flights of stairs leading up to the great **lantern tower** and rooftop, from where you can survey the landscaped grounds and marvel at the exuberant jumble of cupolas, turrets, chimneys and lightning rods.

🛏 p145

Eating & Sleeping

Chinon ❶

🛏 Hostellerie
Gargantua
Historic Hotel €

(📞02 47 93 04 71; www.hotel-gargantua.com;
73 rue Haute St-Maurice; d €55-81; 📶) Superior
rooms with fireplaces or château views are
worth the extra cash at this turret-topped
medieval mansion with spiral staircases, pitch-
dark wood and solid stone.

Langeais ❷

🍴 Au Coin
des Halles
Traditional French €€

(📞02 47 96 37 25; www.aucoindeshalles.com;
9 rue Gambetta; menus lunch €16-19, dinner
€24-49; 🕙lunch Fri-Tue, dinner Thu-Tue) Enjoy
bargain-priced gourmet lunches on the terrace
at this elegant family-run bistro paces from
Langeais' château.

Amboise ❻

🍴 Auberge
de Launay
Traditional French €€

(📞02 47 30 16 82; www.aubergedelaunay.com;
Le Haut Chantier, Limeray; menus €19.50-38;
🕙lunch Tue-Fri, dinner Mon-Sat) This renowned
country inn 8km east of Amboise incorporates
herbs and vegetables from the kitchen garden
into classic meat, fish and poultry dishes,
accompanied by a superb wine list, divine
artisanal cheese platters and desserts like
wine-poached pears.

🍴 La Fourchette
Traditional French €

(📞06 11 78 16 98; 9 rue Malebranche; lunch/
dinner menus €15/24; 🕙lunch Tue-Sat, dinner
Fri & Sat) Chef Christine's down-to-earth home
cooking makes you feel like you've been invited
to her house for lunch; daily specials include
spare ribs, roast chicken and veal stew.

🛏 Le Manoir
Les Minimes
Design Hotel €€€

(📞02 47 30 40 40; www.manoirlesminimes.com;
34 quai Charles Guinot; d €131-205, ste €290;
❄ @ 📶) This riverside pamper-palace would put
most châteaux to shame. The best rooms have
tall windows opening onto Loire or castle views.

🛏 Au Charme Rabelaisien
B&B €€

(📞02 47 57 53 84; www.au-charme-rabelaisien.
com; 25 rue Rabelais; d €92-175; 🕙late Mar-Oct;
📶🏊) Three comfy rooms share a grassy yard,
a swimming pool and free enclosed parking at
this centrally located haven.

Chaumont-sur-Loire

🍴 La Madeleine
de Proust
Traditional French €€

(📞02 54 20 94 80; 33 rue du Maréchal Leclerc;
menus €21-28; 🕙lunch Wed-Sun, dinner daily)
Fresh local produce features in dishes such
as crispy pan-fried trout with herb-sautéed
zucchini at this unpretentious eatery below
Château de Chaumont.

Cheverny ❽

🛏 La Levraudière
B&B €

(📞02 54 79 81 99; www.lalevraudiere.fr; 1 chemin
de la Levraudière; d €66-69) Amid 3 hectares of
grassland, this peaceful and meticulously kept
19th-century farmhouse offers crisp linens and
delicious breakfasts with homemade jams.

Chambord ❾

🛏 Hôtel Grand St-Michel
Hotel €€

(📞02 54 20 31 31; www.saintmichel-chambord.
com; place St-Louis; d €60-106; @) This faded
two-star hotel directly opposite Château de
Chambord offers the unforgettable experience
of wandering the château grounds alone at
dawn or dusk, observing deer and wild boars in
the adjacent park.

Rochemenier Explore incredible
underground troglodyte farmsteads

Caves & Cellars of the Loire

12

This tour of caves, wine cellars and châteaux explores the best of the western Loire Valley, home to habitations troglodytiques (cave dwellings) and some of France's finest food and wine.

TRIP HIGHLIGHTS

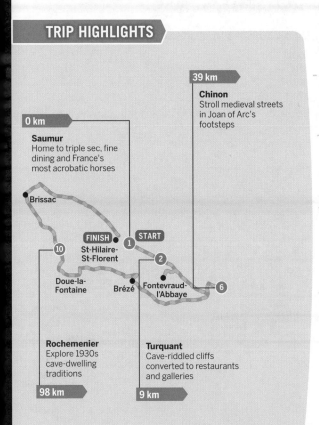

39 km

Chinon
Stroll medieval streets in Joan of Arc's footsteps

0 km

Saumur
Home to triple sec, fine dining and France's most acrobatic horses

Brissac

FINISH — **1** — **START**

St-Hilaire-St-Florent

2

10

Doue-la-Fontaine — Brézé — Fontevraud-l'Abbaye — **6**

Rochemenier
Explore 1930s cave-dwelling traditions

98 km

Turquant
Cave-riddled cliffs converted to restaurants and galleries

9 km

3 DAYS
160KM / 100 MILES

GREAT FOR...

BEST TIME TO GO

May for greenery; September and October for harvest.

ESSENTIAL PHOTO

Turquant's cliff face, with converted cave dwellings and windmill.

BEST FOR WINE-TASTING

The 15km stretch between St-Hilaire-St-Florent and Montsoreau.

147

Caves & Cellars of the Loire

The Loire Valley's soft, easily excavated *tuffeau* (limestone) has been interwoven with local culture for millennia. From Merovingian quarries that did a booming international trade in early Christian sarcophagi, to medieval and Renaissance châteaux, to modern restaurants, mushroom farms and wine cellars adapted from cave dwellings, this tour offers an introduction to local troglodyte culture as well as ample opportunities to savour the region's renowned gastronomy and wines.

TRIP HIGHLIGHT

❶ Saumur

Start your tour in sophisticated Saumur, one of the Loire Valley's great gastronomic and viticultural centres.

For an overview of the region's wine producers, along with free tastings, head to the riverside **Maison du Vin** (7 quai Carnot; ⏰10.30am-12.30pm & 3-6pm Tue-Sat). Next, explore Saumur's other claim to fermented fame at **Distillerie Combier** (www.combier.fr; 48 rue

Beaurepaire; adult €4; ⊘3-5 guided visits per day, 10am-12.30pm & 2-7pm Tue-Sun), where triple sec liqueur was invented in 1834; tours of the still-functioning distillery offer an evocative, behind-the-scenes look at gleaming century-old copper stills, vintage Eiffel machinery and fragrant vats full of Haitian bitter oranges. Around town, make sure to try Saumur's iconic aperitif, *soupe saumuroise* – made with triple sec, lemon juice and sparkling wine.

Other Saumur highlights include the fairy-tale 13th-century **Château de Saumur** (www.ville-saumur.fr/visites.cfm; adult/child €9/5; ⊘10am-1pm & 2-5.30pm Tue-Sun Apr-Oct) and the **École Nationale d'Équitation** (☎02 41 53 50 60; www.cadrenoir.fr; rte de Marson; guided visits adult/child €7/5; ⊘mornings Tue-Sat & afternoons Mon-Fri Apr–mid-Nov), a renowned equestrian academy that's long been responsible for training France's elite Cadre Noir cavalry division and Olympic riding teams. Take a one-hour guided visit (four to 10 daily), or book ahead for one of the not-to-be-missed **Cadre Noir presentations** (adult/child €16/9), semi-monthly 'horse ballets' that show off the horses' astonishing discipline and acrobatic manoeuvres.

✕ ⮞ p154

The Drive » East of Saumur, the D947 meanders 10km through the towns of Souzay-Champigny and Parnay, home to several tasting rooms,

including Château Villeneuve, Clos des Cordeliers, Château de Parnay and Château de Targé. Troglodyte dwellings pockmark the cliff face to your right as a hilltop windmill signals your arrival in Turquant.

TRIP HIGHLIGHT

② Turquant

Backed by chalk-coloured, cave-riddled cliffs, picturesque Turquant is a showcase for the creative adaptation of historic troglodyte dwellings. The town's 'main street' runs parallel to the D947, past a handful of art galleries, restaurants and other enterprises featuring designer windows and colourful doors wedged into the cliff face. Turn right off the main road to **Le Troglo des Pommes Tapées** (letroglodespommestapees.fr; 11 rue des Ducs d'Anjou; adult/child €6/3.50; ⊘2-6.30pm Tue, 10am-12.30pm & 2-6.30pm Wed-Sun mid-Feb–mid-Nov), a giant cave house whose owners have revived the ancient art of oven-drying and painstakingly hammering apples into

N 0 — 10 km
0 — 5 miles

●Gizeux

Parc Naturel Régional Loire Anjou Touraine

CENTRE

A85

Bourgueil

Île St-Martin

Rigny-Ussé

28 km to 1

Indre

●Huismes

11

D751

D751

⑥ Chinon
p180

Forêt de Chinon

⑦
Musée Rabelais

La Roche-Clermault

Vienne

LINK YOUR TRIP

1 Essential France
Head east to Chambord to join this country-wide circuit of iconic French sights.

11 Châteaux of the Loire
In Chinon, connect to this classic tour of the Loire Valley's most famous châteaux.

CHICUREL ARNAUD/GETTY IMAGES ©

the local delicacy known as *pommes tapées*. Guided cave tours are followed by tastings of dried apples simmered in red wine. Turquant's *tuffeau* (limestone) cliffs have also been adapted for use as wine cellars by producers such as **La Grande Vignolle** (www.filliatreau.com) and **Domaine des Amandiers** (www.domaine-des-amandiers. com).

 p154

The Drive » It's just a 3km hop, skip and jump to Montsoreau along the D947 and D751. Alternatively, follow the narrow Route des Vins (parallel and slightly south of the D947) to the 16th-century windmill Moulin de la Herpinière, then continue into Montsoreau via tiny Chemin de la Herpinière.

❸ Montsoreau

Looming impressively above the Loire, **Château de Montsoreau** (www.chateau-montsoreau.com; adult/child €9/6; ⊙10am-7pm May-Sep, 2-6pm Apr, Oct–mid-Nov & weekends Mar, closed mid-Nov–Feb) was built in 1455 by one of Charles VII's advisers, and later immortalised in Alexandre Dumas' novel, *La Dame de Monsoreau*. The crowning attraction here is the dazzling view from the rooftop, extending from the Loire's confluence with the Vienne to the domes and turrets of Saumur. On weekends, enjoy

free wine tasting in the castle's cellars.

Nearby, the **Maison du Parc** (www.parc-loire-anjou-touraine.fr; 15 av de la Loire; ⊙9.30am-7pm) offers information on the Parc Naturel Régional Loire-Anjou-Touraine, which protects 2530 sq km of the surrounding landscape.

p154

The Drive » Follow the D751 1km southeast into Candes-St-Martin, enjoying pretty river views on your left.

❹ Candes-St-Martin

Recognised as one of France's prettiest villages, Candes-St-Martin occupies an idyllic spot at the confluence of the Vienne and the Loire Rivers. A long-time pilgrimage site, the town's 12th- to 13th-century **church** venerates the spot where St Martin died in 397. Wander down to the benches overlooking the waterfront along rue du Confluent (a pleasant spot for a picnic), or follow the brown 'Panorama Piétons' signs above the church for higher-altitude perspectives.

The Drive » Snake 6km south along the D751, D7 and D947, following signs for Fontevraud-l'Abbaye. From the D7/D947 junction, a worthwhile 800m detour leads northwest to the artisanal soap factory Savonnerie Martin de Candre.

❺ Abbaye de Fontevraud

This huge 12th-century complex was once one of Europe's largest ecclesiastical centres. The highlight here is the massive, movingly simple **abbey church**, notable for its soaring pillars, Romanesque domes and the polychrome tombs of four Plantagenets: Henry II, King of England (r 1154–89); his wife Eleanor of Aquitaine (who retired to Fontevraud after Henry's death); their son Richard the Lionheart; and Isabelle of Angoulême. Adjacent

Chinon The village's hilltop château

buildings include a cavernous, multi-chimneyed kitchen, prayer halls, a barrel-vaulted refectory and exhibits on Fontevraud's use as a prison from the French Revolution until 1963.

The Drive ›› Backtrack 5km to the D751 and follow it 13km southeast toward Chinon. Immediately after crossing the Vienne River, take the D749 east 3km, paralleling the riverfront into town.

TRIP HIGHLIGHT

6 Chinon

Renowned for its hilltop château and charming medieval quarter (see our walking tour, p180), the riverside village of Chinon is home to several fine restaurants and AOC red wines, making it a prime candidate for an overnight stay. For customised half-day tours of nearby wine-growing regions, including Chinon, Cravant, Saumur-Champigny, St-Nicolas-de-Bourgeuil and Touraine, contact bilingual Chinon native **Alain Caillemer** (02 47 95 87 59; dcaillemer@rand. com; half-day tours per couple €75).

✗ 🛏 p154

The Drive ›› Zigzag 8km southwest of Chinon through lovely rolling farmland along the D749A, D751E, D759, D24 and D117, following signs for La Devinière.

- - - - - - - - - - -

7 Musée Rabelais

Set among fields and vineyards with sweeping views to the private château of Coudray Montpensier, **La Devinière** is the birthplace of François Rabelais – doctor, Franciscan friar, theoretician and author – and the inspiration for his five satirical Gargantua and Pantagruel novels. The farmstead's rambling buildings hold the **Musée Rabelais** (www.musee-rabelais.fr; adult/child €5/4; ⊙10am-12.30pm & 2-5pm daily, closed Tue Oct-Mar), featuring early editions of Rabelais' work and a Matisse portrait of the author. The winding cave network underneath hosts rotating special exhibitions.

The Drive » Follow the D117 8km west through the gorgeous village of Seuilly, home to an 11th-century abbey, then continue 13km west-northwest along the D48, D50, D310, D110 and D93 into Brézé.

- - - - - - - - - -

❽ Château de Brézé

Off-the-beaten-track **Château de Brézé** (www.chateaudebreze.com; adult/child €11/6; ⊙10am-6.30pm Apr-Sep, to 6pm Tue-Sun Oct-Mar, closed Jan) sits atop an extensive network of subterranean rooms and passages that account for more square footage than the castle itself. A self-guided tour takes you through the original troglodyte dwelling directly under the château, then crosses a deep moat to other caves adapted by the castle's owners for use as kitchens, wine cellars and defensive bastions. Finish your visit with a scenic climb to the château's rooftop, followed by a *dégustation* (tasting) of Saumur wines from the surrounding vineyards.

The Drive » Chart a meandering 22km course through relatively flat farm country into Doué-la-Fontaine via the D93, D162, D163 and D960.

- - - - - - - - - -

❾ Doué-la-Fontaine

At the southeastern edge of this mid-sized town, stop to visit the fascinating **Troglodytes et Sarcophages** (📞06 77 77 06 94; www.troglo-sarcophages.fr; adult/child €4.80/3.30; ⊙2.30-7pm daily Jun-Aug, Sat & Sun May, closed Sep-Apr), a Merovingian quarry where sarcophagi were produced from the 6th to the 9th centuries and exported via the Loire as far as England and Belgium. In summer book ahead for atmospheric lantern-lit evening **tours** (adult/child €7.50/5.50).

Near by, **Les Perrières** (www.ville-douelafontaine.fr/perrieres; adult/child €4.50/3; ⊙2-6.30pm Tue-Sun Apr-Oct) is a vast network of 18th- and 19th-century stone quarries sometimes called the 'cathedral caves' due to their lofty sloping walls that resemble Gothic arches.

The Drive » Skirt the southern edge of Doué-la-Fontaine via the D960 for 4km, then continue 5km north on the D761 to the Rochemenier exit. Follow signs the remaining 1.5km into Rochemenier.

- - - - - - - - - -

TRIP HIGHLIGHT

❿ Rochemenier

In peaceful countryside northwest of Doué-la-Fontaine, the museum-village of **Rochemenier** (www.troglodyte.info; adult/child €5.50/3; ⊙9.30am-7pm Apr-Oct, 2-6pm Sat & Sun Nov, Feb & Mar) preserves the remains of two troglodyte farmsteads that were inhabited until the 1930s, complete with houses, stables and an underground chapel. Throughout the complex, farm tools and photos of former residents evoke the hard-working spirit and simple pleasures that defined life underground for many generations. Displays in the last room focus on international cave-dwelling cultures, including places as far-flung as China and Turkey.

🛏 p155

The Drive » Return to the D761, then follow it 15km northwest to Brissac-Quincé, where signs direct you 1.5km further to the château.

- - - - - - - - - -

⓫ Château de Brissac

France's tallest castle, the imposing **Château de Brissac** (www.chateau-brissac.fr; guided tours adult/child €10/4.50; ⊙10am-12.15pm & 2-6pm Wed-Mon Apr-Oct) is spread over seven storeys and 204 rooms. Built by the Duke of Brissac in 1502, the château has an elegant interior filled with posh furniture, ornate tapestries, twinkling chandeliers and

DETOUR:
ANGERS

Start ⑪ Château de Brissac

Historic seat of Anjou's powerful counts and dukes, bustling Angers revolves around the impressive **Château d'Angers** (angers.monuments-nationaux.fr; 2 promenade du Bout-du-Monde; adult/child €8.50/free; ⊙9.30am-6.30pm May-Aug, 10am-5.30pm Sep-Apr). The castle's walls of blue-black schist loom above the Maine River, ringed by gardens, battlements and 17 watchtowers. Inside is one of Europe's great medieval masterpieces, the **Tenture de l'Apocalypse**. Commissioned around 1375, this stunning 104m-long series of tapestries illustrates scenes from the Book of Revelation, complete with the Four Horsemen of the Apocalypse, the Battle of Armageddon and the seven-headed Beast.

Opposite the château, taste and learn about the region's well-regarded wines at the **Maison du Vin de l'Anjou** (mdesvins-angers@vinsdeloire.fr; 5bis place du Président Kennedy; ⊙2.30-7pm Mon, 10am-1pm & 2.30-7pm Tue-Sat). Afterwards stroll through Angers' pedestrianised centre, where you'll find cafes, restaurants, art museums and the fabulous **Maison d'Adam** (place Ste-Croix), a remarkably well-preserved medieval house decorated with bawdy carved figurines.

To get here, head 28km northwest from Brissac on the D748, A87 and A11, following signs for Angers-Centre.

luxurious bedrooms – even a private theatre. Around the house, 8 sq km of grounds are filled with cedar trees, 19th-century stables and a vineyard, boasting three AOC vintages; free tastings are included in the guided visit.

🛏 p155

The Drive » Follow the D55 6km northeast, then wind 15km east-southeast on the D751 through forests and sunflower fields to rejoin the Loire at Gennes. From here, a particularly scenic stretch of the D751 follows the Loire's sandy banks 12km to St-Hilaire-St-Florent. Along the way, the small towns of St-Georges-des-Sept-Voies (p155) and Chênehutte-Trèves-Cunault (p155) offer enticing eating and sleeping options.

- - - - - - - - - - - -

⑫ St-Hilaire-St-Florent

This western suburb of Saumur is crowded with wineries and cave-based attractions. At the **Musée du Champignon** (Mushroom Museum; www.musee-du-champignon.com; D751; adult/child €8/6; ⊙10am-7pm mid-Feb–mid-Nov), learn oodles of mushroom facts and trivia as you wander deep into a cave where countless varieties of fungi are cultivated; next door, **Pierre et Lumière** (www.pierre-et-lumiere.com; D751; adult/child €8/6; ⊙10am-7pm Apr-Sep, to 12.30pm & 2-6pm Feb, Mar, Oct & Nov) displays intricate limestone sculptures of famous Loire Valley monuments. East towards Saumur, a host of tasting rooms invites you to sample local AOC and AOP vintages including Crémant de Loire and Saumur Brut; well-established wineries along this route include **Ackerman** (www.ackerman.fr), **Gratien et Meyer** (www.gratienmeyer.com), **Langlois Château** (www.langlois-chateau.fr) and **Veuve Amiot** (www.veuveamiot.fr).

The Drive » A quick 3km scoot along the D751 and D161 returns you to downtown Saumur.

Eating & Sleeping

Saumur ❶

🍴 Le Gambetta — Gastronomic €€

(📞02 41 67 66 66; www.restaurantlegambetta. com; 12 rue Gambetta; lunch menus €23.50-28.50, other menus €30-96; ⊗lunch Tue & Thu-Sun, dinner Tue & Thu-Sat) This fantastic regional restaurant combines refined elegance with knock-your-socks-off creativity. The parade of dishes ranges from exquisitely presented classics (rosemary-and-thyme roasted pork) to unexpectedly delicious innovations (wasabi *crème brûlée*). Several menus include wine pairings, and all are punctuated by surprise treats from the kitchen.

🍴 L'Escargot — Traditional French €€

(📞02 41 51 20 88; 30 rue du Maréchal Leclerc; menus €18-33; ⊗lunch Thu, Fri, Sun & Mon, dinner Thu-Mon) A Saumur fixture for over half a century, this place is all about traditional recipes done really well: *escargots* with garlic, parsley and 'three butters' (flavoured with herbs, walnuts and Roquefort); red mullet with fresh thyme, olive oil and vegetables; or a frozen triple sec soufflé with *crème anglaise* and berry coulis.

🛏 Château de Verrières — Castle Hotel €€€

(📞02 41 38 05 15; www.chateau-verrieres. com; 53 rue d'Alsace; r €170-240, ste €280-310; 🛜🏊) Every room is unique, but the feel is universally plush and regal at this impeccable 1890 château, ensconced within the woods and ponds of a 1.6-hectare English-style park. Features include antique writing desks, original artwork, wood panelling, fantastic bathrooms and free parking. Some rooms have views of the sun rising over Saumur's château.

🛏 Château de Beaulieu — B&B €€

(📞02 41 50 83 52; www.chateaudebeaulieu.fr; 98 rte de Montsoreau; d €85-120, ste €140-200; 🛜🏊) Irish expats Mary and Conor welcome you to their sprawling home with a glass of *crémant* (sparkling wine), delicious homemade breakfasts and a wealth of friendly advice on surrounding attractions. The mood among the generally gregarious clientele is one of extended family. Sun yourself by the pool or play billiards in the grand salon. Parking is free.

Turquant ❷

🍴 L'Hélianthe — Traditional French €€

(📞02 41 51 22 28; www.restaurant-helianthe. fr; ruelle Antoine Cristal; lunch/dinner menus €21/30; ⊗lunch & dinner Thu-Tue Apr–mid-Nov, lunch Sat & Sun, dinner Fri-Sun mid-Nov–Mar) At this troglodyte eatery dug into the cliffside, the menu revolves around traditional ingredients including river fish and 'ancient vegetables' (Jerusalem artichokes, beets, rutabagas, sweet potatoes etc).

🛏 Demeure de la Vignole — Design Hotel €€

(📞02 41 53 67 00; www.demeure-vignole.com; 3 impasse Marguerite d'Anjou; d €105-145, ste €150-260; 🛜🏊) This upscale hideaway, built partially into a cliff face above Turquant, offers four gorgeously redecorated troglodyte rooms and a subterranean swimming pool.

Montsoreau ❸

🍴 Le Saut aux Loups — Regional Cuisine €€

(📞02 41 51 70 30; www.troglo-sautauxloups. com; rte de Saumur; menus €19.50-23.50; ⊗lunch daily late Feb–mid-Nov, plus dinner Fri & Sat mid-Jun–mid-Sep) Tuck into fresh fungi at this troglodyte restaurant, then take a tour (€5.90) of the adjacent caves.

Chinon ❻

🍴 Les Années 30 — Traditional French €€

(📞02 47 93 37 18; www.lesannees30.com; 78 rue Voltaire; menus €27-43; ⊗lunch & dinner Thu-Mon) Expect the kind of meal you came to France to eat: exquisite attention to flavours and detail, served up in relaxed intimacy. The interior dining room is golden-lit downstairs and cool blue upstairs, with twin fireplaces enhancing the cosy atmosphere; in summer dine under the street-side pergola, in the heart of Chinon's old quarter.

🛏 Hôtel Diderot
Hotel €

(☎02 47 93 18 87; www.hoteldiderot.com; 4 rue de Buffon; s €46-68, d €56-86; 🛜) Draped with roses and crammed with polished antiques, this gorgeous town house is run by a friendly trio of siblings who impart the kind of glowing charm you'd expect of a much pricier hotel. Breakfast includes a rainbow of homemade jams, plus locally produced goat cheese with honey and 'crack-your-own' walnuts. Parking is €7 on site, or free down the street.

Rochemenier ⑩

🛏 Les Délices de la Roche
B&B €

(☎02 41 50 15 26; www.delicesdelaroche. com; s/d €50/55; 🛜) Friendly young hosts Henri and Sabrina rent out five simple rooms in the peaceful countryside adjacent to Rochemenier's troglodyte village. The adjoining restaurant serves dinner (€22) with advance reservations.

Château de Brissac ⑪

🛏 Château de Brissac
B&B €€€

(☎02 41 91 22 21; www.chateau-brissac.fr; r €390; 🖭) Sleep in a canopied bed surrounded by 16th-century Flemish tapestries, then wake up to breakfast served by the Marquis and Marquise de Brissac themselves! The four opulently decorated guest rooms in France's tallest château offer an unparalleled insider's look at this fabulous country estate, owned

since 1502 by the Cossé-Brissac family, whose relatives include the Veuve Clicquot of Champagne fame, and whose guests have included King Louis XIII.

St-Georges-des-Sept-Voies

🍴 Auberge de la Sansonnière
Traditional French €€

(☎02 41 57 57 70; www.auberge-sansonniere. com; menus €18-41; 🕐lunch Tue-Sun, dinner Tue-Sat) Surrounded by sunflower fields, this old stone country inn with wood-beamed dining room serves exquisite traditional French menus that emphasise fresh local fish and vegetables.

Chênehutte-Trèves-Cunault

🍴 La Cave aux Moines
Regional Cuisine €€

(☎02 41 67 95 64; www.cave-aux-moines.com; menus €20-24; 🕐lunch & dinner daily mid-Jun–mid-Sep, lunch Sat & Sun, dinner Fri-Sun rest of year) Deep inside a limestone cave, this unique restaurant 9km northwest of Saumur specialises in mushrooms, snails and *fouées* (fire-baked breads).

🛏 La Prieuré
Historic Hotel €€€

(☎02 41 67 90 14; www.grandesetapes.fr; Chênehutte-les-Tuffeaux; r €135-282; 🛜🖭) Commanding stunning views of the Loire from its hilltop perch, this hotel occupies a 12th-century priory with luxurious château-style embellishments. The 25 hectares of grounds include hiking trails through the forest, rose gardens, a swimming pool and a kids' play area.

The Auvergne Experience the wild
beauty of this volcanic landscape

Volcanoes of the Auvergne

13

Green pastures and volcanic scenery feature on this tour of the Parc Naturel Régional des Volcans d'Auvergne. Get ready for great hiking, hearty mountain meals and acclaimed cheeses.

TRIP HIGHLIGHTS

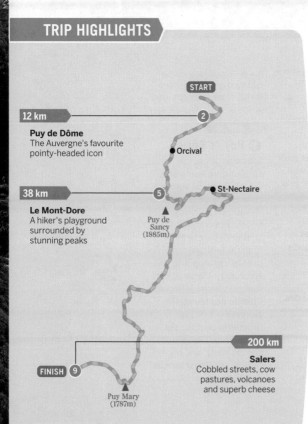

START

12 km ── **2**

Puy de Dôme
The Auvergne's favourite pointy-headed icon

● Orcival

38 km ── **5**

● St-Nectaire

Le Mont-Dore
A hiker's playground surrounded by stunning peaks

▲ Puy de Sancy (1885m)

200 km

Salers
Cobbled streets, cow pastures, volcanoes and superb cheese

FINISH **9**

▲ Puy Mary (1787m)

4 DAYS
200KM / 125 MILES

GREAT FOR...

BEST TIME TO GO
May to September for warm weather and snow-free trails.

 ESSENTIAL PHOTO
The symmetrical crags of Roches Tuilière and Sanadoire framing the lush greenery below Col de Guéry.

 BEST FOR FAMILIES
The volcanic theme park Vulcania.

157

13 Volcanoes of the Auvergne

Aeons ago, Europe's biggest volcanoes shaped the landscape of south-central France, blowing their tops with awe-inspiring force. On this trip you'll experience the wild beauty of the Auvergne's vestigial volcanoes – Puy de Dôme, Puy de Sancy and Puy Mary – but you'll also discover a tamer Auvergne whose picturesque patchwork of eroded cinder cones and verdant pastures is home to family-friendly hiking trails, symphonies of cowbells and some of France's finest cheeses.

❶ Vulcania

For a dramatic introduction to volcano-land, start at this educational, highly entertaining **theme park** 15km west of Clermont-Ferrand. The brainchild of two French geologists, it has such highlights as the dynamic 3-D film **Awakening of the Auvergne Giants**, depicting volcanic eruptions complete with air blasts and water spray, and the **Cité des Enfants** (Kids' City), with activities specially geared to three- to seven-year-olds.

The Drive » Head southeast 7km along the D941 to the D942, where full-on views of

Puy de Dôme beckon you 2km southwest to the junction with the D68 at the mountain's base.

TRIP HIGHLIGHT

❷ Puy de Dôme

Towering above the surrounding landscape, the symmetrical **volcanic cone** of Puy de Dôme (1464m) was already an iconic Auvergnat landmark long before the Romans built a temple to Mercury atop it in the 1st century. Climb to the summit via the 45-minute **Chemin des Muletiers** footpath (following the contours of the old Roman road), or hop aboard spiffy new cog railway the **Panoramique des Dômes** (www.pano ramiquedesdomes.fr;

adult/child €9.50/3.80; ⏰8am-7.30pm). Either way, you'll be rewarded with stunning views of the Chaîne des Puys, a 40km expanse of extinct cinder cones stretching to the horizon. The summit is also prime hang-gliding territory; operators such as **Aero Parapente** (📞06 61 24 11 45; www. aeroparapente.fr; ⏰Apr-Oct) will take you soaring over the surrounding countryside for €80.

The Drive 》 The 17km drive to Orcival skirts Puy de Dôme's southern flanks on the D942, then continues southwest on the D216 and D27, passing through increasingly hilly and pastoral countryside dotted with lovely stone and slate barns.

❸ Orcival

Backed by a leafy green hillside and bisected by a rushing stream, photogenic Orcival

LINK YOUR TRIP

36 Cave Art of the Vézère Valley

Detour four hours west of Le Mont-Dore to discover France's oldest cave art.

37 Dordogne's Fortified Villages

Explore centuries-old castles and fortified villages along the Dordogne River, three hours downstream from Le Mont-Dore.

clusters around a gorgeous Romanesque church that houses one of the Auvergne's most famous *vierges noires* (black Virgins typical of the region). An object of veneration throughout the year, she's paraded through the streets with special fanfare on Assumption Day (15 August). The town also springs to life on Saturday morning, when a colourful market fills the main square. In summertime, head 2km north of town to visit the elegant grounds of **Château de Cordès** (www.chateau-cordes-orcival.com; adult/child €3/free; ⏰10am-noon & 2-6pm daily Jul & Aug, 2-6pm Sun May & Jun), laid out by Versailles garden designer Le Nôtre.

🛏️ p163

The Drive » The D27 climbs 8km through verdant hills and evergreen forest to a spectacular viewpoint just before Col de Guéry (1268m), where the dramatic volcanic crags Roche Tuilière (1288m) and Roche Sanadoire (1286m) rise in perfect symmetry from the farmland below.

- - - - - - - - - - - -

④ Col de Guéry

This mountain pass, flanked by the Auvergne's highest lake, offers varied opportunities for outdoor recreation. A 7km loop trail leads to splendid views over the headwaters of the Dordogne River, while chilly **Lac de Guéry** (1250m) offers excellent fishing for trout and perch. Purchase fishing licences (€6 per day) at the Auberge du Lac de Guéry on the lakeshore.

🍴 p163

The Drive » Spellbinding mountain views unfold as you approach the Massif du Sancy, a wall of peaks that's often snowcapped late into the season. A sinuous 9km drive along the D983 and D996 drops you straight into downtown Le Mont-Dore.

- - - - - - - - - - - -

TRIP HIGHLIGHT

⑤ Le Mont-Dore

Ringed by rugged peaks at the heart of the Parc Naturel Régional des Volcans d'Auvergne, this historic spa town makes a great base for exploring the surrounding high country. A **télépherique** (gondola; one-way/return €6.90/9.10; ⏰9am-12.10pm & 1.30-5pm mid-Apr–Sep) whisks hikers through a landscape of precipitous crags to the foot of **Puy de Sancy** (1885m), France's tallest volcano; across town, a tortoise-slow but creakily atmospheric 1890s-vintage **funiculaire** (funicular; rue René Cassin; one-way/return €3.90/5.20; ⏰10am-12.10pm & 2-5.40pm mid-May–Sep) lumbers up to Salon du Capucin, an upland plateau where well-marked trails fan out in all directions. Several fine hikes and mountain-biking routes

also start in downtown Le Mont-Dore, including the **Chemin de la Grande Cascade**, which leads to a 32m-high waterfall.

For route guides and high-resolution topo maps, visit the tourist office, in a riverside park downtown. Nearby streets are filled with outdoors-oriented shops and purveyors of local charcuterie and cheeses such as **La Boutique du Bougnat** (1 rue Montlosier; ⏰9am-12.30pm & 3-7pm).

🍴 🛏️ p163

The Drive » Begin with a spectacular traverse of 1451m Col de la Croix St-Robert,

Puy de Dôme A hiker heads up the mountain

passing through 17km of wide-open high country along the D36. Next jog 6km downhill along the D637, enjoying pretty views of the Chaudefour Valley and Lac de Chambon, popular with boaters, hikers and campers. Finally follow the D996 9km past Murol's hilltop castle into St-Nectaire.

- - - - - - - - - - - -

6 St-Nectaire

Tiny St-Nectaire is famous for its 12th-century Romanesque church, stunningly set against a mountain backdrop, and its herds of happy bovines, who make this one of the Auvergne's dairy capitals. From the upper town

(St-Nectaire-le-Haut), climb 3km on the D150 to **La Ferme Bellonte** (www.st-nectaire.com; Farges; ⊙ milking 6.30-7.30am & 4.30-5.30pm, cheese making 8.30-10am Tue-Sat & 6-7.30pm daily, cave tours 10am-noon & 2-5pm), a working farm that offers free milking and cheese-making demonstrations twice daily, plus guided tours of the caves across the street where the cheese is aged.

🛏 p163

The Drive » Follow the D996 7km downstream to tiny Rivallet, then head southwest 15km on the D978 into Besse, watching

on the left for the medieval cliff dwellings Les Grottes de Jonas, which include a chapel, spiral staircases and a manor house carved directly into the rock.

- - - - - - - - - - - -

7 Besse-en-Chandesse

Basalt-brick cottages, cobbled lanes and a lovely old belfry are reason enough to visit this pretty mountain village, but hikers and mountain bikers will also appreciate the fine network of trails surrounding **Lac Pavin**, a crater lake 6km west of town. For a taste of mountain culture, visit during the **Transhumance de la Vierge Noire**, when local cows are herded to rich upland pastures on 21 July and back downhill in late September, accompanied by street fairs and fireworks.

The Drive ❱❱ Leave the Massif du Sancy behind and head south 82km towards the wilder, less populated Monts du Cantal. A curvy course through farmland and river valleys along the D978 and D678 leads to a supremely scenic, sustained climb along the D62 and D680, bringing you face to face with Puy Mary, southernmost of the Auvergne's three classic peaks.

⑧ Puy Mary

Barely wide enough to accommodate parked cars, the vertiginous mountain pass of Pas de Peyrol (1589m) hugs the base of pyramid-shaped Puy Mary (1787m), the Cantal's most charismatic peak. A trail, complete with staircases for the steeper sections, leads to the summit (about one hour round-trip). At the trailhead, the **Maison du Site** (www.puymary.fr; ⊙mid-May–mid-Nov) sells IGN's 1:75,000 *Monts du Cantal* topo map and several local hiking guides, including Les Sentiers d'Emilie dans le Cantal, which highlights kid-friendly walks.

 p163

The Drive ❱❱ The 20km descent along the D680 switchbacks steeply through a wonderland of high-country scenery before plunging into fragrant evergreen forest and following a long ridgeline into Salers.

 TRIP HIGHLIGHT

⑨ Salers

Pretty Salers perches on a hilltop surrounded by rolling fields full of long-horned brown cattle that produce the region's eponymous AOC cheese. With a compact core of 16th-century stone buildings and long views up towards Puy Mary, it's a relaxing place to linger. Find park information at **Maison de la Ronade** (place Tyssandier d'Escous; teas €2.90; ⊙3.30-6.30pm) on the picturesque central square, where the elderly owner serves 120 varieties of tea in his bookshelf-lined 15th-century drawing room. Local day hikes range from an easy 75-minute circuit of the stone-walled pastures surrounding town to high-mountain rambles through wide-open country around the base of 1592m-high **Puy Violent**. Another 2.5km walk from town leads to the **Maison de la Salers** (www.maisondelasalers. fr; adult/child €7/4.50; ⊙10am-noon & 2-6pm Feb-Oct), where videos, exhibits and a tasting room introduce visitors to Salers' cheese-making culture.

🍴 🛏 p163

CHEESE COUNTRY

The Auvergne produces some of France's finest cheeses, including five Appellation d'Origine Contrôlée (AOC) and Appellation d'Origine Protégée (AOP) varieties: the semihard, cheddar-like Cantal and premium-quality Salers, both made from the milk of high-pasture cows; St-Nectaire, rich, flat and semisoft; Fourme d'Ambert, a mild, smooth blue cheese; and Bleu d'Auvergne, a powerful, creamy blue cheese with a Roquefort-like flavour.

To taste them on their home turf, follow the signposted **Route des Fromages** (www.fromages-aop -auvergne.com) linking local farms and producers. A downloadable map is available on the website.

Local cheeses figure strongly in many traditional Auvergnat dishes, including *aligot* (puréed potato with garlic and Tomme cheese) and *truffade* (sliced potatoes with Cantal cheese), usually served with a huge helping of *jambon d'Auvergne* (local ham).

Eating & Sleeping

Orcival ❸

🛏 Hôtel Notre Dame   Hotel €

(📞04 73 65 82 02; s €42, d €49-53, menus €13-26; 📶) The seven snug refurbished rooms at this family-run hotel are serenaded by the *basilique*'s bells tolling next door and the rushing stream out back. Breakfasts at its rustic restaurant include homemade blueberry preserves and a tempting selection of local cheeses.

Col de Guéry ❹

🍴 Auberge du Lac de Guéry   Auvergnat €€

(www.auberge-lac-guery.fr; d incl breakfast/half-board/full board €80/128/156, menus €21-42; 🕙lunch Thu-Tue, dinner daily) In an unbeatable position right on the lakeshore, this cosy country inn serves fresh fish straight from the lake.

Le Mont-Dore ❺

🍴 La Golmotte   Auvergnat €€

(www.aubergelagolmotte.com; D996; menus €16-37; 🕙lunch & dinner daily) This mountainside eatery 3km above town is a perfect spot to get introduced to *truffade* (sliced potatoes with Cantal cheese), *aligot* (puréed potato with garlic and Tomme cheese and other Auvergnat classics.

🛏 Grand Hôtel   Hotel €

(📞04 73 65 02 64; www.hotel-mont-dore.com; 2 rue Meynadier; s/d/q €59/69/89; 📶) Built in 1850, this ultracentral and newly renovated Le Mont-Dore landmark provides more comfort and style than its budget prices would imply. Boutiquey bedrooms, including some two-room family suites, come with thick duvets, deep tubs and new wood flooring. There's also a sauna and Jacuzzi (€5 extra).

St-Nectaire ❻

🛏 Le Chastel Montaigu   B&B €€

(📞04 73 96 28 49; www.lechastelmontaigu.com; d €140-150; 🕙Apr-Oct) Head 11km east of St-Nectaire on the D996 to this fairy-tale castle on its own private hilltop. Rebuilt from ruins using authentic medieval materials, the four rooms are filled with heavy stone, rich fabrics and antique wall hangings. One has its own private turret terrace, and all have blindingly good views across the valley. Minimum two-night stay.

Puy Mary ❽

🛏 Auberge d'Aijean   B&B €

(📞04 71 20 83 43; www.auberge-puy-mary.com; La Gandilhon, Lavigerie; d €52-56, q €100-105) With front-row views of Puy Mary, this rustic inn 8km below the summit is a perfect high-country base.

Salers ❾

🍴 La Martille   Auvergnat €€

(www.restaurant-salers.fr; rue de la Martille; menus from €18; 🕙lunch & dinner daily) Head to La Martille's pleasant outdoor terrace for solid, reasonably priced Auvergnat dishes: Salers steaks, stuffed cabbage, and the full line-up of meat, cheese and potato fare.

🛏 Hôtel Saluces   Hotel €€

(📞04 71 40 70 82; www.hotel-salers.fr; rue de la Martille; d €68-99; @📶) A stone's throw from Salers' pretty central square, the town's nicest hotel offers nine spacious rooms with modern amenities in a historic stone building with a sunny interior courtyard.

Vézelay A lovely hilltop village rises from lush, rolling countryside

Medieval Burgundy

14

Fortified hill towns, medieval monasteries, exquisite Romanesque capitals and multicoloured tiled roofs share the stage with rolling vineyards and verdant hiking trails on this idyllic meander.

TRIP HIGHLIGHTS

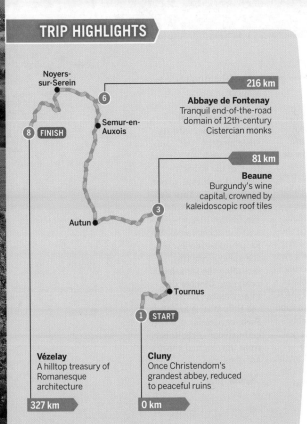

216 km

Abbaye de Fontenay
Tranquil end-of-the-road domain of 12th-century Cistercian monks

81 km

Beaune
Burgundy's wine capital, crowned by kaleidoscopic roof tiles

Noyers-sur-Serein

Semur-en-Auxois

Autun

Tournus

START

FINISH

Vézelay
A hilltop treasury of Romanesque architecture

327 km

Cluny
Once Christendom's grandest abbey, reduced to peaceful ruins

0 km

6 DAYS
327KM / 203 MILES

GREAT FOR...

BEST TIME TO GO

From May wildflower season through to the October wine harvest.

ESSENTIAL PHOTO

Vézelay's sinuous sweep of stone houses crowned by a hilltop basilica.

BEST FOR OUTDOORS

The riverside walking trails around Noyers-sur-Serein.

165

14 Medieval Burgundy

Between the Middle Ages and the 15th century, Burgundy saw a tremendous flowering of ecclesiastical architecture, from Cistercian and Benedictine monasteries to Romanesque basilicas, coupled with active patronage of the arts by the powerful Dukes of Burgundy. This medieval meander shows you all the highlights, while mixing in opportunities for wine tasting and walking in the gorgeous rolling countryside that makes Burgundy one of France's most appealing regions.

- - - - - - - - - - - - -

TRIP HIGHLIGHT

❶ Cluny

Built between 1088 and 1130, the monumental Benedictine **Abbaye de Cluny** (cluny.monuments-nationaux.fr; adult/child €9.50/free; ⏰9.30am-6pm Apr-Sep, to 7pm Jul & Aug, to 5pm Oct-Mar) – Christendom's largest church until the construction of St Peter's in Rome – once held sway over 1400 monasteries stretching from Poland to Portugal. Today you'll need a good imagination to conjure up the abbey's 12th-century glory, but its fragmentary remains, bordered by the giant shade trees of the grassy **Parc Abbatial**, are a delightful place to wander.

Get oriented at the **Musée d'Art et d'Archéologie**, with its scale model of the Cluny complex and 3-D 'virtual tour' of the abbey's original medieval layout, then climb the **Tour des Fromages** (adult/child €2/free; ⏰10am-12.30pm & 2.30-5pm, closed Sun Nov-Mar) for a bird's-eye view of the abbey's remains, including the striking octagonal **Clocher de l'Eau Bénite** (Tower of the Holy Water) and the **Farinier** (Granary), where eight splendid capitals from the original church are displayed.

 p171

The Drive » Head 13km north along the D981 to Cormatin, with its Renaissance-style château, then squiggle 25km east along the D14 past Chapaize's 11th-century Église St-Martin, Ozenay's château and the medieval hill town of Brancion before descending into Tournus.

- - - - - - - - - - - -

② Tournus

Tournus' superb 10th- to 12th-century Benedictine abbey, **Abbatiale St-Philibert** (⊙8.30am-7pm), makes a striking first impression, with its austere Romanesque façade peeking out through a medieval stone gate flanked by twin rounded towers; its apse holds an extremely rare 12th-century **floor mosaic** of the calendar and the zodiac, discovered by chance in 2002. The medieval centre also boasts fine restaurants – good for a lunch stop.

✗ p171

LINK YOUR TRIP

11 Châteaux of the Loire

Three hours west of Vézelay, explore the Loire Valley's classic châteaux.

15 Route des Grands Crus

Switch gears in Beaune to discover Burgundy's best wines.

The Drive » From Tournus, zip 56km straight up the A6 to Beaune.

TRIP HIGHLIGHT

❸ Beaune

Burgundy's prosperous and supremely appealing viticultural capital, Beaune, is surrounded by vineyards producing an impressive array of appellations including Côte de Nuits and Côte de Beaune. Sipping local vintages at sunset on a cafe terrace here is one of France's great pleasures. For a grand tour of the region's renowned wineries, see p173.

The architectural jewel of Beaune's historic centre is the **Hôtel-Dieu des Hospices de Beaune** (www.hospices-de-beaune. com; rue de l'Hôtel-Dieu; adult/child €7/3; ⊙9am-

5.30pm), a 15th-century charity hospital topped by stunning turrets and pitched rooftops covered in multicoloured tiles. Interior highlights include the barrel-vaulted **Grande Salle** with its dragon-embellished beams; an 18th-century **pharmacy** lined with ancient flasks; and the multipanelled 15th-century Flemish masterpiece **Polyptych of the Last Judgement**.

 p171

The Drive » A super-scenic 49km drive along the D973 weaves southwest through gorgeous vineyard country, climbing past La Rochepot's striking 13th-century castle before turning due west to Autun.

❹ Autun

Two millennia ago, Autun (Augustodunum)

was one of Roman Gaul's most important cities. Its next heyday came 1100 years later, when **Cathédrale St-Lazare** (place du Terreau; ⊙8am-7pm) was built to house St Lazarus' sacred relics. Climb through the old city's narrow cobblestone streets to see the cathedral's fantastical Romanesque capitals and famous 12th-century **tympanum** depicting the Last Judgement, carved by Burgundy's master sculptor Gislebertus. Across the street, the **Musée Rolin** (5 rue des Bancs; adult/child €5/free; ⊙9.30am-noon & 1.30-6pm Wed-Mon) houses Gislebertus' precociously sensual masterpiece, the *Temptation of Eve,* alongside Gallo-Roman artefacts and modern paintings.

↻ DETOUR: DIJON

Start ❸ Beaune

Long-time capital of medieval Burgundy, Dijon was the seat of power for a series of enlightened dukes who presided over the region's 14th- and 15th-century golden age, filling the city with fine art and architecture. From Beaune follow the D974 42km north through the vineyards into downtown Dijon, then park and explore the city's treasures on foot.

Topping the list of must-see attractions are the 13th-century **Église Notre Dame** (place Notre-Dame) with its remarkable façade of pencil-thin columns and leering gargoyles; the **Palais des Ducs et des États de Bourgogne** (place de la Libération), the Burgundy dukes' monumental palace, which also houses Dijon's superb art museum, the **Musée des Beaux-Arts** (mba.dijon.fr; tours adult/child €6/3; ⊙10am-5pm Wed-Mon); and the **historic mansions** that line surrounding streets, especially rue des Forges, rue Verrerie, rue Vannerie and rue de la Chouette.

For complete coverage of this engaging city, see Lonely Planet's *France* guide.

LOIRE VALLEY & CENTRAL FRANCE **14** MEDIEVAL BURGUNDY

Abbaye de Fontenay The medieval abbey's arched interior

Roman treasures around town include the town gates **Porte d'Arroux** and **Porte St-André**, the 16,000-seat **Théâtre Romain**, the **Temple de Janus** and the **Pierre de Couhard**, a 27m-high remnant of a Gallo-Roman pyramid.

Autun makes an excellent base for exploring the nearby **Parc Naturel Régional du Morvan** (www.parcdumorvan. org); the park's website offers downloadable hiking, biking and equestrian itineraries.

The Drive » The D980 runs 70km north from Autun to Semur-en-Auxois; halfway along, there's a fine collection of Romanesque capitals at Saulieu's 12th-century Basilique de St-Andoche.

- - - - - - - - - - - -

⑤ Semur-en-Auxois

Perched on a granite spur, surrounded by a hairpin turn in the Armançon River and guarded by four massive pink-granite bastions, Semur-en-Auxois was once an important religious centre boasting no fewer than six monasteries.

Pass through the two concentric medieval gates, **Porte Sauvigne** and **Porte Guillier**, onto pedestrianised **rue Buffon**, where you can sample a few *semurettes* (local dark-chocolate truffles) at **Pâtisserie Coeur** (les-semurettes.com; 14 rue Buffon; ⊙8am-7pm Tue-Sun) before continuing west to **Promenade du Rempart** for panoramic views from atop Semur's medieval battlements.

Semur is especially atmospheric at night, when the ramparts are illuminated, and around Pentecost, when the **Fêtes Médiévales du Roi Chaussé** fill the streets with medieval-themed parades and markets.

The Drive » Follow the D980 20km north into Montbard,

169

then hop 2km east on the D905 before joining the sleepy northbound D32 for the idyllic 3km home stretch into Fontenay.

TRIP HIGHLIGHT

⑥ Abbaye de Fontenay

Founded in 1118 and restored to its medieval glory a century ago, the Unesco-listed **Abbaye de Fontenay** (www. abbayedefontenay.com; adult/child €9.50/5.50, incl guided tour €11.50/6.50; ◷10am-noon & 2-5pm) offers a fascinating glimpse of the austere, serene surroundings in which Cistercian monks lived lives of contemplation, prayer and manual labour. Set in a bucolic wooded valley, the abbey includes an unadorned Romanesque church, a barrel-vaulted monks' dormitory, landscaped gardens and Europe's first metallurgical factory, with a remarkable water-driven forge from 1220.

From the parking lot, the **GR213 trail** forms part of two verdant walking circuits: one to Montbard (13km return), the other (11.5km) through Touillon and Le Petit Jailly. Maps and botanical field guides are available in the abbey shop.

The Drive ⟫ Backtrack to the D905, follow it 14km west-northwest to Rougemont, then take the westbound D956 21km into Noyers.

⑦ Noyers-sur-Serein

Tucked into a sharp bend in the Serein River, picturesque medieval Noyers is surrounded by pastureland and wooded hills. The town's cobbled streets, accessed via two imposing **stone gateways**, lead past 15th- and 16th-century gabled houses, wood and stone archways and several art galleries.

Noyers is a superb base for **walking**. Just outside the clock-topped southern gate, **Chemin des Fossés** threads its way between the Serein and the village's 13th-century fortifications, 19 of whose original 23 towers still remain. The 9km **Balade du Château**, marked in red, follows the Serein's right bank past an utterly ruined château.

In summer, the **Rencontres Musicales de Noyers** (www. musicalesdenoyers.com) bring classical concerts and jazz sessions to town.

✕ 🛏 p171

The Drive ⟫ Snake 14km southward through the peaceful Serein valley via the D86, then head 11km west on the D11 from Dissangis to Joux-la-Ville before charting a southwest course down the D32, D9, D606 and D951 for the final 24km run into Vézelay.

TRIP HIGHLIGHT

⑧ Vézelay

Rising from lush rolling countryside and crowned by a venerable medieval basilica, Vézelay is one of France's loveliest hilltop villages. Founded in the 9th century on a former Roman and then Carolingian site, the magnificent **Basilique Ste-Madeleine** (www. basiliquedevezelay.org) gained early fame as a starting point for the Santiago de Compostela pilgrimage route. Among its treasures are a 12th-century **tympanum**, with a carving of an enthroned Jesus radiating his holy spirit to the Apostles; several beautifully carved Romanesque **capitals**, including the Mystical Mill, which depicts Moses grinding grain into a flour sack held by St Paul; and a mid-12th-century **crypt** reputed to house one of Mary Magdalene's bones. Concerts of sacred music are held here from June to September.

The **park** behind the basilica affords wonderful views and walking access to the verdant Vallée de Cure. From **Porte Neuve**, Vézelay's old town gate, a footpath descends via the 12th-century chapel of **La Cordelle** to the village of **Asquins**. Another nice walk is the **Promenade des Fossés**, which circumnavigates Vézelay's medieval ramparts.

✕ 🛏 p171

Eating & Sleeping

Cluny ❶

✗ La Table d'Héloïse Burgundian €€

(☎03 85 59 05 65; www.hostelleriedheloise.
com; rte de Mâcon; menus €19-49; ☺lunch
Fri-Tue, dinner Mon, Tue & Thu-Sat) Dine on the
light-filled riverside veranda at this charming
family-run restaurant serving traditional
Burgundian fare including tender Charolais
steak, *fricassée d'escargots* (snail stew) and
sensational homemade desserts.

🛏 Le Clos de l'Abbaye B&B €

(☎03 85 59 22 06; www.closdelabbaye.fr;
6 place du Marché; d/tr/q/ste €70/85/105/170;
📶) This handsome old house beside the abbey
offers four comfortable, colour-coordinated
bedrooms and a lovely, kid-friendly garden. The
hosts help guests discover the region's little-
known treasures.

Tournus ❷

✗ Le Bourgogne Burgundian €€

(☎03 85 51 12 23; 37 rue du Dr Privey; menus
from €21; ☺lunch & dinner Thu-Mon) A few steps
south of the abbey, this husband-and-wife team
serves delicious, authentic and well-priced *cuisine
bourguinonne* (Burgundy cuisine), accompanied
by an excellent selection of local wines.

Beaune ❸

✗ Caves Madeleine Traditional French €

(☎03 80 22 93 30; 8 rue du Faubourg Madeleine;
mains €12-25, lunch menus €15; ☺lunch
& dinner Mon-Wed & Sat, dinner Fri) At this
convivial restaurant, locals tuck into French
classics such as *blanquette de veau* (veal stew)
at long shared tables surrounded by wine racks.

🛏 Hôtel des Remparts Historic Hotel €€

(☎03 80 24 94 94; www.hotel-remparts-beaune.
com; 48 rue Thiers; d €80-160; 🅿❄📶) Set

around two delightful courtyards, rooms in
this 17th-century town house have red-tiled or
parquet floors and simple antique furniture;
the nicest come with exposed beams and a
fireplace. Parking is €10.

Noyers-sur-Serein ❼

✗ Les Millésimes Burgundian €€

(☎03 86 82 82 16; www.maison-paillot.com;
place de l'Hôtel de Ville; menus €23-42; ☺lunch
& dinner Tue-Sun, closed Jan-Mar) This culinary
haven in a meticulously restored medieval
house with large fireplace specialises in *terroir*
(regional) creations ranging from *jambon au
chablis* (ham flavoured with Chablis wine) to
tourte à l'Époisses (pie with Époisses cheese).

🛏 Moulin de la Roche B&B €

(☎03 86 82 68 13; www.bonadresse.com/
bourgogne/le-moulin-de-la-roche.htm; rte
d'Auxerre; d €70-80; 🅿📶) Housed in a
renovated mill (complete with a millwheel in the
living room!), this welcoming two-room B&B
sits on three gorgeous hectares overlooking the
River Serein.

Vézelay ❽

✗ Le Bougainville Traditional French €€

(☎03 86 33 27 57; 26 rue St-Etienne; menus
€26-31; ☺lunch & dinner Thu-Mon; 🥗)
The smiling owner serves rich French and
Burgundian specialities alongside a *menu du
jardinier* featuring lighter vegetarian options.

🛏 Cabalus Historic Hotel €

(☎03 86 33 20 66; www.cabalus.com; rue
St-Pierre; d €58) Just below the cathedral, this
supremely atmospheric 12th-century abode
offers four spacious rooms with sturdy beams,
ancient tiles and stone walls.

Burgundy *Sensational vineyards set amid historic surrounds*

Route des Grands Crus

15

The picture-book Route des Grands Crus laces together Burgundy's most reputed vineyards. And, yes, opportunities abound for pleasurable wine tasting in historic surrounds.

TRIP HIGHLIGHTS

START
● Gevrey-Chambertin

2

● Nuits-St-Georges

7 km

Château du Clos de Vougeot
A magnificent wine-growing estate

29 km

Beaune
The opulent capital of Burgundian wines

5

8

7

● Pommard

39 km

Château de La Rochepot

● Puligny-Montrachet

FINISH

Château de Meursault
Wine tasting in a grandiose setting

St-Romain
Sensational views and a bucolic atmosphere

45 km

2 DAYS
62KM / 38 MILES

GREAT FOR...

BEST TIME TO GO

May, June, September and October for a symphony of colour and quiet roads.

📷 ESSENTIAL PHOTO

The views from the cliffs that tower above St-Romain are hallucinogenic.

✅ BEST FOR FOODIES

Beaune is a great place to try Burgundian specialities like snails.

173

15 Route des Grands Crus

Swinging from Gevrey-Chambertin to Puligny-Montrachet, this route is like a 'greatest hits' of Burgundy, with its bucolic views, patchwork of immaculate hand-groomed vines, atmospheric wine cellars and attractive stone villages. If you're looking for an upscale wine château experience, you've come to the right place. Now is your chance to sample some of the most prestigious reds and whites in the world.

1 Gevrey-Chambertin

Kick-start your epicurean adventure by visiting this picturesque village, which enjoys a world-class reputation among wine enthusiasts – it produces nine out of the 32 Grands Crus wines from Burgundy. All are reds made from pinot noir.

The Drive » From Gevrey-Chambertin it's a relaxed drive along the D122 to Château du Clos de Vougeot, 7km south via Morey St-Denis and Chambolle-Musigny.

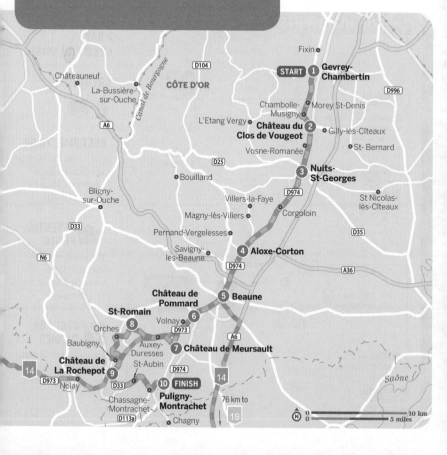

❷ Château du Clos de Vougeot

An essential stop on the Route des Grands Crus, the magnificent wine-producing **Château du Clos de Vougeot** (📞03 80 62 86 09; www.closdevougeot. fr; Vougeot; adult/child €4/3.10; ⏱9am-5.30pm) is regarded as the birthplace of Burgundian wines. Originally the property of the Abbaye de Cîteaux, 12km southeast from here, the 16th-century country castle served as a getaway for the monks, who stored their equipment and produced their wines here for several centuries. Tours uncover the workings of enormous wine presses and casks.

LINK YOUR TRIP

 14 Medieval Burgundy

It's easy to combine this trip with our itinerary focusing on medieval Burgundy, either from Beaune or La Rochepot.

 19 Beaujolais Villages

In the mood for more full-bodied wines? Motor 1¼ hours south to Villefranche-sur-Saône and make your way up to Roche de Solutré.

The Drive ≫ Pick up the D974 to Nuits-St-Georges, 4.5km south via Vosne-Romanée.

❸ Nuits-St-Georges

It's worth spending a little time in attractive Nuits-St-Georges. Splashed around town are a dozen domaines selling superb reds and whites, but an essential port of call on any wine-tasting itinerary is **L'Imaginarium** (📞03 80 62 61 40; www.imaginarium -bourgogne.com; av du Jura; adult/child €8/5; ⏱2-7pm Mon, 10am-7pm Tue-Sun). This gleaming modern museum is a great place to learn about Burgundy wines and winemaking techniques. It's fun and entertaining, with movies, exhibits and interactive displays.

Architecture buffs should take a look at the appealing 17th-century **belfry** of the former town hall and the Romanesque **Église St-Symphorien**, slightly away from the town centre.

The Drive ≫ Continue along the D974 towards Beaune. After passing through the village of Ladoix-Serrigny, look out for the sign to Château Corton-André on the right. It's a 10-minute drive from Nuits-St-Georges (11.5km).

❹ Aloxe-Corton

Surrounded by manicured vineyards, tiny Aloxe-Corton is a real charmer. It's

great for wine lovers, with producers handily scattered around the village. A good starting point is **Domaines d'Aloxe-Corton** (📞03 80 26 49 85; place du Chapitre; ⏱10am-1pm & 3-7pm Thu-Mon Apr–mid-Nov), a polished wine shop representing several makers of the terrific Aloxe-Corton *appellation* (delectable reds and whites).

No visit to Aloxe-Corton would be complete without visiting the high-flying **Château Corton-André** (📞03 80 26 28 79; www.pierre-andre. com; ⏱10am-1pm & 2.30-6pm). With its splendid cellars and tiled roofs, it's a wonderful place for a tasting session in atmospheric surrounds.

🛏 p179

The Drive ≫ Pick up the busy N74 to Beaune, 5.5km due south.

❺ Beaune

Beaune's *raison d'être* and the source of its *joie de vivre* is wine: making it, tasting it, selling it, but most of all, drinking it. Consequently Beaune is one of the best places in all of France for wine tasting.

The amoeba-shaped old city is enclosed by thick stone **ramparts**, which are lined with overgrown gardens and ringed by a pathway that makes for a lovely stroll.

The most striking attraction of Beaune's old city is the magnificent **Hôtel-Dieu des Hospices de Beaune** (see p168).

Underneath Beaune's buildings, streets and ramparts, millions of dusty bottles of wine are being aged to perfection in cool, dark cellars. The bacchanalian **Marché aux Vins** (www. marcheauxvins.com; 2 rue Nicolas Rolin; admission €10; 9.30-11.30am & 2-5.30pm Sep-Jun, 9.30am-5.30pm Jul & Aug) is a one-stop shop to taste, learn about and buy Burgundy wines. Using a *tastevin* (a small silver cup), sample an impressive 15 wines in the candle-lit former Église des Cordeliers and its cellars. Another venerable winery is **Bouchard Père & Fils** (www.bouchard-pereetfils.com; 15 rue du Château; 10am-12.30pm & 2.30-6.30pm Mon-Sat, 10am-12.30pm Sun Apr-Nov, 10am-12.30pm & 2.30-5.30pm Mon-Sat Dec-Mar), housed in a medieval fortress.

✕ ⊨ p179

The Drive » Take the D974 (direction Autun), then the D973 to Pommard (5.5km).

- - - - - - - - - - - - - -

❻ Château de Pommard

For many red wine lovers, a visit to the superb **Château de Pommard** (☎03 80 22 12 59; www.chateaudepommard.

com; 15 rue Marey-Monge; guided tours incl tasting adult/child €21/free; 9.30am-6pm Apr-Nov) is the ultimate Burgundian pilgrimage. The impressive cellars contain many vintage bottles.

The Drive » Follow signs to Meursault (5km), via Volnay. Château de Meursault is signposted in the centre of the village.

TRIP HIGHLIGHT

❼ Château de Meursault

One of the most elegant of the Route des Grands Crus châteaux, **Château de Meursault** (☎03 80 26 22 75; www.chateau-meursault.com; rue Moulin-Foulot; admission incl tasting €15; 9.30am-noon & 2.30-6pm Sep-Jun, 9.30am-6pm Jul & Aug) has beautiful grounds and produces prestigious white wines. You'll be struck by the 14th-century cellars.

✕ p179

The Drive » From the centre of Meursault, follow signs to Auxey-Duresses and Nolay (D23), then signs to Auxey-Duresses and St-Romain (D17E). Then take the D973 (direction Auxey-Duresses). Leaving Auxey-Duresses, take the D17E to Auxey-le-Petit and St-Romain (6.5km from Meursault).

- - - - - - - - - - - - - -

TRIP HIGHLIGHT

❽ St-Romain

Off-the-beaten-path St-Romain is a bucolic village situated right

CHARLES O'REAR/CORBIS ©

where vineyards meet pastureland, forests and cliffs. For drop-dead views over the village and the valley, drive up to the panoramic viewpoint (it's signposted), which is perched atop a cliff near the ruins of a castle.

✕ ⊨ p179

The Drive » Pass through St-Romain and follow signs to

St-Romain Oak wine barrels being made for Burgundy vineyards

Falaises along the D17, then turn left onto the D17 (direction Falaises, Orches, Baubigny). It's a lovely drive with scenic vistas until you reach Baubigny. In Baubigny take the D111D to La Rochepot. It's an 8km drive from Meursault.

---

⑨ Château de La Rochepot

With its conical towers and multicoloured tile roofs rising from thick woods above the ancient village of La Rochepot, the **Château de La Rochepot** (☎03 80 21 71 37; www.larochepot. com; La Rochepot; adult/ child €8/4; ⊙10am-5.30pm Wed-Mon) is a dream come true for photographers and history buffs. This marvellous medieval fortress offers fab views of surrounding countryside.

The Drive ⟩⟩ Look for the D973 (direction Nolay); after 200m look for the left-hand turn onto the D33 that plunges down to St-Aubin. In St-Aubin turn left onto the D906 (direction Chagny), and eventually turn left onto the D113A to Puligny-Montrachet (10km from La Rochepot). It's a journey of 10km.

BURGUNDY WINE BASICS

Burgundy's epic vineyards extend approximately 258km from Chablis in the north to the Rhône's Beaujolais in the south and comprise 100 Appellations d'Origine Contrôlée (AOC). Each region has its own appellations and traits, embodied by a concept called *terroir* – the earth imbuing its produce, such as grapes, with unique qualities.

Here's an ever-so-brief survey of some of Burgundy's major growing regions:

» **Côte d'Or vineyards** The northern section, the **Côte de Nuits**, stretches from Marsannay-la-Côte (near Dijon) south to Corgoloin and produces reds known for their robust, full-bodied character. The southern section, the **Côte de Beaune**, lies between Ladoix-Serrigny and Santenay and produces great reds and great whites. Appellations from the area's hilltops are the **Hautes-Côtes de Nuits** and **Hautes-Côtes de Beaune**.

» **Chablis & Grand Auxerrois** Four renowned chardonnay white-wine appellations from 20 villages around Chablis. Part of the **Auxerrois vineyards**, **Irancy** produces excellent pinot noir reds.

» **Châtillonnais** Approximately 20 villages around Châtillon-sur-Seine producing red and white wines.

» **Côte Chalonnaise** The southernmost continuation of the Côte de Beaune's slopes is noted for its excellent reds and whites.

» **Mâconnais** Known for rich or fruity white wines, like the Pouilly-Fuissé chardonnay.

Want to Know More?

Take a class!

École des Vins de Bourgogne (☏03 80 26 35 10; www.ecoledesvins-bourgogne.com; 6 rue du 16e Chasseurs, Beaune) Offers a variety of courses.

Sensation Vin (☏03 80 22 17 57; www.sensation-vin.com; 1 rue d'Enfer, Beaune; ⊘10am-7pm) Offers introductory tasting sessions (no appointment needed) as well as tailor-made courses.

---

⑩ Puligny-Montrachet

Puligny-Montrachet makes a grand finale to your trip. Beloved of white wine aficionados (no reds in sight), this bijou appellation is revered thanks to five extraordinary Grands Crus. At the **Caveau de Puligny-Montrachet** (☏03 80 21 96 78; www.caveau-puligny.com; 1 rue de Poiseul; ⊘9.30am-noon & 2-8pm Mar-Oct) you can sample various local wines in a comfortable and relaxed setting. This wine bar–cellar is run by knowledgeable Julien Wallerand, who provides excellent advice (in decent English).

🛏 p179

Eating & Sleeping

Aloxe-Corton ④

⚑ Villa Louise Hôtel   Hotel €€

(☎03 80 26 46 70; www.hotel-villa-louise.fr;
9 rue Franche; d €100-195; P @ 🛜 🏊) This
tranquil mansion houses elegant, modern
rooms, each of them dreamily different. The
expansive garden stretches straight to the edge
of the vineyard and a separate gazebo shelters
the sauna and pool. Genteel Louise Perrin
presides, and has a private *cave* (wine cellar)
perfect for wine tastings.

Beaune ⑤

✖ Le P'tit
Paradis   Modern Burgundian €€

(☎03 80 24 91 00; 25 rue Paradis; menus €28-
36; ⊗lunch & dinner Thu-Mon) This intimate
restaurant on a narrow medieval street is known
for *cuisine elaborée* (creatively transformed
versions of traditional dishes) made with fresh
local products.

✖ Loiseau des
Vignes   Gastronomic €€€

(☎03 80 24 12 06; 31 rue Maufoux; menus
€20-95; ⊗lunch & dinner Tue-Sat) A culinary
shrine. Expect stunning concoctions ranging
from caramelised pigeon to *quenelles de sandre*
(dumplings made from pike fish), all exquisitely
presented. In summer, the verdant garden is
a plus.

⚑ Abbaye de
Maizières   Historic Hotel €€

(☎03 80 24 74 64; www.beaune-abbaye
-maizieres.com; 19 rue Maizières; d €118-190;
❄ @) This character-laden establishment
inside a 12th-century abbey oozes history, yet
most rooms have been luxuriously modernised.
Some rooms boast Cistercian stained-glass
windows and exposed beams; those on the
top floor offer views over Beaune's famed
multicoloured tile roofs.

Meursault ⑦

✖ Le Chevreuil –
La Maison de la
Mère Daugier   Modern Burgundian €€

(☎03 80 21 23 25; place de la République; menus
€23-58; ⊗lunch & dinner Mon, Tue & Thu-Sat)
Chef Tiago is known for his creative take on
regional staples. The dining room's country-
chic, with plenty of light, wood and stone for
that down-home feel, and the menu takes the
cream of traditional Burgundian and gives it a
21st-century spin.

St-Romain ⑧

✖ Les Roches   Burgundian €€

(☎03 80 21 21 63; www.les-roches.fr; Bas
Village; menus €29; ⊗lunch & dinner Mon &
Thu-Sun) In the heart of the village, this sweet
little spot with a pleasant outdoor setting
serves farm-fresh fare and well-executed
Burgundian specialities, including snails and
bœuf bourguignon.

⚑ Domaine Corgette   B&B €€

(☎03 80 21 68 08; www.domainecorgette.
com; rue de la Perrière; d €85-110; P 🛜) The
sun-drenched terrace at this renovated winery
looks out on the dramatic cliffs. Tucked in the
centre of the village, its rooms are light and airy,
and retain classic touches like fireplaces and
wooden floors. Good English is spoken.

Puligny-Montrachet ⑩

⚑ La Maison
d'Olivier Leflaive   Boutique Hotel €€€

(☎03 80 21 37 65; www.olivier-leflaive.com;
place du Monument; d €160-220; ⊗closed Jan)
Occupying a tastefully renovated 17th-century
village house, this 13-room venture delivers top
service and classy comfort, and there's an on-
site restaurant. Best of all, it offers personalised
wine tours and tastings. Perfect for wine lovers.

STRETCH YOUR LEGS
CHINON

Start/Finish Hostellerie Gargantua

- - - - - - - - - - - - - - - - - - -

Distance 3km

- - - - - - - - - - - - - - - - - - -

Duration Three hours

This relaxed walk leads you through Chinon's medieval centre from one end to the other, visiting both the lower town and the historic castle above, culminating in a scenic stroll along the cave-riddled cliff face to the east.

Take this walk on Trips

Hostellerie Gargantua

Renowned author François Rabelais (c 1483–1553) grew up in Chinon; this atmospheric **hotel** (73 rue Haute St-Maurice), housed in a Gothic palace that once served as headquarters for the king's representative in Chinon, is one of several places bearing Rabelais-related names that you'll find scattered throughout the old town. On the same street, look for the **Hôtel du Gouverneur**, an impressive town house with a double-flighted staircase ensconced behind a carved gateway.

The Walk >> Head east a few paces along rue Haute St-Maurice to the museum on the opposite side of the street.

Musée d'Art et d'Histoire

This small municipal **museum** (44 rue Haute St-Maurice; adult/child €3/free; 2.30-6.30pm Wed-Mon May–mid-Sep, 2-6pm Fri-Mon mid-Sep–mid-Nov & mid-Feb–Apr, closed mid-Nov–mid-Feb) has a collection of Chinon-related art and archaeological finds dating from prehistory to the 19th century, including a painting of Rabelais by Delacroix. Outside the museum is the intersection of two medieval streets, whose half-timbered buildings are said to have housed Joan of Arc while she awaited her audience with the dauphin Charles.

The Walk >> Continue east along rue Haute St-Maurice, which soon changes its name to rue Voltaire. Look for the Caves Painctes de Chinon in the cliff face to your left.

Caves Painctes de Chinon

Hidden at the end of a cobbled alleyway off rue Voltaire are the **Caves Painctes de Chinon** (impasse des Caves Painctes; admission €3; guided tours 11am, 3pm, 4.30pm & 6pm Tue-Sun Jul & Aug), a network of former quarries that were converted into wine cellars during the 15th century. Local winegrowers run tours of the *caves* (wine cellars) in summer.

The Walk >> Return to rue Voltaire, then walk diagonally across the street to La Cave Voltaire.

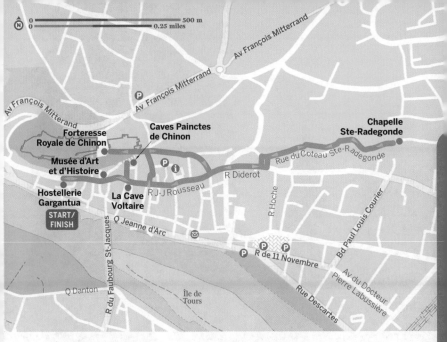

La Cave Voltaire

A great place for a mid-afternoon snack or an evening drink, **La Cave Voltaire** (www.lacavevoltaire.fr; 13 rue Voltaire) stocks over 200 wines from the Chinon region and beyond. Tasty platters of local cheese and charcuterie are served with hearty fresh bread at pavement tables with nice views up to Chinon's castle.

The Walk >> Follow rue Voltaire three blocks east into Chinon's picturesque main square, place du Général de Gaulle, then turn left (uphill) two blocks and take the free elevator to the upper town. Once up top, turn left and climb to the castle.

Forteresse Royale de Chinon

Chinon's star attraction is this fabulous castle (www.forteresse-chinon.fr; adult/child €7.50/5.50; ⏱9.30am-7pm May-Aug, to 5pm or 6pm rest of year). The 12th-century **Fort St-Georges** and **Logis Royal** (Royal Lodgings) date from the Plantagenet court of Henry II and Eleanor of Aquitaine, while the 14th-century **Tour de l'Horloge** (Clock Tower) houses exhibits commemorating Joan of Arc's

1429 meeting with the future Charles VII. For stupendous panoramas, climb atop the 13th-century **Fort du Coudray**.

The Walk >> Descend rue du Puy des Bancs to rue Jean-Jacques Rousseau, turn left and continue two blocks to St-Mexme church. Climb left of the church on rue de Pitoche, then follow rue du Coteau Ste-Radegonde 500m past cave-pockmarked cliffs to Chapelle Ste-Radegonde.

Chapelle Ste-Radegonde

Surrounded by abandoned troglodyte dwellings, this mystical, half-ruined medieval **chapel** (rue du Coteau Ste-Radegonde; adult/child €3/free; ⏱3-6pm Sat & Sun May, Jun & Sep, 3-6pm Wed-Mon Jul & Aug) is built partly into a cave, accessed by a red door in an old stone wall. The chapel's 12th-century 'Royal Hunt' fresco is said to represent members of the Plantagenet royal family; inside, a staircase descends to a subterranean spring associated with a pre-Christian cult.

The Walk >> Retrace your steps to Hostellerie Gargantua via St-Mexme church, rue Jean-Jacques Rousseau and place du Général de Gaulle.

181

Alps & Eastern France

FROM THE RHÔNE RIVER TO EUROPE'S HIGHEST MOUNTAIN, eastern France is a crazy quilt of inspirational landscapes.

Our five itineraries head in all directions from Lyon. To the northwest, narrow roads snake through the vine-covered Beaujolais; to the south, the Rhône flows through increasingly sunny country past Gallo-Roman ruins, medieval hilltop fortresses and precipitous gorges.

East lie the mountains: the Jura, land of Comté cheese and golden wine; the Vercors' poppy-strewn plateaus and limestone peaks; Haute-Provence's lavender fields and multihued canyons; and, towering high above, the Alps, where France's most spellbinding high-country scenery revolves around hulking Mont Blanc.

The Jura Cross-country skiing (Trip 16)
PRISMA BILDAGENTUR AG/ALAMY ©

Rhône Valley Gorges de l'Ardèche (Trip 20)

The Jura 5 Days
16 Mellow out amid bucolic highlands and rolling vineyards in this off-the-beaten-track region. (p187)

Classic Trip
Alpine Adventure 6 Days
17 Revel in France's high-country grandeur, from lakeside Annecy to top-of-the-world Chamonix. (p195)

Foothills of the Alps 6 Days
18 Hike verdant meadows and rugged canyons where the Alps and Provence meet. (p205)

Beaujolais Villages 2 Days
19 Explore the unhurried villages, gentle landscapes and renowned reds of the Beaujolais. (p213)

Rhône Valley 5 Days
20 Follow eastern France's great river from Lyon's bistros to Orange's Roman theatre. (p221)

 DON'T MISS

Château-Chalon
This is the perfect spot to sample the Jura's distinctive 'yellow' wine. Stay in a turreted B&B on Trip **16**

Bonneval-sur-Arc
Hidden on Europe's highest mountain pass, this village in Vanoise National Park is a nature-lover's hideaway. Escape here on Trip **17**

Gîte d'Alpage de la Molière
Homemade raspberry pie and spectacular mountain views welcome hikers at this eatery. Rest your feet here on Trip **18**

Domaine des Vignes du Paradis – Pascal Durand
This family-run domaine welcomes visitors. Stop in to sip award-winning St-Amour reds on Trip **19**

Sentier Aval des Gorges
Driving the Gorges de l'Ardèche scenic route is spectacular. Discover this easy-to-miss trail on Trip **20**

The Jura A waterfall skims mossy rocks in this region of wild terrain

The Jura **16**

On this trip through the extraordinarily diverse Jura region, you'll examine magnificent citadels, explore some of the wildest terrain in France, discover yellow wine and enjoy the mellow Jura vibe.

TRIP HIGHLIGHTS

0 km

Besançon
Seek out the Vauban citadel and the stellar Musée des Beaux-Arts

1 START

85 km

Arbois
Learn about the local speciality wine, *vin jaune*, in this bucolic village

3

115 km

Château-Chalon
Peer over the precipice in picturesque Château-Chalon

6

FINISH
● Les Rousses

205 km

Parc Naturel Régional du Haut-Jura
Act like an explorer in one of the least known corners of France

7

5 DAYS
227KM / 141 MILES

GREAT FOR...

BEST TIME TO GO
Come between June and September, when the sun shines. Avoid the freezing winter.

 ESSENTIAL PHOTO

Snap the hawks' view from the top of the Telesiège Val Mijoux.

 BEST FOR FAMILIES

Exploring the highlands of the Parc Naturel Régional du Haut-Jura.

MICHAEL BUSSELLE/GETTY IMAGES ©

187

16 | The Jura

Bleak and often cold, the high Jura mountains stand as a total contrast to the cheery lowlands, famed for buttercup-coloured wine. And 'contrast' sums up this trip well. One day can see you checking out Egyptian mummies, another will see you sampling local cheeses and still another will have you dangling above the earth in a chairlift. Despite all that, the Jura remains one of the least visited territories in France.

TRIP HIGHLIGHT

1 Besançon

Home to a monumental Vauban citadel and France's first public museum, and birthplace of Victor Hugo and the Lumière brothers, Besançon has an extraordinary background and yet, remarkably, despite charms such as its graceful 18th-century old town and first-rate restaurants, it remains something of a secret.

The Unesco-listed **Citadelle de Besançon** (www.citadelle.com, in French; rue des Fusillés de la Résistance; adult/child €9.20/6.10; ⊙9am-6pm)

is a formidable feat of engineering, designed by the prolific Vauban for Louis XIV in the late 17th century. Inside (and included in the ticket price) are a number of **museums**.

Founded in 1694, the **Musée des Beaux-Arts et d'Archéologie** (www.musee-arts-besancon.org, in French; 1 place de la Révolution; adult/child €5/free; ⊙9.30am-noon & 2-6pm Wed-Mon) is France's oldest museum. The stellar collection includes such archaeological exhibits as Egyptian mummies, neolithic tools and Gallo-Roman mosaics, and boasts a cavernous drawing cabinet with 5500 works including

Dürer, Delacroix, Rubens, Goya, Matisse and Rodin masterpieces.

✗ ⨳ p193

The Drive 》 From Besançon you can opt for the fast A36 (51km, 45 minutes) or the marginally slower but more enjoyable D673 (46km, 55 minutes) to Dole.

---

② Dole

Almost every town in France has at least one street, square or garden named after Louis Pasteur, the great 19th-century chemist who invented pasteurisation and developed the first rabies vaccine. In the Jura it is even more the case, since the illustrious man was a local lad: he was born in 1822 in the

LINK YOUR TRIP

15 Route des Grands Crus

Need a drink before starting our Jura tour? Combine it with our Route des Grands Crus drive; its starting point of Gevrey-Chambertin is 62km from Dole along the A39.

17 Alpine Adventure

If the heights of the Jura appeal then you'll love our Alpine Adventure, which begins in Lyon, a 135km drive from Mijoux down the A42.

well-preserved medieval town of Dole.

A scenic stroll along the Canal des Tanneurs in Dole's historic tanner's quarter brings you to Pasteur's childhood home, **La Maison Natale de Pasteur** (www.musee -pasteur.com; 43 rue Pasteur; adult/child €5/free; ☉10am- noon & 2-6pm Mon-Sat, 2-6pm Sun), now an atmospheric museum housing exhibits including his cot, first drawings and university cap and gown.

The Drive ›› It's a 45-minute, 37km doddle down the D905 and D469 to Arbois.

TRIP HIGHLIGHT

❸ Arbois

The bucolic village of Arbois is well worth a visit. In 1827 the Pasteur

family settled here, and Louis' laboratory and workshops are on display at **La Maison de Louis Pasteur** (83 rue de Courcelles; adult/child €6/3; ☉guided tours 9.45-11.45am & 2-6pm, closed mid-Oct–Mar).

If science is a bit too dusty for you then may we tempt you with a glass of wine? Arbois sits at the heart of the Jura wine region, renowned for its *vin jaune*. The history of this nutty 'yellow wine' is told in the **Musée de la Vigne et du Vin** (www. juramusees.fr; adult/child €3.50/2.80; ☉10am-noon & 2-6pm Wed-Mon), housed in the whimsical, turreted Château Pécauld. Afterwards clear your head by walking the 2.5km-long **Chemin**

des Vignes trail, which wends its way through the vines. It starts from the steps next to the Château Pécauld.

 p193

The Drive ›› Clamber steeply uphill for five minutes (3km) along the D246 to reach the spectacularly situated village of Pupillin.

- - - - - - - - - - - -

❹ Pupillin

High above Arbois is tiny Pupillin, a cute yellow- brick village famous for its wine production. Some 10 *caves* (wine cellars) are open to visitors.

The Drive ›› Head southwest out of Pupillin on the N83 and in 15 minutes (9km) you'll have dropped to the small town of Poligny.

LIQUID GOLD

Legend has it that *vin jaune* (yellow wine) was invented when a winemaker found a forgotten barrel, six years and three months after he'd initially filled it, and discovered its contents miraculously transformed into a gold-coloured wine.

A long, undisrupted fermentation process gives Jura's signature wine its unique characteristics. Savagnin grapes are harvested late and their sugar-saturated juices left to ferment for a minimum of six years and three months in oak barrels. A thin layer of yeast forms over the wine, which prevents it from oxidising, and there are no top-ups to compensate for evaporation (called *la part des anges* – 'the angels' share'). In the end, 100L of grape juice ferments down to 62L of *vin jaune* (lucky angels), which is then bottled in special 0.62L bottles called *clavelin*. *Vin jaune* is renowned for its ageing qualities, with prime vintages easily keeping for more than a century. A 1774 vintage, a cool 220 years old at the time, was sipped by an awestruck committee of experts in 1994.

La Percée du Vin Jaune (www.percee-du-vin-jaune.com) festival takes place annually in early February to celebrate the first tasting of the vintage produced six years and three months earlier. Villages take it in turn to hold the two-day celebrations, at which the new vintage is blessed and rated, and street tastings, cooking competitions, cellar visits and auctions keep *vin jaune* aficionados fulfilled.

HERVE HUGHES/GETTY IMAGES ©

Arbois View across a vineyard

❺ Poligny

Need a little cheese to accompany all that wine? Comté is the indisputable cheese king of the Jura, and the small town of Poligny is the 'capital' of an industry that produces 40 million tonnes of the venerable foodstuff a year. Learn how 450L of milk is transformed into a 40kg wheel of the tangy cheese, smell some of its 83 aromas, and have a nibble at the **Maison du Comté** (www.maison-du-comte.com; av de la Résistance; adult/child €4/2.50; ⌚guided tours 2pm, 3.15pm & 4.30pm, closed Nov-Mar). Dozens of *fruitières* (cheese cooperatives) are open to the public. Poligny's **tourist office** (☎03 84 37 24 21; www.ville-poligny.fr; place des Déportés; ⌚9am-12.30pm & 1.30-5.30pm Mon-Fri, 9am-12.30pm & 2-5pm Sat) stocks an abundance of info on cheesemakers and wineries in the region.

🛏 p193

The Drive » Take the D68 out of town, and after about 4km veer right onto the D96. After a further 4km, make a sharp right onto the D5 and cruise through pretty countryside into Château-Chalon. It's 15km in total.

TRIP HIGHLIGHT

❻ Château-Chalon

Despite a name that conjures up images of grand castles, Château-Chalon is actually a pocket-sized medieval village of honey-coloured stone perched on a hilltop and surrounded by vineyards known for their legendary *vin jaune*.

🛏 p193

The Drive » Leave Château-Chalon in a northeasterly direction on the D5 and then double back to the D70 and the town of Lons-le-Saunier.

HOT BOX, CHRISTMAS ICE & JESUS

It's hot, it's soft and it's packed in a box. Vacherin Mont d'Or is the only French cheese to be eaten with a spoon – hot. Made between 15 August and 15 March with *lait cru* (unpasteurised milk), it derives its unique nutty taste from the spruce bark in which it's wrapped. Connoisseurs top the soft-crusted cheese with chopped onions, garlic and white wine, wrap it in aluminium foil and bake it for 45 minutes to create a *boîte chaude* (hot box). Only 11 factories in the Jura are licensed to produce Vacherin Mont d'Or.

Mouthe, 15km south of Métabief Mont d'Or, is the mother of *liqueur de sapin* (fir-tree liqueur). *Glace de sapin* (fir-tree ice cream) also comes from Mont d'Or, known as the North Pole of France due to its seasonal subzero temperatures (record low: -38°C). Sampling either is rather like ingesting a Christmas tree. Then there's *Jésus* – a small, fat version of *saucisse de Morteau* (Morteau sausage), easily identified by the wooden peg on its end, attached after the sausage is smoked with pinewood sawdust in a traditional *tuyé* (mountain hut).

From here the D52, D470 and D436 will be your route into the high-mountain bliss of the Parc Naturel Régional du Haut-Jura and the village of Lajoux. In total it's 90km and 1½ hours.

TRIP HIGHLIGHT

❼ Parc Naturel Régional du Haut-Jura

Experience the Jura at its rawest in the Haut-Jura Regional Park, an area of 757 sq km stretching from Chapelle-des-Bois in the north almost to the western tip of Lake Geneva.

A great place to start is the **Maison du Parc** (www.parc-haut-jura.fr; Lajoux; adult/child €5/3; ◷10am-12.30pm & 2-6pm Tue-Fri, 2-6pm Sat & Sun), a visitor centre with an interactive sensorial museum that explores the region and its history through sound, touch and smell. The Maison du Parc is in the village

of Lajoux, 19km east of St-Claude and 5km west of Mijoux on the Swiss border.

The Drive » From the Maison du Parc the D436 will have you switchbacking 5km down the valley into the village of Mijoux.

❽ Mijoux

From close to the small ski resort of Mijoux there are some fabulous panoramas of Lake Geneva embraced by the French Alps and Mont Blanc. For the best views, ride the **Telesiège Val Mijoux** (chairlift; adult/child return €7/4.50; ◷10.30am-1pm & 2.15-5.30pm Sat & Sun mid-Jul–late Aug) from Mijoux or drive to the **Col de la Faucille** (7km along the D936), high above the village.

The Drive » It's a 20-minute, 22km drive along the D936 and D1005 to Les Rousses through forest and pastureland.

❾ Les Rousses

The driving tour comes to a close in the resort of Les Rousses, on the northeastern edge of the park. This is the park's prime sports hub for winter (skiing) and summer (walking and mountain biking) alike. The resort comprises four small, predominantly cross-country ski areas: Prémanon, Lamoura, Bois d'Amont and the village Les Rousses. Find out more at the **Maison du Tourisme** (Fort des Rousses; ◷9am-noon & 2-6pm Mon-Sat, 9.30am-12.30pm Sun), home to the **tourist office** (☏03 84 60 02 55; www.lesrousses.com, in French) and the **ESF** (☏03 84 60 01 61; www.esf-lesrousses.com) ski school.

Eating & Sleeping

Besançon ❶

✘ Le Saint-Pierre   Modern French €€€

(📞03 81 81 20 99; www.restaurant-saintpierre.
com, in French; 104 rue Battant; menus €38-70;
🕙lunch & dinner Mon-Fri, dinner Sat) Crisp
white tablecloths, exposed stone and subtle
lighting are the backdrop for intense flavours,
such as lobster fricassee with spinach and herb
ravioli, which are expertly paired with regional
wines. The three-course *menu marché* including
wine and coffee is excellent value at €38.

🛏 Charles Quint Hôtel   Historic Hotel €€

(📞03 81 82 05 49; www.hotel-charlesquint.
com; 3 rue du Chapître; d €89-145; 📶🏊) This
discreetly grand 18th-century town house
turned nine-room boutique hotel is sublime,
with period furniture, sumptuous fabrics, a
garden with a tiny swimming pool and a wood-
panelled dining room. Find it slumbering in the
shade of the citadel, behind the cathedral.

Arbois ❸

✘ La Balance
Mets et Vins   Regional Cuisine €€

(📞03 84 37 45 00; 47 rue de Courcelles; menus
€16.50-36.50; 🕙lunch & dinner Thu-Mon,
lunch Tue; 🍴) With its lunches favouring local,
organic produce, La Balance Mets et Vins

provides the perfect coda to a wine-loving trip.
Its signature *coq au vin jaune et aux morilles*
casserole and crème brûlée doused in *vin jaune*
are must-tastes, as are the wine menus with
five glasses of either Jurassien wine (€17) or *vin
jaune* (€25).

Poligny ❺

🛏 Hôtel de la Vallée Heureuse   Hotel €€

(📞03 84 37 12 13; www.hotelvalleeheureuse.
com; rte de Genève; s €95-125, d €125-150,
q €175, menus €28-65; 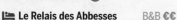) You will indeed
be *heureuse* (happy) to stumble across this
beautifully converted 18th-century mill, which
sits in riverside parkland and affords gorgeous
forest and mountain views. The country retreat
has tastefully decorated rooms and a restaurant
specialising in Jurassien cuisine.

Château-Chalon ❻

🛏 Le Relais des Abbesses   B&B €€

(📞03 84 44 98 56; www.chambres-hotes-jura.
com; rue de la Roche; d €75, dinner €25) At this
turreted *chambre d'hôte* (B&B), Agnès and
Gérard have attractively decorated the rooms
with hardwood floors, romantic canopy beds
and Asian antiques. They are both fine cooks
and dinner is an absolute treat, whether it's
in the elegant dining room or on the terrace
overlooking the countryside.

The Alps Breathtaking Mont Blanc
views from on top of the world

Classic Trip

Alpine Adventure

17

Combining take-your-breath-away grandeur with a delightful dose of French mountain culture, France's Alps provide a stunning and incomparable setting for a summer road trip.

TRIP HIGHLIGHTS

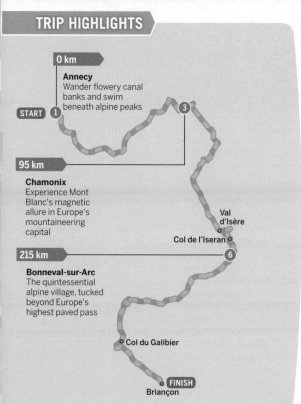

0 km

START 1

Annecy
Wander flowery canal banks and swim beneath alpine peaks

3

95 km

Chamonix
Experience Mont Blanc's magnetic allure in Europe's mountaineering capital

Val d'Isère

Col de l'Iseran

6

215 km

Bonneval-sur-Arc
The quintessential alpine village, tucked beyond Europe's highest paved pass

Col du Galibier

FINISH
Briançon

6 DAYS
363KM / 225 MILES

GREAT FOR...

BEST TIME TO GO
Mid-June to mid-September – mountain passes are snow-free.

 ESSENTIAL PHOTO

Alpine crags and colourful boats reflected in the lake at Annecy.

 BEST TWO DAYS

The section between Annecy and Chamonix: the French Alps' most classic scenery.

195

Classic Trip

17 | Alpine Adventure

A study in superlatives, this outdoorsy ramble through the heart of the French Alps runs from Annecy (France's prettiest lake) to Mont Blanc (western Europe's highest peak) to Col de l'Iseran (Europe's highest mountain pass) to Bonneval-sur-Arc (one of France's most beautiful villages). Along the way you'll have ample opportunities for high-adrenaline mountain adventure – hiking, mountain biking, white-water rafting, vertigo-inducing cable-car rides and crossings of the French Alps' most spectacular passes.

TRIP HIGHLIGHT

1 Annecy

There's no dreamier introduction to the French Alps than Annecy. The mountains rise steep, wooded and snow-capped above startlingly turquoise Lac d'Annecy, providing a sublime setting for the medieval town's photogenic jumble of geranium-strewn houses, romantic canals and turreted rooftops.

Summer is the prime time to visit, when everyone is outdoors, socialising at pavement cafes, swimming in the lake (among Europe's purest) and boating, walking or cycling around it. Evening street performers feature during July's **Les Noctibules** festival, and there are lakeside fireworks during August's **Fête du Lac**.

Wander through the narrow medieval streets of the **Vieille Ville** (Old Town) to find the whimsical 12th-century **Palais de l'Isle** (3 passage de l'Île; adult/child €3.50/1.50; ◷10.30am-6pm) on a

triangular islet in the Canal du Thiou. Next stroll the tree-fringed lakefront through the flowery **Jardins de l'Europe**, linked to the popular picnic spot **Champ de Mars** by the graceful **Pont des Amours** (Lovers' Bridge) and presided over by the perkily turreted **Château d'Annecy** (rampe du Château; adult/child €5/2.50; ⏱10.30am-6pm).

Cycling paths encircle the lake, passing by several pretty **beaches** en route. **Boats** (per hr €15-50) can be hired along the canal-side quays, and several companies offer **adventure sports**. For details, visit Annecy's **tourist office** (📞04 50 45 00 33; www.lac-annecy. com; Centre Bonlieu; ⏱9am-6.30pm Mon-Sat, to 12.30pm & 1.45-6pm Sun).

✗ 🏠 p203

LINK YOUR TRIP

16 The Jura

Discover the tamer pleasures of eastern France's 'other' mountains, three hours north of Annecy.

18 Foothills of the Alps

Join this nature-lover's jaunt through high-country plateaus and dramatic canyons, two hours west of Briançon.

Classic Trip

The Drive >> This 70km drive starts with a pretty southeastern run along Annecy's lakeshore, passing through the wildlife-rich wetlands of Bout du Lac on the lake's southern tip before continuing east on the D1508, then northeast on the D1212 and D909 into St-Gervais.

② St-Gervais-les-Bains

Basking in the shadow of Mont Blanc, St-Gervais-les-Bains is a postcard-perfect Savoyard village, centred on a baroque church and old-fashioned carousel.

Panoramic **hiking trails** in the Bettex, Mont d'Arbois and Mont Joly areas head off from town. Some of the best mountain-biking terrain is marked between Val d'Arly, Mont Blanc and Beaufortain.

For spirit-soaring mountain views with zero effort, board the **Tramway du Mont Blanc** (rue de la Gare; return to Bellevue/Mont Lachat €27.50/30.50; ☉9am-4.50pm), France's highest train. Since 1913 it has been labouring up to Bellevue (1800m) in winter and Mont Lachat (2113m) in summer.

Train buffs will also love the narrow-gauge **Mont-Blanc**

Express (www.ter-sncf.com), which trundles along a century-old rail line from St-Gervais-Le Fayet station to Martigny in Switzerland. For info, enter 'Mont-Blanc Express' into the website's 'Rechercher sur le site' pane.

🛏 p203

The Drive >> The 24km route to Chamonix follows the D902, N205 and D243 into the heart of the Alps.

TRIP HIGHLIGHT

③ Chamonix

An outdoors playground of epic proportions, Chamonix sits directly at the foot of western Europe's highest peak, the pearly white massif of Mont Blanc (4810m).

Climbers with the necessary skill, experience and stamina flock here for the incomparable **Mont Blanc ascent**. If you're not quite ready to scale 'the big one', consider circumnavigating it on the classic six- to 10-day **Tour du Mont Blanc**, which takes in majestic glaciers and peaks in France, Italy and Switzerland; local outfitters organise excursions including half-board in *refuges* (mountain huts), lift tickets and luggage transport. Other peak experiences include Chamonix's dozens of **day hikes** (p199), the

unforgettable cable-car ascent to **Aiguille du Midi** (p202) and the **train ride** (adult/child/family €26.40/22.30/79.20) to France's largest glacier, the glistening 200m-deep **Mer de Glace** (Sea of Ice).

Chamonix has an unparalleled menu of adrenaline sports including **rafting**, **canyoning**, **mountain biking** and **paragliding** down from the heights of Planpraz (2000m) or Aiguille du Midi (3842m). For details, visit the **tourist office** (☎04 50 53 00 24; www.chamonix.com; 85 place du Triangle de l'Amitié; ☉8.30am-7pm).

🍴 🛏 p203

The Drive >> From Chamonix, take the E25 southeast 17km through the Mont Blanc Tunnel into Italy. From the Aosta/Courmayeur exit, continue 31km southwest back towards France along the SS26. Once across the border, follow the D1090 and D84 southwest, then the D902 southeast for a total of 40km into Val d'Isère.

④ Val d'Isère

This world-renowned, end-of-the-valley resort is home to the gargantuan Espace Killy skiing area, named after French triple Olympic gold medallist Jean-Claude Killy. Even in July, you can ski the **Pisaillas Glacier** above town, though many summer visitors also come to hike, mountain bike and enjoy off-season hotel discounts.

HIKING CHAMONIX

Chamonix boasts 350km of spectacular high-altitude trails, many reached by cable car. In June and July there's enough light to walk until at least 9pm. Here are a few recommended walks to get you started.

» Lac Blanc From the top of **Les Praz l'Index Télépherique** (cable car; one-way/return €20/24) or at **La Flégère** (€12/14), the line's midway point, gentle 1¼- to two-hour trails lead to 2352m Lac Blanc, a turquoise-coloured lake ensnared by mountains. Stargazers can overnight at the **Refuge du Lac Blanc** (☑04 50 47 24 49; dm incl half-board €49; ☺mid-Jun–Sep), a wooden chalet favoured by photographers for its top-of-Europe Mont Blanc views.

» Grand Balcon Sud This easygoing trail skirts the western side of the valley, stays at around 2000m and commands a terrific view of Mont Blanc. Reach it on foot from behind Le Brévent's *télécabine* station.

» Grand Balcon Nord Routes starting from the Plan de l'Aiguille include the challenging Grand Balcon Nord, which takes you to the dazzling Mer de Glace, from where you can walk or take the Montenvers train down to Chamonix.

The trails weaving into the nearby valleys of **Parc National de la Vanoise** are a hiker's dream. For more of a challenge, play among the peaks at neighbouring La Daille's two **via ferrata** fixed-rope routes.

Mountain biking (VTT) is big in Val, especially since the resort hosted stages of the UCI World Cup in 2012. Five lifts offer cyclists access to 16 downhill routes, seven endurance runs and two cross-country circuits. Bike rental is available at local sport shops. **Bureau des Guides** (☑06 14 62 90 24; www.guides-montagne -valdisere.com) arranges guided hiking, mountain biking, canyoning and rock-climbing excursions.

Visit the **tourist office** (☑04 79 06 06 60; www. valdisere.com; place Jacques Mouflier; ☺8.30am-7.30pm)

for details on family-friendly activities, from donkey trekking to farm visits.

 p203

The Drive » Prepare for a dizzying climb as you leave Val d'Isère, steeply switchbacking 17km up the D902 to Col de l'Iseran.

- - - - - - - - - - - - -

⑤ Col de l'Iseran

No doubt about it, you're really far above sea level here! Indeed, the D902 over Col de l'Iseran (2770m) is the highest paved through road in Europe. Meteorological conditions at the summit are notoriously fickle – witness the Tour de France stage that was supposed to pass through here on 8 July 1996 but had to be rerouted due to snow and -5°C temperatures!

The Drive » Spellbinding views unfold as you navigate the D902's hairpin turns 14km downhill into Bonneval-sur-Arc.

✓ TOP TIP: WINTER DRIVING

Parts of this route (notably the northern stretches around Annecy and Chamonix) are accessible to drivers in winter, but the high mountain passes further south are strictly off-limits outside summer. See p422 for further notes on driving in the French mountains.

Classic Trip

⑥ Bonneval-sur-Arc

Heralded as one of the *plus beaux villages de la France* (prettiest villages in France), this high mountain hamlet is filled with stone and slate cottages that wear their winter preparations proudly (notice all the woodpiles up on 2nd-floor porches).

Bonneval makes a tranquil base for exploring the 530-sq-km **Parc National de la Vanoise** (www.parcnational -vanoise.fr), whose rugged snowcapped peaks, mirror-like lakes and vast glaciers dominate the landscape between the Tarentaise and Maurienne Valleys.

This incredible swath of wilderness was designated France's first national park in 1963, protecting habitat for marmots, chamois and France's largest colony of ibexes, along with 20 pairs of golden eagles and the odd bearded vulture.

The park is a hiker's heaven between June and September. The **Grand Tour de Haute Maurienne** (www.hautemaurienne.com), a seven-day hike around the upper reaches of the valley, takes in national-park highlights. For information on local day hikes, visit Bonneval-sur-Arc's **tourist office** (☎04 79 05 95 95; www.bonneval -sur-arc.com; ⊙9am-noon & 2-6.30pm Mon-Sat).

🛏 p203

The Drive » Cruise 55km down the Arc River valley on the D902 through Lanslebourg and Modane to St-Michel de Maurienne, then climb 35km through the ski resort of Valloire to the ethereal heights of Col du Galibier.

⑦ Col du Galibier

The signposts say you're simply crossing the departmental border from Savoie into the Hautes Alpes. The landscape says that you've entered another universe. Col du Galibier (2642m) is a staggeringly beautiful Alpine pass, whose forbidding remoteness may make you feel like the last living person on earth. To the west lies the Parc National des Écrins, a 918-sq-km expanse of high

LOCAL KNOWLEDGE
ERIC FAVRET, MOUNTAIN GUIDE, COMPAGNIE DES GUIDES DE CHAMONIX

The best-ever Mont Blanc view? No hesitation: the Traverse from Col des Montets to Lac Blanc. I love swimming in mountain lakes, so I like to stop at Lac des Chéserys, just below, where it's quieter: what's better than a swim in pure mountain water, looking at Mont Blanc, the Grandes Jorasses and Aiguille Verte? This is what I call mountain landscape perfection!

Left: Canal du Thiou and château, Annecy
Right: Val d'Isère ski resort

mountain wilderness. Stop and savour the top-of-the-world feeling before returning to the squiggling ribbon of roadway below.

The Drive » Despite the distance on the signpost (35km), the incredibly twisty and scenic descent into Briançon on the D902 and D1091 feels longer; stupendous views will stop you in your tracks every couple of minutes. Enjoy every horn-tooting, head-spinning, glacier-gawping moment, with views of thundering falls, sheer cliffs and jagged peaks razoring above thick larch forests.

8 **Briançon**

Perched astride a high rocky outcrop, the

fairy-tale walled city of Briançon affords views of the snowcapped Écrins peaks from almost every corner. The centre's Italian ambience is no coincidence; Italy is just 20km away.

Briançon's old town is a late-medieval time capsule, its winding cobbled lanes punctuated by shuttered, candy-coloured town houses and shops selling whistling marmots. The steep main street, **Grande Gargouille**, links two town gates, **Porte de Pignerol** and **Porte d'Embrun**. Crowning the old city is the massive **Fort du Château**. Daily **guided walks** are run by **Service du Patrimoine** (☑04 92 20 29 49; Porte de Pignerol; adult/ child €7/5.50; ⊙2-5.30pm Mon, 9am-noon & 2-5.30pm Tue-Fri).

Briançon's biggest drawcard is its Unesco-

listed ensemble of 17th- and early-18th-century structures designed by pioneering French military architect Vauban, including the old town's signature **star-shaped fortifications**, the coral-pink **Collégiale Notre Dame et St Nicolas**, several nearby **forts** and the **Pont d'Asfeld** bridge.

There are outstanding **hiking** opportunities in the mountains of nearby **Parc National des Écrins** (www.ecrins-parcnational.fr). Pick up maps and info at the **Maison du Parc** (☑04 92 21 08 49; place du Médecin-Général Blanchard; ⊙2-6pm Mon-Fri). For guided treks, glacier traverses, mountain biking, rafting, kayaking, canyoning and *via ferrate,* check with **Bureau des Guides et Accompagnateurs** (☑04 92 20 15 73; www.guides -briancon.fr).

AIGUILLE DU MIDI

A jagged needle of rock rearing above glaciers, snowfields and rocky crags, 8km from the hump of Mont Blanc, the Aiguille du Midi (3842m) is one of Chamonix's most distinctive landmarks. If you can handle the height, don't miss taking a trip up here; the 360-degree views of the French, Swiss and Italian Alps are breathtaking.

All year round the vertiginous **Téléphérique de l'Aiguille de Midi** (place de l'Aiguille du Midi; adult/child return to Aiguille du Midi €45.60/38.50, Plan de l'Aiguille €26.40/22.30; ⊙8.30am-4.30pm), one of the world's highest cable cars, climbs to the summit. Halfway up, Plan de l'Aiguille (2317m) is a terrific place to start hikes or paraglide. In summer you'll need to obtain a boarding card (marked with the number of your departing *and* returning cable car) in addition to a ticket. Bring warm clothes; even in summer the temperature rarely rises above -10°C up top!

From the Aiguille du Midi, between late June and early September you can continue for a further 30 minutes of mind-blowing scenery – think suspended glaciers, spurs, seracs and shimmering ice fields – in the smaller bubbles of the **Télécabine Panoramique Mont Blanc** (adult/child return from Chamonix €70/59.20; ⊙8.30am-3.30pm) to Pointe Helbronner (3466m) on the Franco–Italian border.

Eating & Sleeping

Annecy ❶

✕ L'Esquisse — Regional Cuisine €€

(☎04 50 44 80 59; www.esquisse-annecy.fr; 21 rue Royale; menus lunch €19-22, dinner €29-60; ☺lunch & dinner Mon, Tue & Thu-Sat) Book ahead at this intimate six-table bistro, whose owners' passion shines through in the service, wine list and menus singing with integral flavours, from wild mushrooms to spider crab.

🛏 Hotel Splendid — Boutique Hotel €€

(☎04 50 45 20 00; www.hotel-annecy-lac. fr; 4 quai Eustache Chappuis; s/d €109/121; ✳🛜🚹) 'Splendid' sums up the lakefront position of this friendly, family-oriented hotel, with breezy views from its boutique-chic, parquet-floored rooms.

St-Gervais-les-Bains ❷

🛏 Les Dômes de Miage — Campground €

(☎04 50 93 45 96; www.camping-mont-blanc. com; 197 rte des Contamines; campsites €23-28.50; ☺May–mid-Sep; 🛜) Mont Blanc is your wake-up call at this beautifully set, well-equipped campground with on-site restaurant and playground.

Chamonix ❸

✕ Les Vieilles Luges — Traditional French €€

(☎06 84 42 37 00; www.lesvieillesluges.com; Les Houches; menus €20-35; ☺lunch & dinner daily) At this dreamy 250-year-old farmhouse, reached via a scenic 20-minute hike from Maison Neuve chairlift, Julie and Claude spoil you with their home-cooked bœuf bourguignon and creamy farçon (prepared with potatoes, prunes and bacon). Magic!

🛏 Auberge du Manoir — Hotel €€

(☎04 50 53 10 77; aubergedumanoir.com, in French; 8 rte du Bouchet; s €109-122, d €126-176, q €178; 🛜🚹) Ablaze with geraniums in summer, this beautifully converted farmhouse has it all: pristine mountain views, quaint but never cloying pine-panelled rooms, an outdoor hot tub and a bar. Tasty breakfasts feature fruit, homemade yoghurt, cakes and tarts.

Val d'Isère ❹

✕ L'Étable d'Alain — Savoyard €€

(☎04 79 06 13 02; www.fermedeladroit.com, in French; mains €22-29; 🚹) Feast on deliciously gooey fondues and raclette (an Alpine speciality consisting of boiled potatoes and melted cheese) at this attractively converted stable, watched by cud-chewing cows in the family dairy barn next door.

🛏 Chalet Hôtel Sorbiers — Hotel €€

(☎04 79 06 23 77; www.hotelsorbiers -valdisere.com; Val Village; s/d/tr/q summer €75/104/141/152; 🛜🚹) This cosy, chalet-style hotel has a sunny garden and well-kept rooms with wood trappings, balconies and Jacuzzi bathtubs. Ample breakfasts include fresh pastries, eggs and bacon.

Bonneval-sur-Arc ❻

🛏 Auberge d'Oul — B&B €

(☎04 79 05 87 99; www.auberge-oul.com; dm/d/q incl breakfast €25/58/104, incl half-board €36/80/148) Smack on the village square, this flowery-balconied, slate-walled gîte (self-catering cottage) has one seven-person dorm and three rustic but spotless rooms; add a few euros for home-cooked mountain meals.

Gorges du Verdon Paddle the
magnificent emerald waters

Foothills of the Alps

18

This exhilarating outdoor adventure links two gorgeous, wild landscapes – the high green meadows and peaks of the Vercors, and the rugged canyon country of the Alpes de Haute Provence.

TRIP HIGHLIGHTS

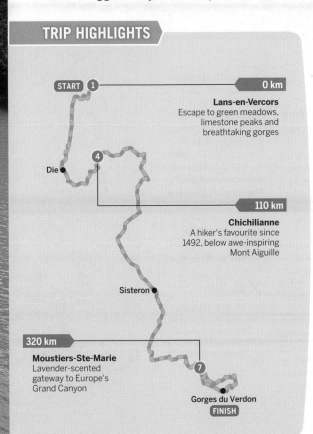

START **1** — **0 km**

Lans-en-Vercors
Escape to green meadows, limestone peaks and breathtaking gorges

Die

4

110 km

Chichilianne
A hiker's favourite since 1492, below awe-inspiring Mont Aiguille

Sisteron

320 km

Moustiers-Ste-Marie
Lavender-scented gateway to Europe's Grand Canyon

7

Gorges du Verdon
FINISH

**6 DAYS
475KM / 295 MILES**

GREAT FOR...

BEST TIME TO GO
June and September, for good weather without peak summer crowds.

 ESSENTIAL PHOTO
The dizzying view of the Gorges du Verdon from Belvédère de l'Escale.

 BEST FAMILY HIKE
The high-country loop from La Molière, near Lans-en-Vercors.

18 Foothills of the Alps

In the transition zone between the Alps and Provence lie some of France's most magnificent and least explored landscapes. Extending from the Vercors plateau to the Verdon River, this trip starts in poppy-strewn pastures where cowbells jingle beneath limestone peaks and ends among the lavender fields and arid gorges of Haute Provence. Along the way, there's plenty of outdoorsy excitement for the entire family.

❶ Lans-en-Vercors

Pristine Lans-en-Vercors (elevation 1020m) is idyllically set among the gently rolling pastures, plateaus and chiselled limestone peaks of the 1750-sq-km **Parc Naturel Régional du Vercors**, 28km southwest of Grenoble. With stunning vistas and wildlife including marmots and chamois, the park draws families seeking low-key outdoor adventure. Hikers of any age will enjoy the easy, supremely scenic 7km high-country loop from **La Molière** to **Pas de Bellecombe**, with its built-in lunch stop at Gîte d'Alpage de la Molière (p211). To reach the trailhead, go 20km north of Lans-en-Vercors via Autrans, following the D106 and a partly unpaved forest road. Alternatively, **Accompagnateurs Nature et Patrimoine** (☎04 76 95 08 38; www.accompagnateur-vercors.com) offers **guided walks** (full day adult/child €26/19) throughout the Vercors.

✕ ⊨ p211

The Drive » Follow the D531 southwest from Lans-en-Vercors, descending to enter the magnificent Gorges de la Bourne after about 10km.

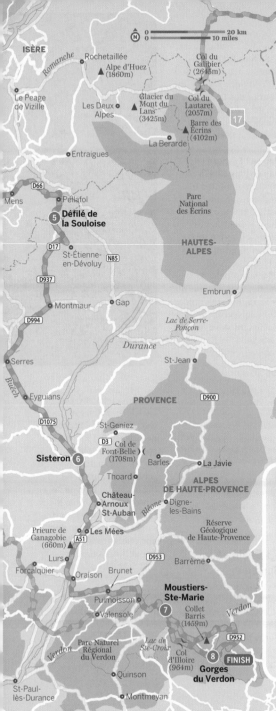

2 Gorges de la Bourne

Cliff walls up to 600m high crowd in around the main road in this magical stretch of gorges cut by a rushing river coming off the Vercors plateau. Watch for narrow turnouts alongside the roadway where you can pull off and admire the views.

The Drive » Near the end of the gorges, bear left on the D103 and proceed 20km south through the pretty mountain villages of St-Julien-en-Vercors and St-Martin-en-Vercors. At St-Agnan-en-Vercors continue 5km south on the D518 to the Grotte de la Luire.

3 Grotte de la Luire

The Vercors was a hotbed of the French Resistance in WWII. This **cave** (adult/child €7/4.50; ☺10am-6pm Jul-Sep, tours 11am, 2pm & 3.30pm Wed, Sat

LINK YOUR TRIP

17 **Alpine Adventure**
Head northeast from Lans-en-Vercors to explore France's most awe-inspiring peaks.

22 **Lavender Route**
Wander the purple-fringed back roads of Provence, west of Moustiers-Ste-Marie.

& Sun May, Jun & Oct) outside the town of St-Agnan-en-Vercors served as a field hospital for Resistance fighters for five days in July 1944 before German troops raided it, killing many patients on site and taking the rest to Grenoble to be shot or deported. Memorial plaques mark the site, and lantern-lit tours are offered in summer.

The Drive ≫ The D518 travels 30km south to Die, culminating in a switchbacking descent from Col de Rousset. The D93 and D539 continue southeast 14km through sun-drenched farmland to Châtillon-en-Diois, a good lunch stop (p211). The final 31km stretch along the D120 and D7 snakes over Col de Menée (1457m) to Chichilianne, affording spellbinding views of Mont Aiguille en route.

TRIP HIGHLIGHT

❹ Chichilianne

Its lovely hayfields strewn with red poppies in late spring, Chichilianne has deep roots in mountaineering history, dating back to 1492 when Antoine Deville scaled massive cube-shaped Mont Aiguille by order of King Charles VIII (accompanied by stonemasons and master carpenters who helped build ladders and attach ropes!). Long nicknamed the 'inaccessible mountain', and celebrated by writers such as Rabelais, Mont Aiguille continues to capture the imagination of all who venture near.

Superb high-country hikes around Chichilianne include the **Sentier des Charenches** up Mont Aiguille's southern flanks, and the six-hour loop to the Vercors plateau via **Pas de l'Essaure** and **Pas de l'Aiguille** (look for the monument to Resistance fighters who battled the Nazis at these high altitudes). Lower-elevation walks in surrounding valleys include the family-oriented 5km loop, **Sentier des Artisans de la Terre**. For trail guides and maps, visit the **Maison du Mont Aiguille** (📞04 76 34 44 95; www.maisondumontaiguille.fr).

🛏 p211

The Drive ≫ Follow the D7 and D526 east 17km to Mens, then cruise another 19km east on the D66 through hayfields backed by the Dévoluy massif's sawtooth ridgeline. Wind 8km south on the D66A and D537, descending to the Souloise River. Just before the bridge, turn left onto the D217, following signs for 'Sources des Gillardes' and parking at the trailhead.

❺ Défilé de la Souloise

Forming the border between the *départements* of Isère and Hautes Alpes, the sheer-faced **Souloise Gorge** is an idyllic spot to get out and stretch your legs. From the parking area, an easy there-and-back hike (200m each way) leads to the **Sources des Gillardes**, France's second-largest natural spring. Alternatively, continue downriver on the delightful **Canyon de l'Infernet** trail, through fragrant evergreen forest sandwiched between grey and orange rock walls. About 1km along, cross a bridge and loop back up the opposite bank to the parking area.

The Drive ≫ Follow the D537 and D937 south through tiny St-Disdier, enjoying stunning views of the Massif de Dévoluy's austere rocky face, punctuated by the pencil-shaped spire of the

GUIZIOU FRANCK/HEMIS.FR/GETTY IMAGES ©

Chichilianne The village backed by mountains

11th-century Mère Église. Zigzag south along the D117 (5km southeast), D17 (7km southwest) and D937 (16km south over Col de Festre). From here, follow the D994, D1075 and D4075 south 54km into Sisteron.

- - - - - - - - - - - - - -

⑥ Sisteron

Perched on a promontory high above the Durance River, Sisteron's stunner is its **citadel** (www.citadelledesisteron.fr; adult/child €6.10/2.70; ☉9am-6pm Apr–mid-Nov). For centuries this imposing fortress guarded the strategic narrow passage between Dauphiné and Provence – though Napoléon did somehow sneak past here

with 1200 soldiers after escaping Elba in 1815! Today it still commands bird's-eye perspectives of Sisteron's medieval streets, the eye-catching stratified rock face **Rocher de Baume** and the Durance Valley beyond. Architectural highlights include a 13th-century *chemin de ronde* (parapet walk) and a powder magazine designed by French military architect Vauban. On summer evenings the hilltop comes alive with open-air dance and classical-music concerts during the **Festival des Nuits**

de la Citadelle (www.nuitsdelacitadelle.fr).

🛏 p211

The Drive » Zip 39km down the A51 to Oraison. Take the D4 (5km), D907 (10km) and D108 (4km) southeast, climbing through Brunet to the Valensole plateau. Cruise 7km east through lavender fields on the D8, take the D953 (4km) into Puimoisson (passing roadside lavender stand Maison du Lavandin), and wind 14km into Moustiers-Ste-Marie along the D56 and D952.

- - - - - - - - - - - - - -

TRIP HIGHLIGHT

⑦ Moustiers-Ste-Marie

Nicknamed Etoile de Provence (Star of

209

DRIVING THE GORGES DU VERDON

This spine-tingling drive is one of France's classic road trips. A complete circuit of the Gorges from Moustiers-Ste-Marie involves 140km (about four hours without stops) of relentless hairpin turns on precarious rim-side roads, with spectacular scenery around every bend. The only village en route is La Palud-sur-Verdon (930m). In summer, expect slow traffic; opportunities to pass are rare.

From Moustiers, aim first for the **Route des Crêtes** (D952 & D23; ⊘closed 15 Nov–15 Mar), a 23km-long loop with 14 lookouts along the northern rim – ensure you drive the loop clockwise: there's a one-way portion midway. En route, the most thrilling view is from **Belvédère de l'Escale**, an excellent place to spot vultures. After rejoining the D952, the road corkscrews eastward, past **Point Sublime**, which overlooks serrated rock formations dropping to the river.

Return toward Moustiers via the **Corniche Sublime** (D955 to D90, D71 and D19), a heart-palpitating route along the southern rim, passing landmarks including the **Balcons de la Mescla** (Mescla Terraces) and **Pont de l'Artuby**, Europe's highest bridge.

Provence), enchanting Moustiers-Ste-Marie straddles the base of towering limestone cliffs – the beginning of the Alps and the end of Haute-Provence's rolling prairies. Winding streets climb among tile-roofed houses, connected by arched stone bridges spanning the picturesque creek (Le Riou) that courses through the village centre.

A 227m-long chain bearing a shining gold star stretches high above the village, legendarily placed there by the Knight of Blacas upon his safe return from the Crusades. Below the star, the 14th-century **Chapelle Notre Dame de Beauvoir** (guided tours adult/child €3/free) clings to the cliff ledge like an eagle's nest. A steep trail climbs beside a waterfall to the chapel, passing 14

stations of the cross. On 8 September, a 5am Mass celebrates the Virgin Mary's nativity, followed by flutes, drums and breakfast on the square.

✕ ⊨ p211

The Drive » The trip to Gorges du Verdon is a classic; see the boxed text above.

- - - - - - - - - - - - - -

❽ Gorges du Verdon

Dubbed the Grand Canyon of Europe, the breathtaking **Gorges du Verdon** slice 25km through Haute-Provence's limestone plateau. The narrow canyon bottom, carved by the Verdon's emerald-green waters, is only 8m to 90m wide; its steep, multihued walls, home to griffon vultures, rise as high as 700m – twice as tall as the Eiffel Tower! One of France's most scenic drives takes in

staggering panoramas from the vertigo-inducing cliffside roads on either side (see the boxed text).

The canyon floors are only accessible by foot or raft. Dozens of blazed trails traverse untamed countryside between Castellane and Moustiers, including the classic **Sentier Martel**, which uses occasional ladders and tunnels to navigate 14km of riverbanks and ledges. For details on 28 walks, pick up the excellent English-language *Canyon du Verdon* (€4.70) at Moustiers' **tourist office** (☎04 92 74 67 84; www.moustiers.fr; ⊘daily, hours vary). Rafting operators include **Guides pour l'Aventure** (www.guidesaventure.com) and **Aboard Rafting** (www.rafting-verdon.com).

Eating & Sleeping

Lans-en-Vercors

✖ Gîte d'Alpage
de la Molière Regional Cuisine €€

(📞06 09 38 42 42; gitedelamoliere.
aufilduvercors.org; menus €15-28; ⏱lunch
daily Jun-Sep) High above Lans-en-Vercors, this
welcoming trailside refuge with incomparable
views serves simple mountain fare (savoury
vegetable tarts, salad with smoked trout,
and raspberry, blueberry and walnut pies) on
umbrella-shaded picnic tables astride an Alpine
meadow.

🛏 À la Crécia Farmstay €

(📞04 76 95 46 98; www.gite-en-vercors.com,
in French; 436 Chemin des Cléments; s/d/
tr/q €58/63/78/93, dinner €19) Goats, pigs
and poultry rule the roost at this renovated
16th-century, solar-powered farm. Rooms are
stylishly rustic with beams, earthy hues and
mosaic bathrooms. Dinner is a feast of farm-
fresh produce.

Châtillon-en-Diois

✖ Restaurant
du Dauphiné Regional Cuisine €€

(📞04 75 21 13 13; place Pierre Dévoluy; menus
€15-25; ⏱lunch & dinner Mon-Sat) Bright
Provençal sunlight, purple shutters and a
flowery, tree-shaded front terrace make this
roadside eatery a delightful lunch stop. The
food is equally divine – from leg of local lamb to
savoury Moroccan stew to fish simmered with
citrus, star anise and fresh herbs.

Chichilianne ❹

🛏 Au Gai Soleil de Mont-Aiguille Hotel €

(📞04 76 34 41 71; www.hotelgaisoleil.com;
r €45-67; 📶) At the foot of charismatic Mont
Aiguille, this simple inn has fabulous views,
superb access to local hiking routes, a rustic
country restaurant and a spa and Jacuzzi for
soaking weary muscles at trail's end.

Sisteron ❻

🛏 Le Mas St-Joseph B&B €

(📞04 92 62 47 54; www.lemassaintjoseph.
com; Châteauneuf-Val-St-Donat; s/d/tr/q
€58/64/83/102; ⏱Apr-Oct; 🐕) This converted
farmhouse with hot tub and shared kitchen
sits on a pastoral hillside, 14km southwest of
Sisteron along the D951. Wooden beams and
stone walls make the whitewashed rooms feel
extra special. Tables d'hôte (set menus at a fixed
price) including wine cost €22.

Moustiers-Ste-Marie ❼

✖ La Ferme Ste-Cécile Gastronomic €€

(📞04 92 74 64 18; www.ferme-ste-cecile.com;
D952; menus €28-38; ⏱lunch Tue-Sat, dinner
Tue-Sun) The delicious culinary surprises
served on the terrace of this authentic ferme
auberge (farm restaurant) may include the
thinnest slice of Roquefort and pear warmed in
filo pastry, or foie gras wrapped in sweet quince.
This is a meal for connoisseurs, from a chef who
expects you to linger.

✖ La Treille Muscate Provençal €€

(📞04 92 74 64 31; www.la-treille-muscate.
com; place de l'Église; lunch/dinner menus from
€20/29; ⏱lunch Fri-Tue, dinner Fri-Wed) This
mid-village terrace restaurant offers exceptional
Provençal cooking with a fabulous view.

🛏 Le Petit Ségriès Farmstay €

(📞04 92 74 68 83; www.gite-segries.fr; r incl
breakfast €69-79; P 📶 ⬛) Sylvie and Noël
offer five colourful, airy rooms in their rambling
country farmhouse outside Moustiers. Family-
style tables d'hôte featuring fresh lamb, rabbit
and mountain honey (€21, including wine) are
served at a massive chestnut table.

Mont Brouilly *A petite hilltop chapel sits atop vast vineyards*

Beaujolais Villages

19

With its lush green hills, cute villages and well-tended vineyards, Beaujolais is a landscape painting come to life. Explore its quaint localities, taste some excellent wines and enjoy the hush.

GÉRARD LABRIET/PHOTONONSTOP/CORBIS ©

TRIP HIGHLIGHTS

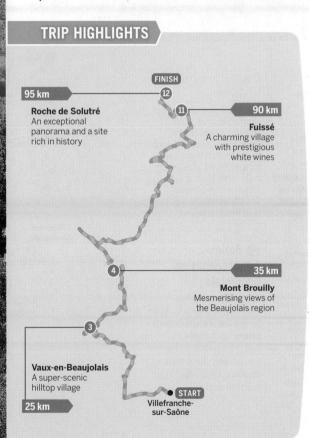

FINISH
12

95 km

Roche de Solutré
An exceptional panorama and a site rich in history

11

90 km

Fuissé
A charming village with prestigious white wines

4

35 km

Mont Brouilly
Mesmerising views of the Beaujolais region

3

Vaux-en-Beaujolais
A super-scenic hilltop village

25 km

START
● Villefranche-sur-Saône

2 DAYS
95KM / 59 MILES

GREAT FOR...

BEST TIME TO GO
April to June, September and October for a patchwork of colours.

ESSENTIAL PHOTO
Enjoy a panorama over the entire region from Mont Brouilly.

BEST FOR FOODIES
Vaux-en-Beaujolais prides itself on its Michelin-starred restaurant.

213

19 Beaujolais Villages

Ah, Beaujolais, where the unhurried life is complemented by rolling vineyards, beguiling villages, old churches, splendid estates and country roads that twist into the hills. Once you've left Villefranche-sur-Saône, a rural paradise awaits and a sense of escapism becomes tangible. Be sure to factor in plenty of time for wine tasting.

① Villefranche-sur-Saône

Your trip begins with a stroll along lively Rue Nationale, where you'll find most of the shops and the Gothic **Collégiale Notre-Dame des Marais**, which boasts an elegant façade and a soaring spire. An excellent starting point for oenophiles, the **tourist office** (☎04 74 07 27 40; www.villefranche -beaujolais.fr; 96 rue de la Sous-Préfecture; ☺9am-6pm Mon-Sat May-Sep, 10am-5pm Mon-Sat Oct-Apr) houses the **Espace des Vins du Beaujolais**, where you'll have the chance to learn about and sample the Beaujolais' 12 AOCs (Appellations d'Origine Contrôlée).

The Drive » At a roundabout about 800m south of the Collégiale, look out for the brown sign to 'Route des Vins du Beaujolais'. Pass through Gleizé, Lacenas, Denicé, St-Julien and Blacé before reaching Salles-Arbuissonas en Beaujolais. Count on a good half-hour to cover the 16km trip.

② Salles-Arbuissonnas en Beaujolais

As you pass through Salles-Arbuissonnas, keep an eye out for the superb **priory** (adult/child €4.50/ free; ☺10am-12.30pm & 2-5pm Apr-Oct) and the adjoining **cloister**, which date from the 12th century.

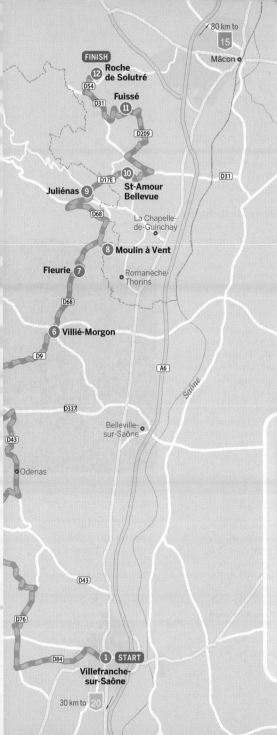

80 km to 15

Mâcon

FINISH

12 **Roche de Solutré**

D54

D31 **Fuissé**

11

D209

10

D17E **St-Amour Bellevue**

Juliénas 9

D68

La Chapelle-de-Guinchay

D31

8 **Moulin à Vent**

Fleurie 7

Romanèche-Thorins

D68

6 **Villié-Morgon**

D9

A6

D337

Belleville-sur-Saône

D43

Odenas

Saône

D43

D76

D84 1 START

Villefranche-sur-Saône

30 km to 20

The Drive » Continue along the D35 to Vaux-en-Beaujolais (6.5km).

- - - - - - - - - - - -

TRIP HIGHLIGHT

3 Vaux-en-Beaujolais

The village of Vaux-en-Beaujolais emerges like a hamlet in a fairy tale. You can't but be dazzled by the fabulous backdrop – it's perched on a rocky spur ensnared by a sea of vineyards. Don't leave Vaux without enjoying the fruity aroma of Beaujolais-Villages (the local appellation) at **La Cave de Clochemerle** (☏04 74 03 26 58; www. cavedeclochemerle.com; ⏰10am-12.30pm & 3-8pm), housed in atmospheric cellars.

✕ ⌂ p219

 LINK YOUR TRIP

15 **Route des Grands Crus**

For more wine tasting and rolling vineyards, make a beeline for the Route des Grands Crus, which unfolds south of Dijon. Head to Mâcon and follow signs to Dijon.

20 **Rhône Valley**

For a change of scene, head to Lyon (via Mâcon) and discover the hidden gems of the Rhône Valley.

The Drive ›› Take the D133 to Le Perréon, then follow signs to St Étienne des Oullières and Odenas. In Odenas, follow signs to Mont Brouilly (13km from Vaux-en-Beaujolais).

TRIP HIGHLIGHT

❹ Mont Brouilly

It would be a crime to explore the Beaujolais and not take the scenic road that leads to Mont Brouilly (485m), crowned with a small chapel. Hold on to your hat and lift your jaw off the floor as you approach the lookout at the summit – the view over the entire Beaujolais region and the Saône valley will be etched in your memory forever.

The Drive ›› Drive down to St-Lager, then take the D68 to Cercié and continue along the D337 to Beaujeu (9km from Mont Brouilly).

❺ Beaujeu

The historic Beaujolais wine capital, Beaujeu is an enchanting spot

to while away a few hours. The **Caveau des Beaujolais-Villages** (☎04 74 04 81 18; place de l'Hôtel de Ville; ◷10.30am-1pm & 3.30-8pm daily May-Sep, closed Mon Oct-Apr), located in the basement of the tourist office, is a great place to sip some excellent Beaujolais-Villages and Brouilly. It's also worth popping your head into the rewarding **Les Sources du Beaujolais** (☎04 74 69 20 56; place de l'Hôtel de Ville; museum adult/child €6/3; ◷10am-7pm Jul & Aug, to noon & 2-6pm Wed-Mon Mar-Jun & Sep-Dec), across the square from the tourist office. Housed in a wonderful Renaissance building, this produce shop hosts a small museum that focuses on traditional Beaujolais life and customs.

The Drive ›› Head to Lantignié along the D78 and continue to Régnié-Durette, where you'll see signs to Villié-Morgon. The full drive covers just over 9km.

WHEN BEAUJEU GOES WILD

A colourful time to motor in Beaujeu is around the third week in November. At the stroke of midnight on the third Thursday (ie Wednesday night), the *libération* (release) or *mise en perce* (tapping; opening) of the first bottles of cherry-bright Beaujolais Nouveau is celebrated around France and the world. In Beaujeu there's free Beaujolais Nouveau for all as part of the **Sarmentelles de Beaujeu** – a giant street party that kicks off on the Wednesday leading up to the Beaujolais Nouveau's release for five days of wine tasting, live music and dancing.

❻ Villié-Morgon

Morgon wine, anybody? Expand your knowledge of the local appellation with a tasting session at the vaulted **Caveau de Morgon** (☎04 74 04 20 99; Château de Fontcrenne; ◷10am-noon & 2-6pm Mar-Dec), which occupies a grandiose 17th-century château in the heart of

Roche de Solutré Rocky outcrop above vineyards

town – it can't get more atmospheric than that.

🛏 p219

The Drive ≫ From Villié-Morgon, it's a relaxed 10km drive to Fleurie via Chiroubles. Follow the D18 and the D86 to Chiroubles, then signs to Fleurie.

- - - - - - - - - - -

7 Fleurie

Beaujolais' rising star, Fleurie red wines are said to be sensuous, offering a combination of floral and fruity notes. A superb experience, **Château du Bourg** (🖉04 74 69 81 15, 06 08 86 49 02; www.chateau-du-bourg.com; Le Bourg; 🕑by reservation), run by the Matray brothers (ask for Denis, who speaks passable English), offers free tastings in a cool bistro-like setting and can arrange vineyard tours and cellar visits on request (€12). Tip: Grille-Midi, its signature vintage, is unforgettable.

🍴 p219

The Drive ≫ Take the D68 towards Chénas; after about 3km turn right onto the D68E towards Romanèche Thorins and you'll soon reach Moulin à Vent. It's a 4km drive from Fleurie.

⑧ Moulin à Vent

Reason itself to visit this drowsy hamlet is the heritage-listed **Moulin à Vent** (Windmill). Dubbed the 'King of Beaujolais', the Moulin à Vent appellation is a particularly charming wine to sample in situ: its **Caveau du Moulin à Vent** (☑03 85 35 58 09; ⊙10am-12.30pm & 2.30-7pm daily Jul & Aug, 10am-12.30pm & 2.30-6pm Thu-Mon Sep-Jun), across the road from the windmill, provides a prime wine-tasting opportunity.

The Drive ⟫ From Moulin à Vent retrace your route back towards Chénas and take the D68 to Juliénas. It's an easy 6.6km drive.

⑨ Juliénas

One of the best-kept secrets in Beaujolais is this delightful village famed for its eponymous vintage. A beauty of a castle, the 16th-century **Château de Juliénas** (☑06 85 76 95 41; www.chateaudejulienas.com; ⊙by reservation) occupies a delightful estate; tours can be arranged by phoning ahead. No doubt you'll be struck by the cellars, the longest in the region. Tours can be followed by an *aperi'vin* (tasting and snacks; €16). Another atmospheric venture set in a château, **La Cave des Producteurs** (☑04 74 04

41 66; www.cave-de-julienas.fr; ⊙by reservation) is a large cooperative which can organise vineyard tours and cellar visits.

✗ ▭ p219

The Drive ⟫ Follow the road to St-Amour Bellevue along the D17E and the D486ter (3.5km from Juliénas).

⑩ St-Amour Bellevue

Not to be missed in St-Amour: the **Domaine des Vignes du Paradis – Pascal Durand** (☑03 85 36 52 97; Le Bourg; www.saint-amour-en-paradis.com; ⊙10am-6pm). This award-winning domaine run by the fifth generation of vintners welcomes visitors to its intimate cellars and sells St-Amour wines at unbeatable prices.

✗ ▭ p219

The Drive ⟫ Follow the D186 towards Chânes. In Bourgneuf, take the D31 to St-Vérand. From St-Vérand, follow signs to Chaintré and continue to Fuissé. It's a 10km trip from St-Amour.

TRIP HIGHLIGHT

⑪ Fuissé

If you like peace, quiet and sigh-inducing views, you'll love this absolutely picturesque stone town nestled in a small valley carpeted by manicured vineyards. You've now left Beaujolais – Fuissé is part of Burgundy. It's famous for its prestigious

whites of the Pouilly-Fuissé appellation. You can attend tastings at various cellars around town or, for the ultimate experience, at the magnificent **Château de Fuissé** (☑03 85 35 61 44; www.chateau-fuisse.fr; Le Plan; ⊙10am-6pm Apr-Sep, 10am-noon & 2-4pm Oct-Mar).

The Drive ⟫ From Fuissé follow signs to Chasselas along the D172. After about 3.5km, turn right onto the D31 (direction Tramayes). Drive another 2km to a right-hand turn onto the D54 (direction Solutré-Pouilly). Count on 15 minutes for the 7km trip.

TRIP HIGHLIGHT

⑫ Roche de Solutré

A lovely 20-minute walk along the Sentier des Roches will get you to the top of the rocky outcrop known as the Roche de Solutré (493m), from where Mont Blanc can sometimes be seen, especially at sunset. For some cultural sustenance, make a beeline for the nearby **Musée de Préhistoire de Solutré** (☑03 85 35 85 24; www.musees-bourgogne.org; Solutré; adult/child €3.50/free; ⊙10am-6pm Apr-Sep, 10am-noon & 2-5pm Oct-Mar), which displays finds from one of Europe's richest prehistoric sites.

✗ p219

Eating & Sleeping

Vaux-en-Beaujolais ③

🛏 Auberge de Clochemerle   Hotel €

(📞04 74 03 20 16; www.aubergedeclochemerle.
fr; rue Gabriel Chevallier; d €78-85, menus €37-
72; ⊘restaurant lunch Thu-Sun, dinner Wed-
Mon Jun-Aug, lunch & dinner Wed-Sun Sep-May;
P 🛜) A pleasant combination of modern and
traditional, this atmospheric hotel has seven
stylishly refitted rooms, some with vineyard
views. Dining at its Michelin-starred restaurant
is a treat.

Villié-Morgon ⑥

🛏 Château de Bellevue   B&B €€

(📞04 74 66 98 88; www.chateau-bellevue.fr;
Bellevue; d €95-160; P 🛜) For the ultimate
château experience, you can't do better than
this attractive venture nestled amid seas of
vineyards. Françoise Barret will welcome you
in perfect English (she has lived in the US) and
offer you a personalised tour of the winery and
the cellars.

Fleurie ⑦

🍴 Auberge du Cep   Traditional French €€

(📞04 74 04 10 77; place de l'Église; mains
€18-25; ⊘lunch & dinner Tue-Sat) Traditional
cooking at its best. Feast on regional
specialities such as pike-perch, snails, perfectly
fried frogs' legs, and rosy tenderloin of
Charolais beef (France's best) in a rustic dining
room.

Juliénas ⑨

🛏 Chez La Rose   Hotel €€

(📞04 74 04 41 20; www.chez-la-rose.fr; Le
Bourg; d €85-110, ste €110-170, menus €21-52;
⊘restaurant lunch Wed, Sat & Sun, dinner Tue-
Sun; P ❄ 🛜 🍽) This charming inn features
13 rooms in various buildings scattered around
the village. They're all equipped to the highest
standard, but the vast suites are the ones to
aim for. Dinner at the restaurant is a gourmet
affair, with standouts like *coq au vin de Juliénas*
(chicken cooked in Juliénas wine) and Charolais
beef fillet.

St-Amour Bellevue ⑩

🛏 L'Auberge
du Paradis   Boutique Hotel €€€

(📞03 85 37 10 26; Le Bourg; d €140-240,
menus €60; ⊘restaurant dinner Wed-Sun;
P ❄ 🛜 🍽) Beaujolais' iconic, much-beloved
inn occupies a village house restyled into an
urban-chic, design-led boutique hotel. Oh, and
there's the fantastic restaurant – the creative,
inspired cooking (expect top-quality ingredients
served with a symphony of spices) draws diners
from afar.

🛏 Le Paradis de Marie   B&B €€

(📞03 85 36 51 90; www.leparadisdemarie.
com; Le Bourg; d €85, caravans €95; 🛜) Have
a decadently bucolic rest at this relaxing place,
a lovingly restored stone mansion exquisitely
situated not far from the main street. The
five rooms open onto a courtyard, while the
romantically furnished gypsy caravan in the
garden will please those in search of an offbeat
experience.

Solutré ⑫

🍴 La Courtille
de Solutré   Traditional French €€

(📞03 85 35 80 73; www.lacourtilledesolutre.
fr; Le Bourg; menus €23-36; ⊘lunch daily,
dinner Tue-Sun Jul & Aug, lunch Wed-Sun, dinner
Wed-Sat Sep-Jun) Chef Adrien Yparraguirre
does traditional dishes exceptionally well, with a
creative twist. Sit on the shady terrace or head
into the rustic-chic interior.

Quenelles de brochet Indulge in a Rhône Valley gourmet speciality

Rhône Valley

20

The mighty Rhône flows from the Alps to the Mediterranean. Trace its course from Lyon to Provence, visiting gourmet restaurants, Gallo-Roman ruins and spectacular river gorges along the way.

TRIP HIGHLIGHTS

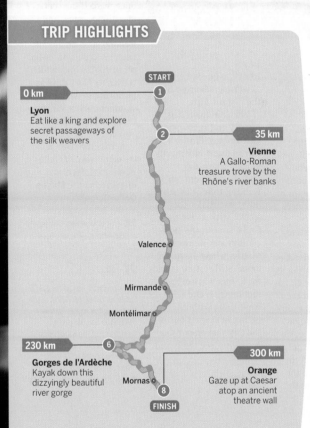

START

0 km — ①

Lyon
Eat like a king and explore secret passageways of the silk weavers

② — **35 km**

Vienne
A Gallo-Roman treasure trove by the Rhône's river banks

Valence

Mirmande

Montélimar

230 km — ⑥

Gorges de l'Ardèche
Kayak down this dizzyingly beautiful river gorge

Mornas ⑧

300 km

Orange
Gaze up at Caesar atop an ancient theatre wall

FINISH

5 DAYS
300KM / 186 MILES

GREAT FOR...

BEST TIME TO GO

June and July for festivals in the Roman theatres of Lyon, Vienne and Orange.

 ESSENTIAL PHOTO

The Pont d'Arc, a stunning stone archway over the Ardèche River.

BEST FOR FOODIES

Lyon's beloved *bouchons* (convivial neighbourhood bistros).

221

20 | Rhône Valley

Food and history are recurring themes on this multifaceted meander down the Rhône, from the fabled eateries of Lyon to the Gallo-Roman museum at Vienne, the nougat factories of Montélimar and the ancient theatre at Orange. As you work your way downriver to Provence, you'll also encounter imposing hilltop fortresses, slow-paced southern villages and one of France's prettiest river gorges.

TRIP HIGHLIGHT

❶ Lyon

This strategic spot at the confluence of the Rhône and Saône Rivers has been luring people ever since the Romans named it Lugudunum in 43 BC. Climb Fourvière hill west of town to witness the successive waves of human settlement, spread out in chronological order at your feet: a pair of Gallo-Roman theatres in the foreground, Vieux Lyon's medieval cathedral on the Sâone's near banks, the 17th-century *hôtel de ville* (town hall) on the peninsula between the rivers, and, beyond the

Rhône, modern Lyon's skyscrapers backed by the distant Alps.

With its illustrious history and renowned gastronomy, France's third-largest city merits at least a two-day visit. Supplement our walking tour of Lyon's quintessential sights (p228) with a visit to Croix Rousse, the 19th-century silk-weaver's district where Jacquard looms still restore fabrics for France's historical monuments, and don't leave town without eating in at least one of the city's incomparable *bouchons* (see the boxed text, p226).

 p227

The Drive ❯❯ Shoot 33km down the A7 to Vienne, enjoying close-up views of the Rhône en route.

TRIP HIGHLIGHT

❷ Vienne

France's Gallo-Roman heritage is alive and well in this laid-back riverfront city, whose back streets hide a trio of jaw-dropping ruins: the 1st-century-BC **Temple d'Auguste et de Livie**, with its splendid Corinthian columns; the **Pyramide de la Cirque**, a 15.5m-tall obelisk that once pierced the centre of a hippodrome; and the 1st-century-AD **Théâtre Romain** (adult/child €2.70/ free; ☉9.30am-1pm & 2-6pm, closed Mon Sep-Mar), relives its glory days as a performance venue each summer during Vienne's two-week **jazz festival** (www.jazzavienne.com).

Across the river, a treasure trove of Gallo-Roman artefacts is displayed at the **Musée Gallo-Romain** (www. musees-gallo-romains.com; D502, St-Romain-en-Gal; adult/child €4/free; ☉10am-6pm Tue-Sun).

 p227

The Drive ❯❯ Follow the D386, D1086 and D86 for 48km south, threading the needle between the Rhône and the pretty mountains of the Parc Naturel Régional du Pilat. At Sarras cross the bridge to St-Vallier, then continue 32km south on the N7 through classic Côtes du

Rhône wine country around Tain l'Hermitage into Valence.

----

❸ Valence

With its warm weather, honey-coloured light and relaxed cadence, it's easy to see why Valence advertises itself as the northern gateway to Provence. At lunchtime, make a beeline for **Le 7** (p227), a stylish eatery with an excellent wine list that's part of the Pic family's award-winning, multigenerational restaurant empire, or pack yourself a picnic at the Pic-affiliated gourmet grocery, **L'Épicerie** (210 av Victor Hugo; ◷9am-7pm Mon-Sat, to 12.30pm Sun). Afterwards visit **Maison Nivon** (17 av Pierre Semard; suisses €2.20; ◷6am-7pm Tue-Sun) for a *suisse,* Valence's classic orange-rind-flavoured pastry in the shape of a Swiss Vatican guard. Around the corner, gawk at the

⑤ LINK YOUR TRIP

13 Volcanoes of the Auvergne

Head west of Lyon for this pastoral meander among ancient green peaks.

21 Roman Provence

From Orange, head northeast and further south to delve deeper into Roman ruins.

223

allegorical sculpted heads adorning the façade of the wonderful 16th-century **Maison des Têtes** (57 Grande Rue).

 p227

The Drive ≫ Cruise 28km south along the N7, then wind 5km through orchard-covered hills on the D57 into Mirmande.

④ Mirmande

Surrounded by pretty orchard country, this hilltop gem of stone houses and sleepy medieval streets was once a major centre of silkworm production. It then became an artists' colony in the 20th century, when Cubist painter André Lhote made his home here. Volcanologist-cinematographer Haroun Tazieff later served as the town's mayor, adding to Mirmande's cultural cachet and earning it recognition as one of *les plus beaux villages de la France* (France's prettiest villages).

With a couple of charming hotels, Mirmande makes an inviting overnight stop. Activities include browsing for treasures at **Porte des Gaultiers** (www.portedesgaultiers. fr), an artsy boutique by the arched 14th-century town gate, and wandering up to the 12th-century Romanesque **Église de Ste-Foy**, where concerts

and art exhibits are held in summertime and beautiful Rhône Valley views unfold year-round.

🛏 p227

The Drive ≫ Snake 12km southeast on the D57 over Col de la Grande Limite (515m) into medieval Marsanne, then continue 17km southwest into Montélimar on the D105 and D6.

⑤ Montélimar

An obligatory stop for sweet tooths, Montélimar is famous for its delectable nougat made from almonds, lavender honey, pistachios, sugar, egg white and vanilla. To taste this sweet delight at the source, visit one of Montélimar's small producers, such as **Diane-de-Poytiers** (www.diane-de -poytiers.fr; 99 av Jean-Jaurès; ⏰8am-noon & 2-5.30pm Tue-Sat Jul & Aug, Mon-Fri rest of yr). Afterwards burn off the calories with a climb to **Château des Adhémar** (chateaux.ladrome.fr; adult/child €3.50/free; ⏰10am-noon & 2-6pm Apr-Oct, 2-6pm Wed-Mon Nov-Mar), whose 12th-century fortifications hold a Romanesque chapel and a rotating series of art exhibits.

The Drive ≫ Follow the D73 southwest for 10km across the Rhône into Viviers, follow the river 15km south into Bourg-St-Andéol, then squiggle 30km along the D4 past St-Remèze's lavender museum to Vallon-Pont-d'Arc, western gateway to the Gorges de l'Ardèche.

`TRIP HIGHLIGHT`

⑥ Gorges de l'Ardèche

These steep and spectacular limestone gorges cut a curvaceous swath through the high scrubland along the Ardèche River, a tributary of the Rhône. The real showstopper,

Mornas Église Notre-Dame du Val-Romigier

near the gorges' western entrance, is the **Pont d'Arc**, a sublimely beautiful natural stone arch. Stop here to camp, swim or join one of the many paddling tours down the river. Further east, the **Sentier Aval des Gorges** descends steeply for 2km to the heart of the gorges, granting hikers access to two primitive campgrounds at Bivouac de Gournier and Bivouac de Gaud. For information about local flora, fauna and recreational opportunities, visit the **Maison de la Réserve** (☎04 75 98 77 31; www. gorgesdelardeche.fr).

🛏 p227

The Drive » From Vallon-Pont-d'Arc, the breathtaking D290 zigzags for 29km along the canyon's rim, with 11 viewpoints revealing dazzling vistas of horseshoe bends, and kayakers in formation far below. Exiting the gorges, take the D200 for 2km south through pretty medieval Aiguèze, then continue 22km southeast across the Rhône into Mornas via the D901, D6086, D994 and N7.

- - - - - - - - - - -

7 Mornas

Perched on some precipitous cliffs, the

225

BOUCHONS

A *bouchon* might be a 'bottle stopper' or 'traffic jam' elsewhere in France, but in Lyon it's a cosy, traditional bistro specialising in regional cuisine. *Bouchons* originated in the early 1900s when many bourgeois families had to let go their in-house cooks, who then set up their own restaurants.

Kick-start your meal with a *communard*, an aperitif of red Beaujolais wine and *crème de cassis* (blackcurrant liqueur), then move on to a *pot* – a 46cL glass bottle adorned with an elastic band to prevent drips – of local Brouilly, Beaujolais, Côtes du Rhône or Mâcon.

Next comes the entrée, perhaps *tablier de sapeur* (breaded, fried tripe), *salade lyonnaise* (green salad with bacon, croutons and poached egg), or *caviar de la Croix Rousse* (lentils in creamy sauce). Hearty main dishes include *boudin noir aux pommes* (blood sausage with apples), *quenelles de brochet* (pike dumplings in a creamy crayfish sauce) and *andouillette* (sausage made from pigs' intestines).

For the cheese course, choose between *fromage blanc* (a cross between cream cheese and natural yoghurt); *cervelle de canut* ('brains of the silk weaver'; *fromage blanc* mixed with chives and garlic, a staple of Lyon's 19th-century weavers); or local St Marcellin ripened to gooey perfection.

Little etiquette is required in *bouchons*. Mopping your plate with a chunk of bread is fine, and you'll usually sit elbow to elbow with your fellow diners at tightly wedged tables (great for practising your French!).

11th- to 14th-century **Forteresse de Mornas** (www.forteresse-de-mornas.com; guided tour adult/child €8/6; ⊗tours 11am, 2pm, 3pm, 4pm, 5pm daily Jul & Aug, Sat & Sun Apr-Jun & Sep) makes a dramatic backdrop for the pretty village below. Built by the medieval Counts of Toulouse, it commands outstanding views west to the Rhône and east to Mont Ventoux. A trail climbs 137 vertical metres from the village past the 12th-century Romanesque **Église Notre-Dame du Val-Romigier** to the fortress, where costumed guides offer historical re-enactments. Medieval fever also grips Mornas in September during **La Médiévale de Mornas**, a popular annual festival and crafts market.

🛏 p227

The Drive » Zip 12km southeast down the N7 into Orange, whose magnificent 2000-year-old Arc de Triomphe provides a fitting welcome.

TRIP HIGHLIGHT

❽ Orange

Sun-drenched Orange is a dream destination for fans of ancient ruins. The city's outstanding **Théâtre Antique** (www.theatre-antique.com; adult/child €8.50/6.50; ⊗9am-6pm, to 4.30pm Nov-Feb), one of only three Roman theatres in the world with a perfectly preserved stage wall, shines brightest during summer performances such as the epic international opera festival **Chorégies d'Orange** (www.choregies.asso.fr; tickets €50-240). North of town, Orange's second Roman treasure is the exquisitely carved 1st-century-AD **Arc de Triomphe**. For sleeping and eating listings in Orange, see p242.

Eating & Sleeping

Lyon ❶

✖ Café des Fédérations   Bouchon €€

(☎04 78 28 26 00; www.lesfedeslyon.com; 8-10 rue Major Martin; lunch/dinner menus from €19/25; ☻lunch & dinner Mon-Sat) Black-and-white photos of old Lyon hang on wood-panelled walls at this Lyonnais classic. From hearty appetisers (lentils in mustardy sauce, *rosette de Lyon* sausage) to a perfect *baba au rhum* (rum-soaked yeast cake) for dessert, this is *bouchon* dining at its finest.

✖ Le Bouchon des Filles   Bouchon €€

(☎04 78 30 40 44; 20 rue Sergent Blandan; menus €25; ☻dinner daily, lunch Sun) The light, fluffy *quenelles* (flour, egg and cream dumplings) at this contemporary *bouchon,* run by an enterprising crew of young women with deep roots in the local food scene, are as good as you'll find anywhere in Lyon.

⌂ Cour des Loges   Hotel €€€

(☎04 72 77 44 44; www.courdesloges.com; 2-8 rue du Bœuf; d/ste from €250/530; ✲@☎☒) Stylish historic details (Italianate loggias) meet modern comforts (an on-site spa) at this exquisite hotel composed of four 14th- to 17th-century houses wrapped around a *traboule* (secret passageway).

Vienne ❷

✖ La Pyramide   Gastronomic €€€

(☎04 74 53 01 96; www.lapyramide.com; 14 bd Fernand-Point; lunch menus €62, dinner menus €117-172; ☻lunch & dinner Thu-Mon) In an apricot-coloured villa with powder-blue shutters, this foodie favourite is helmed by double-Michelin-starred local chef Patrick Henriroux, whose high-end *menus* (set-priced meals) feature lobsters, foie gras, black truffles, scallops and other seasonal treats. His adjacent Espace PH3 offers simpler food at more down-to-earth prices.

Valence ❸

✖ Le 7   Bistro €€

(☎04 75 44 15 32; www.pic-valence.com; 285 av Victor Hugo; menus €18-30; ☻lunch & dinner daily) Anne-Sophie Pic, France's only three-Michelin-star female chef, reigns over Valence gastronomy, as her father and grandfather did before her. *Menus* at her top-of-the-line Restaurant Pic run from €90 to €330, but if your pockets aren't quite that deep, this elegantly relaxed bistro next door serves fab *menus* at a fraction of the price.

Mirmande ❹

⌂ L'Hôtel de Mirmande   Hotel €€

(☎04 75 63 13 18; www.hotelmirmande.fr; d €80-140; ☎) A haven of tranquillity, this simple hotel has friendly staff and a perfect location in the gorgeous stone-walled heart of the village.

Gorges de l'Ardèche ❻

⌂ Camping du Pont d'Arc   Campground €

(☎04 75 88 00 64; www.campingdupontdarc.com; campsites from €21) Adjacent to stunning Pont d'Arc, this tree-shaded three-star campground has its own riverside beach and offers boat trips down the gorges.

Mornas ❼

⌂ Le Manoir   Hotel €€

(☎04 90 37 00 79; www.hotel-le-manoir.com; N7; d €57-100; ☎) With views straight up to Mornas' imposing fortress, this roadside inn blends Provençal country charm with proximity to Orange's more urban attractions.

STRETCH
YOUR LEGS
LYON

Start/Finish Basilique Notre Dame de Fourvière

Distance 3km

Duration 2½ hours

Stroll through two millennia of Lyonnais history, from the Gallo-Roman settlement of Lugudunum to Lyon's avant-garde 20th-century opera house; along the way, three secret medieval passageways and a pedestrian bridge across the Saône River are thrown in just for fun.

Take this walk on Trip

Basilique Notre Dame de Fourvière

Start at this massive hilltop **basilica** (www.fourviere.org; place de Fourvière; ⊘8am-7pm), whose terrace offers stunning panoramas of Lyon, the Rhône and Saône Rivers, and even distant Mont Blanc on clear days.

The Walk ≫ Head southwest along rue Roger Radisson for 250m to the Gallo-Roman Museum.

Musée de la Civilisation Gallo-Romaine

Ancient Gallo-Roman artefacts from the Rhône Valley are displayed at this hillside **museum** (www.musees-gallo-romains.com; 17 rue Cléberg; adult/child €4/free; ⊘10am-6pm Tue-Sun). Next door are two ancient Roman theatres, the 10,000-seat **Théâtre Romain** and the smaller **odéon**.

The Walk ≫ Descend rue Cléberg 200m, then turn left into leafy Parc des Hauteurs, following the main path downhill 400m to Montée St-Barthélémy. Turn right and continue downhill 200m on Montée des Chazeaux to rue St-Jean, then turn right and walk 50m to the cathedral.

Cathédrale St-Jean

This partly Romanesque, partly Flamboyant Gothic **cathedral** (place St-Jean, 5e; ⊘8am-noon & 2-7pm) was built between the late 11th and early 16th centuries. Don't miss the **astronomical clock** in the north transept, which chimes elaborately at noon, 2pm, 3pm and 4pm daily.

The Walk ≫ Walk 50m north on rue St-Jean, then turn left and walk 50m along rue de la Bombardé, stopping at house number 14 (on your right).

Traboules

Throughout Vieux Lyon, secret passages known as **traboules** (from the Latin *transambulare*, 'to walk through') wind through apartment blocks and courtyards, up stairs and down corridors, connecting streets with one another in unexpected ways. In all, 315 passages link 230 streets, with a combined length of 50km.

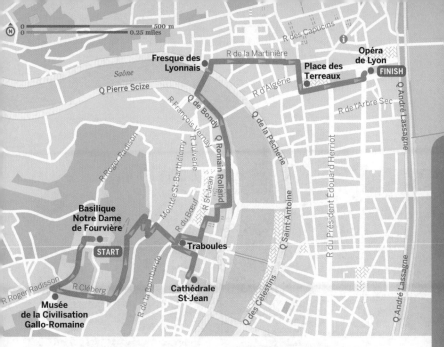

Some *traboules* date from Roman times, while others were constructed by *canuts* (silk weavers) in the 19th century to transport silk in inclement weather. Resistance fighters found them equally handy during WWII.

The Walk » Enter the *traboule* at number 14 and navigate to its exit at 31 rue du Boeuf; next, open the door at 27 rue du Boeuf and cross to 54 rue St-Jean; finally, cross from 27 rue St-Jean to 6 rue des Trois Maries. Now follow the Sâone River 600m north and cross the Passerelle St-Vincent pedestrian bridge to Lyon's most famous mural.

Fresque des Lyonnais

Well-known Lyonnais peer out from this seven-storey **mural** (cnr rue de la Martinière & quai de la Pêcherie), including loom inventor Joseph-Marie Jacquard, superstar chef Paul Bocuse and the yellow-haired Little Prince, created by author-aviator Antoine de St-Exupéry.

The Walk » Head 400m east on rue de la Martinière, then go south one block on rue Paul Chenavard into place des Terreaux.

Place des Terreaux

The centrepiece of Lyon's beautiful **central square** is a 19th-century **fountain** sculpted by Frédéric-Auguste Bartholdi (of Statue of Liberty fame). Fronting the square's eastern edge is the ornate **hôtel de ville** (town hall).

The Walk » From the south side of place des Terreaux head 250m east on rue Joseph Serlin to the Opéra.

Opéra de Lyon

Lyon's neoclassical 1831-built **opera house** sports a striking semi-cylindrical glass-domed roof, added in 1993 by renowned French architect Jean Nouvel. On summer evenings, free jazz concerts are performed under the arches up front.

The Walk » From Hôtel de Ville station, where you're now standing, ride the metro three stops back to Vieux Lyon station, then return to Fourvière via funicular.

Provence & Southeast France

WITH ITS SHIMMERING COAST AND RUSTIC PROVENÇAL HEART, the Mediterranean south has a timeless allure. Driving here you'll travel through wildly divergent landscapes: cinematic coastline, rugged hinterland and bucolic valleys.

The Cote d'Azur's glamorous cities, deep-blue Med and chic hilltop villages never fail to delight. Inland, you'll weave between fragrant fields, forested gorges and Roman ruins. Skip over the sea to the unspoilt island delights of Corsica or be engulfed in the lush green wetlands of the Camargue.

Along the way you'll connect with the poets, painters and writers who flocked here during the 20th century, chasing sun and inspiration.

Cote d'Azur Corniche de l'Estérel (Trip 24)
RUTH TOMLINSON/GETTY IMAGES ©

Provence & Southeast France

Roman Provence 7 Days
21 Provence's impressive Roman treasures line up along this leisurely drive. (p235)

Lavender Route 4–5 Days
22 The region at its prettiest, with flowery fields and rustic villages. (p245)

Classic Trip
The Corniches 3 Days
23 Not one but *three* thrilling coastal roads – the ultimate French drive. (p253)

Classic Trip
Riviera Cruising 7 Days
24 The best beaches, cities, villages and nature along the Med coast. (p263)

Modern Art Meander 7 Days
25 A cross-region route that traces the haunts of modern art's greatest. (p273)

Southern Seduction en Corse 10 Days
26 This jaunt along Corsica's southern coast takes in plenty of history. (p283)

Corsican Coast Cruiser 5 Days
27 Discover western Corsica's majestic mountain peaks and covetable sandy coves. (p293)

The Camargue 4 Days
28 Loop through the wild, lush wetlands where bulls and white horses roam. (p303)

DON'T MISS

The Road up Mont Ventoux

Relive 14 gruelling Tour de France ascents from behind the wheel. Feel the cycling love on Trip 22

Le Merenda, Nice

The simple, sunny, bold standards at this tiny bistro are Nice on a plate. Sample on Trips 23 24 25

Hôtel Nord-Pinus, Arles

What other hotel (or city) boasts embedded Roman columns and bullfighters' trophies? Visit on Trips 21 25 28

Orange's Roman Arc de Triomphe

This monument's detailed carvings are a fascinating peek into what got your average Roman foot soldier excited. Get close on Trip 21

Pastis

Always ask for this aniseed-flavoured liqueur by brand. We like the herbal Henri Bardouin or the spicy Janot. Sip on Trips 21 22 23 24 25 28

Mont Ventoux Cycling to the observatory

Nimes *Architectural awe awaits at Temple de Diane*

BETHUNE CARMICHAEL/GETTY IMAGES ©

Roman Provence

21

Survey Provence's incredible Roman legacy as you follow ancient routes through the region's river gorges and vineyards, gathering provisions as you go.

TRIP HIGHLIGHTS

30 km

Pont du Gard
Aqueduct of dizzying scale, magnificently sited

Vaison-la-Romaine
FINISH

5

2

175 km

Théâtre Antique
A soaring stage conjures up Rome's splendour

START
Nîmes

1

St-Remy de Provence

95 km

3

Place du Forum
Bustling city square with Roman treasures below

Maison Carrée
A 1st-century-AD temple, beautiful and totally intact

0 km

7 DAYS
205KM / 127 MILES

GREAT FOR...

BEST TIME TO GO

Ruins open year-round, but avoid August's heat and crush.

 ESSENTIAL PHOTO

The Pont du Gard, illuminated every night in summer.

☑ **BEST FOR CULTURE**

Balmy nights at Orange's Théâtre Antique are magic; July includes the Chorégies d'Orange.

235

21 Roman Provence

Provence was where Rome first truly flexed its imperial muscles. Follow Roman roads, cross Roman bridges and grab a seat in the bleachers at Roman theatres and arenas. Thrillingly, you'll discover that most of Provence's Roman ruins aren't ruins at all. Many are exceptionally well preserved, and some are also evocatively integrated into the modern city. With Provence's knockout landscape as a backdrop, history never looked so good!

TRIP HIGHLIGHT

1 Nîmes

Nîmes' bizarre coat of arms – a crocodile chained to a palm tree! – recalls the region's first, but definitely not last, horde of sun-worshipping retirees. Julius Caesar's loyal legionnaires were granted land here to settle after hard years on the Nile campaigns. Two millennia later, their ambitious town blends seamlessly with the bustling, workaday French streetscapes

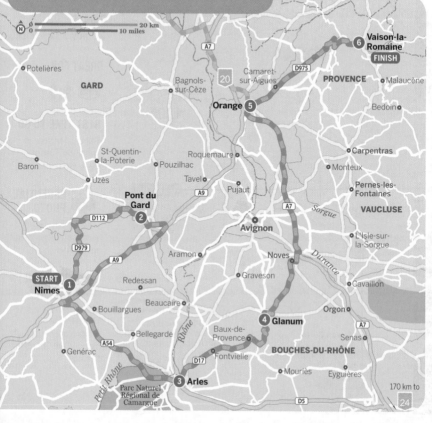

of the modern city. An impressively intact 1st-century-AD **Amphitheatre** (adult/child €7.80/4.50; 9am-6.30pm) makes for a majestic traffic roundabout. Locals nonchalantly skateboard or window-shop on the elegant place that's home to an astonishingly beautiful and preciously intact 1st-century-AD temple, the **Maison Carrée** (place de la Maison Carrée; adult/child €4.50/3.70; 10am-6.30pm). Skip the 22-minute film and instead stroll over to the elegant **Jardins de la Fontaine**. The remains of the **Temple de Diane** are in its lower northwest corner and a 10-minute uphill walk brings you to the crumbling, 30m-high

LINK YOUR TRIP

20 Rhône Valley
Join up with this trip in Orange for several great Roman sites in Vienne, and Lyon's Roman theatres and great Gallo-Roman museum.

24 Riviera Cruising
The Cote d'Azur shares the Roman treasures, and many of them are in superb locations; head east from Arles to Aix, then take the E80 to Cannes to join this trip.

TOP TIP: PADDLING THE RIVER GARD

Get your first glimpse of the Pont du Gard from the river by paddling 8km downstream from Collias, 4km west of the D981. **Kayak Vert** (04 66 22 80 76; www.canoefrance.com/gardon) and **Canoë Le Tourbillon** (04 66 22 85 54; www.canoe-le-tourbillon.com), both based near the village bridge, rent out kayaks and canoes (€20 per person for two hours) from March/April to October.

Tour Magne (adult/child €2.70/2.30; 9.30am-6.30pm). Built in 15 BC as a watchtower and display of imperial grunt, it is the only one that remains of several that once spanned the 7km-long ramparts.

✗ 🛏 p242

The Drive » The D6086 is direct, but sacrifice 15 minutes, and take route d'Uzés (D979). This way, leave Nîmes' snarly traffic behind and suddenly find yourself on a quiet stretch of winding road skirting grey rocky gorges and past honey-stone villages. Cut east via Sanilhac-Sagriès on the D112, then turn off at Begude's roundabout.

- - - - - - - - - - - - - -

TRIP HIGHLIGHT

2 Pont du Gard

You won't get a sneak peek of the **Pont du Gard** (04 66 37 50 99; www.pontdugard.fr; parking €18, after 8pm €10; 7am-1am) on approach. Nature (and clever placement of car parks and visitor centres) has created one bravura reveal. Spanning the gorge is a magnificent three-tiered aqueduct, a marvel of 1st-century engineering. It was built around 19 BC by Agrippa, Augustus' deputy, and it's huge: the 275m-long upper tier, 50m above the Gard, has 35 arches. Each block (the largest weighs over 5 tonnes) was hauled in by cart or raft. It was once part of a 50km-long system that carried water from nearby Uzès down to thirsty Nîmes. It's a 400m wheelchair-accessible walk from car parks on both banks of the river to the bridge itself, with a shady cafe en route on the right. Swim upstream for unencumbered views, though downstream is also good for summer dips, with shaded wooden platforms set in the flatter banks. Want to make a day of it? There's **Museo de la romanité**, an interactive, information-based museum, plus a children's area, and a peaceful 1.4km botanical walk, Mémoires de Garrigue.

✗ 🛏 p242

The Drive >> Kayaking to the next stop would be more fun, and more direct, but you'll need to hit the highway for 40 minutes to Arles – the A9 that skirts back towards Nîmes and then the A54.

- - - - - - - - -

TRIP HIGHLIGHT

③ Arles

Arles, formerly known as Arelate, was part of the Roman Empire from as early as the 2nd century BC. It wasn't until the 49–45 BC civil war, however, when nearby Massalia (Marseille) supported Pompey (ie backed the wrong side), that it became a booming regional capital.

The town today is delightful, Roman cache or no, but what a living legacy it is. **Les Arènes** (Amphithéâtre; adult/child incl Théâtre Antique €6.50/ free; ☺9am-7pm) is not as larges as Nîmes', but it is spectacularly sited and occasionally still sees blood spilled, just like in the good old gladiatorial days (it hosts bullfights and *courses Camarguaises*, which is the local

variation). Likewise the 1st-century **Théâtre Antique** (☎04 90 96 93 30; bd des Lices, enter on rue de la Calade; incl in Amphithéâtre admission; ☺9am-7pm) is still regularly used for alfresco performances.

Just as social, political and religious life revolved around the forum in Arelate, the busy plane-tree-shaded **place du Forum** buzzes with cafe life today. Sip a pastis here and spot the remains of a 2nd-century temple embedded in the façade of the **Hôtel Nord-Pinus**. Under your feet are **Cryptoportiques** (place du Forum; adult/child €3.50/free; ☺9am-noon & 2-7pm) – subterranean foundations and buried arcades. Access the underground galleries, 89m long and 59m wide, at the **hôtel de ville** (town hall; place de la République).

Emperor Constantin's partly preserved 4th-century private baths, the **Thermes de Constantin** (rue du Grand Prieuré; adult/child €3/free; ☺9am-noon & 2-7pm), are a few minutes' stroll

JIM RICHARDSON/GETTY IMAGES ©

away, next to the quai. Southwest of the centre is **Les Alyscamps** (adult/child €3.50/free; ☺9am-7pm), a necropolis founded by the Romans and adopted by Christians in the 4th century. It contains the tombs of martyr St Genest and Arles' first bishops. You may recognise it: Van Gogh and Gauguin both captured the avenues

ROMAN PROVENCE SWAT LIST

» *The Roman Provence Guide* (Edwin Mullins)

» *The Roman Remains of Southern France* (James Bromwich)

» *Southern France: An Oxford Archaeological Guide* (Henry Cleere)

» *Ancient Provence: Layers of History in Southern France* (Jeffrey Wolin)

Site Archéologique de Glanum Ancient Roman triumphal arch

of cypresses on canvas (though only melancholy old Van Gogh painted the empty sarcophagi).

✖ 🛏 p242, p281, p309

The Drive » Take the D17 to Fontvielle, then turn off and follow the D78F/D27A to Baux-de-Provence, then the D5. This minor detour takes you past beautiful dry white rocky hills dotted with scrubby pine; the trip will still only take around 45 minutes. There's on-site parking at Glanum. If heading into St-Rémy, there's parking by the tourist office (parking Jean-Jaurès) and north of the periphery (parking Général-de-Gaulle).

----

4 Glanum

Such is the glittering allure of the gourmet delis, interiors boutiques and smart restaurants that line St-Rémy-de-Provence's circling boulevards and place de la République that a visit to the **Site Archéologique de Glanum** (📞04 90 92 23 79; http://glanum. monuments-nationaux.fr/en; rte des Baux-de-Provence; adult/child €7/4.50, parking €2.20; ⏰9.30am-6.30pm daily Apr-Sep, 10am-5pm Tue-Sun Oct-Mar) is often an afterthought. But

the **triumphal arch**
(AD 20) that marks
Glanum's entrance, 2km
south of St-Rémy, is far
from insignificant. It's
pegged as one of France's
oldest and is joined by
a towering **mausoleum**
(30–20 BC). Walk down
the main street and
you'll pass the mainstays
of Roman life: baths, a
forum and marketplace,
temples and town
villas. And beneath all
this Roman handiwork
lies the remnants of
an older Celtic and
Hellenic settlement,
built to take advantage
of a sacred spring. Van
Gogh, as a patient of the

neighbouring asylum,
painted the olive orchard
that covered the site
until its excavation in the
1920s.

 p242, p281

The Drive » It's the A7 all
the way to Orange, 50km of
nondescript driving if you're not
tempted by a detour to Avignon
on the way.

TRIP HIGHLIGHT

⑤ Orange

It's often said if you can
only see one Roman
site in France, make it
Orange. And yes, the
town's Roman treasures
are gobsmacking and

unusually old; both are
believed to have been
built during Augustus
Caesar's rule (27 BC–AD
14). Plus, while Orange
may not be the Provençal
village of popular
fantasy, it's a cruisy,
decidedly untouristy
town, making for good-
value accommodation
and hassle-free
sightseeing (such as
plentiful street parking
one block back from the
theatre).

At a massive 103m
wide and 37m high, the
stage wall of the **Théâtre
Antique** (www.theatre
-antique.com; adult/child
€8.50/6.50, 2nd child free;

SALVE, PROVINCIA GALLIA TRANSALPINA

It all starts with the Greeks. After founding the city of Massalia, now Marseille, around 600 BC, they spent the next few centuries establishing a long string of ports along the coast, planting olives and grapes as they went. When migrating Celts from the north joined forces with the local Ligurians, resistance to these booming colonies grew. The Celto-Ligurians were a force to be reckoned with; unfortunately they were about to meet ancient history's biggest bullies. In 125 BC the Romans helped the Greeks defend Massalia, and swiftly took control.

Thus begins the Gallo-Roman era and the region of Provincia Gallia Transalpina, the first Roman *provincia* (province), the name from which Provence takes it name. Later Provincia Narbonensis, it embraced all of southern France from the Alps to the Mediterranean and the Pyrenees.

Roads made the work of empire possible, and the Romans quickly set about securing a route that joined Italy and Spain. Via Aurelia linked Rome to Fréjus, Aix-en-Provence, Arles and Nîmes; the northbound Via Agrippa followed the Rhône from Arles to Avignon, Orange and onwards to Lyons. The Via Domitia linked the Alps with the Pyrenees by way of the Luberon and Nîmes.

With Julius Caesar's conquest of Gaul (58–51 BC), the region truly flourished. Under the emperor Augustus, vast amphitheatres, triumphal arches and ingenious aqueducts – the ones that propel this trip – were constructed. Augustus celebrated his final defeat of the ever-rebellious Ligurians in 14 BC, with the construction of the monument at La Turbie (p255) on the Cote d'Azur.

The Gallo-Roman legacy may be writ large and loud in Provence, but it also persists in the everyday. Look for it in unusual places: recycled into cathedral floors or hotel façades, in dusty cellars or simply buried beneath your feet.

⊙9am-6pm Mar-Oct, to 4.30pm Nov-Feb) dominates the surrounding streetscape. Minus a few mosaics, plus a new roof, it's one of three in the world still standing in their entirety, and originally seated 10,000 spectators. Admission includes an informative, if a bit overdramatic, audio guide, and access to the **Musée d'Orange** (☑04 90 51 17 60; museum only adult/child €5.50/4.50; ⊙9.15am-7pm summer, shorter hours in winter) across the road. Its collection includes friezes from the theatre with the Roman motifs we love: eagles holding garlands of bay leaves, and a cracking battle between cavalrymen and foot soldiers.

For bird's-eye views of the theatre – and phenomenal vistas of rocky Mont Ventoux and the Dentelles – follow montée Philbert de Chalons, or montée Lambert, up **Colline St-Eutrope**, once the ever-vigilant Romans' lookout point.

To the town's north, the **Arc de Triomphe** stands on the ancient Via Agrippa (now the busy N7), 19m high and wide, and a stonking 8m thick. Restored in 2009, its richly animated reliefs commemorate 49 BC Roman victories with images of battles, ships, trophies, and chained, naked and utterly subdued Gauls.

🛏 p243

The Drive » Northeast, the D975 passes through gentle vineyard-lined valleys for 40 minutes, with views of the Dentelles de Montmirail's limestone ridges along the way (the D977 and D23 can be equally lovely). Parking in Vaison can be a trial; nab a spot by the tourist office (place du Chanoine Saute), or try below the western walls of the Cité Médiévale, if you don't mind a walk.

– – – – – – – – – – – –

❻ Vaison-la-Romaine

Is there anything more telling of Rome's smarts than a sturdy, still-used Roman bridge? Vaison-la-Romaine's pretty little **Pont Romain** has stood the test of time and severe floods. Stand at its centre and gaze up at the walled, cobbled-street hilltop Cité Médiévale, down at the fast-flowing River Ouvèze.

Vaison-la-Romaine is tucked between seven valleys and has long been a place of trade. The ruined remains of **Vasio Vocontiorum**, the Roman city that flourished here between the 6th and 2nd centuries BC, fill two central **Gallo-Roman sites** (adult/child €8/3.50; ⊙closed Jan). Dual neighbourhoods lie on either side of the tourist office and av du Général-de-Gaulle. The Romans shopped at the colonnaded boutiques and bathed at **La Villasse**, where you'll find **Maison au Dauphin**, which has splendid marble-lined fish ponds.

In **Puymin**, see noblemen's houses, mosaics, a workmen's quarter, a temple, and the still-functioning 6000-seat **Théâtre Antique** (c AD 20). To make sense of the remains (and gather your audio guide), head for the **archaeological museum**, which revives Vaison's Roman past with incredible swag – superb mosaics, carved masks, and statues that include a 3rd-century silver bust and marble renderings of Hadrian and his wife, Sabina. Admission includes entry to the soothing 12th-century Romanesque cloister at **Cathédrale Notre-Dame de Nazareth** (cloister €1.50; ⊙10am-12.30pm & 2-6pm, closed Jan & Feb), a five-minute walk west of La Villasse and, like much of Provence, built on Roman foundations.

🍴🛏 p243

Eating & Sleeping

Nîmes ❶

✕ Au Plaisir des Halles — French €€

(📞04 66 36 01 02; 4 rue Littré; mains €24-30; 🕐Tue-Sat) Ingredients here are the freshest available. The lunchtime three-course *menu* (set-priced meal; €20) is excellent value. Consider ordering local-speciality *brandade* (whipped salted codfish). There's a great list of Languedoc wines.

🛏 Jardins Secrets — Boutique Hotel €€€

(📞 04 66 84 82 64; www.jardinssecrets.net; 3 rue Gaston Maruejols; d from €200; 🅟🛜❄) Yes, it has a secret garden, and a very lushly planted one at that. Tucked away in a central town house, this is a small, deliciously luxurious hotel, with toile de Jouy drapes, classical murals, random curiosities, French windows and claw-foot baths. A rare find in down-to-earth Nîmes.

🛏 Royal Hôtel — Hotel €

(📞04 66 58 28 27; www.royalhotel-nimes.com; 3 bd Alphonse Daudet; r €60-80; 🅟🛜) This raffishly bohemian, 21-room hotel is eternally popular. Many rooms overlook dynamic place d'Assas – an invigorating view, but summer nights are noisy. Light sleepers should book patio rooms.

Pont du Gard ❷

✕ Lisa M — Modern French €€€

(📞04 66 22 92 12; www.lisam.fr; 3 place de la Madone, Vers-Pont-du-Gard; menus €58; 🕐dinner Wed-Sun) A chef with a very contemporary culinary ethos turns out light, seasonal, often exotically spiced dishes in an atmospheric village house that was once a convent. Up the wonderful staircase are two beautiful sandstone-clad rooms (double €140). Terraces look onto the delightfully sleepy village (as does the rooftop plunge pool); you'll never know the Pont is so close. Note: it can be tricky to find.

🛏 La Maison — B&B €€

(📞04 66 81 25 151; www.chambres-provence. com; place de l'Eglise, Blauzac; s/d from €105/120; 🛜❄) This B&B makes a tranquil base halfway between Uzès and the Pont, and offers mountain views, a pretty garden and a pool. The Ferrara room is especially charming, though all rooms use a nice mix of local, Asian and contemporary furnishings.

Arles ❸

✕ L'Autruche — Modern French €€

(📞04 90 49 73 63; 5 rue Dulau; lunch menu €18, mains €29; 🕐lunch & dinner Tue-Sat) This modern, inviting restaurant run by husband and wife team Fabien and Ouria assembles perfect market-fresh dishes. Dishes are creative but earthy, while desserts are extravagant.

🛏 Hôtel Arlatan — Historic Hotel €€

(📞04 90 93 56 66; www.hotel-arlatan.fr; 26 rue du Sauvage; d €85-157, apt €177-247; 🕐mid-Mar–mid-Nov; 🅟@🛜❄) The heated swimming pool, pretty garden and plush rooms decorated with antique furniture are just some of the things going for this hotel. Oh, and, yes, those foundations visible through a glass floor in the lobby are Roman.

Glanum ❹

✕ La Cuisine des Anges — Bistro €€

(📞04 90 92 17 66; www.angesetfees-stremy. com; 4 rue du 8 Mai 1945; lunch/dinner menu €14/27; 🕐lunch Mon-Sat, dinner daily Jun-Aug, lunch & dinner Thu-Sat, dinner Sun Sep-May, closed Nov; 🛜) Light, simple Provençal dishes derive from organic local ingredients at this cosy village bistro with a wood-floored dining room and zinc-topped tables. Upstairs is a *chambre d'hôte*, Le Sommeil des Fées, with five B&B rooms (€74 to €94).

✕ Taberna Romana — Bistro €€

(📞04 90 92 65 97; www.taberna-romana.com; rte des Baux; menus €16-26; 🕐10am-6.30pm Tue-Sun Apr-Oct) Drinks come with a panorama over the ruined city of Glanum, or you can settle in for lunch with a history geek–pleasing menu that revives ancient Roman recipes, including legionnaires' favourites like honeyed red wine, pork balls and spiced beans.

🛏 Hotel de l'Image   Boutique Hotel €€

(☏04 90 92 51 50; www.hotel-image.fr; 36 bd Victor Hugo, St-Remy; d from €130; ❄ 🛜 🏊) Conveniently located on the southern side of St-Rémy's circling boulevard, this midsize, modern place has smart rooms adorned simply with contemporary photography. The perfect extra if you're here in the hot, hectic days of summer: a 2-hectare park facing the Alpilles.

Orange ❺

🛏 Le Glacier   Hotel €€

(☏04 90 34 02 01; www.le-glacier.com; 46 cours Aristide Briand; d €50-110; ❄ @ 🛜) All 28 rooms are individually decorated, and impeccably maintained by charming owners, who pay attention to detail. Also rents bikes (half-/full day €12/16) and has secure, free bike parking.

🛏 Hôtel l'Herbier d'Orange   Hotel €

(☏04 90 34 09 23; www.lherbierdorange. com; 8 place aux Herbes; s/d/tr incl breakfast €59/69/79; ❄ @ 🛜 🛗) Bright high-ceilinged rooms, sparkling bathrooms and friendly enthusiastic owners place this small basic hotel a notch above. Evening aperitif included.

🛏 Camping Le Jonquier   Campground €

(☏04 90 34 49 48; www.campinglejonquier. com; 1321 rue Alexis Carrel; per 2 people €20-26; ☺Easter-Sep; @ 🛜 🏊 🛗) Good for active travellers: pool, minigolf, tennis, Ping Pong, hot tub...and very handy to the Arc de Triomphe.

Vaison-la-Romaine ❻

✕ Le Bateleur   Provençal €€

(☏04 90 36 28 04; www.le-bateleur.com; 1 place Théodore Aubanel; lunch menus €17-22, dinner menus €27-40; ☺closed Mon, dinner Sun & Thu) The best seats at this simple Provençal dining room overlook the river, but you'll need no distractions from the beautifully presented regional cooking. Lunch includes wine and coffee.

✕ La Lyriste   Provençal €€

(☏04 90 36 04 67; 45 cours Taulignan; menus €18-36; ☺Wed-Sun) The contemporary Provençal menu at this charming bistro emphasises seasonal regional ingredients in dishes ranging from *bourride* (fish stew) to a foie-gras tasting *menu* (€36). In summer book a table on the terrace.

🛏 Hôtel Le Burrhus   Design Hotel €

(☏04 90 36 00 11; www.burrhus.com; 1 place de Montfort; d €55-87; 🛜) On Vaison's vibrant central square, this hotel may look quaint, but its 38 rooms have ultramodern decor with designer fittings, original artwork and mosaic bathrooms. No elevator. Parking (€7) must be booked ahead.

🛏 L'Évêché   B&B €€

(☏04 90 36 13 46; http://eveche.free.fr; rue de l'Évêché; d €92-140) With groaning bookshelves, vaulted ceilings, higgledy-piggledy staircase and intimate salons, this five-room *chambre d'hôte,* in the medieval city, is a treat. Loan bikes are complimentary.

🛏 Camping du Théâtre Romain   Campground €

(☏04 90 28 78 66; www.camping-theatre.com; chemin de Brusquet; per 2 people €21; ☺mid-Mar–mid-Nov; 🛜 🏊) Opposite the Théâtre Antique, with a good pool. Some patches are nicely tree-shaded, others are very sunny.

Lavender Sunrise intensifies the purple hue near Valensole

Lavender Route

22

Banish thoughts of grandma's closet. Get out among the purple haze, sniff the heady summer breezes and navigate picturesque hilltop towns, ancient churches and pretty valleys.

TRIP HIGHLIGHTS

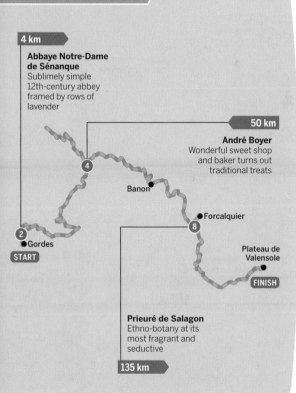

4 km

Abbaye Notre-Dame de Sénanque
Sublimely simple 12th-century abbey framed by rows of lavender

50 km

André Boyer
Wonderful sweet shop and baker turns out traditional treats

4

Banon

Forcalquier

8

2
●Gordes

START

Plateau de Valensole

FINISH

Prieuré de Salagon
Ethno-botany at its most fragrant and seductive

135 km

4–5 DAYS
210KM / 130 MILES

GREAT FOR...

BEST TIME TO GO

July is purple prime time, but June's blooms still impress.

 ESSENTIAL PHOTO

The road just north of Sault is a particularly stunning spot.

 BEST FOR OUTDOORS

Mont Ventoux has brilliant hiking trails and is hallowed ground for cycling fans.

245

Lavender Route

The Luberon and Vaucluse may be well-trodden (and driven) destinations, but you'll be surprised at how rustic they remain. This trip takes you to the undoubtedly big-ticket (and exquisitely beautiful) sights but also gets you exploring back roads, sleepy villages, big skies and one stunner of a mountain. And yes, past fields, and fields of glorious purple blooms.

1 Gordes

The tiered village of Gordes sits spectacularly on the white-rock face of the Vaucluse plateau. It's a traditional base for those on the lavender trail, high on many tourists' must-see lists, and a favourite with posh Parisians. Gordes' star attraction is its 11th-century château, though doing laps in the cliff-side pool at the **Bastide de Gordes** can't be too bad. In truth, the thrill lies in glimpsing the village from a slight

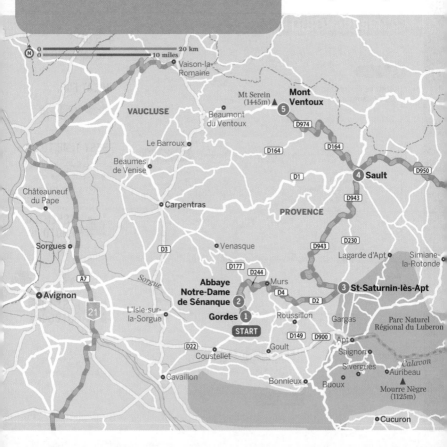

distance – come sunset, the village glows gold.

 p251

The Drive >> Head northwest of Gordes off the D177 with 4km of perfect Provence out your window. The descent down to the abbey is narrow, treacherous in rain, and tricky in sunshine when everyone is blinded by the lavender and pulls over. And yes, if you can, do pull over for a photograph.

TRIP HIGHLIGHT

2 Abbaye Notre-Dame de Sénanque

Isolated and ridiculously photogenic, this 12th-century Cistercian **abbey** (☎ 04 90 72 05 72; www.senanque.fr; guided tour in French adult/child/family €7/3/20; ☺ tours by reservation) is famously framed by lavender from mid-June through July. The abbey was founded in 1148 and is still home to a small number of monks. The cloisters have a haunting, severe beauty; reservations are essential to visit inside but out of high season they can be made on-site (conservative dress and silence are required). Tours begin around 10am,

so for some tranquil time with the lavender, arrive well before then.

The Drive >> The way out of the abbey has you heading north. Continue up the D177 then turn right onto the D244 and follow the signs to Murs, a very winding 9.5km drive accompanied by wheat fields and vineyards. From here it's about 25 minutes to the next stop.

---

3 St-Saturnin-lès-Apt

St-Saturnin-lès-Apt is a refreshingly ungentrified village, with marvellous views of the surrounding Vaucluse plateau punctuated by purple fields – climb to the **ruins** atop the village for a knockout vista. At **Moulin à Huile Jullien** (www.moulin-huile-jullien.com; rte d'Apt; ☺ Mon-Sat) see how olives are milled into

LINK YOUR TRIP

18 Foothills of the Alps

Swap rolling hills for spectacular gorges and then alpine air: take the D6 and D852 to Moustiers-Ste-Marie, or drop in at Sisteron from Forcalquier.

21 Roman Provence

From Roman Provence's last stop in Vaison-la-Romaine, it's a gorgeous drive to Gordes via Carpentras and Venasque.

TOP TIP: LAVENDER: FINDING THE GOOD OIL

When shopping for oil, the sought-after product is fine lavender (in French, *lavande fine;* in Latin, *L. officinalis*), not spike lavender *(L. latifolia)* or the hybrid lavandin *(Lavandula x intermedia)*. The latter are higher in camphor; they're used in soaps and body-care products but rarely in fine perfumery. They're also used to adulterate true lavender oil. Look for oil that's clearly labeled and lacks a harsh camphor note.

oil (with honey and oil tastings thrown in). See *lavande fine* growing at **Château du Bois** (☎04 90 76 91 23; www.lechateaudubois. com), a winding, but gorgeous, drive 20km to the northeast, with 800,000 sq metres of peaceful plantings. (Note, this is a farm only; the shop and museum is in Coustellet.)

✖ 🛏 p251

The Drive ≫ Spot the pretty 17th-century windmill, Le Château les Moulins, 1km north, off the D943 toward Sault, then look out for the magnificent views of the red-tinged escarpment and the rust-coloured village of Roussillon. The views of Mont Ventoux only get more spectacular as you approach Sault, a 35-minute drive away.

TRIP HIGHLIGHT

④ Sault

This drowsily charming, isolated hilltop town mixes its lavender views with plum orchards and scattered forest. Town hot spot is **André Boyer** (☎04 90 64 00 23; place de

l'Europe), keeping farmers, cyclists and mountaineers in honey and almond nougat since 1887; its lavender marshmallows and the local speciality *pognes* (an orange-scented brioche) are also must-tries. Head to **GAEC Champelle** (☎04 90 64 01 50; www.gaec-champelle.fr; rte de Ventoux), a roadside farm stand northwest of town, whose products include great buys for cooks. The lavender up here is known for its dark, OK...deep purple, hue.

The Drive ≫ This is one great 25km. Head out of town on the D164; when you hit the D974, fields give way to dense, fragrant forest (impromptu picnic, perhaps?). Above the tree line, strange spots of Alpine scrub are gradually replaced by pale bald slopes. These steep gradients have often formed a hair-raising stage of the Tour de France – the road is daubed with Tour graffiti and many fans make a brave two-wheeled homage.

----

⑤ Mont Ventoux

If fields of flowers are intoxicating, Mont

Ventoux (1912m) is awe-inspiring. Nicknamed *le géant de Provence* – Provence's giant – its great white hulk is visible from much of the region. *Le géant* sparkles all year round – once the snow melts, its lunar-style limestone slopes glimmer in the sun. From its peak, clear-day vistas extend to the Alps and the Camargue.

Even summer temperatures can plummet by 20°C at the top; it's also twice as likely to rain; and the relentless mistrals blow 130 days a year, sometimes exceeding 250km/h. Bring a cardigan and scarf!

The Drive ≫ Go back the way you came to Sault, then head east to Banon on the D950 for another 40 minutes.

----

⑥ Banon

A tasty, nonfloral diversion: little village, big cheese. Bustling Banon is famous for its chèvre de Banon, a goat's-milk cheese wrapped in a chestnut leaf. Fromagerie de Banon sells its cheese at the Tuesday-morning market, and at wonderful cheese-and-sausage shop **chez Melchio** (☎04 92 73 23 05; place de la Règublique; ☺8am-7pm Jul & Aug, 8am-12.30pm & 2.30-6.30pm Wed-Sun Sep-Jun), which is unbeatable for picnic supplies. Tuck into cheese-and-charcuterie plates at **Les Vins au Vert** (04 92 75 23 84; www.lesvinsauvert.com; rue Pasteur; mains €12-16; ☺ Wed-Sun); make reservations for Thursday to Saturday nights.

The Drive » Follow the D950 southeast for 25km to Forcalquier, as the scenery alternates between gentle forested slopes and fields.

- - - - - - - - -

⑦ Forcalquier

Forcalquier has an upbeat, slightly bohemian vibe, a holdover from 1960s and '70s, when artists and back-to-the-landers arrived, fostering a now-booming organics ('*biologiques*' or bio) movement. Saffron is grown here, absinthe is distilled, and the town is also home to the L'Université Européenne des Senteurs & Saveurs (UESS; European University of Scents and Flavours). To see it all in action, time your visit for the Monday morning market.

Climb the steep steps to Forcalquier's gold-topped **citadel** and octagonal **chapel** for more sensational views; on the way down note the once-wealthy seat's ornately carved wooden doorways and grand bourgeois town houses. Prefer to work your senses overtime? UESS' **Couvent des Cordeliers** (04 92 72 50 68; www.

Prieuré de Salagon A 13th-century priory near Mane

couventdescordeliers.com) conducts workshops (€40 to €50) in perfume making, wine tasting, and aromatherapy in Forcalquier's 13th-century convent.

 p251

The Drive » Find yourself in a gentle world, all plane-tree arcades, wildflowers and, yes, lavender. Around 4km south on the D4100 you'll come to our next stop, just before the pretty town of Mane.

- - - - - - - - -

TRIP HIGHLIGHT

⑧ Prieuré de Salagon

This beautiful 13th-century priory, located on the outskirts of Mane, is today home to a garden museum, the **Jardins Salagon** (04 92 75 70 50;

✔ TOP TIP: BEST PRODUCE MARKETS

The Luberon (p250) has groaning markets run from 8am to 1pm; they're particularly thrilling in summer.

Monday Forcalquier

Tuesday Apt, Gordes, St-Saturnin-lès-Apt

Wednesday Gargas

Thursday Roussillon

Friday Bonnieux, Lourmarin

Saturday Apt, Manosque

Sunday Coustellet, Villars

CHRIS HELLIER/ALAMY ©

www.musee-de-salagon.com; adult/child €7/5; ⊙10am-8pm daily Jun-Aug, to 6pm Wed-Mon Sep-Apr, closed Jan; 🖐). This is ethno-botany at its most poetic and sensual: wander through recreated medieval herb gardens, fragrant with native lavender, mints and mugworts. The bookshop is inviting, too.

The walled town of **Mane** is lovely for strolling. Or for a mysterious, potentially curative detour, visit remote **Église de Cháteauneuf**, where a hermit church sister concocts natural remedies and makes jam. Head 800m south of Mane to the Hôtel Mas du Pont Roman, then turn right and either park and walk, or drive the bumpy final 3km. Be warned: the good sister doesn't always reveal herself. Just in

case, bring a picnic and consider it an adventure.

The Drive » Get on the D13, then follow the signs to the D5, for about 30 minutes.

- - - - - - - - - - -

⑨ Manosque

Manosque has two lovely fountains and a historic cobblestoned core, but the traffic and suburban nothingness make visiting a nuisance. Why swing by? Just southeast is the home of **l'Occitane** (www.loccitane.com; Zone Industrielle St-Maurice; ⊙10am-7pm Mon-Sat), the company that turned traditional lavender-, almond- and olive oil–based Provençal skincare into a global phenomenon. Factory tours can be booked through the **tourist office** (📞04 92 72 16 000); the shop offers a flat 10% discount, and the odd bargain.

The Drive » Leave the freeways and ring roads behind and cross the Durance River towards the quieter D6 (from where it will take around 20 minutes to reach the town of Valensole); make sure you check the rear-view mirrors for mountain views to the northwest as you do.

- - - - - - - - - - -

⑩ Plateau de Valensole

Things get very relaxed once you hit the D6, and the road begins a gentle climb. Picnic provisions packed, wind down your windows. This dreamily quiet plateau has Provence's greatest concentration of lavender farms, and a checkerboard of waving wheat and lavender rows stretch to the horizon, or at least until Riez. Fine picnic spots and photo ops are not hard to find.

DETOUR: THE LUBERON

Start: ⑧ Prieuré de Salagon

The Luberon's other, southern, half is equally as florally blessed. Lavender carpets the **Plateau de Claparèdes** between **Buoux** (west), **Sivergues** (south), **Auribeau** (east) and **Saignon** (north). Cycle, walk or motor through the lavender fields and along the northern slopes of **Mourre Nègre** (1125m) – the Luberon's highest point, accessible from **Cucuron**. The D113 climbs to idyllic lavender distillery **Les Agnels** (📞04 90 74 34 60; www.lesagnels.com; rte de Buoux, btwn Buoux & Apt; free tours mid-Jul–mid-Aug), which distils lavender, cypress and rosemary. The small on-site spa has a lavender-scented swimming pool. Stay at **Chambre de Séjour avec Vue** (📞04 90 04 85 01; www.chambreavecvue.com; rue de la Bourgade; r €80-100) in tiny, hip Saignon, which perches on high rocky flanks, its narrow streets crowning a hill ringed with craggy scrub and petite lavender plots, with incredible vistas across the Luberon to Mont Ventoux.

Eating & Sleeping

Gordes ❶

✕ Le Mas Tourteron   Gastronomic €€€

(☏04 90 72 00 16; www.mastourteron.com; chemin de St-Blaise; menus from €35; ☺lunch & dinner Wed-Sat, lunch Sun) Surrounded by flourishing gardens, the stone dining room has a cosy, boho-chic feel, befitting chef Elisabeth Bourgeois' cooking. Menus are inventive and seasonal, with legendary desserts and an impressive wine menu. It's signposted off the D2, 3.5km south of Gordes. Reservations essential.

🛏 Le Mas de la Beaume   B&B €€

(☏04 90 72 02 96; www.labeaume.com; entrance Gordes village; d €125-180; 🛜🚫) In a stunning hilltop locale at the village's edge, this impeccable five-room place is like a Provençal postcard come to life (never mind summertime traffic over the garden wall). Think yellow-washed stone walls and bunches of lavender dangling from wood beams. Plan a lie-in; breakfast is delivered to your room.

🛏 Auberge de Carcarille   Hotel €€

(☏ 04 90 72 02 63; www.auberge-carcarille. com; rte d'Apt; r €88-115, lunch menus €20, dinner menus €35 to €50; ❄🛜🚫🐾) Tucked in a valley 3km east of Gordes, this mid-size, great-value hotel has spotless if conservatively decorated rooms, and a big garden. Consider half-board: the restaurant serves good regional cooking.

St-Saturnin-lès-Apt ❸

✕ Le Restaurant L'Estrade   Bistro €

(☏04 90 71 15 75; 6 av Victor Hugo; menus from €15) Word of mouth keeps this super-friendly village restaurant buzzing. The menu showcases the season's freshest ingredients – simple stuff but expertly prepared. A good lunch stop; call ahead to secure a table.

🛏 Mas de Cink   Self-Contained €€

(☏06 11 99 80 88; www.lemasdecink.com; Hameau des Blanchards; per 3 nights from €200, per week €300-900; ❄🛜🚫) Apartments evocatively blend northern contemporary cool with earthy Provençal comfort in this sprawling old farmhouse and barn. All have fully equipped kitchens, and a couple are suitable for larger groups. Private terraces and trellised outdoor dining areas overlook a wild garden, lavender fields and vineyards. Happy, lazy days!

Forcalquier ❼

✕ Restaurant Le 9   Provençal €€

(((☏04 92 75 03 29; www.le9-forcalquier.fr; av Jean Giono; lunch menus €13-18, dinner menus €20-26; ☺daily Jul & Aug, Thu-Mon Sep-Jun). High up behind the citadel, with a panoramic terrace, Le 9 is Forcalquier's most reliable address with fresh-from-the-farm ingredients transformed into bold bistro fare. On Fridays there's a classic grand aïoli. Make reservations.

🛏 Couvent des Minimes   Luxury Hotel €€€

(☏04 92 74 77 77; www.couventdesminimes -hotelspa.com; Chemin des Jeux de Mai, Mane; r from €235; ❄🛜🚫) The Pays de Forcalquier's only top-end digs occupies a beautiful sandstone convent, with a l'Occitane spa and an aromatic garden. Luxe rooms are nicely textural (though entry-level ones are tiny). Le Cloître serves up a wonderfully creative, locally sourced menu on a lovely terrace in summer (the dining room proper is a tad corporate). Check online for last-minute half-price room rates.

Roquebrune *Glorious coastal views over terracotta roofs*

Classic Trip

The Corniches

23

This trio of spectacular coastal roads makes for one of the world's most cinematic drives. There are glamorous towns ahead, and some vertiginous bends. Get ready for a jaw-dropping experience.

TRIP HIGHLIGHTS

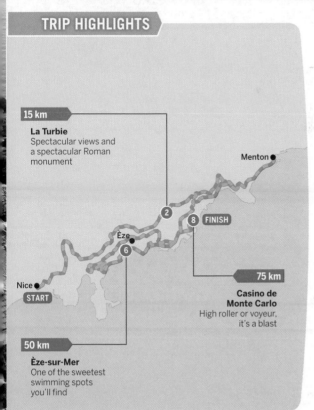

15 km

La Turbie
Spectacular views and a spectacular Roman monument

Menton

2

8 FINISH

Èze

6

Nice
START

75 km

Casino de Monte Carlo
High roller or voyeur, it's a blast

50 km

Èze-sur-Mer
One of the sweetest swimming spots you'll find

3 DAYS
75KM / 47 MILES

GREAT FOR...

BEST TIME TO GO
Avoid August's traffic, but otherwise enjoy winter or summer.

ESSENTIAL PHOTO
Under Augustus' Trophée des Alpes in La Turbie, with Monaco far beneath you.

BEST FOR GLAMOUR
Pull up a cliffside seat for aperitifs on Château Eza's charming stone terrace.

Classic Trip

23 | The Corniches

Don't save the best for last. Say goodbye to Nice from on high, and head onto Napoléon's cliff-hanging Grande Corniche, taking its sweep all the way to the Italian border. Come to your senses as you skim the waterfront on the Corniche Inférieure (aka Basse Corniche), then there are more bedazzling vistas along the Moyenne Corniche before your triumphal entry into Monaco. There's method to the double-back madness — it's all about eastbound views.

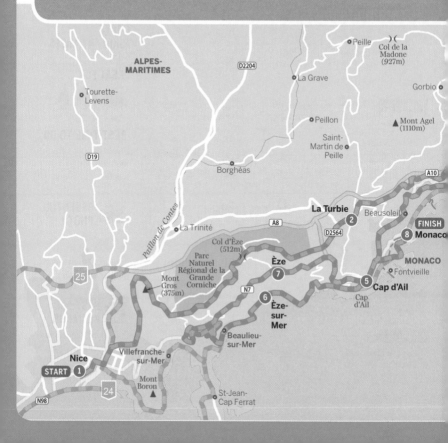

① Nice

You'll begin your trip in Nice (a great place to sleep and gather snacks and supplies), heading out through Riquier on the D2564. The trip, and the thrilling views, officially begins at **l'Observatoire de Nice** (☎04 92 00 30 11; bd de l'Observatoire; adult/child €6/3) up on the summit of Mont Gros. Take it all in, wander the beautiful parkland and get ready to *really* drive.

✕ ⊨ p271, p310, p415

The Drive » This is, without a doubt, 12 spectacular kilometres. Note that the Parc Naturel Départemental de la Grande Corniche will be on your left and stretches almost all the way to La Turbie. Pull over and make use of its picnic tables and dozens of hilly trails – Guides RandOxygène (www.randoxygene.org) has maps.

LINK YOUR TRIP

24 Riviera Cruising
Join this trip at Cap Ferrat or Nice to continue the Cote d'Azur adventure.

25 Modern Art Meander
Combine these routes between Menton and Nice to discover more modern art treasures.

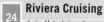
TRIP HIGHLIGHT

② La Turbie

If you were approaching from the east, you might mistake the **Trophée des Alpes** (18 av Albert le; adult/student/child €5.50/4/free; ◷10am-1pm & 2.30-5pm)

Ste-Agnès

LIGURIA
Mortola

A10

Garavan

④ **Menton**

SS1

Ventimiglia

p257

Roquebrune-Cap-Martin

N7

Carnolès

Cap Martin

Cap Martin

Roquebrune-Cap-Martin

③

Ligurian Sea

MEDITERRANEAN SEA

N
0 ――――――― 10 km
0 ――――――― 5 miles

Tue-Sun) for a nuclear reactor or a concrete smelter, so gigantic is its scale. From the west, though, you can't miss the stunning classical façade. Yes, it's a triumphal Roman monument! Built by Emperor Augustus in 6 BC to celebrate his victory over the remaining Celto-Ligurian Alpine tribes that had resisted Roman sovereignty, this amazing tower teeters on the highest point of the old Roman road. It's a joy to visit, with dramatic views of Monaco, and a wooded park setting.

La Turbie often plays bridesmaid to Èze's bride, but it's something of an insider favourite; it's a real town going about its business, nonchalantly blessed with one of the world's most sublimely lovely locations. It's a magical place for a meal or, even better, an overnight stay.

✗ p261

The Drive ≫ Monte Carlo may sparkle and beckon below, but keep your eyes on the road; the principality will keep for another day. Stay on the D2564 to skirt Monaco for another amazing 10km, then turn right into the D52 to Roquebrune.

③ Roquebrune-Cap-Martin

This village of two halves feels a world away from the urban glitz of nearby Monaco: the coastline around Cap Martin remains relatively unspoilt, as if Roquebrune had left its clock on medieval time. The historic half of the town, Roquebrune itself, sits 300m high on a pudding-shaped lump. It towers over the Cap, but they are, in fact, linked by innumerable, *very* steep steps.

The village is delightful, free of tack, and there are sensational views of the coast from the main village square, **place des Deux Frères**. Of all Roquebrune's steep and tortuous streets, **rue Moncollet** – with its arcaded passages and stairways carved out of rock – is the most impressive. Scurry upwards to find architect Le Corbusier's grave at the **cemetery** at the top of the village (in section J, and, yes, he did design his own tombstone).

The Drive ≫ Continue along the D52 towards the coast, following promenade du Cap-Martin all the way along the seafront to Menton. You'll be there in 10 minutes, traffic permitting.

CABANON LE CORBUSIER

On a rocky parcel of land between the railway line and the sea, surrounded by eucalypts, **Cabanon Le Corbusier** (promenade Le Corbusier, Cap Martin; guided tours €8; ⏲ guided tours only 10am Tue & Fri), French architect Le Corbusier's midcentury beach shack, draws design pilgrims from around the world. Come for the architecture, but also for a glimpse of the Riviera that drew the creative classes long before the days of super-yachts and Michelin-star dining.

The *cabanon* was designed using the Modulor, a mathematical benchmark based on the height of a man with his arms held up. It's tiny, and yet a perfect distillation of Corbusier's high Modernist ideals, a place created in which to live a simple, sensual life. It was the only building he ever designed for himself; he declared it 'extravagant in comfort and gentleness'.

Visits are only possible with two-hour guided tours run by the Roquebrune-Cap-Martin **tourist office** (☎ 04 93 35 62 87; www.roquebrune-cap-martin.com; 218 av Aristide Briand).

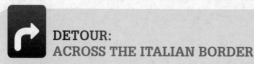

DETOUR:
ACROSS THE ITALIAN BORDER

Start: ❸ Menton

Menton's leafy 'suburbs' reach right to the border with Italy, so getting two countries out of your Côte d'Azur jaunt is simple and highly recommended.

Join hordes of bargain-conscious French shoppers heading to Ventimiglia (Vintimille in French) for the daily **produce market**. Stock up on fruit and fabulous deli and baked goods, such as mozzarella-stuffed peppers, chard tarts, parmesan and *tallegio* cheeses, and *bresaola* (air-dried salt beef). The larger **Friday market** sprawls along the seafront for more than 1km, offering fresh produce as well as general market stalls. It's so popular it routinely results in border gridlock. Unless you're keen to pick up imitation leather goods and bargain clothes, go another day. The town is also known for its cheap alcohol outlets, a good bet for spirits and aperitifs, but not so great for wine.

Hey, you're in Italy! That means pasta for lunch, so head to **Pasta & Basta** (☎39 184 230878; 20/A Via Marconi, Maria San Giuseppe, Ventimiglia; mains €15-20; ⏱lunch & dinner Tue-Sun, lunch Mon; ☻) via the underpass before the town to the perpetually redeveloping port area (don't ask when it will be finished). Various house-made fresh pasta can be matched with a large menu of sauces. Go for a Ligurian speciality: Genovese pesto or *salsa di noci* (a pesto-like blond walnut sauce), and wash it down with a carafe of local white, such as a pale and refreshing *pigato*.

If you've got time, head down the valley to **Dolceaqua**, a steeply sited medieval charmer. If you'd prefer to lunch here, the cute wine bar **Re** (☎39 184 205085; Via del Castello 34; 10.30am-10pm Wed-Mon) does regional standards like borage-stuffed ravioli with a glass of wine and coffee for €10. It's marvellous how essentially Italian it all feels, when you'll be back in France in mere minutes.

For further information, see our *Italy's Best Trips* guide.

---

❹ Menton

Menton's townscape reads like a history book. Its hilltop **Vieille Ville** (old city) is Ligurian to its core, a veritable mini-Genoa, while its sprawling gardens and belle èpoque mansions are a legacy of its 19th-century Brit invasion (it was *the* place to cough your last, darling). Meander the historic quarter all the way to the **Cimetière du Vieux Château** (montée du Souvenir; ⏱7am-8pm May-Sep, to 6pm Oct-Apr) for great views. From place du Cap a ramp leads to the south's grandest baroque church, the Italianate **Basilique St-Michel Archange** (place de l'Église St-Michel; ⏱10am-noon & 3-5.15pm Mon-Fri, 3-5.15pm Sat & Sun), its creamy façade flanked by a towering steeple.

Menton's famed sunny microclimate is a botanist's dream, and there are many historic gardens to wander, including the **Jardin Botanique Exotique du Val Rahmeh** (www.jardins -menton.fr; av St-Jacques; adult/child €8.50/free; ⏱10am-12.30pm & 3.30-6.30pm Wed-Mon) where terraces overflow with exotic fruit-tree collections, and the beautiful, once abandoned **Jardin de la Serre de la Madone** (☎04 93 57 73 90; www. serredelamadone.com; 74 rte de Gorbio; adult/student/child €8/4/free; ⏱10am-6pm Tue-Sun), overgrown with rare plants. The tourist office's dedicated **garden website** (www.jardins-menton.fr) has a comprehensive list and opening times.

✕ ⤶ p261

The Drive » Leave Menton on the D6007, the Moyenne

Classic Trip

Corniche, skirting the upper perimeter of Monaco. Veer left onto the D37 and follow the signs to Cap d'Ail, around a 30-minute trip all up.

- - - - - - - - - - - - - -

5 Cap d'Ail

Ditch the car for a day, hang out on hedonist's favourite **Plage Mala** (a tiny gravel cove where a couple of restaurants double up as private beach and cocktail bars) or do some spectacular coastal walking. Monaco's stretch aside, you can hike the 13km along the **Sentier du Littoral** between Cap d'Ail and Menton without passing a car. Follow the rugged coastline from Mala to Plage Marquet in the Fontvieille neighbourhood of Monaco. The path then picks up at the other end of Monaco, in Larvotto,

from where you can walk to Menton along the beaches and wooded shores of Cap Martin, including the beautiful **Plage Buse**. The walk is easy going (although often tricky in bad weather) and well marked; walk small sections and include beach stops and lunch. This is also a good place to stay overnight if you're shy of Monaco's hotel rates.

🛏 p261

The Drive » Take the D6098 west out of Cap d'Ail for 5km, passing through the giant headland via a tunnel, and then emerge on the coast at Èze-sur-Mer on av de la Liberté.

- - - - - - - - - - - - - -

TRIP HIGHLIGHT

6 Èze-sur-Mer

Èze-sur-Mer can seem a bit dull from the road. But do pull up on av de la

Liberté and find a park. Keep your eyes peeled for the underpass, near the main bus stop, which takes you to the beach, hidden behind a row of cute old beach houses. It's a sweet, intimate stretch of pebbles fronted by a gentle cove and bookended with dark mountains. Head to one of the low-key beach clubs, such as friendly **Papaya Beach** (☎04 93 01 50 33; www.papayabeach.fr; 28 av de la Liberté; ☺Easter-Oct), and sit back and watch the odd luxury yacht bobbing beyond the pontoon. There's a nice public strip here, too.

The Drive » Continue towards Cap Ferrat. Past Beaulieu-sur-Mer's marina, turn into the D133 at the roundabout (signposted Èze village/Moyenne Corniche). Turn right after 4km into the Moyenne Corniche; another

---

LOCAL KNOWLEDGE
LEE (LINO) LATEGAN-MCGREGOR, REAL ESTATE AGENT, NICE

Cheap and chic does exist on the Riviera, even in Monaco. Lounge about on imported sand with the glitterati on the beach along av Princess Grace, then head up to quaint L'Estragon in Monaco-Ville for €9 pizzas and an evening stroll. Want to party with the rich and famous? La Rascasse in Monaco's port has happy hour every night until 11pm – that's €7 cocktails in one of the area's coolest, and hottest, outdoor DJ bars.

Left: Marina, Menton
Right: Monte Carlo

1km or so along are a number of safe spots to stop and admire the view. From here it's around 10 minutes to Èze. Turn right to park at the Fragonard sign.

----

⑦ Èze

This rocky little village perched on an impossible peak is the jewel in the Riviera crown. The main attraction is technically the **medieval village**, with small higgledy-piggledy stone houses and winding lanes (and, yes, galleries and shops). It's undoubtedly delightful but it's the ever-present views of the coast that are truly mesmerising. They just get more spectacular from **Jardin d'Èze** (adult/child €4/free; ☺9am-sunset), a surreal cactus garden at the top of the village, so steep and rocky it may have been purpose-built for mountain goats. It's also where you'll find the old castle ruins; take time to sit, draw a deep breath and gaze, as few places on earth offer such a panorama.

On your way down, look for some horrible histories remnants: the village back door, known as the **Moor's Gate**, where the Saracens invaded in the 8th century; and a strategically placed hole near the village entrance

where boiling oil and shot were launched.

You've already dipped your toes in the Med at Èze-sur-Mer, but if you're up for it, scamper back down via the *steep* **chemin de Nietzsche** (45 minutes one way); this German philosopher wrote parts of *Thus Spoke Zarathustra* while staying in Èze and enjoyed a daily walk down this uber-path.

Èze gets *very* crowded between 10am and 5pm; if you prefer a quiet wander, plan to be here early in the morning or before dinner. Or even better, stay in the village.

✕ 🛏 p261

The Drive ⟫ Stay on the D6007 for the 20-minute descent into Monte Carlo. Avoid temptation to make like Mark Webber when you see your first red and white marked shoulders – this is F1 territory. The Casino de Monte Carlo is well signposted; there's a massive underground car park opposite the fountain, by allées des Boulingrins.

TRIP HIGHLIGHT

⑧ Monaco

This confetti principality squeezed into just 200 hectares is fabulous, absurd, banal and delicious all at once. Come to be part of the gilded, giddy circus or just play voyeur; either way, it's a blast. For conspicuous consumption at its most naked and theatrical, head to the **Casino de Monte Carlo** (www.montecarlocasinos.com; place

du Casino; Salon Europe/Salons Privés €10/€20; ☺Salon Europe noon-late daily, Salons Privés from 4pm Thu-Sun), or for a ringside seat on the action take an outside table at the historic **Café de Paris** (www.montecarloresort.com; place du Casino; mains €17-53; ☺7am-2am).

Take in the city from the **Jardin Exotique** (www.jardin-exotique.mc; 62 bd du Jardin Exotique; adult/child €7/3.70; ☺9am-dusk), where succulents and cacti tumble down the slopes of Moneghetti through a maze of paths, stairs and bridges.

Keen sailor Albert I, great-grandfather of the current Prince Albert, established the **Musée Océanographique de Monaco** (www.oceano.org; av St-Martin; adult/child €13/6.50; ☺9.30am-7pm); its centrepiece **aquarium** features a 6m-deep lagoon, and it's as absorbing as it is huge.

Head to **Le Rocher**, Monaco's old quarter, for a sense of the original town, if not for its souvenir shops and ice-cream sellers. Perfect for an early-evening stroll, or for added royal pomp, time your visit to coincide with the 11.55am **changing of the guard** at the Grimaldi palace; the Carabiniers du Prince sport high helmets with fetching red tassels. To get here, park at the port and take the path up through the shady **Jardins St-Martin**.

✕ 🛏 p261

Eating & Sleeping

La Turbie ②

✕ Café de la Fontaine
Modern French €€

(☎04 93 28 52 79; 4 av Général de Gaulle; mains €13-18; ⊙lunch & dinner Tue-Sun) This inconspicuous village bistro often doesn't get a second glance. Take a tip from the clued-up Monégasques: it's where Michelin-starred chef Bruno Cirino's gets back to his culinary roots with simple dishes like osso bucco à la Niçoise.

Menton ④

✕ Maison Martin et Fils
Modern French €€

(☎04 93 35 74 67; www.martin-et-fils -restaurant06.fr; 7 rue des Marins; menus from €16) Come for a house-made menu that highlights local specialities such as zucchini-flower beignets and soca (chickpea fritter)-wrapped burgers. Tucked behind Menton's covered market.

⛭ All Seasons Menton
Design Hotel €€

(☎04 92 10 95 25; www.all-seasons-hotels.com; 10 rue Villarey; d/f €90/140; ❄@🔊) This little chain hotel gets it right. Bright accented rooms with balconies are comfortable, bathrooms are slick and staff are charming. Online discounts are generous.

Cap d'Ail ⑤

⛭ Hôtel Normandy
Hotel €€

(☎04 93 78 77 77; www.hotelnormandy.no; 6 allée des Orangers; d from €89; 🔊). Rooms here have real charm with their simple, old-school furniture and venetian mirrors; some have amazing sea views.

Èze ⑦

✕ Château Eza
Gastronomic €€€

(☎04 93 41 12 24; www.chateaueza.com; rue de la Pise; mains €39-65) This 10-bed hotel has an excellent Michelin-starred gastronomic restaurant where the seasonal menu will impress as much as the views. The cute stone bar is open to the public, and the staff is welcoming.

⛭ Domaine Pins Paul
B&B €€

(☎04 93 41 22 66; www.domainepinspaul.fr; 4530 av des Diables Bleus; d €175; ❄🔊🏊) Swim in the pool with panoramic views of the sea and Èze village. Rooms in this grand Provençal bastide (fortified town) are beautiful and the surrounding fragrant woods perfect for a stroll.

Monaco ⑧

✕ Bouchon
Bistro €€

(☎97 77 08 80; www.bouchon.mc; 11 av Princesse Grace, Monte Carlo; mains €21-32; ⊙7am-11pm) This Lyonnais bouchon (bistro) might be a box-ticker (we could be in Manhattan), but its dark charm works. Standards are done 'correctly' and a weekly changing lunch menu is a bargain at €17. Bonus: they'll make you a big salad or omelette outside lunch and dinner time.

✕ Tip Top
Pizzeria €

(11 rue Spélugues, Monte Carlo; mains €12-24; ⊙24hr; ☎) This is where Monégasques gather all night long for pizza, pasta and gossip, and it's a good late-night bet in a town that can be surprisingly sleepy.

⛭ Columbus
Boutique Hotel €€€

(☎92 05 90 00; www.columbushotels. com; 22 av des Papalins, Monte Carlo; d from €230; ❄@🔊🏊) Smart Fontvieille rooms, beautifully decorated in designer greys, elegant striped fabrics and 'back to nature' bathrooms. All have little balconies and views.

Nice Stroll along sun-kissed cours Saleya for a mellow Riviera vibe

Classic Trip

Riviera Cruising

24

This seductive Riviera route takes you to the coast and its dazzling, decadent cities, and inland to its clutch of chic hilltop villages. Along the way there are some deliciously serene surprises.

TRIP HIGHLIGHTS

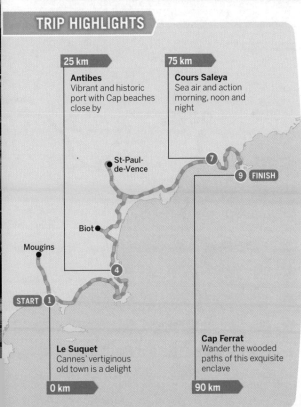

25 km

Antibes
Vibrant and historic port with Cap beaches close by

75 km

Cours Saleya
Sea air and action morning, noon and night

St-Paul-de-Vence

 7

9 FINISH

Biot

Mougins

 4

START 1

Le Suquet
Cannes' vertiginous old town is a delight

0 km

Cap Ferrat
Wander the wooded paths of this exquisite enclave

90 km

7 DAYS
85KM / 53 MILES

GREAT FOR...

BEST TIME TO GO

June or September – you'll avoid the crowds but still can swim.

ESSENTIAL PHOTO

On the 22 red-carpeted steps leading up to the cinema at the Palais des Festivals in Cannes.

BEST FOR OUTDOORS

Find a secluded spot for a divine dip on Cap Ferrat's west coast.

263

24 Riviera Cruising

From the glitz of Cannes to the hushed wealth of Cap Ferrat, you'll discover the Riviera of Picasso, F Scott Fitzgerald and a million paparazzi pictures. But this is not just a landscape of the imagination. Along the way, the sun-kissed cuisine of Nice will enchant, the sea will sparkle, and you'll breathe in the scent of wooded isles and feel the cobbles of hilltop villages beneath your feet.

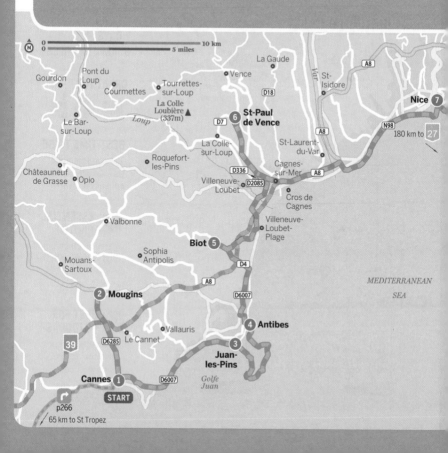

MEDITERRANEAN SEA

TRIP HIGHLIGHT

❶ Cannes

Join the hard-to-faze Cannois who come to **bd de la Croisette** (aka La Croisette) to stroll beneath the celebrated palms (at night all is bathed in coloured lights). It's often heaving, sometimes it's verging on vulgar, but La Croisette is *always* exhilarating.

Take in the sweep of the bay and the Estérel mountains, and drop into the elegant **Hotel Martinez** or the **Carlton InterContinental** for tea. Walk west and you'll hit the imposing **Palais des Festivals** (Festival Palace; bd de la Croisette; 1½hr guided tours adult/child €3/free; ⊙tours 2.30pm Jun-Apr), host of the world's most glamorous film festival.

Head further west and you'll hit old Cannes. Follow **rue St-Antoine** and snake your way up **Le Suquet**, Cannes' atmospheric original village. Pick up the region's best produce at **Marché Forville** (⊙7am-1pm Tue-Sun), a couple of blocks back from the port.

Not seduced? Natural beauty is all around; peace-seeking locals head to the **Lérins**, two islands a 20-minute boat ride away. Tiny and traffic-free, they're fragrantly forested, perfect for walks or a picnic. Boats for the islands leave from quai des Îles, on the western side of the harbour: **Riviera Lines** (www. riviera-lines.com; adult/child return €12/7.50) to Île Ste-Marguerite; **Compagnie Planaria** (www.cannes -ilesdelerins.com; adult/child €13/6) to Île St-Honorat.

✕ 🛏 p271

The Drive » Head directly north on the D6285 (bd Carnot) from central Cannes. Mougins is 15 minutes away if you clear the bd de la Farage in good time.

❷ Mougins

Picasso lived in little Vieux Mougins from 1961 until his death. These days it's an elite Anglo-expat favourite, with prestigious hotel-restaurants, great golfing and France's most sought-after international school. Happily, despite its pristine pulchritude, it's far from intimidating and has plenty to see.

The **Musée d'Art Classique de Mougins** (www.mouginsmusee.com; 32 rue Commandeur; adult/student/child €15/8/5; ⊙9.30am-7pm Tue-Sun Nov-Mar, to 8.30pm daily Apr-Oct) contains 600 works spanning 5000 years. The concept? Juxtapose antiquities with seminal modern works to

Ville Franche ❽

Èze
N7 Èze-sur-Mer
Beaulieu-sur-Mer
St-Jean-Cap Ferrat
D6098
❾ **Cap Ferrat**
FINISH

 LINK YOUR TRIP

27 **Corsican Coast Cruiser**

For some fabulous contrasts, take the ferry to Île Rousse from Nice, a six-hour crossing.

39 **Atlantic to Med**

Jump on this trip in Nice for a cross-France coast-to-coast adventure.

illuminate how ancient civilisations inspired neoclassical, modern and contemporary art. On a different scale completely, but exciting in its own way, **Musée de la Photographie André Villers** (Porte Sarrazine; admission free; ⏲10am-12.30pm & 2-7pm Tue-Fri, 11am-7pm Sat & Sun) has

fascinating black-and-white photos of Picasso and others of his Riviera milieu, and also hosts excellent temporary exhibitions.

At the **Les Jardins du MIP** (www.museesdegrasse.com; 979 chemin des Gourettes, Mouans-Sartoux; adult/child €3/free; ⏲10am-6pm Apr-Oct), a living extension of Grasse's **Musée International de la Parfumerie**, you can pick, rub and smell your way around its

plant collection that's organised by olfactory families (woody, floral, ambered, fougère etc).

🍴 p271

The Drive ≫ Double back towards Cannes, turning left into bd d'Alsace, continuing along bd Vautin and bd Alexandre III, following the signs on to the D6007. The av des Frères Roustan, before Golfe Juan, skirts the waterfront, turning into the bd du Littoral, which takes you right into Juan-les-Pins, a 30-minute drive if you don't hit a traffic snarl.

DETOUR:
CORNICHE DE L'ESTÉREL & ST-TROPEZ

Start ❶ Cannes

St Tropez might be the destination but this detour is just as much about the journey. West of Cannes, take the winding **Corniche de l'Estérel** (also called Corniche d'Or, the 'Golden Coast'; the N98). The Touring Club de France opened this narrow and tortuous 30km road in 1903 for driving pleasure as much as for utility: the views are spectacular, and small summer resorts and dreamy inlets are dotted along it. It gets very busy in summer – if you're in a hurry take the N7 or A8 instead.

Around 10km along, at **Le Trayas**, the rugged jewel-like *calanques* (tiny coves) begin. Behind you the wild country of Massif de l'Estérel rises up, its beautiful red slopes dotted with gnarly oaks, juniper and wild thyme. Beaches run the gamut of possibilities: sandy, pebbled, nudist, cove-like, you name it. But wherever you go, the sea remains that crystal-clear turquoise and deep blue.

You'll then reach the towns of **St Raphael** and **Fréjus**, both with good sleeping and eating options. Visit the Roman ruins in Fréjus or wander its old town's maze of pastel buildings, then head back to the coast road for a final hour.

Brigitte Bardot came to St Tropez in the '50s and transformed the peaceful fishing village into a sizzling jet-set favourite. Tropeziens have thrived on their sexy image ever since. At the **Vieux Port**, yachts like spaceships jostle for millionaire moorings, famous faces shop for K Jacques' Tropezien sandals, cashed-up kids dance until dawn at **Nikki Beach** (www.nikkibeach.com/sttropez; rte de l'Epi) and the restaurants are really fabulous, if only you weren't picking up the tab.

There is another side to this village trampled by 100,000 visitors a day in summer. Out of season, you'll find the St Tropez of mesmerising quaint beauty and 'sardine scales glistening like pearls on the cobblestones' that charmed Guy de Maupassant (1850–93). It's perfect for meandering cobbled lanes in the old fishing quarter of **La Ponche** or sipping pastis at a **place des Lices** cafe.

③ Juan-les-Pins

Be prepared for an initial let-down if your imagined Juan-les-Pins is the one of vintage tinted postcards, all *palazzo* pants and picture hats. Today the 'strip' is far less cinematic, with only a few traces of its early-20th-century architecture and the glamour turned down a notch. Spend some time here, though, and Juan's old-fashioned knack for fun and relaxation are winning. Get to know its charming little bars, shops and restaurants in the town's pedestrianised heart behind **av Maupassant**, settle in at a beach club or head to the western end of **bd du Littoral** where there's a small public patch of soft sand and showers.

✕ 🛏 p280

The Drive >> You could gun this in 20 minutes, but we suggest taking your time. Head south, hugging the coast, taking in the manicured lawns and rugged seascapes. Stop for a drink with literary ghosts at Hotel Cap du Eden Roc. Cut across bd Kennedy to the east coast, lingering in Plage de la Salis for a swim or an unbeatable view of Antibes and beyond. Antibes is just a short hop along the waterfront.

TRIP HIGHLIGHT

④ Antibes

With its harbour full of pleasure boats, its 16th-century ramparts and narrow cobblestoned

streets festooned with flowers, Vieux Antibes is the quintessential Mediterranean port. The **Musée Picasso** (p277) is a highlight, both for its location and collections. Don't miss the views from the sea walls, from sprawling Nice to the snowy peaks of the Alps. If you're here in the morning, the excellent **Marché Provençal** (cours Masséna; ⊙7am-1pm Tue-Sun Sep-Jun, daily Jul & Aug) will be in full swing.

✕ 🛏 p271, p280

The Drive >> Brave the traffic on the D6007 and turn left on the roundabout onto the D4 (after about 4.5km), then head directly to Biot; with luck this should be a 20-minute stretch.

PINK WINE TIME

At the end of a long day's drive, you've undoubtedly earned an *apéro* – a pre-dinner drink. So what's on the menu?

The wine of the south is rosé. Banish thoughts of sickly sweet new-world styles. The pink stuff here is dry, fresh and crisp. Under French law it cannot be a blend; rather, it's made in the same manner as reds and with dark-skinned grapes, but with far shorter skin contact. Depending on the magic combination of grape and timing, the colour of rosé runs a glorious spectrum from the most delicate pinks to warm deep salmons.

There are several Provençal Appellations d'Origine Contrôlée (AOCs), including the Cote de Provence itself, which takes in St Tropez. The only super local appellation is the tiny Bellet, high in the hills 10 minutes northwest of Nice.

Enjoyed your first *pichet* (little jug) and want to taste more? In Nice, talk to the *cavistes* (cellarmen) at **Cave de la Tour** (3 rue de la Tour), or in Antibes try wine bar **Les Sens** (🕿04 93 74 57 06; 10 rue Sade; ⊙10am-midnight Tue-Sat).

---

⑤ Biot

This 15th-century hilltop village is as fashionable and well-to-do as its hinterland neighbours but retains the air of a real town – it's a lovely place for a laid-back stroll or lingering in the village square. It was once an important earthenware manufacturer (and one-time headquarters of the Knights Templar, then the Knights of Malta), but today it is known for its signature bubbled glasswork. The famous **Verrerie de Biot** (🕿04 93 65 03 00; www.verreriebiot.com; chemin des Combes; ⊙9.30am-6pm Mon-Sat, 10.30am-1.30pm & 2.30-6.30pm Sun) is at the

WHY THIS IS A CLASSIC TRIP
DONNA WHEELER, AUTHOR

This legendary drive is one that we can all imagine (flash car and film-star beau, right?). But the experience surpasses cliché – it's infinitely richer, and brims with history, culture and natural beauty. Spend a dreamy day with the monks on Île St-Honorat or a few hours poring over the collection at Mougins' Musée de la Photographie André Villers and you'll see what I mean.

Top: St-Paul de Vence
Left: Vieux Nice
Right: Harbour, Cannes

DOUGLAS PEARSON/GETTY IMAGES ©

SANDRA RACCANELLO/SIME/4CORNERS ©

foot of the village – watch skilled glass-blowers at work and browse their galleries and shop. Back down on the road to Antibes is the **Musée National Fernand Léger** (p277).

The Drive » Leave Biot on the D4; after 1.4km turn left into chemin des Cabots. Continue as it winds down onto the D6007. After 3km turn left into D2085 (av du Grasse). Dogleg to the D336 (the av des Alpes), then veer right onto rte des Cerres to St-Paul de Vence. St-Paul is closed to traffic; car parks fill up in high season.

⑥ St-Paul de Vence

Strolling the narrow streets is how you'll pass the time in picturesque St-Paul: the village has been beautifully preserved and the panoramas from the ramparts are stunning. The main artery, **rue Grande**, is lined with shops and galleries. The highest point in the village is occupied by the **Église Collégiale**; the adjoining **Chapelle des Pénitents Blancs** was redecorated by Belgian artist Folon.

St-Paul was a favoured haunt of artists; today the village claims a Rolling Stone, philosopher prince Bernard Henri Levy and actress Arielle Dombasle. The **tourist office** (☎04 93 32 86 95; www.saint-paul devence.com; 2 rue Grande; ☺10am-7pm) runs themed guided tours (1½ hours, adult/child €5/free) that

Classic Trip

delve into the town's illustrious past.

🍴 🛏 p280

The Drive » You'll return the way you came, then jump on the A8 to Nice. Take exit 50 for the Promenade des Anglais, an 18km drive. There's a real thrill following the Baie des Anges – the beach vibe is instantly intoxicating.

TRIP HIGHLIGHT

❼ Nice

With its unusual mix of real-city grit, old-world opulence, year-round sunshine and exceptional location, Nice pleases everyone from backpackers to romance-seeking couples and families. If you're suffering glam-overload on this trip, kick back at a cafe on cours Saleya in **Vieux Nice** or relax on a bench on the legendary **Promenade des Anglais** and clock an epic sunset.

Eating options are some of the best you'll find in France, the nightlife is buzzing and the art scene is thriving. In fact, civic pride is at an all-time high with a new garden set to snake its way up the **Promenade du Paillon**, and bars, restaurants and shops popping up in the rapidly gentrifying port area. This is a great

base, with a good range of hotels.

🍴 🛏 p271, p280, p310

The Drive » At the port get on the D6098 to Ville Franche. As you climb up the hill, don't miss the fantastic historic architecture and the sparkling blue of the Mediterranean. There's car parking on your right, just before the exit to the old town.

❽ Ville Franche

Heaped above a postcard-perfect harbour, this picturesque village overlooks the Cap Ferrat peninsula and, with its deep *rade* (harbour), is the port of call for supersized cruise ships. Walk down into the 14th-century **vieille ville** (old city). Its tiny, evocatively named streets, broken by twisting staircases and glimpses of the sea, is reason enough to visit and it feels so Italian you'll find yourself saying *'ciao'* to the local old ladies perched on their front steps. Don't miss arcaded **rue Obscure**, an ancient fully enclosed street, a block in from the water.

Artist Jean Cocteau managed to convince local fishermen to let him paint the neglected 14th-century **Chapelle St-Pierre** (admission €2.50; ⏰10am-noon & 2-6pm Wed-Mon). He transformed it with a barrage of mystical frescos and a beautiful pattern.

🛏 p271

The Drive » Head back onto the D6098, skirting the bay on high, for a spectacular 10-minute drive. After 2km, turn right onto the D25 to reach the entrance of Cap Ferrat.

TRIP HIGHLIGHT

❾ Cap Ferrat

As you head down this narrow isthmus you leave the coast's crowds behind and enter the fragrant and leafy, walled realm of the ultrawealthy.

The best way to experience the Cap (besides an invite from Bill Gates or Bono) is to swing by the **tourist office** (☎04 93 76 08 90; www. saintjeancapferrat.fr; 59 av Denis Séméria; ⏰9am-4pm Mon-Fri) and grab a trail map. There are some 14km of easygoing eucalyptus-scented paths skirting the exquisite coastline.

Villa Santo Sospir (☎04 93 76 00 16; www. villasantosospir.fr; 14 av Jean Cocteau; admission €12; ⏰by appointment), tucked away on the Cap's far point, was the home of actress Francine Weisweiller. Jean Cocteau, whilst a houseguest, covered the walls with his signature mythological illustrations. The views and interiors are stunning, and the villa has a touching human scale and warmth. Tours are led by Weisweiller's former nurse and friend, and delightfully peppered with anecdotes about her and Cocteau's exploits.

Eating & Sleeping

Cannes ❶

✗ Mantel — Modern European €€

(📞04 93 39 13 10; www.restaurantmantel.com; 22 rue St-Antoine; menus €25-38; ⏱Fri-Mon, dinner Tue & Thu) Discover why Noël Mantel is the hotshot of the Cannois gastronomic scene at his refined old-town restaurant. Service is stellar and the seasonal cuisine spot on (poached octopus *bourride*-style is Cannes on a plate).

🛏 Hôtel Le Canberra — Boutique Hotel €€

(📞04 97 06 95 00; www.hotel-cannes-canberra.com; 120 rue d'Antibes; d from €155; ❄@🛜🏊) Wow, a Cannes hotel that's reasonably priced, glamorous and intimate. A couple of blocks back from La Croisette, Le Canberra impresses with impeccable service, black marble bathrooms and a heated pool (April to October).

Mougins ❷

✗ L'Amandier — Modern French €€

(📞04 93 90 00 91; www.amandier.fr; 48 av Mallet; menus from €29; ⏱Fri-Tue) Young chef Denis Fétisson has brought Roger Vergé's baby back to its former glory. Set in an old mill, it's considered casual in these parts, but comes with chandeliers and breathtaking views. Various themed *menus* (fixed-price meals) let you shape your culinary experience.

✗ La Cave de Mougins — Delicatessen, Wine Bar €

(www.lacavedemougins.com; 50 av Charles Mallet) Come for the stunning vaulted ceiling, events-packed calendar (tastings, 'meet the winemakers' evenings, little concerts etc) and atmospheric terrace. During the day, nibble on pâté and cheese platters with a glass of wine.

Antibes ❹

🛏 Hôtel La Jabotte — B&B €€

(📞04 93 61 45 89; www.jabotte.com; 13 av Max Maurey; s/d €124/142; ❄🛜) Just 10 rooms and an individual sense of style give this hotel a charming *chambre d'hôte* feel. It's only 50m from the sea at Salis and a 20-minute stroll from Vieil Antibes. Complimentary breakfast is served on the garden patio.

Nice ❼

✗ La Merenda — Niçois €€

(4 rue Raoul Bosio; mains €12-15; ⏱Mon-Fri) Simple, on-the-money Niçois cuisine by former Michelin-starred chef Dominique Le Stanc draws the crowds to this hectic, pocket-sized bistro. No credit cards, no phone bookings.

🛏 Hôtel La Pérouse — Boutique Hotel €€€

(📞04 93 62 34 63; www.hotel-la-perouse.com; 11 quai Rauba Capeu; d from €195; ❄@🛜🏊) A small, genteel, hushed hotel built into the rock cliff next to Tour Bellanda. Bright front rooms have magnificent views out to sea; others look over the lemon trees and pool. Service here is far from stuffy, but exceptionally attentive. A bargain in winter.

Ville Franche ❽

🛏 Hôtel Welcome — Boutique Hotel €€€

(📞04 93 76 27 62; www.welcomehotel.com; 3 quai Amiral Courbet; d from €192; ❄@🛜) Teetering on the edge of Ville Franche's picturesque port, the Welcome has 35 individually decorated rooms, some Cocteau-themed, others Provençal, others art deco; all share sea views

St-Paul de Vence *Stop in for top art at impressive Fondation Maeght*

Modern Art Meander

25

Provence is where many 20th-century artists found their greatest source of inspiration. Cross this photogenic, good-time region and discover its vibrant, creative history along the way.

TRIP HIGHLIGHTS

50 km

Fondation Maeght
Impressive 20th-century collection with equally outstanding sculpture garden

0 km

Musée Jean Cocteau
Unique artist's vision in fascinating contemporary architecture

St-Remy-de-Provence
FINISH

Arles

START

③ ② ①

Biot
Antibes

⑧

225 km

Atelier Paul Cézanne
Postimpressionist master's evocative studio

30 km

Musée National Marc Chagall
Exuberant huge oils, stained glass and mosaics

**7 DAYS
340KM / 211 MILES**

GREAT FOR...

BEST TIME TO GO
Winter – how it used to be done.

 ESSENTIAL PHOTO

A snap in the bar of La Colombe d'Or is a nice trophy for art groupies.

 BEST TWO DAYS

Concentrate on Picasso on the Cote d'Azur, or combine Van Gogh and Cézanne in Provence proper (Arles, Aix and St-Rémy).

273

25 | Modern Art Meander

There's a particular kind of magic that happens when you connect with a work of art in the place it was created. This trip includes the region's stellar art museums, but also takes you to the bays, beaches, fields, hilltop eyries, bars and bustling boulevards where the Modern masters lived, worked and partied. And it's all bathed in Provence's glorious, ever-inspirational light.

TRIP HIGHLIGHT

❶ Menton

Menton is known for two things: lemons and an exceptionally sunny climate. The recent opening of the **Musée Jean Cocteau Collection Séverin Wunderman** (2 quai Monléon; adult/child €6/free; ⊘10am-6pm Wed-Mon) will give Menton a new claim to fame. The artist-poet Jean Cocteau was an honoured adopted son of the town; the collection focuses mainly on Cocteau's illustrations, but

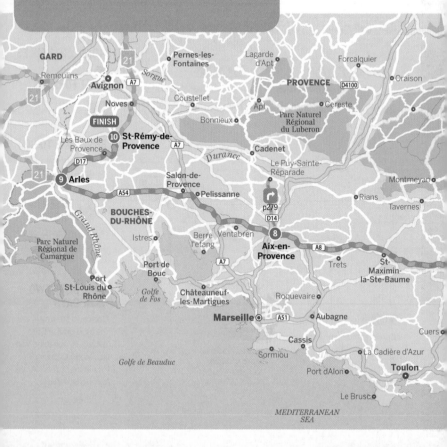

also includes his poetic, experimental films. You can catch delightful glimpses of palms and sparkling sea from slashes in the skin of Rudy Ricciotti's architecturally ambitious building. Cocteau decorated the local **Salle des Mariages** (Registry Office; place Ardoïno; adult/child €2/free; ☺8.30am-noon & 2-4.30pm Mon-Fri) in 1957, and don't miss his rendering of France's official mascot, Marianne.

✕ ⌂ p261, p280

The Drive » Take the coast road – the gorgeous basse

corniche – for about 45 minutes via Roquebrune St-Martin.

- - - - - - - -

TRIP HIGHLIGHT

② Nice

The Cote d'Azur capital is home to two iconic

museums. The **Musée National Marc Chagall** (www.musee-chagall.fr; 4 av Dr Ménard; adult/child €7.50/5.50; ☺10am-5pm Wed-Mon Oct-Jun, to 6pm Jul-Sep) houses the largest public collection of

LINK YOUR TRIP

21 Roman Provence

The 20th-century artists were inspired by this heritage; join in Arles or St-Rémy (and the sunflower therapy around Nîmes is sweet).

23 The Corniches

Cruise the three spectacular roads at the Cote d'Azur's heart, between this trip's two stops Nice and Menton, with art galore.

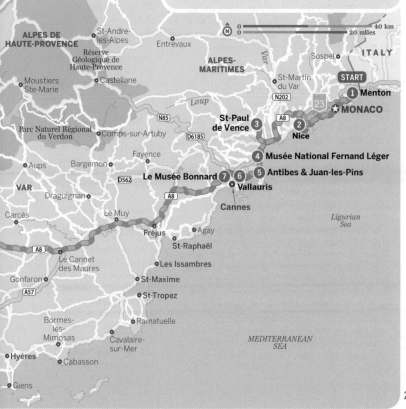

works by Marc Chagall, including monumental paintings, tapestries and glasswork. It's set in an impressive contemporary space perched high over the city. Up in the leafy quarter of Cimiez, the **Musée Matisse** (www. musee-matisse-nice.org; 164 av des Arénes de Cimiez; ☉10am-6pm Wed-Mon) overlooks an olive-tree-studded park and Roman ruins. Its beautiful Genoese villa houses a charming, if slightly underwhelming, permanent collection.

Do also make the most of Nice's burgeoning antiques and vintage scene. Browse **rue Delfy** and the streets running from place Garibaldi towards the port. The most serious dealers can be found in **rue Segurane** and the **puce** (flea market; cnr rue Robilant & quai Lunel).

 p271, p280, p310

The Drive » The coast road between Nice and Cannes is often gridlocked, so jump on the A8 to Cagnes-sur-Mer, about a 15-minute drive, then exit to the D336 to St-Paul de Vence. From here on, the inland run is pretty. Signs to Fondation Maeght appear 500m before the entrance to the village.

- - - - - - - - - - - - -

③ St-Paul de Vence

Chagall, Picasso, Soutine, Léger and Cocteau 'discovered' this hilltop medieval village and were joined by the showbiz set, such as Yves Montand and Roger Moore. Chagall is buried in the **cemetery** at the village's southern end (immediately to the right as you enter).

St-Paul's fortified core is beautifully preserved but gets overrun in high summer. Escape to the **pétanque pitch**, just before the entrance to the village proper, where many a tipsy painter or tousled film star has had a spin.

Below the village, the **Fondation Maeght** (www.fondation-maeght.com; 623 chemin des Gardettes; adult/student/child €14/9/free; ☉10am-6pm) has one of the largest private collections of 20th-century art in Europe, in a Sert-designed building that's a masterpiece itself. There's a Giacometti courtyard, sculptures dotted across the deeply terraced gardens, coloured-glass windows by Braque and mosaics by Chagall.

Head north to **Vence** and look for the blue-and-white ceramic roof tiles of Matisse's **Chapelle du Rosaire** (www.vence.fr/the-rosaire-chapel.html; 466 av Henri Matisse; adult/child €4/2; ☉2-5.30pm Mon, Wed & Sat, 10-11.30am & 2-5.30pm Tue & Thu). Inside, an architecturally stark space is dominated by madly playful **stained-glass windows** in glowing blue, yellow and green, while sketchy, almost brutal, Stations of the Cross are rendered on tile; the artist declared

---

DIY ART COLLECTION: BROCANTE BROWSING

OK, it's highly unlikely you'll come across an obscure Picasso etching for a song. Those New York decorators and Parisian dealers will have got there first. But the *brocante* (vintage and antique) markets of Provence do continue to turn up interesting midcentury ceramics, paintings and works on paper. Banish the thought of excess baggage: these are trip mementos you'll treasure for life.

Get up early and join the locals (a regular mooch around the *puce* – flea market – is an integral part of French life), with dealers at their most charming and chatty first thing in the morning. **Isle sur La Sorgue** (an hour's drive northwest of Aix-en-Provence) is known for its sprawling stalls, and runs each weekend. Both **Nice** and **Aix-en-Provence** also have weekly meets (Nice's cours Saleya hosts on Monday mornings, Aix's on Tuesday, Thursday and Saturday on place Verdun). **Arles** holds one on the first Wednesday of the month on the bd des Lices.

---

it 'the fruit of my whole working life'.

✕ ⊨ p280

The Drive » Head back the way you came to Cagnes, then go south for 10 minutes towards Antibes. The Musée Léger is just inland from the freeway, 2km before Biot. Look out for its brown sign.

`TRIP HIGHLIGHT`

④ Musée National Fernand Léger

Just below the charming little village of Biot, the **Musée National Fernand Léger** (www. musee-fernandleger.fr; Chemin du Val de Pòme, Biot; adult/ child €5.50/free; ☉10am-6pm Tue-Sun May-Oct, to 5pm Nov-Apr) has an excellent monograph collection that captures Léger's wonderful intellectual curiosity as well as his arresting visual style.

The Drive » Head directly across the coast and then south to Antibes for about 15 minutes.

⑤ Antibes & Juan-les-Pins

'If you want to see the Picassos from Antibes, you have to see them in Antibes.' So said the artist himself.

Picasso and Max Ernst were captivated by this pretty port town (as was a restless Graham Greene). Do as Picasso commanded, and head to the **Musée Picasso** (www.antibes-juanlespins.

Aix-en-Provence Atelier Paul Cézanne

com; Château Grimaldi, 4 rue des Cordiers; adult/student/ child €6/3/free; ☉10am-noon & 2-6pm Tue-Sun) in the 14th-century Château Grimaldi, his studio after WWII. Look for works featuring the serenely beautiful face of Françoise Gilot, Picasso's partner of 10 years (he met Gilot in an Antibes' restaurant).

Park to explore Vieux Antibes, then hop in the car to clock **Hôtel du Cap Eden Roc**. This summer favourite of Hemingway, Picasso and others featured as the thinly disguised, fictional Hôtel des Étrangers in F Scott Fitzgerald's *Tender Is the Night* (1934).

✕ ⊨ p271, p280

The Drive » Take the D6107 out of Antibes, and connect with the D6007, parallel to the coast, a 20-minute trip.

⑥ Vallauris

Picasso discovered this potters' village in 1947, along with his own passion for clay. He produced thousands of works here for the next eight years (many on display at the Musée Picasso in Antibes) as well as his last great political composition, a collection of dramatic murals, now part of the **Musée Picasso La Guerre et la Paix** (☏04 93 64 71 83; www.musee-picasso-vallauris.fr; place de la Libération; adult/child €3.25/ free; ☉10am-noon & 2-5pm Wed-Mon). Picasso left Vallauris another gift: a dour bronze, **L'Homme au Mouton**, on place Paul Isnard (adjoining place de la Libération). But his greatest legacy was the revival of the centuries-old local ceramics industry; exuberant '60s pieces by the likes of Roger Capon are now highly collectable, and the town is today dotted with potteries.

The Drive » The D803 will get you out of Vallauris, then to the Chemin des Collines to Le Cannet, a 6km flit.

The Drive » Make sure you're fed and fuelled up before hitting the A8 west, with a 1½-hour drive to Aix-en-Provence. Once there, head north on the ring road, eyes peeled for the D14 exit, then veer right into the av Paul Cézanne. Note, the street is steep and there's no marked parking.

❼ Le Musée Bonnard

Pierre Bonnard's luminous, quiet, intensely personal paintings are often overlooked in the fast and furious narrative of the avant-garde. Bonnard had a base in Le Cannet from 1922, and lived here almost continuously during the last decade of his life. The collection at **Le Musée Bonnard** (🕿04 93 94 06 06; www. museebonnard.fr; 16 bd Sadi Carnot, le Cannet; adult/child/family €5/3/10; ⏱ 10am-8pm Apr-Oct, 10am-6pm Oct-Apr) includes fascinating early pieces and ephemera, but it's the local light and colour of the artist's mature works that are truly unforgettable, for fans and new converts alike.

TRIP HIGHLIGHT

❽ Aix-en-Provence

Oil renderings by post-impressionist Paul Cézanne of the hinterland of his hometown are forcefully beautiful and profoundly revolutionary, their use of geometric layering to create depth making way for the abstract age to come. For art lovers, Aix is hallowed ground.

The painter's last studio, **Atelier Paul Cézanne** (www.atelier -cezanne.com; 9 av Paul Cézanne; adult/child €5.50/2; ⏱10am-noon & 2-6pm, closed Sun winter), 1.5km north of town, has been painstakingly preserved. The painterly clutter is set-dressed, yes, but it's still a sublimely evocative space with soaring iron windows and sage walls

washed with a patina of age. Further up the hill **Terrain des Peintres** (opposite 62 av Paul Cézanne) is a wonderful terraced garden from where Cézanne, among others, painted Montagne Ste-Victoire.

Visits to his other two sites must be booked ahead on the official **tourism website** (www. aixenprovencetourism. com): **Le Jas de Bouffan** (🕿04 42 16 10 91; adult/child €5.50/2), his country manor west of the centre, and his rented cabin at **Les Carrières de Bibémus** (Bibémus Quarries; 🕿04 42 16 10 91; adult/child €6.60/3.10), by a quarry on the edge of town. The latter is where he produced most of his sublime Montagne Ste-Victoire paintings.

The city's excellent **Musée Granet** (www. museegranet-aixenprovence.fr; place St-Jean de Malte; adult/child €4/free; ⏱11am-7pm Tue-Sun) has nine of Cézanne's paintings, though often not on display at the same time (ironically, back in the day, the then director turned down donations by the painter himself).

✕ 🛏 p281

The Drive » For this one-hour drive, start by getting back onto the A8 and head towards Salon-de-Provence; just before the town, take the A54 (aka E80) to Arles. Note that the N113 merges with this road from St-Martin-de-Crau.

TOP TIP: JEAN COCTEAU TRAIL

The dreamy work of Jean Cocteau makes a wonderful mini-trip itinerary. See his murals at Villa Santo Sospir (p270), and discover more of his Cote d'Azur legacy on the **Route Jean Cocteau** (www. le-sud-jean-cocteau.org).

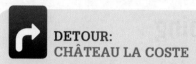

DETOUR:
CHÂTEAU LA COSTE

Start: ❽ **Aix-en-Provence**

Hello 21st century! If you're partial to site-specific installation, don't miss **Château la Coste** (☏04 42 61 92 92; www.chateau-la-coste.com; 2750 Route de la Cride, Le Puy Sainte Réparade; art walk adult/child €12/free; ☺ art walk & wine shop 10am-7pm).

Taking a traditional domaine surrounded by wooded hills, Irish property developer Paddy McKillen has created one of the south's most compelling, and idiosyncratic, contemporary art collections. A 90-minute walk takes you out into the landscape, discovering works by artists such as Andy Goldsworthy, Sean Scully, Tatsuo Miyajima and Richard Serra. In all there are 20 pieces, with more to come. McKillen also has chosen a roll-call of starchitects to design the modern structures: a 'floating' gallery/visitors centre is by Tadeo Ando, and the cellars by Jean Nouvel. Book ahead for a guided cellar visit.

If you don't have time for the hike, taste excellent organic whites, reds and rosés in the shop, and lunch at the casual restaurant between a Louise Bourgeois spider and an Alexander Calder – bliss!

From Aix, take the D14 north. The road splits after 10km, but stay on the D14, which becomes a flawless country drive. Château la Coste is well signposted from there.

❾ Arles

Let's get this out of the way: though he painted 200-odd canvases in Arles, there's no Vincent Van Goghs to see. Instead, come to retrace the streetscapes that fill his bursting canvases, like the **cafe** from *Café Terrace at Night* (1888), which still sits on the place du Forum. Pick up a detailed Van Gogh walking map from the tourist office.

Arles today has an enduring creative vibe and a booming art and artisan scene, concentrated southwest of place du Forum and towards the *quai*.

It's also host to an exciting international photography festival, **Les Rencontres d'Arles Photographie** (www.rencontres-arles.com) running from early July to September.

✖ 🛏 p242, p281, p309

The Drive ❯❯ From Arles head to the D17. This is a 45-minute direct drive, but the Alpilles landscape is one worth slowing down for. Join the D5 after 20km or so, then the Monastère St-Paul de Mausole is 2km before town.

❿ St-Rémy-de-Provence

St-Rémy might be chic, but like Arles, it hasn't got a Van Gogh. A couple of kilometres south of the town, though, the **Monastère St-Paul de Mausole** (☏04 90 92 77 00; www.cloitresaintpaul-valetudo.com; adult/child €4/3, guided tour €8; ☺9.30am-7pm Apr-Sep, 10.15am-5pm Oct-Mar) is a tranquil, if terribly poignant, part of the Van Gogh story. The painter admitted himself to the asylum here in 1889, and his stay proved to be one of his most productive periods (it was here that he painted his irises). View a reconstruction of his room and stroll the gardens and Romanesque cloister that feature in several of his works.

✖ 🛏 p242, p281

Eating & Sleeping

Menton ①

🛏 Hôtel Victoria   Design Hotel €€

(📞04 93 35 65 90; www.hotel-victoria.fr; 7 promenade du Cap Martin, Roquebrune-Cap-Martin; s/d from €134/144; ❄ @ 🛜) Fans of Modernist design (Eileen Gray and Le Corbusier in particular) make a beeline for this sensational hotel. Blue and white rooms reference the looping, graphic signature of the great architect, the lobby and restaurant feature some original furniture and lithographs. All rooms are on the 1st floor and those facing the sea have balconies.

Nice ②

🍴 Chez Palmyre   Niçois €

(📞04 93 85 72 32; 5 rue Droite; menu €15; ⏱lunch & dinner Mon-Fri) A new chef has breathed new culinary life into this fabulously atmospheric little restaurant, seemingly unchanged for its long life, and turns out Niçois standards with a light hand. Service is sweet, the price is fantastic; book ahead, even for lunch.

🛏 Hôtel Windsor   Boutique Hotel €€

(📞04 93 88 59 35; www.hotelwindsornice.com; 11 rue Dalpozzo; d €120-175; ❄ @ 🛜 ▨) A super-central belle-époque façade hides this fun, friendly hotel (not to mention its lush tropical garden). There are artist-designed, conceptual rooms, and ones with sweet water-washed murals; check the website to see which suits your style.

🛏 La Moma   B&B €€

(www.moma-nice.com; 5 av des Mousquetaires; d €100; 🛜) A homey, stylish and creative place to stay, with well-connected artist hosts, and two beautifully decorated, if small, guest rooms. A great choice to avoid negotiating Nice traffic – it's located to the city's north with easy access to the A8, and is only a few tram stops away from the centre.

St-Paul de Vence ③

🍴 Le Tilleul   Modern French €€

(📞04 93 32 80 36; place du Tilleul; menu €25, mains €18-25; ⏱lunch & dinner; 🍴) Under the shade of a big *tilleul* (linden) tree, this is a gem. Considering its location on the ramparts, it could have easily plumbed the depths of a typical tourist trap; instead, beautifully presented dishes (such as saffron mussel gratin with melting leeks) grace your table.

🍴 La Colombe d'Or   Traditional French €€€

(📞04 93 32 80 02; www.la-colombe-dor.com; place de Gaulle; mains €30-55; ⏱lunch & dinner mid-Dec–Oct; 🛜) Once upon a time, impoverished artists paid for meals here in kind (a Léger mosaic here, a Picasso painting there) and writer James Baldwin propped up the bar. If you can score a table, it's as fabulous as it sounds. The menu is surprisingly, comfortingly uncomplicated (terrines, rabbit stew, carpaccio). It's also a hotel (double €310) with a lovely pool, heated year-round, and *objet*-clad rooms.

Antibes & Juan-les-Pins ⑤

🍴 Le Broc en Bouche   Modern French €€

(📞04 93 34 75 60; 8 rue des Palmiers; mains €15-30; ⏱closed Tue dinner & Wed) No two chairs, tables or lights are the same at this lovely bistro: instead, every item has been lovingly sourced from salvage. The same level of care and imagination goes into the cuisine that combines Provençal and oriental flavours.

🛏 Mademoiselle   Hotel €€

(📞04 93 61 31 34; www.hotelmademoiselle.com; 109 av du Docteur Dautheville, Juan-les-Pins; d €120; 🛜 ▨) Stay over in Juan to grab some beach time at this stop. This design-conscious hotel fronts a central town house with a cute tearoom, bringing Parisian cool to the Riviera. Generous details abound (after a long day on the road, you may just find fresh-baked samples from the on-site pastry chef by your bed).

Aix-en-Provence ⑧

✖ Amphitryon — Provençal €€

(☎04 42 26 54 10; www.restaurant-amphitryon.
fr; 2-4 rue Paul Doumer; menus €25-40; ⊙Tue-
Sat) Run by a fiery duo, Amphitryon enjoys
a solid reputation among Aix's bourgeoisie,
particularly in summer for its market-driven
creative cooking and cloister-garden. Attached
is the Comptoir de l'Amphi (mains €12 to €18).

🛏 Hôtel Cézanne — Design Hotel €€€

(☎04 42 91 11 11; http://cezanne.hotelaix.com;
40 av Victor Hugo; d €179-249; ❋ @ 🛜) Aix's
cutest little design hotel is light and clean lined.
Tip: the less expensive 'luxe' rooms are more
charming than the suites. Reserve ahead for
free parking.

Arles ⑨

✖ Le Gibolin — Bistro €€

(☎04 88 65 43 14; 13 rue des Porcelet; menu
€25; ⊙lunch & dinner Mon-Sat Jun-Sep, Wed-
Sat Oct-May) Delight in consummate home
cooking while the friendly patroness bustles
between tables. A cute shopfront in one of Arles'
coolest 'hoods, it's a wine bar too so expect
expert local pairings.

🛏 Hôtel Nord-Pinus — Hotel €€€

(☎04 90 93 44 44; www.nord-pinus.com; place
du Forum; d €160-310; 🛜) Like St-Paul's La
Colombe d'Or, the Nord-Pinus is more than a
hotel: it's living theatre. Lounge, corridors and
stairwells are lined with vintage bullfighting
posters, photographs by and of past guests
(some famous, others notorious) and evocative
Arlesian artefacts. Moody-hued rooms
are spacious, with original tiled floors and
enormous baths and balconies. The bar here
screams lost weekend. (Parking is an extra
€18.)

St-Rémy-de-Provence ⑩

✖ Mas de l'Amarine — Modern French €€

(☎04 90 94 47 82; www.mas-amarine.com;
ancienne voie Aurélia; mains €28-36, r from
€250) Five minutes east of town by car, this
design-oriented *auberge* is filled with fashion-
forward details that complement the stylised
cooking. Many ingredients come from the
magnificent gardens surrounding the former
farmhouse. Reservations essential. Upstairs are
five bright, special rooms.

🛏 La Maison du Village — Boutique Hotel €€€

(☎04 32 60 68; www.lamaisonduvillage.com;
10 rue du 8 Mai 1945; d €170-210; ❋ 🛜) This
hotel is St-Rémy all over – exclusive, eclectically
stylish and appealing to all the senses. Gorgeous
rooms come in a number of configurations and
there's an on-site Diptyque shop.

Plage de Palombaggia Corsica's postcard-perfect coastal idyll

Southern Seduction en Corse

26

From edgy urban vibe to tranquil green lanes and cliff-carved coastline, this trip takes history fiends and culture vultures on a dramatic spin around the best of southern Corsica.

TRIP HIGHLIGHTS

150 km

Plage de Palombaggia
Slip into serene turquoise waters on Corsica's most photographed beach

Ajaccio
START

FINISH
● Solenzara

● Col de Bavella

Porto-Vecchio

● Sartène

Filitosa
Admire the handiwork of prehistoric man on Corsica
50 km

Bonifacio
Test your nerves and fitness on the terrifying Aragon staircase
130 km

**10 DAYS
260KM / 160 MILES**

GREAT FOR...

BEST TIME TO GO

Spring or late summer to beat the crowds on the coast road and heat on the beach.

ESSENTIAL PHOTO

The cliffs of Bonifacio snapped afloat a boat.

BEST FOR HEART-POUNDING HIKES

The Col de Bavella is hot, but nothing beats the hike down the king's staircase in Bonifacio.

26

Southern Seduction en Corse

Starting with your foot on the pedal in the Corsican capital, this 10-day journey ducks and dives along the island's most dramatic coastal roads and mountain passes in southern Corse (Corsica). Mellow green hikes, gold-sand beaches and crisp turquoise waters to break the drive and stretch your legs are never far away, and for archaeology buffs there's the added bonus of some of France's most extraordinary prehistoric sites.

❶ Ajaccio

Napoléon Bonaparte's hometown and the capital of France's ravishing Île de Beauté aka Corsica, this charismatic city on the sea thoroughly spoils with fine art in **Palais Fesch** (www.musee-fesch. com; 50-52 rue du Cardinal Fesch; adult/child €8/5; ⏱10.30am-6pm Mon, Wed & Sat, noon-6pm Thu, Fri & Sun, to 8.30pm Fri Jul & Aug) and a beautiful bay laced with palm trees. Afterwards hike 12km west to **Pointe de la Parata** to watch

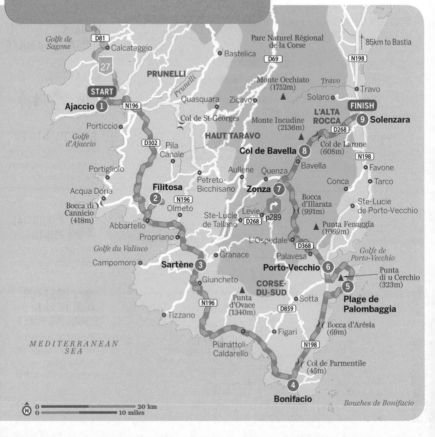

the sunset turn the **Îles Sanguinaires** (Bloody Islands) vivid crimson. Later, savour drinks beneath the stars on a trendy waterfront terrace at Port Tino Rossi.

 p290, p301

The Drive » From Ajaccio port, pick up the N193 and subsequent N196 to Bonifacio. After 12km turn right onto the D302, direction Pila Canale (a brown sign reads 'Filitosa'), and prepare for the sudden grand view of Ajaccio city below as the road climbs. Bear right onto the D255 and wind along peaceful green lanes via the D55, D355, D757 and D57 to Filitosa.

TRIP HIGHLIGHT

❷ Filitosa

Nowhere is more evocative of ancient Corsican civilisation than this archaeological

LINK YOUR TRIP

23 The Corniches
Pop your car on the ferry in Bastia and sail to Nice for more mountainous, hairpin-laced *corniches* (coastal roads) with giant blue views.

27 Corsican Coast Cruiser
Completely smitten? Motor north from Ajaccio and up to Île Rousse to cruise the island's west coast.

site ripe with olive trees, pines and the intoxicating scent of *maquis* (herbal scrub). Visit around noon when the sun casts dramatic shadows on the carved statues and menhirs woven around trees and circling sheep pastures.

Corsica developed its own megalithic faith around 4000 BC to 3000 BC, and many of the stones at **Filitosa** (☎04 95 74 00 91; www.filitosa.fr; adult/child €6/4; ☺8am-sunset Easter-Oct) date from this period. The menhirs are particularly unusual, including some with detailed faces, anatomical features like rib cages, even swords and armour.

The Drive » Wind your way back to the D57 and meander south to the sea along the D157 to join the southbound N196 just north of Propriano. Count on about 40 minutes to cover the 30km trip to Sartène.

TRIP HIGHLIGHT

❸ Sartène

With its ramshackle granite houses, shaded shabby streets and secretive alleys, this sombre town evokes the rugged spirit of rural Corsica, notorious for banditry and bloody vendettas in the 19th century.

A colourful time to motor in is on Good Friday during the **Procession du Catenacciu**, celebrated since the Middle Ages.

Barefoot, red-robed and cowled, the Catenacciu (literally 'chained one'; penitent) lugs a massive 35kg wooden cross through town in a re-enactment of Christ's journey to Calvary. The rest of the year, cross and 17kg penitent chain hang inside **Église Ste-Marie** (place Porta).

Don't leave without filling your picnic hamper with cheese, sausage, honey and wine from **La Cave Sartenaise** (place Porta; ☺daily Apr-Oct).

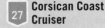 p290

The Drive » From Sartène it is an easy one-hour drive along the southbound N196 to Bonifacio. Slow down along the final leg – coastal views are glittering and you might well want to jump out for a dip.

TRIP HIGHLIGHT

❹ Bonifacio

With its glittering harbour, incredulous clifftop perch and stout citadel teetering above the cornflower-blue waters of the **Bouches de Bonifacio**, this Italianate port is an essential stop. Sun-bleached town houses, dangling washing lines and murky chapels secreted in a postcard web of alleyways hide within the old citadel, while down at the harbour, kiosks tout must-do boat trips through gin-clear waters to **Îles Lavezzi**.

MICHAEL BUSSELLE/GETTY IMAGES ©

Park at the harbour and walk up **montée du Rastello** and **montée St-Roch** to the citadel gateway with 16th-century drawbridge. Inside is the 13th-century **Bastion de l'Étendard** (adult/child €2.50/free; ⊙9am-7pm Mon-Fri, 10am-6pm Sat & Sun Apr-Oct) with a history museum. Stroll the ramparts to **place du Marché** and **place de la Manichella** for jaw-dropping views of the legendary cliffs. Then hike down the **Escalier du Roi d'Aragon** (King of Aragon's stairway; adult/child €2.50/free; ⊙9am-7pm Mon-Fri, 10am-6pm Sat & Sun Apr-Oct), a steep staircase cut into the southern cliff-face to the water. Legend says its 187 steep steps were carved in a single night by Aragonese troops during the siege of 1420. In truth, the steps led to an underground freshwater well, in a cave on the seashore.

✕ ⊨ p290

The Drive » From the harbour, head north along the N198 towards Porto-Vecchio. Count on about 45 minutes to cover the 35km from Bonifacio to the Plage de Palombaggia turn-off, signposted on the large roundabout south of Porto-Vecchio town proper.

- - - - - - - - - - -

TRIP HIGHLIGHT

⑤ Plage de Palombaggia

When it comes to archetypal 'idyllic beach',

Bonifacio Habour backed by the citadel

it's impossible to think past immense **Plage de Palombaggia**, the pine-fringed beach that stars on most Corsica postcards. (Imagine sparkling turquoise water, long stretches of sand edged with pine trees and splendiferous views over the **Îles Cerbicale**. Melting into its southern fringe are the equally picture-perfect expanses of sand and lapping shallow waters of **Plage de la Folacca**. This irresistible duo is sure to set your heart aflutter.

✗ 🛏 p291

The Drive >> Join route de Palombaggia in its anticlockwise loop around the peninsula, afterwards joining the busy N198 briefly for its final sprint into Porto-Vecchio. Spend a pleasant hour mooching along at a relaxed, view-savouring pace.

- - - - - - - - - - - - - - -

❻ Porto-Vecchio

Shamelessly seductive and fashionable, Porto-Vecchio is the Corsican St-Tropez, the kind of place that lures French A-listers and wealthy tourists. Its picturesque backstreets, lined with restaurant terraces and designer shops, has charm in spades – presided over with grace by the photogenic ruins of an old Genoese citadel.

Small and sleepy by day, Porto-Vecchio sizzles

in season when its party reputation dons its dancing shoes and lets rip for a hot night out. Cafes and bars cluster place de la République and along the seafront. On the town's southern outskirts, **Via Notte** (www.vianotte.com; rte de Porra; 🕐 daily May-Sep), with 5000-odd revellers and superstar DJs most summer nights, is the hottest club in Corsica and one of the most famous in the Med.

✗ p291

The Drive >> Leave Porto-Vecchio by the winding D368 and follow it through the heavily wooded Forêt de l'Ospédale – excellent walks and picnic spots – to the rural hamlet of L'Ospédale (1000m), 18km northeast. Continue on the same road through more forest and loads more exhausting wiggles to Zonza, 20km north again. It'll take a good hour for the entire journey.

- - - - - - - - - - - - - - -

❼ Zonza

The chances are you've had a temporary surfeit of superb seascapes, so take a couple of days out to explore the **Alta Rocca** wilderness, a world away from the bling and glitz of the coast. At the south of the long spine that traverses Corsica, the area is a bewildering combination of dense, mixed evergreen–deciduous forests and granite villages strung over rocky ledges.

No mountain village plunges you more dramatically into its heart than Zonza, a hamlet overshadowed by the iconic **Aiguilles de Bavella** (Bavella Needles), granite pinnacles like shark's teeth that jab the skyline at an altitude of more than 1600m. Hiking is the thing to do in this wild neck of the woods.

🛏 p291

The Drive >> Allow up to half an hour for the go-slow, bend-laced drive that climbs slowly and scenically up from Zonza to the mountain pass at 1218m, 10km north.

- - - - - - - - - - - - - - -

❽ Col de Bavella

No number of hairpins or sheer drops can prepare you for the spectacular drama that awaits you atop the Bavella Pass (1218m), the perfect perch for marvelling close-up at the **Aiguilles de Bavella**. Depending on the time of day and weather, these gargantuan granite spikes glimmer red, gold, crimson, ginger or dark broody burgundy.

Short and long hikes are a dime a dozen, and when the drinking in of outdoor action and intoxicating alpine views is done, there is unforgettable feasting on roasted baby goat and wild pig stew at the **Auberge du Col de Bavella** (📞04 95 72 09 87; www.auberge-bavella.com;

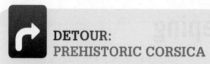

DETOUR:
PREHISTORIC CORSICA

Start **7** Zonza

This short but startling loop dives into the heart of ancient Corsica. To create a perfect weekend, combine it with an overnight stay at the island's best boutique-farm spa.

From Zonza drive 9km south along the D268 to **Levie**, unexpected host to the **Musée de l'Alta Rocca** (adult/child €5.50/3; 9.30am-6pm daily May-Oct, 10am-5pm Tue-Sat Nov-Apr), a local history and ethnographical museum.

Continue south along the D268 and after 3km turn right onto rte du Pianu (D20), a narrow lane signposted 'Cucuruzzo Capula Site Archéologique'. Soon after you arrive at **A Pignata** (04 95 78 41 90; www.apignata.com; rte du Pianu; d incl half-board €180-260, tree house €300; Apr-Oct;), a chic mountain retreat where you can gorge on Alta Rocca mountain views crossed by swirling clouds from a poolside chaise longue. Fronted by brothers Antoine and Jean-Baptiste, the farmhouse spa with vegetable garden and pigs (that become the most mouth-melting charcuterie) is class. Its 18 rooms are contemporary and its restaurant (*menu* €40) is the best in southern Corsica. For heaven on earth, go for the impossibly romantic tree house for two.

Next morning, continue along the same D20 road for five minutes to the **Site Archaéologique Cucuruzzo Capula** (04 95 78 48 21; www.cucuruzzu.fr; adult/child €5.50/3; 9.30am-7pm Jun-Sep, to 6pm Apr, May & Oct), 3.7km in all from the D268. Allow two hours to explore the archaeological site. Enthralling for kids and adults alike, an evocative 3km interpretive trail takes you on foot between giant boulders coloured bright green with moss to the Bronze Age *castelli* (castles) of Cucuruzzu and Capula. Along the way kids can duck into the earliest natural-rock shelters used by prehistoric man (he was small) and poke around the remaining rooms of a stronghold where, a few centuries later, man butchered wild boar, cooked broth, spun wool and fashioned thongs from stretched animal skins.

Backtrack to the D268 and turn left (north) back to Levie and beyond to Zonza.

place de la Fontaine; mains €13-21, menu €24; lunch & dinner Apr-Oct) on the pass. If you want to stay overnight, the Corsican inn has dorm beds (per person including half-board €36).

The Drive » Steady your motoring nerves for relentless hairpins on the perilously steep descent along the D268 from the Col de Bavella to the Col de Larone, 13km northeast, and onwards north through the hills to Solenzara on the coast. Allow at least an hour for the entire 30km trip.

9 Solenzara

The town itself is not particularly worthy of a postcard home. What gives this seaside resort on Corsica's eastern coast natural appeal is its handsome spread of sandy beaches and the journey to it – one of the most stunning (and nail-biting) drives on Corsica. So steep and narrow is the road in places that it's not even single lane, while hazy views of the tantalising Mediterranean far below pose an unnerving distraction. Once through the thick pine forest of the **Forêt de Bavella**, the road drops across the **Col de Larone** (608m) to eventually meet the banks of the **River Solenzara**. When the extreme driving gets too much, pull over and dip your toes in the crystal-clear river water – there are swimming and picnic spots aplenty.

Eating & Sleeping

Ajaccio ❶

✕ Le 20123 — Corsican €€

(☎04 95 21 50 05; www.20123.fr; 2 rue du Roi de Rome; menus €34.50; ⏰dinner Tue-Sun) You won't find many more character-filled places in Corsica than this fabulous country inn with village fountain and twinkling night stars. Everyone feasts on the same four-course *menu*, built from local produce and traditional recipes, and – most fabulously of all – unchanged for 25 years.

✕ U Pampasgiolu — Corsican €€

(☎04 95 50 71 52; 15 rue de la Porta; mains €15-30; ⏰dinner Mon-Sat) The rustic arch-vaulted dining room of this Ajaccio institution is packed with punters nearly every night of the week. They come for the first-rate Corsican food made from carefully chosen ingredients. Go à la carte, or choose from the *planche spuntinu* (snack selection) or *planche de la mer* (fish and seafood selection) for a great assortment of Corsican specialities served on wooden platters.

🛏 Hôtel Kallisté — Hotel €€

(☎04 95 51 34 45; www.hotel-kalliste-ajaccio. com; 51 cours Napoléon; s/d €77/95; ✴@🛜) Find this functional but stylish hotel a short walk along Ajaccio's main shopping street. Should you require wheels, the hotel conveniently shares its ground-floor reception space with a couple of car-hire companies, and covered parking is free. Rooms are all exposed brick, neutral tones and terracotta tiles, and the morning starts well with a copious buffet breakfast for just €4.

Sartène ❸

🛏 Domaine de Croccano — B&B €€

(☎04 95 77 11 37; www.corsenature.com; rte de Granace, D148; d €79-90; ⏰Jan-Nov) Some 3.5km out of town on the road to Granace, this lovely old farmhouse is surrounded by fields with grazing horses. As well as cooking up old-fashioned rooms and homemade breakfasts, the owners run guided horse-riding rambles amid the *maquis*, all with stunning views over Sartène and the sea.

Bonifacio ❹

✕ Domaine de Licetto — Corsican €€

(☎04 95 73 19 48; www.licetto.com; rte du Phare de Pertusato; menu incl drinks €38; ⏰dinner Mon-Sat Apr–mid-Oct) For an authentic Corsican experience, this place is hard to beat. The gargantuan, no-choice, five-course *menu* is a culinary feast based on local ingredients sourced from small-scale farmers. *Menu* stalwarts include lamb and *aubergines à la bonifacienne*. It's right in the *maquis*, on the way to Phare de Pertusato.

✕ Kissing Pigs — Corsican €€

(☎04 95 73 56 09; quai Banda del Ferro; mains €9-15; ⏰lunch & dinner daily) Soothingly positioned by the harbour, this widely acclaimed restaurant and wine bar serves savoury fare in a seductively cosy interior, complete with wooden fixtures and swinging sausages. It's famous for its cheese and charcuterie platters. For the indecisive, the combination *moitié-moitié* (half-half) is perfect. The Corsican wine list is another hit.

🛏 Domaine de Licetto — Hotel €€

(☎04 95 73 03 59; www.licetto.com; rte du Phare du Pertusato; s €55-85, d €70-105, q €115-175; ⏰Apr-Oct) Tucked in the *maquis* a couple of kilometres east of Bonifacio, this motel is lovely. Its seven minimalist rooms sport stylish bathrooms, well-chosen furnishings and private terraces with table and chairs to enjoy the surrounding peace and quiet. Best up, dump the car and walk into town – along the panoramic clifftop coastal path.

🛏 Hôtel Genovese — Design Hotel €€€

(☎04 95 73 12 34; www.hotel-genovese.com; rte de Bonifacio; d €210-250; ⏰Oct-Mar; ✴🛜✻) Chic and stylish, this uber-cool hotel built on the ramparts is hard to resist. Its swimming pool is the last word in pool design, interior furnishings are bright and fresh, and each of its 14 rooms is different. Spoil yourself.

Plage de Palombaggia ❺

✖ Tamaricciu Mediterranean €€

(☎04 95 70 49 89; www.tamaricciu.com; rte de Palombaggia; mains €15-32; ☺lunch Apr, May & Sep, lunch & dinner Jun-Aug) **Complete** a perfect day in beach paradise with an *apéro* and dinner at the hippest of the beach dining spots scattered on the Palombaggia sands. This address screams St-Tropez with its chic wooden-decking terrace and first-class views of the turquoise surf. Cuisine is lots of grilled fish beautifully presented.

🛏 A Littariccia B&B €€

(☎04 95 70 41 33; www.littariccia.com; rte de Palombaggia; d €85-220; ▣) Find bucolic bliss at this attractive B&B that boasts a *faaabulous* location. Your heart will lift at the dreamy views over the Med; your soul will find peace in the six button-cute rooms; and your body will relax in the small pool. Not all rooms come with sea view.

🛏 Le Belvédère Hotel €€

(☎04 95 70 54 13; www.hbcorsica.com; rte de Palombaggia; d €210-255; ☺mid-Apr–Dec; ❄ @ 🛜 ▣) Built from an old family estate tucked between eucalyptuses, palm and pine on the seashore, this 15-room hotel is divine. Decor is an exotic mix of stone, wood, marble and wrought iron. Public areas lounge between natural rock and sand, and the sea-facing pool? You'll be hard-pushed to move.

Porto-Vecchio ❻

✖ A Cantina Di L'Orriu Traditional French €

(☎04 95 25 95 89; www.orriu.com; 5 cours Napoléon; mains €14-24; ☺lunch & dinner May-Sep) Gourmets will be in heaven at this *bar à vin*, with an atmospheric old-stone interior packed to the rafters with sausages and cold meats hung up to dry, and cheeses. Lunch platters range from light to feisty, and the *formules aperitives* (pre-dinner drinks with nibbles) are inspired. Don't miss the fresh Brocciu cheese sold in season in the adjoining boutique.

Zonza ❼

🛏 Chez Pierrot B&B €€

(☎04 95 78 63 21; d incl half-board €110) Southern Corsica's most idiosyncratic venture, this multifaceted address – *gîte*, B&B, restaurant and equestrian centre – is run by the charismatic Pierrot, at home here since childhood. Find it on Plateau de Ghjallicu, 5km uphill from Quenza, 10km from Zonza.

🛏 Hameau de Cavanello B&B €€

(☎04 95 78 66 82; www.locationzonza.com; s/d €77/89; 🛜 ▣) This reliable sleep with cosy rooms and wonderful pool nesting in hectares of green meadows and forests is 2km from Zonza (in the direction of Col de Bavella).

Corsica Rocky coastline and
alluring blue waters near Ajaccio

Corsican Coast Cruiser

27

Few coastlines are as ravishing or varied as the seashore ribbon that unfurls on this five-day trip around western Corsica. For some daredevil action, detour inland to the island's deepest canyon.

TRIP HIGHLIGHTS

10 km

Tramway de la Balagne
Discover the secret cove of your dreams aboard the rickety Trembler

Île Rousse
START

Calvi

20 km

Le Matahari
Lunch on the sand at one of Corsica's most coveted beach dining spots

90 km

Porto
Cruise from Porto to the dazzling Réserve Naturelle de Scandola

100 km

Les Calanques de Piana
See red, blazing red, between fantastic rock formations

Ajaccio
FINISH

5 DAYS
185KM / 115 MILES

GREAT FOR...

BEST TIME TO GO
April to July and September for quiet roads and blue-sky views.

ESSENTIAL PHOTO
Snap blazing-red rock formations at Les Calanques de Piana.

BEST FOR BOAT TRIPS
Set sail from Porto for some of Corsica's most breathtaking coastal scenery.

Corsican Coast Cruiser

Keep both hands firmly on the wheel during this high-drama ride along Corsica's hairpin-laced west coast. Dangerously distracting views out the window flit from glittering bay and bijou beach to sawtooth peak, blazing-red rock and *maquis*-cloaked mountain; while the road – never far from the dazzling big blue – gives a whole new spin to the concept 'Go Slow': you won't average much more than 35km/h for the duration of the trip.

❶ Île Rousse

Sun-worshippers, celebrities and holidaying yachties create buzz in this busy beach town straddling a long, sandy curve of land backed by mountains and herb-scented *maquis*.

Begin the day on Île Rousse's central tree-shaded square, **place Paoli**, overlooked by the 21 classical columns of the Greek Temple–styled **food market**, built around 1850. Get lost in the rabbit warren of old-town alleys around the square, and at noon sip a pre-lunch aperitif on the terrace of venerable **Café des Platanes** (place Paoli)

and watch old men play boules.

Later, take a sunset stroll past a Genoese watchtower and lighthouse to the russet-coloured rock of **Île de la Pietra**, from which the town, founded by Pascal Paoli in 1758, gets its colourful name. Sea kayaking around the promontory and its islets is an outdoor delight.

🍴 🛏 p300

The Drive » From the roundabout at the western end of town, pick up the N197 towards Calvi; buy fresh fruit for the journey from the open-air stall signposted 'Marche Plein Air' on the roundabout.

TRIP HIGHLIGHT

❷ Alagajola

This gloriously old-fashioned, bucket-and-spade address makes a great base. Its golden-sand beach is one of Corsica's longest and loveliest, and budget accommodation options are superb. If your idea of luxury is drifting off to the orchestra of crashing waves, and frolicking on the sand in pyjamas fresh out of bed at dawn, there is no finer place to stay.

Next morning, jump aboard the *trinighellu* (trembler) aka the **Tramway de la Balagne**, a dinky little seaside train that trundles along sand-covered tracks between Île Rousse and Calvi, stopping on request only at hidden coves and bijou beaches en route.

🛏 p300

The Drive » Continue towards Calvi on the coastal N197 and in the centre of Lumio, 6km south of Algajola, turn right following signs for 'Plage de l'Arinella'. Twist 2.6km downhill past leafy walled-garden *residences secondaires* to the turquoise water lapping onto Plage de l'Arinella.

TRIP HIGHLIGHT

❸ Plage de l'Arinella

If there is one crescent of sand in Corsica you must not miss, it's this serene,

rock-clad cove with one of Corsica's finest beach restaurants and dramatic views of the citadel of Calvi. Lunch here is a trip highlight.

From the stylish, shabby-chic interior of **Le Matahari** (📞04 95 60 78 47; www.lematahari.com; mains €20-30; 🕐 lunch Tue-Sun Apr, Sep & Oct, lunch & dinner daily May-Aug) to the big windows looking out to Calvi beyond the waves, this hip beach spot is one very special hideaway. Wooden tables, strung on the sand and topped with straw parasols, immediately evoke a tropical paradise, while cuisine is creative – think penne *à la langouste* (lobster), squid, fresh *morue* (codfish) or a

 LINK YOUR TRIP

25 Modern Art Meander

Sail by car ferry from Ajaccio to Nice and follow in the footsteps of Picasso, Van Gogh and others along the mythical French Riviera.

26 Southern Seduction en Corse

Corsica is so seductive you might well find yourself extending your trip with this 10-day motor from Ajaccio around the island's southern tip to Porto on the east coast.

simple tuna steak pan-fried to pink perfection.

The Drive ❯❯ Motor back up the hill to join the coastal N197 and continue south for another 15 minutes, around the Golfe de Calvi, to Calvi. The best spot to park is at the top of town, across from the entrance to the citadel.

The Drive ❯❯ Across from the citadel, pick up the coastal road D81B signposted 'Rte de Porto – Bord de Mer'. Before driving off, don't miss the old shabby square shaded by rare Ombu trees with gnarled and knotted trunks, and sweet honey-producing flowers.

JOHANNA HUBER/SIME/4CORNERS ©

④ Calvi

Basking between the fiery orange bastions of its 15th-century citadel and the glittering waters of a moon-shaped bay, Calvi feels closer to the chichi sophistication of a French Riviera resort than a historic Corsican port. Palatial yachts and private cruisers jostle for space along its harbourside, while high above the quay the watchtowers and battlements of the town's Genoese stronghold stand guard, proffering sweeping views inland to Monte Cinto (2706m).

Set atop a lofty promontory, Calvi's massive fortified **citadel** has fended off everyone down the centuries, from Franco-Turkish raiders to Anglo-Corsican armies. Wraparound views from its five feisty bastions certainly have the wow-factor, and **Chez Tao** (rue St-Antoine; ☺Jun-Sep), a wildly hip and lavish music bar around since 1935, is the spot to lap them up, cocktail in hand.

 p300

⑤ Pointe de la Ravelleta

Within seconds of leaving town, you're deep in the hot sun-baked *maquis* (herbal scrubland), with a low stone wall being the only separator between white-knuckled passenger and green drop down to emerald water below. After 4km the magnificent cape of Pointe de la Ravelleta – the nearest Corsican point to the French mainland – pops into view, with a toy-like white lighthouse at its tip and dusty walking trails zigzagging between the scrub and the ocean. Park and indulge in a signposted 1.5km hike to **Chapelle Notre Dame de la Serra** or a 20-minute sea-bound stroll for lunch at **Mara Beach** (☎04 95 65 48 30; Plage de l'Alga; mains €15-20; ☺lunch Apr-Oct), a Robinson Crusoe–style beach hut in a turquoise-water creek.

The Drive ❯❯ Continue south on the D81B. After the *champ de tir* (military shooting range), savour a brief reprieve from the big coastal views as the road ducks inland between the mountainous 703m hulk of Capu di a Veta

Porto Promontory and beach

(left) and fields of grazing sheep (right). At the first road fork, 35km south of Calvi, bear right along the D81 signposted 'Galeria 5km, Porto 49km', and at the second fork, bear left.

⑥ Col de la Croix

Having driven for a good hour around relentless hairpins, you might be tempted to stop on **Col de Palmarella** (406m), a mountain pass with fine views of the W-shaped bay of the Golfe de Girolata far below. Pull over to photograph the blazing blue Mediterranean ensnared by the flaming-red rock of **Punta Rossa** (right), the dollhouse-sized hamlet of Girolata tucked in the creek of the bay, and the menacing dark green of forested **Capo d'Osani** (left). But save the picnic lunch and sun-fuelled siesta for **Col de la Croix** (260m), about 10km further south.

Park in the car park and pick up the dusty footpath behind the snack bar signposted *'Panorama – Table d'Orientation'.* Climbing gently uphill for 20 minutes through typical Corsican *maquis*, the path suddenly staggers out of the Mediterranean bush into a mind-blowing panorama of fiery red and smouldering black-green capes, blue bay and the spaghetti road you've successfully navigated to get here. An orientation

table tells you what's what.

Back at the roadside *buvette* (snack bar), longer walking trails lead downhill to the seaside hamlet of **Girolata** (1¾ hours, 7km) and to **Plage de Tuara** (45 minutes).

The Drive » Count on a good half-hour of relentlessly bend-laced motoring to cover the 25km from Col de la Croix south to Porto. The final five minutes reward you with a sudden dramatic narrowing of the road and dramatic roadside rock formations that flame a brilliant red. Go even slower than slow.

TRIP HIGHLIGHT

⑦ Porto

The crowning glory of the west coast, Porto sits sweet at the foot of a thickly forested valley trammelled on either side by crimson peaks. Split by a promontory, the village itself is topped by a restored **Genoese tower** (adult €2.50; ⊙9am-9pm Jul & Aug, 11am-7pm Sep-Jun) built in the 16th century to protect the gulf from Barbary incursions. Scale the russet-coloured rocks up to the square tower, take in the tiny local-history exhibition inside, then stroll to the bustling marina where a footbridge crosses the estuary to a eucalyptus grove and pebble beach. April to October, boats sail from the marina to the shimmering seas around the magnificent,

Unesco-protected marine reservation of the **Réserve Naturelle de Scandola**.

 p300

The Drive » Cruise 12km south along the same coastal D81 towards the village of Piana. When you see red you know you've hit the next stop.

TRIP HIGHLIGHT

⑧ Les Calanques de Piana

No amount of hyperbole can capture the astonishing beauty of these sculpted cliffs teetering above the Golfe de Porto. Rearing up from the sea in staggering scarlet pillars, teetering columns, towers and irregularly shaped boulders of pink, ochre and ginger, Les Calanques flames red in the sunlight and is among Corsica's most iconic, awe-inspiring sights. And as you sway around switchback after switchback along the rock-riddled 12km stretch of the D81 south of Porto towards the village of **Piana**, one mesmerising vista piggy-backs another.

For the full technicolour experience of this natural ensemble of gargantuan proportion, park up and savour Les Calanques on foot. Several trails wind their way around these dramatic rock formations unwittingly shaped like

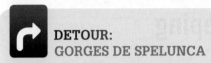

DETOUR:
GORGES DE SPELUNCA

Start ❼ Porto

If you crave a break from blue, head inland to the hills to **Ota** and **Évisa**, a twin set of enigmatic mountain villages that dangle defiantly above a plunging canyon blanketed with thick woods of pine, oak and chestnut. Quintessentially Corsican, these magical mountain hideaways are a haven for hikers, positioned halfway along the **Mare e Monti hiking trail** and within striking distance of Corsica's answer to the Grand Canyon, the unforgettable **Gorges de Spelunca**.

Until the D84 was carved out from the mountainside, the only link between the two villages was a tiny mule track via two Genoese bridges, the **Ponte Vecchju** and **Ponte Zaghlia**. The trail between the villages is a fantastic day hike (five hours return), winding along the valley floor past the rushing River Porto and soaring orange cliffs, some more than a kilometre high. Or follow the shorter two-hour section between the bridges; pick up the trail at the arched road-bridge 2km east of Ota.

Carpeting the slopes east of Évisa is **Forêt d'Aïtone**, home of Corsica's most impressive stands of *laricio* pines. These arrow-straight, 60m-high trees once provided beams and masts for Genoese ships.

South of Porto, the D84 wiggles direct to Évisa, 22km east and a good 30 minutes of go-slow, blind-bend driving. Or opt for the narrower, slower D12 to the north that detours to the village of Ota before hooking up with the same D84.

dogs' heads, dinosaurs and all sorts; trails start near **Pont de Mezzanu**, a road bridge on the D81 about 3km north of Piana. Afterwards, splurge on lunch at Corsica's most mythical hotel, **Les Roches Rouges** (p300).

The Drive ›› Driving drama done with, it is a relatively easy 70km drive south along the D81 to the Corsican capital of Ajaccio.

- - - - - - - - - - - - -

❾ Ajaccio

Corsica's capital is all class – and seduction. Commanding a lovely sweep of the bay, the city breathes confidence and has a real whiff of the Côte d'Azur. Mosey around the centre with its mellow-toned buildings and vibrant cafe culture, stroll the marina and trendy beach-clad route des Sanguinaires area, and congratulate yourself on arriving in the city – several hundred hairpin bends later – in one piece!

Napoléon Bonaparte was born here in 1769, and the city is dotted with sites relating to the diminutive dictator. The **Salon Napoléonien** (www.musee-fesch.com; av Antoine Sérafini; adult/child €2.30/1.50; ☺2-5.45pm Mon, 9-11.45am & 2-5.45pm Tue-Fri Jun-Sep, 9-11.45am & 5.45pm Mon-Fri Oct-May) displays Napoléonic medals, portraits, busts and a frescoed ceiling of Napoléon and entourage; and his childhood home is now the **Maison Bonaparte** (www.musee -maisonbonaparte.fr; 18 rue St-Charles; adult/child €7/5.50; ☺10.30am-12.30pm & 1.15-6pm Tue-Sun).

The Oscar for most fascinating museum goes to Ajaccio's fine arts museum, established by Napoléon's uncle, inside **Palais Fesch** (www. musee-fesch.com; 50-52 rue du Cardinal Fesch; adult/child €8/5; ☺10.30am-6pm Mon, Wed & Sat, noon-6pm Thu, Fri & Sun, to 8.30pm Fri Jul & Aug). France's largest collection of Italian paintings outside the Louvre hangs here.

✕ ⊨ p290, p301

Eating & Sleeping

Île Rousse ❶

✗ U Libecciu — Seafood €€

(☑04 95 60 13 82; www.ulibecciu.com; rue Notre-Dame; mains €15-28; ⊘lunch & dinner daily Apr-Oct) Named after Corsica's westerly wind, this address is hip. Cuisine is creative (mussels cooked in Cap Corse liqueur are to die for), desserts are famously decadent, and, should you be wondering what's up with the empty 1919 rum bottles on the shelves, the house *cocktail du siècle* mixes rum, strawberries and basil to sweet perfection.

🛏 Hôtel Le Splendid — Hotel €

(☑04 95 60 00 24; www.le-splendid-hotel.com; av Comte Valéry; s €60-95, d €74-105, tr €102-145, q €130-184; [@][⊠]) The Splendid is splendid in value, attitude and proximity to the beach (footsteps away). The tiny pool for a dip, the generous breakfast buffet and the free parking are icing on the cake. Look for the pretty pink building and giant palm trees a block from the seafront promenade.

Alagajola ❷

🛏 L'Escale — Bungalows, Self-Contained €

(☑04 95 60 60 80; www.lescale.biz; Plage d'Aregno; d €50-80; ⊘Apr-Oct) Beach bums rejoice! This cluster of 20 self-catering apartments and 50 spick-and-span rooms – with bathroom, comfy bed, terrace and five-star sea view – sit inside low-lying cream bungalows plump on the sand, at the northern end of Alagajola on Alegno Beach.

🛏 Hôtel de la Plage Santa Vittoria — Hotel €€

(☑04 95 35 17 03; www.hotelplage-vittoria -corse.com; d €76-118, with sea view €80-128; ⊘Apr-Oct) With a history dating to 1870 and a flawless sea view, this family run affair on the sand is Alagajola's peachiest hotel choice.

Calvi ❹

✗ A Candella — Traditional Corsican €€

(☑04 95 65 42 13; 9 rue Ste-Antoine; mains €15-25; ⊘lunch & dinner daily Apr-Oct) One of a handful of addresses to eat within the citadel, A Candella stands out for its romantic, golden-hued terrace of stone with pretty flowers in pots and olive trees. The sea view is the most marvellous you could ever hope for.

🛏 Hôtel Le Magnolia — Hotel €€

(☑04 95 65 19 16; www.hotel-le-magnolia.com; rue Alsace Lorraine; d €70-150; ⊘Apr-Nov; [❄][@][🖤]) An oasis from the harbourside fizz, this attractive mansion sits behind a beautiful high-walled courtyard garden pierced by a handsome magnolia tree. Pretty much every room has a lovely outlook – Calvi rooftops, garden or sea – and connecting doubles makes it an instant hit with families.

Porto ❼

✗ Hôtel-Restaurant Le Maquis — Traditional Corsican €€

(☑04 95 26 12 19; www.hotel-lemaquis.com; cnr D214 & D81; mains €20-30, d €94-114; ⊘lunch & dinner daily Apr-Oct) This character-filled eatery in a granite house high above the harbour is much loved by locals and tourists alike. The food's a delight, with a tempting menu based on traditional Corsican cooking. There's a cosy all-wood interior but, for preference, reserve a table on the balcony – brilliant views! There are also some rooms available.

Piana

🛏 Les Roches Rouges — Historic Hotel €€

(☑04 95 27 81 81; www.lesrochesrouges. com; D81; s €102-123, d €114-136, tr €156-176, q €177-213; ⊘Apr-Oct; [🖤]) Built in 1912 on the northern fringe of Piana village, vintage Red Rocks remains one of Corsica's quirkiest addresses. Faded grandeur at its best, a meal in its gourmet restaurant or a room with sea view is worth every cent. At the very least partake in a drink on the romantic stone terrace to savour the truly extraordinary coastal vista.

Ajaccio 9

✗ L'Altru Versu   Gastronomic €€

(☎04 95 50 05 22; www.laltruversu.com; rte des Sanguinaires, Les Sept Chapelles; mains €20-30; ☺lunch & dinner daily Jun-Sep, Tue-Sun Oct-May; ❄) Ajaccio's top-notch restaurant belongs to the creative Mezzacqui brothers who are passionate gastronomes and excellent singers – they hitch on their guitars and serenade guests each Friday and Saturday night.

✗ Le Bilboq – Chez Jean Jean   Seafood €€€

(☎04 95 51 35 40; 1 rue du des Glacis; mains around €50; ☺dinner daily) In business for decades, this Ajaccio icon is famous for *langouste aux spaghetti* (lobster with spaghetti; €12 per 100g), eaten al fresco in a tiny pedestrian street. Knock it all down with a well-chosen Corsican wine, and enter seventh heaven.

⊨ Palazzu u Domu   Hotel €€€

(☎04 95 50 00 20; www.palazzu-domu.com; 17 rue Bonaparte; d €220-270; ❄@⊚) Bold contemporary design inside the historic 1760 mansion of Duke Pozzo di Borgo is what Ajaccio's stylish four-star hotel, footsteps from the water, is all about. The bijou patio garden in the heart of old Ajaccio is an irresistible touch.

Stes-Maries-de-la-Mer *Pretty pink flamingoes dot the lush landscape*

The Camargue

28

Take this semicircular tour from Arles to the coast and loop back again to experience Provence at its most wild, lush and lovely. Welcome to a watery, dreamlike landscape that's like no other.

TRIP HIGHLIGHTS

**4 DAYS
190KM / 118 MILES**

35 km

Église des Stes-Maries
A 12th-century church housing the town's namesakes

START/FINISH
①

0 km

Place Paul Doumer
Possibly Provence's hippest square

Étang de Vaccarès ●

● Le Sambuc

⑤

③

105 km

Salin de Badon
Flamingos swoop over wetlands as you walk

Le Point ●
de Vue

125 km

⑦

Plage de Piémanson
End-of-the-earth feel with miles of windswept beach

GREAT FOR...

BEST TIME TO GO
May, July and September – if you like it hot and can handle a mosquito or two.

ESSENTIAL PHOTO
Point de Vue for its salty backdrop and flocks of flamingos taking flight.

BEST FOR ROMANTICS
Dinner by the hearth in the timber-beamed 17th-century kitchen of Mas de Peint.

303

28 The Camargue

Leave Arles and the highway behind and suddenly you're surrounded by the Camargue's great yawning green, and an equally expansive sky. It won't be long until you spot your first field of cantering white horses, or face off with a black bull. This is not a long trip, but one that will plunge you into an utterly unique world of cowboys, fishermen, beachcombers, the Roma and all their enduring traditions.

TRIP HIGHLIGHT

1 Arles

Befitting its role as gateway to the Camargue, Arles has a delightfully insouciant side. Long home to bohemians of all stripes, it's a great place to hang up your sightseeing hat for a few languorous hours (or days). Soak it in from the legendary bar at the Hôtel Nord-Pinus (p281), with its bullfighting trophies and enthralling photography collection, or pull up a

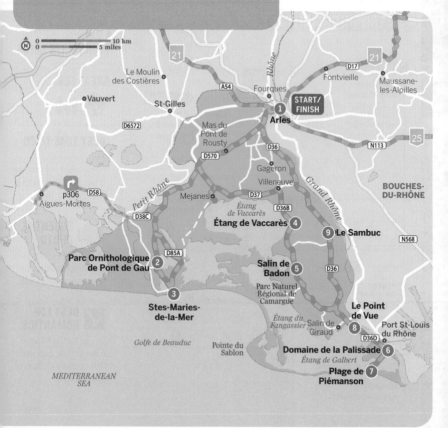

table on lively **place Paul Doumer**, where Arles' new generation makes its mark. Make a beeline for Saturday-morning's **market** (bd des Lices) and pack a Camargue-worthy picnic basket with local goats' cheese, olives and *saucisson d'Arles* (bull-meat sausage), or do likewise on Wednesday mornings on bd Émile Combes.

With precious little parking within the old town, unless you're staying at a hotel with a garage (usually an expensive extra), opt for the secure municipal facilities on bd des Lices (€7 per day).

 p309, p242, p281

The Drive » Take the D35A across the Grand Rhône at the Pont de Trinquetaille, then follow signs to the D570 – you'll soon be in no doubt you've entered the Camargue. Continue south on the D570 until Pont de Gau,

4km before you hit the coast, around 30 minutes all up.

2 Parc Ornithologique de Pont de Gau

Itching to get in among all that green? **Parc Ornithologique de Pont de Gau** (☎04 90 97 82 62; www.parcornithologique. com; Pont de Gau; adult/child €7/4; ☺9am-sunset), a 60-hectare bird park, makes for a perfect pit stop. As you meander along 7km of trails, flamingos pirouette overhead; while the pink birds can't help play diva, the marshes here also secret every bird species that call the Camargue wetlands home, including herons, storks, egrets, teals and raptors.

The Drive » Continue south on the D570. The last stretch of road into Stes-Maríes-de-la-Mer is dotted with stables – little-white-horse heaven, so get out your camera.

3 Stes-Maries-de-la-Mer

Apart from a stretch of fine sand beaches – some 30km – the main attraction at this rough-and-tumble beach resort is the hauntingly beautiful **Église des Stes-Maries** (place de l'Église), a 12th-century church that's home to a statue of Sara-la-Kali, or black Sara. The crypt

houses her alleged remains, along with those of Marie-Salomé and Sainte Marie-Jacobé, the Maries of the town's name. Shunned by the Vatican, this paleo-Christian trio has a powerful hold on the Provençal psyche, with a captivating back story involving a boat journey from Palestine and a cameo from Mary Magdalene. Sara is the patron saint of the *gitans* (Roma people), and each 24 May, thousands come to town to pay their respects and party hard. Don't miss the ex-voto paintings that line the smoke-stained walls, personal petitions to Sara that are touching and startlingly strange in turns.

This town is the easiest spot to organise *promenades à cheval* (horseback riding); look for Fédération Française d'Equitation (FFE) accredited places, such as the friendly **Les Cabanes de Cacharel** (☎04 90 97 84 10; www.cabanesdecacharel. com) on the easterly D85A.

 p309

The Drive » The scenic D85A rejoins the D570, then, after 10 minutes or so, turn right into the D37. Stop at Méjanes for supplies or to visit the legendary fish restaurant Le Mazet du Caccarés. The D36B dramatically skims the eastern lakeshore; it's a 20-minute journey but is worth taking your time over.

 LINK YOUR TRIP

21 Roman Provence

Slot in the Camargue trip's loop south from either Nîmes or Arles.

25 Modern Art Meander

Need some culture after all this nature? Start in Arles.

④ Étang de Vaccarès

This 600-sq-km lagoon, with its watery labyrinth of peninsulas and islands, is where the wetlands are at their most dense, almost primordial. Much of its tenuous shore forms the **Réserve Nationale Camargue** and is off-limits, making the wonderful nature trails and wildlife observatories at **La Capelière** (☏04 90 97 00 97; www.reserve-camargue. org; adult/child €3/1.50; ☺9am-1pm & 2-6pm Apr-Sep, Wed-Mon Oct-Mar; 🚹) particularly precious. The 1.5km-long **Sentier des Rainettes** (Tree-Frog Trail) takes you through tamarisk woodlands and the grasses of brackish open meadows.

The Drive ⟫ Continue on the D36B past Fiélouse for around 10 minutes.

TRIP HIGHLIGHT

⑤ Salin de Badon

Before you leave **La Capelière**, grab your permits for another outstanding reserve site, once the **royal salt works** (adult/child €3/1.50). Around the picturesque ruins are a number of observatories and 4.5km of wild trails – spy on flamingos wading through springtime iris. True birdwatchers mustn't miss a night in the **gîte** (dm €12) here, a bare-bones cottage in a priceless location.

The Drive ⟫ Continue south until you meet the D36, turning right. Stop in Salin de Giraud for bike hire and fuel (there's a 24/7 gas station) or visit the salt works. The D36 splits off to cross the Rhône via punt, but you continue south on the D36D, where it gets exciting: spectacular saltpans appear on your right, the river on your left.

⑥ Domaine de la Palissade

Along the D36D, **Domaine de la Palissade** (☏04 42 86 81 28; www.palissade.fr; rte de la Mer; adult/child €3/free; ☺9am-5pm Apr-Oct, 9am-5pm Wed & Sun Nov-Feb) organises **horse treks** (from 1hr adult/ child €16/14) where you'll find yourself wading across brackish lakes and through a purple haze of sea lavender. It will also take you around lagoons and scrubby glasswort on foot, or give you a free map of the estate's marked walking trails. Don't forget to rent binoculars; best €2 you'll spend this trip!

DETOUR: AIGUES-MORTES

Start ③ Stes-Maries-de-la-Mer

Located over the border from Provence in the Gard, Aigues-Mortes sits a winding 28km northwest of Stes-Maries-de-la-Mer at the Camargue's far western extremity. Its central axis of streets often throngs with tourists, and shops spill out Camargue-themed tack, but the town is none the less magnificent, set in flat marshland and completely enclosed by rectangular ramparts and a series of towers. Come sundown, things change pace, and its squares are a lovely place to join locals for a relaxed *apéro* (pre-dinner drink). Established by Louis IX in the mid-13th century to give the French crown a Mediterranean port, it was from here that the king launched the seventh Crusade (and persecuted Cathars). The **Tour de Constance** (adult/child €6.50/free; ☺10am-7pm May-Aug, 10am-5.30pm Sep-Apr) once held Huguenot prisoners; today it's the start of the 1.6km wall-top circuit, a must-do for heady views of salt mountains and viridian plains. Park on bd Diderot, on the outside of the northwestern wall.

Camargue horses

The Drive » The next 3.7km along the rte de la Mer is equally enchanting, with flocks of birds circling and salt crystals flashing in the sun. Stop when you hit the sea.

TRIP HIGHLIGHT

❼ Plage de Piémanson

Just try and resist the urge to greet the Med with a wild dash into the waves at this lovely, windswept beach. Unusually, camping is allowed here from May to September, and hundreds of campervans line up along the dunes for the duration of the *belle saison*. It's a scene that's as polarising of opinion as it is spectacular. Basic facilities and a patrolled section of sand are right at the end of rte de la Mer; head east for the popular nudist beach.

The Drive » Backtrack north along the D36, just before Salin de Giraud, look for a car park and a small black shack on your right.

----

❽ Le Point de Vue

This lookout provides a rare vantage point to take in the stunning scene of pink-stained

307

the D570 heading to Arles, a 25km stretch in all.

TOP TIP:
ARLES SAVVY

Grab *Arles For Cool Tourists!*, a folding brochure with a simple city map and spot-on listings of restaurants, bars and shops. It also covers the Camargue.

salins (saltpans) and soaring crystalline mountains. As fruitful as it is beguiling, this is Europe's largest salt works, producing some 800,000 tonnes per year. A small shop (the aforementioned black shack) sells *sel de Camargue* (Camargue salt) by the pot or sack, bull sausages and tins of fragrant local olive oil.

The Drive » Heading north on D36 for 20 minutes, Le Mas de Peint is on your right before Le Sambuc, while La Chassagnette's fork and trowel shingle is on the left to its north.

⑨ Le Sambuc

This sleepy town's outskirts hide away a couple of the region's best restaurants and its most upscale lodgings. *Manadier* (bull estate

owner) Jacques Bon, son of the family who owns hotel Le Mas de Peint, hosts Camargue farm-life demonstration days, **Journées Camarguaises** (☎04 90 97 28 50; www. manade-jacques-bon.com; adult/child incl lunch €38/19; ⊙monthly in summer), with music, *gardians* (cowboys) doing their thing and *taureau au feu de bois* (bull on the barbie). But if it's boots-'n'-all *gardian* style you're after, pull up a stool at the roadside **Café du Sambuc** (rte du Sambuc): bull couscous and a jug of rosé for loose change, *and* staff adorned with horse and Camargue cross tattoos.

✕ ⮐ p309

The Drive » Continue north on the D36, where you'll re-meet

⑩ Arles

Back in Arles, visit the magnificent **Les Arènes** (Roman Amphithéâtre; adult/child incl Théâtre Antique €6.50/free; ⊙9am-7pm). Buy tickets for concerts at the **Bureau de Location** (box office; ☎08 91 70 03 70; www.arenes-arles.com; ⊙9.30am-noon & 2-6pm Mon-Fri, 10am-1pm Sat). Note, the Camargue take on the bullfight, the *course Camarguaise*, does not end in bloodshed. Well, not much. Rather, *razeteurs,* brave amateurs wearing skin-tight white shirts and trousers, snatch rosettes and ribbons tied to the horns of the *taureau* with a sharp comb. Victory is never as certain as the fact that, at some point, the bull will charge and the *razeteurs* will leap the arena's barrier, and the crowd will cheer.

✕ ⮐ p309

Eating & Sleeping

Arles ① ⑩

✖ Le Galoubet — Modern French €€

(📞04 90 93 18 11; 18 rue Docteur Fanton; lunch/dinner menu €18/27; ⊙dinner Mon, lunch & dinner Tue-Sat) With one simple room and a romantic trellised terrace, this restaurant hits the sweet spot between casual and considered. The staff is warm and the chef confidently handles both delicate sauced dishes and the region's big-flavoured favourites.

🛏 Hôtel de l'Amphitheatre — Historic Hotel €€

(📞04 90 96 10 30; www.hotelamphitheatre.fr; 5-7 rue Diderot; s/d/tr/q from €57/67/117/137; ❄ @ 🛜) Set in an exquisitely earthy 17th-century town house, suites have pretty terraces and rooftop views, and guests of all budgets can enjoy courtyard breakfasts in summer and a roaring fire in winter.

🛏 La Pousada — B&B €€

(📞 06 74 44 39 77; www.lapousada.net; 9 rue Croix Rouge; s/d €90/115; ⊙Mar-Nov; @🛜) A chic little guesthouse that combines evocative pan-Mediterranean decor with excellent extras for independent-minded travellers: there's a kitchen and a selection of local produce for purchase, as well as bicycles and library.

Stes-Maries-de-la-Mer ③

✖ La Cabane aux Coquillages — Seafood €

(rue Théodore Aubanel; menu from €18.50; ⊙lunch & dinner Mar-Nov) Come to this pocket-sized fish shop for crustaceans; half-a-dozen oysters (as nature intended them, ie with a glass of crisp white wine) cost €8.50.

🛏 L'Auberge Cavalière — Farmstay €€

(📞04 90 97 88 88; www.aubergecavaliere.com; rte d'Arles/D570; d €145-190, tr €145-180; ❄ @ 🛝 🏠) These thatched-roof cottages along a lake edge woo with manicured grounds and a restaurant (menus €32 to €38) serving up homemade bread, bull steaks and biodynamic produce. Find it set back from the D570 about 1.5km north of Stes-Maries-de-la-Mer.

🛏 Mas de la Fouque — Design Hotel €€€

(📞04 90 97 81 02; www.masdelafouque.com; rte du Petit Rhône/D38; d from €230; 🛜🛝) A few minutes' drive from Stes-Maries central, this newly refurbished ecosensitive hotel on the Étang des Launes feels deliciously remote. Decoration is a very 'now' combination of local vide grenier (car-boot sale) finds, posh midcentury pieces, and locally sourced linens and matting. Yes, there's a spa.

Le Sambuc ⑨

✖ La Chassagnette — Gastronomic €€€

(📞04 90 97 26 96; www.chassagnette.fr; menus from €85, mains €35; ⊙lunch & dinner daily Jul & Aug, Thu-Mon Apr-Oct, Thu-Sun Nov-Mar) Ducasse prodigy Armand Arnal cooks up a stunningly creative menu and grows much of the organic produce himself; beautiful terraces are draped to keep mosquitoes at bay.

🛏 Le Mas de Peint — Gastronomic €€€

(📞04 90 97 20 62; www.masdepeint.com; d/ste from €260/395; ⊙mid-Mar–mid-Nov; ❄🛜🛝) This is the ultimate in gentrified rustic quarters. The atmospheric wood-beamed kitchen restaurant (lunch/dinner menu from €39/55; lunch Sat & Sun, dinner Fri-Wed) and casual poolside place are open to nonguests.

STRETCH YOUR LEGS
NICE

Start/Finish Hotel Negresco, Promenade des Anglais

Distance 7km

Duration 2.5 hours

Get to know Nice's bustling heart with this walk that begins with a seaside stroll, then takes you into the tangled alleys of the old town and finally up and over the city's soaring headland to the port. Along the way shop, eat and drink with the fun-loving Niçois.

Take this walk on Trips

Promenade des Anglais

Nice to a tee, the Prom seductively blends hedonism with history, pumping beach clubs with quiet seaside gazing. Why 'Anglais'? English expats paid out-of-work citrus farmers to build the Prom in 1822 – a civic win-win. Don't miss the palatial façades of belle époque Hôtel Negresco and art deco Palais de la Méditerranée.

The Walk » Turn up av de Verdun past palms and posh shops to the place Masséna. Take in the elegant Italian architecture, then head down the steps. Take rue de l'Opéra, a quick walk to our next stop.

Rue St-François de Paule

Window-shop, pick up snacks or do your take-home gift hit in one go on this elegant street just back from the seaside. First stop: **Moulin à Huile d'Olive Alziari** (www.alziari.com.fr; 14 rue St-François de Paule) for superb local olive oil, tapenade (olive spread) and olives. Head west to the florid **Opera House**; across the road is **Henri Auer Confiserie** (www.maison-auer.com; 7 rue St-François de Paule), a film-set-perfect sweet shop; pick up *amandes enrobé* (cocoa-dredged chocolate-covered almonds).

The Walk » Continue on past soap sellers and wine bars and into the open square. This eventually becomes cours Saleya.

Cours Saleya

A top tourist destination that remains Niçois to the core, this bustling market square does different moods according to the hour. Greet the day with espresso and a banter with the produce and flower sellers, lunch with locals or get rowdy after dark with the town's cool kids and students.

The Walk » Any of the streets running away from the beach take you to rue de la Préfecture.

Vieux Nice

Soak in the labyrinthine streets of Nice's old town, stumbling upon Baroque gems like **Cathédrale Ste-**

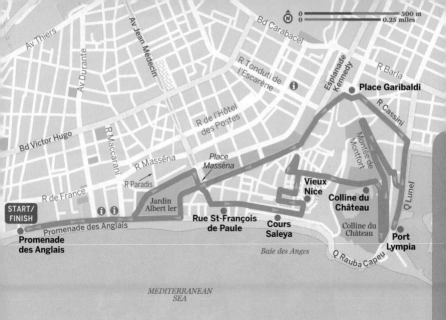

Réparate (place Rossetti). Stop to eat – book **Le Bistrot d'Antoine** (☑04 93 85 29 57; 27 rue de la Préfecture; mains €13-18; ⊙lunch & dinner Tue-Sat), or grab an apéritif at **Les Distilleries Idéales** (24 rue de la Préfecture; ⊙9am-12.30am) and snack at **Lou Pilha Leva** (10 rue Collet; ⊙9am-midnight). Grab the best gelato this side of the border at **Fenocchio** (2 place Rossetti; ⊙9am-midnight).

The Walk ≫ Take the stairs at rue Rossetti (or the lift at rue des Ponchettes). Skip the next stop if you can't face the climb and instead follow quai Rauba Capeu around the headland, passing the massive war memorial on the way.

Colline du Château

On a rocky outcrop towering over Vieux Nice, the **Parc du Château** (⊙8am-6pm winter, to 8pm summer) offers a panorama of the whole city – Baie des Anges on one side, the port on the other. Fabulous for picnics (there's a waterfall) or let kids loose in the playground.

The Walk ≫ Take the Montée de Montfort down the hill. Turn right and wander back along pretty rue Ségurane down to quai Lunel, stopping at the Marché aux Puces on the way.

Port Lympia

Be prepared for yacht envy. Want to get out on the water for a better gawp? In summer **Le Passagin** (⊙10am-7pm) will ferry you across the mouth of the port.

The Walk ≫ Skirt the water and then head up rue Cassini or rue Bonaparte to take in the port's increasingly hip shops and bars.

Place Garibaldi

Named for Italian patriot Giuseppe Garibaldi, who was born in Nice, this stately Italianate square is a low-key favourite of locals, who come to sit in its cafes, eat gelato, visit its indie cinema and meet at the fountain. Kick back with them at **Café Turin** (www. cafedeturin.fr; mains from €15; ⊙8am-10pm), oysters and icy rosé optional.

The Walk ≫ Head back to the start directly along bustling bd Jean Jaurès, soon to be lined with spectacular gardens.

Pyrenees & Southwest France

PEAKS TO PLAINS, VALLEYS TO VILLAGES, MOUNTAINS TO MED: the southwest encompasses the French landscape in all its drama and diversity. Stretching from the dog's-tooth peaks of the Pyrenees all the way to the scrubby, sun-baked plains of the Languedoc, it's a region that's made for driving.

In the west, you'll meander across mountain passes and delve into remote valleys where life still feels timeless and traditional. As you move east, you'll discover the two sides of the Languedoc: Bas-Languedoc, with its flat plains, sprawling vineyards and laid-back coastal cities, and Haut-Languedoc, home to the wild hills and rocky gorges of the Parc National des Cévennes.

Pyrenees View of the hills from a ruined fortress (Trip 32)
GIOVANNI SIMEONE/SIME/4CORNERS ©

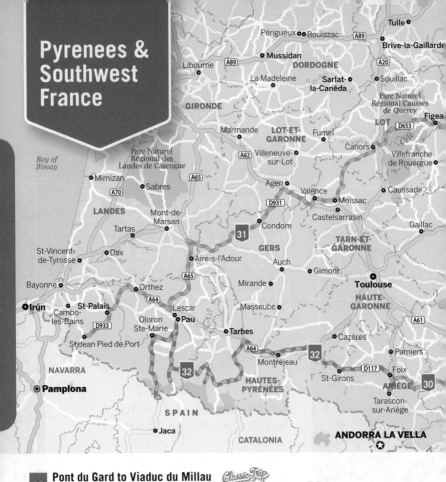

Pyrenees & Southwest France

DON'T MISS

Le-Puy-en-Velay

Climb inside a giant statue of the Virgin Mary for views across this Auvergnat town. Take them in on Trip 31

Lac de Gaube

One of the Pyrenees' finest trails leads to the glittering Lac de Gaube. Catch the cable car to the trail on Trip 32

Chaos de Montpellier-le-Vieux

An otherworldly landscape of limestone pillars has been created here by centuries of natural erosion. Walk among it on Trip 29

Col d'Aubisque

The col is one of the Pyrenees' highest road passes. Competitors in the Tour de France have to pedal it, so count yourself lucky to just drive it on Trip 32

Roquefort

Descend into murky, mould-covered cellars to find out how this pungent fromage is made. Sample a piece on Trip 29

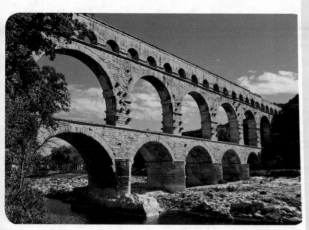

Pont du Gard (Trip 29)

Viaduc de Millau *Gravity-defying bridge that's stunning by night*

Pont du Gard to Viaduc du Millau

29

This trip begins and ends with a river, traversing hills and gorges in between. Start at the Pont du Gard, France's greatest Roman aqueduct, and finish by crossing the space-age Viaduc du Millau.

TRIP HIGHLIGHTS

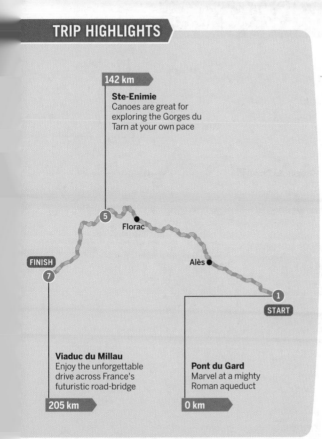

142 km

Ste-Enimie
Canoes are great for exploring the Gorges du Tarn at your own pace

Florac

Alès

FINISH
7

START
1

Viaduc du Millau
Enjoy the unforgettable drive across France's futuristic road-bridge

205 km

Pont du Gard
Marvel at a mighty Roman aqueduct

0 km

5 DAYS
205KM / 128 MILES

GREAT FOR...

BEST TIME TO GO
April to July.

 ESSENTIAL PHOTO

The Pont du Gard from your boat on the river.

 BEST FOR FAMILIES

Canoeing through the towering cliffs of the Gorges du Tarn.

317

29

Pont du Gard to Viaduc du Millau

Languedoc's known for its fine coastline and even finer wines, but on this trip you'll explore a different side to this peaceful corner of France. Inland, the landscape climbs into the high hills and river ravines of the Parc National des Cévennes, beloved by walkers, kayakers and nature-lovers alike. The scenery is truly grand, but keep your eyes on the tarmac, as some of the roads are hairy.

TRIP HIGHLIGHT

❶ Pont du Gard

The trip begins 21km northeast of Nîmes at the **Pont du Gard** (www.pontdugard.fr), France's finest Roman aqueduct. At 50m high and 275m long, and graced with 35 arches, it was built around 19 BC to transport water from Uzès to Nîmes. A **museum** (◷9am-7pm) explores the bridge's history, and walking trails wind through the surrounding scrubland,

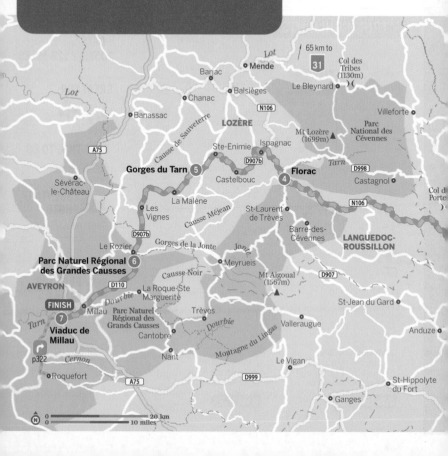

offering some of the best views of the bridge.

There are car parks on both riverbanks, about 400m from the bridge. Parking costs a flat €5; admission for up to five people costs €18.

Crowds can be large in summer; consider visiting in the evening, since parking is free after 7pm and the bridge is impressively illuminated after dark.

The Drive » Drive northwest from the Pont du Gard along the D981 for 15km to Uzès.

② Uzès

Northwest of the Pont du Gard is Uzès, a once-wealthy medieval town that grew rich on the proceeds of silk, linen and, bizarrely, liquorice. It's also home to the **Duché Château** (www.duche-uzes.fr; admission €12, incl guided tour adult/12-17yr/7-11yr €17/13/11; ☻10am-noon & 2-6pm), a castle that belonged to the powerful Dukes of Uzès for more than 1000 years. You can climb to the top of the Tour Bermonde for a

magnificent view across the town's rooftops.

If you've got a sweet tooth, don't miss the nearby **Musée du Bonbon** (Pont des Charrettes; adult/child €7/4; ☻10am-1pm & 2-6pm daily Jul-Sep, Tue-Sun Feb-Jun & Oct-Dec), a candy museum belonging to the Haribo brand. Join in with a tasting session, or just pick up some treats for the road.

📖 p323

The Drive » Continue through the countryside along the D981. Alès is 33km northwest; the Mine Témoin and the Train Vapeur des Cévennes are both well signed.

③ Alès

A short drive across wooded countryside brings you to Alès, once one of France's main coal-mining centres. The last mine closed down

🔗 LINK YOUR TRIP

21 Roman Provence
Our tour through southern France's Gallo-Roman legacy also passes through Pont du Gard, so it's a perfect add-on.

31 Cheat's Compostela
Our Chemin de Compostela drive is an ideal route back to the Atlantic Coast. It starts 180km northeast of Millau in Le Puy-en-Velay.

in 1986, but at the **Mine Témoin** (www.mine-temoin. fr; chemin de la Cité Ste-Marie; adult/child €8/5; ⊘9.30am-12.30pm & 2-6pm Mar–mid-Nov) there are more than 700m of murky tunnels to explore. Equipped with a safety helmet, you catch the rattling cage into the darkness. It's an experience that's definitely not designed for claustrophobes. Tours are in French, but English guidebooks are available.

If you fancy a break from driving, a trip aboard the **Train à Vapeur des Cévennes** (www.trainavapeur.com; adult/ child return €14/9; ⊘Apr-Oct) is just the ticket. This vintage steam train chugs 13km between St-Jean du Gard and Anduze, a journey of 40 minutes. En route, you'll stop at a 150-year-old bamboo garden called the **Bambouseraie de Prafrance** (www. bambouseraie.com; adult/child €8.60/5.10; ⊘9.30am-7pm, closed Dec-Feb).

The Drive » The 66km stretch of the N106 between Alès and Florac is a memorable drive, slowly looping up through the forested hillsides into the high Cévennes. Petrol stations are few and far between, so remember to fill your tank.

- - - - - - - - - - -

④ Florac

Northwest from Alès, you'll begin the long, winding drive up into the **Parc National des Cévennes** (www.

cevennesparcnational.fr). Created in 1970, this wild expanse of hills, gorges and empty plateaus covers 910 sq km of Upper Languedoc. Famously featured in Robert Louis Stevenson's classic 1878 travelogue, *Travels with a Donkey in the Cévennes,* it's still a remote and sparsely populated landscape, home to rare species including vultures, beavers, otters, roe deer and golden eagles.

The riverside town of Florac makes an ideal base, draped along the west bank of Tarnon River, a tributary of the Tarn. There's not much to see in town, but it's a good place to stretch your legs: Florac's **Maison du Parc** (☎04 66 49 53 01; www.cevennesparcnational. fr; ⊘9am-6.30pm Jul & Aug, 9.30am-12.15pm & 1.30-5.30pm Mon-Fri Oct-Apr), sells information kits (€5 each) describing various circular hikes from town.

🛏 p323

The Drive » Head on from Florac along the N106, and keep your eyes open for the sharp left turn onto the D31. The road teeters along the edge of the gorge as it passes through Ispagnac and tracks the river to Ste-Énimie, 28km from Florac.

- - - - - - - - - - -

TRIP HIGHLIGHT

⑤ Gorges du Tarn

West of Florac, the rushing River Tarn has carved out a series of sheer slashes into the

limestone known as the Gorges du Tarn. Running southwest for 50km from Ispagnac, this spectacular ravine provides one of Languedoc's most scenic drives. In summer the cliffside road becomes one long traffic jam, though – you'll find spring or autumn are more relaxing times to travel.

Until the road was constructed in 1905,

Gorges du Tarn Paddlers along the limestone ravine

the only way through the gorges was by boat. Piloting your own kayak is still the best way to experience the scenery; the villages of **Ste-Enimie** and **La Malène** both have lots of companies offering river trips.

p323

The Drive » The cliff-side D907B runs all the way to Le Rozier, 36km to the southwest of Ste-Énimie. It's a superbly scenic drive, so don't rush, and leave ample time for photo ops. When you get to Le Rozier, crawl your way up the hairpin bends of the D29 and turn left onto the D110 to the Chaos de Montpellier-le-Vieux, another 9km.

- - - - - - - - - -

6 Parc Naturel Régional des Grandes Causses

Around the gorges of the western Cévennes, the Rivers Tarn, Jonte and Dourbie have created four high *causses* ('plateaux' in the local lingo): Sauveterre, Méjean, Noir and Larzac, each slightly different in geological character. You could spend several days touring along the tangled roads that cut between them, but the D996 along the **Gorges de la Jonte**

DETOUR:
ROQUEFORT

Start: ❼ Millau

The village of Roquefort, 25km southwest of Millau via the D992 and the D999, is synonymous with its famous blue cheese, produced from the milk of local ewes who live in natural caves around the village. Marbled with distinctive blue-green veins caused by microscopic mushrooms known as penicillium roquefort, this powerfully pungent cheese has been protected by royal charter since 1407, and was the first cheese in France to be granted AOC (Appéllations d'Origines Contrôlées) status in 1925.

There are seven AOC-approved producers in the village, three of which (La Société, Le Paipillon and Gabriel Coulet) offer cellar visits and tasting sessions. The cellars of four other producers (Roquefort Carles, Le Vieux Berger, Vernières Frères and Les Fromageries Occitanes) aren't open to the public, but they all have shops where you can sample the village's illustrious cheese.

is particularly detour-worthy.

South of Le Rozier is the **Chaos de Montpellier-le-Vieux** (www.montpellierlevieux. com; adult/child €5.95/4.80; ☺9am-7pm Jul & Aug, 9am-5.30pm Mar-Jun & Sep-Nov), where centuries of erosion have carved out a landscape of amazing limestone formations, often given fanciful names, such as the Sphinx and the Elephant. Three walking trails cover the site, or you can cheat and catch the tourist train (adult/child €3.85/2.90) instead.

The Drive » Continue along the narrow D110 towards Millau, 18km to the southwest. There are a couple of great roadside lookouts on the way, as well as a

trail to the top of the local peak known as Puncho d'Agast.

- - - - - - - - - - - -

TRIP HIGHLIGHT

❼ Viaduc du Millau

Finish your road trip with a spin over the gravity-defying **Viaduc de Millau** (www. leviaducdemillau.com; ticket €8.60), the famous road bridge that hovers 343m above the River Tarn. Designed by the British architect Norman Foster, the bridge contains over 127,000 cu metres of concrete and 19,000 tonnes of steel, but somehow still manages to look like a gossamer thread, seemingly supported by nothing more than seven needle-thin pylons.

It's such a wonderful structure, it's worth seeing twice. Begin with the drive across: head north of Millau on the D911, and then turn south onto the A75 motorway.

Once you've crossed the bridge, turn off at exit 46, and loop back to Millau along the D999 and D992, which passes directly underneath the bridge and gives you an unforgettable ant's-eye view. En route, you'll pass the bridge's visitor centre, **Viaduc Éspace** (☺10am-7pm Apr-Oct, to 5pm Nov-Mar).

🛏 p323

Eating & Sleeping

Uzès ②

🛏 Hostellerie Provencale   Hotel €€

(📞04 66 22 11 06; www.hostellerieprovencale.com; 1-3 rue de la Grande Bourgade; d €98-148; 🛜) This nine-room hotel shimmers with the colours of Provence: terracotta floors, butter-yellow walls, and patches of exposed stone. The downstairs restaurant, La Parenthèse, serves regional cuisine. Breakfast is pricey: €13 in the restaurant, €16 on the terrace.

🛏 Château d'Arpaillargues   Hotel €€€

(📞04 66 22 14 48; www.chateaudarpaillargues.com; rue du Château; d €125-240; 🛜🏊) A regal residence in an 18th-century château once occupied by Frank Liszt's muse, Marie de Flavigny. Rooms have period features such as fireplaces, beams and flagstone floors. There's a solid restaurant, too. It's 4km from Uzès.

Florac ④

🛏 Grand Hôtel du Parc   Hotel €

(📞04 66 45 03 05; www.grandhotelduparc.fr; 47 av Jean Monestier; r €52-72; ⏾mid-Mar–mid-Nov; 🛜🏊) Shuttered and spacious, this venerable hotel has 55 pleasant rooms, but the main selling points are the gardens, terrace and outdoor pool.

🛏 La Ferme de la Borie   Farmstay €

(📞04 66 45 10 90; www.encevennes.com; La Salle Prunet; d €38-47, tw €48-59, tr €58-71, meals €12-15; ⏾Mar-Nov) Run by organic farmer Jean-Christophe Barthes, who'll happily show you how to make cheese, jams or the perfect rustic loaf. Meals are available, too. To get here, turn right onto the narrow C4, signed La Borie, about a kilometre southeast of Florac on the N106.

Gorges du Tarn ⑤

🛏 La Pause   B&B €

(📞05 65 62 63 06; www.hebergement-gorgesdutarn.com; rte de Caplac; s €42, d €53-58, f €75-102; 🏊) At the gorges' southern end in Le Rozier, La Pause has three rooms in pinks and yellows, plus a couple of suites. Breakfast jams – fig, quince, cherry and more – are homemade by your hostess, Pierrette Espinasse.

🛏 Manoir de Montesquiou   Hotel €€

(📞04 66 48 51 12; www.manoir-montesquiou.com; r €82-117, ste €150; 🛜) This 16th-century manor overlooks the bridge in La Malène. The rooms are trad – half-tester beds, antique furniture – and some are reached via the house's spiral staircase. Ask about half-board deals.

Millau ⑦

🛏 Château de Creissels   Castle Hotel €€

(📞05 65 60 16 59; www.chateau-de-creissels.com; r new wing €71-85, old wing €108; ⏾Mar-Dec; 🛜) In Creissels, 2km southwest of Millau on the D992, this castle offers old-style rooms in its 12th-century tower, plus modern ones in the wings. Regional cuisine is served in the brick-vaulted cellar or on the garden terrace.

🛏 Hôtel La Capelle   Hotel €

(📞05 65 60 14 72; www.hotel-millau-capelle.com; 7 place de la Capelle; d €39-61, f €49-90; ❄🛜) Budget hotel in a former leather factory, with boxy rooms decked out in crimson bedspreads and generic wallpapers. It's short on wow, but the cheap rates appeal.

Foix Dusk descends on turreted Château des Comtes de Foix

The Cathar Trail

From the fairy-tale towers of Carcassonne to the tumbledown walls of Montségur, this cross-country trip explores the main Cathar strongholds of sunbaked southwest France.

TRIP HIGHLIGHTS

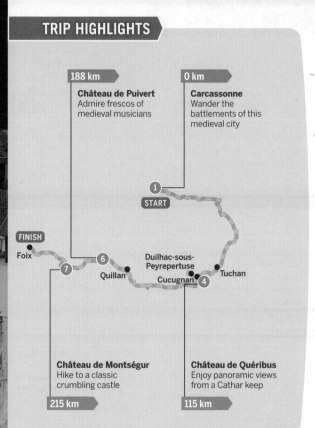

188 km
Château de Puivert
Admire frescos of medieval musicians

0 km
Carcassonne
Wander the battlements of this medieval city

1
START

FINISH
Foix

6

7

Duilhac-sous-Peyrepertuse
Quillan
Cucugnan

Tuchan

4

Château de Montségur
Hike to a classic crumbling castle

215 km

Château de Quéribus
Enjoy panoramic views from a Cathar keep

115 km

---

3 DAYS
247KM / 153 MILES

GREAT FOR...

BEST TIME TO GO
September to November when the summer heat has passed.

 ESSENTIAL PHOTO
The view from the ramparts of Carcassonne.

 BEST FOR HISTORY
Go in search of the Holy Grail in Montségur.

DOUG PEARSON/GETTY IMAGES ©

30 The Cathar Trail

The parched land between Perpignan and the Pyrenees is known as Le Pays Cathare (Cathar Land), a reference to the Christian order who escaped persecution here during the 12th century. Their legacy remains in a string of hilltop castles, flanked by sheer cliffs and dusty scrubland. Most can be reached after a short, stiff climb, but this is wild country and hot as hell in summer, so be sure to pack a hat.

TRIP HIGHLIGHT

❶ Carcassonne

Jutting from a rocky spur of land, and ringed by battlements and turrets, the fortress of Carcassonne was one of the Cathars' most important strongholds. After a notorious siege in August 1209, the castle crumbled into disrepair, but was saved from destruction in the 19th-century by Viollet-le-Duc, who rebuilt the ramparts and added the turrets' distinctive pointy roofs.

These days Carcassonne is one of the Languedoc's biggest tourist draws, and its cobbled streets can feel uncomfortably crowded in summer. Try and time your visit for early or late in the day when the hordes have headed home.

✖ 🛏 p331

The Drive » From Carcassonne, take the A61 east for 36km towards Narbonne. Turn off at exit 25, signed to Lezignan-Corbières, and follow the D611 across the sunbaked countryside for 46km. Just before you reach Tuchan, look out for a white sign with a blue castle pointing to 'Aguilar'. Drive up this minor track to the car park.

- - - - - - - - - - - - - -

② Château d'Aguilar

When the Albigensian Crusade forced the Cathars into the mountains between France and the province of Aragon, they sought refuge in a line of frontier strongholds. The first of these is the **Château d'Aguilar** (Tuchan; adult/child €3.50/1.50; ⏱9am-7pm Apr–mid-Sep, 11am-5pm mid-Sep–Nov), which squats on a low hill near the village of Tuchan. It's the smallest

of the castles, and is crumbling fast – but you can still make out the six corner turrets along with the hexagonal outer wall.

The Drive » Take the D611 through Tuchan, emerging from the narrow streets onto dry, vine-covered slopes. You'll reach a roundabout; turn left onto the D14, signed to Padern and Cucugnan. After 15km, note the turn-off to the Château de Quéribus on the D123 as you bypass Cucugnan. Continue 9km northwest towards Duilhac-sous-Peyrepertuse. There's an easy-to-miss left-hand turn to the Château de Peyrepertuse just before the village.

- - - - - - - - - - - - - -

③ Château de Peyrepertuse

The largest of the Cathar castles is **Peyrepertuse** (www.chateau-peyrepertuse

LINK YOUR TRIP

31 Cheat's Compostela

Make a longish detour off our version of the Chemin de St-Jacques by driving southeast of Moissac for 165km to Carcassonne, with an optional stop in Toulouse en route.

32 The Pyrenees

Foix sits on the eastern edge of the Pyrenees, so our Pyrenean tour makes a natural next stage – although you'll have to do it in reverse.

.com; Duilhac-sous-Peyrepertuse; adult/child €8.50/3, audio guide €4; ☺9am-8pm Apr-Sep, shorter hr rest of yr), with a dizzying drop of 800m on either side. Several of the original towers and many sections of ramparts are still standing. In July and August the castle holds falconry displays and a two-day medieval festival, complete with knights in period armour.

The Drive ››› Backtrack along the D14 for 9km to the turn-off onto the D123 near Cucugnan. The road twists and turns steeply into the dusty hills. Keep your eyes peeled for the Quéribus turn-off as you drive another 3km uphill.

TRIP HIGHLIGHT

➍ Château de Quéribus

Perilously perched 728m up on a rocky hill, **Quéribus** (www.cucugnan.fr; Cucugnan; adult/child €5/3, audio guide €4; ☺9am-8pm Jul & Aug, 9.30am-7pm Apr-Jun & Sep, 10am-5pm Oct-Mar) was the site of the Cathars' last stand in 1255. Its interior structure is fairly well preserved:

the **Salle du Pilier** inside the central keep still features its original Gothic pillars, vaulting and archways. There's also a small house that has been converted into a theatre, and shows a film documenting the story of the castle through the eyes of one of the castle's curates.

The top of the keep is reached via a narrow staircase and offers a truly mind-blowing view stretching to the Mediterranean and the Pyrenees on a clear day.

The Drive ››› Drive back down to the turn-off, and turn left. Continue along this road (the D19) for 8km to the small town of Maury. Take the D117 for 25km to Lapradelle. The next castle is signed from here, another 3km south.

➎ Château de Puilaurens

If it's the classic hilltop castle you're after, **Puilaurens** (Lapradelle; adult/child €4/2; ☺9am-8pm Jul & Aug, 10am-7pm Jun & Sep, to 5pm rest of yr) is it. With its turrets and lofty location, it's perhaps the most dramatic of the

Cathar fortresses, and boasts all the classic medieval defences: double defensive walls, four corner towers and crenellated battlements. It's also said to be haunted by the White Lady, a niece of Philippe le Bel.

The Drive ››› Backtrack to the D117 and follow it west for 36km to Puivert, skirting through hills, fields and forests. Just before you reach the village, there's a sharp right turn to the château, near a white barn. It is 1km further up a steep track.

TOP TIP:
PASSEPORT DES SITES DU PAYS CATHARE

This pass is available from local tourist offices and gives discount admission to 20 local sites, including all the main Cathar castles and the abbeys at St-Hilaire, Lagrasse and Villelongue.

Carcassonne The city viewed across autumnal trees

TRIP HIGHLIGHT

⑥ Château de Puivert

Built during the late 12th century, the **Château de Puivert** (www.chateau-de
-puivert.com; adult/child
€5/3; ☺9am-7pm May–
mid-Nov, 10am-5pm Sun-Fri
mid-Dec–Apr) belonged to the aristocratic Congost family, who were high-profile members of the Cathar movement. It was besieged in 1210 by Thomas Pons de Bruyères-le-Chatel, who subsequently took control of the castle and oversaw its redevelopment.

Camped on a 605m-high promontory, Puivert still boasts much of its medieval footprint. Five of the eight corner towers remain, and the central keep has four vaulted rooms including the **Salle des Musiciens**, decorated with frescos of medieval troubadours – including a flautist, guitarist, bagpiper, tambourine man and hurdy-gurdy player.

The Drive ❯❯ Take the D117 west of Puivert for 13km to Bélesta. As you drive through town, spot signs to 'Fougax et B/Querigut/Château de Montségur'. The village is another 14km further,

spectacularly perched above the forested slopes; follow the winding road past the village until you see the castle's roadside car park.

TRIP HIGHLIGHT

⑦ Château de Montségur

For the full Monty Python medieval vibe – not to mention a good workout – tackle the steep 1207m climb to the ruins of the **Château de Montségur** (www.
montsegur.fr; adult/child
€4.50/2; ☺9am-7pm Jul &
Aug, 10am-5pm Mar-Jun, Sep
& Oct, 11am-4pm Dec-Feb). It was here, in 1242, that

WHO WERE THE CATHARS?

In many ways, the Cathars were the fundamentalists of their day: a sect of ultra-devout Christians known for their rigid beliefs and disdain for the teachings of the established church.

Their name derives from the Greek word *katharos*, meaning 'pure'. They believed that though humans were fundamentally evil, salvation could be attained through religious devotion.

Preaching in *langue d'oc*, the local tongue, the Cathars believed in a form of reincarnation, rejected the doctrine of original sin, welcomed women into prominent roles, and remained profoundly critical of the worldliness and corruption of the mainstream church. The most devout of all were the *parfaits* (perfects), who abstained from sex and ate a strict vegetarian diet.

The Cathars' anti-establishment beliefs inevitably placed them on a collision course with Catholic Rome. In 1208, local lords embarked on a bloody crusade sanctioned by Pope Innocent III. After long sieges, the major Cathar centres in Béziers, Carcassonne, Minerve and the fortresses of Montségur, Quéribus and Peyrepertuse were taken and thousands of people were burned as heretics (in Béziers alone, as many as 20,000 faithful are thought to have been slaughtered). The bloodletting continued until 1321, when the burning of the last 'perfect', Guillaume Bélibaste, marked the end of Catharism in Languedoc.

The useful **Pays Cathare** (www.payscathare.org) website has plenty of background history on the Cathars, and details major sites.

the Cathar movement suffered its heaviest defeat; attacked by a force of 10,000 royal troops, the castle fell after a gruelling nine-month siege, and 220 of the defenders were burnt alive when they refused to renounce their faith.

Montségur has also been cited as a possible location for the Holy Grail, which was supposedly smuggled out of the castle in the days before the final battle.

The original castle was razed to rubble after the siege, and the present-day ruins largely date from the 17th century.

The Drive » Continue on the D117, turning onto the busy D20 to Foix, 32km northwest.

- - - - - - - - - - - -

🔟 Foix

Complete your trip through Cathar country with a visit to the **Château des Comtes de Foix** (05 61 05 10 10; adult/child €4.50/3.30; ⏰10am-6pm summer, shorter hr rest of yr), nestled among the foothills of the Pyrenees. It's in a more complete state of repair than many of the Cathar fortresses you've seen, and gives you some idea of how they may have looked in their medieval heyday.

✕ 🛏 p331, p349

Eating & Sleeping

Carcassonne

✕ Au Comte Roger   French €€

(☎04 68 11 93 40; www.comteroger.com; 14 rue Saint-Louis; lunch menu €19-27, dinner menu €38; ⏱lunch & dinner) Starched tablecloths, a pergola-covered patio and nouvelle cuisine–style dishes presented with flair by chef Pierre Mesa make this the best option in La Cité for sit-down dining – just don't expect the portions to be large.

⊨ Hotel du Château   Hotel €€€

(☎04 68 11 38 38; www.hotelduchateau.net; d €120-280; ❄ 🖥 🛗 🏨) You get the best of both worlds at this flashy hotel: knockout night-time views of La Cité's amber ramparts, coupled with the convenience of staying outside the walled town. The 16 rooms are snazzily finished with wood, exposed stone and boutique-style furnishings, and you can admire wonderful castle views from the heated pool and Jacuzzi.

⊨ La Maison Vieille   B&B €€

(☎04 68 25 77 24; www.la-maison-vieille.com; 8 rue Trivalle; d €85; 🖥 🏨) Charm oozes out of every nook and cranny at this amber-stone B&B. The rooms are enormous, and decorated in supremely good taste: Barbecane in soothing blues, Cité with exposed brick, Prince Noir with a white sofa and roll-top bath. Breakfast is served in the courtyard garden.

⊨ Bloc G   B&B €€

(☎04 68 47 58 20; www.bloc-g.com; 112 rue Barbacane; d €90-120; 🖥) Not what you'd

expect in Carcassonne – a trendy, minimalist B&B that wouldn't look out of place in Paris' fashionable quarters. It's part bistro, part design gallery, part *'chambres urbaines'* – the decor is stripped back to the minimum, with stark white walls offset by arty prints and retro bits of furniture.

Foix ⑧

⊨ Château de Beauregard   Hotel €€

(☎05 61 66 66 64; www.chateaubeauregard. net; av de la Résistance, St-Girons; d €120-160, ste €160-200; 🖥 🛗) If you've always wanted to play lord of the manor, try this opulent château complex in St-Girons, halfway between St-Gaudens and Foix along the D117. Topped by turrets and surrounded by 2½ hectares of private gardens, it's full of quirky touches (such as bathrooms hidden away in the castle's corner towers). Throw in a garden pool, a candlelit spa and a superb Gascon restaurant, and you have a castle getaway par excellence.

⊨ Hôtel les Remparts   Hotel €€

(☎05 61 68 12 15; www.hotelremparts.com; 6 cours Louis Pons Tarde; r €80-120; 🖥) This is one of the area's smartest hotels, a nine-room beauty in Mirepoix that's awash with decorative tics (rough stone, twisted willow, stripped-wood floors), and boasts a delightful breakfast salon with its original beams and chimney. Young chef Nicolas Coutand has turned the restaurant into a notable dining destination, too.

Cahors Medieval Pont Valentré once defended the walled town

Cheat's Compostela

31

Follow in the footsteps of pilgrims on this holiest of road trips, which follows one of the main routes across France en route to Santiago de Compostela in Spain.

TRIP HIGHLIGHTS

**7 DAYS
725KM / 450 MILES**

GREAT FOR...

BEST TIME TO GO
May to September, to make the most of the summer sunshine.

ESSENTIAL PHOTO
Being dwarfed beside Le Puy's huge statue of the Virgin Mary.

BEST FOR CULTURE
Comparing the tympanum (decorative arch) of churches in Condom, Cahors and Moissac.

0 km
Le Puy-en-Velay
Puff your way around this volcanic town in the Massif Central

349 km
Cahors
Explore Cahors' shady old city and Romanesque cathedral

Saugues ①
START

Agen ④ ② Espalion

FINISH
⑦ Pau

St-Jean Pied de Port
Look out from the ramparts towards the Spanish border

725 km

Conques
Wander around the classic pilgrimage church of St-Foy

220 km

333

31

Cheat's Compostela

During the Middle Ages, countless pilgrims undertook the long trek along the Chemin de St-Jacques, as it's known in France, in the hope of earning spiritual salvation and some extra brownie points in the afterlife. We've chosen to follow one of the oldest routes between Le Puy-en-Velay and St-Jean-Pied-de-Port: on the way you'll visit iconic churches, historic cities and a giant iron statue of the Virgin Mary.

TRIP HIGHLIGHT

❶ Le Puy-en-Velay

Your journey begins at the striking town of Le Puy-en-Velay, where pilgrims would traditionally have earned a blessing at the Unesco-listed **Cathédrale Notre-Dame** (www.cathedraledupuy.org; cloister adult/child €7.50/free; ⏰9am-noon & 2-5pm, to 6.30pm in summer). Among the Romanesque archways and Byzantine domes is a statue of St Jacques

himself, the patron saint of Compostela pilgrims.

While you're here, it's well worth visiting Le Puy's other ecclesiastical sights. Perched on the top of an 85m-high volcanic pillar is the **Chapelle St-Michel d'Aiguilhe** (www.rochersaintmichel.fr; adult/child €3/1.50; ⏰9am-6.30pm), Le Puy's oldest chapel (established in the 10th century). Carved directly into the rock, its cave-like atmosphere and 12th-century frescos create an otherworldly atmosphere.

On another nearby peak is an enormous cast-iron statue of the Virgin Mary, aka **Notre Dame de France** (adult/child €4/2.50; ⏰9am-6pm). A creaky spiral staircase winds its way to the top of the 22.7m-tall, 835-ton statue; you can peep out through portholes for dizzying vistas over town.

✕ ⌂ p339

The Drive ≫ From Le Puy to Conques, it's a scenic half-day drive of around 220km. Take the twisty D589, passing through the spectacular Gorges de l'Allier to Saugues. Follow the D989 under the A75 highway, then join the D921 to Espalion. The last stretch along the D920, D107 and D141 tracks the course of the Lot River, turning briefly onto the D910 to Conques.

- - - - - - - - - - - - -

TRIP HIGHLIGHT

❷ Conques

The next stop for medieval pilgrims would have been Conques – or more specifically, the **Abbey Church of St-Foy**, built to house the holy relics of its namesake saint, a young woman martyred during the 4th century. In fact, the relics proved so popular that the original 8th-century church had to be rebuilt with extra chapels, a higher roof and a viewing gallery to accommodate the pilgrim traffic.

It's a classic example of a pilgrimage church: simple and serene, with architectural flourishes

LINK YOUR TRIP

32 **Pyrenees**
For fantastic mountain scenery, veer off 140km south of Condom at Pau to begin our Pyrenees trip.

38 **The Lot Valley**
You can do two trips in one by incorporating our trip through the beautiful Lot Valley as your route from Cahors to Figeac.

kept to a minimum. It's laid out to a cruciform (cross-shaped) design, the traditional layout for pilgrimage churches. Also note the elegant columns, decorated with scenes from the life of St Foy.

Outside, look out for the **tympanum** (decorative arch) above the main doorway depicting the Day of Last Judgment – a popular theme for Compostela churches.

The Drive >> Backtrack north to the Lot River and turn left onto the D42. Follow signs to Decazeville, then turn west onto the D840 to Figeac, just over 54km from Conques.

- - - - - - - - - - - -

❸ Figeac

During the Middle Ages, riverside Figeac was a major ecclesiastical centre. All the four monastic orders (Franciscans, White Friars, Dominicans and Augustinians) were established here, and the town had a large hospice for accommodating pilgrims (later turned into Figeac's hospital, appropriately named Hôpital St-Jacques).

Though most of Figeac's monastic buildings were torn down during the Revolution, a few still remain. On place Vival, there's an arcaded 13th-century building that was part of Figeac's lost abbey; it's now home to the tourist office.

You can pick up a leaflet called *Les Clefs de la Ville* (€0.30), which details the town's other medieval buildings. **Rue de Balène** and **rue Caviale** offer rich pickings; they're lined with 14th- and 15th-century houses, many with stone carvings and open-air galleries on the top floor, once used for drying leather.

🛏 p405

The Drive >> The prettiest drive to Cahors is along the D662, which runs for a scenic but slow 75km along a dramatic gorge carved out by the Lot River (a trip covered in detail on p399). A faster alternative is via the D13 and D653, which takes about an hour from Figeac.

- - - - - - - - - - - -

TRIP HIGHLIGHT

❹ Cahors

Now best known for its wine, the walled city of Cahors once earned a lucrative trade from passing pilgrims. A prosperous (and well-protected) city, Cahors also has an impressive Romanesque cathedral, the **Cathédrale St-Étienne** (⊘ cloister Jun-Sep), which is similar in style to the Cathédrale St-Front in Périgueux. Consecrated in 1119, the cathedral's airy nave is topped by two huge cupolas which, at 18m wide, are the largest in France.

Some of the frescos are from the 14th century, but the side chapels

DEA/A. DAGLI ORTI/GETTY IMAGES ©

and carvings in the cloister mainly date from the 16th century. On the cathedral's north façade is another carved **tympanum**, depicting Christ surrounded by fluttering angels and pious saints.

At the top of the old city, the **Tour du Pape Jean XXII** (3 bd Léon Gambetta) was part of a 14th-century mansion belonging to Jacques Duèse, who went on to become Pope John XXII.

Cahors' medieval bridge, the **Pont Valentré**, was part of the town's defences during the 14th century.

Conques Tympanum detail, Abbey Church of St-Foy

🍴 🛏 p405

The Drive » The D653 travels 61km southwest to Moissac, passing through a delightful landscape of woods, fields and sleepy villages.

⑤ Moissac

Moissac's crowning glory is the monumental **Abbaye St-Pierre** (place Durand de Bredon), one of France's finest Romanesque abbeys. Above the south portal is yet another marvellous **tympanum**: completed in 1130, it depicts St John's vision of the Apocalypse, with Christ flanked by the Apostles, angels and 24 awestruck elders.

Outside, the columns of the **cloister** (adult/child €5/3.50; 🕘9am-7pm) are topped with carved capitals depicting foliage, figures or biblical scenes. Sadly, the Revolution took its toll – nearly every face is smashed.

Entry to the abbey is via the **tourist office** (www.moissac.fr; 6 place Durand de Bredon; 🕘9am-7pm).

🛏 p339

The Drive » The easiest route for the 85km trip to Condom travels west on the D813 to Valence, crosses the river and then joins the A62 highway (toll charge). Take exit 7 onto the D931, a much quieter road that meanders through rural countryside all the way to Condom.

- - - - - - - - - - - - -

⑥ Condom

Despite its snigger-inducing name, Condom actually has nothing to do with contraceptives – its name dates from Gallo-Roman times, when it was known as Condatomagus.

Established as a Roman port on the River Baïse, the town's Flamboyant Gothic **Cathédrale St-Pierre** (place St-Pierre) was the

CHEMIN DE ST-JACQUES

Ever since the 9th century, when a hermit named Pelayo stumbled across the tomb of the Apostle James (brother of John the Evangelist), the Spanish town of Santiago de Compostela has been one of Christendom's holiest sites.

The pilgrimage to Santiago de Compostela is traditionally known as the Camiño de Santiago (Chemin de St-Jacques in French; Way of St James in English). Early pilgrims were inspired to undertake the arduous journey in exchange for fewer years in purgatory. Today the reward is more tangible: walkers or horse riders who complete the final 100km to Santiago (cyclists the final 200km) qualify for a Compostela Certificate, issued on arrival at the cathedral.

The modern-day GR36 roughly follows the Via Podensis route from Le Puy. Find out more at www.webcompostella.com and www.csj.org.uk.

main point of interest for pilgrims. The tentlike cloister, covered by a vaulted roof was designed to offer them wet-weather protection while they were waiting to pay their religious dues.

Condom's other claim to fame is as the home of Armagnac, a potent brandy brewed since medieval times as a medicinal tonic, but now drunk as an after-dinner *digestif*. There are many distilleries around town, but one

of the best is **Armagnac Ryst-Dupeyron** (36 rue Jean Jaurès; ⊙10am-noon & 2-6.30pm Mon-Fri), where you can taste vintage brandies in a turn-of-the-century cellar.

Nearby, the teeny **Musée de l'Armagnac** (2 rue Jules Ferry; adult/child €2.20/1.10; ⊙10am-noon & 3-6pm) has a small collection of vintage Armagnac-making equipment.

✖ 🛏 p339

The Drive » The last stretch to St-Jean Pied de Port is an epic 230km via the A65 and A64 highways, so you might like to break it up by combining it with stops detailed in our tours of the Pyrenees (p341) or the Atlantic Coast (p407).

- - - - - - - - - - - - - -

TRIP HIGHLIGHT

❼ St-Jean Pied de Port

Your pilgrimage ends at the walled town of St-Jean Pied de Port, the last stop for Compostela pilgrims on French soil before crossing the Spanish border, 8km away.

With its cobbled lanes and impressive ramparts, it's one of southwest France's most authentically medieval towns, so it makes a fitting end to your trip. The foundations of the **Église Notre Dame du Bout du Pont** are said to be as old as the town itself, but the building itself was rebuilt in the 17th century.

While you might be ending your pilgrimage here, spare a thought for the real pilgrims – for them, there's still another 800km to go before they reach journey's end at Santiago de Compostela's famous cathedral.

Eating & Sleeping

Le Puy-en-Velay ❶

✖ La Parenthèse   Regional Cuisine €€

(📞04 71 02 83 00; 8 av rue de la Cathédrale; menus €19-27; ⊘lunch & dinner Mon-Fri) This cosy spot serves traditional dishes such as *tartare de saumon et lentilles vertes du Puy* (smoked salmon with Le Puy lentils) and sizzling pots of *aligot* (cheesy, garlicky potato purée).

✖ François Gagnaire   Gastronomic €€€

(📞04 71 02 75 55; www.francois-gagnaire -restaurant.com; 4 av Clément-Charbonnier; menus €28-145; ⊘lunch Wed-Sun, dinner Tue-Sat; 🛗) Book well ahead for François Gagnaire's flagship restaurant. The no-holds-barred *inspiration gourmande,* including wines, costs €145.

🛏 Hôtel du Parc   Hotel €€

(📞04 71 02 40 40; www.hotel-du-parc-le-puy. com; 4 av Clément Charbonnier; d €92-114, ste €159-199; ❄ @ 🛜) Minimalist-chic rooms and stylish suites are the norm at this 15-room hotel, adjacent to François Gagnaire's Michelin-starred restaurant.

🛏 Hôtel Le Régina   Hotel €€

(📞04 71 09 14 71; www.hotelrestregina.com; 34 bd Maréchal Fayolle; s €58-75, d €65-95, ste €101-123; ❄🛜🛗) Topped by a neon-lit art deco turret, the Régina's rooms are individually decorated (our favourite is room 207, with its pop art Chrysler building mural), and some have air-conditioning.

Moissac ❺

🛏 Le Moulin de Moissac   Hotel €€

(📞05 63 32 88 88; www.lemoulindemoissac. com; esplanade du Moulin; d €89-166, mains €18-55; 🛜) Housed in a 15th-century grain mill

overlooking the Tarn, rooms at this riverside hotel have French windows opening onto river-view balconies. Elsewhere, you'll find a waterside restaurant, a smart sauna-spa and a cellar-style Jacuzzi.

🛏 Au Château   B&B €€

(📞05 63 95 96 82; www.au-chateau-stn.com; St Nicolas de la Grave; r €62-116; ❄🛜🛁🛗) This village B&B 10km south of Moissac offers five enormous rooms, which blend modern touches (wood floors, flat-screen TVs, funky fabrics) into the house's 18th-century shell. There's a heated pool and it's very family-friendly.

Condom ❻

✖ La Table des Cordeliers   Gastronomic €€€

(📞05 62 68 43 82; www.latabledescordeliers.fr; 1 rue des Cordeliers; menus €25-67; ⊘Tue-Sat) Overseen by Eric Sampietro, one of the region's culinary big-hitters, Condom's top gastronomic restaurant is housed in a former chapel complete with vaulted arches and cloister garden.

🛏 Les Trois Lys   Hotel €€

(📞05 62 28 33 33; www.lestroislys.com; 38 rue Gambetta; d €130-190, menus €40-45; ❄🛜🛁) Pricey, but if it's antiques and architecture you're after, this is the town's premier proposition. There are 10 rooms set around the 18th-century mansion, and a classy restaurant downstairs.

🛏 Hôtel Continental   Hotel €

(📞05 62 68 37 00; www.lecontinental.net; 20 rue Maréchal Foch; s from €45, d from €49, menus €21-29; 🛜) This waterfront hotel offers great value, with spick-and-span rooms and an excellent restaurant. Front rooms overlook the river but suffer from road noise; garden rooms are quieter.

Lac de Gaube *Sapphire-tinted lake beneath peaks of snowy splendour*

Classic Trip

Pyrenees

32

Traversing hair-raising roads, sky-top passes and snow-dusted peaks, this trip ventures deep into the unforgettable Pyrenees. Buckle up – you're in for a roller coaster of a drive.

TRIP HIGHLIGHTS

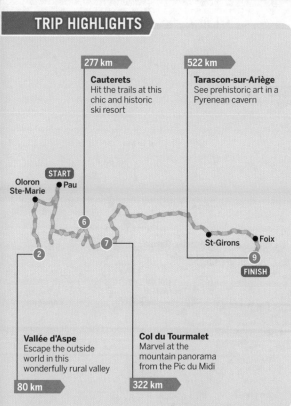

277 km

Cauterets
Hit the trails at this chic and historic ski resort

522 km

Tarascon-sur-Ariège
See prehistoric art in a Pyrenean cavern

Oloron
Ste-Marie

START
Pau

6

7

St-Girons   Foix

9

FINISH

2

Vallée d'Aspe
Escape the outside world in this wonderfully rural valley

80 km

Col du Tourmalet
Marvel at the mountain panorama from the Pic du Midi

322 km

7 DAYS
522KM / 324 MILES

GREAT FOR...

BEST TIME TO GO

June to September, when the road passes are open.

 ESSENTIAL PHOTO

Standing on top of the Pic du Midi.

 BEST FOR OUTDOORS

Hiking to the Lac de Gaube near Cauterets.

Classic Trip

32 Pyrenees

They might not have the altitude of the Alps, but the Pyrenees pack a mighty mountain punch, and if you're an outdoors-lover, you'll be in seventh heaven here. With quiet villages, rustic restaurants, spectacular trails and snowy mountains galore, the Pyrenees are a wild adventure — just remember to break in your hiking boots before you arrive.

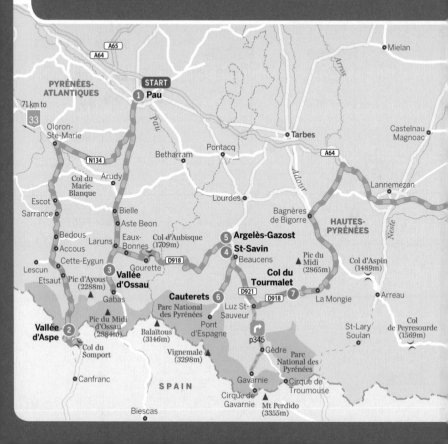

1 Pau

Palm trees might seem out of place in this mountainous region, but Pau (rhymes with 'so'), has long been famed for its mild climate. In the 19th century this elegant town was a favourite wintering spot for wealthy Brits and Americans, who left behind many grand villas and smart promenades.

Its main sight is the **Château de Pau** (www.musee-chateau-pau. fr; adult/18-25yr €6/4.50, incl temporary exhibitions €8/6.50; ⏰9.30am-12.30pm & 1.30-6.45pm, garden longer hr), built by the monarchs of Navarre and transformed into a Renaissance château in the 16th century. It's home to a fine collection of Gobelins tapestries and Sevres porcelain.

Pau's tiny old centre extends for around 500m around the château, and boasts many

LINK YOUR TRIP

30 The Cathar Trail
From Foix, it's only a short drive from the mountains before you reach the heart of the Cathar lands and its amazing châteaux.

33 Basque Country
This Pyrenean trip makes a natural extension of our themed trip through the French Basque country. From St-Jean Pied de Port, it's 71km to Oloron-Ste-Marie, or 103km to Pau.

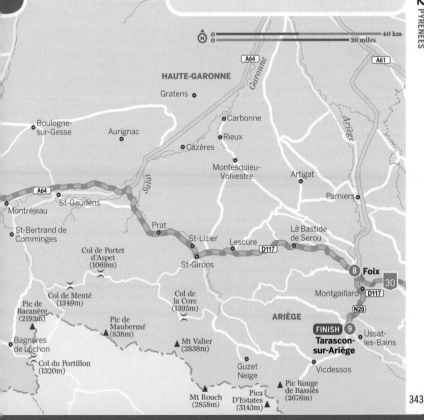

Classic Trip

attractive medieval and Renaissance buildings.

Note that street parking in Pau is nearly all *payant* (chargeable), so it's worth choosing a hotel with its own car park.

✕ ⊨ p349

The Drive ›› To reach the Vallée d'Aspe from Pau, take the N193 to Oloron-Ste-Marie. The first 30km are uneventful, but over the next 40km south of Oloron the mountain scenery unfolds in dramatic fashion, with towering peaks stacking up on either side of the road.

TRIP HIGHLIGHT

② Vallée d'Aspe

The westernmost of the Pyrenean valleys makes a great day trip from Pau. Framed by mountains and bisected by the Aspe River, it's awash with

classic Pyrenean scenery. The main attraction here is soaking up the scenery. Allow yourself plenty of time for photo stops, especially around pretty villages such as **Sarrance**, **Borcé** and **Etsaut**.

Near the quiet village of **Bedous**, it's worth detouring up the narrow road to **Lescun**, a tiny hamlet perched 5.5km above the valley, overlooking the peak of **Pic d'Anie** (2504m) and the cluster of mountains known as the **Cirque de Lescun**.

The valley comes to an end 25km further south near the **Col du Somport** (1631m), where a controversial tunnel burrows 8km under the Franco-Spanish border. The return drive to Pau is just over 80km.

The Drive ›› To reach the Vallée d'Ossau from Pau, take the N134 south of town, veering south onto the D934 towards Arudy/Laruns. From Pau to Laruns, it's about 42km.

③ Vallée d'Ossau

More scenic splendour awaits in the Vallée d'Ossau, which tracks the course of its namesake river for a spectacular 60km. The first part of the valley as far as Laruns is broad, green and pastoral, but as you travel south the mountains really start to pile up, before broadening out again near Gabas.

Halfway between Arudy and Laruns, you can spy on some of the Pyrenees' last griffon vultures at the **Falaise aux Vautours** (Cliff of the Vultures; www.falaise-aux-vautours.com; adult/child €7/5; ⊙10.30am-12.30pm & 2-6.30pm, closed Jan & Mar). Once a common sight, these majestic birds have been decimated by habitat loss and hunting; they're now protected by law. Live CCTV images are beamed from their nests to the visitors centre in Aste-Béon.

The ski resort of **Artouste-Fabrèges**, 6km east of Gabas, is linked by cable car to the **Petit Train d'Artouste** (www.train-artouste.com; adult/child €22.50/18), a miniature mountain railway built for dam workers in the 1920s. The train is only open between late May and September; reserve ahead and allow four hours for a visit.

THE TRANSHUMANCE

If you're travelling through the Pyrenees between late May and early June and find yourself stuck behind a cattle-shaped traffic jam, there's a good chance you may have just got caught up in the Transhumance, in which shepherds move their flocks from their winter pastures up to the high, grassy uplands.

This ancient custom has been a fixture on the Pyrenean calendar for centuries, and several valleys host festivals to mark the occasion. The spectacle is repeated in October, when the flocks are brought back down before the winter snows set in.

The Drive » The D918 between Laruns and Argelès-Gazost is one of the Pyrenees' most breathtaking roads, switchbacking over the lofty Col d'Aubisque. The road feels exposed, but it's a wonderfully scenic drive. You'll cover about 52km, but allow yourself at least 1½ hours. Once you reach Argelès-Gazost, head further south for 4km along the D101 to St-Savin.

- - - - - - - - - - - -

❹ St-Savin

After the hair-raising drive over the Col d'Aubisque, St-Savin makes a welcome refuge. It's a classic Pyrenean village, with cobbled lanes, quiet cafes and timbered houses set around a fountain-filled main square.

It's also home to one of the Pyrenees' most respected hotel-restaurants, **Le Viscos** (☑05 62 97 02 28; www.hotel-leviscos.com; 1 rue Lamarque; r €99-123, full board €67, menus €27-89; ❋ 🛜), run by celeb chef Jean-Pierre St-Martin, known for his blend of Basque, Breton and Pyrenean flavours (as well as his passion for foie gras). After dinner, retire to one of the cosy country rooms and watch the sun set over the snowy mountains.

🛏 p349

The Drive » From St-Savin, travel back along the D101 to Argelès-Gazost. You'll see signs to the Parc Animalier des Pyrénées as you approach town.

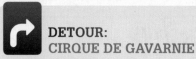

DETOUR:
CIRQUE DE GAVARNIE

Start: ❻ Cauterets

For truly mind-blowing mountain scenery, it's well worth taking a side trip to see the Cirque de Gavarnie, a dramatic amphitheatre of mountains 20km south of Luz-St-Saveur. It's a walk of about two hours from the village, and you'll need to bring sturdy footwear.

There's another spectacular circle of mountains 6.5km to the north, the **Cirque de Troumouse**. It's reached via a hair-raising 8km toll road (€4 per vehicle; open April to October). There are no barriers and the drops are really dizzying, so drive carefully.

- - - - - - - - - - - -

❺ Argelés-Gazost

Spotting wildlife isn't always easy in the Pyrenees, but thankfully the **Parc Animalier des Pyrénées** (www.parc-animalier-pyrenees.com; adult/child €12/8; ⏱9.30am-6pm Apr-Oct) does all the hard work for you. It's home to a menagerie of endangered Pyrenean animals including wolves, marmots, lynxes, giant ravens, vultures, racoons, beavers and even a few brown bears (the European cousin of the grizzly bear).

The Drive » Take the D921 south of Argelès-Gazost for 6km to Pierrefitte-Nestalas. Here, the road forks; the southwest branch (the D920) climbs up a lush, forested valley for another 11km to Cauterets.

- - - - - - - - - - - -

TRIP HIGHLIGHT

❻ Cauterets

For alpine scenery, the century-old ski resort of Cauterets is perhaps the signature spot in the Pyrenees. Hemmed in by mountains and forests, it has clung on to much of its *fin-de-siècle* character, with a stately spa and grand 19th-century residences.

To see the scenery at its best, drive through town along the D920 (signed to the 'Pont d'Espagne'). The road is known locally as the **Chemins des Cascades** after the waterfalls that crash down the mountainside; it's 4 miles of nonstop hairpins, so take it steady.

At the top, you'll reach the giant car park at **Pont d'Espagne** (Spanish Bridge; per day €5.50, over 12 hr €8). From here, a combination *télécabine* and *télésieg*e (adult/child €11.50/9.50) ratchets up the mountainside allowing access to the area's trails – including the popular hike to the

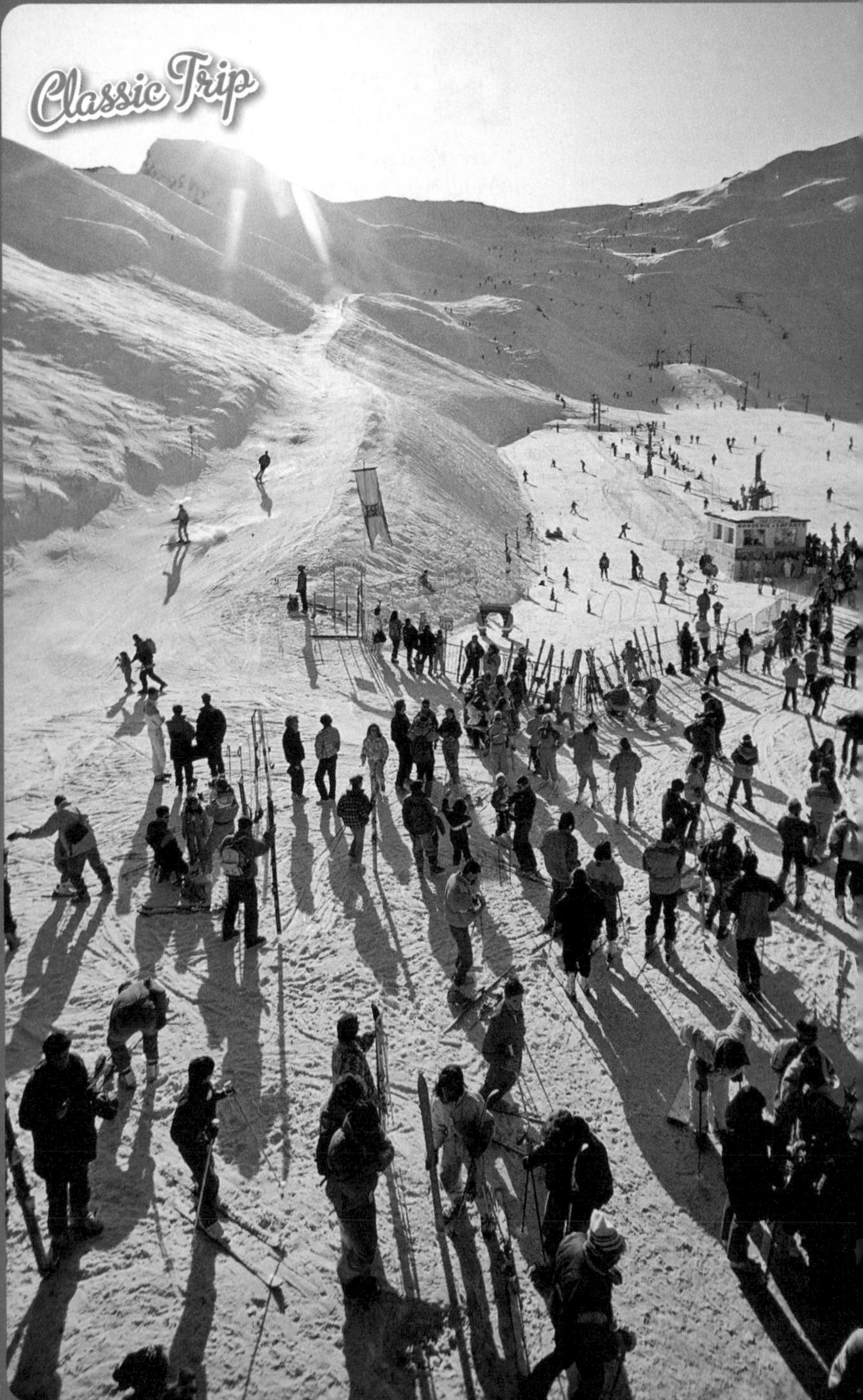
Classic Trip

sapphire-tinted **Lac de Gaube**.

🛏 p349

The Drive » After staying overnight in Cauterets, backtrack to Pierrefitte-Nestalas, and turn southeast onto the D921 for 12km to Luz-St-Saveur. The next stretch on the D918 is another mountain stunner, climbing up through Barèges to the breathtaking Col du Tourmalet.

TRIP HIGHLIGHT

7 Col du Tourmalet

Even in the pantheon of Pyrenean road passes, the Col du Tourmalet commands special respect. At 2115m, it's the highest road pass in the Pyrenees, and usually only opens between June and October. It's often used as a punishing mountain stage in the Tour de France, and you'll feel uncomfortably akin to a motorised ant as you crawl up towards the pass.

From the ski resort of La Mongie (1800m), a cable car climbs to the top of the soaring **Pic du Midi** (www.picdumidi. com; adult/child €32/22; ⏰9am-7pm Jun-Sep, 10am-5.30pm Oct-May). This high-altitude observatory commands otherworldly views – but it's often blanketed in cloud, so make sure you check the forecast before you go.

The Drive » The next stage to Foix is a long one. Follow the D918 and D935 to Bagnères-de-Bigorre, then the D938 and D20 to Tournay, a drive of 40km. Just before Tournay, head west onto the A64 for 82km. Exit onto the D117, signed to St-Girons. It's another 72km to Foix.

8 Foix

Foix is a quiet mountain town, but it's an excellent base for exploring the eastern Pyrenees. Looming above town is the triple-towered **Château des Comtes de Foix** (☎05 61 05 10 10; adult/child €4.50/3.30; ⏰10am-6pm summer, shorter hr other times), constructed in the 10th century as a stronghold for the counts of Foix. The interior is rather bare, but there's a small museum, and the view from the battlements is glorious. There's usually at least one daily tour in English in summer.

Afterwards, head 4.5km south to **Les Forges de Pyrène** (☎05 34 09 30 60; adult/child €8/4.70;

WHY THIS IS A
CLASSIC TRIP
OLIVER BERRY, AUTHOR

The craggy peaks of the Pyrenees are home to some of France's rarest wildlife and most unspoilt landscapes, and every twist and turn in the road seems to reveal another knockout view – one of my personal favourites is the amazing road over the Col d'Aubisque, which feels closer to flying than driving. I love the traditional way of life here, too. Visit during the Transhumance (see p344) to be treated to one of France's great rural spectacles.

Left: Cauterets ski resort
Right: Château de Pau

ESCUDERO PATRICK/GETTY IMAGES ©

Classic Trip

🕑10am-7pm summer, shorter hr other times) a fascinating 'living museum' that explores Ariège folk traditions. Spread over 5 hectares, it illustrates traditional trades such as glass blowing, tanning, thatching and nail making, and even has its own blacksmith, baker, and cobbler.

📑 p349, p331

The Drive » Spend the night in Foix, then head for Tarascon-sur-Ariège, 17km south of Foix on the N20. Look out for brown signs to the Parc de la Préhistoire.

TRIP HIGHLIGHT

❾ Tarascon-sur-Ariège

Thousands of years ago, the Pyrenees were home to thriving communities of hunter-gatherers, who used the area's caves as shelters and left behind many stunning examples of prehistoric art.

Near Tarascon-sur-Ariège, the **Parc de la Préhistoire** (📞05 61 05 10 10; Tarascon-sur-Ariège; adult/child €9.90/6; 🕑10am-6pm) provides a handy primer on the area's ancient past. It's a mix of multimedia exhibits and hands-on outdoor displays, exploring everything from prehistoric carving to the art of animal-skin tents and ancient spear-throwing.

About 6.5km further south, the **Grotte de Niaux** (📞05 61 05 88 37; adult/child €9.40/5.70; 🕑tours hourly 10.15am-4.15pm, extra tours in summer) is home to the Pyrenees' most precious cave paintings. The centrepiece is the **Salon Noir**, reached after an 800m walk through the darkness and decorated with bison, horses and ibex. To help preserve the delicate paintings, there's no artificial light inside; you're given a torch as you enter. The cave can only be visited with a guide. From April to September there's usually one daily tour in English at 1.30pm. Bookings are advisable.

ROAD PASSES IN THE PYRENEES

The high passes between the Vallée d'Ossau, the Vallée d'Aspe and the Vallée de Gaves are often closed during winter. Signs are posted along the approach roads indicating whether they're *ouvert* (open) or *fermé* (closed). The dates given below are approximate, and depend on seasonal snowfall.

Col d'Aubisque (1709m; 🕑May-Oct) On the D918, linking Laruns in the Vallée d'Ossau with Argelès-Gazost in the Vallée de Gaves. An alternative that's open year-round is the D35 between Louvie-Juzon and Nay.

Col de Marie-Blanque (1035m; 🕑May-Oct) The shortest link between the Vallée d'Aspe and the Vallée d'Ossau is the D294, which corkscrews for 21km between Escot and Bielle.

Col du Pourtalet (1795m; 🕑most of the year) The main crossing into Spain generally stays open year-round except during periods of exceptional snowfall.

Col du Tourmalet (2115m; 🕑Jun-Oct) Between Barèges and La Mongie, this is the highest road pass in the Pyrenees. If you're travelling east to the Pic du Midi (for example from Cauterets), the only alternative is a long detour via Lourdes and Bagnères-de-Bigorre.

Eating & Sleeping

Pau ❶

✕ Le Majestic   Traditional French €€

(📞08 92 68 06 89; 9 place Royale; lunch menus €15-24, dinner menus €28-39; 🕐lunch & dinner Mon-Sat) Top-notch French cuisine on central place Royale. The atmosphere is formal – ice-white tablecloths, razor-sharp napkins – but it suits the sophisticated food, heavy on quality ingredients such as turbot, sea bass, Bigorre pork and Pyrenean lamb.

🛏 Hôtel Bristol   Hotel €€

(📞05 59 27 72 98; www.hotelbristol-pau. com; 3 rue Gambetta; s €75-91, d €82-99, f €110-120; 🛜) Pau's best midrange option, in a quintessentially French 19th-century building that offers surprisingly modern rooms. Cool whites are the keynote, but stripy fabrics, throws and modern art liven things up considerably. Ask for a balcony overlooking the mountains.

🛏 Hôtel Roncevaux   Hotel €€

(📞05 59 27 08 44; www.hotel-roncevaux.com; 25 rue Louis Barthou; d €82-160; 🛜) Modern, business-orientated hotel that's part of the Logis chain. There are four room categories, from 'Confort' to 'Luxe' – 'Grand Confort' are the best compromise between price and comfort.

St-Savin ❹

🛏 Hôtel des Rochers   Hotel €

(📞05 62 97 09 52; www.lesrochershotel.com; 1 place du Castillou; d/tr/f €57/78/95; 🛜) If you can't get a room at Le Viscos (p345), this cute hotel in St-Savin makes a useful fall-back. It has plain rooms, friendly owners and a decent restaurant with home-cooking and valley views from the dining room.

Cauterets ❻

🛏 Hôtel du Lion d'Or   Hotel €€

(📞05 62 92 52 87; www.liondor.eu; 12 rue Richelieu; d €88-147; 🛜) This sweet alpine-style hotel, under the Logis umbrella, oozes mountain character. Knick-knacks and curios are dotted throughout the building, and the restaurant serves up classic Pyrenean cuisine in cosy surroundings.

🛏 Hôtel-Restaurant Astérides-Sacca   Hotel €€

(📞05 62 92 50 02; www.asterides-sacca.com; 11 bd Latapie-Flurin; r €52-76; 🕐closed Oct & Nov) This *grande-dame* hotel is on Cauteret's prettiest street, lined with well-preserved 19th-century buildings and often used as a film set. Rooms come in checks or floral fabrics, and the restaurant is splendid.

Foix ❽

🛏 Hôtel Restaurant Lons   Hotel €€

(📞05 34 09 28 00; www.hotel-lons-foix.com; 6 place Dutilh; r from €55, menus €18.50-25.70) A traditional and very cosy Logis-affiliated hotel in the middle of Foix, in a super spot overlooking the river. Rooms are fairly functional, but the river-view restaurant serves solid regional cuisine.

🛏 Auberge les Myrtilles   B&B €

(📞05 61 65 16 46; www.auberge-les-myrtilles. com; Salau; r €63.50-67.50, with half-board €91.50-96.50; 🛜🐾) This mountain retreat in Salau 10km west of Foix, is tailor-made for active types: owners Anouk and René are mad-keen hikers and bikers. Expect simply furnished rooms and a beamed restaurant serving filling Ariègeois cuisine: try the local speciality of *azinat*, a hot pot of sausage, duck and vegetables.

STRETCH YOUR LEGS
TOULOUSE

Start Place Wilson

Finish Quai de la Daurade

Distance 3km

Duration Three hours

Known to the locals as 'La Ville Rose' (The Pink Town), the vibrant city of Toulouse has a sun-baked southern air, a reminder that Languedoc lies just to the south. It's France's fourth-largest city, and is well worth a stroll for its buzzing markets, cafe culture and atmospheric old quarter.

Take this walk on Trips

Les Halles Victor Hugo

Start on place Wilson and head along rue Victor Hugo to Toulouse's covered **food market** (www.marchevictorhugo.fr; place Victor Hugo; ⊗ around 8am-5pm), where shoppers stock up on fresh meat and veg. Look out for the long, curly *saucisse de Toulouse,* the city's trademark sausage.

For a quintessentially Toulousien experience, join the locals at the busy **restaurants** (menus €10-20; ⊗ lunch Tue-Sun) on the 1st floor.

The Walk » Follow rue du Périgord, then head north along rue du Taur.

Basilique St-Sernin

This **basilica** (place St-Sernin; ⊗ 8.30am-noon & 2-6pm Mon-Sat, 8.30am-12.30pm & 2-7.30pm Sun) is one of France's finest Romanesque structures. It's topped by a soaring spire and octagonal tower, and inside is the tomb of St Sernin himself, sheltered beneath a sumptuous canopy. The basilica was an important stop on the Chemin de St-Jacques pilgrimage route.

The Walk » Head south on rue du Taur all the way to place du Capitole.

Place du Capitole

At the end of rue du Taur, you'll emerge onto **place du Capitole**, Toulouse's grand main square, where Toulousiens turn out on sunny evenings to sip a coffee or an early aperitif.

On the eastern side is the 128m-long façade of the **Capitole**, the city hall, built in the 1750s. Inside is the Théâtre du Capitole, one of France's most prestigious opera venues. To the south are the alleys of the **Vieux Quartier**, the heart of old Toulouse.

The Walk » Take rue de la Pomme, which runs southwest to another cafe-lined square, place St-Georges. Before you reach it, turn right onto rue des Arts, then right onto rue de Metz, where you'll find the museum entrance.

Musée des Augustins

Toulouse's fabulous fine arts **museum** (www.augustins.org; 21 rue de Metz; adult/child

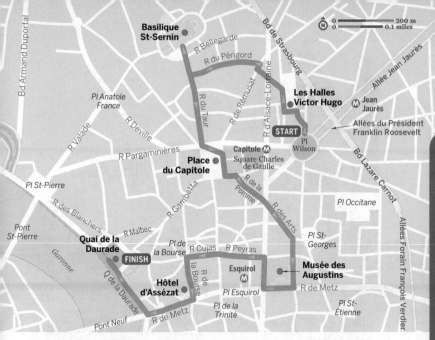

€3/free, temporary exhibitions €6/free; 10am-6pm, to 9pm Wed) **spans the centuries from the Roman era through to the early 20th century. The highlights are the French rooms, with Delacroix, Ingres and Courbet representing the 18th and 19th centuries, and Toulouse-Lautrec and Monet among the standouts from the 20th-century collection. It's in a former Augustinian monastery, and its two 14th-century cloister gardens are postcard pretty.**

The Walk » Turn right onto rue d'Alsace-Lorraine, then left onto rue Peyras. Follow this street to place de la Bourse, then turn left along rue de la Bourse.

Hôtel d'Assezat

This area has some of Toulouse's most elegant *hôtels particuliers,* private mansions built during the 16th and 17th centuries. Among the finest is the **Hôtel d'Assezat**, built for a woad merchant in 1555. It now houses a private art collection belonging to the **Fondation Bomberg** (www.fondation

-bemberg.fr; place d'Assézat; 10am-12.30pm & 1.30-6pm Tue-Sun, to 9pm Thu). The 1st floor is mainly devoted to the Renaissance, while impressionism, pointillism and other 20th-century movements occupy the upper floor.

The Walk » Walk onto rue du Metz and follow it to the elegant Pont Neuf, spanning the Garonne. Turn left onto quai de la Daurade.

Quai de la Daurade

Toulouse looks its best when seen from the water. From March to October, scenic **boat cruises** run along the Garonne from the quai de la Daurade; in summer, some boats also travel onto the Canal du Midi.

The two main companies are **Les Bateaux Toulousains** (www.bateaux-toulousains.com) and **Toulouses Croisières** (www.toulouse-croisieres.com). Trips cost around €8/5 per adult/child for an hour's cruise.

The Walk » From quai de la Daurade, follow rue Malbec and rue Gambetta back towards place Wilson.

Atlantic Coast & Western France

THE ATLANTIC COAST IS WHERE FRANCE GETS BACK TO NATURE. Much more laid-back than the Med, this is the place to slow the pace right down.

Driving through this region is all about quiet country roads winding through vine-striped hills, glimpsed views of dead-at-noon villages and the occasional foray into energetic cities such as Bordeaux.

The region's wine is famous worldwide, and to wash it down you'll find fresh-from-the-ocean seafood wherever you go and plenty of regional delicacies including snails in the north, foie gras further south and, in the unique Basque regions, chilli-tinted dishes filled with hints of Spain.

Biarritz Turreted house perched on rocky coastline (Trips 33, 39)
SHAUN EGAN/GETTY IMAGES ©

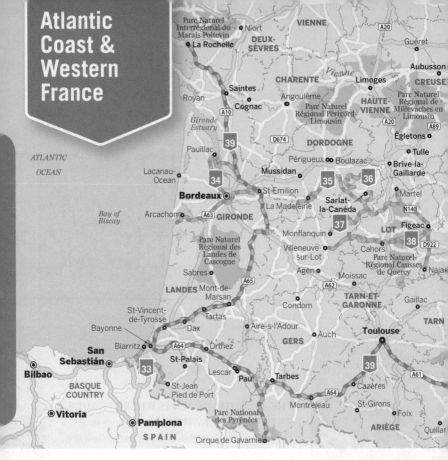

Atlantic Coast & Western France

La Roque Gageac A barge passes the village on the Dordogne River (Trip 35)

 DON'T MISS

St-Cyprien

An expert resident in the village offers truffle hunts. Accompany the hounds on Trip 35

Musée National de la Préhistoire

A brilliant place to do your homework on the Vézère Valley's cave art. Bone up on Trip 36

Domme

Explore this spectacular hilltop village, with its views over the Dordogne valley. Take it all in on Trip 37

Najac

This fairytale castle offers some of the most breathtaking views in southwest France. Explore it on Trip 37

Tapas

Tuck into these tasty bites and wonder whether you're in France, Spain or somewhere else altogether. Indulge yourself on Trip 33

Basque Country *Bayonne festival antics in Basque red and white*

ALEX GRIFFITHS/ALAMY ©

Basque Country **33**

Feisty and independent, the Basque Country is famous for the glitzy resort of Biarritz. But on this tour you'll also fall for delightful fishing ports, chocolate-box villages and jade-green rolling hills.

TRIP HIGHLIGHTS

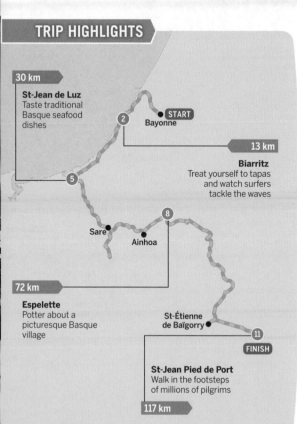

30 km

St-Jean de Luz
Taste traditional Basque seafood dishes

2 **START**
Bayonne

13 km

Biarritz
Treat yourself to tapas and watch surfers tackle the waves

5

8

Sare
Ainhoa

72 km

Espelette
Potter about a picturesque Basque village

St-Étienne de Baïgorry

11
FINISH

St-Jean Pied de Port
Walk in the footsteps of millions of pilgrims

117 km

7 DAYS
117KM / 73 MILES

GREAT FOR...

BEST TIME TO GO

September and October offer the best combination of weather and low crowds.

ESSENTIAL PHOTO

Looking across Grande Plage in Biarritz from the southern headland.

BEST FOR CULTURE

Absorbing the Basque spirit of old Bayonne.

357

33 Basque Country

Driving into the village of Espelette you'll be struck by how different everything is from other parts of the country. The houses are all tarted up in the red and white of Basque buildings, streamers of chilli peppers hang from roof beams, and from open windows comes a language you don't recognise. As you'll discover on this tour, being different from the rest of France is exactly how the proud Basques like it.

TRIP HIGHLIGHT

① Bayonne

Surrounded by sturdy fortifications and splashed in red and white paint, Bayonne is one of the most attractive towns in southwest France. Its perfectly preserved old town and shoals of riverside restaurants are an absolute delight to explore.

Inside the **Musée Basque et de l'Histoire de Bayonne** (☎05 59 59 08 98; www.musee-basque.com; 37 quai des Corsaires; adult/

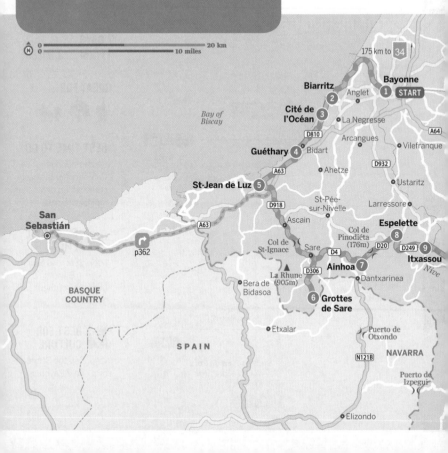

child €6.50/free; ⏱10am-6.30pm) the seafaring history, traditions and cultural identity of the Basque people are all explored.

The twin towers of Bayonne's Gothic **Cathédrale Ste-Marie** (⏱10-11.45am & 3-6.15pm Mon-Sat, 3.30-6.15pm Sun, cloister 9am-12.30pm & 2-6pm) soar above the city. Construction began in the 13th century, and was completed in 1451.

✖ p363

The Drive » Bring a towel because we're taking the 13km

Adour
A64
Briscous Bardos
La Bastide Clairence
Hasparren
Bonloc
Mendionde D22
Louhossoa
Hélette
D918
Bidarray Iholdy
Irissarry
Ossès
PYRÉNÉES-ATLANTIQUES
D948
Irouléguy
10 D15 St-JeanPied de Port 31
St-Étienne de Baïgorry 11 D933
FINISH

(25 minute) beach-bums route to Biarritz. Follow the River Adour out of Bayonne down allée Marines and av de l'Adour. At the big roundabout turn left onto bd des Plages and take your pick from any of the beaches along this stretch. This road will eventually lead into Biarritz.

TRIP HIGHLIGHT
2 Biarritz

As ritzy as its name suggests, this stylish coastal town took off as a resort in the mid-19th century when Napoléon III and his Spanish-born wife, Eugénie, visited regularly. Along its rocky coastline are architectural hallmarks of this golden age, and the belle-époque and art deco eras that followed. Although it retains a high glamour quotient (and high prices to match), it's also a magnet for vanloads of surfers, with some of Europe's best waves.

Biarritz' raison d'être is its fashionable beaches, particularly the central **Grande Plage** and **Plage Miramar**, which are lined end to end with sunbathing bodies on hot summer days.

For a look under the waves, check out the **Musée de la Mer** (☎05 59 22 75 40; www.museedelamer.com; esplanade du Rocher de la Vierge; adult/child €13/9.50; ⏱9.30am-midnight Jul & Aug, shorter hr rest of year), rich in underwater life from the Bay of Biscay and beyond.

For life further afield, have a poke about the stunning collections of Asian art at the **Musée d'Art Oriental Asiatica** (☎05 59 22 78 79; www.museeasiatica.com; 1 rue Guy Petit; adult/student/child €7/5/3; ⏱10.30am-6.30pm Mon-Fri, 2-7pm Sat & Sun).

✖ 🛏 p363

The Drive » It's a 4km, 10-minute drive south out of Biarritz down rue Gambetta and rue de Madrid to the Cité de l'Océan. On the way you'll pass some fantastic stretches of sand just calling for you to dip a toe in the sea or hang-ten on a surfboard.

LINK YOUR TRIP

31 Cheat's Compostela

From St-Jean Pied de Port work your way in reverse through our cheat's version of this ancient spiritual journey.

34 Heritage Wine Routes

From Bayonne it's a 192km pine tree–scented drive to the capital of wine, Bordeaux, and the start of our wine tour.

❸ Cité de l'Océan

We don't really know whether it's fair to call Biarritz's new showpiece, **Cité de l'Océan** (📞05 59 22 75 40; www.citedelocean. com; 1 av de la Plage; adult/child €10.50/7; ⏱10am-10pm), a mere 'museum'. At heart it's a museum of the ocean but in reality this is entertainment, cutting-edge technology, theme park and science museum all rolled into one spectacular attraction. Inside the eye-catching building you'll learn how the ocean was born and watch giant squid and sperm whales do battle.

The Drive ⟫ It's an easy 6km drive down the D911 (av de Biarritz) and the D810, passing through the village of Bidart, to the ocean views of pretty Guéthary. Traffic can be awful.

❹ Guéthary

Built onto cliffs overlooking the ocean south of Biarritz, this red and white seaside village has gained a reputation as the Basque Country's chichi resort of choice for the jet set. The pebble beach below the village offers safe bathing for all the family while the offshore reefs offer some exceptional surf for the brave.

The Drive ⟫ It's another seriously traffic-clogged 7km down the D810 to St-Jean de Luz. This short hop should only take 10 minutes but it rarely does! Sadly, there's no worthwhile alternative route.

TRIP HIGHLIGHT

❺ St-Jean de Luz

If you're searching for the quintessential Basque seaside town – with atmospheric narrow streets and a lively fishing port pulling in large catches of sardines and anchovies that are cooked up at authentic restaurants – you've found it.

St-Jean de Luz' beautiful banana-shaped sandy **beach** sprouts stripy bathing tents from June to September. The beach is sheltered from Atlantic swells and is among the few child-friendly beaches in the Basque Country.

With plenty of boutique shops, little cafes and pretty buildings, walking the streets of the pedestrianised town centre is a real pleasure. Don't miss the town's finest church, the **Église St-Jean Baptiste** (rue Gambetta; ⏱8.30am-noon & 2-7pm), which has a splendid interior with a magnificent baroque altarpiece.

✕ 🛏 p363

The Drive ⟫ The 15km, 20-minute, drive down the D918 and D4 to Sare is a slow road through the gorgeous gentle hills of the pre-Pyrenees. From the village of Sare, which is well worth a wander, hop onto the D306 for a further 7km (10 minutes) to the Grottes de Sare.

---

❻ Grottes de Sare

Who knows what the first inhabitants of the **Grottes de Sare** (www.grottesdesare.fr; adult/

TAPAS ON THE SEASHORE

The influence of Spain is everywhere in the French Basque country, and that includes the cuisine. All the Basque coastal towns have a tapas bar or two, but in Biarritz the pickings are especially rich. The following are our favourites:

Bar Jean (5 rue des Halles; tapas €1-2) The most original, and delicious, selection of tapas in the city is served up with a flamenco soundtrack.

Le Comptoir du Foie Gras/Maison Pujol (1 rue du Centre; tapas €1) This quirky place morphs from a shop selling jars of outstanding foie gras in the day to a tapas bar in the evening. Expect the tapas to be foie gras heavy.

Bar du Marché (📞05 59 23 48 96; 8 rue des Halles; tapas €1-2.50) First opening its doors in 1938, this is another authentic tapas bar beside the market.

VALISCHKAPHOTO/GETTY IMAGES ©

Bayonne

child €8/4; ⊙10am-7pm) –
who lived some 20,000
years ago – would make
of today's whiz-bang
technology, including
lasers and holograms,
during the sound-and-
light shows at these
caves. Multilingual
45-minute tours take
you through a gaping
entrance via narrow
passages to a huge
central cavern adorned
with stalagmites and
stalactites.

The Drive ≫ To get to our
next stop, Ainhoa, retrace your
steps back to Sare and then
jump onto the D4. After 14km
and 20 minutes it's job done. If
you're feeling adventurous you
could weave your way there on
any number of minor back roads
or even cross briefly into Spain
and drive via the lovely village of
Zugarrmurdi.

❼ Ainhoa

Beautiful Ainhoa's
elongated main street
is flanked by imposing
17th-century houses,
half-timbered and
brightly painted. The
fortified **church** has the
Basque trademarks of an
internal gallery and an
embellished altarpiece.

✖ p363

The Drive ≫ It's 6km down
the D20 to our next halt,
Espelette.

TRIP HIGHLIGHT

❽ Espelette

The whitewashed Basque
town of Espelette is
famous for its dark-red
chillies, an integral
ingredient in traditional
Basque cuisine. In
autumn the walls of the
houses are strung with
rows of chillies drying
in the sun. To learn
more about the chillies,
and taste and buy chilli
products visit **l'Atelier
du Piment** (☎05 59 93 90
21; www.atelierdupiment.com;
admission free; ⊙9am-7pm)
on the edge of town.

🛏 p363

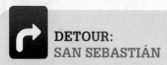

DETOUR:
SAN SEBASTIÁN

Start: ⑤ St-Jean de Luz

Spain, and the elegant and lively city of San Sebastián, is just a few kilometres along the coast from St-Jean de Luz and put simply, San Sebastián is not a city you want to miss out on visiting. The town is set around two sickle-shaped beaches, at least one of which, **Playa de la Concha**, is the equal of any city beach in Europe. But there's more to the city than just looks. With more Michelin stars per capita than anywhere else in the world, and arguably the finest tapas in Spain, many a culinary expert has been heard to say that San Sebastián is possibly the worlds best food city.

By car from St-Jean de Luz, it's just a short 20-minute jump down the A64 (and past an awful lot of toll booths!), or you can endure the N10, which has no tolls but gets so clogged up that it will take you a good couple of hours to travel this short distance.

The Drive ≫ It's an exceedingly pretty 6km (10 minutes) down the D249 to the cherry capital, Itxassou.

- - - - - - - - - -

⑨ Itxassou

Famed for its cherries, as well as the beauty of its surrounds, Itxassou is a classic Basque village that well rewards a bit of exploration. The cherries are used in the region's most famous cake, gateau Basque, which is available pretty much everywhere you look throughout the Basque Country.

The Drive ≫ It's 28km (about 30 minutes) down the D918 and D948 to St-Étienne de Baïgorry. On the way you'll pass the village of Bidarry, renowned for its white-water rafting, and some pretty special mountain scenery.

- - - - - - - - - -

⑩ St-Étienne de Baïgorry

The riverside village of St-Étienne de Baïgorry

is tranquillity itself. Like so many Basque settlements, the village has two focal points: the **church** and the **fronton** (court for playing *pelota,* the local ball games). It's the kind of place to while away an afternoon doing nothing very much at all.

The Drive ≫ It's a quiet 11km (20 minute) drive along the rural D15 to our final stop St-Jean Pied de Port. The thirsty will be interested to know that the hills around the village of Irouléguy, which you pass roughly around the halfway point, are home to the vines that produce the Basque Country's best-known wine.

- - - - - - - - - -

TRIP HIGHLIGHT

⑪ St-Jean Pied de Port

At the foot of the Pyrenees, the walled town of St-Jean Pied de Port was for centuries the last stop in France for pilgrims heading south over the Spanish border

and onto Santiago de Compostela in western Spain. Today it remains a popular departure point for hikers attempting the same pilgrim trail.

St-Jean Pied de Port isn't just about hiking boots and God though; its old core, sliced through by the River Nive, is an attractive place of cobbled streets and geranium-covered balconies. Specific sights worth seeking out include the **Église Notre Dame du Bout du Pont**, which was thoroughly rebuilt in the 17th century. Beyond Porte de Notre Dame (the main gate into the old town) is the photogenic **Vieux Pont** (Old Bridge), the town's best-known landmark.

✕ p363

Eating & Sleeping

Bayonne ❶

✖ La Feuillantine   Gastronomic €€€

(☎05 59 46 14 94; www.lafeuillantine-bayonne.
com; 21 quai Amiral Dubourdieu; menus €25-67,
mains €25) This colourful riverside place
might be quite small, but the culinary skills of
chef Nicolas Bertegui have received virtually
universal praise in the mainstream French
media.

Biarritz ❷

✖ Casa Juan Pedro   Seafood €

(☎05 59 24 00 86; Port des Pêcheurs; mains
€7-10) Down by the old port is this cute little
fishing-shack restaurant. The gregarious
atmosphere ensures that you can wash down
your tuna, sardines or squid with plenty of
friendly banter from both the staff and other
customers.

⌂ Hotel de Silhouette   Designer Hotel €€€

(☎05 59 24 93 82; www.hotel-silhouette-biarritz.
com; 30 rue Gambetta; d from €220; ✻🛜) This
fabulous hotel has designer rooms that have a
dollop of big-city attitude, but in order to remind
you that the countryside is close at hand there
are a couple of 'sheep' in the garden.

St-Jean de Luz ❺

✖ Buvette des Halles   Seafood €

(☎05 59 26 73 59; bd Victor Hugo; dishes €7-14;
⊙6am-2pm & 7-11pm, closed Tue Sep-Jun)
Tucked into a corner of the covered market, this
minuscule restaurant serves goat's cheese,
Bayonne ham, grilled sardines, fish soup,
mussels and much more outside beneath the
plane trees between June and September. The
rest of the year you can eat tucked up inside,
but go early for the best pickings.

⌂ La Devinière   Boutique Hotel €€

(☎05 59 26 05 51; www.hotel-la-deviniere.
com; 5 rue Loquin; d €120-180; 🛜) You have to
love a place that forsakes TVs for antiquarian
books. Beyond the living room, with its piano
and comfy armchairs, there's a delightful small
patio equipped with lounges, and the rooms are
stuffed full of antique furnishings including old
writing desks.

Ainhoa ❼

✖ Ithurria   Basque €€€

(☎05 59 29 92 11; www.ithurria.com; d from
€135, menus €39-62; 🅿✻🛜🏊) For a
memorable meal, stop at the Michelin-starred
Ithurria, set inside an old pilgrims' hostel.
Superb local dishes and an impressive wine list
will put a smile on your face.

Espelette ❽

⌂ Maison d'hôte Irazabala   B&B €

(☎06 07 14 93 61; www.irazabala.com; 155
Mendiko Bidea; s/d €60/80; 🛜) This beautiful
Basque farmhouse is situated in the middle of
wild flower meadows and offers breathtaking
views over a raised rumple of green mountains.
The four rooms are easily the equal of the
setting and you'll struggle to tear yourself away
from the garden. It's a short way out of town
(follow signs for the campsite, after which it's
signed).

St-Jean Pied de Port ⓫

✖ Chez Arrambide   Gastronomic €€€

(menus €42-110, mains €30-52; ⊙closed Tue
Sep-Jun) This twin-Michelin-starred restaurant,
inside the (overpriced) Hôtel Les Pyrénées, is
where chef Firmin Arrambide works wonders
(such as truffle and foie-gras lasagne) with
seasonal market produce.

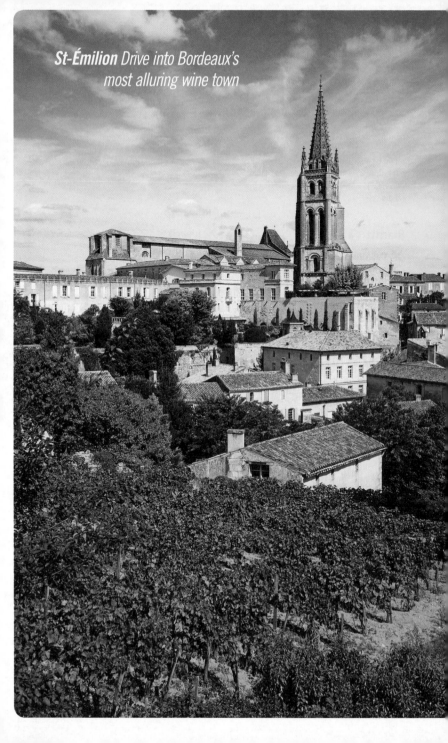

St-Émilion *Drive into Bordeaux's most alluring wine town*

Heritage Wine Routes

34

This is the trip for those who appreciate the finer things in life: great wine, fabulous regional cuisine and gentle driving through glorious vine-ribboned countryside studded with grand châteaux.

TRIP HIGHLIGHTS

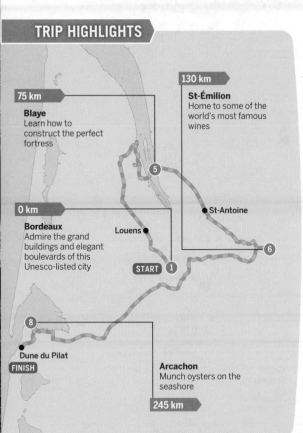

130 km

St-Émilion
Home to some of the world's most famous wines

75 km

Blaye
Learn how to construct the perfect fortress

● St-Antoine

0 km

Bordeaux
Admire the grand buildings and elegant boulevards of this Unesco-listed city

Louens ●

START ①

⑤

⑥

⑧

Dune du Pilat
FINISH

Arcachon
Munch oysters on the seashore

245 km

5 DAYS
245KM / 152 MILES

GREAT FOR...

BEST TIME TO GO
September and October: the grape harvest takes place, oysters are in season

ESSENTIAL PHOTO
Over the red roofs of St-Émilion from the place des Créneaux.

BEST FOR FOODIES
Slurping fresh oysters at Bordeaux's Marché des Capucins.

365

34 Heritage Wine Routes

10am: The southern sun warms your face and you're standing in a field surrounded by vines heavy with ready to burst grapes. 1pm: Cutlery clinks, tummies sigh in bliss and you're on a gastronomic adventure in a top-class restaurant. 7pm: Toes in the sand and Atlantic breeze in the hair and you down an oyster in one. All this and more awaits you on this refined culinary trip.

TRIP HIGHLIGHT

❶ Bordeaux

Stately Bordeaux is a city of sublime food, even better drink and long, lazy sun-drenched days. It's true that for a city of its size and standing, actual physical tourist attractions are somewhat thin on the ground, but come here with an empty tummy and eye for fine architecture and you'll find that Bordeaux more than satisfies your cravings.

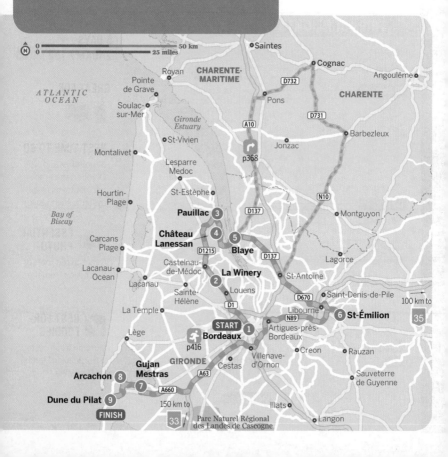

Gallo-Roman statues and relics dating back 25,000 years are among the highlights at the impressive **Musée d'Aquitaine** (20 cours Pasteur; permanent exhibitions free, temporary exhibitions adult/student/child €5/2.50/free; ⊙11am-6pm Tue-Sun). Upstairs is a small collection of statues and masks from the former French African and Oceania colonies. Ask to borrow an English-language catalogue.

The **tourist office** (☐05 56 00 66 00; www.bordeaux-tourisme.com; 12 cours du 30 Juillet; ⊙9am-7.30pm Mon-Sat, 9.30am-6.30pm Sun) runs a packed program of bilingual Bordeaux city tours, including a wheelchair-accessible two-hour

LINK YOUR TRIP

Basque Country

33 From Arcachon drive 182km through the forests of Les Landes to Bayonne and our Spanish-flavoured Basque Country tour.

Gourmet Dordogne

35 Slip some truffle hunting into your wine tour. From St-Émilion it's a mere 100km to Périgueux and our Gourmet Dordogne drive.

morning walking tour (adult/child €8.50/6; ⊙10am Mon, Tue, Thu, Fri & Sun) and a **night-time walking tour** (adult/child €16/11) that takes in Bordeaux' floodlit buildings and monuments. Contact the tourist office for details of dozens of other tour options, including gourmet food and wine tours as well as river cruises in the warmer months. All tours take a limited number of participants; reserve ahead.

For more on things to see in the city see our walking tour, p416.

🍴 🛏 p372

The Drive » It's a 23km trip along the D1 from Bordeaux to La Winery. Technically this should take around 40 minutes, but traffic around Bordeaux can be dreadful so allow a bit longer.

- - - - - - - - - - - - - -

② La Winery

Part giant wine shop, part grape-flavoured theme park, and part wine museum, **La Winery** (☐05 56 39 04 90; www.lawinery.fr; Rond-

Point des Vendangeurs, D1) is a vast glass-and-steel wine centre that mounts concerts and contemporary-art exhibits alongside various fee-based tastings, including innovative ones that determine your *signe œnologique* ('wine sign') costing from €16 (booking required). It stocks over 1000 different wines.

The Drive » It's 29km (30 minutes) from La Winery to Pauillac along the D1215, which becomes ever more rural.

- - - - - - - - - - - - - -

③ Pauillac

Northwest of Bordeaux, along the western shore of the Gironde Estuary – formed by the confluence of the Garonne and Dordogne Rivers – lie some of Bordeaux' most celebrated vineyards. On the banks of the muddy Gironde, the port town of Pauillac is at the heart of the wine country, surrounded by the distinguished Haut-Médoc, Margaux and St-Julien appellations.

TOP TIP: OYSTERS AT CAPUCINS

A classic Bordeaux experience is a Saturday morning spent slurping oysters and white wine from one of the seafood stands at **Marché des Capucins** (6 oysters & glass of wine €6; ⊙7am-noon). Afterwards you can peruse the stalls while shopping for the freshest ingredients to take on a picnic.

The Pauillac wine appellation encompasses 18 *crus classés* including the world-renowned Mouton Rothschild, Latour and Lafite Rothschild. The town's tourist office houses the **Maison du Tourisme et du Vin** (☑05 56 59 03 08; www.pauillac-medoc.com; ⊗9.30am-7pm Mon-Sat, 10am-1pm & 2-6pm Sun), which has information on the area's many châteaux and how to visit them.

The Drive » It only takes about 15 minutes to cover the 10km between Pauillac and the next stop. Take the D2 south out of Pauillac for 7.3km and then turn right towards Lachesnaye, continue for around 1.5km, and then turn right up to Château Lanessan.

④ Château Lanessan

There are so many châteaux around here with such a confusing web of opening times and visiting regulations that it can be hard to know where to begin. One of the easiest to visit is **Château Lanessan** (☑05 56 58 94 80; www.lanessan. com; Cussac-Fort-Medoc; ⊗advance reservation), which offers daily hour-long tours throughout the year including ones tailored to children and hard-to-please teenagers; advance reservations required.

The Drive » Getting to Blaye involves splashing over the River Gironde on a car ferry – how exciting! Return to the D2 and

MICHAEL BUSSELLE/ROBERT HARDING/GETTY IMAGES ©

DETOUR: COGNAC

Start: ⑤ Blaye

On the banks of the River Charente amid vine-covered countryside, the picturesque town of Cognac, home of the double-distilled spirit that bears its name, proves that there's more to southwest France than just wine.

The best-known Cognac houses are open to the public, running tours of their cellars and production facilities, and ending with a tasting session. The **tourist office** (☑05 45 82 10 71; www.tourism-cognac. com; 16 rue du XIV Juillet; ⊗9.30am-7pm Mon-Sat, 10am-4pm Sun) can give advice on current opening hours of each Cognac house.

It's 85km from Blaye to Cognac, much of which is along the A10 highway. From Cognac you can cut down to stop 6, St-Émilion, in two hours on the D731 followed by the busy N10.

head south to Lamarque where you hop on-board the ferry (passenger/car €3.20/13.70, departures every 1½ hours in July and August) for the short crossing to Blaye. It's 11km from the château to the ferry.

TRIP HIGHLIGHT

⑤ Blaye

If you want a lesson in how to build a protective citadel, then the spectacular **Citadelle**

Paulliac Wine casks are inspected in a vineyard cellar

de Blaye (admission free) is about as good an example as you could hope to find. Largely constructed by that master fortress-builder Vauban in the 17th century, it was a key line of defence protecting Bordeaux from naval attack. It was inscribed onto the Unesco World Heritage List in 2008. **Guided tours** (adult/ child €5/3; ⊘2.30pm daily Jun-Sep) in English are available through the tourist office.

The Drive » From Blaye to St-Émilion is a simple 50km drive. From Blaye take the D137 toward St-André de Cubzac, where you join the D670 to Libourne. After a bit of time stuck in traffic you continue down to St-Émilion. It should take an hour but traffic means it will probably take longer!

TRIP HIGHLIGHT

⑥ St-Émilion

The medieval village of St-Émilion perches above vineyards renowned for producing full-bodied red wines and is easily the most alluring of all the region's wine towns.

The only way to visit the town's most interesting historical sites is with one of the tourist office's varied **guided tours** (adult €7-14, child free).

The tourist office organises two-hour afternoon **château visits** (adult/child €14/free). It also runs various events throughout the year, such as **Les Samedis de l'Oenologie** (adult €77; ☻Sat), which combines a vineyard visit, lunch, town tour and wine-tasting course.

For a fun and informative introduction to wine tasting, get stuck into some 'blind' tastings at **L'École du Vin de St-Émilion** (www.

vignobleschateaux.fr; 4 rue du Clocher; tasting course €29; ☻3pm Apr-Oct, by reservation Nov-Mar). The adjacent **Maison du Vin** (place Pierre Meyrat; class €21; ☻mid-Jul–mid-Sep) also offers bilingual 1½-hour wine-tasting classes.

Reserve all tours in advance.

 p372

The Drive ≫ To get to the next stop you've simply no option but to endure the ring road around Bordeaux. Make sure you don't do this at rush hour! Head toward Bordeaux on the N89, then south down the A63 following signs to Arcachon and then Gujan Mestras. It's a 100km journey that should, but probably won't, take an hour.

- - - - - - - - - - - -

7 **Gujan Mestras**

All that wine must be giving you a giddy head by now (and frankly that's not great on a driving tour) so let's take a break from the grape and head to the seaside to eat oysters in the area around Gujan Mestras. Picturesque oyster ports are dotted around the town, but the best one to visit is **Port de Larros**, where locally harvested oysters are sold from wooden shacks. To learn more about these

---

ON THE WINE TRAIL

Thirsty? The 1000-sq-km wine-growing area around the city of Bordeaux is, along with Burgundy, France's most important producer of top-quality wines.

The Bordeaux region is divided into 57 appellations (production areas whose soil and microclimate impart distinctive characteristics to the wine produced there) that are grouped into seven families, and then subdivided into a hierarchy of designations (eg *premier grand cru classé,* the most prestigious) that often vary from appellation to appellation. The majority of the Bordeaux region's reds, rosés, sweet and dry whites and sparkling wines have earned the right to include the abbreviation AOC (Appellation d'Origine Contrôlée) on their labels, indicating that the contents have been grown, fermented and aged according to strict regulations that govern such viticultural matters as the number of vines permitted per hectare and acceptable pruning methods.

Bordeaux has more than 5000 châteaux, referring not to palatial residences but rather to the properties where grapes are raised, picked, fermented and then matured as wine. The smaller châteaux sometimes accept walk-in visitors, but at many places, especially the better-known ones, you have to make advance reservations. Many close during the *vendange* (grape harvest) in October.

Whet your palate with the Bordeaux tourist office informal introduction to wine and cheese courses (adult €25) where you sip three different wines straight from the cellar and sup on cheese.

Serious students of the grape can enrol at the **École du Vin** (Wine School; ☎05 56 00 22 66; www.bordeaux.com; 3 cours du 30 Juillet), within the Maison du Vin de Bordeaux, across the street from the tourist office. Introductory two-hour courses (adult €25) are held Monday to Saturday from 10am to noon between July and September.

delicious shellfish, the small **Maison de l'Huître** (adult/child €4.50/2.50; ⊙10am-12.30pm & 2.30-6pm Mon-Sat) has a display on oyster farming, including a short film in English.

The Drive ⟫ It's 10, sometimes traffic-clogged, but well-signposted, kilometres from Gujan Mestras to Arcachon.

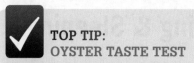

TOP TIP: OYSTER TASTE TEST

Oysters from each of the Bassin d'Arcachon's four oyster-breeding zones hint at subtly different flavours. See if you can detect these:

Banc d'Arguin – milk and sugar

Île aux Oiseaux – minerals

Cap Ferret – citrus

Grand Banc – roasted hazelnuts

TRIP HIGHLIGHT

8 Arcachon

The seaside town of Arcachon has lured bourgeois Bordelaise since the end of the 19th century. Its four little quarters are romantically named for each of the seasons, with villas that evoke the town's golden past amid a scattering of 1950s architecture.

Arcachon's sandy beach, **Plage d'Arcachon**, is flanked by two piers. Lively **Jetée Thiers** is at the western end. In front of the eastern pier, **Jetée d'Eyrac**, stands the town's turreted **Casino de la Plage** built by Adalbert Deganne in 1953 as an exact replica of Château de Boursault in the Marne. Inside, it's a less-grand blinking and bell-ringing riot of poker machines and gaming tables.

On the tree-covered hillside south of the Ville d'Été, the century-old **Ville d'Hiver** (Winter Quarter) has over 300 villas ranging in style from neo-Gothic through to colonial.

For a different view of Arcachon and its coastline, take to the ocean waves on one of the boat cruises organised by **Les Bateliers Arcachonnais** (UBA; ☎05 57 72 28 28; www.bateliers-arcachon. com; Île aux Oiseaux adult/ child €15/10, Banc d'Arguin adult/child €20/14). It offers daily, year-round cruises around the **Île aux Oiseaux**, the uninhabited 'bird island' in the middle of Arcachon bay. It's a haven for tern, curlew and redshank, so bring your binoculars. In summer there are regular all-day excursions (11am to 5.30pm) to the **Banc d'Arguin**, the sand bank off the Dune du Pilat.

✕ ⩗ p373

The Drive ⟫ Dune du Pilat is 12km south of Arcachon down the D218. There are restrictions on car access in summer for the last part of the route.

9 Dune du Pilat

This colossal sand dune (sometimes referred to as the Dune de Pyla because of its location in the resort town of Pyla-sur-Mer) stretches from the mouth of the Bassin d'Arcachon southwards for almost 3km. Already the largest in Europe, it's spreading eastwards at 4.5m a year – it has swallowed trees, a road junction and even a hotel.

The view from the top – approximately 114m above sea level – is magnificent. To the west you can see the sandy shoals at the mouth of the Bassin d'Arcachon, and dense dark-green pine forests stretch from the base of the dune eastwards almost as far as the eye can see.

Eating & Sleeping

Bordeaux ❶

✖ La Tupina — Regional Cuisine €€€

(☎05 56 91 56 37; www.latupina.com; 6 rue Porte de la Monnaie; menus €18-65, mains €27-45) Filled with the aroma of soup simmering inside an old *tupina* ('kettle' in Basque) over an open fire, this place is feted far and wide for its seasonal southwestern French specialities such as a mini-casserole of foie gras and eggs or goose wings with potatoes and parsley. It's a 10-minute walk upriver from the city centre.

✖ Le Cheverus Café — Bistro €

(☎05 56 48 29 73; 81-83 rue du Loup; menus from €11.40; ⊙Mon-Sat) In a city full of neighbourhood bistros, this is one of the most impressive. It's friendly, cosy and chaotically busy (be prepared to wait for a table at lunchtime). The food tastes fresh and home-cooked and it dares to veer slightly away from the bistro standards of steak and chips. The lunch *menus*, which include wine, are an all-out bargain.

✖ La Boîte à Huîtres — Oysters €€

(☎05 56 81 64 97; 36 cours du Chapeau Rouge; lunch menu €19, 6 oysters from €10) This rickety, wood-panelled little place feels like an Arcachon fisherman's hut. It's a sensation that's quite appropriate because this is by far the best place in Bordeaux to munch on fresh Arcachon oysters. Traditionally they're served with sausage but you can have them in a number of different forms, including with that other southwest delicacy, foie gras.

🛏 Ecolodge des Chartrons — B&B €€

(☎05 56 81 49 13; www.ecolodgedeschartrons. com; 23 rue Raze; incl breakfast s €96-118, d €98-134; 🛜) The owners of this *chambre d'hôte* have stripped back and lime-washed the stone walls of an old town house, scrubbed the wide floorboards and polished up the antique furniture to create a deliciously pleasant place, hidden away in a little side street off the quays in Bordeaux' Chartrons wine merchant district. There's nearby street parking.

🛏 L'Hôtel Particulier — Boutique Hotel €€€

(☎05 57 88 28 80; www.lhotel-particulier.com; 44 rue Vital-Carles; apt from €97, d from €168; 🛜) When you step into this fabulous boutique hotel and find a thousand eyes staring at you from the reception walls, and lampshades made only of feathers, you realise you've stumbled upon somewhere special. The rooms don't disappoint and are highly extravagant affairs with huge fireplaces, carved ceilings, free-standing bath tubs and quality furnishings throughout.

🛏 Les Chambres au Coeur de Bordeaux — B&B €€

(☎05 56 52 43 58; www.aucoeurdebordeaux.fr; 28 rue Boulan; s/d incl breakfast from €85/95; 🛜) This recently renovated town house is now a swish B&B run very much along the lines of a small boutique hotel. Its five charming rooms are a very Bordeaux-appropriate mix of the old and the new, and each evening a free aperitif is offered at 7pm.

St-Émilion ❻

✖ Restaurant Hostellerie de Plaisance — Gastronomic €€€

(☎05 57 55 07 55; www.hostellerie-plaisance. com; place du Clocher; menus €105-150; ⊙lunch Tue-Fri, lunch & dinner Sat) Award-winning chef Philippe Etchebest cooks up food like you've never had before at his double-Michelin-starred restaurant housed in a dining room of eggshell blue and white gold inside the hotel of the same name. The 'discovery menu' allows you to do just that in about eight courses. Advance reservations essential.

✖ L'Huîtres Pie — Seafood €€

(☎05 57 24 69 71; 11 rue de la Porte Bouqueyre; menus €22-52; ⊙closed Tue & Wed) Arcachon oysters and other seafood feature heavily in the dishes on offer here, but if slippery shellfish don't do it for you, tuck into one of the hearty meat or fish dishes. You can eat inside or outside on the pleasant olive-shaded courtyard.

🛏 Grand Barrail
Historic Hotel €€€

(📞05 57 55 37 00; www.grand-barrail.com; rte de Libourne/D243; r from €320; ❄🌐🏊) Grand doesn't even begin to describe this immense 1850-built château, 3km from the village, with its decadent on-site spa, stone-flagged heated swimming pool and regal rooms. Undoubtedly the best seat in its restaurant (*menus* from €29) is the corner table framed by 19th-century stained glass that would make the average church green with envy.

🛏 Hôtel-Restaurant
du Palais Cardinal
Historic Hotel €€

(📞05 57 24 72 39; www.palais-cardinal. com; place du 11 Novembre 1918; s €71-142, d €88-166; 🌐🏊) Run by the same family for five generations, this hotel puts a little more thought into its dress sense than many St-Émilion hotels. The heated pool is set in flower-filled gardens and framed by sections of the original medieval town-wall fortifications, dating from the 13th century. Its well worth partaking in the gastronomic fare served at its restaurant.

Arcachon ⑧

✕ Aux Mille
Saveurs
Traditional French €€

(📞05 56 83 40 28; 25 bd du Général Leclerc; menus €19-50; 🕐closed Wed & dinner Sun & Tue) In a light-filled space of flowing white table cloths, this genteel restaurant is renowned for its traditional French fare artistically presented on fine china.

🛏 Hôtel le Dauphin
Historic Hotel €€

(📞05 56 83 02 89; www.dauphin-arcachon.com; 7 av Gounod; s/d from €112/122; ❄🌐🏊) Don't miss this late-19th-century gingerbread place with patterned red-and-cream brickwork. An icon of its era, it's graced by twin semicircular staircases, magnolias and palms. Plain but spacious rooms are well set up for families. Parking is free.

🛏 Park Inn
Design Hotel €€

(📞05 56 83 99 91; www.parkinn.fr; 4 rue du Professeur Jolyet; d from €155; ❄🌐) Arcachon's version of this chain is utterly distinctive, thanks to its vivid swirled carpet, candy-striped curtains and primary-coloured modular furniture. It's a bit like bouncing around in a preschoolers' playroom.

Black truffles *Savour the star ingredient of Dordogne gastronomy*

Gourmet Dordogne

35

The Dordogne is definitely a place that thinks with its stomach. This foodie tour indulges in the region's gastronomic goodies, from walnuts and truffles to fine wine and foie gras.

TRIP HIGHLIGHTS

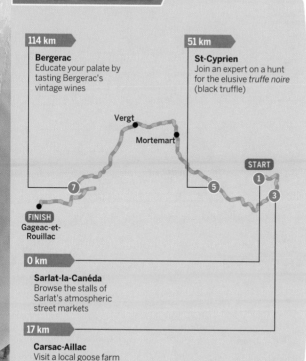

114 km

Bergerac
Educate your palate by tasting Bergerac's vintage wines

51 km

St-Cyprien
Join an expert on a hunt for the elusive *truffe noire* (black truffle)

Vergt

Mortemart

START

FINISH
Gageac-et-Rouillac

0 km

Sarlat-la-Canéda
Browse the stalls of Sarlat's atmospheric street markets

17 km

Carsac-Aillac
Visit a local goose farm and try some foie gras

3 DAYS
138KM / 85 MILES

GREAT FOR...

BEST TIME TO GO

September and October for harvest markets; December and March for truffle season.

 ESSENTIAL PHOTO

A picnic among the endless vines surrounding Bergerac.

 BEST FOR FOODIES

Shop till you drop at Sarlat's chaotic street market.

35 Gourmet Dordogne

If you enjoy nothing better than soaking up the sights, sounds and smells of a French market, you'll be in seventh heaven in the Dordogne. This region is famous for its foodie traditions, and immersing yourself in its culinary culture is one of the best — and tastiest — ways to experience life in rural France.

TRIP HIGHLIGHT

1 Sarlat-la-Canéda

Start in the honey-stoned town of Sarlat-la-Canéda, which hosts a wonderful **outdoor market** on Saturday mornings. Local farmers set up their stalls on the cobbled place de la Liberté, selling seasonal treats such as cèpe mushrooms, duck terrines, foie gras, walnuts and even *truffes noires* (black truffles). There's also an atmospheric **night**

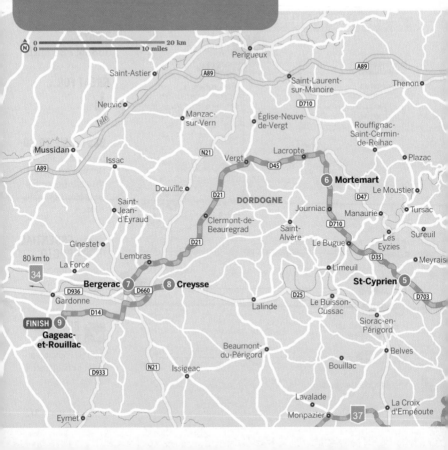

market (🕐6-10pm) on Thursdays from mid-June to September, and **truffle markets** (🕐Sat morning) from December to February.

Even if you're not here on market day, you can shop for foodie souvenirs at Sarlat's **covered market** (🕐8.30am-2pm daily), housed in the converted Église Ste-Marie. While you're here, don't miss a trip up the tower in the **panoramic lift** (adult/child €5/4; 🕐Apr-Dec), overlooking Sarlat's slate rooftops.

✕ 🛏 p381

The Drive ❯❯ Travel 9km east of Sarlat on the D47 towards the village of Sainte-Nathalène. You'll pass walnut groves and wooded copses lining the roadsides. The Moulin de la Tour is on a back road north of the village, signed to Proissans, Salignac and St-Crépin-et-Carlucet; you'll see the sign after another 1.5km.

---

② Sainte-Nathalène

One of the Dordogne's most distinctive flavours is the humble *noix* (walnut). It's been a prized product of the Dordogne for centuries, and is still used in many local recipes – cakes, puddings, pancakes and breads, as well as liqueurs and *huile de noix* (walnut oil). At the **Moulin de la Tour** (📞05 53 59 22 08; www.moulindelatour.com; 🕐9am-noon & 2-6pm Mon-Sat), the region's last working watermill, you can watch walnut oil being made and stock up with nutty souvenirs. Don't miss the *cerneaux de noix au chocolat*

(chocolate-covered walnuts) and *gâteau de noix* (walnut cake).

The Drive ❯❯ Backtrack to the junction in Sainte Nathalène, turn left and follow road signs to St-Vincent-Le-P/RD704. Continue along this minor road until you reach the D704A. Cross straight over and follow white signs to Le Bouyssou. It's a drive of 8km or 15 minutes.

TRIP HIGHLIGHT

③ Carsac-Aillac

Alongside black truffles, the Dordogne is famous for its foie gras (fattened goose liver). As you drive around, you'll see duck and goose farms dotted all over the countryside, many of which offer guided tours and *dégustation* (tasting).

L'Elevage du Bouyssou (📞05 53 31 12 31; elevage.bouyssou@wanadoo.fr; 🕐shop 8am-6pm, tours 6.30pm daily) is a family-run farm to the north of Carsac-Aillac. If it's your kind of thing, owners Denis and Nathalie Mazet run tours and

LINK YOUR TRIP

34 Heritage Wine Routes

The hallowed vineyards of Bordeaux lie 96km to the west of Bergerac along the D936.

37 Dordogne's Fortified Villages

Most of the region's best *bastides* (fortified towns) lie to the south of the Dordogne River. Head south from La Roque Gageac for 6km to begin in Domme.

demonstrate *la gavage* – the controversial force-feeding process that helps fatten up the goose livers. You can also buy homemade foie gras in the shop.

The Drive » Travel south from Carsac-Aillac and turn left onto the D703 for 12km towards La Roque Gageac. You'll have lovely views across the river, and the banks are lined with medieval villages dangling over the water. Stop for photos at the Cingle de Montfort viewpoint, which overlooks a picturesque bend backed by a medieval château.

- - - - - - - - - - - - - -

④ La Roque Gageac

The lovely D703 tracks the course of the Dordogne River and passes through a string of lovely riverside villages, including La Roque Gageac.

If you feel like burning off some of the calories acquired on this trip, the village is an ideal place to do it: several companies hire out kayaks and canoes for exploring the river, including **Canoë Dordogne** (☑05 53 29 58 50; www.canoe-dordogne.fr; canoe & kayak trips €6-24) and **Canoë Vacances** (☑05 53 28 17 07; www. canoevacances.com; La Peyssière; canoeing €10-20).

✖ p381

The Drive » From La Roque Gageac, St-Cyprien is 15km further west along the river. It's a gorgeous drive that passes several medieval châteaux (see p396) en route. Once you reach

St-Cyprien, continue north on the D49 for another 6.5km, and look out for the easy-to-miss right turn to Lussac/Péchalifour.

- - - - - - - - - - - - - -

TRIP HIGHLIGHT

⑤ St-Cyprien

In the village of St-Cyprien you can indulge in another of the Dordogne's great gastronomic gems – the *perle noire* of the Périgord, otherwise known as the black truffle. At **Truffière de Péchalifour** (☑05 53 29 20 44; www.truffe-perigord.com), expert Édouard Aynaud offers hour-long truffle-hunting trips (🕙11am Tue-Sat Jul & Aug) assisted by his keen-nosed hounds. The best time to visit is during truffle season from December to March, when he runs half-/full-day trips around the *truffières* (truffle-growing areas) that include a chance to try the rarefied fungi over a picnic lunch.

If you have time, stop at the nearby **Domaine de la Voile Blanche** (☑05 53 29 57 34; www.domaine -voie-blanche.com), where the Dalbavie family run tours around their vineyard.

The Drive » From Lussac, backtrack to the D35 and turn northwest towards the bustling town of Le Bugue, following signs to Périgueux onto the D710. It's about 13km to Mortemart; there's a sign to the boar farm just before the village.

LOUIS-LAURENT GRANDADAM/GETTY IMAGES ©

- - - - - - - - - - - - - -

⑥ Mortemart

Next up is **Les Sangliers de Mortemart** (☑05 53 03 21 30; www.elevage -sangliers-mortemart. com; adult/child €3/1.50; 🕙10am-7pm summer, 1-5pm winter), where you can see wild boars being raised in semi-freedom on a farm just outside Mortemart. These

Truffle hunting A farmer and his pig searching for truffles

porky cousins of the modern pig were once common across France, but their numbers have been reduced by habitat restriction and hunting.

The boars are fed a rich diet of *chataígnes* (chestnuts), which gives the meat a distinctive nutty, gamey flavour. It's a key ingredient in the hearty stew known as *civet de sanglier,* as well as pâtés and country terrines. Naturally enough, there's a farm shop where you can buy boar-themed goodies.

The Drive » From Mortemart, the nicest drive to Bergerac follows the D45 and D21, a drive of 51km through classic Dordogne countryside. Once you reach town, leave your car in the car park on quai Salvette, and walk towards the centre along rue des Récollets.

TRIP HIGHLIGHT

⑦ Bergerac

It's not as famous as Bordeaux and St-Émilion, but Bergerac is still an essential stop for wine-lovers. Vineyards carpet the countryside around town, producing rich reds, fragrant whites and fruity rosés – but with 13 AOCs (Appéllations d'Origines

TRUFFLE SECRETS

Few ingredients command the same culinary cachet as the *truffe noire* (black truffle), variously known as the *diamant noir* (black diamond) or, hereabouts, the *perle noire du Périgord* (black pearl of the Périgord). The gem references aren't just for show, either: a vintage truffle crop can fetch as much as €1000 per kilogram at seasonal markets.

A subterranean fungus that grows naturally in chalky soils (especially around the roots of oak trees), this mysterious mushroom is notoriously capricious; a good truffle spot one year can be bare the next, which has made farming them practically impossible.

The art of truffle-hunting is a closely guarded secret; it's a matter of luck, judgement and experience, with specially trained dogs (and occasionally pigs) to help in the search.

The height of truffle season is between December and March, when special truffle markets are held around the Dordogne, including in Périgueux and Sarlat.

Contrôlées), and more than 1200 wine-growers, the choice is bewildering.

Thankfully, the town's **Maison des Vins** (☏05 53 63 57 57; www.vins-bergerac. fr; 1 rue des Récollets; ⏱10am-12.30pm & 2-7pm) knows all the best vintages, offers wine-tasting courses and organises vineyard visits. You could spend at least another couple of days touring the local vineyards, using Bergerac as a base.

✕ ⌕ p381

The Drive ≫ Creysse is 9km east of Bergerac along the D660.

---

⑧ Creysse

Many Bergerac vineyards are open to the public, including the prestigious

Château de Tiregand
(☏05 53 23 21 08; www. chateau-de-tiregand.com; tours adult/child €3/2), which is mainly known for its Pécharmant wines; it runs tours and tasting sessions in its cellars. English tours run at 2.30pm from June to August.

The Drive ≫ South of Bergerac, you'll really start to get out into wine country, with vineyards and châteaux lining the roadsides. Gageac-et-Rouillac is 15km southwest of Bergerac off the D14, not far from Saussignac. Take the D936 west of town, and look out for the left turn onto the D15.

---

⑨ Gageac-et-Rouillac

Bergerac's largest vineyards lie to the

south of town. Driving round among the rows of vines is a pleasure in itself, especially if you indulge in a bit of *dégustation*. The village of Gageac-et-Rouillac is home to **Clos d'Yvigne** (☏05 53 22 94 40; www.closdyvigne.com; Gageac et Rouillac), a small vineyard run by Patricia Atkinson, a British expat who moved to France in 1990. She arrived knowing next to nothing about winemaking; since then, she's tripled the vineyard's size and written about her experiences in two bestselling books. Phone ahead to make sure the vineyard's open.

Eating & Sleeping

Sarlat-la-Canéda ❶

✗ Le Grand Bleu — Gastronomic €€€

(☎05 53 29 82 14; www.legrandbleu.eu; 43 av de la Gare; menus €36-65; ⊙lunch Thu-Sun, dinner Tue-Sat) Run by head chef Maxime Lebrun, this Michelin-starred restaurant is known for creative cuisine that makes maximum use of luxury produce: truffles, lobster, turbot and St-Jacques scallops all feature, and every *menu* starts with a *mise-en-bouche* treat.

✗ Jardins de Harmonie — Traditional French €€

(☎05 53 31 06 69; www.lesjardinsdharmonie. com; mains €21-35, menus €22-48; ⊙lunch & dinner Thu-Mon) This upmarket restaurant has a gorgeous setting, with table lamps, crimson chairs and white linen crammed in between rough stone walls. The food is classic French with contemporary touches: foie gras with Madagascan vanilla, or duck breast smoked in tea.

⌂ Villa des Consuls — B&B €€

(☎05 53 31 90 05; www.villaconsuls.fr; 3 rue Jean-Jacques Rousseau; d €82-103, apt €124-184; @🛜) Despite its Renaissance exterior, the enormous rooms here are modern through and through, with shiny wood floors, sofas and original roof trusses. Self-catering apartments are dotted round town, all offering period plushness.

⌂ La Maison des Peyrat — Hotel €€

(☎05 53 59 00 32; www.maisondespeyrat.com; Le Lac de la Plane; r €56-103) This beautifully renovated 17th-century house, formerly a nun's hospital and later an aristocratic hunting lodge, is set on a hill about 1.5km from the town centre. The 11 generously sized rooms are plain, but ooze country charisma. The restaurant's very good, too.

La Roque Gageac ❹

✗ La Belle Étoile — Traditional French €€

(☎05 53 29 51 44; www.belleetoile.fr; Le Bourg; d €55-75, ste €130, menus €26-42; ⊙Apr-Oct; 🛜) A great place to eat (and stay) is this waterfront hotel-restaurant known for its sophisticated French food. Local specialities such as truffles, walnuts and foie gras feature heavily, and there's a vine-shaded terrace for when the weather's fine.

Bergerac ❼

✗ La Ferme de Biorne — Regional Cuisine €€

(☎05 53 57 67 26; www.biorne.com; menus €19-23; ⊙Tue-Sun Apr-Oct) This rural *ferme auberge* (farm restaurant), 12km northwest of Bergerac, raises its own birds for the restaurant table, including goose, quail and duck. Definitely book ahead. Cosy *gîtes* (€300 to €980 for four people) are also available.

✗ L'Imparfait — Regional Cuisine €€

(☎05 53 57 47 92; www.imparfait.com; 6-10 rue des Fontaines; menus €26-32; ⊙lunch & dinner) Chef Hervé Battiston has made this sweet little restaurant a real local favourite, thanks to artful French food served up in a pretty 12th-century cloister. It's popular, so reserve ahead.

⌂ Château les Merles — Boutique Hotel €€€

(☎05 53 63 13 42; www.lesmerles.com; d €150-200, ste €155-240, apt €225-340; @🛜🅿) Behind its 19th-century neoclassical façade, this boutique château 15km east of Bergerac is a study in modish minimalism, with elegantly monochrome rooms and a ravishing fusion restaurant (five-/eight-course *menu* £41/49). There's even a 9-hole golf course.

⌂ Château Les Farcies du Pech' — B&B €€

(☎06 30 19 53 20; www.vignoblesdubard. com; Hameau de Pécharmant; d €110; ⊙mid-Mar–mid-Nov) Part of a conglomerate of four renowned wineries, this beautiful château-vineyard is the choice for oenophiles. All five rooms scream rustic chic, with original stonework and hardwoods for vintage character. The owner, Marie, will gladly arrange tours of local vineyards.

Vézère Valley *Explore prehistory at Musée National de Préhistoire*

Cave Art of the Vézère Valley

36

The limestone caves of southwest France contain some of Europe's finest examples of prehistoric art. This tailored trip explores the most famous ones, including the frescos of the Grotte de Lascaux.

TRIP HIGHLIGHTS

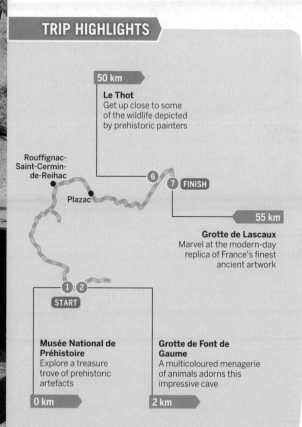

50 km

Le Thot
Get up close to some of the wildlife depicted by prehistoric painters

Rouffignac-Saint-Cermin-de-Reihac

Plazac

6

7 FINISH

55 km

Grotte de Lascaux
Marvel at the modern-day replica of France's finest ancient artwork

1 **2**

START

Musée National de Préhistoire
Explore a treasure trove of prehistoric artefacts

Grotte de Font de Gaume
A multicoloured menagerie of animals adorns this impressive cave

0 km

2 km

3 DAYS
196KM / 122 MILES

GREAT FOR...

BEST TIME TO GO

April to June, when most caves are open, but the summer crowds haven't arrived.

ESSENTIAL PHOTO

The minimalist façade of the Musée National de Préhistoire.

BEST FOR FAMILIES

The prehistoric zoo at Le Thot contains ancient animals such as bison, reindeer and ibex.

383

36 Cave Art of the Vézère Valley

This trip feels like catching a time capsule into the prehistoric past. Hidden deep underground in the murky caves of the Vézère and Lot Valleys, Cro-Magnon people left behind a spectacular legacy of ancient artworks, ranging from rock sculptures to multicoloured murals – and this is one of the few places in the world where it's possible to see their work up close.

TRIP HIGHLIGHT

❶ Les-Eyzies-de-Tayac

This small one-street tourist town is right in the middle of the Vézère Valley, 9km northwest of Sarlat-la-Canéda. Most of the area's major caves are within half-an-hour's drive, so it makes a useful base for exploring, and for a quick primer on prehistoric art there's nowhere better than the **Musée National de Préhistoire** (☎ 05 53 06 45 45; www.musee-prehistoire

-eyzies.fr; 1 rue du Musée; adult/child €5/3, 1st Sun of month free; ⏰9.30am-6pm, closed Tue), home to France's most comprehensive collection of prehistoric artefacts. Inside you'll find lots of fascinating Stone Age tools, weapons and jewellery, as well as animal skeletons and original rock friezes taken from the caves themselves: look out for the famous one of a bison licking its flank. Panels are mostly in French, but explanatory sheets in English are available.

🛏 p389

The Drive » To get to Font de Gaume from Les-Eyzies, follow the D47 east towards Sarlat, and look out for the brown signs pointing to Font de Gaume.

LINK YOUR TRIP

35 **Gourmet Dordogne**

It's easy to combine this trip with our gourmet guide to the Dordogne – take the D47 to Sarlat-la-Canéda.

38 **The Lot Valley**

From Cabrerets, you'll be roughly halfway along our Lot Valley route, 3km west of St-Cirq Lapopie and 32km east of Cahors.

TRIP HIGHLIGHT

➋ Grotte de Font de Gaume

Now you've got the background, it's time to see some real cave art. Just 1km northeast of Les-Eyzies is **Font de Gaume** (☎05 53 06 86 00; fontdegaume@monuments-nationaux.fr; adult/child €7.50/free; ⏰9.30am-5.30pm mid-May–mid-Sep, 9.30am-12.30pm & 2-5.30pm mid-Sep–mid-May, closed Sat year-round), an underground cavern that contains the only multicoloured paintings still open to the public. Around 14,000 years ago, the prehistoric artists created a gallery of over 230 animals, including reindeer, horses, mammoths and bears, as well as a dramatic 'Chapelle des Bisons' (Bison Chapel). Reservations are essential: the 45-minute tours are usually in French, but English tours are offered in summer.

The Drive » Continue along the D47 for 1km from Font de Gaume and turn off at the brown sign for the Grotte de Combarelles.

➌ Grotte des Combarelles

Prehistoric artists weren't just skilful painters – they also knew how to sculpt. About 1.5km further east of Font de Gaume, this narrow **cave** (☎05 53 06 86 00; fontdegaume@monuments-nationaux.fr; adult/child €7.50/free; ⏰same as Font de Gaume) contains many engravings that cleverly use the natural contours of the rock to sculpt the animals' forms: look out for mammoths, horses, reindeer and a mountain lion that seems to leap out from the rock face. The cave's walls are also covered with geometric symbols and shapes that have so far eluded interpretation. Six- to eight-person group tours last about an hour and can be reserved through the Font de Gaume ticket office.

The Drive » Travel 1km further east of Combarelles, then turn left onto the twisty D48. You'll travel into a pleasant wooded valley. Continue for 7km, following the road up the hillside towards the Cap Blanc car park. The museum entrance is a short walk downhill along a rough track.

➍ Abri du Cap Blanc

This ancient **sculpture gallery** (☎05 53 06 86 00; adult/child €7.50/free; ⏰10am-6pm mid-May–mid-Sep, 10am-noon & 2-6pm mid-Sep–mid-May, closed Sat year-round) makes a fascinating comparison with Combarelles. It was used as a natural shelter 14,000 years ago by Cro-Magnon people, who left behind an amazing 40m-long frieze of

DOZIER MARC/GETTY IMAGES ©

horses and bison, carved directly into the rear wall of the cave using flint tools. Originally the cave would have been open to the elements, but it's now housed inside a modern museum.

The Drive » Backtrack to Les-Eyzies, then follow the D47 northwest along the valley, turning right onto the D32 after about 11km. The road becomes narrower and travels through scrubby woodland. Follow the signs to the 'Grotte Préhistorique de Rouffignac' for another 7km.

- - - - - - - - - - - - -

⑤ Grotte de Rouffignac

After staying overnight in Les-Eyzies, get an early start at the astonishing **Grotte de Rouffignac** (☏05 53 05 41 71; www.grottederouffignac. fr; adult/child €6.50/4.20;

⏰9am-11.30am & 2-6pm Jul & Aug, 10am-11.30pm & 2-5pm rest of yr), often known as the 'Cave of 1000 Mammoths' thanks to its plethora of painted pachyderms. The paintings are spread along the walls of a subterranean cavern that stretches for 10km – fortunately, you visit aboard a rickety electric train, so there's no chance of getting lost. Along the way is an amazing frieze of 10 mammoths in procession. You'll also see many hollows in the cave floor, scratched out by long-extinct cave bears. Tickets are sold at the cave entrance; wrap up warm, as it's chilly below ground.

The Drive » From the Grotte de Rouffignac, retrace your route to the D32, and follow

---

DETOUR:
GROTTE DE PECH MERLE

Start: ① Les-Eyzies-de-Tayac

To complete your cave tour, it's worth taking the longish 92km trip southeast to the **Grotte de Pech-Merle** (☏05 65 31 27 05; www.pechmerle.com; adult/child €9/5; ⏰9.30-noon & 1.30-5pm Apr-Oct), one of only a handful of decorated caves to be discovered around the Lot Valley. It contains galleries of mammoths, goats and bison, as well as a famous panel featuring two dappled horses. Most haunting of all, the cave's walls are covered with human hand tracings, as well as a set of footprints, left behind by an adolescent artist between 15,000 BC and 10,000 BC.

Guided tours are in French, but explanatory sheets in English are available. Reserve ahead, as visitor numbers are limited to 700 per day.

Grotte de Lascaux Cave painting detail

PREHISTORY 101

If you're visiting the cave paintings around the Vézère, it helps to know a little about the artists who created them. Most of the paintings date from the end of the last ice age, between 20,000 BC and 10,000 BC, and were painted by Cro-Magnon people – descendants of the first *Homo erectus* settlers who arrived from North Africa between 700,000 BC and 100,000 BC.

Cro-Magnon people lived a hunter-gatherer lifestyle, using caves as temporary hunting shelters while they followed their prey (including mammoths, woolly rhinoceros, reindeer and aurochs, an ancestor of the modern cow).

Generally, they painted the animals they hunted using mineral paints derived from magnesium and charcoal (black), ochre (red/yellow) and iron (red). Although no one is certain what the purpose of the paintings was, it's assumed they served some kind of magical, religious or shamanic significance.

Painting seems to have ceased around 10,000 BC, about the same time that humans settled down to a more fixed lifestyle of farming and agriculture.

signs to Montignac, making turns onto the D6 and D45. Northeast of Thonac, turn onto the D706 and look out for the sign to Le Thot shortly afterwards.

- - - - - - - - - - - -

TRIP HIGHLIGHT

6 Le Thot

It's well worth visiting **Le Thot** (☑05 53 50 70 44; www.semitour.com; adult/child €7/4.50, joint ticket with Grotte de Lascaux €12.50/8.50; ◎10am-7pm Jul & Aug, 10am-6pm Apr-Jun & Sep-early Nov, 10am-12.30pm & 2-5.30pm rest of yr, closed Jan), where you can see some of the real-life beasts depicted by prehistoric artists – including reindeer, stags, horses, ibex and European bison. Sadly, though, you'll have to put

up with fibreglass models of extinct species such as woolly mammoths.

The Drive » Turn back onto the D706 and head towards Montignac, about 10km northeast. Once you reach town, cross the bridge and follow av du 4ème Septembre, then look out for brown signs to the Grotte de Lascaux, perched on a hilltop 1km south of town.

- - - - - - - - - - - -

TRIP HIGHLIGHT

7 Grotte de Lascaux

Sometimes known as the Sistine Chapel of cave art, the **Grotte de Lascaux** (☑05 53 51 95 03; www.semitour.com; adult/child €9.50/6; ◎9am-8pm Jul & Aug, 9.30am-6pm Apr-Jun & Sep-early Nov, 10am-12.30pm & 2-5.30pm rest of yr, closed Jan) is home to France's most

famous – and finest – prehistoric paintings.

The 600-strong menagerie is vividly depicted in shades of red, black, yellow and brown, ranging from reindeer, aurochs, mammoths and horses to a huge 5.5m-long bull, the largest cave drawing ever found.

The original cave has been closed to the public since 1963, but a painstaking replica has been created nearby. There are several guided tours every hour, including several in English. From April to October, tickets are sold *only* at the ticket office next to Montignac's tourist office.

Eating & Sleeping

Sarlat-la-Canéda

🛏 Plaza Madeleine   Hotel €€
(📞05 53 59 10 41; www.hoteldelamadeleine
-sarlat.com; 1 place de la Petite Rigaudie;
d €99-179; ❄🛜🛗) Smack bang in the centre
of town, this elegant shuttered hotel has
benefited from a much-needed decorative
overhaul, and it now offers an attractive mix of
modern and traditional. Classy rooms subtly
evoke a bygone era, with vintage phones and
shuttered windows, while a solarium and Finnish
sauna create a modern boutique feel.

🛏 Hôtel St-Albert   Boutique Hotel €
(📞05 53 31 55 55; www.hotel-saintalbert.eu;
place Pasteur; d €55-96; 🛜) A small, chic hotel
with the barest of boutique touches: chocolate-
and-cream tones and posh bath goodies make
it feel closer to a metropolitan crash pad than
an old-town *auberge*, but rooms are on the small
side.

Les-Eyzies-de-Tayac ❶

🛏 Hôtel des Glycines   Hotel €€
(📞05 53 06 97 07; www.les-glycines-dordogne.
com; 4 av de Laugerie; d €95-165, ste €195-235;
❄🛜🛗) Les-Eyzies' old post house has been
converted into this posh pad. Rooms range from
cream-and-check 'classics' to full-blown private
suites, complete with private terrace and
garden outlook. Avoid the 'courtyard rooms',
which overlook the main road out of Les-Eyzies.
The hotel's gastronomic restaurant (*menus*
from €45) is a suitably pampering affair –
gourmets should go for the *menu truffe* (€95).

🛏 Hôtel Le Cro-Magnon   Hotel €€
(📞05 53 06 97 06; www.hostellerie-cro-magnon.
com; 54 av de la Préhistoire; d €82-95; 🌣closed
Dec-Feb; 🛜🛗) This wisteria-clad hotel has
been around since the 1850s and was often
used as a base by pioneering prehistorians. It's
more modern these days. Although the flowery
rooms have a touch of the chain hotel about
them, the corridors built straight into the rock
face add quirky appeal. Dining is good value in
the beam-ceilinged restaurant.

Montignac ❻

🛏 Hostellerie la Roseraie   Hotel €€
(📞05 53 50 53 92; www.laroseraie-hotel.com;
11 place des Armes; d €85-185; 🌣Apr-Oct;
🛜🛗) The name's the giveaway: this mansion
in Montignac boasts its own gorgeous rose
garden, set around box-edged grounds and
a palm-tinged pool. Rococo rooms certainly
aren't cutting edge, but they're lovely if you like
rosy pinks, floral patterns and garden views.
Truffles, chestnuts, pork and guinea fowl find
their way onto the seasonal menu, and on warm
summer nights the canopy-shaded terrace is an
utter delight.

🛏 Hotel le Lascaux   Hotel €
(📞05 53 51 82 81; www.hotel-lascaux.jimdo.
com; 109 av Jean-Jaurès; d €62-92; 🛜) Despite
the old-timey candy-stripe awnings, rooms at
this family-owned hotel are bang up to date,
with cool colour schemes, distressed wood
furniture and sparkling bathrooms. The superior
rooms have more space, and some overlook the
shady back garden.

Rocamadour Piligrimage town clinging precariously to the cliffside

Dordogne's Fortified Villages

37

The Dordogne spoils for choice with its hilltop history. This trip links some of the region's distinctive bastides (fortified villages) and medieval castles, and takes in holy Rocamadour.

TRIP HIGHLIGHTS

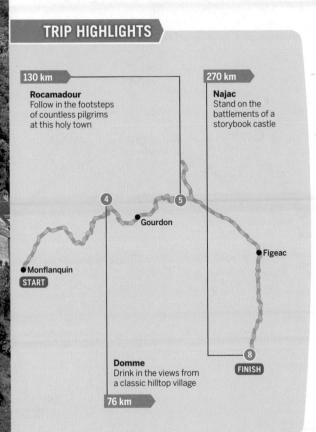

130 km

Rocamadour
Follow in the footsteps of countless pilgrims at this holy town

270 km

Najac
Stand on the battlements of a storybook castle

④

● Gourdon

⑤

● Figeac

● Monflanquin
START

Domme
Drink in the views from a classic hilltop village

⑧
FINISH

76 km

**5 DAYS
270KM / 168 MILES**

GREAT FOR...

BEST TIME TO GO

April to July, to make the most of the spring weather.

📷 **ESSENTIAL PHOTO**

Looking out across the Dordogne valley from Domme's spectacular *belvédère*.

✔ **BEST FOR HISTORY**

Najac's hilltop castle is a classic example of medieval military architecture.

37

Dordogne's Fortified Villages

The Dordogne may be a picture of tranquillity now, but during the Middle Ages it was frequently a battleground. The Dordogne River marked an important strategic frontier between English and French forces during the Hundred Years War, and the area's many châteaux and fortified villages remain as a reminder of this war-torn past. Most distinctive of all are the *bastide* towns, encircled by defensive walls and protected by sturdy ramparts.

❶ Monflanquin

Founded in 1256, this small *bastide* makes an excellent place to start your tour of France's defensive architecture. Founded in 1256, it has the classic *bastide* structure: a rectangular layout, a grid of straight streets, and an arcaded market square, with a church tucked into one corner. Originally the town would have also been ringed by ramparts, but these have long since been plundered. The central place des Arcades

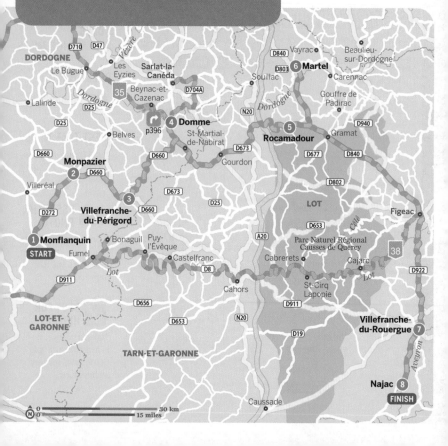

still hosts its weekly market on Thursday morning, just as it has done since the Middle Ages.

The Drive » The quickest route to Monpazier heads 22km northwest across quiet farmland, following the minor D272. You'll pass into woodland near Vergt-de-Biron, and then turn right onto the D2 towards Monpazier.

❷ Monpazier

Monpazier is perhaps the best example of *bastide* architecture in southwest France. It's crisscrossed by arrow-straight streets, all of which lead to the market square on **place Centrale**, lined by arcaded walkways and tall houses built from lemon-yellow stone. In one corner, there's an old *lavoir* that was still being used for washing

LINK YOUR TRIP

35 Gourmet Dordogne

Head north from Domme for 14km along the D46 to link up with our gastronomic road trip around the Dordogne.

38 The Lot Valley

This trip combines well with our route along the Lot Valley – just turn off at Figeac.

clothes right up to the end of the 19th century.

The town itself was founded in 1284 by a representative of Edward I (king of England and duke of Aquitaine). It had a turbulent time during the Wars of Religion and the Peasant Revolts of the 16th century, but despite numerous assaults it survived the centuries remarkably unscathed. Most unusually of all, its defensive walls are still largely intact.

The Drive » Take the D660 east from Monpazier, and follow it for 21km through the countryside.

❸ Villefranche-du-Périgord

The amber town of Villefranche-du-Périgord once occupied an important strategic position on the frontier between the historic regions of Agen and Quercy. It was founded in 1261 by Alphonse de Poitiers, a brother of the French king Louis IX, and still possesses most of its medieval layout, including the original arcaded square, pillared marketplace and fortified church, all of which date from the 13th century. It's a bit off the beaten track and a touch neglected in spots, which means its often much quieter than some of the area's better-known *bastides*.

The Drive » The drive to Domme is particularly pleasant, veering across hilltops and passing through oak and beech woodland. Start on the minor D57 towards Besse, turning onto the D60 at St-Pompont, followed by the D46 to Domme – it's just over 33km in all, or 40 minutes. Parking is tricky in the village, so leave your car outside the walls and walk up.

TRIP HIGHLIGHT

❹ Domme

For panoramic views, there's nowhere in the Dordogne that can top Domme. Teetering on an outcrop high above the river valley, this hilltop *bastide* still boasts most of its 13th-century ramparts as well as three original fortified gateways.

Approached via a tortuous switchback road from the valley below, it's the perfect defensive stronghold – a fact not lost on Philippe III of France, who founded the town in 1281 as a bastion against the English. The town's clifftop position is best appreciated from the esplanade du Belvédère and the adjacent promenade de la Barre, which both offer an unforgettable outlook across the valley.

🛏 p397

The Drive » The most pleasant route to Rocamadour travels southeast via the D46 and the towns of St-Martial-de-Nabirat and Gourdon. From here, pick up the twisty D673, which crosses underneath the A20 motorway. Soon afterwards there's a wonderful windy section with fine views across the Ouysse River and the cliffs around Rocamadour. Most of Rocamadour's car parks are above the old city in L'Hospitalet. All in, the journey covers 54km.

TRIP HIGHLIGHT

⑤ Rocamadour

Clinging precariously to a rocky cliffside, the holy town of Rocamadour looks like something out of *Lord of the Rings*. It's been an important pilgrimage destination since the Middle Ages thanks to the supposedly miraculous powers of its *Vierge Noire* (Black Madonna), which is now housed in the Chapelle de Notre Dame, one of several chapels that make up the town's **Sanctuaires** (Sanctuaries).

The old town itself (known as La Cité) consists of one long medieval thoroughfare, overflowing (just as in the pilgrims' day) with souvenir shops and touristy restaurants. One of the medieval gateways is still standing at the end of the Grande Rue.

From here, a stone staircase switchbacks up the cliff to the Sanctuaries, emerging next to Rocamadour's 14th-century **château** (admission €2; ⊙8am-9pm). During the Middle Ages, pilgrims would have climbed the steps on their knees as a demonstration of piety, but these days you can cheat by catching a combo lift and cable car.

The Drive ≫ From the town's main car parks in L'Hospitalet, head north along the D873 and follow the signs to Martel, 22km away.

⑥ Martel

Known as *la ville aux sept tours* (the town of seven towers) thanks to its turret-topped skyline, this delightful village was the ancient capital of the Vicomte de Turenne. It's crammed with fascinating architecture, best seen around the place de la Halle. The **covered market** still boasts many of its medieval roof beams, and one of the town's namesake towers can be seen above the **Palais de la Raymondi** (built for a 13th-century tax collector but now home to the village's tourist office). You'll spot the other towers as you wander round town, including **La Tour Tournemire**, a square tower which once served as a prison, and the **Cordeliers Tower**, the only remains of a 13th-century Franciscan monastery. Try to time your visit with the lively markets on Wednesday and Saturday.

🛏 p397

The Drive ≫ Spend the night in Martel, then pick up the D840

GUY CHRISTIAN/GETTY IMAGES ©

Martel Place de la Halle covered market

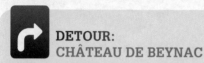

DETOUR:
CHÂTEAU DE BEYNAC

Start ④ Domme

The riverbanks of the Dordogne are lined with medieval châteaux, mostly built as defensive fortresses during the 12th and 13th centuries. One of the most dramatic is the **Château de Beynac** (www.beynac-en-perigord.com; Beynac-et-Cazenac; adult/child €7.50/3.20; ⏰10am-6pm or 7pm Apr-Oct, to 5pm Jan-Mar, closed Nov & early Dec), a clifftop castle 10km northwest of La Roque, protected by 200m cliffs, a double wall and double moat. From the battlements, there's a dizzying view over the picture-perfect village of **Beynac-et-Cazenac**, which featured in the Lasse Hallström movie *Chocolat* (2000), starring Johnny Depp and Juliette Binoche.

There are several other châteaux to explore nearby. Situated 4.5km southwest is the **Château de Castelnaud** (www.castelnaud.com/uk; adult/child €8.20/4.10; ⏰9am-8pm Jul & Aug, 10am-6pm or 7pm Feb-Jun & Oct–mid-Nov, 2-6pm mid-Nov–Jan), another quintessential castle that houses a museum of medieval warfare.

Another 4km further is the **Château de Milandes** (www.milandes.com; Castelnaud-la-Chapelle; adult/child €9/5.80; ⏰9.30am-7.30pm Jul & Aug, 10am-6.30pm or 7pm Apr-Jun & Sep-Oct), which was famously owned by the glamorous African-American music-hall star Josephine Baker (1906–75), who bought it in 1936.

all the way to Figeac, a historic riverside town that makes a good spot to stop for coffee and cake. From here, continue south on the D922 to Villefranche de Rouergue. Plan on covering the 95km in 1¾ hours.

⑦ Villefranche de Rouergue

Villefranche's origins as a *bastide* are barely recognisable beneath the modern roads and busy shopping streets – it's only once you get right into the old town that they become apparent. At the centre is the arcaded **place Notre Dame** – another typical example of a *bastide* square. Nearby is the square-pillared 15th-century

Collégiale Notre Dame, with its never-completed bell tower and choir stalls, ornamented with a menagerie of comical and cheeky figures.

The Drive » The D922 continues all the way to Najac, 23km south of Villefranche.

TRIP HIGHLIGHT

⑧ Najac

If you were searching for a film set for Camelot, you've found it. Najac's soaring hilltop **castle** (adult/child €4.50/3; ⏰10.30am-7pm Jul & Aug, 10.30am-1.30pm & 3-5pm, 6pm or 7pm Mar-Jun & Sep-Nov) looks as if it's fallen from the pages of a fairy tale: slender towers

and fluttering flags rise from the battlements, surrounded on every side by dizzying *falaises* (cliffs) dropping to the Aveyron River far below.

The castle is reached via a steep 1.2km-long cobbled street from **place du Faubourg**, the village's central square. It's a masterpiece of military planning: its clifftop position meant it was practically unassailable, and it became a key stronghold during the Middle Ages. Its architecture is beautifully preserved, and the view from the central keep is simply superb.

✕ ⛉ p397

Eating & Sleeping

Domme 4

La Guérinière   B&B €€

(📞05 53 29 91 97; www.la-gueriniere-dordogne.
com; Cénac et St-Julien; d €80-95; 🛜🅿)
Surrounded by 6-hectare grounds complete
with a tennis court, rooms at this family-friendly
chambre d'hôte are all named after flowers:
our faves are Mimosa, with its sloping roof and
Chinoiserie wardrobe, and the supersize Bleuet
room. Book ahead for the *table d'hôte* dinner
(€25 including wine), using mostly organic
produce. It's about 5km south of Domme along
the D46.

L'Esplanade   Hotel €€

(📞05 53 28 31 41; www.esplanade-perigord.
com; rue du Pont-Carral; d €120-160, menus €35-
70; ❄🛜) Teetering on the edge of Domme's
ramparts, this family-owned hotel has two main
selling points: a top-notch country restaurant
and truly mindboggling valley views. Rooms are
frilly and frippy, decorated in pastel shades and
upholstered armchairs.

Martel 6

Château de Termes   B&B €€

(📞05 65 32 42 03; www.chateau-de-termes.
com; St-Denis-lès-Martel; gîtes per night €59-110,
per week €250-490; 🅿) This family-friendly
gîte complex is set around a cute mini-château.
It has something to suit all needs: spacious,
countrified rooms, and two- to six-person *gîtes*
available nightly or by the week. It's very kid-
friendly – with badminton, ping-pong, skittles
and heated pool – and the owners can help
organise canoe hire and horse-riding trips.

Manoir de Malagorse   B&B €€€

(📞05 65 27 14 83; www.manoir-de-malagorse.
fr; Cuzance; d €150-180, ste €280-310) Situated
8km northwest of Martel in quiet Cuzance, this
period house is a chic combo of sleek lines,
soothing colours and fluffy fabrics: some rooms
feature worn roof trusses, others polished
wooden floors; all are gorgeous. The five-course
home-cooked dinner (€42) is superb.

Relais Sainte-Anne   Hotel €€€

(📞05 65 37 40 56; www.relais-sainte-anne.
com; d €95-155, ste €185-275; 🛜🅿) The pick
of places to stay in the village itself, with 16
individually decorated rooms that blend country
comforts with contemporary flair. Its restaurant
utilises produce directly from Martel's markets.

Najac 8

La Salamandre   Regional Cuisine €€

(📞05 65 29 74 09; rue du Barriou; menus
€18-36; ☺lunch & dinner Tue-Sun) Simple but
charming, this little restaurant is a treat for its
local dishes and wonderful panoramic terrace
overlooking the castle.

Oustal del Barry   Hotel €€

(📞05 65 29 74 32; www.oustaldelbarry.com;
place du Faubourg; s €49, d €59-77, menus €19-
43.50, cooking courses incl 4 nights half-board
€400; ❄) The best place to stay in Najac, a
wonderfully rustic *auberge*, with haphazard
rooms filled with trinkets and furniture to match
its timber-framed façade. Even if you're not
staying here, be sure to stop by its country
restaurant, renowned for its traditional
southwest cuisine.

St-Cirq-Lapopie *The Lot's famously photogenic hilltop village*

The Lot Valley

38

This scenic drive snakes along a plunging canyon carved out by the Lot River. It's bookended by the riverside towns of Figeac and Villeneuve-sur-Lot, and veers through wine country.

TRIP HIGHLIGHTS

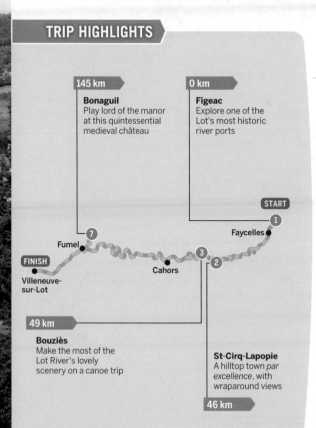

145 km

Bonaguil
Play lord of the manor at this quintessential medieval château

0 km

Figeac
Explore one of the Lot's most historic river ports

START

Faycelles

7 Fumel

FINISH

Villeneuve-sur-Lot

3
2

Cahors

49 km

Bouziès
Make the most of the Lot River's lovely scenery on a canoe trip

St-Cirq-Lapopie
A hilltop town *par excellence*, with wraparound views

46 km

3 DAYS
181KM / 113 MILES

GREAT FOR...

BEST TIME TO GO

March to June, when the valley's at its most tranquil.

ESSENTIAL PHOTO

Standing on top of St-Cirq-Lapopie's sky-top ruined château.

BEST FOR FAMILIES

Paddling down the Lot River in a canoe from Bouziès.

38 The Lot Valley

For river scenery, the Lot is right up there alongside the Loire and the Seine. Over countless millennia, it's carved its way through the area's soft lemon-yellow limestone, creating a landscape of canyons, ravines and cliffs, best seen on the zigzagging 80km-odd section between Figeac and Cahors. It's a journey to savour: take your time, pack a picnic and soak up the vistas.

TRIP HIGHLIGHT

❶ Figeac

The riverside town of Figeac has a rough-and-ready charm that makes a refreshing change after many of the Lot's prettified towns. Traffic buzzes along the river boulevards and the old town has an appealingly lived-in feel, with shady streets lined with ramshackle medieval and Renaissance houses, many with open-air galleries on the top floor (once used for drying leather).

Founded by Benedictine monks, the town was later an important medieval trading post and pilgrims' stopover.

Figeac is also famous as the birthplace of François Champollion (1790–1832), the Egyptologist and linguist whose efforts in deciphering the Rosetta Stone provided the key for cracking Egyptian hieroglyphics. Explore his story at the **Musée Champollion** (www.musee-champollion.fr; place Champollion; adult/child €5/2.50; ⊙10.30-12.30pm & 2-6pm Wed-Mon Apr-Jun, Sep & Oct, 10.30am-6pm daily Jul & Aug, 2-6pm Wed-Mon Nov-Mar).

🛏 p405

The Drive » The corkscrew drive west of Figeac along the D662 is a classic, tracking the course of the Lot River all the way to Cahors. The 46km stretch to St-Cirq-Lapopie is particularly scenic, at some points cut directly into the cliffside, at others snaking along the peaceful riverbanks. Take it slow and enjoy the drive.

- - - - - - - - - - - - - -

TRIP HIGHLIGHT

❷ St-Cirq-Lapopie

This famously photogenic hilltop village teeters at the crest of a sheer cliff, high above the Lot. It's a delightful tangle of red-roofed houses, cobbled streets and medieval buildings, many of which now house potteries and artists' studios. The village is essentially one long, steep main street; at the top is the ruined **château**, which has a magnificent viewing terrace that overlooks the whole Lot Valley. It's a magical setting, but be warned: if it's peace and tranquillity you're looking for, you won't find it in high summer.

There are two pricey car parks at the top of the village, but it's more sensible to take advantage of the free one at the bottom of the hill and follow the pedestrian trail up to the main street.

✗ 🛏 p405

LINK YOUR TRIP

31 Cheat's Compostela

This route intersects with our road-trip version of the Chemin de St-Jacques at Cahors and Figeac.

37 Dordogne's Fortified Villages

Our *bastide* tour begins at Monflanquin, 20km north of Villeneuve-sur-Lot.

The Drive » Head downhill from St-Cirq-Lapopie, cross the river and rejoin the D662. Bouziès is 3km west.

③ Bouziès

Just west of St-Cirq, this riverside hamlet is an ideal place to get out on the water – either on a boat cruise or under your own steam. **Les Croisères de St-Cirq-Lapopie** (📞05 65 31 72 25; www.lot-croisieres.com) runs regular river cruises on its small fleet of boats, including aboard an open-topped *gabarre,* a flat-bottomed barge that was once the traditional mode of river transport in this region of France.

Alternatively, if you prefer to act as your own captain, **Kalapca** (📞05 65 24 21 01; www.kalapca.com/uk; half-/full day €30/40) hires out kayaks and canoes, perfect for experiencing the gorgeous river scenery at your own pace. Trip lengths range from 4km to 22km; rates include minibus transport to your chosen start-point.

The Drive » The twisty route west to Cahors is another fine drive, travelling for 28km along the gorge and affording dramatic views nearly all the way. There are plenty of pleasant places to stop for a picnic by the river. Once you reach Cahors, follow signs to the 'Centre-Ville'. Parking is free along the river and on place Charles de Gaulle.

④ Cahors

Nestled in a U-shaped *boucle* (curve) in the Lot, Cahors is the area's main city. With its balmy weather and scarlet-stone buildings, it has the air of a sunbaked Mediterranean town. Pastel-coloured buildings line the shady squares of the old medieval quarter, crisscrossed by a labyrinth of alleyways, cul-de-sacs and medieval quays. It's also an important winegrowing area, with vineyards stretching out across the surrounding hills.

The town's main landmark is the impressive **Pont Valentré**, one of France's most iconic medieval bridges. Built as part of the town's defences in the 14th century, the parapets projecting from two of its three tall towers were designed to allow defenders to drop missiles on attackers below. It's also worth stepping inside the **Cathédrale St-Étienne**, Cahors' beautiful 12th-century cathedral, a harmonious blend of Romanesque and Gothic styles.

✕ ⟚ p405

The Drive » Head west of town via the D8, following signs to Luzech and Pradines.

GIUGLIO GIL/GETTY IMAGES ©

⑤ Luzech

Downstream from Cahors, the lower Lot twists its way through the rich **vineyards** of the Cahors AOC (Appellation d'Origine Contrôlée) region. It's up to you whether you wish to take advantage of the signs offering *dégustation* (tasting). Otherwise,

Figeac Visitors explore an exhibit at the Musée Champollion

carry on along the road, passing the dams at Luzech, whose medieval section sits at the base of a *donjon* (keep), and **Castelfranc**, with a dramatic suspension bridge.

The Drive » West of Luzech, stay on the minor D8, which hugs the south bank of the river. The road affords super vistas of the local vineyards and the river's many hairpin curves.

You'll reach Puy l'Évêque after 36km, or around 45 minutes' driving.

- - - - - - - - - - - - -

⑥ Puy l'Évêque

On a rocky hillside above the northern bank of the Lot, Puy l'Évêque was one of the most important medieval ports in the Lot Valley, and its quays are lined with once-grand merchants'

houses – some have been carefully restored; others are a little worse for wear. The old town is also well worth a stroll, with many fine stone mansions and tumbledown medieval buildings, best appreciated from the road bridge that spans the Lot just outside town.

The Drive » To get to the Château de Bonaguil, continue

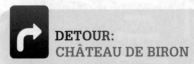

DETOUR:
CHÂTEAU DE BIRON

Start: **7** **Bonaguil**

If you enjoyed the castle architecture of Bonaguil, you might like to cut across country to the nearby **Château de Biron** (www.semitour.com; adult/child €7/4.50; ⊙10am-7pm Jul & Aug, 10am-5pm or 6pm Feb-Nov, closed Dec & Jan), a glorious mishmash of styles, having been fiddled with by eight centuries of successive heirs. It's particularly notable for its slate turrets, state rooms and double loggia staircase, supposedly modelled on one at Versailles; the oldest part of the castle is the 12th-century keep.

It's had mixed fortunes over the centuries, and was finally sold in the early 1900s to pay for the extravagant lifestyle of a particularly irresponsible heir. It's since featured in countless films, including Luc Besson's *Jeanne d'Arc* (Joan of Arc; 1999) and Bernard Tavernier's *La Fille d'Artagnan* (D'Artagnan's Daughter; 1994).

west along the D911 for 14km towards Fumel. About 1km east of town, there's a right turn onto the D673, signed to Gourdon/Bonaguil. Follow signs for another 8km, making sure not to miss the left turn onto the D158.

- - - - - - - - - -

TRIP HIGHLIGHT

7 Bonaguil

There's one unmistakeable reason to stop in the village of Bonaguil, and that's to wander round its imposing feudal **château** (📞05 53 71 90 33; www.bonaguil.org; St-Front-sur-Lémance; adult/child €7/4; ⊙10am-7pm Jul & Aug, 10am-12.30pm & 2-5.30pm or 6pm Mar-Jun & Sep-Oct, closed Nov-Feb), a fine example of late-15th-century military architecture, with towers, bastions, loopholes, machicolations and crenellations built directly into the limestone cliffs. Guided tours in English run several times daily in July and August.

The Drive » Loop back onto the D673, making a short detour via the pretty little village of St-Martin-le-Redon if you wish. Follow signs through Fumel onto the D911 all the way to Villeneuve-sur-Lot.

- - - - - - - - - -

8 Villeneuve-sur-Lot

Last stop on the trip is the river town of Villeneuve-sur-Lot, which began life as a *bastide* but has long since been swallowed up by more modern architecture. The centre of the old town is guarded by two medieval gateways, the **Porte de Paris** and the **Porte de Pujols** (the other six are no longer standing); in between runs the main thoroughfare of rue de Paris and the arcaded *bastide*-style square of place Lafayette, surrounded by shops and cafes. Along the river, look out for the **Pont Vieux**, a 13th-century bridge that was supposedly modelled on the Pont Valentré in Cahors, although its defensive towers have disappeared.

Eating & Sleeping

Figeac ❶

🛏 Hostellerie de l'Europe   Hotel €

(☏05 65 34 10 16; www.hotel-europe-figeac.
com; 51 allée Victor Hugo; r €59-75, half-
board per person €54-79, menus €14.50-34;
🕑restaurant lunch Sun-Thu, dinner Sat-Thu;
❄🛜🏊) This efficient Inter Hotel near the
river has an excellent restaurant, La Table de
Marinette. The half-board deals are great value.

🛏 Hôtel La Grézalide   Hotel €€

(☏05 65 11 20 40; www.grezalide.com; Grèzes;
d €77-157, tr €117-137, q €137-177; P🛜🏊)
This rural retreat is 21km west of Figeac near
Grèzes. It's in a 17th-century house set around
a courtyard garden and heated pool. Rooms are
full of period architecture, and the public rooms
are stuffed with sculptures (the owners are both
art aficionados).

St-Cirq-Lapopie ❷

🍴 Le Gourmet
Quercynois   Regional Cuisine €€

(☏05 65 31 21 20; www.restaurant-legourmet
quercynois.com; rue de la Peyrolerie; 🕑lunch &
dinner daily) The village's fanciest table, offering
a *menu* of biblical proportions, from *nougat de
porc* (pork medallions) to country *cassoulet*
(stew). The in-house deli sells treats including
cèpe mushrooms, gingerbread and chestnut
cake.

🛏 Auberge de Sombral   Hotel €

(☏05 65 31 26 08; www.lesombral.com;
r €52-80, menus lunch €15-22, dinner €28.50;
🕑restaurant lunch daily, dinner Fri & Sat; 🛜) In
the centre of St-Cirq-Lapopie is this treacle-
stoned house with seven cosy doubles and a
titchy attic room. The restaurant offers tasty
Quercy cuisine.

🛏 Hôtel Le Saint Cirq   Hotel €€

(☏05 65 30 30 30; www.hotel-lesaintcirq.com;
Tour de Faure; d €68-118, ste €140-160) This
luxurious hotel in Tour de Faure boasts fine
views of St-Cirq-Lapopie. The traditional rooms
are lovely, with tiled floors and French windows
onto the garden, but it's the 'Seigneurale'
rooms which really dazzle: sunken baths,
slate bathrooms and all. It's about 1km east of
St-Cirq.

Cahors ❹

🍴 Le Bergougnoux   Traditional French €

(☏05 65 35 62 92; 77 Rue Bergougnoux;
menus lunch €12, dinner €16; 🕑lunch & dinner
daily) Country cuisine *à la grande mère* is the
speciality of this homely eatery, secreted along
a backstreet in the old town. Sophisticated it
isn't, but for *pot au feu* (hot-pot) or *suprême de
poulet* (creamy chicken), it's just the ticket.

🍴 Le Marché   Fusion €€

(☏05 65 35 27 27; www.restaurantlemarche.
com; 27 place Jean-Jacques Chapon; menus
lunch €16-19, dinner €23-40; 🕑lunch & dinner
Tue-Sat) This contemporary restaurant dabbles
in French-meets-fusion flavours such as satay
tuna and roast beef in soy marinade.

🛏 Hôtel Jean XXII   Hotel €

(☏05 65 35 07 66; www.hotel-jeanxxii.com; 2
rue Edmond-Albé; s €51, d €62-69, tr €76; 🛜)
Next to the Tour Jean XXII, this excellent little
hotel mixes original stone and wood with a dash
of metropolitan minimalism.

🛏 Grand Hôtel Terminus   Hotel €€

(☏05 65 53 32 00; www.balandre.com; 5 av
Charles de Freycinet; d €77-100, ste €130-160,
menus €18-75; 🕑lunch Tue-Sat, dinner daily;
❄🛜) Built c 1920, Cahors' venerable station
hotel evokes an air of faded grandeur. Its
chandelier-lit restaurant, Le Balandre, serves
classic French food and runs cooking courses.

La Rochelle Arcaded walkways and luminous limestone façades

Classic Trip

Atlantic to Med

39

Salty Atlantic ports, pristine mountain vistas, the heady bouquet of fine wine, reminders of Rome and Hollywood glam: this classic trip from sea to sea takes you through the best of southern France.

TRIP HIGHLIGHTS

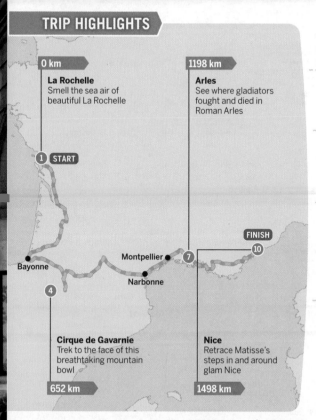

0 km

La Rochelle
Smell the sea air of beautiful La Rochelle

1198 km

Arles
See where gladiators fought and died in Roman Arles

1 START

Bayonne

4

Montpellier **7**

Narbonne

FINISH **10**

Cirque de Gavarnie
Trek to the face of this breathtaking mountain bowl

652 km

Nice
Retrace Matisse's steps in and around glam Nice

1498 km

10 DAYS
1498KM / 931 MILES

GREAT FOR...

BEST TIME TO GO

Spring or autumn, for fine weather without the summer crowds.

📷 ESSENTIAL PHOTO

Pose like a film star on the steps of Palais des Festivals et des Congrès in Cannes.

☑ BEST FOR FAMILIES

La Rochelle, with child-friendly attractions and stunning looks.

Classic Trip

39 Atlantic to Med

In May the film starlets of the world pour into Cannes to celebrate a year of movie-making. Let them have their moment of glam – by the time you've finished scaling Pyrenean highs, chewing Basque tapas, acting like a medieval knight in a turreted castle and riding to the moon in a spaceship, you too will have the makings of a prize-winning film.

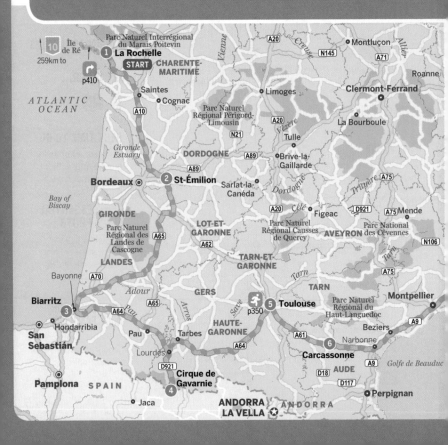

1 La Rochelle

Known as La Ville Blanche (the White City), La Rochelle is home to luminous limestone façades, arcaded walkways, half-timbered houses and ghoulish gargoyles glowing in the bright coastal sunlight. One of France's foremost seaports from the 14th to the 17th century, it remains a great seafaring centre and one of the most attractive cities in France.

There are several **defensive towers** (adult/child €8.50/free; ⏰10am-6.30pm) around the harbour area that once served to protect the town at night in times of war. They can be climbed for stunning views.

La Rochelle's number-one tourist attraction is the state-of-the-art **aquarium** (www.aquarium -larochelle.com; quai Louis Prunier; adult/child €14.50/11; ⏰9am-11pm). Highlights include UFO-like rays and fearsome sharks, teeth-gnashing piranhas, timid turtles and the bizarre half-newt, total fish mudskippers.

✗ ⏚ p415

The Drive » Using the main A10 toll road it's 187km (about 2½ hours) to St-Émilion. Turn off the A10 at exit 39a, signed for Libourne. Skirt this industrial town and follow the D243 into St-Émilion.

2 St-Émilion

Built of soft honey-coloured rock, the medieval village of St-Émilion produces some of the world's finest red wines. Visiting this pretty town, and partaking in some of the tours and activities on offer, is the easiest way to get under the (grape) skin of Bordeaux wine production.

The tourist office runs several **guided**

LINK YOUR TRIP

10 Breton Coast

The wind-swept coast of Brittany is a wild tonic to the south's refined atmosphere. Drive three hours north of La Rochelle to pick up the trip in Vannes.

23 The Corniches

Starting in Nice, where this trip ends, the Corniches drive takes you through the glitz and glamour of the French Riviera.

Classic Trip

tours (adult/child €7-14/free) as well as two-hour afternoon **château visits** (adult/child €14/free). Be sure to reserve ahead.

The Drive » The obvious route from St-Émilion to Biarritz is down the N10 via Bordeaux, but it's likely to be slow going for the next couple of years thanks to major road works. Instead, take the D670 to Sauveterre-de-Guyenne, the D672 to Langon, the A65 to Mont-de-Marson and the D824 toward Dax before joining the A63 to Biarritz. It's 257km (about 3½ hours).

❸ Biarritz

This coastal town is as ritzy as its name makes out. Biarritz boomed as a resort in the mid-19th century due to the regular visits by Napoléon III and his Spanish-born wife, Eugénie. Along its rocky coastline are architectural hallmarks of this golden age, and the belle époque and art deco eras that followed.

Biarritz is all about its fashionable beaches, especially the central **Grande Plage** and **Plage Miramar**. In the heat of summer, you'll find them packed end to end with sun-loving bathers.

The Drive » It's 208km (2¾ hours) to the village of Gavarnie. Take the A64 toll road, turn off at exit 11 and take the D940 to Lourdes (worth a look for its religious Disneyland feel), then continue south along the D913 and D921.

TRIP HIGHLIGHT

❹ Cirque de Gavarnie

The Pyrenees certainly doesn't lack impressive scenery, but your first sight of the Cirque de Gavarnie is guaranteed to raise a gasp. This breathtaking mountain amphitheatre is one of the region's most famous sights, sliced by thunderous waterfalls

DETOUR: ÎLE DE RÉ

Start ❶ La Rochelle

Bathed in the southern sun, drenched in a languid atmosphere and scattered with villages of green-shuttered, whitewashed buildings with red Spanish-tile roofs, Île de Ré is one of the most delightful places on the west coast of France. The island spans just 30km from its most easterly and westerly points, and just 5km at its widest section. But take note: the secret's out and in high season it can be almost impossible to move around and even harder to find a place to stay.

On the northern coast about 12km from the toll bridge that links the island to La Rochelle is the quaint fishing port of **St-Martin-de-Ré**, the island's main town. Surrounded by 17th-century fortifications (you can stroll along most of the ramparts), the port town is a mesh of streets filled with craft shops, art galleries and sea-spray ocean views.

The island's best **beaches** are along the southern edge – including unofficial naturist beaches at **Rivedoux Plage** and **La Couarde-sur-Mer** – and around the western tip (northeast and southeast of Phare-des-Baleines). Many beaches are bordered by dunes that have been fenced off to protect the vegetation.

From La Rochelle it's 24km and a half-hour drive to St-Martin-de-Ré via a very expensive toll bridge (€8 mid-September to mid-June, €16 mid-June to mid-September).

and ringed by sawtooth peaks, many of which top out at over 3000m.

There are a couple of large car parks in the village of Gavarnie, from where it's about a two-hour walk to the amphitheatre. Wear proper shoes, as snow lingers along the trail into early summer. Between Easter and October you can clip-clop along on a horse or donkey (around €25 for a round-trip).

The Drive » Retrace your steps to Lourdes, then take the N21 toward Tarbes and veer off onto the A64 toll road to reach Toulouse. It takes nearly three hours to cover the 228km.

⑤ **Toulouse**

Elegantly situated at the confluence of the Canal du Midi and the Garonne River, the vibrant southern city of Toulouse is often known as La Ville Rose, a reference to the distinctive hot-pink stone used to build many of its buildings.

Toulouse's magnificent main square, **place du Capitole**, is the city's literal and metaphorical heart. To the south of the square is the city's **Vieux Quartier** (Old Quarter), a tangle of lanes and leafy squares.

The sky's the limit at the fantastic **Cité de l'Espace** (☎08 20 37 72 33; www.cite-espace.com/ en; av Jean Gonord; adult €19.50-23, child €14-15;

🕗9.30am-7pm mid-Jul–Aug, 9.30am-5pm or 6pm Sep-Dec & Feb–mid-Jul, closed Jan). Since WWII, Toulouse has been the centre of France's aerospace industry, developing many important aircraft (including Concorde and the Airbus A380) as well as components for many international space programs. The museum brings this interstellar industry vividly to life through hands-on exhibits including a shuttle simulator, a planetarium, a 3-D cinema and a simulated observatory.

For more on the city, see p350.

✕ 🍽 p415

The Drive » It's an easy 95km (one hour) down the fast A61 to Carcassonne. Notice how the vegetation becomes suddenly much more Mediterranean about 15 minutes out of Toulouse.

⑥ **Carcassonne**

Perched on a rocky hilltop and bristling with zigzagging battlements, stout walls and spiky turrets, from afar the fortified city of Carcassonne looks like something out of a children's storybook and is most people's perfect idea of a medieval castle.

Today around four million tourists a year stream through the city gates in search of knights in armour and damsels

in distress. Instead they find a lot of tacky souvenir shops. Even so, this is a fascinating place to explore, and, when it's bathed in afternoon sunshine and highlighted by dark clouds, Carcassonne is simply breathtaking.

The Drive » Continue down the A61 to the Catalan-flavoured town of Narbonne, where you join the A9 (which can get very busy in summer) and head east to Nîmes. From there the A54 will take you into Arles. Allow just over two hours to cover the 223km and expect lots of toll booths.

TRIP HIGHLIGHT

⑦ **Arles**

Arles' poster boy is the celebrated impressionist painter Vincent van Gogh. If you're familiar with his work, you'll be familiar with Arles: the light, the colours, the landmarks and the atmosphere, all faithfully captured. But long before Van Gogh rendered this grand Rhône River locale on canvas, the Romans valued its worth. Today it's the reminders of Rome that are probably the town's most memorable attractions.

At **Les Arènes** (Amphithéâtre; adult/child incl Théâtre Antique €6.50/ free; 🕗9am-7pm) slaves, criminals and wild animals (including giraffes) met their dramatic demise before a jubilant 20,000-strong

WHY THIS IS A CLASSIC TRIP
STUART BUTLER, AUTHOR

The scenic highlight of this trip is undoubtedly the Pyrenees. Many people would say that the Cirque de Gavarnie is, if you'll excuse the pun, the high point, but for an even more heart-wrenching view try the nearby Cirque de Troumouse. To reach it involves a stomach-churning drive that's absolutely not for vertigo sufferers. The turnoff is signed near the village of Gèdre, 6.5km north of Gavarnie.

Top: Canal du Midi, Carcassonne
Left: Rue St-Ferréol, Marseille
Right: Les Arènes, Arles

crowd during Roman gladiatorial displays.

The **Théâtre Antique** (☎04 90 96 93 30; bd des Lices, enter on rue de la Calade; admission incl in Amphithéâtre ticket; ⏱9am-7pm), which dates from the 1st century BC, is still regularly used for alfresco concerts and plays.

✗ ⇋ p415

The Drive » From Arles take the scenic N568 and A55 route into Marseille. It's 88km (an hour's drive) away.

- - - - - - - - - - - - - -

8 Marseille

With its history, fusion of cultures, *souq*-like markets, millennia-old port and *corniches* (coastal roads) along rocky inlets and sun-baked beaches, Marseille is a captivating and exotic city.

Ships have docked for more than 26 centuries at the city's birthplace, the colourful Vieux Port (Old Port), and it remains a thriving harbour to this day. Guarding the harbour are **Bas Fort St-Nicolas** on the south side and, across the water, **Fort St-Jean**, founded in the 13th century by the Knights Hospitaller of St John of Jerusalem. At the time of writing, the national **Musée des Civilisations de l'Europe et de la Méditerranée** (Museum of European & Mediterranean Civilisations;

Classic Trip

📞04 96 13 80 90; www.
musee-europemediterranee.
org; ⏰1-7pm Wed, Thu & Sat)
was getting set to open a
brand-new 40,000-sq-m
state-of-the-art museum
here in 2013.

From the Vieux
Port, hike up to the
fantastic history-woven
quarter of **Le Panier**,
dubbed Marseille's
Montmartre as much
for its sloping streets
as its artsy ambience.
It's a mishmash of lanes
hiding artisan shops,
ateliers (workshops) and
terraced houses strung
with drying washing.

The Drive » To get from
Marseille to Cannes take the
northbound A52 and join the
A8 toll road just east of Aix-en-
Provence. It's 181km and takes
just under two hours.

⑨ Cannes

The eponymous film
festival only lasts for
two weeks in May, but
thanks to regular visits
from celebrities the buzz
and glitz are in Cannes
year-round.

The imposing **Palais
des Festivals et des
Congrès** (Festival Palace;
bd de la Croisette; guided
tours adult/child €3/free)
is the centre of the
glamour. Climb the red
carpet, walk down the
auditorium, tread the
stage and learn about
cinema's most prestigious
event on a **guided tour**
(adult/child €3/free; ⏰2.30pm
Jun-Apr). The 1½-hour
tourist-office-run tours
take place several times a
month, except in May.

The Drive » Leave the
motorways behind and weave
along the D6007 to Nice, taking
in cliffs framing turquoise
Mediterranean waters and the
yachties' town of Antibes. It's

31km and, on a good day, takes
45 minutes.

TRIP HIGHLIGHT

⑩ Nice

'Most people come here
for the light. Me, I'm from
the north. What moved
me are January's radiant
colours and luminosity of
daylight.' The words are
Matisse's, but they could
be those of any painter –
or, in fact, of any visitor
who comes to Nice, for
it's true: the light here
is magical. The city has
a number of world-class
sights, but the star
attraction is probably the
city itself. Atmospheric,
beautiful and photogenic,
it's a wonderful place to
stroll or watch the world
go by, so make sure you
leave yourself plenty of
time to soak it all in.

For more on the city,
see p310.

✗ p415

DETOUR:
AIX-EN-PROVENCE

Start ⑦ Arles

Aix-en-Provence is to Provence what the Left Bank is to Paris: an enclave of bourgeois-
bohemian chic. Art, culture and architecture abound here. A stroller's paradise, the
highlight is the mostly pedestrian old city, **Vieil Aix**. South of cours Mirabeau, **Quartier
Mazarin** was laid out in the 17th century, and is home to some of Aix's finest buildings.
Place des Quatre Dauphins, with its fish-spouting **fountain** (1667), is particularly
enchanting. Further south still is the peaceful **parc Jourdan**, home to the town's
Boulodrome Municipal, where locals gather beneath plane trees to play *pétanque*.

From Arles it's a simple 77km (one-hour) drive down the A54 toll road to Aix-en-
Provence. To rejoin the main route take the A51 and A7 for 32km (30 minutes) to
Marseille.

Eating & Sleeping

La Rochelle ❶

🍴 Le Soleil Brille Pour
Tout Le Monde   International, Vegetarian €

(📞05 46 41 11 42; 13 rue des Cloutiers; menus/
mains from €13/9.50; 🕑lunch & dinner Tue-
Sat; 🍴) There's a distinctly bohemian air to
this excellent little place, decked out in hippy
colours. Some highly original dishes originate
from the kitchen, many of them inspired by
the tropical French islands of Réunion and
Martinique.

🛏 Trianon de la Plage   Historic Hotel €€

(📞05 46 41 21 35; www.hoteltrianon.com; 6 rue
de la Monnaie; r €80-111,; 🕑closed Jan; P🛜) A
fading world of art deco stained-glass windows,
curly-whirly staircases, a grand dining room and
multihued rooms dominate this character-laden
hotel. The in-house restaurant (mains €15 to
€18) has well-priced, high-quality meals.

Toulouse ❺

🍴 Chez Navarre   Regional Cuisine €€

(📞05 62 26 43 06; 49 Grande Rue Nazareth;
menus €13-20; 🕑lunch & dinner Mon-Fri) Fancy
rubbing shoulders with the locals? Then this
wonderful *table d'hôte* is definitely the place,
with honest Gascon cuisine served up beneath
a creaky beamed ceiling at communal candlelit
tables.

🛏 Les Bains Douches   Hotel €€€

(📞05 62 72 52 52; www.hotel-bainsdouches.
com; 4 & 4bis rue du Pont Guilhemery; d €140-
210, ste €280-330; ✳) If it's style you want, it's
style you'll find at this ubercool establishment:

shimmering chrome, sleek surfaces, statement
light fittings and a salon-bar that wouldn't
look out of place in Paris' more fashionable
arrondissements.

Arles ❼

🍴 Le Cilantro   Provençal €€€

(📞04 90 18 25 05; www.restaurantcilantro.com;
31 rue Porte de Laure; mains €41; 🕑lunch Tue-
Fri, dinner Tue-Sat; 🍴) Chef Jérome Laurant, a
born-and-bred local lad, runs this hot spot and
combines local ingredients with world spices
to create accomplished dishes from local beef,
fish and duck.

🛏 Hôtel de
l'Amphithéâtre   Historic Hotel €€

(📞04 90 96 10 30; www.hotelamphitheatre.fr;
5-7 rue Diderot; s/d/tr/q from €57/67/117/137;
✳@🛜) Crimson, chocolate, terracotta and
other rich earthy colours dress the exquisite
17th-century stone structure of this stylish
hotel, with narrow staircases, roaring fire and
alfresco courtyard breakfasts.

Nice ❿

🍴 Le Chantecler   Gastronomic €€€

(📞04 93 16 64 00; www.hotel-negresco-nice.
com; Le Negresco, 37 promenade des Anglais;
menus €90, mains €55-68; 🕑dinner Wed-Sun,
lunch Sun) Make sure you're in a grand mood if
you're going to splash out at this two-Michelin-
star restaurant: every dish is the most exquisite
creation, both in cuisine and presentation,
and there's a seemingly endless succession of
appetisers, palate cleansers and petits fours.

STRETCH YOUR LEGS
BORDEAUX

Start/Finish Cathédrale St-André

Distance 5km

Duration 1½ hours

Bordeaux looks good. In fact it looks so good that it has been granted World Heritage status. With pedestrian-friendly streets and stately architecture, this is a city made for exploring on foot. This walking tour reveals the city at its finest.

Take this walk on Trips

Cathédrale St-André

Lording over the city, the cathedral dates from 1096, but most of what you see today was built in the 13th and 14th centuries. Next door is the gargoyled, 50m-high Gothic belfry, **Tour Pey-Berland** (adult/child €5.50/free; ⊘10am-1.15pm & 2-6pm Jun-Sep, shorter hours rest of year), erected between 1440 and 1466.

The Walk ≫ Head up rue Elisée Reclus and turn right to enter the small but elegant Jardin de la Mairie, where you'll find the Musée des Beaux-Arts.

Musée des Beaux-Arts

The evolution of Occidental art from the Renaissance to the mid-20th century is on view at this **museum** (20 cours d'Albret; ⊘11am-6pm mid-Jul–mid-Aug). Occupying two wings of the 1770s-built Hôtel de Ville (city hall), the museum was established in 1801; highlights include 17th-century Flemish, Dutch and Italian paintings.

The Walk ≫ Continue down cours d'Albret, across place Gambetta and onto cours Georges Clemenceau. At place Tourny turn left onto rue Fondaudège and then take the second right.

Jardin Public

For art of a different sort take a stroll through these gorgeous **gardens** (cours de Verdun). On sunny days it can seem as though half of Bordeaux has come to feed the ducks here.

The Walk ≫ Exit the park via cours de Verdun, then head down cours du Maréchal Foch, turn left onto rue Ferrére and continue to CAPC.

CAPC Musée d'Art Contemporain

Built in 1824 as a warehouse for French colonial produce such as coffee, cocoa, peanuts and vanilla, the cavernous Entrepôts Lainé building creates a dramatic backdrop for cutting-edge modern art at the **CAPC** (rue Ferrére, Entrepôt 7; ⊘11am-6pm Tue & Thu-Sun, to 8pm Wed). The contrast between the works on display here and those in the Musée des Beaux-Arts could hardly be greater.

The Walk >> Follow the river along the quai des Chartrons to the esplanade des Quincones. Walk through this square, past the Girondins monument, and continue 100m down cours du 30 Juillet to the Maison du Vin de Bordeaux.

Bar du Vin

Time for a drink? In Bordeaux there's only one place to wet the whistle. Wine's holy of holies, the **Bar du Vin** (3 cours du 30 Juillet; glasses of wine from €2; ⏰11am-10pm Mon-Sat), inside the hallowed **Maison du Vin de Bordeaux**, is the place to come for a tipple with people who really know their wine from their beer.

The Walk >> With a wine-induced skip in your step continue 150m down Bordeaux's swankiest street to the magnificent Grand Théâtre.

Grand Théâtre

Designed by Victor Louis (of Chartres cathedral fame), this 18th-century theatre is a breathtaking venue for operas, ballets and classical-music concerts. Guided behind-the-scenes

tours of the building (€3) are possible on Wednesday and Saturday afternoons at 3pm, 4pm and 5pm.

The Walk >> Turn left behind the theatre and walk down the attractive cours du Chapeau Rouge, home to a number of decent restaurants. Turn right and walk along the waterfront to place de la Bourse.

Place de la Bourse & Quai de la Douane

Surrounded by magisterial public buildings that attest to Bordeaux's 18th-century wealth is the **place de la Bourse**. Opposite, the quai de la Douane has been given a facelift and now incorporates playgrounds and a wafer-thin 'swimming pool' that hot and sticky young Bordelaise roll about in during summer.

The Walk >> Head up rue Fernand Philippart to place du Parlement with its numerous cafes, then weave along rue du pas-St-George, rue St-Siméon and rue de la Merci to turn left onto rue de Cheverus and back to the cathedral.

417

ROAD TRIP ESSENTIALS

France Driving Guide

With stunning landscapes, superb highways and one of the world's most scenic and comprehensive secondary road networks, France is a road-tripper's dream come true.

DRIVING LICENCE & DOCUMENTS

Drivers must carry the following at all times:

➡ passport or an EU national ID card

➡ valid driving licence (*permis de conduire*; most foreign licences can be used in France for up to a year)

➡ car-ownership papers, known as a *carte grise* (grey card)

➡ proof of third-party liability *assurance* (insurance)

An International Driving Permit (IDP) is not required when renting a car but can be useful in the event of an accident or police stop, as it translates and vouches for the authenticity of your home licence.

Road Trip Websites

AUTOMOBILE ASSOCIATIONS

RAC (www.rac.co.uk/driving-abroad/france) Info for British drivers on driving in France.

CONDITIONS & TRAFFIC

Bison Futé (www.bison-fute.equipement.gouv.fr)

Les Sociétés d'Autoroutes (www.autoroutes.fr)

ROUTE MAPPING

Mappy (www.mappy.fr)

Via Michelin (www.viamichelin.com)

INSURANCE

Third-party liability insurance *(assurance au tiers)* is compulsory for all vehicles in France, including cars brought from abroad. Normally, cars registered and insured in other European countries can circulate freely. Contact your insurance company before leaving home to make sure you're covered, and to verify whom to call in case of a breakdown or accident.

In a minor accident with no injuries, the easiest way for drivers to sort things out with their insurance companies is to fill out a *Constat Amiable d'Accident Automobile* (accident report), a standardised way of recording important details about what happened. In rental cars it's usually in the packet of documents in the glove compartment. Make sure the report includes any proof that the accident was not your fault. If it *was* your fault you may be liable for a

Local Expert: Driving Tips

France driving tips from Bert Morris, Research Consultant for IAM (www.iam.org. uk) and former Motoring Policy Director for the AA:

➡ First thing if you're British: watch your instinct to drive on the left. Once I was leaving a supermarket using the left-turn exit lane. I turned by instinct into the left lane of the street and nearly had a head-on collision. My golden rule: when leaving a parking lot, petrol station or motorway off-ramp, do it on the right and your instinct to stay right will kick in.

➡ French law says to give way to traffic on the right, even when you're on a main road. So I advise people to ease off on the foot whenever you get to a junction.

➡ Never go below a third of a tank, even if you think there's cheaper petrol further down the road; sometimes the next station's a long way off. My approach is, don't fret about cost; you're on holiday!

hefty insurance deductible/excess. Don't sign anything you don't fully understand. If necessary, contact the **police** (☑17).

French-registered cars have their insurance-company details printed on a little green square affixed to the windscreen (windshield).

HIRING A CAR

To hire a car in France, you'll need to be older than 21, with an international credit card. Drivers under 25 usually must pay a surcharge.

All car-hire companies provide mandatory third-party liability insurance, but prices and conditions for collision-damage waiver insurance (CDW, or *assurance tous risques*) vary greatly from company to company. Purchasing the CDW can substantially reduce the *franchise* (deductible/excess) that you'll be liable for if the car is damaged or stolen, but car-hire companies sometimes charge exorbitant rates for this protection; if you travel frequently, sites like insurance4carhire.com may provide a cheaper alternative. Your credit card may also cover CDW if you use it to pay for the rental; verify conditions and details with your card issuer.

Arranging your car hire from home is usually considerably cheaper than a walk-in rental, but beware of online offers that don't include CDW or you may be liable for up to 100% of the car's value.

Be sure your car has a spare tyre (it's not uncommon for rentals to be missing these).

International car-hire companies:

Avis (www.avis.com)

Budget (www.budget.com)

Europcar (www.europcar.com)

Hertz (www.hertz.fr)

National-Citer (www.nationalcar.com)

Sixt (www.sixt.com)

French car-hire companies:

ADA (www.ada.fr)

DLM (www.dlm.fr)

France Cars (www.francecars.fr)

Locauto (www.locauto.fr)

Renault Rent (www.renault-rent.com)

Rent a Car Système (www.rentacar.fr)

Internet-based discount brokers:

Auto Europe (www.autoeurope.com)

DriveAway Holidays (driveaway.com.au)

Easycar (www.easycar.com)

Holiday Autos (www.holidayautos.co.uk)

Rental cars with automatic transmission are rare in France; book well ahead for these.

For insurance reasons, rental cars are usually prohibited on ferries, for example to Corsica.

BRINGING YOUR OWN VEHICLE

Any foreign motor vehicle entering France must display a sticker or licence plate identifying its country of registration. Right-hand-drive vehicles brought from the UK or Ireland must have deflectors affixed to the headlights to avoid dazzling oncoming traffic.

MAPS

Michelin's excellent, detailed regional driving maps are highly recommended as a companion to this book, as they will help you navigate back roads and explore alternative routes; IGN's maps are ideal for more specialised activities such as hiking and cycling. Look for both at newsagents, bookshops, airports, supermarkets, tourist offices and service stations along the autoroute.

➡ **Institut Géographique National** (IGN; www.ign.fr) Publishes regional fold-out maps as well as an all-France volume, *France – Routes, Autoroutes*. Has a great variety of 1:50,000-scale hiking maps, specialised

cyclocartes (cycling maps) and themed maps showing wine regions, museums etc.
➡ **Michelin** (boutiquecartesetguides.miche lin.fr) Sells excellent, tear-proof yellow-orange 1:200,000-scale regional maps tailor-made for cross-country driving, with precise coverage of smaller back roads.

ROADS & CONDITIONS

France has one of Europe's densest highway networks. There are four types of intercity roads:

➡ **Autoroutes** (highway names beginning with A) Multilane divided highways, usually with tolls *(péages)*. Generously outfitted with rest stops.

➡ **Routes Nationales** (N, RN) National highways. Some sections have divider strips.

Road Distances (KM)

	Bayonne	Bordeaux	Brest	Caen	Cahors	Calais	Chambéry	Cherbourg	Clermont-Ferrand	Dijon	Grenoble	Lille	Lyon	Marseille	Nantes	Nice	Paris	Perpignan	Strasbourg	Toulouse
Bordeaux	184																			
Brest	811	623																		
Caen	764	568	376																	
Cahors	307	218	788	661																
Calais	164	876	710	339	875															
Chambéry	860	651	120	800	523	834														
Cherbourg	835	647	399	124	743	461	923													
Clermont-Ferrand	564	358	805	566	269	717	295	689												
Dijon	807	619	867	548	378	572	273	671	279											
Grenoble	827	657	1126	806	501	863	56	929	300	302										
Lille	997	809	725	353	808	112	767	476	650	505	798									
Lyon	831	528	1018	698	439	755	103	820	171	194	110	687								
Marseille	700	651	1271	1010	521	1067	344	1132	477	506	273	999	314							
Nantes	513	326	298	292	491	593	780	317	462	656	787	609	618	975						
Nice	858	810	1429	1168	679	1225	410	1291	636	664	337	1157	473	190	1131					
Paris	771	583	596	232	582	289	565	355	424	313	571	222	462	775	384	932				
Perpignan	499	451	1070	998	320	1149	478	1094	441	640	445	1081	448	319	773	476	857			
Strasbourg	1254	1066	1079	730	847	621	496	853	584	335	551	522	488	803	867	804	490	935		
Toulouse	300	247	866	865	116	991	565	890	890	727	533	923	536	407	568	564	699	205	1022	
Tours	536	348	490	246	413	531	611	369	369	418	618	463	449	795	197	952	238	795	721	593

➼ **Routes Départementales** (D) Local highways and roads.

➼ **Routes Communales** (C, V) Minor rural roads.

The latter two categories, while slower, offer some of France's most enjoyable driving experiences.

Motorcyclists will find France great for touring, with high-quality roads and stunning scenery. Just make sure your wet-weather gear is up to scratch.

Note that high mountain passes, especially in the Alps, may be closed from as early as September to as late as June. Conditions are posted at the foot of each pass ('*ouvert*' on a green background means open, '*ferme*' on a red background means closed). Snow chains or studded tyres are required in wintry weather.

ROAD RULES

Enforcement of French traffic laws has been stepped up considerably in recent years. Speed cameras are increasingly common, as are radar traps and unmarked police vehicles. Fines for many infractions are given on the spot.

Speed Limits

Speed limits outside built-up areas (unless signposted otherwise):

➼ **Undivided N and D highways** 90km/h (80km/h when raining)

➼ **Non-autoroute divided highways** 110km/h (100km/h when raining)

➼ **Autoroutes** 130km/h (110km/h when raining)

Unless otherwise signposted, a limit of 50km/h applies in *all* areas designated as built up, no matter how rural they may appear. You must slow to 50km/h the moment you come to a town entry sign; this speed limit applies until you pass a town exit sign with a diagonal bar through it.

You're expected to already know the speed limit for various types of roads; that's why most speed-limit signs begin with the word *rappel* (reminder). You can be fined for going as little as 10km over the speed limit.

Alcohol

➼ The blood-alcohol limit is 0.05% (0.5g per litre of blood) – the equivalent of two glasses of wine for a 75kg adult.

➼ Police often conduct random breathalyser tests. Penalties can be severe, including imprisonment.

Motorcycles

➼ Riders of any two-wheeled motorised vehicle must wear a helmet.

➼ No special licence is required to ride a motorbike whose engine is smaller than 50cc, which is why rental scooters are often rated at 49.9cc.

➼ As of 1 January 2013, all riders of motorcycles 125cc or larger must wear high-visibility reflective clothing measuring at least 150 sq cm on their upper bodies.

Child Seats

➼ Up to age 10 (or 1.4m tall), children must use a size-appropriate child seat or booster.

Priority to the Right

Under the *priorité à droite* (priority to the right) rule, any car entering an intersection from a road on your right has the right of way. Don't be surprised if locals courteously cede the right of way when you're about to turn from an alley onto a highway, yet boldly assert their rights when you're the one zipping down a main road.

Priorité à droite is suspended on some main roads marked with a yellow diamond-shaped sign. The same sign with a diagonal bar through it reinstates the *priorité à droite* rule.

At roundabouts where you don't have the right of way (ie the cars already in the roundabout do), you'll see signs reading *vous n'avez pas la priorité* (you do not have right of way) or *cédez le passage* (yield/give way).

Driving Problem-Buster

I can't speak French; will that be a problem? While it's preferable to learn some French before travelling, French road signs are mostly of the 'international symbol' variety, and English is increasingly spoken among the younger generation. Our Language chapter can help you navigate some common roadside emergency situations; in a worst-case scenario, a good attitude and sign language can go a long way.

What should I do if my car breaks down? Safety first: turn on your flashers, put on a safety vest (legally required, and provided in rental-car glove compartments) and place a reflective triangle (also legally required) 30m to 100m behind your car to warn approaching motorists. Call for **emergency assistance** (☎112) or walk to the nearest orange roadside call box (placed every 2km along French *autoroutes*). If renting a vehicle, your car-hire company's service number may help expedite matters. If travelling in your own car, verify before leaving home whether your local auto club has reciprocal roadside-assistance arrangements in France.

What if I have an accident? For minor accidents you'll need to fill out a *constat amiable d'accident* (accident statement, typically provided in rental-car glove compartments) and report the accident to your insurance and/or rental-car company. If necessary, contact the **police** (☎17).

What should I do if I get stopped by the police? Show your passport (or EU national ID card), licence and proof of insurance. See our Language chapter for some handy phrases.

What's the speed limit in France and how is it enforced? Speed limits (indicated by a black-on-white number inside a red circle) range from 30km/h in small towns to 130km/h on the fastest *autoroutes*. If the motorbike police pull you over, they'll fine you on the spot or direct you to the nearest gendarmerie to pay. If you're caught by a speed camera (placed at random intervals along French highways), the ticket will be sent to your rental-car agency, which will bill your credit card, or to your home address if you're driving your own vehicle. Fines depend on how much you're over the limit.

How do French tolls work? Many French *autoroutes* charge tolls. Take a ticket from the machine upon entering the highway and pay as you exit. Some exit booths are staffed by people; others are automated and will accept only chip-and-PIN credit cards or coins.

What if I can't find anywhere to stay? During summer and holiday periods, book accommodation in advance whenever possible. Local tourist offices can sometimes help find you a bed during normal business hours. Otherwise, try your luck at national chain hotels such as Etap and Formule 1 (p427), which are typically clustered at *autoroute* exits outside urban areas.

➡ Children under 10 cannot ride in the front seat (unless the back is already occupied by other children under 10).

➡ A child under 13kg must travel in a backward-facing child seat.

Other Rules

➡ All passengers, including those in the back seat, must wear seat belts.

➡ Mobile phones may be used only if equipped with a hands-free kit or speakerphone.

➡ Turning right on a red light is illegal.

France Playlist

Bonjour Rachid Taha and Gaetan Roussel

Coeur Vagabond Gus Viseur

La Vie en Rose Édith Piaf

Minor Swing Django Reinhardt

L'Americano Akhenaton

Flower Duet from Lakmé Léo Delibes

De Bonnes Raisons Alex Beaupain

➡ All vehicles driven in France must carry a high-visibility safety vest, a reflective triangle, a spare set of headlight bulbs and (as of 1 July 2012) a portable, single-use breathalyser kit. Non-compliant drivers are subject to fines.

For pictures and descriptions of common French road signs, see the inside back cover.

PARKING

In city centres, most on-the-street parking places are *payant* (metered) from 9am to 7pm Monday to Saturday (sometimes with a midday break). Buy a ticket at the nearest *horodateur* (coin-fed ticket machine) and place it on your dashboard with the time stamp clearly visible. Bigger cities also have public parking garages.

FUEL

➡ Diesel (*gazole* or *gasoil*) – €1.35/L; many cars in France run on diesel.

➡ *Essence* (gas/petrol), or *carburant* (fuel) – €1.50/L for 95 unleaded (SP95).

➡ Filling up (*faire le plein*) is most expensive at *autoroute* rest stops, cheapest at hypermarkets.

➡ When renting a car, ask whether it runs on *gazole* or *essence*.

➡ At the pump, diesel nozzles are generally yellow, unleaded gas nozzles green.

➡ Many petrol stations close on Sunday afternoon; even in cities, staffed stations are rarely open late.

➡ After-hours purchases (eg at hypermarkets' fully automatic 24-hour stations) can only be made with a credit card that has an embedded PIN chip. If you don't have a chip-and-PIN card, try to get one from your card company before leaving home; chip-and-PIN cards are also required at many toll booths and train-ticket dispensers throughout France.

SATELLITE NAVIGATION SYSTEMS

Sat-nav devices can be helpful in navigating your way around France. They're commonly available at car-rental agencies, or you can bring your own from home. Accuracy is more dependable on main highways than in small villages or on back roads; in rural areas, don't hesitate to fall back on common sense, road signs and a good Michelin map if your sat nav seems to be leading you astray.

SAFETY

Never leave anything valuable inside your car, even in the boot (trunk). Note that thieves can easily identify rental cars, as they have a distinctive number on the licence plate.

Theft is especially prevalent in the south. In cities like Marseille and Nice, occasional aggressive theft from cars stopped at red lights is also an issue.

RADIO

For news, tune in to the French-language France Info (105.5MHz), the multilanguage RFI (738kHz or 89MHz in Paris) or, in northern France, the BBC World Service (648kHz) and BBC Radio 4 (198kHz). Popular national FM music stations include **NRJ** (www.nrj.fr), **Skyrock** (www.skyrock.fm) and **Nostalgie** (www.nostalgie.fr).

In many areas, Autoroute Info (107.7MHz) has round-the-clock traffic information.

France Travel Guide

GETTING THERE & AWAY

AIR

International Airports

Rental cars are available at all international airports listed below.

Paris Charles de Gaulle (CDG; www.aeroportsdeparis.fr)

Paris Orly (ORY; www.aeroportsdeparis.fr)

Aéroport de Bordeaux (www.bordeaux.aeroport.fr)

Aéroport de Lille (www.lille.aeroport.fr)

Aéroport Lyon-Saint Exupéry (www.lyonaeroports.com)

EuroAirport (Basel-Mulhouse-Freiburg; www.euroairport.com)

Aéroport Nantes Atlantique (www.nantes.aeroport.fr)

Aéroport Nice Côte d'Azur (societe.nice.aeroport.fr)

Aéroport International Strasbourg (www.strasbourg.aeroport.fr)

Aéroport Toulouse-Blagnac (www.toulouse.aeroport.fr)

CAR & MOTORCYCLE

Entering France from other parts of the EU is usually a breeze – no border checkpoints and no customs – thanks to the Schengen Agreement, signed by all of France's neighbours except the UK, the Channel Islands and Andorra. For these three, old-fashioned document and customs checks are still the norm when exiting France (as well as when entering from Andorra).

Channel Tunnel

The Channel Tunnel (Chunnel), inaugurated in 1994, is the first dry-land link between England and France since the last ice age.

High-speed **Eurotunnel Le Shuttle** (www.eurotunnel.com) trains whisk cars and motorcycles in 35 minutes from Folkestone through the Chunnel to Coquelles, 5km southwest of Calais. Shuttles run 24 hours, with up to three departures an hour during peak time. LPG and CNG tanks are not permitted; gas-powered cars and many campers and caravans have to travel by ferry.

Eurotunnel sets its fares the way budget airlines do: the earlier you book and the lower the demand for a particular crossing, the less you pay; same-day fares can cost a small fortune. Fares for a car, including up to nine passengers, start at £30.

SEA

P&O Ferries (www.poferries.com) and **DFDS Seaways** (www.dfdsseaways.co.uk) both operate regular trans-Channel car ferry service from England to France (primarily from Dover to Calais, with less frequent services from Dover to Dunkirk). **Brittany Ferries** (www.brittanyferries.com) offers additional services from Plymouth, Portsmouth and Poole to the French ports of Roscoff, St-Malo, Cherbourg and Caen.

Ferry companies typically offer discounts for advance booking and/or off-peak travel. Seasonal demand is a crucial factor (Christmas, Easter, UK and French school holidays, July and August are especially busy), as is the time of day (an early-evening ferry can cost much more than one at 4am).

For the best fares, check **Ferry Savers** (www.ferrysavers.com).

TRAIN

Rail services link France with virtually every country in Europe. The **Eurostar** (www.eurostar.com) whisks passengers from London to Paris in 2¼ hours.

You can book tickets and get train information from **Rail Europe** (www.raileurope.com). In France ticketing is handled by the national railway company **SNCF** (www.sncf.com). High-speed train travel between France and the UK, Belgium, the Netherlands, Germany and Austria is covered by **Railteam** (www.railteam.co.uk) and **TGV-Europe** (www.tgv-europe.com).

Avis (www.avis.fr), in partnership with **SNCF** (www.voyages-sncf.com/train/train-avis), has rental-car agencies in most major French railway stations. Cars booked through the SNCF website may be picked up from an SNCF representative after hours if the Avis office is closed.

DIRECTORY A–Z

ACCOMMODATION

Be it a fairy-tale château, a boutique hideaway or floating pod on a lake, France has accommodation to suit every taste, mood and pocket.

Categories

Budget covers everything from hostels to small, simple family-run places; midrange means a few extra creature comforts such as satellite TV and free wi-fi; and top-end places stretch from luxury five-star palaces with air conditioning, pools and restaurants to boutique-chic chalets in the Alps.

Costs

Accommodation costs vary wildly between seasons and regions: what will buy you a night in a romantic *chambre d'hôte* (B&B) in the countryside may only get you a dorm bed in a major city or high-profile ski resort.

Reservations

Midrange, top-end and many budget hotels require a credit-card to secure a reservation. Tourist offices can often advise on availability and reserve for you, sometimes charging a small fee.

Seasons

➡ In ski resorts, high season is Christmas, New Year and the February-March school holidays.

➡ On the coast, high season is summer, particularly August.

➡ Hotels in inland cities often charge low-season rates in summer.

➡ Rates often drop outside the high season – in some cases by as much as 50%.

➡ In business-oriented hotels in cities, rooms are most expensive from Monday to Thursday and cheaper over the weekend.

➡ In the Alps, hotels usually close between seasons, from around May to mid-June and from mid-September to early December; many addresses in Corsica only open April to October.

B&Bs

For charm, it's hard to beat privately run *chambres d'hôte* (B&Bs), available throughout rural France. By law a *chambre d'hôte must* have no more than five rooms and breakfast must be included in the price; some hosts prepare home-cooked evening meals *(table d'hôte)* for an extra charge of €20 to €30. Pick up lists of *chambres d'hôte* at local tourist offices, or consult the websites below:

Bienvenue à la Ferme (www.bienvenue-a-la-ferme.com) Farmstays.

Chambres d'hôtes de Charme (www.guidesdecharme.com) Boutique B&Bs.

Chambres d'Hôtes France (www.chambresdhotesfrance.com)

en France (www.bbfrance.com) B&Bs and *gîtes* (self-catering cottages).

Fleurs de Soleil (www.fleursdesoleil.fr) Stylish *maisons d'hôte,* mainly in rural France.

Gîtes de France (www.gites-de-france.com) France's primary umbrella organisation for B&Bs and *gîtes*. Search for properties by region,

---

Practicalities

➡ **Time** France uses the 24-hour clock and is on Central European Time, which is one hour ahead of GMT/UTC. During daylight-saving time, from the last Sunday in March to the last Sunday in October, France is two hours ahead of GMT/UTC.

➡ **TV & DVD** TV is Secam; DVDs are zone 2; videos work on the PAL system.

➡ **Weights & Measures** France uses the metric system.

Sleeping Price Ranges

The following price ranges refer to a double room with private bathroom in high season (breakfast is not included, except at B&Bs).

€   less than €80

€€   €80–180

€€€   more than €180

theme (with kids, by the sea, gourmet, etc), activity (fishing, wine tasting etc) or facilities (pool, dishwasher, fireplace, baby equipment etc).

Guides de Charme (www.guidesdecharme. com) Upmarket B&Bs.

Samedi Midi Éditions (www.samedimidi. com) *Chambres d'hôte* organised by location or theme.

Camping

Camping is extremely popular in France. There are thousands of well-equipped campgrounds, many considerably placed by rivers, lakes and the sea. Gîtes de France and Bienvenue à la Ferme coordinate camping on farms.

➡ Most campgrounds open March or April to late September or October; popular spots fill up fast in summer, when it's wise to book ahead.

➡ Economisers should look out for local, good-value but no-frills *campings municipaux* (municipal campgrounds).

➡ Many campgrounds rent mobile homes with mod cons like heating, kitchen and TV.

➡ Camping 'wild' in nondesignated spots (*camping sauvage*) is illegal in France.

➡ Campsite offices often close during the day.

Websites with campsite listings searchable by location, theme and facilities:

Camping en France (www.camping.fr)

Camping France (www.campingfrance.com)

Guide du Camping (www.guideducamp ing.com)

HPA Guide (http://camping.hpaguide.com)

Hostels

Hostels in France range from spartan rooms to hip hang-outs with perks aplenty.

➡ In university towns, *foyers d'étudiant* (student dormitories) are sometimes converted for use by travellers during summer.

➡ A dorm bed in an *auberge de jeunesse* (youth hostel) costs from €10.50 to €28 depending on location, amenities and facilities; sheets are always included, breakfast more often than not.

➡ Hostels by the sea or in the mountains sometimes offer seasonal outdoor activities.

➡ French hostels are 100% non-smoking.

Hotels

We have tried to feature well-situated, independent hotels that offer good value, a warm welcome, at least a bit of charm and a palpable sense of place.

Hotels in France are rated with one to five stars, although the ratings are based on highly objective criteria (eg the size of the entry hall), not the quality of the service, the decor or cleanliness.

➡ French hotels rarely include breakfast in their rates. Unless specified otherwise, prices quoted don't include breakfast, which costs around €7/10/20 in a budget/midrange/top-end hotel.

➡ A double room generally has one double bed (sometimes two singles pushed together!); a room with twin beds (*deux lits*) is usually more expensive, as is a room with a bathtub instead of a shower.

➡ Feather pillows are practically nonexistent in France, even in top-end hotels.

➡ All hotel restaurant terraces allow smoking; if you are sensitive to smoke sit inside or carry a respirator.

Chain Hotels

Chain hotels stretch from nondescript establishments near the *autoroute* (motorway, highway) to central four-star hotels with character. Most conform to certain standards of decor, service and facilities (air conditioning, free wi-fi, 24-hour check-in etc), and offer competitive rates as well as last-minute, weekend and/or online deals. Countrywide biggies include:

Book Your Stay Online

For more accommodation reviews by Lonely Planet authors, check out http://hotels.lonelyplanet.com. You'll find independent reviews, as well as recommendations on the best places to stay. Best of all, you can book online.

B&B Hôtels (www.hotel-bb.com) Cheap motel-style digs.

Best Western (www.bestwestern.com) Independent two- to four-star hotels, each with its own local character.

Campanile (www.campanile.com) Good-value hotels geared up for families.

Citôtel (www.citotel.com) Independent two- and three-star hotels.

Contact Hôtel (www.contact-hotel.com) Inexpensive two- and three-star hotels.

Etap (www.etaphotel.com) Ubiquitous chain.

Formule 1 (www.hotelformule1.com) Nondescript roadside cheapie.

Ibis (www.ibishotel.com) Midrange pick.

Inter-Hotel (www.inter-hotel.fr) Two- and three-star hotels, some quite charming.

Kyriad (www.kyriad.com) Comfortable midrange choices.

Novotel (www.novotel.com) Family-friendly chain.

Première Classe (www.premiereclasse.com) Motel-style accommodation.

Sofitel (www.sofitel.com) Range of top-end hotels in major French cities.

ELECTRICITY

European two-pin plugs are standard. France has 230V at 50Hz AC (you may need a transformer for 110V electrical appliances).

230V/50Hz

FOOD

Food-happy France has a seemingly endless variety of eateries; categories listed below are found throughout the country: The Eating & Sleeping sections of this guide include phone numbers for places that require reservations (typically higher-end bistros or family-run enterprises such as *tables d'hôte*).

➜ **Auberge** Country inn serving traditional fare, often attached to a B&B or small hotel.

➜ **Ferme auberge** Working farm that cooks up meals – only dinner usually – from local farm products.

➜ **Bistro** (also spelt *bistrot*) Anything from a pub or bar with snacks and light meals to a small, fully fledged restaurant.

➜ **Brasserie** Much like a cafe except it serves full meals, drinks and coffee from morning until 11pm or later. Typical fare includes *choucroute* (sauerkraut) and *moules frites* (mussels and fries).

➜ **Restaurant** Born in Paris in the 18th century, restaurants today serve lunch and dinner five or six days a week.

➜ **Cafe** Basic light snacks as well as drinks.

➜ **Crêperie** (also *galetterie*) Casual address specialising in sweet crêpes and savoury *galettes* (buckwheat crêpes).

➜ **Salon de Thé** Trendy tearoom often serving light lunches (quiche, salads, cakes, tarts, pies and pastries) as well as black and herbal teas.

➜ **Table d'hôte** (literally 'host's table') Some of the most charming B&Bs serve *table d'hôte* too, a delicious homemade meal of set courses with little or no choice.

Eating Price Ranges

The following price ranges refer to a two-course set menu (ie entrée plus main course or main course plus dessert), with tax and service charge included in the price.

€   less than €20

€€ €20–40

€€€ more than €40

GAY & LESBIAN TRAVELLERS

The rainbow flag flies high in France, a country that left its closet long before many of its European neighbours. *Laissez-faire* perfectly sums up France's liberal attitude towards homosexuality and people's private lives in general. Paris, Bordeaux, Lille, Lyon, Montpellier and Toulouse are among the many cities with thriving gay and lesbian scenes. Attitudes towards homosexuality tend to be more conservative in the countryside and villages. France's lesbian scene is less public than its gay male counterpart.

Publications

Damron (www.damron.com) Publishes English-language travel guides, including the *Damron Women's Traveller* for lesbians and the *Damron Men's Travel Guide* for gays.

Spartacus International Gay Guide (www.spartacusworld.com) A male-only guide with more than 70 pages devoted to France, almost half of which cover Paris. iPhone app too.

Websites

France Queer Resources Directory (www.france.qrd.org) Gay and lesbian directory.

French Government Tourist Office (www.us.franceguide.com/special-interests/gay-friendly) Information about 'the gay-friendly destination par excellence'.

Gay France (www.gay-france.net) Insider tips on gay life in France.

Gayscape (www.gayscape.com) Hundreds of links to gay- and lesbian-related sites.

Gayvox (www.gayvox.com/guide3) Online travel guide to France, with listings by region.

Tasse de Thé (www.tassedethe.com) A *webzine lesbien* with lots of useful links.

INTERNET ACCESS

➡ Wireless (wi-fi) access points can be found at major airports, in many hotels and at some cafes.

➡ Some tourist offices and numerous cafes and bars tout wi-fi hot spots that let laptop owners hook up for free.

➡ To search for free wi-fi hot spots in France, visit www.hotspot-locations.co.uk or www.free-hotspot.com.

➡ Internet cafes are becoming less rife, but at least one can still be found in most large towns and cities. Prices range from €2 to €6 per hour.

➡ If accessing dial-up ISPs with your laptop, you'll need a telephone-plug adaptor, available at large supermarkets.

MONEY

ATMs

Known as *distributeurs automatiques de billets* (DAB) or *points d'argent* in French, ATMs are the cheapest and most convenient way to get money. Those connected to international networks are ubiquitous and usually offer an excellent exchange rate.

Cash

You always get a better exchange rate in-country, but if arriving in France by air or late at night, you may want to bring enough euros to take a taxi to a hotel.

Credit & Debit Cards

➡ Credit and debit cards, accepted almost everywhere in France, are convenient and relatively secure and usually offer a better exchange rate than travellers cheques or cash exchanges.

➡ Credit cards issued in France have embedded chips – you have to type in a PIN to make a purchase.

➡ Visa, MasterCard and Amex can be used in shops and supermarkets and for train travel, car hire and motorway tolls, though some places (eg 24-hour petrol stations, some autoroute toll machines) only take French-style credit cards with chips and PINs.

➡ Don't assume that you can pay for a meal or a budget hotel with a credit card – enquire first.

➡ Cash advances are a supremely convenient way to stay stocked up with euros, but getting cash with a credit card involves both fees (sometimes US$10 or more) and interest – ask your credit-card issuer for details. Debit-card fees are usually much less.

Moneychangers

➡ In Paris and major cities, *bureaux de change* (exchange bureaus) are open longer hours, give faster and easier service and often have better rates than banks.

➡ Some post-office branches exchange travellers cheques and banknotes; most won't take US$100 bills.

Tipping Guide

By law, restaurant and bar prices are *service compris* (include a 15% service charge), so there is no need to leave a *pourboire* (tip). If you were extremely satisfied with the service, however, you can – as many locals do – leave a small 'extra' tip for your waiter or waitress.

bars	round to nearest euro
hotel cleaning staff	€1-1.50 per day
hotel porters	€1-1.50 per bag
restaurants	5-10%
taxis	10-15%
toilet attendants	€0.20-0.50
tour guides	€1-2 per person

OPENING HOURS

Below are standard hours for various types of business in France (note that these can fluctuate by an hour either way in some cases). For individual business listings in this book, we've only included opening hours where they differ significantly from these standards:

banks	9am-noon & 2-5pm Mon-Fri or Tue-Sat
bars	7pm-1am Mon-Sat
cafes	7am or 8am-10pm or 11pm Mon-Sat
nightclubs	10pm-3am, 4am or 5am Thu-Sat
post offices	8.30am or 9am-5pm or 6pm Mon-Fri, 8am-noon Sat
restaurants	lunch noon-2.30pm, dinner 7-11pm six days a week
shops	9am or 10am-7pm Mon-Sat (often with lunch break noon-1.30pm)
supermarkets	8.30am-7pm Mon-Sat, 8.30am-12.30pm Sun

PUBLIC HOLIDAYS

The following *jours fériés* (public holidays) are observed in France:

New Year's Day (Jour de l'An) 1 January.

Easter Sunday and Monday (Pâques and lundi de Pâques) Late March/April.

May Day (Fête du Travail) 1 May.

Victoire 1945 8 May – commemorates the Allied victory in Europe that ended WWII.

Ascension Thursday (Ascension) May – celebrated on the 40th day after Easter.

Pentecost/Whit Sunday and Whit Monday (Pentecôte and lundi de Pentecôte) Mid-May to mid-June – celebrated on the seventh Sunday after Easter.

Bastille Day/National Day (Fête Nationale) 14 July – *the* national holiday.

Assumption Day (Assomption) 15 August.

All Saints' Day (Toussaint) 1 November.

Remembrance Day (L'onze novembre) 11 November – marks the WWI armistice.

Christmas (Noël) 25 December.

SAFE TRAVEL

France is generally a safe place to travel, though crime has risen substantially in recent years. Property crime is much more common than physical violence; it's extremely unlikely that you will be assaulted while walking down the street. Always check your government's travel advisory warnings.

Hunting is traditional and commonplace throughout rural France, and the season runs from September to February. If you see signs reading '*chasseurs*' or '*chasse gardée*' strung up or tacked to trees, think twice about wandering into the area.

Natural Dangers

➡ There are powerful tides and strong under-tows at many places along the Atlantic coast, from the Spanish border north to Brittany and Normandy.

➡ Only swim in *zones de baignade surveillée* (beaches monitored by life guards).

➡ Be aware of tide times and the high-tide mark if walking on a beach.

➡ Thunderstorms in the mountains and the hot southern plains can be extremely sudden and violent.

➡ Check the weather report before setting out on a long walk and be prepared for sudden temperature drops if you're heading into the high country of the Alps or Pyrenees.

➡ Avalanches pose a significant danger in the Alps.

Theft

There's no need to travel in fear, but it is worth taking a few simple precautions against theft.

➡ Break-ins to parked cars are not uncommon. Never leave anything valuable inside your car, even in the boot (trunk).

➡ Aggressive theft from cars stopped at red lights is occasionally a problem, especially in Marseille and Nice. As a precaution, lock your car doors and roll up the windows in major urban areas.

➡ Pickpocketing and bag snatching (eg in dense crowds and public places) are prevalent in big cities, particularly Paris, Marseille and Nice. Be especially vigilant for bag-snatchers at outdoor cafes and beaches.

TELEPHONE

Mobile Phones

➡ French mobile-phone numbers begin with 06 or 07.

➡ France uses GSM 900/1800, which is com-patible with the rest of Europe and Australia but not with the North American GSM 1900 or the totally different system in Japan (though some North Americans have tri-band phones that work in France).

➡ Check with your service provider about roaming charges – dialling a mobile phone from a fixed-line phone or another mobile can be incredibly expensive.

➡ It may be cheaper to buy your own French SIM card – and locals you meet are much more likely to ring you if your number is French.

➡ If you already have a compatible phone, you can slip in a SIM card (€20 to €30) and rev it up with prepaid credit, though this is likely to run out fast as domestic prepaid calls cost about €0.50 per minute.

➡ Recharge cards are sold at most *tabacs* and newsagents.

➡ SIMs are available at the ubiquitous outlets run by France's three mobile-phone compa-nies, **Bouygues** (www.bouyguestelecom.fr), **Orange** (www.orange.com) and **SFR** (www.sfr.com).

Phone Codes

➡ **Calling France from abroad** Dial your country's international access code, then 33 (France's country code), then the 10-digit local number *without* the initial zero.

➡ **Calling internationally from France** Dial 00 (the international access code), the *indicatif* (country code), the area code (without the initial zero if there is one) and the local number. Some country codes are posted in public telephones.

➡ **Directory enquiries** For national *service des renseignements* (directory enquiries) dial 11 87 12 (€1.46 per call, plus €0.45 per minute), or use the service for free online at www.118712.fr.

➡ **Emergency numbers** Can be dialled from public phones without a phonecard.

➡ **Hotel calls** Hotels, *gîtes*, hostels and *chambres d'hôte* are free to meter their calls as they like. The surcharge is usually around €0.30 per minute but can be higher.

➡ **International directory enquiries** For numbers outside France, dial 11 87 00 (€2 to €3 per call).

Phonecards

➡ For explanations in English and other languages on how to use a public telephone, push the button engraved with a two-flags icon.

➡ For both international and domestic calling, most public phones operate using either a credit card or two kinds of *télécartes* (phonecards): *cartes à puce* (cards with a magnetic chip) issued by Orange (formerly France Télécom) and sold at post offices for €8 or €15; and *cartes à code* (cards where you dial a free access number and then the card's scratch-off code), sold at *tabacs*, newsagents and post offices.

➡ Phonecards with codes offer *much* better international rates than Orange chip cards or Country Direct services (for which you are billed at home by your long-distance carrier).

➡ The shop you buy a phonecard from should be able to tell you which type is best for the country you want to call. Using phonecards from a home phone is much cheaper that using them from public phones or mobile phones.

TOILETS

Public toilets around France are signposted WC or *toilettes*. These range from spiffy 24-hour mechanical self-cleaning toilets costing around €0.50 to hole-in-the-floor *toilettes à la turque* (squat toilets) at older establishments and motorway stops. In the most basic places you may need to supply your own paper.

The French are more blasé about unisex toilets than elsewhere, so save your blushes when tiptoeing past the urinals to reach the ladies' loo.

TOURIST INFORMATION

Almost every city, town, village and hamlet has a clearly signposted *office de tourisme* (government-run tourist office) or *syndicat d'initiative* (tourist office run by local merchants). Both can supply you with local maps as well as details on accommodation, restaurants and activities such as walking, cycling or wine tasting. Useful websites:

➡ **French Government Tourist Office** (www.franceguide.com) The low-down on

sights, activities, transport and special-interest holidays in all of France's regions. Brochures can be downloaded online. There are links to country-specific websites.

➡ **Réseau National des Destinations Départementales** (www.fncdt.net) Listing of CRT (regional tourist board) websites.

TRAVELLERS WITH DISABILITIES

While France presents evident challenges for *handicapés* (people with disabilities) – namely cobblestone, cafe-lined streets that are a nightmare to navigate in a wheelchair, a lack of curb ramps, older public facilities and many budget hotels without lifts – you can still enjoy travelling here with a little careful planning.

Whether you are looking for wheelchair-friendly accommodation, sights, attractions or restaurants, these associations and agencies can help:

➡ **Association des Paralysés de France** (APF; www.apf.asso.fr) National organisation for people with disabilities, with offices throughout France.

➡ **Tourisme et Handicaps** (www.tourisme-handicaps.org) Issues the 'Tourisme et Handicap' label to tourist sites, restaurants and hotels that comply with strict accessibility and usability standards. Different symbols indicate the sort of access afforded to people with physical, mental, hearing and/or visual disabilities.

VISAS

For up-to-date details on visa requirements, see the website of the **Ministère des Affaires Étrangères** (Ministry of Foreign Affairs; www.diplomatie.gouv.fr/en) and click 'Coming to France'. Visas are not required for EU nationals or citizens of Iceland, Norway and Switzerland, and are required only for stays greater than 90 days for citizens of Australia, the USA, Canada, Hong Kong, Israel, Japan, Malaysia, New Zealand, Singapore, South Korea and many Latin American countries.

Language

The sounds used in spoken French can almost all be found in English. There are a couple of exceptions: nasal vowels (represented in our pronunciation guides by o or u followed by an almost inaudible nasal consonant sound m, n or ng), the 'funny' u (ew in our guides) and the deep-in-the-throat r. Bearing these few points in mind and reading our pronunciation guides below as if they were English, you'll be understood just fine.

BASICS

Hello.	*Bonjour.*	bon·zhoor
Goodbye.	*Au revoir.*	o·rer·vwa
Yes./No.	*Oui./Non.*	wee/non
Excuse me.	*Excusez-moi.*	ek·skew·zay·mwa
Sorry.	*Pardon.*	par·don
Please.	*S'il vous plaît.*	seel voo play
Thank you.	*Merci.*	mair·see

You're welcome.
De rien. der ree·en

Do you speak English?
Parlez-vous anglais? par·lay·voo ong·glay

I don't understand.
Je ne comprends pas. zher ner kom·pron pa

How much is this?
C'est combien? say kom·byun

ACCOMMODATION

Do you have any rooms available?
Est-ce que vous avez es·ker voo za·vay
des chambres libres? day shom·brer lee·brer

How much is it per night/person?
Quel est le prix kel ay ler pree
par nuit/personne? par nwee/per·son

DIRECTIONS

Can you show me (on the map)?
Pouvez-vous m'indiquer poo·vay·voo mun·dee·kay
(sur la carte)? (sewr la kart)

Where's ...?
Où est ...? oo ay ...

EATING & DRINKING

What would you recommend?
Qu'est-ce que vous kes·ker voo
conseillez? kon·say·yay

I'd like ..., please.
Je voudrais ..., zher voo·dray ...
s'il vous plaît. seel voo play

I'm a vegetarian.
Je suis végétarien/ zher swee vay·zhay·ta·ryun
végétarienne. vay·zhay·ta·ryen (m/f)

Please bring the bill.
Apportez-moi a·por·tay·mwa
l'addition, la·dee·syon
s'il vous plaît. seel voo play

EMERGENCIES

Help!
Au secours! o skoor

I'm lost.
Je suis perdu/perdue. zhe swee·pair·dew (m/f)

Want More?

For in-depth language information and handy phrases, check out Lonely Planet's *French Phrasebook*. You'll find it at **shop.lonelyplanet.com**, or you can buy Lonely Planet's iPhone phrasebooks at the Apple App Store.

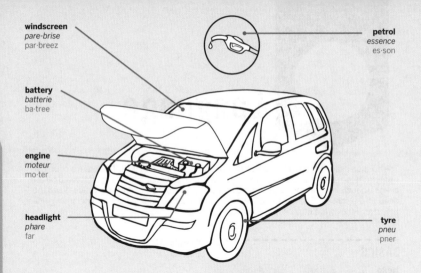

windscreen
pare-brise
par·breez

petrol
essence
es·son

battery
batterie
ba·tree

engine
moteur
mo·ter

headlight
phare
far

tyre
pneu
pner

Signs

Cédez la Priorité	Give Way
Sens Interdit	No Entry
Entrée	Entrance
Péage	Toll
Sens Unique	One Way
Sortie	Exit

I'm ill.
Je suis malade.   zher swee ma·lad

Call the police!
Appelez la police!   a·play la po·lees

Call a doctor!
Appelez un médecin!   a·play un mayd·sun

ON THE ROAD

I'd like to hire a/an ...	*Je voudrais louer ...*	zher voo·dray loo·way ...
4WD	*un quatre-quatre*	un kat·kat
automatic/ manual	*une auto- matique/ manuel*	ewn o·to· ma·teek/ ma·nwel
motorbike	*une moto*	ewn mo·to

How much is it daily/weekly?
Quel est le tarif par jour/semaine?   kel ay ler ta·reef par zhoor/ser·men

Does that include insurance?
Est-ce que l'assurance est comprise?   es·ker la·sew·rons ay kom·preez

Does that include mileage?
Est-ce que le kilométrage est compris?   es·ker ler kee·lo·may·trazh ay kom·pree

What's the speed limit?
Quelle est la vitesse maximale permise?   kel ay la vee·tes mak·see·mal per·meez

Is this the road to ...?
C'est la route pour ...?   say la root poor ...

Can I park here?
Est-ce que je peux stationner ici?   es·ker zher per sta·syo·nay ee·see

Where's a service station?
Où est-ce qu'il y a une station-service?   oo es·keel ya ewn sta·syon·ser·vees

Please fill it up.
Le plein, s'il vous plaît.   ler plun seel voo play

I'd like (20) litres.
Je voudrais (vingt) litres.   zher voo·dray (vung) lee·trer

Please check the oil/water.
Contrôlez l'huile/l'eau, s'il vous plaît.   kon·tro·lay lweel/lo seel voo play

I need a mechanic.
J'ai besoin d'un mécanicien.   zhay ber·zwun dun may·ka·nee·syun

The car/motorbike has broken down.
La voiture/moto est tombée en panne.   la vwa·tewr/mo·to ay tom·bay on pan

I had an accident.
J'ai eu un accident.   zhay ew un ak·see·don

BEHIND THE SCENES

SEND US YOUR FEEDBACK

We love to hear from travellers – your comments help make our books better. We read every word, and we guarantee that your feedback goes straight to the authors. Visit **lonelyplanet. com/contact** to submit your updates and suggestions.

Note: We may edit, reproduce and incorporate your comments in Lonely Planet products such as guidebooks, websites and digital products, so let us know if you don't want your comments reproduced or your name acknowledged. For a copy of our privacy policy visit lonelyplanet.com/privacy.

AUTHOR THANKS

OLIVER BERRY

Biggest thanks go to all my hard-working co-authors, who have helped make this book what it is. Thanks also to Susie, Mo and Gracie Berry, Justin Foulkes and Patrick Desgué for their help with Mont St-Michel, David Levasseur for his assistance on the finer points of Champagne production, and everyone else I met out on *la route*.

STUART BUTLER

I want to thank my wife, Heather, for everything she does and my young son, Jake, who has brought us so much happiness (and sleepless nights!). Thanks to Jake's grandparents and aunties for babysitting during my research for this book. I would also like to thank Rosie Warren in Bordeaux and the good people of France who knowingly or unknowingly helped out on this project.

JEAN-BERNARD CARILLET

A huge thanks to everyone who made these trips a pure joy, including Didier Ferat, Laurent and Bea in Normandy. At Lonely Planet, a big thanks to Jo, Annelies and the carto team for their support. I'm also grateful to *monsieur* Oliver Berry, coordinating author extraordinaire, for his help, tips and support.

GREGOR CLARK

Un grand merci to countless people who shared their love and knowledge of France with me, especially Alisa, Jean-Philippe, Alain, Aline, Andy, Mary, Conor and Gloria. Back home, hugs to my wife, Gaen, and daughters, Meigan and Chloe, who helped me immeasurably in researching the Loire Valley's *châteaux* and *boulangeries*.

DONNA WHEELER

Big love to the Nice gang and to Lino Lategan-McGregor for Monaco nous. Thanks to hospitable Pascal Hauer, Flavie Gil, Brigitte Walzing and Mamashelter Bob. More *mercis* to Jo Cooke, Annelies Mertens and Laura Stansfeld in-house. Final thanks to Joe Guario: that Webber-esque fang outside the Fairmont was really something.

THIS BOOK

This 1st edition of Lonely Planet's *France's Best Trips* guidebook was researched and written by Oliver Berry, Stuart Butler, Jean-Bernard Carillet, Gregor Clark, Donna Wheeler and Nicola Williams. Contributors to this title were Alexis Averbuck, Kerry Christiani, Emilie Filou, Catherine Le Nevez, Chris Pitts and John Vlahides .

This guidebook was commissioned in Lonely Planet's London office, and produced by the following:

Commissioning Editor Joanna Cooke **Coordinating Editors** Sarah Bailey, Susan Paterson **Coordinating Cartographer** Gabriel Lindquist **Coordinating Layout Designer** Wibowo Rusli **Managing Editors** Annelies Mertens, Kirsten Rawlings **Senior Editors** Andi Jones, Catherine Naghten **Managing Cartographers** Anita Banh, Anthony Phelan **Managing Layout Designer** Jane Hart **Assisting Editors** Carly Hall, Helen Koehne, Joanne Newell **Assisting Cartographers** James Leversha, Cameron Romeril

Cover Research Timothy O'Hanlon **Internal Image Research** Aude Vauconsant **Language Content** Branislava Vladisavljevic **Thanks to** Sasha Baskett, Jennifer Bilos, Laura Crawford, Janine Eberle, Ryan Evans, Jennye Garibaldi, Joshua Geoghegan, Liz Heynes, Laura Jane, Jennifer Johnston, David Kemp, Wayne Murphy, Trent Paton, Jessica Rose, Mik Ruff, Julie Sheridan, Amanda Sierp, Laura Stansfeld, Matt Swaine, John Taufa, Diana Von Holdt, Gerard Walker, Juan Winata

NICOLA WILLIAMS

On the road, *merci mille fois* to Corsica aficionado Vincent Lehoux (unsurpassable Ajaccio recommendations); Kasia Dietz and Lindsay Tramuta (Corsica tips by way of Paris); Charlie Johnson (best hidden beach camping); travel-mad husband Matthias and our trilingual tribe (only one case of car sickness during the entire 2500km of extreme hairpins covered).

PUBLISHER THANKS

Climate map data adapted from Peel MC, Finlayson BL & McMahon TA (2007) 'Updated World Map of the Köppen-Geiger Climate Classification', *Hydrology and Earth System Sciences*, 11, 163344.

Cover photographs
Front (clockwise from top): The medieval fortress of Carcassonne, Luigi Vaccarella/4Corners; Vase of sunflowers on a table with an antique chair, Barbara Van Zanten/Lonely Planet Images; A red citroen 2CV car, Ruaridh Stewart/Corbis
Back: Rows of lavender in bloom, Provence, David Tomlinson/ Lonely Planet Images.

INDEX

Jean-Bernard Carillet As a Paris-based (and Metz-born) journalist and photographer, I was delighted to rediscover my own turf. For this Lonely Planet title I couldn't resist the temptation of exploring Burgundy and Beaujolais, if only to sample some of the best wines in the world. I confess a penchant for the Meursault whites (in Burgundy) and the Fleurie reds (in Beaujolais).

My Favourite Trip `8` **Monet's Normandy**
As a Parisian, I regularly set off to coastal Normandy (favourite area: Côte d'Albâtre) to savour a seafood platter.

Gregor Clark My first epic French road tri[p]
Bastille Day at age 20. Nearly broke and hit[ch]
towards my next fruit-picking job, I landed a [?]
lift from a lost tourist and proceeded to spend[?]
night winding through the fireworks-lit streets o[f]
every little village in Haute-Provence. To this day,
I love nothing better than aimlessly wandering
France's back roads in search of hidden villages and
unexpected treasures. I contribute regularly to Lonely
Planet's European and South American guidebooks.

My Favourite Trip `18` **Foothills of the Alps**
for the landscape's beautiful transition from the high-mountain greenery of the Vercors to the arid majesty of the Verdon.

Donna Wheeler I've been visiting France for many years, but I really got to know the south when living just over the border in Turin. I'm the author of several Lonely Planet guidebooks and have published elsewhere on art, architecture and design, history, and food. I'm also a creative consultant and travel experience planner. My Australian childhood was one epic coastal road trip, hunting down the best swimming spots and seafood dinners – something that stood me in good stead for this assignment.

My Favourite Trip `28` **The Camargue** for the wonderful, wayward city of Arles and the wetlands' untamed viridian beauty.

Nicola Williams Originally from Britain, I've lived in France for over a decade. From my hillside house on the southern shore of Lake Geneva, it's a quick and easy motor to the Alps (call me a ski fiend...), Paris (art buff...), southern France (foodie...). For this Lonely Planet title I clocked up 2500km – all at a graceful average speed of 38km/h – on the island of Corsica. I blog at tripalong.wordpress.com and tweet @Tripalong.

My Favourite Trip `26` **Southern Seduction en Corse** The dramatic contrasts in landscape, peaking with that cinematic hike down Bonifacio's Escalier du Roi d'Aragon to the sea's edge, get me every time.

OUR STORY

A beat-up old car, a few dollars in the pocket and a sense of adventure. In 1972 that's all Tony and Maureen Wheeler needed for the trip of a lifetime – across Europe and Asia overland to Australia. It took several months, and at the end – broke but inspired – they sat at their kitchen table writing and stapling together their first travel guide, *Across Asia on the Cheap*. Within a week they'd sold 1500 copies. Lonely Planet was born.

Today, Lonely Planet has offices in Melbourne, London and Oakland, with more than 600 staff and writers. We share Tony's belief that 'a great guidebook should do three things: inform, educate and amuse'.

Oliver Berry My first trip to France was a family holiday to Provence at the age of two, and I've been back many times since while working on Lonely Planet's bestselling *France* guide. I've covered nearly every corner of L'Hexagone on my travels, but I have an especially soft spot for Corsica and the Pyrenees. When not in France, I can usually be found wandering the beaches and clifftops of my home county, Cornwall. I'm also a regular contributor to many other websites, newspapers and magazines, including *Lonely Planet Traveller*. Check out my latest travels at www.oliverberry.com.

My Favourite Trip 32 **Pyrenees** I'm a sucker for wild places, and they don't get much wilder than the snow-dusted mountains and quiet valleys of the Pyrenees.

Stuart Butler My first encounters with southwest France came on family holidays. When I was older I spent every summer surfing off the beaches of the southwest until one day I found myself so hooked on the region that I was unable to leave – I've been here ever since. When not writing for Lonely Planet I hunt for uncharted surf on remote coastlines. The results of these trips appear frequently in the world's surf media. My website is www.stuartbutlerjournalist.com.

My Favourite Trip 33 **Basque Country** I'd never tire of driving this route; bumbling between postcard-pretty villages, strolling Biarritz' waterfront and clambering around the Pyrenean foothills.

Read more about Oliver at: lonelyplanet.com/members/oliverberry

Read more about Stuart at: lonelyplanet.com/members/stuartbutler

 MORE WRITERS

Published by Lonely Planet Publications Pty Ltd

ABN 36 005 607 983
1st edition – Mar 2013
ISBN 978 1 74220 985 2
© Lonely Planet 2013
Photographs © as indicated 2013
10 9 8 7 6 5 4 3 2
Printed in China

Although the authors and Lonely Planet have taken all reasonable care in preparing this book, we make no warranty about the accuracy or completeness of its content and, to the maximum extent permitted, disclaim all liability arising from its use.

MIX
Paper from responsible sources
FSC™ C021741

Paper in this book is certified against the Forest Stewardship Council™ standards. FSC™ promotes environmentally responsible, socially beneficial and economically viable management of the world's forests.

Praise for *Relentless*!

"Parrish writes with the verve and attitude of a New York City cab driver, plunging ahead with barely a glance at oncoming traffic. . . . There's a reason this novel is called *Relentless*."

Bookpage

"Like high-octane jet fuel laced with pure adrenaline, Robin Parrish's *Relentless* is a potent cocktail of adventure and myth—guaranteed to keep you racing through pages long into the night."

T.L. Hines, author of *Waking Lazarus*

"Rather than being a great 'Christian novel,' *Relentless* is a great novel by a very talented Christian writer."

Jenn Wright, hollywoodjesus.com

"If you enjoyed Ted Dekker's *Three*, or Frank Peretti's *Monster*, you will love this book. Non-stop action makes *Relentless* hard to put down!"

Marty Medley, armchairinterviews.com

"*Relentless* is a mystery/action novel like you've never read. There are so many twists and turns, you wonder where you'll wind up next. Parrish feeds us action from beginning to end, and boy what an ending. . . ."

Shane Werlinger, buddyhollywood.com

"*Relentless* drew me relentlessly into the story. . . . Never has the hero's journey been so tangled with conspiracies, secret organizations, age-old mysteries and sword wielding assassins."

H. Michael Brewer, author of *Who Needs a Superhero?* and *Lessons From the Carpenter*

BOOKS BY ROBIN PARRISH

FROM BETHANY HOUSE PUBLISHERS

Relentless

Fearless

RELENTLESS

THE DOMINION TRILOGY: BOOK 1

ROBIN PARRISH

BETHANY HOUSE PUBLISHERS

Minneapolis, Minnesota

Relentless
Copyright © 2006
Robin Parrish

Cover design: Brand Navigation, LLC
Bill Chiaravalle, Russ McIntosh

Cover images: Getty, Photodisc

Cover photography: Steve Gardner, Pixelworks Studio

Published by Bethany House Publishers
11400 Hampshire Avenue South
Bloomington, Minnesota 55438

Bethany House Publishers is a division of
Baker Publishing Group, Grand Rapids, Michigan.

Printed in the United States of America

ISBN-13:   978-0-7642-0345-9
ISBN-10:   0-7642-0345-2

The Library of Congress has cataloged the hardcover edition as follows:

Parrish, Robin.
    Relentless / Robin Parrish.
       p.   cm. — (The Dominion trilogy ; 1)
    ISBN 0-7642-0221-9 (alk. paper)
1. Doppelgängers—Fiction. 2. Psychic ability—Fiction. 3. Conspiracies—
Fiction. 4. Prophecies—Fiction. 5. Supernatural—Fiction. I. Title. II. Series:
Parrish, Robin. Dominion trilogy ; 1.

    PS3616.A7684R45   2006
    813'.6—dc22

                                                            2006011317

**Dedicated to the memory of
Michael Wayland Parrish**

*You would have loved this story, Dad.
I miss you.*

PROLOGUE

Somewhere in the world, an unbearable cry pierced the darkness.

It was the sound of pain.

The sound of birth.

And the sound of death.

It was a sound that would change *everything*. . . .

Collin Boyd stepped off the Metro bus on his way to work, and across the street he saw *himself* strolling down the sidewalk.

A stubborn but warm February rain was pouring hard across the concrete canyons of downtown. His foot had landed ankle-deep in a drainage puddle, and his half-broken umbrella wasn't extending as it should. But the umbrella, which had rarely seen use, quickly fell out of his hands and he no longer noticed the rain. His eyes were fixed, his head turning slowly to follow the other man down the opposite side of the street.

It wasn't until someone shouted from behind that he finally got his legs moving again.

The man he watched with rapt attention weaved his way casually through the crowd, headed in the direction of Collin's workplace. He wasn't a man who merely *resembled* Collin. He *was* him. The same face, the same body, the same walk. He wore the clothes and raincoat Collin had put on that morning. He carried Collin's briefcase.

It was only then that Collin noticed he no longer *had* his briefcase. When had he seen it last? On the bus? Before that? He'd been so groggy all morning, he couldn't place it.

And what was that on the man's wrist? Collin clenched a hand around his own wrist, feeling for what was missing.

He's wearing Granddad's bracelet . . .

That line of thought was gone once the other man began fussing with the piece of unruly hair up front that Collin could never seem to keep in place.

This impostor wasn't a twin or duplicate. He was *him*, in every way. Every look, every gesture, every expression. And he was walking to work in the rain, under L.A.'s towering skyscrapers, brushing shoulders with countless citizens and tourists.

As if everything were exactly as it should be.

Without ever deciding to, Collin moved his legs. He crossed the bustling downtown street, just aware enough of the cars, buses, and bicycles zipping by to dodge them. But his eyes remained on the man who looked like him, who checked his watch—*No, that's* my *watch*, he reminded himself—and then picked up his pace, apparently realizing he was about to be late for work.

Late for my *work*, Collin stupidly thought again, his mind spinning.

This was a lie. It had to be a lie.

A twisted joke.

But then, who would play such a prank? He hadn't had any close friends since childhood, and even then he knew that his "friends" had been forced to play with him by the orphanage staff. He couldn't think of a single acquaintance he had now who had anything resembling a sense of humor.

Collin increased his own speed, tailing his doppelganger from about fifteen paces behind. The impossibility of the situation seemed like an absurd thing to think about right now as he spied on himself walking to work in the rain, yet nothing else entered his mind.

It couldn't be impossible if he was looking right at it.

What am I supposed to say if I catch up to him?

Maybe he's my clone. Are they cloning humans yet? Eh, I don't know.

He's living my life. He's walking in my shoes on his way to my job, living my life.

Did he steal *my life?*

Maybe I'm sitting somewhere in a padded room right now. "Careful there, honey," the kind nurse is saying to my slack-jawed, vacant expression. "You're drooling all over your straitjacket . . ."

Collin's adrenaline surged, and the confusion of the moment was overpowered by a rising agitation.

The other man approached a street corner, and even though the light on the other side was blinking DON'T WALK, he crossed anyway, nearly jogging.

Collin broke into a run and hit the crosswalk full bore. He was halfway across, his eyes still following his quarry, when a blaring horn filled his ears, followed by the metallic screech of brakes. He barely managed to jump backward a few feet before a Metro bus filled the space where he'd just been standing. The angry driver shouted a few choice phrases in Collin's direction, followed by an emphatic hand gesture.

Collin gave a dazed wave. As the bus chugged slowly along, passing within inches of his face, his stunned reflection gazed back at him in the glass windows as they passed by.

He didn't recognize the man in the glass.

Time seemed to shudder. The sounds of vehicles, store owners, tourists, businesspeople, and even planes flying overhead all fell away, until he heard nothing but the rush of blood surging past his ears and pounding in his temples. There was nothing wrong with his eyes, but he couldn't seem to get them to focus. And he felt a sharp pain in his stomach, as if he might vomit.

Somehow he stumbled his way across the street and managed to hold on to his breakfast—*Did I* have *breakfast?*—and stopped to rest on the sidewalk, the chase erased from his thoughts.

The rain had stopped. He stood under the small canvas awning of a tiny high-end boutique with a floor-to-ceiling storefront window. He looked up, expecting to see mannequins on the other side of the glass, but instead, reflected back at him, was a man he'd never seen before.

Everything about his appearance was unfamiliar. He was taller, appeared to have a rather meaty, athletic build, and he wore high-end clothes much too rugged and in style for Collin's taste. Gone was the tiny, balding spot on top of his head, replaced now by thick brown locks trimmed neatly above his ears. He wasn't wearing his glasses—in fact, he didn't seem to need them. He had a few days' growth of facial hair. Even his flabby midsection was missing.

I've gone mad.

He stared at his reflection for minutes on end, unable to do anything else.

Who am I?

That other man—he's me. And I'm . . . not.

Did we switch?

A stranger looked through his eyes, taking him in.

And not just any stranger, it occurred to him. He was as close to a perfect specimen of manhood as Collin allowed might exist. An absence of creases around the eyes and a naturally pleasant expression indicated a calm, confident, well-adjusted individual. One who was clearly bogged out of his mind at the moment, but still.

Collin admired this man a minute more, unable to remove his eyes from the reflection, barely even remembering to breathe. He never noticed the slender, short brunette standing behind his shoulder, also taking in his reflection, until she whistled in appreciation.

"Well, *some*body got the deluxe package."

He turned at last to face the intruder. She was in her mid-to-late twenties. Wearing a no-muss T-shirt and jeans. She went without makeup, a rarity for L.A., and there was no jewelry either.

And she wore no shoes.

For a second he wondered if she might be homeless. Yet her clothes were too clean. She was pretty and casual, her long brown locks falling off her shoulders in untamed curls, but her expression was a flashing neon billboard that declared her to be sharp and confident. She nodded at the glass window, and he turned once more to peer at his image.

Despite—or perhaps because of—the jumble of thoughts pouring through his mind, a guttural "Huh?" was all he could get out.

My voice is different.

Deeper.

Why is this girl barefoot?

"Oh, I know," she went on. "You have no idea what's going on. Blah-blah-raving-hysteria-blah. I'm just saying . . . You took a shortcut to the top of the food chain, handsome."

"What?"

She placed her hands on his neck, straightening the collar of his brown leather jacket and then examining his reflection once more. "This is the part where I'm probably supposed to say something about . . . 'stepping through the looking glass.' Isn't it? I don't know, maybe that's wrong—I never dug sci-fi. But I *do* love that jacket," she said, nodding at his coat.

"This . . . isn't science fiction," he choked, surprised to find he'd been holding his breath since she started talking.

"You're not wrong," she replied with a cocked eyebrow and a smirk. "Things are about to get *real* complicated and I have an elsewhere to be, so let me cut to the heavy exposition. Put your listening cap on, sport, 'cause I'm about to give you a cheat sheet.

"You've just been dropkicked into the middle of something *so big* you'd never buy it if I tried to explain it now. So here's the big reveal. Are you listening? 'Cause this is the one thing you absolutely *gotta* know: you're being watched, right now, this very minute. Several *groups* of people are keeping tabs on your every snap, crackle, and pop. *Everything you do* from this moment on will blip their radars. So be careful. Though you don't have to fear them *all*."

"Watching me? How? Why?" he stammered, trying and failing to keep up with the barefoot girl's barrage of information. His heart thudded madly in his chest, his breaths coming in sudden heaves.

She ignored him and continued. "One group is out to help you. They're not the worry. The other group'll kill you the first chance they get. Don't give 'em one."

"*Kill* me?" he asked, his eyes darting about aimlessly, searching for people watching him . . .

All he saw were bored pedestrians going about their business.

His stomach lurched, and he swallowed bile.

The girl nodded. She'd been toying with him at first, but suddenly she turned somber. "Don't bother looking. This particular less-than-philanthropic group has hired one of the best to do their dirty work, and he knows how to stay hidden. His name is Konrad. I'm sure he's watching you with his own two peepers as we speak."

"But . . . but . . . shouldn't I just go to—"

"The cops?" she finished for him, eyebrows raised. "*That* conversation would go well. 'Say, Officer, did you ever see *Invasion of the Body Snatchers*?'"

He opened his mouth, but no words came out.

She knows.

"But what *is* all this? What's going on?" he nearly yelled after collecting himself. "Why is this happening to me? I'm no one! *Why me?*"

She was silent for a moment, studying him. Finally she spoke, looking deep into his eyes. "It has to be you."

"But *why?*"

"Because you're a player now."

"A player?" he faltered. "We're playing? Playing what?"

She was shorter than Collin, yet somehow she managed to look down on him like a lost toddler in a department store. "Don't follow Collin—the old you."

Wait, his name wasn't Collin anymore? He was Collin Boyd. He knew that as certain as he knew he was standing here.

Which, given how nuts he seemed to have gone, wasn't all that reassuring.

But no, of course Collin wouldn't be his name anymore.

New body, new name.

His thoughts were coming too fast now, his eyes still looking into surrounding windows, buildings, cars, pedestrians walking by . . .

"*Listen* to me," she said, grabbing him by the shoulders and forcing him to focus. "*Don't go near* who you used to be. Get out of town and *just keep going*. Don't slow down. Don't stop. Your life is in danger if you do. Every minute you stay in one place brings Konrad that much closer to you. So you should *go*. Right now."

Still he'd didn't move. Just stood there, eyes wide with fear and brow knitted in deep confusion. A small part of him bristled at being given orders by a stranger. None of this made sense and leaving was out of the question until it did.

The barefoot girl let out a deep breath with just a hint of annoyance. When she opened her mouth, she spoke slower, as if enunciating to someone hard of hearing. "I know this is confusing; it will get easier for you. It *will*. But you don't have time to be stubborn right now. And you're *so* not ready to know yet, anyway. Just *go. Now!*"

She stood there watching him, unblinking, unmoving, waiting for him to move. He thought he detected a trace of concern, or perhaps urgency, on her face. Mostly she appeared put out by his refusal to start running.

He glanced over her shoulder in the direction of the office where he worked, and in the distance the old him, the other man—Collin Boyd— was nowhere, probably already inside. The new him had no idea whether or not to trust this strange woman, but there was an urgency in her voice that was hard to ignore. Still, his frustration was palpable as he glanced back at her.

"I'm not ready to know?" he asked. "Know *what*?"

"What's to come," she said without hesitation.

He bored his eyes into hers, but she never blinked. He found it extremely annoying.

She frowned. "Well, I gotta jet. Keep standing here if you want, but don't come crying to me when you're dead."

With that, she turned and flitted off into the busy throng. The rain had stopped just in time for her exit, which he also found annoying.

He started to call after her, but she was long gone. He didn't know what to say anyway.

He didn't even know her name.

With something she said still tugging at his mind, he reached inside his coat pocket in a mechanical, mindless way and pulled out a fine leather wallet he'd never seen before. Opened it.

Inside was a wad of crisp, clean hundred-dollar bills.

There was also a driver's license bearing the name GRANT M. BORROWS. It was the first time he'd seen or heard the name. Whoever this Grant Borrows was, apparently that's who he was now.

The gravity of the situation struck him all at once, and the world began spinning wildly beneath his feet. It was spiraling out of control, and his stomach churned once more.

He caught the eye of a woman who passed him by, entering the clothing store behind him, and as their eyes met, she . . . *smiled* at him.

That was new.

Another brushed his shoulder exiting the store and actually apologized with a sheepish, overly friendly "I'm so sorry!"

Grant began to hyperventilate. No one *ever* looked him in the eye. He'd spent most of his life cultivating the ability *not* to be noticed. Now it felt like everyone was looking him up and down.

Admiring what they saw.

An old Volkswagen van passed by the sidewalk where he stood, and it backfired loudly like a gunshot, snapping him back to the moment.

Somewhere out there—where he would never see—a man named Konrad was watching him. Possibly moving closer. Meaning to kill him. Perhaps he had a gun with Grant in its sights right now.

Grant Borrows ran.

2

Dr. Daniel Cossick had just arrived at his second-floor lab and placed his key into the lock when the door burst open from the inside and a breathless, red-faced brunette stood before him. He sighed. His assistant Lisa always arrived early, and she had a tendency to get excited over little things, so this was nothing new.

"Doctor Cossick! I just registered a spike of *three-point-seven*," she said, eyes wide with excitement.

Every other thought in Daniel's mind vanished into black. He forgot his keys, forgot his briefcase, forgot everything but the three words he'd just heard. *Three-point-seven.*

Three-point-seven!

He dropped everything and ran after her down the dilapidated hall. Lisa flew into the "lab"—a makeshift facility they'd built themselves in an abandoned building in the Warehouse District—with Daniel following and made for the middle of a modest white room overflowing with odd machinery. The atmosphere was alive with mechanical whirrs and beeps, pungent odors, and the occasional fizz of air or fire. Few visitors could stomach being in the room because the odors were so strong and the sounds so constant, but Daniel and Lisa had grown accustomed to it. They both practically lived here, conducting their search.

Always searching.

In the center of the room was the lab's largest piece of equipment, a massive mechanism that looked like half a giant metal sphere had been mounted on top of a collection of circuitry, wires, and semiconductors. It hummed quietly, almost vibrating, but nothing moved because stillness was crucial. It was approximately four feet in diameter and full of a thick, silver liquid that rose almost to the rim.

"My own potion of mercury mixed with a few other potent elements," Daniel would explain to potential investors, though visitors to the lab were increasingly rare. The liquid itself was inconsequential; it was there to provide mass at the correct density that would measure what they were looking for. The mercury mixture usually remained at a flat calm. Daniel had built special dampeners into the undercarriage to prevent shaking of any kind. Even an earthquake could not jar it, unless the whole building was to topple.

But it would shake if there was a *shimmer*.

And a shimmer was what they were searching for.

If Lisa was correct, a three-point-seven would be the largest event Daniel had ever witnessed. By far.

She motioned to the computer station adjacent to the device and pointed at the screen, grinning from ear to ear.

"Look at that!" She chewed on a nail, watching his every move.

He pulled out his glasses and, hands shaking, slipped them on, his eyes never leaving the monitor. There it was. The device had recorded a three-point-seven spike roughly seven minutes ago. His heart fluttered.

"Location?" he asked, without looking up.

"Already on it," she said, still smiling. "Take another ten or twenty minutes to triangulate."

Daniel nodded, studying the dozens of numbers that appeared on the screen. He did some math in his head and then his entire body stiffened, alarmed.

"Close," he said, still staring at the screen. "Less than three miles from here."

He stood, his eyes out of focus, his mind elsewhere. "Downtown," he mumbled to no one, wiping his hands against the sweater he wore.

He seemed to snap to attention, but still didn't look at her. "Get me that location the moment you have it." He began walking away, toward the other end of the hall, to the only other room they'd retrofitted into the building: his office.

"Dr. Cossick?" Lisa called.

He turned around distractedly. "Yes?"

"This is really it, isn't it?" she asked, holding her breath. She was beaming, excited beyond words.

He forced a modest smile for her benefit, but then turned and continued walking.

"I hope not."

Home turned out to be a different neighborhood than Grant had ever known. Instead of his utilitarian apartment, his cab ride steered him into the canyons of downtown amid the shadows of skyscrapers. The Wagner Building was a new high-rise on Wilshire, a few blocks from the famous old Library Tower and L.A.'s Central Library itself where he'd visited once or twice as a child. The key Grant found in his jacket pocket alongside the wallet unlocked the elevator up to the penthouse floor and then slid smoothly into the apartment's front-door lock.

Before opening the door, a twinge of apprehension tingled in his mind, returning his thoughts to the strange barefoot girl he'd met on the street and her warning to get out of town. Which he had completely ignored. Grant *had* hailed a cab, but as soon as he saw the address on the wallet, all thoughts of fleeing were abandoned. He couldn't resist finding out more about this person he'd somehow become.

And a small part of him did it just to spite the girl and her stupid bare feet.

He pushed open the door to the penthouse and saw a shadowy room ahead. His hand felt around on the inside wall until he found the light switch and flipped it on.

Spread out before him was a bachelor's paradise. Black leather furnishings. Spacious surroundings. Giant flatscreen plasma TV. A desk at the far end of the room featured a sleek, stainless steel computer. Speakers from a massive stereo system were situated throughout the room. Chic floor lamps stood at corners like sentries. Modern art adorned the clean, white walls. To the immediate left of the front door was a fully outfitted kitchen with appliances that bore the stainless-steel sheen of restaurant-quality machinery. Beyond the kitchen was a fully-furnished dining room. Somewhere down the long hall beyond the living room was probably a bedroom, a bathroom, and who knew what else.

He stepped inside and continued to gape. But instincts he couldn't explain were telling him something was wrong. It was the middle of the day, and all of the drapes around the room were closed tight. The pillows on the sofa were perfectly arranged. Everything in the kitchen was exactly where it belonged. The apartment looked as if it had never been used. Not one thing was out of place.

Except for the doormat on which he stood, which was crooked by less than an inch.

He put it together a second too late.

The door slammed shut behind him just as someone grabbed his right arm and pressed it into the small of his back. He felt the tip of a knife against his throat.

Without thinking, Grant grabbed the arm holding the knife with his free hand, and twisted it hard. The knife fell to the floor and at the same time, Grant ducked and sent the attacker flying over his left shoulder, where he crashed on the floor in the living room over ten feet away.

Grant couldn't tell which of them was more surprised at what he'd just done—he or the other man, who slumped against the ground. Grant watched the other man fall, but could only stand there numbly, breath caught in his throat. It had all happened so fast.

He had no idea how he'd done it.

His assailant, a short stump of a man clad in a baggy black jump-suit and shin-high black boots who had to be pushing fifty, lay there for a fraction of a second, stunned at Grant's quick reaction. He looked like he was made of solid brick and frowned in a way that looked as though the expression had been permanently etched into his face.

Konrad, Grant guessed.

What did I ever do to you?

But Konrad's pause lasted only a moment, and he rolled back to his feet and pulled a gun out of a shoulder holster in a simple, fluid motion.

"I wasn't told you could do that," Konrad said. His deep, abrasive voice sounded like a jackhammer pounding into pavement. "I'm a col-lector; lack of full disclosure means I get something extra. I'm think-ing . . . *kneecap*." He lowered the gun and pointed it at Grant's leg.

Grant had launched into a dead sprint, instincts taking over. He was outside the apartment door before the first shot was fired. He darted down the corridor, unsure where he was headed. He made it to the end of the hall, where he met a full-length window and a sprawling view of the L.A. skyline that should have been breathtaking. But a second shot shattered the glass, and Grant dove around the corner to his right.

A door marked "STAIRS" that he hadn't noticed earlier waited before him. Grant's heart leapt and he dashed through the door. He made it down the first flight before hearing the door slam open behind him, and he rounded to the next floor, just as Konrad fired again.

A pinching pain sliced through his left leg, and he staggered. But the adrenaline was surging now like nothing he'd felt before, and it kept him from stopping. Rounding the next staircase, he caught sight of the adjoining door, which read "ELEVEN."

Come on, come on. Ten flights.

You can do this.

Down he ran, feet flying over each step. It seemed impossible. Just the other night he'd been talking with his landlady about how quiet and lonely and boring his life was. All he had was his job. She wondered if he brought it on himself but he told her that he'd never asked to be alone. Why bother questioning fate? Yet in the dark of the night it had come to him. How pointless it all seemed, this endless stupid pattern, winding around him tighter and tighter.

His job. Being around other people. His whole life.

It felt like a snake twisting around his neck, tightening its grip, and he'd woken many nights in a sweat, gasping for air.

Now *he* was the snake, winding dizzyingly around and around while breathing became harder and harder . . .

Another shot rang out, closer this time, and he instinctively ducked.

"Did you know that dismemberment isn't always fatal?" Konrad said from above. He wasn't shouting, he was growling, quietly. He was keeping up with Grant's frantic pace, but his words had come as casually as if he were riding an elevator.

Halfway down the next flight, Grant grabbed the middle rail and flung himself over, dropping ten feet to the flight below. He landed solidly, but his leg flashed with a stabbing pain, and he kept going down, rolling to the bottom of the stairs. When he stopped, he noticed that his left pant leg was crimson with blood.

But there was no time to think; he jumped to his feet and darted off again, down, down, down.

Come on! This is taking too long!

More shots clanged off of the center railing. Grant moved to the outside edge of the stairs, staying close to the wall. Another flight. Another. More shots.

Keep moving. You can do this.

Maybe I should just stop, let him finish it. Wouldn't it be easier?

The thought of dying wasn't all that bad . . .

"The trick is sealing off the wound," Konrad's voice echoed in the stairwell. "A needle and string will do, but I find that cauterizing the wound works best. With the proper antibiotics, I can take a man apart one inch at a time. It can last for *weeks* before I even *get close* to the vital organs."

And . . . let's keep running, shall we?

The pain in his leg seared now, and he broke into a cold sweat. He may have been more in shape now than before, but he was still human. And his leg screamed in agony.

At last he made it to the door marked "ONE." He had the door open when another idea came to mind. He pushed the door open as far as it would go, so its hydraulic hinge would require several seconds to pull it closed. Then he hopped on one foot, so as to not leave another blood trail, in the direction of the last flight of stairs, which led to the building's mechanical room.

He stopped halfway down the steps and crouched, listening. Konrad's heavy footfalls faded away, and then he heard the open door above him click shut.

Grant wasted no time. Hurtling himself down the remaining steps, he burst through the mechanical room's door. Frantic, he glanced around the warm, dark, dry room, looking for anything that might help. A broomstick he could use as a weapon, something to lodge against the door. But there was nothing. The small room held the building's massive furnace and myriad other equipment, but little else. Even light seemed to be swallowed up by the space.

He felt his way around the furnace to the right, thinking only of how Konrad wouldn't be thrown off the trail long. There on the right side of the room, he came upon a small locked door. He thought about kicking it, but his leg hurt too deeply so he lowered his shoulder and crashed at it with as much force as he could manage.

To his astonishment, it worked, and he let out a triumphant grunt. A narrow flight of stairs beyond the open door led down. He threw himself down them, legs barely working anymore. At the bottom he slammed his body into a second door and dashed through.

Grant couldn't believe his luck. He was standing in the middle of an enormous subway station, bustling with activity. And not just any station—he knew this place, had been here before. It was the Metro Center Station, just across Figueroa Street from the Wagner Building. He remembered the movie-themed artwork adorning the walls. It felt more like a sterile airport than a subterranean tunnel. Its shiny steel fittings mirrored Grant's dilapidated appearance back at him everywhere he looked.

A Blue Line train bulleted by on the tracks nearest him, its engine piercing the roar of the vast crowd.

Grant looked back at the door he'd just passed through. On this side, it read "EMERGENCY EXIT."

He glanced around the subway, his mind racing. About a hundred feet down the corridor, beyond a swell of pedestrians waiting for the next train, he spotted an escalator that led up to sunlight beyond.

He set off again, forcing his way through the crowd, brushing shoulders and nearly shoving others. But once they got a look at his haggard features and bloodied clothes, most were only too happy to get out of his way. He was limping now, blood still dribbling from his leg onto the floor's brick-colored tiles.

He felt light-headed. *Probably from the blood loss*, some part of his mind registered the sensation.

Grant had just placed one foot on the bottom step when he heard another gunshot, followed by hundreds of screams. Konrad was descending the stairs directly above him, and fast.

Grant hobbled in the opposite direction, trying to run, but the other man jumped from near the bottom of the steps, tackling him from behind. The gun went off again as they grappled for it on the floor. A train pulled up and most of the crowd scrambled into it, many of them still screaming.

Grant threw a punch and was surprised to see it connect.

But Konrad stood up, unfazed, and hoisted Grant to his feet as well. Grant's senses were muddled, feeling more of the pain in his leg now. His newfound reflexes seemed to have slowed when the exhaustion had kicked in. His chest heaved and he couldn't catch his breath. He didn't realize what was happening until it was too late to stop it— the other man had shoved him up against the nearest wall and pinned a bulky arm across his chest.

"I still want my kneecap," he growled, his hot breath inches from Grant's face.

3

"You're not going to kill me," Grant announced, surprised at himself.

Konrad punched him in the face. Grant's head thumped against the tiled wall behind him, and he winced at the pain from his nose and mouth.

"You could have shot me in the apartment," he continued, panting, "but you snuck up behind me with a *knife*. On the stairs, you shot me in the *leg*, not the chest," Grant concluded. "You *want* something."

Konrad smiled the ugliest smile Grant had ever seen. He had perfect teeth, but there was a gruesome malevolence in the expression. "Not bad. But if killing you is the only way of getting what I'm here for . . . I've made my peace with it." His hollow eyes slowly moved down Grant's right arm and landed on his hand, which he looked at hungrily. Grant followed his gaze down to the same spot.

And gasped.

A large gold ring, wider on top than underneath, like the shape of a class ring, rested there on his middle finger. The gold was so smooth it might have been liquid. Not a single scratch could be seen. Inset in the widest part of the band was a dark red gemstone. Odd markings were cut as tiny holes into the sides of the band. Grant had never seen the ring before, but he could tell from the sensation that it had been on his finger for a while.

At least since the bus, he guessed.

"You can have it," Grant said, holding out his hand. The chase had worn him out, strength all but gone, breath coming in shooting waves, along with the pounding of his pulse that he could feel in the pain from his leg. His equilibrium was damaged by the blow to the head, and if Konrad hadn't been pinning him against the wall, he might have collapsed.

"Hold it!" a man screamed from twenty feet down the line, in Grant's line of sight and directly behind Konrad. He looked like some kind of Metro security . . .

Without hesitating or even looking, Konrad fired a shot over his shoulder and the security guard went down. The few remaining pedestrians in the station panicked and ran. Konrad holstered the gun and retrieved a knife from his belt—the same one he'd pressed against Grant's throat in the apartment. Letting go with his other arm, he slammed his fist into Grant's face once again. Something cracked this time, but Grant couldn't be sure if it was his head or the ceramic of the wall. He fought the rising bile in his throat as well as the blackness creeping into the edge of his vision.

Konrad clutched Grant's wrist with a powerful, vice-like grip. The blood drained out of it quickly, and soon Grant could no longer feel it. Konrad curled Grant's other fingers into a fist, until only the middle ring finger remained extended.

"Heh," Grant spat deliriously, eyes half-open. "I'm giving you the finger."

Konrad looked into his eyes. "No," he said, "I'm taking it."

His blade touched the side of Grant's finger, just below the ring, where his finger met his hand, and he started to slice.

Grant's head bucked violently and he clenched his eyes closed tight, gritting his teeth. A blinding pain ripped through his head, and his whole body seized.

No!

Grant heard Konrad gasp and then the whistle of something flying through the air. The man's grip relaxed and when Grant opened his eyes, Konrad was staring, neck craned, across the subway station where something glinted on the wall.

The pain faded as quickly as it had come, and Grant saw his one opportunity. He kneed Konrad viciously in the groin with every bit of strength he had left. Konrad doubled over, coughing and wheezing, then collapsed.

Grant staggered away from the wall, towering over the man. Despite his pain, he felt an unmistakable rush of satisfaction.

"*That* was my kneecap!" Grant shouted in a blind rage. "How'd it feel?!"

His eyes shifted to the gun attached to Konrad's belt and lingered there. He couldn't seem to slow his breathing, giving in to a crazed fit of wrath that erupted from him, swelling through his entire being.

Konrad spoke in a wheeze, sensing Grant's next action. "Think carefully . . ." he whispered, "about your next move."

Grant returned his focus, completely incensed, to the man on the ground, who continued speaking while clutching his privates, his face beet red and tears in his eyes. "I know who you really are," he wheezed with a slight bob in his eyebrows. "And if I can't kill *you* . . . I'll settle for those you care about most."

Grant was a bomb ready to explode, his chest swelling equally from the exertion of standing and the outrage he felt. "There *isn't* anyone I care about," he seethed through gritted teeth.

He kicked Konrad across the face, as hard as he could, and the man on the ground was out cold.

Grant braced himself against the wall, winded and stunned that he'd just beaten this man—whom he could only assume was some sort of mercenary or assassin. Despite his pain and fatigue, the fight had felt quite natural, even intuitive. Most of the time, Grant found he hadn't even known what he was doing until it was done.

How could that be?

A handful of people—those who hadn't run at the sight of Konrad's gun—still hovered, watching him. But his attention shifted away from them to a space across the tracks, where a larger group of people were huddled before a round pillar made of solid concrete. A man in a navy blazer shifted to one side, and Grant saw there, sticking out of the pillar, the hilt of his attacker's knife. The blade was buried deep inside the column.

He hesitated, confused. He couldn't recall how the knife had gotten all the way over there. He thought back to the fight . . . Grant had closed his eyes only for a second when the headache struck, and when he opened them, Konrad's hand was empty, his attention drawn elsewhere.

A shot of blinding pain from his leg wrenched him back to the present.

The girl at the storefront—whoever she was . . . She had been right.

He should have bolted when this all started.

Too late now.

He limped in the direction of the stairs leading up and out.

He had to get out of here, find safety.

If such a thing still existed.

"It looks like you're within twenty meters of the convergence," Lisa said into Daniel's earpiece.

"Okay, I'll take it from here," he replied.

She immediately went radio silent. Thankfully.

He liked Lisa. Well, he *tolerated* her, anyway, as much as he tolerated anyone. But if she weren't whip-smart and an astute lab tech, he never would have been able to abide her endless chatter. He hadn't known her for very long before he realized that she lacked a filter between her brain and her mouth—she simply verbalized every thought that entered her mind.

She was good, though—really good. She often caught things that he was too impatient to notice, and she had a way of pushing their research along avenues of thought that he might not otherwise have considered.

But the constant conversation drove him batty, particularly in the mornings. He preferred the silence of his own thoughts.

Daniel stood on the downtown sidewalk under the midday sun, which had finally broken through the clouds, holding his small device in his hand. It was a simple instrument he'd built from pieces of a Pocket PC and some other materials. Its panel lit up whenever a shimmer—or the residual energy given off by a recent shimmer—was nearby. The closer he got, the brighter it glowed. Lisa said it was essentially a high-tech version of the "you're getting warmer" game.

He marched forward another ten paces and glanced at the device. It was brighter here. He looked up. A bus stop faced him across the street.

It had happened right around here, he was sure of it.

But what was he expecting to find? It had taken much longer than he'd hoped for the lab's past-generation systems to narrow down the shimmer's position. As his rumbling stomach reminded him, it was nearing lunchtime. Whatever event had taken place here, it was long over.

Daniel walked forward, crossing the street and nearing the bus stop, when a high-pitched squeal in his earpiece brought him up short.

"Doct—! It hap—a—n!" Lisa was shouting.

He reached up and massaged his ear. "Say again? *Quietly*?"

"It happened again! Another shimmer! Just now!" she replied.

He froze. *Two in one day.*

One was unprecedented. Two was unimaginable.

"How big?" he shouted, not caring about the people on the street who stopped to stare.

"Hang on, it's processing now . . ."

An impossibly long minute passed, and the light changed. A bicyclist squeaked his horn, so Daniel ran out of the street and under the empty glass bus shelter.

"Well?" he asked impatiently.

"Doctor Cossick, . . ." she whispered, "it was a *seven-point-nine*."

He plopped down on the shelter's plastic bench, aware of nothing around him save his heart pounding madly beneath his chest.

"Where was it?" he finally said.

"Can't tell yet," she mumbled. "It's still triangulating. But *two* of them! *Two shimmers!* Can you *believe* this?"

"Feed me the data," he replied, pulling out a touch-screen device smaller than a laptop. He tapped the screen and looked at the data Lisa was pouring into it by remote. He focused on the numbers and quickly did some preliminary math on the small computer.

When he was finished, he sat back, dropping the pad to his knees.

"I think it's near the Library," he said out loud.

He pulled the smaller device back out of his pocket and turned it on.

Even in the rising midday sun, it glowed ferociously.

4

Grant walked as far as he could before the pain in his leg grew unbearable. It needed dressing, and he had to find someplace safe to hide, get his bearings and consider his options. He'd crossed 110 on West 7th and guessed he was now a mile or so west of the Wagner Building. He'd never been in this part of the city before.

Konrad would wake up soon. Grant wondered if he should have done something more. Perhaps he should have tied Konrad up and thrown him onto one of the moving trains or something. But the people standing around, who'd witnessed the entire fight, had watched him carefully after it was over. Add that weird knife thing to the situation, and he just wanted to get out of there.

He wasn't equipped to deal with what was happening on his own, that much was clear. For that matter, he didn't even know who he was. He'd never heard of this "Grant Borrows." The most likely scenario, he decided, was that somehow, he and this Borrows person had exchanged . . . *lives*.

However impossible that sounded.

He hailed a passing cab and asked the driver—an elderly woman with thin, wiry hair and large horn-rimmed glasses that had lenses set to a high magnification—to take him to the closest drugstore. At the strip mall where she stopped, he handed her three of his crisp hundred-dollar bills, and asked her to please wait. She didn't reply, but her huge eyes got even bigger when he placed the currency into her hand, so he wasn't concerned.

Grant staggered into the store, trying hard not to pass out, and drew expressions from patrons and employees that ranged from puzzled to downright spooked. Most backed away at the sight of him.

Shuffling his way down various aisles, Grant's thoughts lingered bleakly on how he hoped to be waking up any minute now. He picked up a small, brown bottle of peroxide, a roll of gauze, a bottle of Tylenol, and a few snacks. He paid the clerk—whose fearful eyes seemed to silently call for a co-worker to come handle this situation—and asked if they had a restroom.

Once inside the tiny room at the back of the store, he locked the door and rolled his pant leg up to get his first look at the wound on his leg. Or rather, whoever's leg this was. It wasn't a limb he recognized.

It was worse than he'd thought. Much more than a graze. The bullet had torn through one side of his tan, muscular calf and exited straight out the other. He couldn't believe it. There were two holes in his leg. His rear end smacked the floor as he slid down the wall, then he leaned back, took a deep breath, and closed his eyes.

He stayed that way until his breathing slowed.

He eyed the ring on his finger, and timidly touched it with a finger on the other hand. The metal was smooth and warm, and while not exactly store window material, it looked quite old.

Suddenly he tugged at it, alarmed. It wouldn't come off.

He pulled harder.

It wouldn't budge.

At first he thought it was merely stuck, that his finger had swollen. But the ring didn't wiggle *at all*. It was affixed to his finger, as if bonded directly to the skin.

That's why he was going to use a knife, he thought, remembering his struggle in the subway. *Konrad couldn't take the ring off, so he was going to take my whole finger*.

He propped his injured leg up over the open toilet seat, and after a moment's hesitation, poured the peroxide over it. The pain was excruciating, acid bubbling up around the wound and pus pouring out. He turned his leg over and did the same to the other side. He repeated the process several times, until satisfied.

Finally, he stood and popped a few Tylenol in his mouth, then began winding gauze around his leg. Wrap after wrap after wrap.

His mind wandered again, watching the white wrap go round and round. It twisted like the snake in his mind. A pure white snake intent on strangling him . . .

When I woke up this morning, I was Collin Boyd.

Now I'm Grant Borrows.

"My name is Grant Borrows."

"Grant Borrows, nice to meet you."

The white snake spun around its victim again and again. Grant's eyes glazed over, watching it curl and fighting a growing shortness of breath.

I stepped off a bus, found out I was no longer myself, and now I'm cleaning a gunshot wound inside a drugstore bathroom, and there's a ring on my finger that won't come off.

How did I get here?

A few wraps of medical tape would hold the gauze securely in place. He limped painfully to the tiny sink and gazed wearily into the mirror above it.

The handsome man he'd first seen in the store window that morning was still there, looking back at him, but he was a horrible mess now. Bruises on his cheek. Dried blood beneath his nose. His bottom lip was split. Hair disheveled. Eyes dark like a raccoon's. He ran a hand around the back of his head and felt more dried blood, from where it had smacked the concrete wall.

No wonder the store clerk had been terrified. The sudden notion that she might have called the police increased the urgency of his movements.

He poured peroxide over his ring finger where it had been cut, and bandaged it as best he could. He put what remained of his meager supplies in his inside jacket pockets, then washed his hands and face, which provided only a minor improvement. His clothes were still a bloody mess, but he couldn't do anything about it now.

He had to keep moving. He'd stayed in one place too long already. But where to go?

Grant thought again of the barefoot girl and her warning to keep moving. And he thought about Konrad and the last words he'd uttered.

"If I can't kill you . . . I'll settle for those you care about most."

He gasped, and for once, it wasn't from the pain.

Oh no.

He slammed open the door to the bathroom and ran back out to the cab as best he could, adrenaline surging through him once more as the sun waned on the horizon.

If he knows who I really am, then he knows . . .

About her!

"Where to, honey?" the cab driver's squeaky voice intoned.

"UCLA campus," he replied breathlessly, shoving two more hundred-dollar bills into her hands. "Take Wilshire and run every light you have to!"

Amid the panic it occurred to him that however scared he'd been before . . . it was *nothing* compared to what he was feeling now.

Every hair on Julie Saunders' arms and neck stood on end. It was late as she stopped, all alone in the UCLA faculty offices, to lock her office door, the darkness closing in around her.

She had no idea how or why, but she *knew* she was being watched.

Julie made her way quickly down the hall, breathing fast, eyes darting all around. The only sound came from the keychain jangling in her hand.

The feeling was suffocating, as if the air were made of syrup. She trembled visibly as she exited the building and walked out onto the campus grounds. Once outside, she stopped for a moment and collected herself, taking several deep breaths.

The outside air brought some comfort. The lights in most of the dormitories were still on—but that was no indication of the time, considering how late college students stayed up. The outdoor lamps were also on and she could see the front end of her car peeking at her from its perch atop the adjacent parking garage. The little teal Saturn appeared to be all alone up there.

The sense that she was being watched had not gone away.

Just get me home safe, and I'll never stay at work past sundown again, she thought, her heart pounding. But she knew she'd had little choice besides putting in the extra hours. Recent events had put her behind on everything, most especially grading mid-term papers.

Julie wound the stairs to the top of the garage. Beside her car, she fiddled awkwardly with her keys, hands trembling until she found the right one. Once inside, she locked the doors. Starting the engine made her feel better.

As she quietly backed out of her parking space, her pulse began to calm.

Hundreds of feet away, high atop one of the twin bell towers of the campus's auditorium, Konrad lay on his stomach, cradling a sniper rifle that was propped on the brick ledge. His right eye squinted into the telescopic lens as Julie's car slowly shifted into drive and turned toward the downward exit.

The car turned left, and now the driver's side of the car was facing him. Konrad's mouth stretched into a tight smile. He was going to enjoy this just a little more than usual.

He zeroed in on Julie's head and tightened his grip, waiting patiently. He could make the shot while she was in motion, he knew, but the distance was further than he preferred. So he decided to wait. The hunt was the best part, no doubt. But it failed to provide the divine *thirst* that waiting brought.

A ramp led from the garage to the nearest street; she would have to stop there, before turning out onto the main road. And he would be ready.

Inside the car, Julie glanced at the dashboard clock as she spiraled down the exit ramps. *10:43* P.M.

She sighed. So late, and she still had a long drive ahead on the 405. She was going to need help staying awake that long.

Julie passed through the garage's gated entrance and tapped her brakes until she stopped at her exit onto the main road. She leaned into the passenger's side floorboard to find a CD in her purse. She was only halfway over when the glass in the driver's-side door shattered.

She screamed then unlocked her seatbelt and lay all the way over in the passenger's seat. She looked around, unsure of what to do, when another shot popped loudly, punching a hole in the dashboard just above her.

Still hunched flat in the car, she jammed her foot on the gas, unconcerned about any oncoming traffic she might be turning in to. Once the car had gone a full ninety degrees to the right, she sat up and pushed the pedal as far down as it would go, racing along the college's back roads.

No pain. She glanced down to see if she was hurt. No blood stains. She felt her head and her face, which was moist, but she dabbed it with a finger and saw that the liquid was clear. Only then did she realize that she'd been crying since the first shot was fired.

Julie sped her way south along the campus grounds, wiping her face and dodging students. Her muscles were tensed and she was shivering all over.

She snatched her phone and dialed 911.

An hour later, Konrad was still watching.

Through his sniper scope, he could see the woman sitting in a chair. She was plainly worn out and hadn't regained her composure since his attack. He could see her hands shaking slightly as she accepted a cup of coffee from the duty officer.

She was inside the UCLA Police Department building, near the center of the campus. He watched from an office on the top floor of the Gonda Center, a genetic research building just across the street

A street ran between the Center and the campus police headquarters, with cars passing between very infrequently. A few students could be seen here and there walking and talking, even at this ungodly hour. But Konrad had no fear that he might be discovered. The building was locked down and all the lights were out.

If anyone did somehow intrude on him, he'd simply shoot them in the head with the silenced pistol on his hip.

All of this was part of Konrad's contingency plan, of course, made long before he'd shot holes into the woman's car, just as he'd known she would go straight to the police if he missed. He'd been given a complete file on this woman, which was almost as thick as the file for Borrows. She was a good citizen: she paid her taxes on time, she gave regularly to charities, she often worked late at her office.

She cared. She *loved*. She believed that doing right was what mattered.

Of course she would go straight to the police when someone took a shot at her. She'd be "safe" there.

He was unconcerned about his earlier failure to kill her, but it gnawed at him that he hadn't been able to off Borrows yet. Still, setbacks were inevitable. He was a detail person, and this was a possibility he'd planned for. Besides, the woman's movements would prove even *more* predictable in this state.

Best of all, it prolonged the hunt.

And the hunt was all there was.

So he didn't mind waiting, sipping water from a bottle as he kept an eye on her through the rifle scope. She'd just been handed off to another policeman—a man in a suit sitting behind a desk, concern written all over his face—when a bulky, heavyset man in an overcoat—*Classic detective*, Konrad thought—strode into the office and began speaking to the desk officer with his arms crossed. He looked most displeased.

From what Konrad could tell, the police didn't seem keen on releasing the woman until they were convinced she was out of danger, though it looked like this new policeman might be shaking things up.

Whatever.

Improvising wasn't a problem. Neither was patience.

So he watched, and he waited.

Very patiently.

5

Julie had no idea who this guy in the trench coat was, and she couldn't bring herself to care.

All she could think about was how she should feel perfectly safe right now, and yet she didn't. As the two officers in this small room conferred quietly—some kind of jurisdictional dispute, from the sound of it—she was met with the growing sensation that all of the oxygen was very slowly being vacuumed from the room. It was growing steadily warmer, and her heart beat a little faster with each passing minute.

The young UCLA officer finally cleared his throat before smiling again at Julie, as both officers turned to face her. "This is Detective Drexel, and he's going to be taking care of you and looking into your case, Ms. Saunders."

Julie carefully got to her feet. "I just want this to be over. I still can't believe it. Can I go home?"

Drexel smiled at her reassuringly—though his smile looked an awful lot like the face other people make when they're in pain—as he hefted his considerable weight a step forward in her direction. "Very soon, I promise," he attempted to soothe, but his voice was surprisingly nasal and scratchy for such a barrel-chested man. "I need to get your statement on record at my office downtown, which is between here and your house. I won't delay you any longer than I have to."

Julie thought quietly to herself as Drexel ushered her from the room.

"Could it be gang-related?" she asked.

"I doubt it," he replied casually, his hand steering her shoulder through the all-but-empty outer room and toward the front door. "Any of your students unhappy with their grades lately?"

She offered a halfhearted chuckle. "Students are *always* unhappy with their grades, Detective."

"Stop!" Grant screamed from the back seat of the cab.

They'd reached the street outside of the UCLA Police Department. Standing there on the curb in front of the building was a girl. The girl without shoes.

"Wait right here!" Grant shouted, jumping from the cab.

"Honey, I can't park in the middle of the—" the driver called after him, but he ignored her and ran toward the station house.

Grant had just limped through the building's front door, following the shoeless girl inside, when he stopped cold. The young woman was nowhere to be seen, but Julie was right in front of him, being escorted straight toward him from a hallway on the right. She came closer, into the lobby, and their eyes met from ten feet away. She didn't recognize him, of course, but she held his gaze nonetheless. Perhaps it was Grant's bloodied and battered appearance—which was far worse than hers—but there was a peculiar expression on her face as she gazed at him.

Her long black hair was matted, disheveled, and her face gaunt and weary. Bags drooped under her eyes. If Grant hadn't known who she was, he might not have recognized her. A big man in a blue trench coat had his hand on her shoulder, directing her, but now was shifting his attention to Grant, suspicion unmistakable in his features.

Julie didn't look away as they drew closer together from opposite corners of the lobby. Time slid into slow motion for Grant as they came close enough to touch one another. He couldn't bring himself to speak, couldn't think of what to say, how to explain his situation, his appearance, his fear for her life. What *was* there to say? What could possibly escape from his lips that wouldn't sound like the ramblings of a crazy person?

Grant took a step toward them. The cop yanked Julie out of concern, and at the same moment glass exploded from the window to Grant's immediate right. Julie's bulky escort fell sharply to the ground, but Julie herself stopped cold exactly where she stood.

Grant's breath caught in his throat.

It was as if Julie had been frozen and bolted into place, in mid-stride, her eyes still trained on him. She simply . . . *paused* for a long moment, before her eyes rolled up and her entire body went limp. She collapsed to the floor.

Grant snapped out of his reverie and dove to shield her body with his.

The police department had erupted into chaos, officers screaming and shouting. More shots rang out and some fled for cover and others ran out onto the street. The first officer to attempt an exit had been gunned down, and now his body lay just outside the door.

For the hundredth time that day, Grant's thoughts returned to a single notion: *Why is this happening to me?*

The shooting paused, and Grant knew instinctively that the sniper—Konrad, no doubt—had stopped to reload. Depending on the model, there should be somewhere between five and twelve seconds before the shooting resumed.

Grant blinked.

How do I know that?

No time to figure it out now, Grant labored onto his haunches and threw Julie's limp, unconscious form over his shoulder. With his new body, she felt almost weightless. He took off down the hallway she'd just emerged from, a corridor without windows that paralleled the street outside.

The gunfire and chaos continued behind him, but it faded as he made a left, and then a right. He found himself at another entrance on the far right side of the building. Outside, he gently lay Julie on the grass and felt her pulse.

Alive. He scanned her for wounds, found none. Grant hoisted her up again and carried her toward the front corner of the building.

Peeking cautiously around the brick, he spotted a handful of black-suited officers illuminated by streetlamps aiming, pointing, yelling, running, barking into radios. One of them seemed to have spotted where the gunshots were coming from.

Grant's cab had vanished. He wanted to be angry, after all the money he'd given her, but what could he expect?

No transportation.

Cops everywhere.

And Konrad will start shooting again any second.

Now what?

Come on, you weird new reflexes! Kick in again and tell me what to do!

Grant ducked and pulled Julie farther away from the edge of the building as another shot was fired. He couldn't tell where Konrad had aimed this time, but he felt the need to be even farther away from the target area, all the same. It sounded like he had switched to a semi-automatic.

The policemen preparing to enter the Gondo Center were pinned down. Every time one of the men in black got close to the building, more shots would ring out, sometimes connecting with a leg or an abdomen. One fell and pulled himself to safety. Another fell and did not move. Only a pair of policemen remained able to fight, but they were taking cover behind vehicles.

Running out of time. . . !

Approaching the building was a red Jeep with no side doors and its canvas top missing. The Jeep had stopped at the sight of the drama playing out in front of the police station, and Grant seized the opportunity.

He climbed into the vehicle's passenger side, laid Julie across the backseat, and muttered a "sorry" to the stunned young man in the driver's seat as he kicked him out the other side. The boy rolled on the ground, but Grant didn't wait to see what happened next. He dropped into the driver's seat and gunned the engine.

He'd nearly made a clean getaway when the big cop in the blue trench coat burst through the front door and stopped in front of the car, his gun leveled at Grant's head.

"Let 'er go!" he shouted in a pinched voice, his free hand clutching his opposite shoulder, which was bleeding.

But Konrad chose that moment to start firing again, and the cop turned his attention to the faraway window and fired his pistol in that direction instead.

Grant swerved around the cop and immediately heard a shout of "Hold it!" from behind.

He didn't.

Julie moaned again. She was waking up.

Daniel Cossick had seen some strange things in his life—stranger than most could claim—but there were no words for what he was seeing at this moment.

Midnight had come and gone, and he'd just tracked down the source of the second shimmer at last.

Stepping across fresh yellow police tape, he tentatively touched the knife that was wedged into the subway station column. It had dug all the way into the cement, stopped only by its hilt from going in any further.

The subway was far from empty at this time of night, but no one seemed to care that he was taking a closer look.

He was surprised the police hadn't tried to remove the thing from the wall.

Or maybe they *had*, and couldn't.

"What is it? What do you see?" Lisa squawked eagerly in his ear, making him jump.

When he'd settled, he replied quietly, still examining the knife.

"Exactly what we're looking for. Something impossible."

Daniel took a step forward and leaned in close to the weapon, getting as close an impression of it as he could. It looked rather heavy. Probably at least nine inches in length, handle to razor-sharp tip. The hilt was solid and had a comfortable, form-fitted grip.

This was no pocket toy casually left behind. To whoever owned it, this was something of great value. It would not have been left here by choice.

Daniel knew there was little chance of removing it, but he couldn't resist trying. He gripped it with gloved hands, and after glancing around the station to make sure no one was looking, gave it his best King Arthur tug. It was a pointless exercise.

"What does *that* mean?" Lisa asked.

Daniel turned to see the other roped-off area on the opposite side of the tracks. Spots of dried blood were visible on the ground. He twisted to face the pillar in front of him once more.

"It means the Threshold has been breached," he answered somberly, stepping away from the column but never looking away from the knife. "And all bets are off."

6

Grant drove. For hours, much of the time not realizing where he was going.

He had no destination in mind; he just wanted to get Julie away from danger. Eventually he took the 405 to Rosa Parks and then headed east back to the glow of downtown. Traffic buzzed even this late but never bogged down. He almost took the exit back to his penthouse but dismissed it. It was too dangerous.

The stolen Jeep finally came to a stop almost of its own volition at a small park called Hollenbeck Lake. Sunrise was still an hour or two away and Grant tucked the Jeep as far from streetlamps as possible. His mind should've been whirling, trying to decide what to say to Julie when she fully came to, but exhaustion overtook him and he fell into a fitful sleep.

He roused, chilled, when a glint of dawn peeked off to the east.

Julie made groggy noises from the backseat, and Grant carefully scooped her up into his arms, struggling under the weight on his bad leg. Her pocketbook still drooped over one shoulder. He glanced around frantically and spotted a park bench at the edge of the lake.

Even at daybreak he was unsurprised to find a small handful of runners already there, circling the water. Fitness always came first in L.A.

Grant placed Julie gently upon the bench, just as her eyes began to flutter open. He sat opposite her and steadied her, holding her upright.

She looks so tired . . .

Her eyes focused at last, and she screamed.

"Listen to me, Julie—" he started, letting go of her.

"Who are you! What—"

"Julie, listen! You *know* me! You know who I am!"

She was in danger of hyperventilating, but she said nothing, both terror-filled eyes trained on him, taking in his bloodstained, battered appearance. "I—I do?"

Grant was breathing rapidly, too, his thoughts coming faster than his tongue could handle. "I wish I could do this differently," he spoke hurriedly. "But we don't have time. We won't be safe here for long."

Still she looked at him. He forced himself to breathe more slowly as he gazed into her eyes—those eyes he knew so well, so deep, the skin around them creased by long years of tears and laughter. What a life she'd led . . .

He was suddenly overcome with emotion, sitting next to her for the first time in years. And she looked at him with such intense fear.

He took one last, slow, unsteady breath.

"Julie, I'm Collin. I'm *your brother*."

She stood up from the bench, and began backing away from him. Anguish filled her eyes.

She started to say something, but nothing came out. Instead, she just shook her head, unblinking.

Grant stood. "It's the truth. I know you don't recognize me—*I* don't even recognize me—but I *am* the man you knew as Collin Boyd."

"I'm calling the police right now," she said. She pulled a tiny phone out of her pocketbook. She started to dial and turned and walked away from him.

Grant stood and swallowed. If he couldn't convince her now, then they had no chance. There was no time for this. Konrad would be coming. What could he say that she would believe? One obvious thing came to mind, but he'd been avoiding that conversation for twenty-some years . . .

She was still moving away, nearing the shoreline.

There was no choice.

"The day you left the orphanage," he called out, "was the worst day of my life."

Grant had never spoken aloud these thoughts that had tumbled through his mind so many times. The gravity of the moment struck him just then, and his words came out slowly.

Julie stopped walking. Her fingers paused over the phone, but she didn't face him.

"You held me *so* tight before they took you," he gasped, his throat full. "I was *terrified* when you let go. I tried not to show it. For you. I didn't want to make it worse." A tear built up in one eye, and then tumbled down his face. "I knew you felt bad. Maybe worse than I did. But I was *petrified*, Julie."

She stared off into the increasingly bright sky, blinking back tears of her own.

"I never knew Mom. I barely remember Dad. You were the only family I had left."

"This is cruel," she said, shaking her head, still not looking at him. "You're lying, you *heard* this—!"

"You *begged* your new parents," he went on, barely able to choke back his own tears now. "—*pleaded* with them to take me—adopt me, too. But they live in Seattle and they could only take one of us."

She spun around, tears streaming down her cheeks. "I don't believe you," she shouted. "Collin lives in Glendale; he's probably there right now. You *can't* be him!"

His gaze fell, too pained to meet her eyes. "The next time I saw you, four months had passed. *Four months*, Julie. You said you'd tried to visit sooner, that you asked them about it every day." The tears were falling freely now. "But by then it was too late. You *forgot* about me."

"That's not true! I could *never*—!"

He sniffled and continued, "I know . . . now. I know. But I was lost without you." His breaths came in heaves, and he finally raised his eyes again. "When you left at the end of that first visit—you whispered into my ear. Do you remember what you said?"

She watched him warily, hopefully.

"You told me that when we dream, we go to a special place where anything is possible. You said we would make this our—"

"Our safe house," Julie whispered, finishing for him.

"Where we could meet and play together every single night," Grant concluded. "I went there every night in my sleep, or tried to . . . But even there you never came."

Julie's phone fell to the ground.

Crying openly, a hand over her mouth, she walked back to him, staring into his eyes. She stood only inches from him, watching him. Wanting to believe, but dazed and confused. At last her expression softened. "*You* were always there in *my* dreams," she said softly.

They both took choked breaths and then embraced hard, rocking back and forth, holding tight, as morning glowed gold and green all about them.

They never wanted to let go.

"So what do we do about all this?" Julie asked. After he didn't say anything, she prodded. "Collin?"

They were back in the Jeep, and downtown L.A., unusually glossy and clear, beckoned them from dead ahead.

"Grant."

"What?" she asked, distractedly.

"I'm still your brother, but I . . . I'm not Collin anymore. There's too much . . . I can't . . ." His voice, his entire manner had changed. He was focused and severe, but frustrated and tired, struggling for words. "My name is Grant."

"All right, whatever."

Over the last hour at the park, Grant had filled her in on everything that had happened during the last twenty-four hours. All it had done was open a door to questions he couldn't answer.

Creeping ahead in the morning traffic, Julie finally asked the big question. "How can this be possible?"

"Wish I knew."

"So whoever is after me . . . you think it's the same guy that tried to kill you?" Julie asked.

"Hope so."

"That's an odd thing to hope for."

He massaged his forehead. "It would mean I only have one enemy to worry about. On the other hand, maybe there are dozens of people out there hunting me down. I'm willing to bet that what they're after is *this*." He held up the ring. "Or maybe Konrad is just trying to drive me insane. And maybe it's working."

She took a deep breath and shook her head. None of this made sense to her. How could it? None of it made sense to *him*.

"This guy . . . he's never going to give up, is he?" she asked, fearful. "He'll just keep coming, no matter what we do."

"He won't give up."

"Then . . . what do we do?"

"We have to force his hand."

"And just exactly how do we do that?"

"We go where he'll expect me to go next," he said. "And we *finish* this."

She looked at him, alarmed. He saw her shiver, slightly. "Are you *sure* you're my brother? You don't talk like him. Or *think* like him."

"We can't go back to the police," Grant explained as if it were obvious. "You're obviously not safe there, and they'd never believe my story. They think I kidnapped you."

"Which, technically, you did," she agreed.

"Look, I don't know *how* I'm suddenly able to strategize and make with the big plans, but I need you to trust me. Konrad has the advantage. He can pick us off from anywhere if we slow down long enough to give him the chance. So our only option is to engineer a situation where *we* have the advantage."

She studied him, nonplussed. "You're going to draw him out into the open by being *bait* yourself." It wasn't a question; it was disapproval.

"It'll be all right," said Grant, a deadly glint in his eye. "I'll take care of you. I promise."

"It's not me I'm worried about. And I'm not talking about what this Konrad person is capable of, either. You said *you* nearly killed *him* yesterday afternoon."

Grant made no response.

Julie proceeded with caution. "I know you've had . . . episodes . . . in the past, but you were doing better, weren't you?"

"I was," he said, exasperated. "It was just . . . it felt *natural*. I reacted without thinking. I just knew how to stop him. I knew exactly where and how to hit him to knock him unconscious. I don't know how . . . I just knew."

"And aside from this instinct stuff, you've had an hour of sleep in what, thirty-six hours now?"

"What do you want me to *say*!" shouted Grant. "Am I tired? Yes! Am I on edge? *Yes!* Am I a danger to myself? Maybe. To others? Probably! But this guy's not going to stop to let me get some shut-eye, so unless you have a better idea . . ."

She looked away, out her side window. They inched forward in silence for a few minutes. The morning had already gotten hot and without the Jeep's top, the sun beat down. Grant soon felt badly about his outburst, but anger and frustration were the only sources of energy he had left. He'd apologize later. For now . . .

"Will you kill him?" Julie spoke up in a small voice.

"What?"

She wouldn't look at him; still she stared out her window, squinting into the brightness, though he thought he saw a tear falling down her cheek in her reflection. "Will you kill him?" she repeated. "Can you really do that?"

He didn't answer.

7

Grant insisted they wait until nightfall before making another move. They hid the Jeep and spent the day taking cover in tiny Mestizo restaurants, dark bars, and even a library. Anything to stay out of sight. When night fell, they returned to the Jeep and headed to their destination, pulling up to an old brick apartment building in Glendale, where Grant—*Collin*—had lived for the last seven years. It looked exactly as it always had, though it seemed a little smaller to him now.

Grant stared straight ahead at the apartment, unmoving. The sun was a distant memory now, not to be seen again for hours, and the darkness outside echoed the fear creeping in around them.

"Scared?" Julie prompted.

He nodded, fatigue and anxiety contorting his eyes.

"Me too," Julie admitted. She placed a reassuring hand on his shoulder.

"I, uh, . . . I need to know something," he delicately announced.

"Okay," she replied tentatively.

"Did you ever blame me for what happened to Mom?"

Julie shifted in her seat. "How can you even *ask* that? Of course not!"

A pause. "Then why didn't you ever talk about her? To this day, I hardly know anything about Mom at all."

Julie looked away, paused. "I guess it was too hard."

"And Dad?"

She was silent.

"Did he blame me?"

"*Never*," she answered, without hesitation.

The car became as still as the sleepy neighborhood outside. The question had eaten away at Grant in his waking hours for years. All alone in his most vulnerable moments, he would allow himself to think about it for brief snippets of time, before throwing the usual walls back up in front of his emotions.

Sometimes he even cried.

"Thanks," he replied weakly.

"Dad once told me," Julie said suddenly, thoughtfully, "that you were going to be . . . *different*. He said he thought you might grow up and do *important* things, things different from what most people do."

Grant was taken aback. "Why would he say that?"

She thought for a moment, straining her memory. "I forget why, but he had your mental acuity tested—this was only a few months before he died." Her voice sounded far away, as she thought. "I remember him saying that your test results were 'off the charts.'"

"You're kidding. But I was only three."

"I know," she affirmed.

His mind raced. "Thanks for telling me. I had no idea." He took a deep, shuddering breath and blew it out.

"You can do this, Coll—um, Grant. *Whoever* you are, I know you better than anyone and you're stronger than you think you are."

"Sure," he said, despondent.

Out of the corner of his eye he saw her digging through her purse. She produced a tiny pocket knife attached to a keychain. Before Grant could stop her, she folded out the knife and cut a slash across her wrist.

"Julie!" he cried, grabbing her by the arm.

She used her free arm to take a similar swipe at his wrist. It was then he noticed that the cuts were too shallow to sever a vein; the "knife" was little more than a fingernail clipper attachment. The gashes produced just a tiny inkling of blood, surrounded by angry-looking pink swaths of skin, on both of their wrists.

He watched as she pressed her open wound against his. "There, now we've made a pact."

"Are you crazy?"

"Whatever," Julie replied, undeterred. "It's a pact made in blood, so you can't break it. I'm going to hold you to it."

Grant studied her. "And exactly what are we . . . pact-ing?"

"Never surrender to anger or despair, no matter what. Never give up; never give in."

Grant wanted to laugh at how absurd all of this was, but Julie wouldn't let go. "*Promise* me," she said.

"Fine, okay," he said. "I promise."

At Grant's instructions, Julie was to park the Jeep three blocks down the street, turn off the engine, and wait for him there.

He took a deep breath and limped toward the building's front door. He no longer had the keys to his home, of course—like everything else, that other man, the new "Collin," now had them. So he veered to his left, around the side of the building, and looked in his ground-floor apartment window. One glance inside the darkened space told him that his double wasn't home.

Grant took what was left of the gauze out of his pocket and rolled it around one hand and fingers, like a boxer wrapping his fist.

This will either be very butch, or very bloody.

With a quick snap, he punched straight through the bottom middle window pane. It broke loudly, the shards falling into a crinkled heap on the carpet inside. He waited, watching the building's other windows to see if any lights came on. Nothing.

He snaked a hand inside and unlocked the window, slowly pushing up on the frame. The old window groaned and creaked, resisting his efforts. His thoughts returned to all the times over the years he'd attempted to open this same window from the inside, to get some air, and he could never get it to budge. Now, with his newly muscular frame, he could manage it.

Grant hopped up and crawled into the tiny living room, and then pushed the window closed again. He didn't bother turning on the lights. As small and unremarkable as the apartment was, he knew it well, even in the dark. Once his eyes had adjusted to the darkness, he glanced around and noted that everything was exactly as it had been when he'd left for work yesterday morning.

Creeping down the hall past the door to the bedroom, he made sure his doppelganger wasn't asleep or hiding. No one there. He ventured back into the hall and checked the bathroom. Nothing. The closet across from the front door still held his scarf on a hook, exactly as he'd left it yesterday. The kitchenette around the corner was also clear. Even his coffeepot still held the dregs from his last dose of caffeine.

Grant walked from one end of the apartment to the other, and wound up back in the small living room, where he'd entered. It looked like Collin—this new Collin—hadn't even been home yet.

But Grant's curiosity lasted only moments before he heard someone fumbling with keys outside the door.

The lock spun, the door opened, and Collin stepped inside.

He didn't notice Grant at all. He turned and walked in the opposite direction, into the bedroom. A lamp came on, its light shining into the hallway.

Carefully and quietly, Grant stood. He flinched as the pain in his leg returned with a sharp twinge. He stole down the hall, careful to avoid the places in the floor that creaked. Peering around the open bedroom door, he saw Collin frowning into a large, horizontal mirror that hung on the opposite wall.

Grant quietly walked up behind him and looked at him in the mirror. "How was *your* day?" he asked breezily.

The man tensed, but didn't turn. Instead, he gazed at Grant in the mirror. Grant had expected some kind of reaction, but "Collin" merely sighed and shook his head. He sat down on the edge of the bed, still watching the mirror.

Grant observed him for a moment, puzzled, and then the pain in his leg convinced him to have a seat, too.

It felt abnormal, and yet not, at the same time, as they sat there, side-by-side, watching one another in the mirror.

Grant broke the silence. "Do you want to start, or should I?"

They held eye contact.

"They didn't think you would come back here," Collin said. His voice sounded so odd; Grant wasn't used to hearing it from the outside.

"Sure," Grant replied, nodding slowly.

A pause. Neither of them blinked.

"But I knew you would. I said so. No one listens to me."

"I know the feeling," said Grant.

Another pause.

"Looks like you had difficulty getting here," Collin commented, sizing up Grant's bruises and bloodied leg.

"Yeah."

"Then it's a shame you'll be leaving empty-handed. I can't help you."

"Actually," Grant replied, "you've *already* helped me. Until now, I had no idea if you might be some kind of victim in this, just like me. Or if you were involved. Now I know. Things aren't looking especially good for you."

The thought of beating his former self to a bloody pulp sounded oddly appealing just now. Why not just finish himself off? Do the world a favor . . .

"I didn't do this to you," Collin said.

"Then who did?" Grant's voice gained strength.

The other man just stared at him.

"How did it happen? How can this be real?" Grant cried.

"It shouldn't be," Collin looked away. "But it is."

Grant stood, his pulse rising.

"Who are you?"

"No one."

Grant stepped an inch closer, his pulse rising.

"You're me. Just like that. Does that mean I'm *you*?"

Collin shook his head. "That's not how this works. I'm . . . just a . . . volunteer," Collin replied, and then looked up at Grant. "I'm no one important. You're different."

Grant swallowed. "Someone today told me I was a 'player,'" he paused, brow furrowed, studying the other man's reactions. "What are we playing? Am I a pawn in someone's twisted game?"

"I don't know. Please, Grant, for both our sakes, you've got to leave here and never come back."

Grant snapped.

"*What is this?*" he roared. He felt like putting the man's head through the mirror. "What is going on?!"

"I don't have any answers for you," Collin replied, speaking slow and calm. "I don't know the extent of your role."

Grant's head sagged. He rubbed his eyes.

"But if I were to guess," Collin suddenly added, and Grant's head popped up, "I'd say you're much more than a pawn. A knight, maybe. Maybe more."

Grant was breathing fast, thoughts and questions shifting through his brain. Tears formed in his eyes, but he angrily fought them back.

"I want my life back!" he said.

Collin rolled his eyes. "*Sure* you do . . ."

Collin's head whipped violently to the side and Grant was surprised to see that he'd just delivered a brutal backhand across Collin's face. He'd never consciously decided to hit the man; it just came out, along with a primal scream of rage.

"Switch us back!" he shouted.

Collin stood, anger rising in his voice. "Look at this place! You live a solitary life in a tiny apartment. No friends. No family. No connections of any kind. You make less money than you deserve. Your entire *existence* is miserable, and *you know it*! I've had it for less than two days, and I'm ready to *let* you finish me off. Why on earth would you want to come back to *this*?"

Grant was stunned.

Only one answer came to mind. "It's who I am."

Collin was unmoved. "Are you sure?" He paused. "Think about it. You've been given a second chance. It's a blank slate. Do you know how many people would *kill* for what's been handed to you? Grant, this is your chance to live the life you *should* have had."

The notion that this could be a desirable situation had never entered Grant's mind. It barely registered now. "I want to know who did this to me. You *must* know."

Collin nodded. "I'm sure you'll run into them, when the time is right."

"Are 'they' the same ones who hired this man to kill me?"

"No, but I heard about him." He cast another glance at Grant's bloodied pant leg. "Konrad is a contract killer. A single-minded mercenary. I don't know who sent him, but his interest in you doesn't extend beyond his payment. And believe me when I say, he *always* gets paid."

Grant held up his hand, and his eyes fell down upon the ring. "Would his payment include this?"

Collin eyed the ring and smiled a humorless smile.

"Just tell me what it is," Grant said imploringly. "*Please.*"

Collin cocked his head to one side and gazed at him carefully, as if seeing him for the first time.

"It's the answer—"

Something burst through the bedroom window. It flew straight into the mirror, shattering it into hundreds of shards that flew everywhere.

Collin grabbed Grant and pulled him down to the floor.

Coming to a rest next to them both was a broken liquor bottle with a rag sticking out of its hole. The rag was soaked and on fire. Some part of his brain registered that the crude weapon was called a Molotov cocktail. It was an old but effective and inexpensive trick.

The bottle's contents spilled onto the floor, and with a soft *whoosh* the carpet was ablaze. Before they could react, another bottle sailed through the open window and hit the bed. It too was soon covered with flames.

Grant and Collin ran from the room, more bottles raining in after them. As one, they darted for the apartment door. Collin grabbed his cell phone on the way out and dialed 911, shouting into the phone as they ran through the outer hallway.

At the building's front entrance, Collin burst through the main door first, looking back over his shoulder at Grant.

"It's *him*, come on—!"

They both jumped at the sound of gunfire.

Grant instinctively flung himself down on the floor, just inside the door, covering his head with his hands, as more shots were fired from outside. Collin flew back into the doorway and thudded onto the ground. Grant peered over at him. Collin was lying across the threshold, his chest and arms inside and his legs outside. He made no movement, but his weight kept the old steel door from shutting itself.

Blood pooled beneath him.

8

The gunshots stopped. Grant peeked carefully outside. Konrad stood below the front steps, his gun trained and leveled, waiting for Grant to appear in the open doorway.

It was a silent challenge.

Instead of accepting, Grant pulled on Collin's hands, dragging him out of the doorway. Once Collin's body had cleared the entrance, the door shut itself. It was self-locking.

Grant stood and looked down at Collin's body.

His body.

The blood that had once run through his veins was quietly spilling out onto the floor. It had streaked across the threshold, making a trail where Grant had dragged him.

It should have been me, he thought.

Maybe it is me.

Death had come for him, but it hadn't recognized him.

Grant jumped when the man lying on the ground moaned.

"Grant," he whispered. Grant dropped to his knees and put his ear next to Collin's face. "The ring . . ." he wheezed. "The ring is the answer . . ."

"To what? To my questions?" Grant asked desperately.

Collin shook his head resignedly. "To *the* questions. The only *real* questions that have ever *mattered*."

Konrad resumed his gunfire from outside. There were no holes in the big steel door. But Konrad was undeterred. He began pounding on the door with something heavy.

Grant estimated that he had only a few minutes. Maybe seconds. The man outside was terribly strong. Focused. Determined.

And probably not too happy about that whole subway station thing.

"Grant," Collin whispered.

Grant looked back down at him, as the hammering continued.

"Take this. You should keep something . . . from your life . . ." he said, gesturing vaguely with his wrist. It took Grant a moment to realize that he was talking about the bracelet. The one his grandfather had worn and then passed to Grant's father. Grant inherited it after his father's death. It was handmade, roughly cut from a brass shell casing fired during World War II.

Collin slowly removed the bracelet and dropped it into Grant's inside jacket pocket. Grant felt the weight of it drop into his coat, but made no attempt to put it on.

Not now.

The front door was dented. Grant turned to the hallway leading back to his old apartment and saw the orange glow of flames dancing among shadows. The entire building would soon be burning; he was out of time.

He allowed himself one last glimpse of Collin. The man's chest was no longer rising and falling.

Tears formed behind Grant's eyes again, but he wiped his face furiously. *No no no!* Whoever this man had been, he'd just given his life trying to save Grant's. Blinding anger welled up within him.

He stood to watch the door. The pounding had stopped.

"You can't stay in there, and you know it!" Konrad shouted through the door. From the sound of it, only the steel and a handful of inches separated the two of them. "You'll be burned alive if you do!"

He's not wrong, Grant thought. But what was he supposed to do?

"Come out," Konrad lowered his voice, "and I'll finish it quick."

Grant's face burned red. He was breathing fast now, his mind at full speed.

"Or if you want," the man said, "just open the door, and we can do this where it's *warm*." Konrad chuckled.

Grant leaned down to Collin one last time, and grabbed the cell phone from his hand, which was still clutching it. He put it in his outer jacket pocket and then faced the door, standing tall.

"Then come!" he called.

He turned and walked away, down the burning hallway.

The pounding resumed.

"Wake up!" came a shout in Lisa's cheerful voice.

Daniel started, then rose slowly. He'd been slumped over his desk, asleep. Papers stuck to his arms and face, and he carefully peeled them off.

"Lisa," he said groggily, "I pay you for research, not," he yawned, "arrhythmia."

It was dark and quiet outside. The digital clock on his desk read 5:08 A.M.

"You said you wanted to know when I had the results on the knife tests," she said, with raised eyebrows.

He sat up straight, alert, adjusting his glasses. "Right. What did you find?"

"Come look," she said with an air of mystique.

He stood and followed her down the hall to the large laboratory that housed all of their experiments. She followed the right-side wall until she came to a small device hooked up to a tiny television monitor, which was showing wavy, green lines moving rapidly across its black screen.

"When I input the readings you took of the knife," she said, stopping at the monitor, "this is what I got. I would have told you sooner, but I wanted to make sure it wasn't an equipment malfunction."

Daniel focused on the monitor, brow tightened. He glanced at her and then back at the screen.

"What am I looking at?"

"The knife," she replied matter-of-factly.

He frowned, silent. Then he shook his head.

"I expected matter readings," he said with the air of a college professor, "which look nothing like this. This seems more like—"

"Waves of energy," she finished. "Yeah." She merely stared at him, unflinching.

He was silent a moment.

"You're telling me the knife is *radiating* energy?"

"Not quite. Whether it still is or simply was last night when you took the readings, I couldn't say," she replied, followed by a deep breath. "But these readings were not emanating *from* the knife. They *are* the knife."

He stared at her. "That can't be right."

She nodded slowly, smiling again, eyebrows raised. "I know."

Grant waited for his eyes to adjust to the darkness, but they never did. There was nothing to adjust *to*. Everywhere he looked was black.

The loud pounding against the door continued in the distance, but then suddenly stopped with a crash.

He's in.

Grant listened carefully for the sound of footsteps, for any sound at all. But there was nothing. The stench of smoke filled his nose, and he fought the urge to cough.

He craned his head closer to the door, listening carefully, so carefully. He held his breath so he could hear.

The floor creaked nearby. His muscles stiffened.

But then there was nothing except the soft, distant sounds of flames. He relaxed and took a thick, smoke-filled breath.

The door to the tiny broom closet burst open, and Konrad stood on the other side. His gun was inches from Grant's chest.

Konrad's forefinger wrapped around the trigger and tensed. "It's time I got paid," he said, smirking.

A loud gurgling sound came from around the corner, in the kitchen. Konrad turned, startled for a fraction of a second by the bubbling coffee pot. Which was exactly what Grant was waiting for.

He flung his hand straight into Konrad's face, splashing what remained of the peroxide from the drugstore into the mercenary's eyes. Konrad screamed in pain, both hands covering his eyes, and Grant slugged him as hard as he could in the stomach with his other fist. The short man doubled over, down on his knees, roaring in agony and clawing at his face.

Grant dropped the small brown bottle from his hand and kicked Konrad once more in the gut for good measure. Then he ran.

But he only took a step or two before Konrad's powerful hand wrapped around his ankle—the ankle attached to his wounded leg. Grant yelped in pain and went down face-first onto the floor.

He recovered quickly, kicking backward at the other man with his free leg. But Konrad was crazed, unflinching. His eyes were a mess, and he was bearing down, transferring all of his pain to the powerful grip he had on Grant's leg.

Grant wiggled and kicked with his whole body, but it was like being held in stone. Grant twisted and looked in front of him on the floor. The carpet was in flames, a bonfire only inches from his face.

There was nowhere to go.

Grant looked back at the fire on the floor in front of him again.

Konrad's grip tightened further.

A scream escaped his lips, as if it would help. The apartment door to his left flew open with a wooden *crack*, seemingly of its own accord. How Grant longed to run through it, he was only a few feet away . . .

But it was no good. The liquid fueling the flames rolled closer and the fire came with it, close enough for the heat to burn Grant's face and hair.

The liquid!

Grant snapped his head to the right and saw an unbroken bottle that Konrad had flung through the windows.

Intense heat burning his skin was all he could feel as he strained hard to wrap his fingers around the bottle's neck.

And then he had it. He twisted around sharp and fast, and with all of his remaining strength, he brought the bottle down from over his head to crash against Konrad's skull. Blood and liquid fire snaked down through the unconscious man's dark hair and across his face.

The last thing Grant saw of him was Konrad's blistered, broken scalp in flames. Forcing himself to his feet, he coughed through the smoke as he surveyed the place. There was nothing more to be done here. The flames had spread everywhere. Out in the hall, into the other apartments. Everything that he had ever owned was going up in flames.

He couldn't seem to care.

In the distance, he heard sirens, bringing questions that he had no answers for.

He made his way out of the apartment, delirious and unsteady on his feet, but still careful to avoid the flames. They spread faster now, out into the hall, and then out the building's front door and into the night. Julie brought the Jeep to a screeching halt a few feet away and he fell into the back, utterly spent.

"What happened?" she shouted. "Are you okay?"

"If I ever . . . get my hands on . . . the person who did this to me," he panted, on the brink of unconsciousness, *"I'll kill 'em."*

Two days later, across town at Grandview Cemetery, a closed-casket funeral was held for Collin Boyd—for this man who had become the man Grant once was. It was an outdoor service on a brisk, windy day, with just a handful of white folding chairs containing occupants. Julie attended, tears quietly streaming down her face throughout the entire event, but Grant told her he "just couldn't do it." Watching *himself* be buried . . . It was too much, he said, after everything he'd been through the last few days.

But despite his insistence that he would sit this one out, he'd found his way here anyway. He watched the ceremony from a distance, amid a stand of trees on the east side of the cemetery.

The reverend presiding over the funeral had delivered an unusual message. Grant couldn't quite make it all out—something about "a life that's wasted."

Long after everyone had gone and night had fallen, Grant still stood in his spot by the trees, watching the casket sink into the ground. The loud clacking of the coffin mechanically lowering was the only audible sound in the graveyard.

But he could barely make out the wooden box through his red, bleary eyes.

He was consumed with emotions, thoughts, and regrets. This wasn't just his body that was descending into the ground. It was everything he had been, the life he had known. It was gone, all of it. Forever.

He had always coveted his private life. Being by himself was the only time he found peace. But it was also the source of his greatest turmoil.

He was grateful to have his sister as a part of his life again. But even with her there, even though he was used to relative solitude . . . For the first time since childhood, he felt utterly, terrifyingly *alone.*

Collin Boyd was gone. Dead and buried. Grant Borrows was who he was now.

There was no going back.

Everything he thought he understood about life had changed, in less than an instant. The rules of science and nature and human existence were broken. He couldn't be Collin Boyd anymore, but he had no desire to be Grant Borrows, either.

All he really had to call his own were the questions.

So many questions.

Am I living someone else's life? he thought uselessly. *What right do I have to live a life that isn't my own?*

Shouldn't that be me *going into the ground?*

He studied the coffin as it went lower, lower, lower, until it was beyond his ability to see.

Standing alone in the silent darkness, Grant could keep his feelings in check no longer, and he was tired of trying. He broke down, his battered body collapsing into a shuddering heap on the ground, his shoulders shaking violently.

The sound of his sobs filled the graveyard.

But there was something . . .

What was that?

A faint glow caught his attention between haggard breaths. The ring on his finger had become radiant. It was diffuse, like a light shining deep underwater.

It was shimmering.

Miles away, far outside of town, a middle-aged woman with a serene presence and silver hair stood alone in a darkened room.

All of her attention was focused on the ancient object lying on a table in front of her. She studied it with tremendous mental focus, memorizing its every groove, crevice, and pattern. Her finger ran gently over it, rubbing the scarred, craggy surface.

Something in the room began to glow softly. Her eyes shifted to the source of the light as a smile spread across her features.

"At last," she proclaimed, standing upright, "the Bringer has come."

"PHASE ONE COMPLETE," said a voice hiding behind a pair of slumped shoulders that slouched before a bright computer monitor. The computer and its user were accompanied by dozens of others just like them, lining the outer walls of the shadowy room.

A single reply came from a voice somewhere near the center of the vast room. It was a deep, booming voice, punctuated with unmistakable authority. "Activate Phase Two."

"Yes sir," the computer technician replied without taking his eyes from the screen. "Making the call now."

9

The motorcycle snarled down the murky street through late evening fog, a fog as thick as the motorcycle rider's hot breath. The black, gleaming machine was a bloodthirsty predator, nose to the ground in anticipation of a kill. The two tires chewed asphalt at speeds far above the legal limit, leaving the scent of hot rubber in its wake.

But the man who rode the metallic beast wore an expression of unemotional, intense concentration as he stared without blinking into the onrushing wind. No glasses or helmet visor obstructed his view; he had little use for either. Covered in black from collar to foot, he was completely bald and rather short of stature. He favored the simplistic look primarily for its functionality, but also because of the imposing silhouette it formed.

Fear was a powerful weapon. But it wasn't the most powerful one he carried.

Subterfuge, on the other hand, was pointless. It mattered not whether those he hunted saw his face. If they did, it was the last thing they would see in this life.

To those in the darkest corners of society—those who knew of the terrifying things that happened in the world's underbelly—he was known as the Thresher.

This particular chase had lasted a scant few hours. Another hunter might be disappointed by such a weak prey; the Thresher cared little for how long a hunt lasted. Once begun, he would see it through, regardless of how long it took. As a rule, he refused to stop for food, rest, or sleep until his agreed-upon task was complete.

This one would be over in less than five minutes.

Streetlamps passed overhead as fast as a strobe light. He paid them no attention. His eyes were on the narrow main road ahead, long empty in the deep of night. His senses were alert and his muscles tensed.

Each time a side street appeared to his right, he stole a quick look, briefly searching for signs of his prey. It was on the seventh side street he passed that he caught the faintest glimpse of the other biker before the buildings between them again blocked his view.

He bore no weapons save for the contents of a single scabbard secured to his left hip. From the ornate leather sheath he withdrew a sword, which reverberated on the air like a chime. An intricate pattern was pressed into the blade, which bore all the hallmarks of a Japanese *daito*—thin blade, curved upward at the end. The sword was powerfully sharp with a crystallized edge, made entirely of one of the world's strongest metals—save for its unusually long hilt, which was nearly two feet long by itself. The oversized wooden handle was wrapped in overlapping black leather straps.

The Thresher held the sword out to his side in one hand while guiding the motorcycle in the other, eyes still watching the passing streets to the right. His eyes were a glassy void, his breathing slow and cunning. As always, once the hunt was nearing its final moments, he relaxed and allowed himself to become an embodiment of undiluted reflex and instinct.

Suddenly he stood on the bike's foot pegs, calling on every last bit of torque the machine had to offer. It roared in protest but obeyed its master, streaking along the twilight pavement at suicidal speeds. Two more side alleys lay ahead, separated by wide blocks of buildings. And though he had no practical idea of how many seconds there would be before he reached the last of the two, he knew precisely when it would occur. He could feel it approaching . . .

The first street passed, and this time he was almost neck-and-neck with the bright red motorcycle he was chasing. He'd gained a second or two on the other man, which was all he needed. He increased his speed to the machine's last ounce of capability, and at the final moment, preparing to strike, he leaned forward as far as the bike's balance would allow.

Milliseconds before clearing the second alleyway, the Thresher flung the sword down the last street with a brutal swing of his right arm. The thin blade reacted as an arrow springing from a bow, darting through the dirty alleyway.

As the red bike came into view, it passed to the immediate left of a large, rusted-out, double-wide Dumpster. The Thresher's sword passed straight in front of his quarry's line of sight and pierced the side of the Dumpster. The sword's oversized hilt stuck out as a blunt instrument—directly in front of the passing motorcyclist's face.

The driver of the red machine didn't have time to realize what was happening until it was too late.

The Thresher watched as his quarry's head collided violently with the sword's protruding hilt, the man's neck wrenching itself sickeningly backward. He fell from the crimson bike with the unmistakable crack of breaking bones, while the bike continued moving out of sight.

In what seemed like only an instant, the Thresher had retrieved his sword from the Dumpster and was on top of the other man, holding his dazed and battered form in a brutal headlock with one arm. His other hand pressed the razor-sharp side edge of the sword against the man's throat with a tight, back-handed grip. He barely seemed to be exerting himself, with practiced, measured movements that applied only the exact amount of energy and force required, and nothing more.

The man flailed and struggled, but his body was still in shock from the blow, and his coordination faltered.

He spat into the bald man's face.

There was a buzzing sound and the Thresher turned loose of the headlock, yet the sword held the other man steadily in place.

"One move, and I'll sever your windpipe," the Thresher said in a calm, gravelly voice that was every bit as frightening as the sword he held with such perfect stillness. The words were marked with a refined British clip.

The hunted man tried to hold his breath as sweat mingled with his own blood, streaming into his eyes and down his face. He felt the edge of the sword prick the skin around his neck, yet he remained as still as he could manage.

The Thresher wiped the spit from his face and fished into one of his pockets, retrieving a tiny phone. He thumbed it open casually. "Yes?" his serious voice intoned.

"Konrad is finished," said the voice on the other end. "You may proceed."

"Parameters?" the Thresher asked, even though he knew the answer. This was no client calling to offer a job. This was *the* call.

The conversation he'd been waiting *years* for. Quite possibly his entire life for.

"You are hereby endowed with authority and purpose beyond that of any law of man," came the emotionless reply. "Do not stop until your task is complete."

The Thresher hesitated for a faint moment, effortlessly maintaining the sword's pressure against his quarry's neck. "The Secretum is confident? This *is* the time?"

"The appointed hour is at hand," was the slightly annoyed reply. "Your destiny has been written, and so shall it be: *the Bringer shall be slain at the hands of the Thresher*. Find him, and perform your function."

The Thresher snapped the phone shut, sliced his target's head from his shoulders in a powerful back-handed chop, wiped the blood off onto the headless torso's shirt, and sheathed the gleaming sword to his side, all in one elegant precise move.

He was gone without another sound.

10

Grant awoke violently, jerking straight up to a sitting position. He was sweating and breathing hard, and every muscle was tensed. It took several quiet minutes before he could remember where he was.

Or *who* he was.

When he'd finally caught his breath, he frowned; his bed sheet was ripped straight down the middle. He was still clutching the two torn halves in his hands. His leg throbbed, bright sunlight streamed in between the cracks in the blinds, and his thoughts drifted back . . .

Three days had passed since his defeat of the mercenary Konrad. And Julie's fussing over him had become more and more pronounced each day.

The morning after Collin and Konrad had died in the fire, Grant and Julie visited an emergency room in Garden Grove, on the south side of L.A.—to avoid any potential connection with the arson. It was more than two hours after they entered the hospital before Grant had finally seen a doctor.

The terse woman at the check-in desk was most unhelpful. When she requested his insurance card and carrier, he asked if she could find his records in the computer based on his name. She appeared rather miffed by the request, but she complied. He was unable to muster any surprise when she called him and Julie back to the desk to pronounce that no "Grant Borrows" had ever been a patient at any hospital on record. Her tone of voice made it clear how satisfied she was upon making this conclusion.

Grant paid the bill in cash.

That afternoon, at his sister's suggestion, they'd both taken up residence in the Wagner Building's high-rise penthouse. Grant still didn't feel like it was really his, but as Julie had put it, they simply had nowhere else to go. He tried to convince her to go back home; with Konrad dead, she should be safe. But she would hear none of it, determined as she was to look after him.

He'd spent each night tossing and turning in bed, snatching only brief moments of unconsciousness—all of which were filled with nightmares about burning buildings and bottles filled with fire and watching his own funeral from inside the coffin. He'd woken up screaming several times, and Julie repeatedly burst into the room and rushed to his side.

Prescription bottles rested on his nightstand, waiting. They were terribly inviting.

That night after the hospital visit, he'd had to physically lean on Julie just to make it inside the condominium, but she never complained. Two brand-new sets of stitches were biting into his leg on either side, where the bullet holes had been. The doctor had also treated him for a mild concussion, along with his other scrapes, and given him a prescription for pain—the very bottles that were currently holding his attention.

And as he'd done several times over the last three days, he quietly opened the nearest pill bottle so Julie wouldn't hear, and ingested more of the contents. He was consuming more than the recommended dosage—Julie had threatened to hide them if he did it again—but he didn't care.

It was late morning when he emerged from the bedroom to find Julie on the computer in the living room. She didn't look up from the screen as he crossed the hall to the bathroom.

"Hey, you ever heard of an 'Inveo Technologies'?" she called out.

"Who?" he replied, shouting through the closed door.

"Could you come out here, Collin? I think I may be on to something."

Grant swung open the bathroom door and crossed the hallway and living room to stand by her side. "Stop calling me Collin," he grumbled.

"Why do you keep saying that?" she demanded. "You *are* Collin on the inside, right?"

"Collin's dead," he said sourly, but then caught her expression. "*I'm me*, yeah. But Collin's gone. You should know, you went to the funeral."

"So what?" she finally turned to look at him. "You're my *brother*. I don't care if you start growing tentacles out of your nose, you're *always* going to be 'Collin' to me."

Grant frowned and turned away. He entered the kitchen and began rooting around in the refrigerator—which, like the apartment, had been fully stocked when they moved in—for something to eat, making quite a racket. Finally he fished out the milk, found a bowl, and poured himself some cereal at the kitchen's bar. He took a seat on a stool, his back stooped low as he leaned over the bowl to eat.

Julie knew that his bending over had less to do with the food than with what was happening inside his head.

"I'm worried about you."

He looked up, spotted her watching him.

"Please stop this," he said, resignedly.

"I can't help it!" she exclaimed, pent-up frustrations erupting. "You internalize *everything*, you always have!"

"How would *you* know what I've 'always' done? Like you were there to see it." He instantly regretted the outburst.

Julie's lips pressed together. "Even *I* can see that everything—all of this *insanity* that's happening to you—it's eating you alive. And it's eating *me* alive that it's eating *you* alive!"

Grant grimaced. *Women . . .*

"I feel . . . *trapped!*" he said. "Like I've been wrapped in unfamiliar skin, and there's no way to escape it. What am I supposed to do? Go *talk* to somebody? There aren't any specialists for this."

"You could talk to me."

Ah. The real problem.

He stepped out from behind the bar and crossed the room to kneel beside her desk chair. "You *know* I've never been much of a talker, Julie. And honestly . . . I haven't even seen you in *years*—"

"That was *your* choice, not mine—"

"I don't want to *talk*. I don't want to get into how I'm feeling. It's too much right now, I can't . . . process . . ."

"But," she protested, "you have to get past all of this bitterness and anger and frustration."

"No, I don't," he said plainly.

Julie nearly fell out of her chair.

He pressed the issue. "The pain and the hostility are all that's keeping me going. This drive to find answers is the only reason I have for getting out of bed in the morning."

"No, Collin—" she shook her head vehemently—"You can't give in to that."

"Why not?" he stood, frustrated.

"Because I don't want you to be a person who *hates*!" she howled. Tears began to stream down her cheeks. She crumpled further into her chair. "And neither would Mom and Dad. I want you to be the good man I know you are."

"But I'm *not* a good man!" he exploded at last, his face the color of blood.

She wouldn't face him and he looked away angrily, at a loss for words.

Finally he spoke in a small voice. "I killed him. Konrad. I think I really did it."

Julie stood and lifted his head with one hand. "He *was* trying to kill you."

Grant shook his head, inconsolable.

"When you realized that I was in danger," she said slowly, "what was your first instinct? What did you immediately do?" When he refused to answer, she said, "Think about *that* the next time you decide you're not a good person."

She left him standing there to retrieve something from her desk.

When she returned, Grant saw that it was the brass bracelet that Collin had placed inside his jacket before he died. "You are who you decide to be," she said, placing the bracelet on his wrist. "And *I* have decided that you're a kind, good-hearted man who takes after his father."

Grant embraced her, and she hugged him back. When they let go, she could see on his face that he remained unconvinced, uncertain. But there was hope in his eyes for the first time. That was something.

"You never answered my question, by the way," she re-seated herself at the computer. "Who do you know at Inveo Technologies?"

His face was awash in confusion. "I have no idea what you're talking about."

Julie fingered a small business card from the desktop and handed it to him. "I found this in your jacket. With the bracelet."

What?

He'd checked all of his pockets after his first conversation with that weird barefoot girl, and hadn't noticed any business cards anywhere. His jacket had been empty, at least until Collin had put the—

"It was in the same pocket as Granddad's bracelet?"

Julie nodded.

A clue! At last.

Collin had given him more than he thought. He looked again at the card. It read "Carl MacDugall, CEO, Inveo Technologies."

"Looks like some kind of tech company. They've got a big plant here in California, though it's a ways off, northeast of San Bernardino. Near Apple Valley, I think . . ." Julie was saying. She had pulled up Inveo's website and was clicking rapidly through the pages.

Grant began to pace.

"That man—we'll call him Collin for lack of a real name—he meant for me to find this. This company . . . they're involved, they have to be. It's some kind of conspiracy or something. Maybe they've even got the—I don't know, the *technology* or whatever that did this to me."

Julie watched him from a sideways view but said nothing. He couldn't tell whether she was incredulous at his suggestion that technology was responsible for his brand new life, or if she just didn't like where this line of reasoning was headed.

"Maybe I'm supposed to talk to this Carl MacDugall."

"You *really* think he'd give you an audience?" Julie asked, dubious. "Honey, from the looks of this office complex of his, the man could buy *Bill Gates* if he wanted to. What could possibly make him want to talk to you?"

"He *is* involved," Grant protested. "Or Collin wouldn't have given me that card."

"But what good does it do you?" Julie said, examining the card she held between two fingers. "What did he expect you to do, march into this guy's office and demand answers?"

Grant's eyebrows popped up.

"Don't even think about it," Julie warned, and then turned back to her computer monitor. "The front entrance has three guards, so the rest of the place must be major league."

"I can do this. Don't ask me how, I just know I can. This MacDugall guy and I have got to have a conversation."

Julie's ears were burning red, but Grant ignored her. It felt good to be in forward motion again.

"Are you seriously telling me," Julie remarked slowly, "that you're going to try to get an *appointment* to talk to this person?"

"It'd never work," he concluded after some thought, shaking his head. "It would look too suspicious, and besides, I'd have to make something up—some fake story about why I want to see him—and let's face it, I'm a *terrible* liar."

A hint of a smile played at her lips, accompanying memories of awkward attempts he'd made as a toddler to explain how he'd made a terrible mess or "accidentally" let the dog out of the back yard.

"Then where does that leave us?" she asked.

"Only one option I can think of," he said. "But you're *really* not going to like it."

11

"So that morning, four days ago, did you see anything . . . out of the ordinary?" Daniel asked.

The young man on the other side of the counter had been listening to him very intently, but now he rolled his eyes straight up, vacantly, in what Daniel could only assume was some form of concentration.

"It was the morning of that terrible rainstorm . . ." Daniel prodded.

"Oh right," The boy's eyes lit up. "This one dude came in with, like, *the* most criminal toupee ever," he said, laughing. Daniel didn't respond, so he went on. "I kid you not, it was like *moss* on top of his head, man."

Daniel merely stared at him, eyebrows up.

"Does that help?" the boy asked blankly.

Daniel turned and walked out of the coffee shop into the concrete canyons.

Do I attract *the crazy people? Am I putting something out there that* draws *them to me?*

Dry wind whipping around him, he scratched his head of short-cropped hair while surveying the street from side to side. Were there any other stores on this side of the road he hadn't tried yet? He glanced once again down at the bus stop, a few blocks away. *It began there*, he thought. The further he got away from the shimmers' points of origin, the less likely he was to find out where they were coming from. Or rather, *who* they were coming from, as he suspected.

Why can't I find you, whoever you are?

How did you do it, when so many others have failed?

His cell phone vibrated. He flipped it open as he continued walking down the street.

"What have you got?" He knew it was Lisa. No one else ever called him. He'd sent her to check some of the businesses in the upper floors of the larger buildings while he stuck to the storefront shops on ground level.

"One juicy possibility, though it's sort of a dead issue. So to speak."

"What is it?"

"This snotty secretary at a consulting firm said one of their IT guys was killed a few days ago."

Daniel stopped walking.

"Killed how?" he asked.

"She wouldn't say. Not sure if she just didn't know or if she was holding out on me. But she did mention that the guy lived in Glendale, at the site of that towering inferno from a few days ago. So naturally, I'm wondering if he died in the fire."

He was walking again. "Yeah, yeah. I remember that on the news. Did she give you a name?"

"She didn't want to, but I decided to make myself her new best friend until she felt like opening up."

Daniel found himself sympathizing with the woman at the consulting firm. "What's the name?"

"Collin Boyd," she replied.

"Collin Boyd," he repeated thoughtfully.

"You think he's our shimmer guy?" she asked.

"If he is, then the best lead I've ever had just went up in smoke," he replied.

"Let me see what I can find out about the fire and I'll get back to you," Lisa said. She was always up for a challenge.

The elevator dinged and the doors opened to the Wagner Building's spacious parking deck, which extended four floors below the building. Grant exited, purpose in his stride for the first time in days, and was met by a sea of Mercedes, Cadillacs, Ferraris, and Hummers.

A key chain from a kitchen drawer in his apartment looked an awful lot like car keys. Did the apartment come complete with wheels of some sort? If so, it would be here. He pressed the button on the chain.

A *boop-boop* echoed in the cement garage, and he walked toward it. He made the sound again and, turning to his left, saw where it had come from. A metallic navy blue convertible Corvette seemed to be grinning at him, as if it had just rolled off the assembly line and was hungrily waiting for him to rev the engine. He'd loved Corvettes ever since seeing a picture of his father gripping the wheel of a classic 1960 roadster. It seemed like a good omen to find one waiting for him. For the first time in days, he smiled.

"Nice bracelet," called a familiar voice.

"Mm," his shoulders drooped. "Swell."

He turned.

There she was again, leaning against a concrete pillar a few yards away. *Maybe she has a shoe phobia . . . Wonder if there's a name for that?*

Eh, who am I kidding? I don't care.

"What's the inscription say?" she asked, trying to make it out from where she stood.

"None of your business. What do you want?"

"Well, if what I'm hearing is true, you're setting out on a one-way street to badness. Not only am I *not* the only one who knows what you're planning . . . but only fools rush in to a place like Inveo Technologies. It's not a company; it's a *fortress*. Comes with all the extras, including one of the most state-of-the-art security forces in the world. We're talking *guardapalooza*. Even if you somehow managed to sneak in, the only way out of *that* place is with a tag on your toe."

"And just exactly how do know what I'm planning?" Grant's feathers were ruffling with every word she spoke.

"Fish gotta swim. Birds gotta fly. We all got our purpose."

"And keeping up with my itinerary is yours?" he asked.

"Hey, I'm the one who told you to leave town and not look back."

He frowned.

"But your curiosity got the better of you. Don't suppose I can blame you for that." She cocked her head to one side. "By the way, for what it's worth, it looks like you're out of danger. For the moment. That is, aside from this big 'storm the gates' thing you're working on."

"Who *are* you?"

She just smiled.

"If you can't tell me who you are, then why are you helping me?"

"Oh, you're *so cute*," she said as though she were admiring a friend's baby. "Who said I was here to *help* you?"

He frowned. "You helped me find my sister."

"Did I?" she replied thoughtfully. "You sure of that?"

He *had* seen her outside the UCLA police station, hadn't he? Pointing the way to find his sister? Of course he'd seen her.

Right?

"You're really infuriating." He massaged his forehead.

She nodded, unconcerned. "I get that a lot." She squared her shoulders. "Look, I just stopped by to offer congrats, slugger, and a warning. Instead of this Inveo thing, you really should be looking into the other groups that are keeping an eye on you. There's one in particular that frankly, I expected you to have already found . . .

"But anyway, back to the big victory. That's one down. Burned and buried alive. Juicy." Her eyebrows popped up. "Of course, most of the others watching you have little interest in seeing you *dead*, so hopefully you won't always knee-jerk into violence mode. But I should warn you that *very few* of these folks have your best interests at heart. And just because you defeated Konrad doesn't mean that the ones who hired him won't send somebody else to try again."

His eyes met hers, but she maintained a casual expression. "How many?"

She didn't answer. For a moment, he thought she might not have understood the question.

"How many of these groups *are there*, keeping tabs on me?"

She smiled without humor. "Lot more than you think, bucko. But if what you did to ol' Konrad was just the warm-up . . . Can't *wait* to see how you handle the rest," she said, her eyes dancing.

Grant rolled his eyes and stalked to his car. By the time he checked his rearview mirror, she was gone.

Daniel and Lisa waited two days before visiting the burned-out Glendale apartment building. They figured the police and fire marshals would mostly be done by then and a curious bystander could get a look around easier. Only there wasn't much to look at.

Daniel kept a bandana to his nose as he picked his way through the rubble of the burned down apartment building. He and Lisa had been here for hours and still couldn't make head nor tail of anything they found. It was beyond recognition.

Lisa was wandering around, picking up various things and scanning for traces of a shimmer, but nothing spiked. The one part of the building still standing was the central stairwell, an old brick shaft that reached all three floors. Only the first-floor portion of it remained intact.

"What are you thinking?" Daniel asked her as he continued to sift.

"Well . . . it definitely strikes me as odd that nothing—not one single object—survived this fire."

He nodded. "Someone's covered their tracks."

"Didn't the news say it was a gas main or something?" she said, still looking through the debris.

He eyed her. "Don't believe everything you hear on the news."

She grinned.

"If the police lied to the media about the cause of the fire," Daniel said, "then I'd say there's a good chance this Collin Boyd may not be dead, after all. . . . At any rate, I want to know who he is. Would you go round to the back of the building and jot down the license-plate numbers of the cars back there? We can check them later to see if one of them was his."

She nodded and was off.

He continued sifting for a moment before he noticed that a nearby shadow was moving.

"And how did *you* know Mr. Boyd?" a booming voice said.

He looked up. A man stood to his right with an angry frown on his face. A large man whose bulging midsection protruded from a navy blue trench coat, though only his left arm went through one of the sleeves. His right was under the coat, held in place by what looked like a shoulder sling.

"Old friend from college," Daniel lied. He stuck out his hand to the detective. "Daniel Cossick."

"Matthew Drexel," the cop replied, refusing to take Daniel's hand.

"Do you contaminate the crime scenes of *all* of your college buddies' mishaps?"

"Collin was the first," Daniel said nervously. "My assistant and I—we were just . . . curious . . . about the circumstances surrounding his death. The damage here is just . . . mind-boggling . . ." his voice trailed off as he glanced around.

"That kind of curiosity will land you in jail," said the man, with a dour scowl. He adopted an authoritative swagger as he walked closer.

"You're a police officer, then?" Daniel asked.

The man flipped open a badge. "Detective. I'm investigating the arson/homicide on these premises, which I believe to be connected to . . . another case I'm working on."

"So it *was* just the one death, then?" Daniel probed.

"Just one *body*," Drexel replied slowly, still warily watching Daniel.

The detective narrowed his eyes and took another step closer. They were standing in the sun, but to Daniel it felt like a third-degree heat lamp.

Drexel gestured with his chin toward Lisa. "You want to tell Ms. Moneypenny over there to stop rifling through my evidence?"

"What?" Daniel blustered, then caught on. "Oh! Lisa, this nice officer wants you to quit whatever you're doing back there!"

She appeared from behind the central stairwell wall. "You really a cop?" she shouted.

"You really this guy's assistant?" Drexel replied.

Lisa rolled her eyes at his attempted joke, but then was all business. "You better come see this."

Daniel and Detective Drexel both circled the stairwell until they reached Lisa's vantage point. Sticking out from the other side of the wall was a tiny foot with a black shoe on. As they continued to circle, the full body came into view: an elderly woman with graying purplish hair, her short frame lying facedown, unmoving. Her wrinkled face was turned too far to one side, her eyes closed. She still clenched a large, pearl-white purse with both knobby hands.

Drexel's eyes became tiny slits, and he examined the woman for several minutes without approaching. Then he knelt and seized her hand. It was limp. "Hasn't been dead long. And no burn marks, so she definitely didn't die in the fire." He pushed aside her hair. Dark bruises were visible along her neck. "Her neck is snapped," Drexel concluded.

"Either of you know this woman?" he asked softly.

Daniel exchanged a clueless glance with Lisa, but her eyebrows appeared knitted together.

"I think . . . she's the landlady," she said.

Drexel swore. "You sure about that?"

"No," Lisa answered honestly. The way she effortlessly held the larger man's gaze . . . It occurred to Daniel that Lisa wasn't intimidated by Drexel. Not at all.

While *he* had become unhinged the moment the large man had spoken.

But then, she has no reason to be anxious around a policeman. I, on the other hand . . .

"I'm going to need you both to come with me," Drexel was saying, rising to his feet. "Your knowledge of the victim may be . . . *useful* to my case. And frankly, the fact that you knew him at all means that *you* may not be safe—" The detective's phone rang, interrupting his speech. "Excuse me," he mumbled, and turned away, moving back toward his brown sedan. He was trying to keep Daniel and Lisa from hearing, but it was a quiet Sunday morning in the old neighborhood. They clearly made out the words "cut off his *head*?" as Drexel's voice rose involuntarily as he said it.

Lisa carefully and innocently walked to Daniel's side.

"You're white as a sheet," she whispered. "You all right?"

Daniel wiped sweat from his brow with one hand while whispering back to her. He eyed the cop again, who was now speaking on his car radio, the cord snaking out through the side window.

"I think things just got a lot more complicated."

12

Three days later, Grant sat with Julie in a diner across the street from the Inveo Technologies corporate headquarters, trying not to look nervous. It was one of those tiny truck stops stuck in the middle of desert sprawl like a ship bottomed on a dry lake. They were the only non-regulars in the ramshackle building, which looked like it could collapse in on itself at any moment.

But Grant's attention was elsewhere. The barefoot girl had been right again. This was no simple facility he was looking at. It was a *campus*.

Grant and Julie had spent every waking minute carefully considering his covert entry into Inveo. Hours upon hours they pored over books at the local library, on the computer, digging up old architectural plans from county and district records. It wasn't easy, but they needed every last detail they could find. Of particular interest was the structure's layout and security.

The campus was located well outside of L.A., cozied on the gentle slopes of a mountainside, on a big plot of undeveloped land north of Big Bear Lake. A modest town had sprung up around the Inveo plant, but the town was dwarfed by the scale of the plant itself. The entire Inveo property struck Grant as akin to some kind of modern citadel.

And here he was, about to David his way into this Goliath.

Grant and Julie ate breakfast in silence, both nervous at what waited ahead of them. After leaving cash on their table, they stepped out into the arid wind and squinted across the road at their target. The mammoth complex, dozens of high-rise buildings, sprawled over four square miles of land at a sloping angle, essentially a city unto itself. An enormous manufacturing plant was situated in the middle, with other buildings of all sizes surrounding it. The plant was clearly the oldest of the buildings on the grounds, with metal siding, a flat roof, and add-ons stretched outward in every direction. Many of the other buildings were much newer, with sparkling glass on all sides, or modern brick façades.

Grant's eyes fell upon the tallest of these buildings, which was situated closer than any of the others to the diner, only a few hundred yards across the street and behind a tall perimeter fence. It was the executive building, his target.

Julie sat in the driver's seat of the car and Grant knelt next to her, door open.

"What's your job?" he asked Julie.

"Surveillance. Keep the car ready," she recited, steeling herself.

Grant nodded then retrieved a shopping bag out of the blue convertible's trunk. Carrying the bag, he strolled down the street to an abandoned gas station. It was here that he and Julie had struck gold during their research. Yesterday, while surfing the Net, one of their searches turned up a site on urban legends, which contained an entry about Inveo Technologies and a secret exit built long ago as an executive escape. They were about to write off the legend as a myth when another entry claimed to have proof that it really existed, providing step-by-step details on how to access it from the outside. A few urban explorers even claimed to have snuck into the plant and caused a little mischief. The plant being so big, once you were inside, it wasn't hard to blend in with all of the employees if you could simulate their look, they explained.

Behind the decrepit gas station, Grant hefted open a set of wooden storm doors. A set of stairs inside led down to a cellar, where he tugged on a cord overhead to turn on a lone light bulb. He quickly stripped and put on the gray jumpsuit that was inside the bag, along with a matching pair of gloves. His heart pumping like mad, he stuffed his street clothes into the bag and stowed it under the stairs. A tiny earpiece went into his left ear, completely hidden from sight once inside; Julie had acquired a set of them rush delivery from an online store.

"Okay, I'm set," he said.

"You've got eight minutes until shift change," Julie said.

Grant found the door to the tiny closet on his left, just as the Web site had described. Following the instructions exactly, he stepped inside and shut the door behind him, which left him in the dark. To his right, he felt for and found a set of old wooden shelves attached to the wall. So far the instructions were dead on. Counting down, he grabbed the third one from the top and pulled it straight out. It only gave an inch. He pulled similarly on the top shelf, and then pushed it back in.

Straight ahead, a dim light appeared as the wall suddenly swung open.

"Did it work?" Julie said, her voice clear but a bit tinny in his ear.

"Think so," he replied.

"What do you see?"

"A really long hallway. Dark. What should I expect at the other end?"

She was silent a moment. *"I'm not entirely sure . . ."*

"You can't tell from the floor plans?"

"Collin," Julie deadpanned, *"my expertise in this area is summed up in the number of times I've seen Tom Cruise dangling from that wire in* Mission: Impossible. *Give me a break, okay? Hey, you better hurry—there's less than five minutes."*

Abandoning stealth, Grant sprinted down the narrow corridor. A stench like rotten potatoes filled the hallway, which was lit only by individual light bulbs dangling from the ceiling every thirty feet. A few minutes later, following a couple of turns and some more running, he came upon the next door and opened it. Out of breath, he pulled out a tiny flashlight and turned it on.

Stretched out before him was an enormous basement that looked like a vast warehouse. Wooden crates, cardboard boxes, and assorted shelves stacked floor to ceiling filled with more boxes, consumed the space in every direction.

"What do they make here again?"

"New technologies, according to their website. Whatever that means."

He looked to the far left wall and saw his next door. Beyond it, he found a stairwell. So far, so good.

He glanced at his watch again: 5:30.

Time's up.

He bolted up the stairs.

Opening the door to the first floor, he was met by an enormous, bustling lobby, complete with cherry wood accents, marble and carpeted floors, hand-crafted lounge chairs, and a giant glass façade that stretched from the floor to the vaulted ceiling, over three stories high. A behemoth of a receptionist desk stretched forty feet long, with no less than six employees seated behind it. All of them appeared to be speaking into headset telephones. The Inveo logo was emblazoned behind them in a monstrous 3-D art piece that stretched upward the entire three stories; it was a gaudy melting pot of Greek and Roman symbols mixed with high technology, with a stylized "I.T." at the top.

Employees entered and exited the vast atrium, most of those entering making for one of the eight elevators at the far end of the lobby. Grant watched them come and go for a moment, considering how normal their lives were. They were grazing through their day like cows, casual, unconcerned.

Normal.

He'd forgotten what that was like.

This certainly didn't look like the command center for an identity-theft conspiracy.

Grant blended in with the crowd moving toward the elevator, his jumpsuit vaguely resembling that worn by the janitorial staff. As long as no one made a close inspection of his appearance, he'd be fine. The outfit was the least of his worries.

His heart skipped a beat as he approached the crowd inside the concave elevator foyer. This was possibly the riskiest part of his plan. If this didn't work just right, the game was over before it had even begun.

Two sets of elevator doors opened at once and Grant intentionally entered the one that seemed to have more people on board. He squeezed through the tiny, congested space and stood at the back of the elevator.

Craning his neck around those before him, he saw that the panel of buttons was activated by a keycard. As expected. Several of the buttons were already lit up, indicating which floors the car would stop on. But his destination—the floor with Carl MacDugall's office on it—wasn't one of them.

"Um . . ." Grant offering his best embarrassed fumble, "Could you hit sixteen, please?"

The man closest to the panel of buttons turned in surprise. His refined, tailored ensemble stood in stark contrast to Grant's loud coveralls, which he did not fail to notice, offering Grant a quick look up and down. With distaste, he turned back to face the sliding doors.

He pressed the button marked "16" with a pronounced sigh.

Grant breathed a silent sigh of his own, working hard to relax his raging pulse. He ran through his plan once more as the elevator moved up. Julie remained silent in his headpiece, but he could hear her misgivings beneath the dead air.

He knew what she was afraid of. Breaking and entering was one thing. But what if MacDugall refused to talk? Was Grant capable of doing what he must to *make* the man talk?

Guess we'll find out.

The elevator chimed and he exited into a pristine hallway fit for Caesar, complete with ornately-carved Roman pillars. A secretarial pool faced him; most of the desks were empty from the shift change. A few half-glances were cast in his direction from the handful of employees still there, but otherwise no one seemed to take notice of him.

"The hall to your right," Julie said in his ear, though he remembered where to go. A spacious assistant's office at the end of the hall would lead into the vast corner office of Carl MacDugall, chief executive officer.

But he was looking for something else. "Which door is it?" he whispered, then smiled pleasantly at a woman emerging from a rest room on the right.

"Should be the fourth one on your left," Julie answered. *"Assuming they haven't remodeled since the date on these floor plans."*

That's a comforting thought.

The door she directed him to wasn't labeled. There was no way to tell if it was the right one.

But he had no other options. With a deep breath—and a quick glance to both sides to make sure no one was observing him closely— he put his hand on the doorknob and turned it.

To his surprise, it opened. Inside was a lavishly equipped conference room, its centerpiece an oblong mahogany table surrounded by
sixteen leather chairs. Doors were situated on either end of the long
room, leading sideways into other rooms. He marched to the closest
door on his right and opened it.

The next room was a plush office, with more mahogany fixtures,
shelves on all of the walls, a flamboyant, hand-carved wooden desk, an
old fashioned banker's-style desk lamp, and a burgundy wingback
chair. The chair was swiveled in Grant's direction, as if waiting for him.
In it sat an elderly fellow who could only be Carl MacDugall.

Streaks of silver defined his perfectly groomed head of hair, along
with a navy blue pinstripe suit, manicured nails, and black loafers so
shiny Grant found it hard to look directly at them. His brown eyes
were sunken deep. He clutched at his pants with one hand yet gave off
an appearance of being thoroughly unmoved by Grant's entrance.

"Mr. MacDugall, I hope you'll forgive the unexpected entrance," he
began, wasting no time, "but my name is Grant Borrows. Do you know
who I am?"

MacDugall looked him in the eye but hesitated, as if trying to
decide what to say.

"No," he grunted, his eyes still locked on Grant. He wasn't panicking, he was barely even reacting.

This is very, very wrong.

"How about Collin Boyd?" Grant tried again, approaching the desk.
"Ever heard that name?"

"I'm afraid not, young man," MacDugall replied, but quickly gave a
furtive glance in the direction of his secretary's outer office.

Uh-oh.

"You shouldn't be here," the elder man said suddenly.

Grant ran for the receptionist's door. "You knew I was coming!" he
cried. "Who's out there, security?"

He flung the door open, frustration overwhelming all sense of caution.

He froze.

"What do you see?" Julie said breathlessly from his earpiece. *"Who
is it?"*

13

San Diego's coolest winds of the year blew hard across the harbor against the Thresher and his motorcycle, tempting it from the road. But he was undeterred. Distractions were pointless.

He had an appointment with an old contact. It had taken days to track her down. In the end, he found her at an art studio that catered to a rather eclectic clientele.

Which was perfectly in keeping with what he knew about her.

"Everyone's buzzin', man," said Lilly, the girl with the paintbrush and palette, adding a flourish of green to her work. "I don't know who started it, but just last night, more'n once I heard, 'Someone's come, someone who can protect us.'"

She looked completely different from the last time he'd seen her. Her hair was pink and purple, her nose and ears were filled with rings, and one arm bore dozens of plastic charm bracelets.

"Us?" he asked her, even though he knew the answer.

"*Us*, man," she said, as if it were obvious. She splashed yellow and orange in furious swings of her brush. In the three minutes since he had found her, Lilly had taken a four-foot-wide canvas and turned it into an impressionist vista of the Santa Ana mountains. It was so breathtakingly beautiful, even he was taken with it.

"Why do you need protecting?" he asked idly, studying her work.

"I gotta *gift*, dude," Lilly gestured toward her canvas. "People hate anyone who's different. *Tell me* you don't know this."

The Thresher watched as she added magnificent, stringlike clouds over the painting's sunset, mixing gorgeous shades of light red, teal, and a deep purplish tone.

"This man who will protect you, who is he?"

"Never said it was a *guy*," she teased, turning to look at him for the first time. "Don't start in with the chauvinist male superiority crap. Because I will *ditch* you right here and now . . ."

He stepped forward and pressed a wad of greenbacks into her hand.

She offered a fake wounded expression for a moment, but then grinned. "They call him Borrows. Friend of mine told me *everyone's* talking 'Borrows this' and 'Borrows that'."

"Fascinating," he said thoughtfully.

"Liar," she jabbed. "You could care less about anything but whoever you're hunting right now."

He eyed her evenly. Watched her sign her initials to the fresh painting and set the used canvas aside for a fresh one.

"Why do you help me, Lilly?" he asked, genuinely curious. "You know who I am and what I do."

"Dude, I may be gifted, but I ain't exactly rollin' in it. I need the bank."

He resigned himself to her answer, satisfied.

"Now when are you going to ask me what you *really* came to ask me?" she cast a quick glance over her shoulder before returning to her canvas.

"What do you know of the Bringer?" he asked.

Lilly stopped painting and turned.

"I've heard the phrase. Whoever or whatever it is, rumor mill says it's in L.A.," Lilly replied, her eyes falling to his hip.

Los Angeles . . . His mind began formulating the fastest route to the big city.

"I see you're still carrying that overgrown knife of yours . . ."

The Thresher didn't reply, looking blandly into her eyes.

"Thought maybe you would've traded up to a gun or something by now. Kill anybody with it lately?" she asked.

He turned to leave.

"It's not for buttering toast, love."

"Okay, you owe me big for this one," Lisa huffed, marching into Daniel's office.

"What? Did you get something?" he replied, glancing up at her. He was shuffling papers, trying to find his desk, which was beneath them . . . somewhere. Probably.

She sighed, frustrated at his lack of attention.

"Well?" he prodded. He clutched another large stack of papers, opened the filing cabinet to his left, and began sorting them in.

"Do you remember Barry?"

"No," he replied without looking up.

"My ex-boyfriend Barry? We went out for a year before he decided he needed a girlfriend who wasn't smarter than him?"

"Still no."

Lisa frowned. "He's got a job as vault security at the bank's main branch downtown. I had to promise the sleazeball that I'd go out with him again sometime, but he tracked down Collin Boyd's last bank statement for me and . . . *get this*. Collin's cell phone bill is still being paid. The most recent payment—four days ago—was paid by automatic debit."

"How can the phone company collect from a dead man's bank account?"

She smiled for the first time. "Because the payment wasn't taken from Collin's account. The billing was changed a week ago to an account belonging to someone else."

The stack of papers fell from Daniel's hands and fluttered across the floor, as he looked up at her.

"Grant Borrows," she grinned, enjoying his growing excitement.

"We've got his name!" he said, breathlessly.

"Um, hello, *I* got his name," she said. "I'll tell you the rest, but first you have to tell me something."

"*Lisa* . . ." Daniel's eyes scanned the ceiling for nothing. "Don't do this now . . ."

It wasn't the first time she'd used her investigative skills to try and bargain her way into his past. Her growing obsession with knowing everything she could about him was something he found not only inappropriate, but annoying to the highest degree.

When she didn't respond, he sighed. "What is it?" he asked resignedly.

"I just want to know why you do this, that's all," she said innocently, clinging tightly to a manila folder she'd just retrieved from her shoulder bag. "Why you study, well . . . what we study."

"Fine," he grimaced, leaning back in his chair and rubbing his eyes. "I guess it goes back to my mother."

Lisa settled into the chair opposite his desk.

"I never knew my dad. He ran out on her before I was born. And having no siblings, it was just me and Mom for my entire childhood. I had an insatiable curiosity about how things work, but it made me accident-prone—constantly sticking my fingers into electrical sockets or trying to open batteries to see the acid inside or . . . well, you get the idea. But no matter what kind of danger I fell into, I always managed to bounce back. Mom said I was just too curious and stubborn to quit learning—I had no time for anything else.

"I was fifteen when the world changed. Mom was crossing the street on her way home—right in front of our house—when a car hit her doing fifty."

Lisa gasped, yet Daniel continued his story as if giving a clinical dissertation.

"She suffered many injuries, but it was the brain damage that proved irreparable. The doctors told me that she still had brain activity, that she was able to see and comprehend, but the part of her brain that allowed her to communicate had been damaged beyond repair. Essentially, she was still my mother 'in there,' in her head, but she was trapped and couldn't express herself, couldn't *be* herself.

"I became obsessed with the human brain. I received my doctorate in neuroscience. Finding alternative ways of allowing my mother's brain to express itself, beyond normal human interaction, became my obsession. But I went beyond the typical fields and embraced extrasensory studies in addition to my continued work on uncovering the deepest mysteries of the human brain. And I subsequently became the laughingstock of my post-graduate studies. Now will you please hand me that file?"

He could tell he'd surprised her. She placed the file on the desk without a word.

He grabbed it and began scanning through it quickly. "Mm, no picture . . ." he muttered.

Lisa snapped back to reality. "I couldn't find records of any kind for anyone with the name 'Grant Borrows' before five days ago. No medical records. No tax history. Not even a Social Security number. It's undoubtedly a fabricated identity."

"What's this medical discharge report? And how on earth do you get this stuff?"

"I know a guy who knows a guy. The Garden Grove Hospital report you have there is our biggest lead. He was treated there for various injuries the same night as the Glendale fire . . ."

"Let me guess," Daniel interjected. "He was treated for, among other things, burns?"

She nodded. "Along with a minor concussion, various cuts and bruises, and a *bullet wound*."

Daniel whistled. What kind of danger was he about to fall into?

14

Grant was thunderstruck. Confused, and a little dizzy.

Staring back at him wasn't a security guard, a policeman, or even a secretary.

It was a woman. And likely the most beautiful woman he'd ever seen. Blond and cherry-lipped. Blue eyes alive with mischief. Dressed in a worker's jumpsuit not that different from his own, though her curves shaped it into something almost trendy. Her mouth was turned up faintly, in seductive amusement.

"I was starting to think you'd *never* get here," she said in a slight Southern drawl.

Her right arm was out, a gloved hand pointed at him as if a gun. But she held no weapon. She gave a *click* as if cocking a trigger, then slinked her way around Grant, eyes still holding his, until she was past him. At the last moment, she winked.

She slowly walked toward MacDugall, her hand leveled at his head the entire time. "Now you be a good boy," she said to the CEO, "and tell this good-lookin' fella the same thing you told me."

Grant was stupefied. It was ridiculous. Yet MacDugall was watching the woman's every move, her every gesture, as if he fully expected her to pull the gun's imaginary trigger any second.

Grant shifted uncomfortably on his feet, almost feeling sorry for MacDugall.

When MacDugall didn't speak up, she placed the tip of her finger next to his temple.

"O-okay, okay!" he said, beads of sweat visible on his forehead. "I, uh . . . I wasn't lying when I said I don't know you, son. But I know what's *happened* to you."

Grant slowly shuffled back toward the desk, his attention suddenly shifting from the beautiful woman. "Did you do this to me?"

MacDugall shook his head quickly, desperately. "No! I just . . ." He blew out a breath. "We research and develop new technologies here. Of all kinds. On a few rare occasions, we've done some—some highly specialized, custom research—"

The blond woman prodded him with her finger. "Get to the good part already." She rolled her eyes impatiently.

Who was this woman? Why was she *helping* him?

"Quite some time ago, when we were a much smaller operation," MacDugall said, eyes shifting like mad, "we conducted some very . . . next generation research and experimentation on behalf of a well-paying client. It was all kept very quiet, completely off the books."

"What kinds of experiments?" Grant immediately demanded.

"Mr. Evers, the client, asked us to develop technologies—mechanical, pharmaceutical, whatever—capable of *enhancing* the functions of the human body."

The blond woman shot Grant a look as if this revelation vindicated her strange actions.

"Evers . . ." Julie said thoughtfully in Grant's ear.

He turned his head and whispered back, "You know that name?"

"No, I don't think so. Evers . . . Evers . . ." she repeated, as if trying to jar it free from her mind.

"And did you succeed in your experiments?" the blond woman prompted.

"No!" MacDugall cried. "Never! That's what I've been trying to *tell*—"

Grant jumped when a blaring siren wailed out, sounding as though it had filled the entire building.

The woman, suddenly furious, turned to MacDugall and said, "BANG!" He recoiled violently, as if the faux gun in her hand had shot him in the head. But before he realized the truth, she backhanded him into unconsciousness. One of his hands fell limp and Grant could see that MacDugall had pressed some kind of alarm button attached to the underside of the arm on his chair.

It occurred to Grant that he was feeling the same way he'd felt on that first day, a week ago, when he'd found out his life had been changed. Nothing made any sense, and things could *not* get any more bizarre . . .

The next thing he knew, the blond woman had grabbed him by the hand and was dragging him through the secretary's office and out into the hall. "Come *on!*" she sighed, thoroughly exasperated.

The last thing Grant saw of MacDugall's office was a security camera over the door, swiveling to follow him.

Swell.

This was just the best plan ever.

The blond woman led Grant to the elevator area—past the secretarial pool, none of whom seemed to care very much about the sirens—and brandished a screwdriver from one of her pockets. The light above the doors indicated that this car was currently on the fifth floor and going down.

She wedged the flat-head between the doors, prying them open. Then she looked back and winked at Grant. "See ya at the bottom," she said merrily. She stepped off the ledge and fell straight down into the empty shaft.

Grant's breath caught in his throat, not believing what he'd just seen. Was this woman *insane?*

An elevator to his right dinged, opened, and spit out a handful of security guards, decked in military body armor.

There was no time to think.

"Hold it!"

Still wearing his jumpsuit and matching gloves, Grant dove into the empty elevator shaft after the woman, grasping desperately at the center bundle of cables that held the elevator. One look down found him fighting the urge to panic.

Two of the guards stood in the doorway above him. A third knelt and tried reaching down far enough to grab Grant with a powerful hand.

One of the standing guards pulled two items from a belt clip: one he barked into, the other he pointed like a pistol. But it didn't quite look like a pistol.

He fired. Grant ducked. Two small darts grazed his left arm, still attached to the guard's device by long wires.

Oh, of course. Taser.

Grant began making his way down the cable, hand-over-hand. Faster and faster he descended, as the guard above shot at him again.

He had started from the sixteenth floor, but he tried not to think about that, or anything else, except that next handful of cable.

Just take one more handhold. One more.

Come on.

One more.

Adrenaline was pumping hard through his veins when his feet finally touched solid ground. His arms were exhausted and he was covered in sweat, panting hard, but he'd made it.

Except he hadn't. This wasn't the bottom; it was only the top of the elevator car. Above him, he could see shadows still moving from the open door he'd come from. He counted the floors as best he could, estimated that he was around the fourth or fifth floor now.

There was a crack in the door in front of him, less than an inch wide.

She went through here.

If she could, so could he.

He squeezed his fingers through the crack, arms still shaky from the exhausting descent. But he managed to force the doors apart with little difficulty. He found himself a few feet below the floor level, so he had to climb up and roll over onto the marble floor. He lay there for a few moments, catching his breath.

When he looked up, a pristinely groomed woman in an immaculate pantsuit stood nearby, waiting for an elevator car.

She was looking down at him as if he were a leper.

His jumpsuit grimy and wet with sweat, Grant stood slowly, still struggling to breathe. Her bug eyes followed him as he strode by her, and he pointed back at the open elevator shaft.

"Don't ride that one," he said.

Her face blanched as she nodded.

He spotted a men's room nearby and ducked inside, locking the door behind him.

"Don't do this often, do ya, big boy?"

He spun around and there she was—the blond woman from the office. She was leaning back against the sink, untying one of her shoelaces. Once done, she wrestled it out of her shoe. She shoved the string into her pants pocket.

"Still . . . points for makin' it this far," she said, smiling. "You might just be worth savin'."

He leaned over on shaky arms, hands on his knees, and tried to catch his breath, while allowing himself a moment to take her in more fully. She had a rosy complexion and strong cheekbones. Her head was tilted to the side as she studied him with deep-set, unconcerned eyes.

"So you *do* do this sort of thing a lot?" he asked between gasps.

"Zip cord makes the trip down easier," she said, holding out a wadded-up, black nylon rope, clipped to her belt on some kind of pulley.

"*That's* what I forgot when I left the house this morning," he wheezed, still panting.

She acknowledged his sarcasm with a smile. Then she grew serious. "The guards know what floor we're on by now. Time for Plan B."

She turned and stepped into one of the bathroom stalls. He staggered after her.

She stood atop the commode, and had her screwdriver out again, unscrewing the grate from a heating duct in the ceiling.

"You're kidding me, right?" he said, the thought of crawling up into the duct remarkably unappealing.

"Y'reckon?" she said absently.

She loosened a second screw and the grate fell open on hinges. She turned to face Grant again. "Give me a boost," she said.

He paused, uncertain. "Why should I trust you?"

"You shouldn't . . ."

The door handle to the bathroom suddenly jiggled from the other side. Then a knock. "Open up!" a deep voice barked.

". . . but it's me or *them*," she finished matter-of-factly.

Grant made a foothold with his hands and lifted her up into the duct. She scrambled nimbly inside as Grant heard keys jangling outside the door.

"You comin' or what?" her voice called from above.

He looked up to see her hand extending down toward him.

He stepped up onto the toilet seat and took the hand as he heard a key slide into the door's lock.

The bathroom door swung open just as he'd pulled the grate closed.

The blond woman pulled the shoestring out of her pocket and tied the grate closed from inside.

15

They crawled. The going was slow through the tight quarters. She was in front, Grant close behind.

The only thought he could manage right now was that this woman must be from one of the "groups of people" the barefoot girl had warned him about. And stunning or not, he needed to be wary around her.

Aside from that, he also found himself wondering if she might be insane.

He broke the silence first, whispering. "Are you a crazy person?"

"No, but you ain't the first to ask."

"Then what's your story? Who are you? And why are you here? Are you *helping* me?"

"Just keep crawlin', big boy," she whispered back, a smile audible in her voice. "There'll be time for questions *after* today's object lesson."

"Hey," Julie broke in, *"I hate to interrupt the rampant and inappropriate flirting but the situation outside has disintegrated."*

"Like what?" Grant stopped crawling. Through another ventilation grate, he saw and heard at least a dozen security guards march below in fast succession.

"Bad time to quit movin'," the blond woman paused and looked back. "Don't make me regret helping you out."

"Police cars, fire trucks, dozens of security vehicles . . ." Julie replied. *"You name it. All blocking the front entrance."*

That was no problem. He had no intention of going *out* the front entrance.

"And they've barricaded the entire street," Julie added. *"The gas station is blocked—I can't reach it."*

"Perfect."

"You comin' or what?" the blond woman asked in a bored tone of voice.

Grant began crawling again. Something else occurred to him as they moved.

"How did you do that back in the office?" he whispered. "MacDugall wasn't afraid you were going to *scratch* him to death. He really believed you were holding a gun. Didn't he?"

He heard her sigh. "You'd never understand how it works. People trust their eyes too much. It's an easy weakness to exploit."

Grant tried to swallow that. Found that he couldn't.

"So . . . what? You're some kind of—I don't know—illusionist?"

"Sure," she replied, unconvincingly. "Somethin' like that."

They crawled on.

"She is so *full of it,"* Julie said.

Something else occurred to Grant.

"Hey, why not use your mojo on the security guards, so we could just *walk* out of here?" he said.

"If it were *that* simple, d'you think we'd be havin' this conversation?" she replied. "Look, you're *way* out of your depth here, sugar. Leave the escape planning to the professionals."

Fifteen minutes later, they dropped through another grate into a tiny office. It was the first one they'd run across that was empty, and it was a long way from the bathroom. They'd watched from above as guards continued to march vigorously throughout the floor, searching everywhere for the intruders. As soon as they disappeared into another area, a new set of guards emerged and searched the same area all over again.

What are they so eager to keep anyone from finding?

As he dropped down into the office behind her, he caught a glimpse of the woman's eyes scanning the entire room. She turned away, trying not to show it, but he could see her inspecting every inch of the office.

Grant stood in place, watching her. She was nearing the door when he whispered again.

"You're a cat burglar!" he said, the same moment he pieced it together.

"*A what?*" Julie cried in his earpiece, so loud the blond woman could hear it.

She turned to face him, raised an eyebrow. "Me. Ow."

His shoulders dropped and he looked down. "I was trying to convince myself you were some kind of government agent . . ."

She walked closer to him, icy cool gaze and platinum smile still intact. "Government jobs are for bland people who look good in a tie. *Real* fieldwork needs imagination, instinct, cunning. And hey, it pays the bills."

"Right. Because who *wouldn't* rather steal to get ahead."

She offered a fake hurt look. "Hey, I don't take nothin' from nobody who can't afford to lose it. Rare art, antiques, fine jewelry, that sort of stuff. And nobody gets hurt. As long as they leave *me* alone, I leave *them* alone."

Grant was unconvinced. "So . . . you're a criminal with a heart of gold. Like Robin Hood—stealing from the rich."

"Mm-hmm," she nodded, then flashed another smile. "Just without that pesky 'giving to the poor' fixation."

Grant rolled his eyes.

"*This woman is* the Devil," Julie said. "*Why are you helping her?*"

"I'm not!" Grant whispered into his earpiece. "She's helping *me*! I mean, I think she is. It's complicated."

"Remind your friend," the blond woman said, "that if it wasn't for me, you'd've never gotten anything out of ol' MacDugall."

"How did you know I would show up in MacDugall's office?" he asked quietly.

"First we make with the escaping," she said. "Answers come later."

Something else clicked in Grant's mind. "Are you the reason the conference room door was unlocked?"

"*Yes*," she exhaled, annoyed. "Now will you *come on!*"

They made it to the main stairwell without incident and ran down to the first floor. She cracked open the door, and Grant could see through the slit that the gargantuan room was buzzing with activity, even more than before. Dozens of security guards were in the mix now.

He reached over her head and pushed the door shut.

"I know an easier way," he said.

"Oh, really?"

"Oh, really!"

She was dubious, one eyebrow cocked upward. But she had to know the front door was suicide.

"Then impress me, big boy," she said, hands on her hips.

He led the way down the stairs to the basement, along the narrow hall, and into the warehouse-sized room. The main lights were out overhead, but emergency floodlights had been triggered by the alarm. They made their way through crates and boxes until they reached the furthest wall. Grant had to feel around for a few minutes under her wilting gaze before he finally found the hidden doorway. A small pedal on the floor, hidden under a nearby shelf, triggered it open.

Grant walked in and she followed, gazing around the narrow corridor that led back to the gas station. She pushed the door shut behind them.

They walked in silence.

Suddenly Grant jumped and shouted.

She did the same. "What's wrong?"

"My cell phone vibrated. Hasn't happened in a long while."

She turned and walked on.

He pulled the phone open and kept walking, pressing it to his face. "Yeah?"

"Hello. I'm trying to find information about a man named Collin Boyd," a voice on the other end said. A male voice.

Grant's mind froze; that was the last thing he'd expected to hear. Still, this *was* his old cell phone; he'd pulled it off Collin's body in the burning hallway.

He swallowed and rubbed his thumb against the ring again. It was a nervous habit he'd fast developed.

"Collin is dead," he said softly, where the woman couldn't hear.

"Yes, I know," the voice said. "But this phone is registered in his name, is it not?"

"Yes, this is Collin's phone, but—"

"Well, there we are then," the man said, sounding pleased with himself. "There are no coincidences."

"Look, this isn't a good time—"

"Have you, by any chance, seen inanimate objects moving by themselves lately?"

Grant stopped cold. The blonde up ahead of him noticed and turned around to see what he was doing.

"Could you say that again?" Grant said.

"You've seen some strange things happen lately, haven't you? Things you can't explain. Like a hunting knife burying itself deep inside a column made of solid concrete."

Grant was too stunned to answer.

The woman approached him in the corridor. "Come *on*," she whispered. "I can see the exit. We're nearly there!"

Grant ignored her, listening to the phone.

"Fine. Get caught." She turned and walked off without him.

"Whoever you are," the voice on the phone said, "we need to talk. My name is Daniel Cossick. I'm a scientist, and I think I can help you. But know this: you're not just witnessing these strange events—I believe you're *causing* them. Call me back at this number when you're ready to talk."

Grant pulled the phone away from his face and beeped it off, too stunned to think or move.

"Who was that, Collin?" Julie asked.

He heard a door open in the distance and looked up. The woman was already at the gas station cellar, going in.

He walked after her.

Grant soon reached the cellar, passed through the broom closet, grabbed his bag under the stairs, and ran up and out. Night had fallen, and it was growing cold out.

He had just reached the top of the steps when he saw her lying facedown on the ground, near the corner edge of the building.

He ran to her, kneeling down and feeling her pulse. She was alive.

"She's all right, just had a bit of a shock," said a voice above him.

Grant looked up, but it was too late. Torrents of electricity flowed through him and he felt his entire body clench, folding itself into a fetal position until all he knew was darkness.

16

Grant awoke to the sound of screaming.

He noticed he couldn't move before his droopy eyes opened. He was handcuffed to a chair, his ankles shackled around the chair's legs. His chair was near the corner of a vast, dark room with no windows. Two dozen security guards stood around him in a semicircle. Beyond them, he could see security monitors, desks, and gear of all kinds. Enormous digital screens were on every wall, showing scenes from all around the Inveo campus.

This was no security office. It was a full-fledged operations center. *They could coordinate a war from in here if they wanted to*, Grant thought. *What is a new technologies developer doing with this kind of firepower?*

He glanced up at the guards. They were watching him. No, they were watching the blond woman, who was five feet away to his right, also cuffed to a chair. Most of the guards were expressionless, others appeared to be enjoying this.

Her entire body convulsed.

One of the guards had pulled a chair up right in front of her and was using a Taser gun to shock her. *It must be on a lower setting. She's still conscious.*

The two darts from the gun were attached to her stomach and the guard was zapping her over and over. She braced herself, trying not to react, but she couldn't help it. The electricity surged through her, and she shook violently. But she refused to make a sound.

"Aw, come on, I want to hear that girly scream again," the guard with the Taser said, grinning, holding down the switch.

She bit down on her lip, hot tears burning her cheeks, refusing to give in. But he didn't stop until she screamed.

"That wasn't so hard, was it?"

"Hey," Grant said with a slur, "I'm awake . . . My turn now."

The guard barely glanced over. "Sorry," the man grunted. "We're under orders not to harm you."

"What? Why?"

The guard looked back at the woman. "You know, honey," he said, inching closer to her, "you'd probably think this is a high-stress job. It's really not. Sure, big place like this, people are always doing things they shouldn't. Activating emergency exits by going out the *wrong door*—" he tapped the Taser for a second and she jumped—"lighting one up in the bathroom and setting off the *sprinklers*—" another jolt—"parking in the boss's *spot*—" again—"and guess who has to deal with it all?" He glanced around at the other guards in the room. "*We* do."

He sighed. "Now, big, strapping fellas that we are, we signed on to run with a high-risk security task force. But *look* at this place. So much technology, what do they need us for? Instead of keeping this place secure, we end up helping old Mrs. Greenburg to the ladies' room. Do we look like Boy Scouts to you?"

She opened her eyes, panting; sweat was dripping off of her, and her hair was soaked. Grant knew she must've been dying to tell these "boy scouts" *exactly* what they looked like but, to her credit, she was holding her tongue.

"So as you might imagine," the guard continued when she didn't say anything, "when we get our hands on a pair of real-life criminals, caught in a real-life criminal act. . . . well, that's a red-letter day." He smiled and shocked her again. She screamed.

"You call holding and torturing us *legal*?" Grant asked.

"We'd be working in law enforcement if any of us cared about what's 'legal,'" the guard said with a bored expression. His empty eyes stayed on Grant as he Tasered the woman again, calmly holding the button down. A few of the other men in the room chuckled as she shook so hard Grant thought she might break the chair.

He was becoming increasingly frantic each time the woman

received another jolt. She wouldn't be able to withstand this forever. But what could he do? He couldn't even *move*.

His thoughts returned to that strange phone call, and what the man had said.

Was it possible? Was he responsible for the knife in the subway wall? Could he have somehow caused the knife to leave Konrad's hand? It was bizarre, but he had no other explanation.

He strained his memory, trying to remember how it had felt, in the moment. He'd been hit by a wave of panic. It had washed over him accompanied by a cold sweat, and then there had been that mind-splitting headache that lasted for just a second. He remembered closing his eyes with the pain, and when he'd opened them, it was over.

There are no coincidences. That's what the man on the phone had said.

Grant took a long, deep breath.

He closed his eyes and focused on trying to recreate that feeling of overwhelming panic. He thought about being captured, trapped by security guards who were clearly sadistic, and probably had no intention of releasing him.

The panic began to build and he breathed faster.

He thought of the woman seated next to him. The Taser darts embedded into her stomach. The pain she was experiencing. Her waning stamina. Whoever she was, whatever she had done—no one deserved this kind of cold-blooded cruelty. And he was responsible. *He* had led her out that secret exit.

He began to sweat, his chest rising and falling harder. Faster and faster he breathed, the cold panic mounting, until—

A violent pain stabbed through his brain. Someone shouted.

And just as fast as it had happened, the headache was gone.

He opened his eyes to see the guard no longer holding his Taser—he wasn't even in the *chair*. Instead, he had curled up on the floor, clenching his stomach with both hands. Blood was visible between his fingers.

"Holy . . ." one of the other guards muttered. "Get some help! *Go!*" the man shouted. Two of the guards left the room. The one who'd shouted for help knelt down beside the man on the ground. The others had frozen in shock, but now they moved in for a closer look, eyes wide.

Grant looked over at the woman. A hole had been ripped in the side of her jumpsuit, where the pocket was, but otherwise she looked okay, although she was barely conscious and her breathing shallow.

"Forget it," one of the guards said. "We'll take him to medical." The kneeling guard nodded and three others moved in to help pick up the man on the ground.

They hefted him, and he grunted in pain. As they marched toward the door, they passed Grant, and he looked between them at the injured man. He gasped.

The familiar black handle of the blond woman's screwdriver was sticking out of the guard's stomach.

He'd never consciously thought about the man with the Taser gun *or* the screwdriver. He'd just forced himself to panic, and the rest had somehow happened.

"Watch them!" the guard who had knelt down shouted back at the others in the room, as they carried the injured man out.

The remaining dozen or so guards became all business, dispersing throughout the room, some taking up positions at various monitors, one standing in front of Grant and the woman.

Grant began breathing faster.

Could he do it twice? They *had* to get out of here.

Now.

He shut his eyes tight and bore down, clenching every muscle he could. He started to shudder, sweating again. He thought about the man with the screwdriver in his gut and that *he* had somehow caused it . . .

The panic hit again.

His brain seized, much harder this time.

He nearly blacked out.

When Grant opened his eyes, he was lying against the corner wall, on the floor. The cuffs were still around his wrists and ankles, but the chains were broken. He was free!

The pungent odor of burning metal awakened him to the chaos filling the room. The metal chair he had been sitting in was sticking straight out of one of the enormous digital screens across the room, smoke and sparks pouring from the gaping hole. One of the guards reached for a fire extinguisher, the others looked like they were too stunned to react.

That was when Grant noticed they were one short. The guard that had been standing right in front of him was gone. Grant looked across the room at the chair again and saw that the spot where the guard had been standing was directly between the chair and where Grant now lay.

He didn't move for a long moment, looking harder at the broken screen and the chair sticking out of it, as he swallowed the obvious implication.

Finally, he hopped up and moved toward the woman. One of the guards noticed and ran over to him. The guard threw a wide punch and Grant ducked it, bringing his fist up into the guard's stomach. It knocked the wind out of him, and he doubled over. Grant saw a key-chain on the guard's belt loop and he swiftly reached in and grabbed it. Then punched him again in the stomach. The guard toppled over.

The few guards that were left were still attending to the electrical fire or shouting into radios. They seemed to have forgotten about their prisoners in the corner.

Grant found his earpiece on the ground and put it back on.

"You still there?" he whispered.

"What happened? Are you okay?!"

"Tell you later. I'm in a humongous room inside some kind of security bunker. Need a way out."

"All right, hold on." Grant knew she must be checking the floor plans. *"Is there a door at the far corner of the room?"*

"Looks like it."

"Take it."

With a glance at the still-distracted guards, Grant uncuffed the woman and scooped her up in his arms. She was shaking all over, unable to stand. But the look on her face was completely changed. Gone was the playful grin, the seductive eyes. She was aghast, drained of color.

She took in the chair in the screen and then turned back to Grant.

Whatever had happened, Grant realized she'd seen the whole thing.

Grant ran out the door and into a long, dark corridor. He couldn't see to the hallway's end, and the only exit from the hall that was visible was the door he'd just come from.

"What am I looking for?" he asked Julie.

"A door," she replied, as if it were obvious. *"Other end of the hall."*

Grant ran as fast as he could until the end of the hall became visible. There were *two* doors, one to the left, one to the right.

He chose left.

When he opened the door, he nearly dropped the girl.

A small, wide foyer gave way to a massive, O-shaped metal structure.

Grant stepped inside. Neither he nor the blond woman could take their eyes off of the three-story-high mechanism. It looked like a massive bank vault but was probably much thicker and had to weigh over a ton. And just like a vault, there were hinges on one side . . .

A quiet hum filled the room.

Grant was certain this wouldn't appear on Julie's floor plans. Which only made him all the more curious as to what was behind it.

A security panel waited patiently on the right side of the room, for what looked like a keycard, retinal scan, and vocal identification. There was nothing else in the room.

The door itself was flat and smooth.

Grant glanced at the woman in his arms; she was still staring at the big metal door, her eyes wide and taking in the entire thing.

This . . . this was breathtaking. Massive and beyond comprehension.

"What's going on?" Julie cried in his ear. *"Did you find the door?"*

"Uh-huh," he replied, dumbstruck. "We found the door."

17

The blond woman in Grant's arms was gaping at the door as well, but finally she croaked, "We can't stay—they're comin'."

"But . . ." he protested, "we've got to find out what's behind this thing. It could explain *everything* that's happened to me!"

"Then we'll come back for it *later*," she implored. "If they find us, they'll *kill* us. We gotta go!"

"No! We'll never make it this far again! All the answers I'm looking for could be behind this thing!" Something about the size of it was . . . captivating.

"You'll find a way," the woman said slowly.

He didn't hear her.

"Hey." She put her hand on his cheek. "I'll help you find a way. I promise."

For the first time, he transferred his attention away from the door and really looked the blond woman in the eyes. A bright shade of blue, her eyes were soft, round, and absolutely stunning, yet dark and pained from her ordeal. For the first time all evening, he felt like he was seeing the real her.

Finally he nodded, taking one last look at the door. He turned and exited the room, opening the opposite door on the right of the hall. It led to a stairwell, going only up.

They were underground. *Deep* underground, from the look of these stairs.

Grant charged up the steps, adrenaline surging again, flight after flight.

After several minutes, they emerged from a nondescript door into a garage full of minivans, sedans, and golf carts, all marked "Inveo SECURITY." The guards themselves were nowhere to be seen.

"We're in some kind of security garage," Grant reported to Julie.

"Good. If you go out the back door, there's a smaller side entrance to the campus. I can meet you there."

Grant turned; the back garage entrance was open. But no, that wouldn't work. He was sweating, fatigued, and his mind was reeling from the day's events; he couldn't carry his new friend any farther. Besides, the side entrance would no doubt be shut tight, so how was he supposed to . . .

An idea sparked, and Grant dumped the blond woman in the passenger seat of the nearest security van. He found a corkboard hanging from a nearby wall where dozens of key rings, all numbered, waited. A sticker on the rear bumper of the security van said "08." He snatched the corresponding key from the board.

"Julie, change of plan. You start heading back toward L.A. We'll meet up with you shortly."

Grant cranked the van's engine to life and jammed the pedal to the floor. A few guards lurked just outside the exit, and they began screaming at him, but he never slowed, nearly ran them over.

The tires squealed loudly as the van took the corner at full speed, bearing down on the side entrance. It was gated, a barbed wire fence blocking the way along with an enormous metal arm.

"Seatbelt on and head down!" Grant shouted. Still shaking, she fiddled with her seatbelt until it locked; then she leaned over all the way, covering her head with her arms.

A guard emerged from the gatehouse when he saw the van approaching at high speed, but he was far too late.

Grant covered his face with one arm and kept the other on the wheel as the van exploded through the gate with a horrible screeching. Metal grinded and clashed against metal, but it only lasted a moment, and then they were out.

Grant never let up from the gas pedal, the van careening down the road. But the woman was still leaning over in her seat.

He wiped his sweat-soaked face with a dirty sleeve.

"It's okay, we made it," he said, panting.

She slowly sat back up and looked around, rubbing her arms and shivering.

"No we didn't," she said softly.

She was looking behind. He checked the rear-view and saw flashing red-and-blue lights.

He punched the steering wheel in frustration, and the horn blared.

Checking his surroundings, he saw that they were on what had to have been the local main street. It was late, so most of the stores and streets were deserted, save for cruising teenagers and joyriders.

"Are you able to get up on your own?" Grant asked the woman beside him, a plan rapidly formulating.

"I think so," she said uneasily.

"Julie, how far out are you?" *She* should *be on the same road we are . . .*

"Few miles outside of downtown, why?"

"Anywhere nearby where you can pull off the road inconspicuously?"

"Um . . . Yeah, I see a car dealership a few blocks ahead."

"Turn in," Grant commanded, "and shut off the car and all the lights. Wait there."

"Okay . . ." Julie replied, clearly wanting to know more, but not asking.

Grant glanced quickly over each shoulder. "Good, sliding doors on both sides . . ." he mumbled.

"You're not thinkin' what I think you're thinkin' . . ." said the blond woman.

Grant nodded, assuming she was already on the same page with him. "We need something to aim for, something that'll cover our tracks but won't hurt anybody."

"You're crazy," she commented wearily, but quickly joined him in scanning the road for an appropriate target.

The chasing vehicles behind them had crept closer, the leader less than three car's lengths away. Grant couldn't see how many cars there were, but from the noise of all the sirens, it had to be a lot.

They know what we saw underground . . . Grant surmised.

A sign for a car dealership was visible in the distance, on the right side of the road.

"Julie, can you hear sirens?"

"I'll say," she replied. *"Sounds like a* fleet."

"We're in a yellow security van. We're about to pass you," he said. Then he turned to his passenger. "Open the doors."

She nodded and carefully got to her feet in the speeding van, holding tight to seats, the ceiling—whatever she could find.

Just as the second door slid open, the van shot past the car lot like a bullet, police cars and more security vehicles right behind.

"Stand by, Julie . . . *There."*

A rock face on the side of the mountain was ahead on the left, at least a hundred feet from the nearest buildings.

"You ready?!" Grant shouted.

"No," the blond woman replied, "but go on and do it anyway!"

Grant jammed the pedal all the way down and swerved the car just enough so that it would aim for the rock face. When they were three hundred feet away, he turned off the car's headlights, jumped out of his seat, and shouted, "Now!"

She jumped out of the van's right side, and he followed suit on the left, hitting the ground with a hard crack and rolling at an impossible speed. He came to a rest against a wooden road barrier.

Grant looked up just in time to watch the van ram straight into the mountain, generating sparks, fire, and the loudest crash he had ever heard.

Twenty minutes later, Grant was driving the Corvette, the barely conscious blond woman riding shotgun and Julie in the backseat. Grant and his companion were scraped and bruised, but they'd both managed to escape with no broken bones.

"You're insane," Julie huffed. "If I had known what you were going to do—"

"Why do you think I didn't tell you?" he cut her off.

She pouted in the backseat.

His blond companion stirred awake and watched him drive for a very long time before speaking up.

"So what's your name?" she asked in a tired, raspy voice.

"Grant," he replied. "Grant Borrows."

"Well, Grant Borrows," she replied slowly. "I'm Hannah." She held her hand out to him. "And I am very pleased to meet you."

He took her hand and held it. She seemed to take strength from it. She sat up taller in the seat.

They let go and she studied her hand for a moment, lost in thought.

"Grant, I need to ask you something . . . And it might sound a little odd."

She sat back in her seat, relaxing, and began peeling off her gloves.

"Okay . . ." he said, curious, but still watching the road, nervously checking the rear-view for signs of the Inveo security or the police.

Hannah looked down for a moment, and then back up at him.

"You used to be someone else, didn't you?"

His head snapped around. "How do you know that?"

She pulled the glove off from her right hand and lifted it for him to see. Resting there was a gold ring with an inset burgundy gemstone.

"Because *I* used to be someone else."

The Corvette's tires screeched to a halt in the middle of the road.

He took her hand and pulled it closer, biting off his own glove with his teeth. Julie leaned forward from the backseat. Grant compared the two rings. Hers was slightly smaller, and it had none of the etchings or markings on the sides that his had. Otherwise, the two rings were identical.

Grant let go and sat back in the driver's seat, his mind spinning. Hannah and Julie both watched him silently.

"I'm not the only one," Hannah broke the silence. "There're others."

He looked her in the eye and tried to speak, but found himself breathless.

"How many?" he got out.

"I don't know. I know a place where some of them live, or *hide* . . . It's a sort of a . . . commune. People like us, who live . . . *away*. From the rest of the world. A friend of mine runs the place; the same friend who sent me to Inveo to help you. They're the only ones that I know of myself. But I'm told there are many more . . . out there." She gazed out the front window.

Grant put a hand to his forehead and rubbed it. His eyes darted all around, lost in thought.

Suddenly he sat upright and focused his eyes on the road ahead.
He began driving.

"Where?"

"I don't know—"

"No, this group—the commune or whatever. Where are *they*?"

Hannah nodded, exhaling slowly. "Right, I'll let 'em know you'd like to meet—"

"No, *now*. How do I get there?"

"Grant," she hesitated, "these people live in total seclusion from the outside world. And they don't like visitors . . ."

"I don't care!" he shouted. "If this friend of yours knows about me, he might have answers. If he can tell me *anything* about what's happened to me and why . . . And just knowing that I'm not alone, I'm not the only one . . ."

He shook his head.

"*No!*" he cried. His gaze was set dead ahead. "We're going there *now*."

18

An old road snaking deep into a canyon miles outside of Thousand
Oaks led Grant, Julie, and Hannah to a paved driveway. Cracked and
broken cement made the way tough for the Corvette, but eventually
they pulled up to a sturdy-looking gate and a ten-foot-high electric
fence. In the distance stood a large, single-story brick complex.

Being this close to answers raised goosebumps on Grant's arms.
Would this bleak, uninviting place reveal to him all that he longed to
know?

At the edge of the gate nearest the driveway, a surprisingly modern
keycard entry system was mostly obscured from external view by over-
hanging brush. Grant hadn't noticed the high-tech machine until they
were right beside it.

But he was more interested in the building that had just emerged
into sight.

"Is that . . . what I think it is?"

"It used to be a . . . *facility*," Hannah replied uneasily, still sporting
reddened skin and fatigue from her ordeal. "Government abandoned it
and sold the property after the 'deinstitutionalization' of the early '60s.
'Community care' became all the rage afterwards, as I've been told.
Many times."

"What kind of facility?"

"I believe the preferred term is 'mental health institution'," she
replied.

"So it's an insane asylum," he concluded.

"Pretty much. They thought the foliage would soothe the patients."

It was so different than what he was expecting. Grant's eyes searched the front of the edifice for any signs of life, any evidence that this was a place to be excited about visiting. But the doors were solid and what few windows there were, were high off the ground, with iron bars over them. The brick walls were chipping away slowly, entire bricks missing from a few spots.

"You said this friend of yours would be expecting us," Grant prodded.

"Yep," Hannah replied.

"I didn't see you make any calls. How does he know we're coming?"

"Been expecting you, from what I understand, for a long while now. Before you ask, I don't know how that's possible. And by the by—my friend's a 'she', not a 'he'."

"Duly noted."

He parked the Corvette in front of the decaying facility and helped Hannah out of the car. She kept telling him she was fine, but he practically had to carry her up the five or six steps that led to the front door. Julie pulled up the rear, watching both of them warily.

"Dr. Cossick?"

"Yeah," Daniel said absentmindedly, poring over computations on his laptop.

"Detective Drexel is here to see you," Lisa said formally. Then, lowering her voice and scrunching her face, she added, "Guess we didn't pacify him enough the last time?"

Daniel grimaced. *Great*. He quickly shut his laptop.

Lisa showed their guest into Daniel's office, and Daniel rose to shake the man's hand.

Drexel removed his fedora while offering half a haggard smile. The heavyset man had a few days' worth of stubble, and his clothes and trench coat looked like they hadn't seen the inside of a washing machine in years.

Daniel took in all of this in less than a second but decided to politely ignore it.

"How can I help you today, Detective?"

"Well, I'm not sure you can," Drexel began, forcing a cordial smile, "but I hope so." He noticed the business card holder on Daniel's desk and picked one up, pocketing it. "I have this problem."

Daniel returned to his chair, listening. "Related to the Boyd case?"

Drexel nodded. "Boyd's sister was kidnapped not long before the arson on his apartment, you see. And I believe the kidnapper may be the same man who started the fire."

Whoa.

"As you can imagine," the detective continued, "I've been trying to find out who this man is, but I haven't been having much luck."

"I'm sorry to hear that, Detective, but I'm not sure how I can help."

"The name 'Grant Borrows' ring a bell with you?"

Daniel blinked. "No."

"Hmm," Drexel said slowly, showing an exaggerated confusion on his face. "Now that's very odd." He reached inside his coat pocket and pulled out a piece of paper. Unfolding it, his eyes moved back and forth, skimming the document as he continued to speak.

"See, I followed the trail from Mr. Boyd's most recent bank statement to a mobile phone, which is now being paid for by this 'Grant Borrows'. Then I talked to his wireless provider, and a gentleman there was kind enough to run a trace on all of Borrows' recent calls on that phone."

A trickle of sweat formed on the back of Daniel's neck and wiggled its way south.

"Now here's my favorite part," Drexel said, relishing his tale. "The phone has only been used one time since the kidnapping. It was an *incoming* call, and it took place just about three hours ago, much to my surprise."

Daniel tried not to react, but he could feel the blood draining from his face.

"Would you like to know who called him?" Drexel said with complete sincerity.

Daniel sat back in his chair and did his best to stare blankly at the detective.

But instead of reading from the document, Drexel folded the paper and put it back inside his coat. "I think we both know the answer to that question."

Daniel cleared his throat, squared his shoulders. "Detective, are you accusing me of doing something unlawful?"

Drexel smiled. "Right now, I'd say it qualifies as circumstantial. But I *know* you know who this man is. And based on what I've seen of your 'scientific research facility' out there"—he nodded his head in the direction of the lab—"I suspect you're just as interested in finding him as I am. What I can't figure out is *why*."

"And if I *am* looking for this 'Grant Borrows'?"

"Then you and I are destined to be best friends."

"Detective, I don't know this man. I can assure you I have absolutely no information on him, whoever he is." Daniel sat up straight in his chair. "*If* we dialed his phone from the lab, then it must've been an accident."

"Well," Drexel said, still smiling, "you might want to take some time to give that statement some careful consideration, Doctor. You see, you may not know Borrows, and you may not know me, but I know *you*. I checked you out. And I found out about some very interesting things you've been involved with in the past—downright *appalling* things, if you want to know the truth—that I'm sure you wouldn't want anyone else to know. Like maybe that pretty young assistant of yours."

An exaggerated gagging sound resembling a cat with a hairball was heard coming from the outer office.

"I don't have anything to hide, Detective," he said. "We all do things in life we're not proud of. I'm not ashamed of my past. Are you?"

Drexel stood, his wide frame casting a shadow over the entire wall behind him. "You may not be ashamed of your past, but I *know* you're hiding from it. Or maybe someone in it." He put his hat back on his head and moved to go. "Think it over, Doc. That lab o' yours down the hall has a lot of specialized equipment in it. Pretty delicate stuff from the look of it. Nothing you'd want anyone else messing with, I'm guessing. You know, we got a *whole* bunch of science geeks in our forensics unit who'd just *love* to get in there and take all that stuff apart to find out what it does."

Drexel opened the office door. "I'll be in touch," he said, pulling out Daniel's business card and waving it at him.

Daniel stood. "You won't be allowed back in here without a search warrant."

"Don't tempt me," Drexel said, the smug grin still on his face, as he turned and walked out.

Lisa gave Drexel the evil eye as he strolled out of the outer office and down the hall to the exit. When he was safely gone, she wheeled around and burst into Daniel's office.

"He's dirty," she said. Daniel was still standing exactly where Drexel had left him, fuming.

"Oh, I got the feeling he wasn't threatening us for the common good," he replied.

"No," she said, crinkling her nose, "didn't you smell him? He's *dirty*."

"He's got nothing and he knows it. We're not doing anything even *remotely* illegal here. How were *we* supposed to know the man we're investigating is involved in a kidnapping?" He sat back down, mind racing, and then looked back up at her. "We'd better double-check our permits, make sure they're all up-to-date."

She nodded.

"And that file you started on Borrows? Get rid of it."

After Hannah inserted her keycard in the scanner beside the main entrance, Grant pushed open the double doors and was greeted by the dry, musty smell of books. A long hallway stretched before them, but instead of white-painted walls, the hall was crammed floor to ceiling with books. Every shape, every size. Some thick, some as narrow and flimsy as magazines. One stack after another after another, completely covering the walls, as if the building were being supported by the numerous volumes. So many of them . . . Thousands, tens of thousands, that he could see and far more than he could count.

A few of the stacks leaned precariously inward toward the long hallway he now traversed, and Grant was struck by an odd sense of claustrophobia. He couldn't shake the feeling that the walls had sprouted long fingers made of hardbacks and paperbacks that were trying to reach out and touch him.

He was struck by how quiet it was. Nestled deep in the woods, the facility was far away from civilization, but even those who lived here seemed to make very little noise.

The long, dimly lit corridor led the three of them to another set of double doors. These doors were glass on top, with criss-crossed wire inside. They opened suddenly with a flourish as Grant, Julie, and Hannah approached them. A nondescript man and woman stood on either side and motioned for them to enter.

Grant glanced at Hannah, who offered him a reassuring, if weak, nod.

Inside was a large, rectangular room which they had entered near one corner. Lush and soothing with an "old fashioned charm," this room showed the most evidence of renovation of anything Grant had seen so far.

And here too, the walls were stuffed, packed, and jammed with books of every size, shape, and color. Wooden fixtures and a low ceiling added to the "cozy" feel. The area nearest to them appeared to be a lounge of sorts: a pool table, a sofa and bean bags, a few small desks with reading lamps, a handful of laptop computers, and a modest television set.

In the middle of the room was a fireplace made of grayish red bricks, surrounded by wingback chairs and small end tables. A dark crimson rug ran underneath this furniture; it was at least two inches thick, made of long, furry tendrils of string.

There were people everywhere. Dozens of them. The residents, Grant assumed. They looked disarmingly normal, and closer inspection revealed individuals from all walks of life, all social classes, and various races and ages. But he saw no children. And each and every one of them wore a golden ring on their right-hand middle finger.

On the far end of the room, in relative seclusion, sat an ancient-looking desk piled high with dozens—perhaps hundreds—more books. Barely visible behind the mountains of books was the top of a simple desk chair. If one looked hard enough, a small grayish-white mop of hair could be seen leaning against the chair's headrest.

Every person in the room had stopped whatever they were doing as soon as Grant had entered, and now they watched him with great interest. Whispers buzzed like a swarm of bees throughout the room, as the men and women leaned in to one another, all eyes unwavering from Grant.

He absent mindedly rubbed his thumb against the ring.

The woman who had helped open the double doors quickly walked to the desk and stepped behind it, whispering something to the person who sat there.

"Brilliant!" a female voice announced in an impeccable British accent.

A woman emerged from behind the desk. She couldn't have been more than forty-five and was short in stature, yet her nearly all-white hair made her look older. She stood tall—as tall as she could, anyway—as though a metal rod was holding her back straight. Large eyes peered down a pudgy nose over the rims of bifocal glasses to land on Grant, and she walked forward calmly but purposefully, and outstretched her hand.

"Welcome, Mr. Borrows," she said with a gleam in her eyes. "Welcome to the Common Room. My name is Morgan."

The Thresher shoved his motorcycle's kickstand down, and stepped off into dirt.

Ahead he saw a honky-tonk bar that couldn't have been any more stereotypical if it tried. Rust and mold covered the building's exterior in a sort of patchwork of disgusting colors. A bright red neon light flashed the word "BEER" over the door, which was solid, looked rather thick, and had no window to see inside.

He opened the door. A wall of cigarette and cigar smoke, sweat, and stale alcohol rushed at him but did not slow him down.

The interior was even less appealing than the outside. Dingy lights hung low from overhead, illuminating a handful of pool tables, a jukebox, a bar and stools, and a few tables.

The dozen or so patrons turned as he entered, surveying the newcomer who dared intrude on their private haunt. They looked like feral dogs, sniffing to see who had invaded their territory. And not one of them failed to notice the scabbard hanging from his hip.

"I'm looking for Mr. Odell," the Thresher said, to everyone.

"Don't know nobody by that name, son," called a filthy man in a white apron, standing behind the bar. "But weapons ain't allowed in here."

The Thresher scanned the crowd. Nearly every man had the telling bulge of a shoulder gun holster under their jackets. The few who didn't had large knives attached to their hips.

He locked eyes again with the bartender. "I know Mr. Odell is here." He took a menacing step forward, but still spoke calmly. "And I don't like repeating myself."

"What d'ya want with 'im?" someone called out from a murky corner of the room.

"A conversation," the Thresher replied.

"And if he don't feel like talkin'?" another man shouted.

The Thresher slowly and carefully reached for the handle of his sword.

"Then very soon, he will feel differently."

Grant was still speechless from his surroundings. It was a moment before he replied to Morgan. "Um, is 'Morgan' your first name or last?"

"Neither," she replied, offering him a knowing smile. "May I call you Grant?"

"Okay." He gestured. "My sister, Julie."

Morgan acknowledged Julie with a polite nod. "We have a great deal to discuss, Grant, yet I feel as though I know you already," she said in her quick British clip. "Please, please have a seat."

But Grant found himself once again staring at the innumerable volumes covering the walls.

"All these books . . ." he began, taking in his surroundings in wonder.

She gestured to a chair in front of the crackling fireplace. "Oh yes, they are mine. But we'll get to that. Right now, we have more important matters to discuss."

Morgan joined him at the fire in a tall armchair that seemed to recognize her shape and weight. Julie and Hannah took seats not far from the fireplace as well, but it was clear that this conversation was meant for Grant and Morgan. The elder woman watched him intently, waiting for him to speak.

"Who are you people?"

"We are those who must withdraw from society in order to survive it," replied Morgan. "Like you, we have all undergone a drastic change to everything we know. For many of us, secluding ourselves was the only remaining option if we wished to conduct normal lives. The world does not welcome us anymore, so we have *made* a place where we can belong, here, together. In this place, far from the cares of civilization, we are safe."

"Sounds pretty good to me," Grant said, attempting a lighthearted chuckle. "Where do I sign up?"

But Morgan was somber. "That luxury is not available to you."

"Why not?"

"Because . . ." she hesitated, savoring this moment, as though she had waited a lifetime for it . . .

"Because you are the Bringer."

"The what?" Grant asked dumbly.

"Your entire world has changed," Morgan said in her polite diction, the smile gone from her face, replaced by a furrowed brow of concentration. She was concentrating on him, studying his every response and facial tic.

Her statement wasn't a question.

Grant looked down at his feet. He'd liked this woman instantly, and yet . . . there was a lingering sense of perception about her that made him crumple under her gaze.

"Yes, it has," he said.

"You feel like a doormat in a world of boots, I imagine. It began with this," she said, producing her right hand. A sparkling gold ring rested on her middle finger, with an inset burgundy gemstone.

He nodded, then glanced briefly around the room. The others watched with rapt attention, some of them nervously stroking their own rings.

Morgan stared at his ring for a long moment, then shook her head in . . . was that wonder?

"I know you have millions of questions. Or quite possibly more." Her soft eyes twinkled as her face became round and welcoming again. "I am afraid I do not have quite that many answers, but I will tell you all that I can. First, I wonder if you would tell *me* something."

"Okay," he replied tentatively.

"How have you been sleeping of late?"

"I haven't."

"Quite," she nodded thoughtfully. "'And thereby hangs a tale.' You tell yourself the nightmares come from the *trauma* you have endured."

It wasn't a question, but he answered anyway. "Yeah."

Her round eyes were stern, but he detected a hint of compassion in them. "When the truth is that you've learned very quickly how to keep yourself busy, running headlong from one task to the next. No time for sitting idle and putting genuine thought into how you feel. Oh no, can't have that. Because *that* is more frightening than anything in your nightmarish dreams."

Grant wanted to argue with this logic but found that he couldn't.

"Yes, I understand you all too well, Grant," she said with a gentle smile, as if reading his mind. "We've never met, of course. I simply recognize a familiar pattern."

"So you have trouble sleeping, too?"

Morgan smiled again. "As Hamlet said, 'There's the rub.' I *do not* sleep. Ever. Grant, *all* of us here have been through precisely what you're facing now. We know every feeling, every fear, every ridiculous notion that has crossed your mind since this began. *Nothing* makes sense to you right now, does it?"

He shook his head.

She took a deep breath and never moved her eyes away from his. "I like to begin by telling my own story. It seems to help those who come here to know that their experience was not as uncommon as they think."

She leaned back in the chair and collected her thoughts. "It happened rather inconspicuously, really. In my former life, I was a librarian working at the London Library, near St. James Park. As I was leaving work one day, I stopped in the rest room. I caught my reflection in the mirror while washing my hands . . . and I screamed. The reflection I saw was not my own. And a foreign voice was screaming. I had a different face, different clothes. My purse was gone, and had been replaced by a different one, sitting in the same spot on the counter where I'd left mine. No one else entered nor left the rest room while I was inside, so I opened the purse. Within, I found a photo I.D. that matched the woman in the mirror, and a set of keys I didn't recognize."

He nodded. This sounded very familiar.

"After a great deal of study and investigation, I eventually came upon a few others who had also experienced 'the Shift,' as we call it. Most of us had nowhere to go, and many were so traumatized by the shaking of the foundations of their very existence that they lived in mortal fear of what might happen to them next. After all, if one's identity is so malleable, so vulnerable, that it can be taken away in a heartbeat . . . then *anything* is possible. So I decided to create a haven where those like us could gather and be safe. Eventually . . . we found this place."

She grew silent, allowing Grant time to process this.

"How many are here?"

Morgan's shoulders rose in a small shrug. "Perhaps fifty or sixty at any given time. It varies. This building was constructed to hold more than two hundred, but we've never reached even half that capacity. Still most who find their way here never leave."

"But why?"

"You *know* why. They want a place to bury their heads and hope the world will not fall apart on them again. You remember that feeling? That cold ache in the pit of your stomach when you first realized that everything you know had irrevocably changed, forever?"

"I remember," he replied. "But I can't imagine just deciding to run away and hide—not even *trying* to find out what happened and why."

"Of course you can, dear boy," she replied calmly. "You considered it yourself in those first few moments after the Shift. We all do. It's *terrifying* to see everything you are and everything you know, stripped away in a single moment. Your very flesh and blood has been replaced, and some find it very easy to lose their entire identity to that. When the world caves in, you contemplate throwing in the towel. That is the first reaction we all share."

He thought back to his own experience that first day.

"Do not kid yourself, Grant," she said with sad, compassionate eyes. "All that separates you from my friends here is a thin line spread across a scant few seconds. Each of us decides in those first moments: run and hide, or press on. But we all began at the same intersection."

He looked down at the tiny scar on his wrist that Julie had made, then raised his head to meet her eyes. An entire conversation passed silently between them in that look.

Never give up. Never give in. Never surrender to anger or despair.

"As I was saying," Morgan continued, "most, once they come here, decide to stay. Some, like your friend Hannah, come and go as they wish. Our door is always open to those like us, who have nowhere else to go. Often, many of them will gather their intellects together—which are considerable, given the fact that everyone here is a *genius* of one type or another—and spend their time quite literally deliberating and sorting out the vast mysteries of the universe. They call themselves the Loci."

"An asylum full of geniuses," Grant mused. "Genius Loci, I get it. And have they turned up *answers* to any of life's big mysteries?"

"They have."

"Then why not share their answers with the world?"

Morgan gave a sad smile. "It is easier to *learn* about the world than try to save it, is it not?"

Then she sat forward on her chair, bowing her head. He thought she was praying or concentrating at first, but then saw the muscles on her neck were clenched tight. And she was squeezing her eyelids together.

"Morgan!" Hannah cried.

"I'm all right, Hannah," Morgan whispered. "Don't make a fuss." She massaged her temples for a few moments as Hannah edged out of her chair, prepared to jump to the rescue. Morgan finally opened her eyes and sat back in the chair. She looked sideways at Hannah, who was still standing. "But *you* are *not* all right. You have been electrocuted. Severely, from the looks of it. You should see a doctor."

"I'm *fine*," Hannah said forcefully, still watching Morgan with concern. She returned to her chair. "Never better."

Grant watched them both with concern and curiosity, then settled on Morgan.

"I get headaches," she told him quietly.

"She gets *migraines*," Hannah corrected her, loudly.

Morgan's lips curled into a frown. "Migraines, then." She shot a look at Hannah, who held her gaze without flinching. Eventually she looked back to Grant.

"You are overwhelmed," she consoled. "This is a great deal of information to absorb."

"None of it seems to bother *you*," he said abruptly.

"That's because I've been doing this longer than you. Longer than anyone, in point of fact."

He blinked. "You mean—"

Morgan nodded. "To the best of my knowledge, I was the first to undergo the Shift. It was over fourteen years ago that I found someone new in that mirror at the London Library. And I have never encountered another who predates me. I was the very first to have *this*." She held up her ring hand again.

Fourteen years! There were people in this world who had lived for almost fifteen years with what had just happened to him only weeks ago. It was mind-boggling.

His eyes fell upon her ring.

"Tell me about the rings." he said, sitting up straight in his chair now. "Why won't they come off?"

She glanced around the room and then leaned in closer to him. "They *do* come off," she whispered. "But only after the wearer dies."

Grant thought of the contract killer, Konrad, who had wanted his ring. *He knew. He either had to kill me or cut off my finger altogether. Both of which he tried . . .*

"Do the rings trigger the . . . the Shift?" he asked.

"The two *do* always seem to coincide. But all I can tell you with certainty is that, despite their appearance, the rings are *not* made of gold, nor any other precious metal that I can identify. It appears they're comprised of some kind of alloy that's stronger—its molecules packed together more densely—than any metal that exists in nature. They're *so* strong, in fact, that I haven't even been able to chip off any residue for study."

"Are you a scientist?" Grant asked.

Morgan offered a bemused smile. "Hardly. I was born a lover of books and shall die one. I'd rather be spending my time with Dickens and Steinbeck, but in the years after the Shift, I spent much of my time searching the world and researching our civilization's entire wellspring of knowledge to find out all I could about these rings. Unfortunately, I've learned precious little with regard to their origin. But as for what they are . . ." she paused in thought, "I need to *show* you what I've learned, rather than try to explain it. But before we get to that, though, I would ask you to fill in some gaps for me. Tell me how all this began for *you*."

He launched into his story, beginning with the morning he spotted himself, Collin, walking down the sidewalk, and ending with his daring escape from the Inveo plant with Hannah, only hours before.

Morgan watched him with a soft gaze throughout the entire story. She was patient and allowed him to tell it in his own time. When he finished, she looked away for a few minutes.

Finally she looked at him again. "May I see your ring, please?"

He held out his hand.

She adjusted her bifocals until they rested on the very tip of her nose. Gently turning his hand to the side, her eyes narrowed as she studied the ring.

While she was looking at his ring, he glanced at hers. It was just like Hannah's—nearly identical to his own, only slightly smaller and with no markings on the sides.

Morgan let go of him and sat back in her chair, her eyes focusing on him even more intently than before.

"There can be no doubt; you *are* the Bringer. Does anyone else know of what's happened to you, besides your sister?" He caught a trace of urgency in her voice.

He thought for a moment. "There's this weird girl who keeps following me around."

One eyebrow went up. "A girl?"

"She won't tell me who she is. She just keeps popping up and telling me—well, I guess you could call it advice. She's . . , younger than me. Not much I can say about her appearance. Nothing sticks out. Well, except that she's always barefoot."

Morgan's spine straightened as she sat up in her chair. "Barefoot?" She stared at him over the rims of her bifocals once again. "This girl— she had long brown hair? No makeup or jewelry?"

"Sounds right," Grant nodded. "You know her?"

"We have never met," Morgan shook her head, gazing off in thought. "I thought she was something of an urban myth. Someone fitting that description has been spotted a few times in the past, watching those like us, scrutinizing our movements. But the glimpses of her have been so fleeting I ascribed the whole affair to group imagination."

She focused on Grant again. "She actually *spoke* to you?"

He nodded.

"What did she talk about?"

"Odd things . . . I don't know . . . The conversations are always so short. But it seemed like, in some way . . . I think she's trying to help me."

"Hmm," Morgan replied. She leaned back in her chair, lost in thought again.

"You mentioned wanting to show me something . . ." Grant prompted her.

Her attention snapped back to him. "Ah, yes, quite so." Her expression changed and she formed her words slowly and carefully. "I hesitate to say this, Grant, because I realize full well how it will sound to you. But please trust that I would not ask anything of you if it were not of the greatest importance. In this case, I do not see any alternative."

Grant leaned back in his seat, wary. "All right."

"In order to show you what I want to show you," she began, "I need a favor. A very important item was due to be delivered to me, but it was intercepted before I received it. And I need it back. I want *you* to retrieve it for me."

Dread flooded Grant's heart. "What?"

"Morgan, he's no thief!" Hannah said, rising precariously from her chair. "If there's somethin' you need, *I'll* go get it for you."

"Dear, you can't even *walk*," was Morgan's reply. "We haven't time to wait for your recovery."

Morgan spoke to Grant with utmost sincerity. "I promise you, Grant, this won't involve committing any sort of crime. In point of fact, you'll be *resolving* a crime. The object I'm asking you to retrieve belongs to me. I merely need you to it get back."

"What do you know of the Bringer?" the Thresher demanded.

The short, scrawny man he held off of the floor by the lapels of his jacket seemed to balk at this question.

But there was no one around to save him. The bar's remaining patrons were unconscious, resting peacefully on the floor. Apparently this crowd lived for a good brawl, but the Thresher had overpowered the entire room in under two minutes, before rounding on the man he had come here for.

The drunken man dangling in the air drooled beer down his shirt, his eyes over-wide and his expressions exaggerated.

In a flash, the Thresher's sword was out and upheld, ready to strike, as he held the man with one hand.

"I won't ask a second time," his brogue accent intoned, menacingly.

The drunken man stared all-too-obviously at the gold ring upon his own finger. "I heard the phrase before, but that's all, man, I swear," he slurred.

Why must they always resist? the Thresher thought, bored.

"I couldn't help noticing," he observed gently, "that during our entire conversation, you haven't been able to take your eyes off of that golden bauble on your right hand. Which means that to get your *full* attention, I will have to eliminate the offending hand from your field of vision."

The Thresher prepared to swing, but the drunken man shouted, "Wait, wait!"

But the Thresher refused to return his arm to its former position; he held the sword up in striking position, waiting for the other man to continue.

"This guy I know . . ." the drunken man slurred, "he runs with this crowd that squats in some kind of super-secret location. I dunno where they are, man, but he told me they've all been talking about this 'Bringer', and how he's . . . 'on his way' or something."

When the man stopped speaking, the Thresher prompted, "Continue."

"I don't know no more than that, man! Honest!"

The Thresher studied the drunken man, discerning the truth from his features. "If you've lied to me—"

"I'm not that stupid!" the other man bellowed. "You got a *rep*, man! Nobody's gonna disrespect *you*, you're the Thresh—" He broke off suddenly, realizing he'd said more than he'd meant to.

The Thresher brought the sword to rest against the drunken man's throat, and lowered the man far enough that his mouth was right next to the man's ear.

"*How*," he breathed hot air, "do you know *that name*?"

"I-I-I uh, I heard it—" the man blustered.

The Thresher dropped the man to the floor. "From *whom?*" he asked, raising the blade and preparing to strike. Fire had suddenly come to his listless eyes.

But he never got the opportunity to find out more. Something struck the back of his head forcefully, and he collapsed to the floor, unconscious.

20

In the end, Grant hadn't agreed or disagreed. Morning approached and since the job had to be completed under night's cloak everybody decided to discuss again after some rest. Grant and Julie accepted rooms for the evening and soon said farewell. After their departure, Morgan ventured deeper into the asylum, winding her way into a distant back corner to the only occupied room in the wing.

Approaching the door carefully, she knocked on it.

"*Sí?*" a tired, low-pitched Latin voice called out from behind the door.

Morgan entered.

Sitting on the bed was a bronze-skinned woman with a wrinkled face and a serious expression. She was knitting.

They called her Marta, though Morgan had no idea what her original name might have been. She was the oldest of all the Loci at seventy-nine years of age—the oldest Morgan had ever met who had experienced the Shift.

Marta preferred solitude, so she lived alone in this abandoned section of the facility and rarely left her room. Morgan thought back to their first meeting, only a few years ago, when she had asked Marta to come live here. Having nowhere else to go, the old woman had agreed, on one condition: she had no desire to be around others. The Shift had been so traumatic for her at her age that she simply wanted to be left alone.

But occasionally, she would tolerate visits from Morgan, at those times when she had important information.

Marta did not look up as Morgan walked in.

"This man you have brought here. He will learn the truth very soon," the old woman said without greeting or preamble. She spoke in Spanish, as she knew not a single word of English and didn't care to. But Morgan understood her.

Morgan took a seat at a small desk opposite the bed, turning the chair to face Marta.

"What truth is that?" Morgan asked.

"His truth. Who and what he is," Marta said matter-of-factly. *"When that happens, he may become . . . unpredictable."*

"He's *already* unpredictable. Are you saying I should take some kind of precautions?" asked Morgan.

"He will become what he will become. Your actions will change nothing," Marta answered evenly.

"And is he becoming what I believe he is?"

Marta stopped knitting and looked up into Morgan's eyes for the first time. She studied Morgan for a long moment before speaking. *"This man is part of something greater than all of us. Vast and powerful, it reaches back through the fabric of history to the very beginning of time. Those like him have been with us since it all began, in one form or another."*

Morgan frowned. "I need more, dear. If you want me to be on guard, I'm going to need more from you than vague notions about who he's turning into . . ."

"No," Marta said flatly. *"He has* always *been who he is now. But what he is becoming is . . . something else. And it is unavoidable."*

"I don't understand," said Morgan.

Marta sighed. *"There are some storms that even you cannot quell."*

The two women stared at each other for a moment, Morgan wondering, as always, if Marta's intuition could be false. But she'd certainly been proven right many times in the past.

"And if I were you," Marta suddenly said, *"I would discourage him from keeping company with that burglar woman."*

Hannah.

"Why?"

"A friendship forged between them will not end well."

By evening, Grant was gone and Julie paced the Common Room. Hannah had recovered enough to drive Grant to his destination, so here Julie was, all alone in this loony bin with these weird people who just stood around and stared at her.

"I don't like this," Julie finally said, to no one in particular.

"Then we share something in common, dear," Morgan replied from her chair at the fireplace, her eyes glued to the latest hardback to grab her attention. "But I promise you, I would not have asked this of him if it weren't absolutely vital."

"You keep saying that," Julie retorted. "Feeling guilty?"

"Quite so," Morgan answered, without hesitation, looking up from her book for the first time.

Julie frowned, regretful. She shivered, her hand shaking from nerves as she took the seat opposite Morgan in front of the fire.

"You seem nervous," Morgan said, eying Julie with a studious expression.

"Of course I am."

"You wish that you could be with him, to help him," Morgan stated.

"Yeah!" Julie cried, realizing it herself for the first time.

"But this is not the reason you tremble."

Julie blinked, staring wide-eyed at Morgan.

"Tell me," Morgan went on, lowering her voice yet full of compassion, "how long has it been since you were diagnosed?"

Julie was taken aback, though she regrouped fast. "I don't know what you're—"

"My dear, you've been demonstrating minor uncontrollable shakes since you and your brother arrived. I'm no diagnostician, but I *am* well-read, and I recognize the symptoms of Parkinson's when I see them."

Julie was flabbergasted. Tears stung her eyes, but she blinked them back.

"It was about a month ago," she whispered in reply, struggling to keep her composure. "Only a few weeks before my brother and I reunited."

Morgan sighed in sympathy. "Grant doesn't know?"

Julie shook her head, tears spilling out. "*Please* don't tell him. He has enough to worry about, and he *needs* me . . . Frankly, I'm afraid for him. *All the time*. He's been through so much. I feel like I'm desperately holding on to him, trying to pull him back all by myself . . ."

Morgan smiled sensitively. "I won't tell him, dear, you have my word. But if I may offer an unsolicited word of advice: show *confidence* in him. Make him *see* that you have faith he will overcome his obstacles. *That's* what he needs from you now."

"I just don't know what to think about any of this," Julie replied, sniffling. "All this stuff about him and you and the others and those rings. . . . I just don't believe it."

Morgan tilted her head, the faintest hint of a smile forming at the edge of her lips. "Sometimes *belief* is all you really need."

"What am I supposed to believe *in*?" Julie asked, flustered, looking away. She turned back to face Morgan when she felt the elder woman's hand rest on top of hers, quieting its trembling with a gentle, steady grip.

Morgan leaned forward in her chair just slightly. Her eyes twinkled in the firelight.

"Believe," she said softly, "that all that is happening to your brother—*and* to you—is not random."

21

Hannah stopped the convertible three blocks from their destination. All she and Grant could see in every direction were darkened homes in a modest residential development. It was after one; the entire neighborhood should be asleep.

Grant glanced at Hannah, who was behind the wheel.

This is the part where I'm supposed to get out . . .

Hannah took his hand in hers. "It's gonna be okay. You're *way* more capable than ya think you are."

He smiled weakly, insincerely.

"And I don't care *what* Morgan says," Hannah added, "I ain't leaving you here, big boy. I'll be waiting—and *watching*—right here, in case anything goes wrong."

Grant nodded appreciatively and took a deep breath. Hannah handed him a large flashlight, and he got out of the car.

He imagined—or rather *hoped*—that he looked catlike as he crept up the dark sidewalk. The black shirt and pants he'd put on at the asylum helped him blend in with the night—even though the shirt was two sizes too big—but he still felt like he had no idea what he was doing.

How am I supposed to do this? I'm no good at this stuff.

Who is Morgan, anyway?

His thoughts drifted back to that afternoon, when he'd finally emerged from his "cell" at the asylum. Sleep had come only because he was wholly exhausted, but even so, the nightmares remained. After a shower and a little food, he'd found Morgan in the Common Room, chatting with a dozen of the others. Hannah was there, scowling, as was Julie, sitting in one corner alone and fidgeting.

Morgan had spotted him first as he walked in and motioned him forward.

Before she could speak, he blurted out, "Let's just get this over with."

"Of course," she replied. "The task is a simple one. Go to this address"—she handed him a folded-up piece of paper—"and retrieve a small, brown cardboard box, wrapped in brown packing paper and tied with twine. You'll know it when you see it. It will be fairly heavy for its size. Its 'owner' will be occupied this evening."

Grant frowned. "What's in the box?"

"A fragment," she replied. When he was unimpressed, she continued, "You want to know what all of this is about? Why we experienced the Shift and what these rings are doing on our fingers? This little brown box holds the key to answering every one of your questions."

"And this address? What's there?"

"It's a residence out in Van Nuys," she replied calmly, "Beyond that. . . ."

He was nonplussed. "So that's it," he motioned wide with his hands, in desperation. "Go to this mystery address and pick up some nonde-script brown box. It'll be that simple?"

"Of course it won't," Morgan said casually. "Nothing ever is. But I need you to understand something, Grant, and it's very important that you hear me clearly on this: What I want to show you is something I have never shown *anyone*. I hate the idea of testing you as much as you do, but I can't show you what I have to show you until I *know* you are indeed the one meant to see it. And if you can't complete this task, then you are not that person."

Grant swallowed. "That your idea of a pep talk?"

"As a matter of fact, it is," Morgan replied.

Grant opened the paper and read the address; he didn't recognize it. Morgan said it was near the Van Nuys airport.

Grant's head dropped and shook back and forth, his mind swimming.

"Why can't anything ever be simple? Why does everything have to be complicated?" he muttered.

"I think you know why," she replied, unmoved. "And if you don't, you soon will."

He turned to go.

"You can do this, Grant," Morgan said. "I believe in you."

She sounded completely convinced.

Now, in the dead of night, he ducked behind a patch of bushes near the street after spotting the address in question. There was nothing remarkable about it. It was a simple two-story house. A garage on the far end of the house was closed, which meant he couldn't tell if anybody was home. The place wasn't especially large. White siding with charcoal shutters and highlights. Windows all around, on both floors.

It was no different from the many other homes in the neighborhood.

Grant's new instincts offered nothing about break-in techniques, so he focused on the windows. The solid front door didn't look like it would budge anyway.

He tiptoed to the right side of the house, feeling a bit silly, and pushed up on the first window he came to.

Locked.

He tried the next one.

Also locked.

He stole a few quick looks around to make sure there was no activity, and prayed for silence as he punched a fist through the windowpane. The gloves Hannah had given him during their drive protected his skin.

The glass tinkled loudly, and he crouched under the window, waiting a full minute to make sure no one reacted. No lights came on inside the house. No activity from any of the neighboring homes. No alarm went off.

Grant took a deep breath and stood. Reaching in, he unlocked the window, pushed up, and climbed through.

He pulled out the flashlight and flicked it on, sweeping the downstairs area with the tiny light. He was in the dining room. He scanned the table in the middle of the room and then moved on.

The next room looked like it should have been the living room or den, but whoever lived here was using it as some sort of personal space. A large oak desk sat against the far wall, with various disheveled items on top, including a computer buried underneath some of the others. A punching bag hung from the ceiling in the corner to his right. To his left were several bookcases full of books.

He walked to the desk and quietly opened each drawer, shifting things aside and looking for the small cardboard box. Nothing.

He surveyed the floor, the walls. No sign of a safe. The shelves next to the door held dozens of books. One book on the top shelf was enormous, over a foot tall and easily five inches thick.

Grant walked closer. It appeared to be some sort of exhaustive dictionary, but . . .

No one would be that obvious, would they?

He pulled down the oversized book. It was lighter than he'd expected. He opened it.

The book was hollow. A small, brown box tied with twine rested in its cavity, and Grant pulled it out. He held his flashlight up to the box; it was about five inches square, and about an inch thick.

Click.

Grant froze.

He felt the pistol's cool steel on his right ear.

"You don't belong here," a voice growled. The man with the gun reached to the wall beside him with his free hand and turned on the light.

Grant glanced sideways and the two of them locked eyes.

"But then," the man said, "you must hear that a lot."

It was Detective Drexel.

Grant's memory rushed back to Julie's description of him from her encounter at UCLA. Grant had only seen the man once, staring down the barrel of a gun. And here they were again, history repeating itself.

Drexel stepped back and motioned for Grant to turn around fully. Grant complied and they faced one another.

Grant felt the panic begin to rise in his throat, but he closed his eyes and forced himself to be calm. After what had happened at the Inveo security office, he was determined not to let it out again until he could find a way to control it.

"Mr. Borrows," Drexel began with a smug grin, the gun still trained on Grant. "You wouldn't *believe* all the trouble I've gone through to find you. And where do you turn up? Right in my own home."

Grant's thoughts were elsewhere. Having nothing to lose, he held up the box between them. "Did *you* steal this?"

"I'm a *policeman*," Drexel snarled, snatching the box out of Grant's hand. "I don't steal, I *recover evidence*. Who sent you after this?"

Drexel's eyes focused on the box for a split second, and in that second, Grant reacted. He darted left through the open doorway that he'd come in.

Drexel fired but missed.

Grant tore through the house in a straight line for the front door, but just as he reached it, Drexel fired another shot, and this one punched a hole in the front door only inches above Grant's shoulder. He stopped.

"Move and I'll kill you," Drexel's intimidating voice called. "Hands up."

Grant complied. Drexel approached him from behind, taking the box and setting it on a small lamp stand in the hall.

"Breaking and entering is a misdemeanor," he said as he stopped a few feet away. "That'll do for a start." He pulled a pair of handcuffs out of his pants pocket with his free hand. He snapped one cuff into place, and then brought that arm down behind Grant. He grabbed the other arm.

Grant brought a leg up to kick Drexel between the legs; Drexel cried out in pain, and Grant turned and opened the front door, reaching for the latch to the glass outer door.

But before he touched it, an alarm sounded. Floodlights flashed on, both inside and out.

"Don't go," Drexel said lightly. "We're about to have company."

Grant turned to see Drexel holding some kind of panic button in his free hand. The gun was still extended in his other. He had tears in his eyes from the pain, but he was smiling again.

Grant wanted to cover his ears because of the loud blaring of the security sirens, but he was afraid to move. Drexel's entire appearance had suddenly become crazed.

"On your knees, hands behind your head!" he screamed.

Grant dropped to the floor and couldn't keep his hands from

shaking as he laced them behind his neck. Instincts he couldn't control were flooding his mind with techniques to take Drexel down, how to sweep the other man's feet out from under him and pin him to the ground, or how to quickly snatch the gun away. But Drexel had a tight grip on the pistol and his finger was steady on the trigger.

Grant watched as Drexel snatched a radio off of his belt clip and began whispering into it.

"This is Detective Drexel—there's somebody in my house and I think he's armed! I need *backup*!" He threw the radio aside and stepped forward, grinning. "No need to bother with an arrest now. It was only self-defense."

Drexel extended the gun and touched it to the top of Grant's down-turned head.

And Grant panicked.

The entire neighborhood awoke to the sound of a concussive blast, as every window in Drexel's house exploded outward.

NO! STOP!!

Grant came to moments later, curled up on the ground in agony. The pain this time was more intense than anything he'd ever imagined possible, and it had lasted longer.

His eyes gaped wide, his heart racing again. His eyes burned as he blinked them back and stumbled to his feet, taking in the impossible sight before him.

It looked as if a bomb had gone off, only nothing was charred. Every object around him had been overturned or broken. The house still stood, but all of the windows and doors had exploded.

Grant took a few unsteady steps and heard breathing.

He found Drexel lying on his back, over ten feet away down the hall. The gun was nowhere in sight. Drexel was awake, breathing fast, an entirely new look on his face. One Grant hadn't seen on him before. Terror.

He saw Grant coming and his breathing rate increased. The man had a few cuts on his face but didn't look seriously injured.

Grant wasn't faring much better. He was in shock, cold and wobbly, his eyes darting everywhere. It was all he could do not to panic again at the sight of what he had somehow just done.

"I left the-the box on the table . . . r-right there!" the other man stammered, raising an arm to point. "Just take it and get out!"

Grant swallowed as he spotted the box under a pile of rubble that used to be the small end table. He braced himself on the wall as he leaned over to recover it.

Rising again, he stared at the fallen detective for another moment before turning and walking drunkenly down the hall and out the empty doorway.

Drexel raised his head enough to watch Grant go. When Grant was out of sight, he craned to the left and saw his radio on the ground, under a smashed picture frame.

He fished it out with a shaking hand, but didn't get up.

"This is Drexel," he spoke into the radio, out of breath. "Disregard previous call. Repeat: cancel backup. False alarm."

Then something smoldered behind his eyes and he slowly sat upright. He keyed the radio again and his mouth twisted into an angry snarl.

"But get me a forensics unit down here right away. And put an unmarked car at the laboratory of Daniel Cossick. If he *burps*, I want a full report."

22

An hour later, Grant flung the box at Morgan. His fists were balled and shaking, his entire body barely containing his fury.

She caught the box in her hand and examined it. "Nicely done," she said.

"*Nice?*" he nearly spat the word.

Julie had dozed off in her chair in the far corner but jerked awake at Grant's raised voice. She leaped from her chair and began running for Grant, but she stopped when she saw how he looked. He felt the blood in his face, and he knew his stance and expression must have looked threatening.

Hannah stood a safe distance behind Grant, watching closely, but staying out of it.

Morgan was unruffled, examining him. He knew he looked terrible—clothes ripped, hair askew, bruises and dirt all over. Fear and anger writhed through him, and he was barely keeping it contained.

Grant was terrified of what he was capable of, and outraged that she'd forced him to do it.

"You got the job done," she said, appraising him.

"You owe me answers," he said shakily, but he stood up taller. "And they had *better* be worth it."

"Indeed." She looked down, gathering her thoughts. A crowd of residents gathered behind her. "Pose your questions, Grant. And I shall answer."

"*What am I?*"

"You are the Bringer. The fulcrum on which all of our fates will turn."

He didn't blink. "You're going to have to do better than that."

She looked around at the gathered crowd, her expression becoming resolute. She joined her hands in front and then turned back to him, leveling her gaze.

"As it was with each of us, the Shift affected you in ways more than physical. It was mental as well."

"Meaning what? I'm not me anymore?"

"No, you're still you . . . more or less." She paused. "Have you ever heard the statistic that says that humans only use a small percentage of their brains?"

His impatience was boiling over. "I heard it was a *myth* . . ."

She nodded. "The theories posited that anywhere from seventy to ninety percent of the human brain is unused. Those same theories stated that if we were ever to tap into the idle parts of our minds, we might gain enhanced mental skills. Abilities like a photographic memory might become attainable by *everyone*."

Grant's expression was unchanged.

"Most modern scientists," she continued, "have discounted this as nonsense, and they're probably right. But modern science ignores most of what it refuses to understand. These theories have validity and we're the proof. Each of us. Our mental amplifications are as unique as our fingerprints."

Now she had his attention.

"I know how this sounds. And I honestly have no idea *how* it works. I only know that it *does*. However it happens, *something* extra—maybe that extra seventy percent of brain power, maybe something else altogether—is switched 'on' in us when the Shift occurs."

Grant had difficulty swallowing this. "All of them?" he said.

"I have met over one hundred people over the years who wear rings like ours, and the resulting enhancements are different in each and every one of them."

"Different how?"

"A rare few, like Hannah, have stronger, more overt skills. I cannot conceive of how she does it, but through some sort of profound mental persuasion, she's able to convince others that they're seeing things that aren't there."

Grant's mind raced back to everything he'd seen Hannah do at the Inveo plant . . .

"Most of us, however," Morgan went on, "have more mundane skills."

"Like what?"

Beside Morgan stood an elderly man. She smiled at him and placed a hand on his shoulder. "Nigel, what's four hundred thirty-two thousand, six hundred ninety-one *squared*?"

"One hundred eighty-seven billion, two hundred twenty-one million, five hundred one thousand, four hundred eighty-one," he replied without hesitation.

Grant's eyebrows popped up.

"The majority of us have these kinds of talents—unique intuitions or expanded mental capacities based on very normal human functions. Like our human calculator here."

"What about you?" Grant asked, beginning to calm. "What can you do?"

"I can remember everything that happens within my perception with *perfect, absolute clarity*."

"You really *do* have a photographic memory?"

"It's far more than that," she said, speaking plainly and directly. "Every conversation I've heard since the day of the Shift, I can repeat to you *verbatim*. And it goes beyond words. Every smell I've breathed in, I can recall with the precision of a bloodhound. Every surface I've touched, every taste I've sampled. Every sound I've heard. Everything I see. Every word of every book I've read. I remember it all, without error . . . and without effort."

"That's why you have migraines."

She nodded. "And why I don't sleep. My brain simply never stops retaining, working, filing away information. I can catch brief snippets of unconscious rest every now and again, but my mind rarely lets that happen, and I can't explain how, but my body is somehow able to manage with a lack of cognitive rest. I've theorized that perhaps since the body is *regulated* by the mind . . ."

"So the books that line the halls," Grant interjected. "You've read them *all*?"

Morgan smiled a humorless smile. "Are you familiar with the saying, 'The more you eat, the more you *want* to eat'?"

Grant nodded.

"I'm afraid the same axiom applies to knowledge. I have read and memorized every word of every volume you see in this building—save the stack atop my desk. When I say that I am the most well-read person on this planet, it is a statement of fact, and nothing more."

Grant was reeling, trying to process all of this.

Morgan took a deep breath. "I've told you all this, Grant, because it's important that you know what the rest of us can do. I need you to understand *us* before I can explain *you*."

His heart fluttered. "Okay."

"Each of us can do something extraordinary. But of all of the unusual skills that we possess, *none* of us—not one—is as powerful as you."

"I'm different?"

"We're *all* different," she said. "You're *special*."

He swallowed.

"Grant, it's my belief that whatever has happened to us all . . . *We*"—she motioned to herself and the others—"are just the warm-up. *You* are the main event."

"Why?"

"Because *no one* has ever manifested abilities like yours, with genuine, physical power. And more importantly, I base it on that ring on your finger."

He held it up, glanced at it. "It's just like yours. Like *all* of yours."

"It's *similar*," she corrected him. "But the markings etched into the sides are tremendously significant. None of ours have those symbols."

"So? Why does that make *me* Mr. Special?"

Morgan broke away from the others and they parted as she moved toward the fireplace. "Because of *this*," she said. With one foot, she stepped on a brick just in front of the fire, which gave way like a large button.

Grant heard a *click*. The entire fireplace—mantel, bricks, and all—swiveled slowly open, like a door.

"Follow me, please," Morgan said. "Your sister may join us, as well." She retrieved a long wooden match from a box by the fire and stuck it into the fire. When it lit, she entered the dark opening in the wall.

Grant didn't snap out of his astonishment until he felt Julie's hand clasp his. He couldn't see anything at all in the space Morgan had just confidently entered, but he and Julie followed nonetheless. Morgan touched something on the wall—he couldn't see what—and the fireplace behind them swiveled shut again, sealing them into the darkness.

"Don't be frightened," Morgan said gently, as her tiny, flickering light led the way. "No one has ever been down here except me. There are stairs ahead, so watch your step."

Grant found his eyes adjusting to the dark quickly, as he carefully and cautiously got his footing on each new step before placing his weight on it. He also tried to help Julie, who seemed even more unsteady than he was.

As they neared the bottom of the steps, a new question popped into his head.

"Why didn't you invite Hannah to come down with us?"

"She can't be trusted." Immediately she stopped descending the steps and turned, a frown on her face flickering in the candlelight. "I apologize, that was a poor choice of words. I *do* trust her. She's a good friend, she's one of *us*, and she is indebted to me because of a matter that occurred between us several years ago."

"Then—?"

"She's a *thief*. By definition, she does not hold to the same codes and principles inherent in some others. And I make no exaggeration when I say that she is capable of *anything*. You've seen her in action; I'm sure you can attest to this."

Memories of Hannah's exploits again swam inside Grant's mind as they reached the bottom of the stairs and came into what seemed to be some kind of underground laboratory. Only without cement or bricks or even wood. It was more like a cave, carved right out of the earth. The walls around them weren't even perfectly vertical; it looked like huge chunks of the ground had been scooped away, and this small room beneath the asylum was the result.

Candles lined the perimeter of the room. Some of them were

already burning, and she lit a few more.

"This room was here already when we moved in," she said as an aside, "but I had the entrance upstairs specially made. I'm not sure what they might have done in here related to mental patient care, and frankly I don't *care* to know. But I have found it to be an effective vault, even though no electricity runs into here."

A small table almost like a flat podium stood in the middle of the room, and she approached it. The table was covered with a large piece of sandy brown burlap.

"Grant, you are special because your ring is different from all the others. And I know that makes you special, because of *this*." She held up the small box he'd given her, still tied with twine.

He and Julie walked closer as she untied the box. She pulled out the small object inside and held it next to a tall candle on the edge of the center table. They looked closer.

Candlelight danced over a small piece of brown stone, full of tiny, intricate symbols.

"Do you understand now?"

He never moved his eyes from the piece of stone, but whatever she was seeing, he didn't.

"Not really," he said, though Julie was squeezing his hand awfully hard.

"Then I'll bring it into focus for you," she said.

She unwrapped the cloth on the table to reveal a much larger, flat slab of brown stone that matched the one in her hand. It was about eighteen inches across and twelve inches high, with an obvious chunk missing, broken off at an angle in one corner. It too was filled with markings just like the piece in her hand. It was writing of some sort, though Grant had no idea where it might have come from.

Cracks ran through the slab, and he realized that this wasn't merely one piece—it was several small pieces fit together, like a jigsaw puzzle.

Morgan placed the small stone Grant had taken from Drexel's home on the table and slid it into the missing spot in the bottom corner. It fit perfectly. The stone—whatever it was—was now whole, complete.

"Over the last decade, I have studied every resource I can get my hands on—ancient texts, historical records, forgotten libraries—to find out all I can about the rings we wear. Where do they come from? What do they do? How did we get them? And do you know what I found? *Nothing*. No record of what they are or where they came from exists, anywhere in the world.

"Or so I believed," Morgan continued, "until I came upon this artifact, many years ago. It was broken, its pieces scattered across the globe. Collecting and assembling it has been my life's work since the Shift. I have been unable to determine where it came from, but it's *thousands* of years old. Perhaps older. Do you recall what I said earlier, about how the rings have a molecular density greater than any known substance in nature? I've tested the chemical structure of the stone, and its molecular cohesion shows the same density as the rings."

"But it was shattered."

"Yes. Which worries me greatly. The power that could break this stone . . ."

Grant was still confused. "But what does any of this prove?"

"Do you not see it? The symbols on the tablet—look closely. Here," Morgan pointed, "the piece you just retrieved is the final one, and there are more of the symbols there. Grant, a section of the symbols on this tablet match the etchings on your ring *precisely*."

He pulled away from the table, suddenly not liking where this conversation was going. "But . . . if the tablet talks about this ring, and it's as ancient as you say it is, why do you assume that it has anything to do with me? Couldn't *anyone* have worn this ring in all that time?"

A hesitant look shadowed her face. "There's more. I've never quite come up with a complete word-for-word translation, but I've been able to decipher many of the *meanings* behind these symbols. One key area I've decoded is numbers.

"I've discovered a date on the tablet, Grant," she said portentously, taking a step closer to him as he continued to slowly creep backward. "The date refers to you."

"How do you know that?"

"Because it matches the date you experienced the Shift."

Grant moved backward until his back hit the wall. He caused a few of the candles to tumble to the ground, but Morgan ignored them. Julie, meanwhile, was speechless, her eyes bouncing hopelessly between Morgan and Grant.

The date on this ancient hunk of rock matches the date I spotted myself walking down the sidewalk downtown? The day all of this began?

"That's preposterous," he blurted out, but the shock and concern never left his features.

"Whatever is happening to all of us," Morgan said with conviction, "it hinges on you. The Shift. The rings. This tablet. Our enhanced abilities. You are the *key* to it all, Grant."

Grant swallowed and fought the urge to pass out. This wasn't happening, it couldn't be true . . . He shook his head. There were no words, no other response.

She moved closer to him, her eyes piercing his soul.

"The bits of the stone tablet I've been able to translate speak of a 'miracle man' called 'the Bringer,' whose destiny it is to 'shape the future.' That man . . . is *you*."

23

Morning came, and once again Grant had been up all night. Only this time, he had been talking with Morgan. Julie had fallen asleep somewhere along the way. Morgan had no more details or speculation to offer him, but she helped him sort through the stone tablet's implications, and gave him her word that she would always help him with all of the resources at her disposal. She also promised that she would keep working to translate the entire tablet, encouraged now that it was completed and a full translation was possible.

When they finally emerged from the hidden room, the Common Room was louder than usual. There seemed to be a buzz about the room, which for the first time featured no one who stopped to stare at him for long periods of time. Instead, the Loci were coming and going, to and fro, busy little workers. They had purpose in their movements, and Grant realized that all of this commotion was because of him.

They knew, and they understood.

Julie walked away, lost in her own thoughts.

Grant noticed that Hannah was still around, helping with chores and other tasks. He was a little surprised to find himself *encouraged* to see her friendly face, considering Morgan's earlier warning, though he couldn't quite put his finger on when it was he'd begun thinking of her face as "friendly."

Grant was about to break away from Morgan and approach Hannah when Morgan touched his arm and pulled him aside.

"May I ask you one last personal question before you go?" she said quietly.

"Sure."

"Who were you, before all this? Before the Shift?"

"My name was—"

"No no no. I'm not asking for a *name*. Who *were* you? What was your *identity*, your purpose, your path? What was your existence like?"

He looked into her gaze until he could look no more. Finally, he spoke again. "I was . . . alone."

Morgan examined him thoughtfully for a moment. "I thought as much. What would you say was your greatest weakness?"

He looked away, stunned at her forthright manner regarding his deepest, most hidden feelings. "I had some problems, growing up. At the orphanage . . . sometimes I would pick fights with other kids. On purpose. And I almost always *lost*. When I finally got out of that place, I told myself it was all over, and now was my chance to make a clean break, to start again. But there were a few times, in public places . . . when I lashed out. My anger would just build and build . . . until it exploded."

"So you isolated yourself to ward off the temptation," she summed up. "Very noble, in a way. But in all this time, you had no friends?"

"No."

"No family?"

"Just Julie. But I stayed away."

"Acquaintances, co-workers? Not even a pet?"

Grant shook his head.

"My, my," she breathed in deeply, examining him with new eyes. "You embraced it. You allowed it to change the very foundations of who you are."

He breathed faster, old feelings rushing to the surface. "I never *asked* for everyone in my life to run out on me," he huffed. "Why are you asking me about this?"

"Grant, my fate and that of those around us is about to be decided at your hands. I'd like to know if you're more Jekyll or Hyde."

"Morgan!" someone shouted.

They both turned as a tall, thin, black man Grant hadn't yet met stormed through the Common Room doors and marched straight up to

Morgan. He appeared to be ignoring Grant.

"It was *too soon!*" he cried, his eyes twitching wildly behind his oval, wire-rimmed glasses. "How *could* you?!"

The man had short, braided hair and was clearly agitated, gesturing wildly with his arms. He was impossibly thin and couldn't have been more than twenty-three.

Morgan was untroubled by his actions. She merely stared at him.

"Grant, I don't believe you've met Fletcher," Morgan said without taking her eyes off of the newcomer. "You'll have to forgive his . . . *zeal*. He's made it his self-appointed mission to guard the safety of this place and the Loci who live here. His enthusiasm sometimes gets the best of him. But I keep him around because he's a genius."

"I thought you were *all* geniuses, of one kind or another."

"Well, yes. But he's different. Fletcher is capable of multiple thoughts at the same time. He's quite brilliant, capable of seeing patterns and connections that others physically cannot."

Finally Fletcher turned his twitchy frame in Grant's direction, though he barely acknowledged him at all. "I provide the intuition that her vast knowledge of cold facts utterly lacks." He returned his attention to Morgan. "This man could be anyone. How could you take him to see the stone so soon? You don't know *anything* about him!"

"Enough," Morgan said forcefully, her face calm but her volume matching his. "I know *enough*."

"You're jeopardizing our safety by trusting him." His eyes darted back and forth quickly between Grant and Morgan. "He's killed at least one person—*that we know of*—and injured several others. Morgan, he blew up a house, for crying out loud!"

Morgan's lips stretched into a thin frown as Fletcher continued talking for another minute. Her head slowly turned to look in his direction.

"Young man, are you aware that your lips are still moving?" she said, interrupting him.

He fell silent, registering an appalled expression.

"You should look after that," she said, her eyebrows slightly raised.

He glared at her. Then stormed off.

"Don't mind him. You are *always* welcome here, Grant. Though when you stop by, I would thank you to bring me a new book or two, if you can." She offered a knowing smile. "Preferably something rare."

He nodded, and Morgan excused herself.

Hannah noticed the opening and approached. She must have guessed the meaning of the stare Grant couldn't hide because she smiled.

"Sleep makes all things better," she quipped. She grabbed his hand and gave it a little squeeze, and he found himself squeezing back, overwhelmed and grateful to have sympathetic human contact. "You should try it."

"No, I'm glad to be headed home. Though to be honest, I am a little worried," he said sheepishly.

"What, because of those Inveo people?" she replied.

"They can identify us."

"We don't know that anybody other than the security guards ever actually saw our faces, and they were a bunch of psychos, anyway," she replied. "I'm thinkin' the question they have to ask themselves is, do they know more about us, or do we know more about them? We saw their entire operation. Their 'war room' or whatever. Not to mention that enormous door, which leads to God only knows what. I'm guessin' that's not the kinda info they'd want the police or the media to find out about."

"But that's all the more reason for them to come after us," he said.

She sighed, rolled her eyes. "They won't try anything, they'll be too afraid after what you did to them. You certainly struck fear into that detective's heart tonight, too. And if they *do* come after us, I'll just put tarantulas in their dreams." He thought she might be joking, but reconsidered at her expression.

"You can do that?" he said.

"Tip of the iceberg, big boy," she said, breaking into that thousand-dollar smile, with those gorgeous ruby lips and radiant white teeth . . .

Her cell phone rang. She pulled it out and looked at the display.

"Sorry, I've been waiting to hear from a client," she said, and started walking away.

"Remind me to have a talk with you about your line of work sometime," Grant called out.

Still walking, she craned her head around and stuck her tongue out at him, before flashing that big smile again.

The smile that he was finding increasingly pleasant.

On the front doorstep, Hannah opened her ringing phone.

"Yeah?"

She walked lightly down the front steps and glanced at her watch. Then she walked away from the building, along the broken driveway until she was as far away as she dared.

"No, I was just talkin' to him before you called," she said, her voice low.

The voice on the other end responded.

"Yes . . . I understand."

She listened to the phone.

"Trust me . . ." she said, turning back to gaze at the asylum. "He has no idea."

24

"You're not going to get anything out of him," said a man with the name "Hanson" on his nametag. He seemed like a competent kid, but a bit young for a lieutenant. And the way he kept sizing up Drexel's bruises and scrapes was starting to grate. "He hasn't said a word since we brought him in after that 911 call."

"He hasn't met *me*," Drexel replied.

Drexel put his hand on the doorknob to the interrogation room and opened it.

"So . . . the legendary Thresher, caught with his guard down," Drexel said. He began circling the small metal chair in the interrogation room. The bald man sitting within it tensed briefly but said nothing. A bright spotlight shone from above—the only light in the room— and the Thresher's hands were cuffed in plastic restraints behind him.

"Oh, I know all about you," Drexel continued, noting the other man's edge. "It would seem your skills are surpassed only by your legendary status in your line of work. Did you know you're creeping up the FBI's Most Wanted list? Though they never had a picture to go with the profile till now."

The Thresher squared his shoulders, sat upright.

Drexel leaned forward and lowered his voice, so only his captive could hear him speak. "I know what you're looking for. You want the Bringer."

The Thresher turned to face him for the first time. "For your sake, I hope you're going to tell me where to find him."

"Ah, he speaks!" Drexel triumphed. "Idiots here were just telling me how they couldn't get a single word out of you. Now that we're friends, why don't you tell me your real name. To go along with your portrait."

"I have none."

Drexel shrugged. "Never hurts to ask. So how *did* they capture you, anyway?"

"They cheated," the Thresher replied.

"Cheated!" Drexel laughed out loud. "Let me guess, *everyone* who defeats you cheats."

"No one has *ever* defeated me. Your men scored no victory," the Thresher spat. "Where is triumph when you lack the spine to look your opponent in the eye? Those adolescents with guns and nightsticks knew they had no chance of besting me. Just as *you* do. So you seek to intimidate me." He paused then continued with a note of amusement in his voice. "Intimidate . . . *me*."

Drexel slapped him hard across the back of his bald head. "Men in handcuffs shouldn't mock."

He didn't say anything else for a moment, just circled the man for a minute or two. Finally he asked, "Are the rumors true? Do you really get a million per hit, in cash?"

The Thresher made no response.

"What a stash you must have!" Drexel continued. "A man might wonder what you spend that kind of money on."

Still there was no response.

"They say you're real selective about the jobs you'll take," Drexel continued, still walking in a circle around the chair. "But no one's ever been able to figure out what your method of selection is."

The Thresher did not even move in his chair, he simply continued staring straight ahead.

"Ah, well," Drexel resolved. "Back to business at hand, I guess. Let's start with this, my new favorite piece of evidence." Drexel produced the sword from somewhere beyond the room's darkness and continued to circle until he was standing in front of the seated man. He hefted the sword with his good right arm—the other was still in a shoulder brace from his episode at the UCLA office. "Don't suppose you'd care to tell me what these markings on the blade signify?"

The Thresher looked up at Drexel.

He kicked out sharply with his foot, knocking the sword out of Drexel's hand. It arced into the air until the tip was pointing down; soaring downward, the mighty blade sliced through the plastic cuffs and as his hands became free, he caught the sword in one hand at the last second.

The Thresher stood and the sword became a blur of movement. Drexel's belt disappeared from his pants, flying off into the air behind the Thresher. His pants instantly fell around his ankles and he felt a sharp sting across his rear end that could only have come from the flat of the sword's blade. The pain thrust him suddenly forward, but his feet were tangled in the fallen trousers and there was nothing nearby to grab.

As he toppled over, the Thresher caught him by the forehead with a single hand. The arm attached to that hand was outstretched far enough to keep Drexel out of his reach; the Thresher sat on a nearby table calmly, his arm keeping Drexel from falling over without breaking a sweat.

It had all happened much too fast for Drexel to react to. Now he found himself leaning over far, arms flailing madly to get his balance back. He panicked as his bulbous belly touched the sword's edge, which the Thresher held in position by sitting on the hilt, wedging it between himself and the tabletop.

Yet he sat there staring at Drexel with utmost calm.

The Thresher leaned in to whisper a response to Drexel's last question. "You wanted to know what the markings on the blade signify? More than a right waste like you could *ever* comprehend."

Drexel awoke minutes later, surrounded by fellow policemen.

"What happened? Where'd he go?" he stammered.

"Long gone," one of the cops replied. "Looks like he knocked you out somehow."

Drexel came to his feet, not entirely steady, and pulled his pants back up with an angry jolt.

Blood surged through him and pounded against his temples.

That's it, then.

Enough was enough. The department wanted results, and he was going to get them.

No matter what.

He flipped open his phone from one of his pockets and stormed out the door.

"We're moving to Plan B," he said when the ringing stopped. "Do it *now*."

He hung up, withdrew a business card from his pocket, and dialed the number printed on it.

"I've told you already, Detective. I don't know anything about this man you mentioned," Daniel said into his phone, as he walked down the second-floor steps. Drexel had called just as Daniel was leaving the lab; Lisa had gone home hours ago.

"I had no idea," Drexel replied, "ethical scientist types like yourself were so skilled at lying."

Daniel walked out the front door into the cool night air in the warehouse district. It was unusually cold, yet he began to sweat at Drexel's implication. "Detective, I've contacted my lawyer, and I *know* you have no right to search or seize anything on my property without just cause."

Silence met him on the phone line, as he turned around to lock the outside door of the old brick warehouse building.

With a deep snarl, Drexel said, "We'll have to find one then."

Daniel stared at his phone, wondering if that had been a smart move. He'd meant to stave off the other man, but instead he'd somehow challenged him to up his game.

He wondered what else Drexel might have up his sleeve. Anything was possible.

It occurred to him just then how remarkably silent it was, there on the usually busy street behind him. Even the wind had momentarily stopped, holding its breath.

His phone rang again and he jumped.

Lisa . . .

Before he could answer it, he heard a loud crack.

The phone fell out of his hand and he slumped to the ground.

His mind was reacting too slowly, he realized—the crack had been something hitting the back of his head. On his hands and knees, he grabbed the door handle in front of him to steady himself and stand back up. He had a firm grip on it, and he gradually, carefully got to his feet. He turned around.

Something hard swung sideways into him, and he heard another sickening *pop*. He fell again, backward this time, as the wind was knocked out of him and a sharp pain shot through his chest.

Coughing, Daniel looked up through bleary eyes at the three obscure figures that towered over him. He couldn't make out their features. He saw only dark silhouettes. Perhaps they were men wearing hooded sweatshirts. Or perhaps they were wolves, tenderizing their next meal. The nearest one was holding a large metal bat. But as he lay there, none of them moved a muscle.

They watched him.

Daniel raised a hand straight up into the air. "Please, don't . . ." he gasped.

The bat came down again in a flash, this time into his stomach, and it was all he could manage to swallow the rising nausea.

"No—" he tried to say, but it didn't sound right, and he couldn't catch his breath.

One of them grabbed him by his straight brown hair and lifted, forcing him to stand. Daniel flailed his arms about, trying to get the man to let go, but he was facing the wall now and couldn't see what they were doing.

He gasped hard, eyes filled with blood and pain as the bat collided with his legs from behind. He fell yet again, fast and hard, the strength in his legs leaving as violent pain coursed through them.

Somewhere nearby, something was ringing.

What is that. . . ? I know that sound . . .

He fought to remain conscious as he realized it was his phone, still ringing from before. If only he could get his fingers around it . . . He threw an arm out in the direction the sound was coming from, but his eyes were bleary and bloodshot, and suddenly the sound stopped.

And then fists, feet, knees, and the heavy baseball bat descended upon him, all at once. Blows came from all sides, and he knew only pain. It was happening too fast. There was no time to react. One of the men stomped hard on his upturned foot and it twisted to the side with a sharp *snap*.

He couldn't get angry, couldn't be sad. Couldn't be afraid. Couldn't even cry.

He could only *feel*.

Barely holding to consciousness, he was outstretched on his chest now, though he didn't remember turning over. He opened his swollen eyes as much as possible, barely able to see through the haze of agony.

One fierce kick to the face ended that, as he finally, gratefully slipped into nothingness.

25

An accident on the 101 turned the trip back from Las Virgenes Canyon into a wasted afternoon. The winding canyon roads suited the Corvette perfectly while the stalled traffic surrounding them now was like making a Thoroughbred pull a plow. Eventually they growled their way back to the Wagner Building and into the parking garage. Finding a space and setting the brake, Grant said, "I need a plan."

"Agreed," Julie replied. She'd been brooding silently in the passenger seat since leaving the asylum. He thought she might yell on the drive back but she'd sat quiet and serious. It was like it was almost too much and the weight of everything had found her shoulders. The sun had waned in the horizon and vanished once they arrived at home, yet this was the first word she'd uttered during the drive.

"Think I might jot some things down, gather my thoughts, maybe see if I can come up with some idea of what I should do next," he continued. "Want to help?"

"I was wondering if I could borrow the car, actually," she replied. In response to his unspoken question, she said, "I haven't been home in a while. Thought I should check the mail, make sure my bills are caught up. Won't take long."

Something was wrong with this scenario, and Grant didn't have to be her brother to see it. But she was so distant, so withdrawn . . . and his mind was running in a hundred different directions. He didn't press the matter.

"Sure," he tossed her the keys and got out of the vehicle. "See you after a while."

Julie nodded in reply as she scooted over to the driver's seat and started the engine again. She backed out of the parking space and was out of sight in a moment.

Grant shook his head. *What's eating her? Probably everything.*

He'd just reached the door to the parking garage's elevator, glad to be exiting the nighttime shadows, when a voice said, "Nice to see you with some forward momentum."

Terrific. Her *again.*

His barefoot friend sauntered into view from an open stairwell beside the elevator. Her hands were clasped behind her back and she was typically smug.

"Admit it," she said playfully, "you missed me."

"Between escaping death within inches of my life—*twice*—and learning that I may be the culmination of some kind of ancient prophecy . . . no, sorry, you never once crossed my mind."

"Might want to spit that bitter pill back out before you choke on it," she remarked sourly. "So it's true. You had a little meet-'n'-greet with the one and only Morgan herself."

"Why didn't you tell me there were other people out there like me? Why did you let me think I was the only one?"

"You weren't ready to know," she said, dismissing him. "So how are the genius Loci?"

Grant said nothing.

"Morgan and her 'flock' definitely fall into the 'good guy' camp," the girl replied. "I'm sure she seemed eager to help you. But Morgan has her own agenda, just like everybody else. She sees a lot more potential in you than you do. And she may not be wrong."

Grant snorted. "All of this advice. So which camp do *you* fall into? Are you one of the good guys?"

"There are more colors in the crayon box than black and white, hot-shot," she countered. "Everyone's got their own agenda, and I do mean *everyone*. And it's rarely the one they let you see. But I would have *thought* you would've pieced together by now that I'm risking my own life and limb every time I stick my neck out far enough to speak to you."

"Then why *do* you talk to me? Are you manipulating me too?" He sighed, irritated and tired. "Everyone I've met since this began has pulled and prodded and wanted a piece of me."

"But you keep bouncing back, sweetie." She smiled. "That's why I like you. I'm here to watch you. I'm to observe your actions and file reports on your progress. I do the same for the others—the ones I can keep track of, anyway, before they disappear off to Morgan's little hide-away."

"So if you're trying to help me," Grant said, piecing the story together, "which is a violation of your 'orders,' then why not give me anything more to go on? Why all the vague clues?"

"You want something solid? Okay, how about this. Drexel intercepted that fragment of the stone tablet—not to learn anything from it himself, not to foil Morgan's plans—but to lure *you* to his apartment. A plan your new pal Morgan unwittingly accommodated."

"What? But . . ." Grant faltered, "how could he know Morgan would send me to get it?"

"Drexel may be little more than a cop who knows more than he should, but he knows *enough* about Morgan to know that she'd pay *any* price to get that fragment back. Sweetie, seriously, you're starting to worry me. In case you hadn't noticed—and clearly you *haven't*—this entire 'game' you're playing is completely rigged. Has been from the start. The things that have happened to you over the last few weeks may feel random to you, but it's all connected."

Grant's brow furrowed, anger rising once more at the layers upon layers of manipulation he'd been subjected to. He rubbed at the ring's underside.

"If you're going to play to win," the girl said, conviction in her voice, "then you have to go off script. And you've *got* to learn not to take 'no' for an answer. Do you even know what you're capable of?"

"I'm starting to."

"You could probably stand to learn a thing or two from your new girlfriend. Mayhem and anarchy—that's right up her alley, isn't it?"

"Who's swallowing the bitter pill now?"

"The point is, you need to start putting your handy-dandy new skills to work and break down some doors, pal. It's time to stop playing by everyone else's rules."

"Sounds like you're applying to be my coach," Grant joked, but she made no response, positive or negative. He found he was fast warming to the idea of coloring outside the lines. "Okay, then. I want to know your name. And I'm not taking 'no' for an answer."

A smile played at the corner of her lips, and her eyes became narrow openings. But he could tell her annoyance wasn't sincere.

"Fine," she said, pursing her lips. "My name is Alex."

Much to her relief, Julie found her apartment exactly as she'd left it.

But truth be told, she had little interest in checking the mail *or* paying her bills. She bypassed both on her way to the spare room she used for storage.

Boxes, unused and broken appliances, and a multitude of college textbooks crammed the room. So much had been taken from her early in life that now she had a hard time parting with anything. Julie had difficulty finding her footing, as very little of the carpet was visible. Goose-stepping around the poorly organized room was the best she could manage.

"Where is it. . . ?" she mumbled, rifling through box after box.

One hour and thirteen boxes later, she had a eureka moment.
This is it.

Now she could show Grant some cold, hard facts about this conspiracy he was caught up in. She had evidence in her hand that proved that none of what Grant was experiencing would be solved via lunatic prophecies. She'd heard quite enough of Morgan filling her brother's head with bizarre theories for one lifetime, thank you very much.

Julie could handle the "enhanced mental abilities" thing. She could deal with the "Shift." She could even swallow the notion that Morgan had somehow read every single one of the thousands of books lining the walls at the asylum.

But this "Bringer" nonsense was going too far.

Grant had enough on his mind trying to sort out the truth, his anger issues, and even his very identity, without complicating matters with ideas better suited to the realm of mythology.

Leaving the room, she seized three spare college textbooks on her way out.

Morgan would probably enjoy reading these. Just because she's misguided doesn't mean I can't be nice to her.

This is not happening.

Lisa glanced down at the LCD clock on the dashboard of her Honda Civic, which read *3:42* A.M. She looked up, saw that the light had turned green, and jammed her foot down on the gas pedal.

She flew through traffic, swerving around the few cars on the road at this hour with her blinkers flashing like mad. Eyes wide, she gripped the wheel with both hands as the next light turned red, and slammed on the brakes. Her tires squealed as she barely avoided colliding with the car that had already stopped in front of her.

Lisa swallowed, her eyes frantically searching for nothing. It was still dark out, but the streetlights cast an eerie orange glow onto the streets.

Who would do something like this? Her mind raced, recalling the few things Daniel had told her about his past. From what she had been able to glean, she knew that he had once been the golden boy at a megacorporation—though she didn't know which one—working on something revolutionary. It didn't end well, but she knew whatever he had worked on there was somehow related to what the two of them were studying now.

The light turned green and she slammed her foot onto the gas pedal once again, swerving around a massive black SUV.

Her thoughts went back to the phone call she'd received only minutes ago. The woman on the phone, with all the sweetness in the world, evaded Lisa's questions and simply told her, "It would be good if a friend or family member could get here quickly."

They don't usually say that about people who are alive, do they?

Her heart jumped into her throat and soon tears were spilling out of her eyes.

Another light turned red and she stopped once again, now barely able to see through the haze of tears, and she broke down, no longer caring about the light.

The car jarred as something bumped it from behind, and she looked into her rear mirror. The black Expedition had caught up to her, and now the light had turned green.

She was bumped again, a little harder this time.

All right, all right . . .

Lisa hit the gas, but quickly realized she wasn't moving under her own power. The monstrous SUV behind her was *pushing* her down the road, literally bumper to bumper. Bright light poured in from the Expedition's headlamps blinding Lisa off her rearview mirror and she was so taken by surprise that for a second she could do nothing. The two vehicles plowed ahead, gaining frightening speed, as cars passing the other way blared their warning.

A red light ahead finally roused Lisa from her stupor. She didn't know what intersection waited for her, but it was a busy one, and the SUV was pushing her toward it at fifteen, now twenty miles an hour. Cars poured across from either direction and she was headed straight for them.

She had seconds to react. Maybe less.

With too many cars ahead of her in the right-hand lane, Lisa saw her only hope.

Foot off the gas, she waited for two cars to pass headed the other way, and then simultaneously swung the wheel hard to the left and jammed on her brakes.

Squealing tires and the horrendous sound of something tearing at the back of her car filled the air, and the Civic swung into a devastating arc, crossing the double-lines then corkscrewing across the two oncoming lanes before slamming into parked cars outside an Asian grocer.

It was over. It was now 3:45 A.M. and yet Lisa felt like the last few minutes had taken hours.

The SUV!

She whirled to see what had become of the vehicle but it was gone. The light was green at the intersection and now early morning L.A. traffic rolled toward her, slowed to gape, and then headed off. Sirens blared somewhere in the distance. Headed to help her.

She glanced at herself in the mirror. A thin line of blood snaked down her face and both her head and right shoulder ached—she must have banged them sometime but couldn't remember—yet otherwise she felt okay. Daniel was the one who needed help. Daniel was the one in the hospital.

Lisa let up on the brake, which she'd still held slammed to the floor, and offered the Civic some gas. It groaned but moved. The sound of sirens grew closer, but she didn't look back. She pointed her car back toward the hospital and drove, but it was only Daniel's battered, torn face that she could picture in her mind as the car lumbered its way toward him.

26

"Wake up," a voice called out of the darkness. "Collin?"

"Hannah?" Grant mumbled. "Alex?"

"Sorry to disappoint you," Julie replied, sitting on the edge of his bed. "And who's Alex?"

"What time is it?" Grant mumbled, sitting up. He saw that the clock by his bed read *4:22* A.M. "What's going on?"

"I found something I need to show you," she replied, plopping the three heavy college textbooks she'd retrieved onto the bed, where they bounced.

He picked up the first book. *A History of Modern Sociology.*

"Not the books themselves," she said, retrieving a handful of small envelopes from inside. *"These."*

He opened one of the envelopes and unfolded its contents. "Looks like a love letter from Dad to Mom."

She nodded. "About half of what I found are those little love notes, but the rest are formal letters written by Dad to a friend of his, another officer. I think the guy was his superior, but from the letters it sounds like the two of them were close friends. Collin, this man—this friend of Dad's—his name was Harlan *Evers.*"

"Evers?" he replied, groggy. "Where do I know that name?"

"From that guy MacDugall at the Inveo plant. Didn't he say his big, secret customer from years ago was named Evers? I know it's not an uncommon name, but there could be a link."

"Right, right . . ." he began to catch on, but was still too sleepy to catch the implications of what she was saying.

"Here," Julie pulled something small out of her purse and handed it to him, "take a look at this."

It was a small, round piece of engraved metal with an ornate ribbon attached.

"I found that among some of Dad's old things, along with the letters. You remember Dad was an Army tactician, right?"

"Barely."

"Well, he was," she continued, gaining steam. "I looked through his entire service record—the parts that are unclassified, anyway—and Dad was never awarded any medals."

He was examining the medal but stopped at this revelation, catching her eye.

"But Mom was."

Grant sat up straighter. "Mom was in the Army? You never told me that."

"I didn't know," she replied. "Dad never mentioned it. She must have been discharged before we were born. But I read through all of these letters, and it sounds like their mutual Army affiliation was how they met. I'm guessing that when she got out, Dad chose to stay in. I don't know, maybe they decided one of them had to stay home with the kids."

Grant leaned back against the bed's headboard, and looked far away. "Okay . . . So you're thinking that this Harlan Evers man probably knew Mom *and* Dad."

"Right," she nodded. "And I keep thinking about that story I told you, about how Dad had your mental acuity tested when you were very young. If this Evers guy is still alive, maybe he can explain that. At the very least, his connection to Inveo Technologies seems way too coincidental."

It took him a moment to put it together.

"You think he might be able to explain what's happening to me," he concluded.

"At the very least, it would be worth looking into, just to find out if he's still alive."

Everyone in the waiting area gawked as Lisa rushed into the emergency room at full tilt. She came to a sudden stop in the middle of the room, trying to find the admitting desk.

"Daniel Cossick!" she yelled, sprinting to the desk. "Where is he? Is he alive?"

The nurse looked up, and her eyes widened in alarm. Lisa knew. Blood had dried on her face and more than just her shoulder ached now. Her right eye had already started to swell a bit and her entire right leg throbbed. It didn't matter. Only Daniel did.

"Are you the woman I spoke with on the phone?"

"Yes!" Lisa shouted. "I'm Lisa Hazelton! I'm his assistant! Is he all right?!"

"He's in surgery, Ms. Hazelton."—She motioned toward the waiting room—"Please have a seat."

Lisa didn't budge. "What happened? Did they find whoever did this to him?" Her voice was loud enough for the entire emergency room to hear.

"Please sit, before you fall over."

Lisa stared at her for a moment but finally caved and collapsed anxiously into one of the waiting room chairs.

The woman took a seat beside her, sitting on the edge of the couch.

"My name is Evelyn," she said gently. "Does Mr. Cossick have any family that should be notified?"

Lisa shook her head. "His mother lives in a nursing home upstate, but she's not coherent," she said quickly, still staring at the woman.

"As near as we can tell," Evelyn said, "Mr. Cossick—"

"*Doctor* Cossick."

"—was attacked outside a parking garage in the warehouse district."

Lisa nodded impatiently, prodding her to speed up. "Yeah, his lab is on the second floor, it's where we work. Did they take anything?"

"They never entered the building," Evelyn continued, "and we found Dr. Cossick's wallet still in his pants when they brought him in. The police said it looked as if he was leaving for the night, locking up, when several individuals snuck up from behind—we believe there was more than one of them because of the extent of his injuries. A homeless man found him lying on the ground outside the building and believed he was dead. He found your boss's phone on the ground and dialed 911.

But while on the phone, he noticed that Dr. Cossick was still breathing."

"Will he make it?" Lisa asked, quieter.

Evelyn was silent for a moment, as if trying to decide how to say it. She reached out to put a steadying hand on top of Lisa's, but Lisa jerked away.

"His injuries were *extensive*, Ms. Hazelton," she said tentatively. "He's in critical condition."

"*Just tell me* if he's going to live."

Evelyn hesitated, but finally spoke. "He has three broken ribs and a punctured lung. He has a fractured wrist, both of his legs are broken, and his right ankle has been shattered in three places. There are some broken fingers; he's covered in bruises. And he has a severe concussion. The doctor believes there could be brain damage. They've gone to surgery because the doctor feared there could be internal trauma. Normally, we would never risk keeping a patient unconscious this long after a concussion, but the doctor felt there was no—"

"What are his chances?" Lisa whispered. The tears had appeared out of nowhere as the elder woman had listed Daniel's injuries, and were now pouring openly down her face. She made no attempt to wipe them away.

Evelyn spoke slowly. "We won't know until the doctor can assess his internal injuries. If that assessment goes well, then our biggest concern is the concussion and the potential brain damage. He should be out of surgery soon. If he wakes up within a few hours . . . then that's a good sign. But the longer he remains unconscious . . ."

Lisa choked back her tears and sat back in her seat.

"Ms. Hazelton, why don't you come on back and I'll have the attending take a look at your injuries," Evelyn said.

Slowly and carefully, Lisa rose to her feet. She didn't follow Evelyn, however, just crossed the lobby to a restroom on wobbly legs and found an empty stall.

Stepping inside, Lisa locked the door behind her.

She turned around and threw up.

"The General is not available at this time, sir."

"General?" Grant said, then moved the phone's receiver away from his mouth. "He's a *general*?"

Julie shrugged but watched with tremendous interest.

"Perhaps you could tell the General that the son of Frank Boyd, his best friend, would very much like to talk with him."

A pause. "Hold, please, sir."

Grant smirked at his sister as he waited. She rose from the sofa and opened the window blinds. They were high enough that she could see the sun struggling to cut through the morning's haze over the sprawl of the L.A. valley.

There was a knock at the apartment door. Grant and Julie eyed one another quizzically; no one had ever visited them here before.

Julie opened the door.

"Hannah!" Grant called out in surprise. "Um, come on in."

She slipped through the room, dropping a tiny purse on the kitchen counter and seating herself across from Grant in the living room without preamble.

"Thought I'd pop by and see if you needed any help," she said, flashing that gorgeous smile and crossing her legs. "Figured you'd be planning your big re-infiltration of Inveo Technologies about now."

Grant couldn't form a coherent thought in response. He'd never in his life met anyone who flirted as casually as most people breathe.

"How'd you know where we live?" Julie asked accusingly, still standing at the front door but now her arms were crossed.

"I'm a *thief*, cupcake. And I know your names," Hannah paused, tossing her long blond locks out of her face. "Work it out."

Julie opened her mouth, a sarcastic retort prepped and ready, but Grant waved a hand when the gentleman at the military base returned to the phone.

"Sir, I'm sorry, but General Evers says he has no memory of a Frank Boyd."

"That's impossible," Grant replied, his heart rate rising.

"I'm sorry, sir."

"Tell him," Grant said, "he's *going* to help me whether he wants to or not." He hung up.

"That probably wasn't smart," Julie said, warningly.

Grant placed the phone onto its cradle. "He's stonewalling me," his disappointed voice intoned.

"Who is?" Hannah asked.

"Evers. Harlan Evers. We found out who he is. You up for a little cloak-and-dagger?"

She smiled. "Always."

27

Lisa rubbed her eyes, fighting fatigue. She was in the middle of filling out her *fourth* form of the morning—or was it afternoon now? or evening?—having been questioned by the police at length about the car wreck and then patched up by a P.A.

"Dr. Cossick's been taken down to Intensive Care," Evelyn called out softly.

Lisa sprung from her seat and hurried to the counter where the admittance clerk stood. "Can I see him?"

"Follow me."

Evelyn led her down a long, white hall to the left, through a set of locked doors that buzzed before she could open them. Down another hall and inside a door to the right, they came upon eight neat rooms, cloistered about a busy nurses' station. Evelyn led her inside the first one on the right, where a short, squat nurse stood fussing over a gurney.

Lisa's hand flew up to cover her mouth and she felt weak in the knees. The tears came again, but she blinked them back.

"This is Grace," Evelyn said. "She'll be watching over Dr. Cossick until he's moved to his own room." And with that, she swept silently back down the hall.

"How is he?" Lisa stammered, carefully lowering herself into a chair beside the bed. "Will he make it?"

Grace smiled. "He's a fighter. Most folks in his state wouldn't have made it down here at all."

Despite herself, Lisa let out a small, quick laugh. She wiped her eyes and looked at him again. If she hadn't had assurance this was Daniel, she would never have known. There were bandages wrapped around his forehead and his entire face looked like one big, grayish-blue swollen egg. Casts had been applied to his left wrist and both lower legs. A cylindrical metal contraption with needle-like pins sticking out of it enclosed his right ankle. White tape was strapped all across his chest. And everywhere skin was visible, she saw discolorations and scabs.

It was so quiet here. She thought she detected the sound of rain outside, though there were no windows nearby to see out.

"What's that?" she said, pointing. Red stains were seeping through the tape over his chest.

The nurse frowned, knowing the answer would only upset Lisa more. "It's okay, the blood's dried. It's from his incision. They had to explore to make sure everything was okay," she said gently. "They were able to repair the lung, but I'm afraid they had to remove his spleen."

"But he's going to make it, right?"

Grace looked back at Daniel and adjusted his breathing tube. "He'll tell us the answer to that when he's ready."

Rain soaked through Grant's clothes in the night's heavy darkness as his feet pounded the muddy earth and his concentration was focused on only one thing:

Keep going.

Have to keep going.

Grant had never run this hard in his life. Even trying to escape Konrad was nothing like this. He'd been running as fast as his leg would allow for fifteen minutes and even with his new and improved physique, he was nearing exhaustion. It was all he could do not to trip over his own feet.

He tasted dirt when he stumbled and landed face-first while rounding a corner. Staggering back up, he made his way around another building and stopped for a second, leaning over, gasping for air.

There he listened.

The dogs were still barking but it sounded like they'd stopped moving. Then he saw the glow of flashlights from around the corner, and he realized they were closing fast.

That got him moving again.

"Hannah?" he whispered into his earpiece. "Need a little help here!"

"There!" a voice from behind shouted, and Grant ducked into a supply bunker. He heard his pursuer's footfalls come and then go. He breathed a sigh of relief.

The door to the bunker was ratcheted open and his heart skipped a beat.

Hannah stood there, grinning. "Sent those boys an image of you runnin' the other way. That'll keep them for a bit. I think I found the headquarters building, but it ain't gonna be easy to reach. You ready to let loose with the big whammy?"

"The only way I know to unleash it," he replied, "is to panic. I don't think I'll have too hard a time with that tonight."

For an army base that bordered on dilapidated and was rumored to be in danger of closing down, its military police had proven surprisingly severe. The three that were chasing him had brought along two very angry-sounding attack dogs. Grant and Hannah had been forced to split up once inside the compound.

"Here we go," Hannah said, eagerly opening the door.

They dashed.

Rounding a corner, Hannah pointed out a three-story building about five hundred yards away.

A vivid white floodlight blinked into existence from somewhere high above, illuminating their movements like dancers on stage. They ducked around another building just as they heard shouts of "Hold it!"

Grant yelped when a loud gunshot went off and chunks of the corner behind him chipped away.

"Warnin' shot!" Hannah shouted.

Which meant only one thing: he wouldn't be so lucky next time.

Already his legs were weary again, but he poured on the speed, doing his best to keep up with Hannah, who barely seemed to be breaking a sweat.

Another gunshot was fired and he instinctively ducked. The action made him lose his balance and slip in the mud, toppling onto his back. Something hot and wet was running down his right arm, but there was no time to examine it; Hannah was already pulling him to his feet.

"No time to rest, big boy," she said.

I've been shot, he thought, struggling to stand. *Again.*

The headquarters building was only a few hundred meters away now, but more troops were pouring out upon them from all directions. Hannah dragged him further, though he felt like giving up. Their pursuers were close enough that he could hear the dogs breathing.

Have I lost my mind? Trying to storm a military base? I'm not Rambo.

Ahead, dozens of troops were massing in front of the headquarters building, forming a line they would never be able to cross. Still they didn't stop running. More gunshots went off from behind as they approached the ranks of the soldiers ahead, all with automatic weapons trained on them . . .

"DON'T MOVE!" one of them shouted. "Stop or be killed!!"

"You're up," Hannah remarked.

He thought of the building ahead, wondering which window might be Evers' office . . .

Panic flooded his heart just as another shot went off and he let out a primal, terrified scream . . .

Blinding pain shot through his head . . .

He stumbled again . . .

When he opened his eyes, the soldiers had vanished.

No, they weren't gone. They were slumped on the ground, backs against the headquarters building. Unconscious.

"What happened?" he whispered.

"I think ya *swatted* 'em," Hannah replied.

A dozen more MPs appeared and surrounded them in a circle, fingers hair-triggered on their rifles. They were screaming at the intruders to get their hands up and get down on the ground.

"That'll do, boys," said a new player, approaching from the front of the building. He was broad-shouldered and hard-nosed. Though he must've been in his midsixties, he looked as though he could eat a box of cigars for breakfast. "Return to your posts," he barked.

The men lowered their weapons and turned away, some stopping to help the unconscious soldiers at the foot of the building.

"You're Frank's boy?" Evers asked, throwing Grant a stern look.

"I am."

"You *better* be," Evers growled. "Because if you're not, then that means you *stole* that bracelet you're wearing, and I'll have to kill you myself."

Grant glanced down at the bracelet on his wrist.

"*You* come with me," Evers ordered. "Your girlfriend'll have to wait out here."

"She's not—"

"It's all right," Hannah spoke up, and he got the distinct impression she'd interrupted what he was about to say on purpose. "Go on. I'll be fine."

28

Evers led the way up two flights of stairs to his office. It was smaller than Grant would've thought and smelled stale.

"Find a seat, if you can," Evers said, rounding on his desk. Wrinkles around his eyes and mouth spoke of his long years of service to his country. He had a gruff and menacing manner, but there was a look in his eyes that was almost . . . resigned.

Grant looked about and saw the problem. Files, papers, manuals, and other assorted trinkets were filling most of the spaces throughout the room.

"D.C.'s putting me out to pasture as soon as they close us down here," Evers muttered. "Assuming I make it till then."

What does that mean?

Grant moved aside a large stack of folders and sat in the chair they had been occupying. "So you recognize my granddad's bracelet?"

"'Course. Your dad treasured it. I don't remember Frank without it. It wasn't military protocol of course, but he was the best at what he did, so I let him get away with it. His father had made it by hand during *double-u double-u two*."

"So you were his superior officer?" Grant probed.

"That's right. For oh . . . about sixteen years or so. I considered him my protégé. I was grooming him to take my place one day, but that didn't happen."

"Did you know my mother too?"

Evers nodded, his beady eyes trained calmly on Grant. "I was best man at their wedding. Your father was very laid-back; I didn't think he was capable of getting nervous. He proved me wrong that day."

"Were they colleagues? Was my mother in the Army, too? Is that how they met?"

Evers studied him, a trace of a scowl on his lips. "Quit beating around the bush, Grant." Grant's eyes grew as Evers emphasized a name he'd never told him. "Yes, I know what's happened to you, and I know you didn't Battle-of-Normandy your way in here just to get a play-by-play on your parents' courtship. Ask me what you came here for."

But Grant was too stunned to go forward just yet. "How do you know that name? How could you *possibly* know what's happened to me?"

"It was my business at one time to keep tabs on these things. You can't tell from looking around this place, but I've spent most of my life keeping secrets. Trust me when I say I've gotten good at it."

"Tell me about Inveo Technologies."

Evers hesitated, visibly surprised. "Inveo is a dead end. That's not what you really came here for."

Grant was undeterred. "Did you or did you not hire a man named Carl MacDugall at Inveo Technologies to research ways of enhancing the capabilities of the human body?"

Evers sighed. "I did."

"Why?"

"Did MacDugall bother telling you *when* I placed that order?"

"No . . . What difference does it make?"

"All the difference in the world, son. It was right about the same time your father tested your mental acuity." Evers leaned forward. "You see, the bioengineering research at Inveo—I placed the order, yes. But it was done at your *father's* request."

Nine hours passed after Daniel was admitted to the ICU before he stirred.

Lisa let out an enormous sigh of relief when he started twitching his head. She shot out of her seat to stand right next to him.

He tried licking his lips, but the breathing tube was in the way. "Mmm-mm," he moaned.

"It's about time, sleepyhead," she said. She was trying to be cheerful but couldn't quite pull it off. Seeing him this way was overwhelming.

Daniel tried to open his eyes, but they were swollen too badly and he found he couldn't.

Grace, the nurse, left to find the doctor and a few moments later rushed back in, Daniel's surgeon right behind.

"Go ahead," the doctor nodded to Grace.

"Take a deep breath in . . ." she grabbed the tube as Daniel complied, "and blow it out." As he did, she pulled out the tube.

He coughed and gagged then settled.

For a moment, Lisa thought he might have fallen back to sleep. She carefully pushed his mussed hair out of his face.

"Amehgunnaliff?" Daniel mumbled.

The doctor turned to Lisa quizzically.

"Is he going to live?" she whispered.

The doctor smiled. "Yes," he said, carefully checking Grant's vitals, "we think you'll recover just fine. You have a long road ahead, I'm afraid. And you may never get full use of that ankle back. We're going to take good care of you."

"Imalife?" Daniel asked deliriously, as though he hadn't understood the doctor's report.

The doctor smiled. "Yes, you're alive. And we're going to keep you that way." He turned to Lisa and said quietly, "We've asked that a patrolman be posted outside your door, just to be safe."

"Thanks," Lisa said quietly. Then, turning to Daniel, "You hear that? You're going to be okay," she said, a little louder than necessary.

Daniel managed a weak nod.

The doctor told Lisa he'd be back to check in another hour. She returned to her chair beside the bed.

"Do you remember what happened?" she said softly into his ear.

He nodded weakly, and his breath suddenly caught in his throat, before he released it and breathed normally again. Lisa detected a trace of clear fluid around his puffed-up eyes.

"Good thing you're too stubborn and curious to give in to this sort of thing," she tried joking. But she quickly bit her lip as she watched his battered, unrecognizable body inhale and exhale with difficulty. She stretched out a hand to grasp his, but then thought better of it and rested her hand very gently on top of his instead.

She started when his hand came to life and grabbed hers. She had thought he had no strength left in his body, but he was holding frightfully tight.

Lisa looked at his face, and his eyes were still unable to open, but his lips moved. She leaned in closer to hear.

"Don' leaf me," he whispered. "Don' go anywhere, okay?"

Lisa couldn't hold back the flood of emotions pouring into and out of her heart. How often had she wanted to take his hand in hers?

But never like this . . .

Her tears came, and she was glad he couldn't see them or her own injuries.

"Didn't you hear what the doctor said?" She placed her other hand on top of his, smiling sweetly. "We're going to take good care of you."

Grant felt sick to his stomach.

"My *father*? *He* wanted to find ways of enhancing the human body?" It made no sense.

"I don't know exactly *what* he was after," Evers replied. "I headed up a tactical analysis unit that had been granted a wide berth by the Pentagon. One of the projects your father worked on led him to these experiments at Inveo Technologies. And in the years after his death, I came to suspect a number of things about him. One was that maybe he had you tested for the *same project* that he contracted Inveo for."

"I don't understand," Grant shook his head, suddenly full of more questions than he'd come here with. If that was possible.

"Let me back up," Evers said, still eying Grant. "Bet you didn't know I'm your godfather."

Grant's eyebrows popped up.

"I am. Your parents were remarkable people. Your mother, Cynthia, was just a beautiful, beautiful person. And smart as a tack—I actually thought she was smarter than your dad, and that's saying something. I assume you know how she died?"

Grant swallowed. "There were . . ." His throat constricted and he cleared it. "There were complications when I was born."

Evers nodded, examining him. "Most men would have shut down after losing someone that way. Not Frank. He had *such* a strong sense of purpose. He grieved for your mom in his own way, but he kept going. He refused to take any time off, and I saw the pain in his eyes nearly every day, but he continued to serve. And he loved his children very much. He spoke of you constantly."

Evers sighed. Grant said nothing, waiting for the elder man to continue.

"Grant, has it never struck you as *odd* that both of your parents died within a few years of each other?"

"No . . ." Grant replied, disbelieving what he'd just heard. "It didn't strike me as *odd*, it struck me as terrifying."

"Son," Evers said, a trace of compassion in his voice for the first time, "we *all* have that moment in life when something terrible happens for the first time. Something so unexpected, so awful, that it . . . it takes the magic out of the world. Life becomes harder, colder. And everything we do in our lives, from that day on, is our way of coping with that one moment. We stop living and we merely exist. We either choose to move on from that, or we let it consume us."

"I don't believe that," Grant replied, but in truth, his mind was racing, trying to piece together what Evers was insinuating.

"My best friend's death has consumed *me* for much of my life," Evers said. "I couldn't ever get past the odd timing of it all."

"Timing?" Grant said, trying to hold his growing worry inside. "He got clipped by a drunk driver. People die all the time." Grant stared hard at the man. "I'm not sure I understand where you're going with this."

"I was *there* the day your father ordered your mental acuity tested, Grant," Evers replied. "I thought it strange for a three-year-old, but at the time, I figured maybe he was hoping you would turn out to be as smart as your mom. I remember when the results came back so high— I had hoped he'd be ecstatic. But instead he became distant, somber.

"Two months later he died in that horrific car accident. Body wrecked beyond recognition. And now, you have yourself a whole new life and the ability to *think* things into happening. That's an ability that—*I* believe—only someone with as high a mental acuity as yours could ever hope to control."

The room was dead silent. Grant was having trouble remembering to breathe.

"You're not suggesting—"

"I've gone over it in my mind so many times, over the years," Evers replied. "Then when I heard about what happened to you recently . . . it has to be linked. And it can't be an accident."

"You think he was *killed*? Because of me?" Grant exhaled.

Evers let out a humorless laugh. "I'm not nearly as clever as I once was, but I am good at my job. I've been trained to take distinct variables and place them into a cohesive explanation. It's what I do. And when I put the pieces of this puzzle together, *this* is one of the two explanations that I come up with."

"But . . . why? Who would want him dead? And what would it accomplish?"

"Think about it. With your mother dead from childbirth and your father subsequently removed from the equation, what was the result? You. Isolated. Alone. No one to teach you about your future, no one to groom you for your destiny."

"But that would mean my father . . ." Grant slowly realized as he said it, "He knew. He knew what I was going to become."

Evers avoided Grant's eyes. "At the very least, I think he suspected."

Grant sat stunned. "And what was the other explanation?" He could hardly imagine.

Evers' face look concerned. "I don't put much stock in that one."

Grant waited.

"Well, given the timing and the terrible circumstances of the accident. There's the slim chance . . . that the whole thing may have been arranged. To just make it *look* like. . . ."

29

"What aren't you telling me?" Grant said.

"I've already told you too much," Evers replied. It struck Grant that suddenly Evers looked very old. "It won't be long now," he said quietly.

Grant's mind was racing too fast to catch the remark, but once he did, he came crashing to a stop.

"Not long until what?"

"There's more," Evers said, urgency rising into his voice, "*much* more you need to know; I'm sorry I won't get a chance to tell you. But you don't last as long as I have in this business without planning for every possible contingency, and trust me, I have. So did your father."

"I don't understand," said Grant.

"How long has it been, son?" Evers asked, wistful. "How long since you were there? Your parents' old house?"

Grant blinked. "I don't know. More than twenty-five years, I guess."

"Go back."

"What? Why?" The first home he'd ever known—where his father and sister lived with him, before the orphanage—was military housing on an old Army base north of Monterey. Only vague images remained as his memory of the place. "Would the house even still be there?"

"The base is closed, of course," Evers said, undeterred. "It's a museum now. But the houses stand. Empty and rotting, but they stand."

"But why should I go back there?" That old house was the last place Grant wanted to be.

"You're looking for a safe. Your *father's* safe. He kept one, hidden somewhere in the attic. I don't think he ever knew I knew about it. It contained all of his old records and personal files. There's information in those files that—well, it's not exactly what you're searching for, but you need to see it."

A siren began to wail loudly, throughout the entire base. Grant saw flashing lights outside the building and all of the base's floodlights came on.

It hit Grant like a truck. "The sirens are for *you*! This is why you didn't want to talk to me!"

He was on his feet in an instant, but Evers grabbed him by the shoulders and spun him around.

"If you go and find your father's files," Evers said sternly, as if the sirens weren't sounding, "you're going to learn things that will be hard to accept. Things about your parents *and* about yourself. Take it from an old man—sometimes ignorance truly *is* bliss, son. Do you understand what I'm telling you? Think long and hard about whether or not you want to do this. Because once you turn this corner, once you know this truth, there will be no going back. Not ever."

Too much was happening too fast . . .

Evers squared his shoulders and sat back down at his desk. "You should go now," he said quietly. "Looks like the base is closing down a bit earlier than expected . . ."

In a daze, Grant made for the door.

His father could be alive.

His heart surged at the thought, yet all he could feel was sad and lost at the very idea. How could this possibly be true?

Evers shouted, rousing Grant. "Not that way!" He pointed toward the window. "Use the slide. Quickly, now."

Grant had no idea what was happening, but he went to the window as instructed. A large metal box marked "Fire Slide" rested beneath the windowsill. He opened it and found a large bundle of fabric wrapped around dozens of wide metallic rings.

Grant slid the window up and threw the bundle in his arms outward as far as he could. It stretched into a fabric tube that glided to the ground, extending over thirty feet away from the building.

"Good luck, son," Evers said as Grant climbed into the tube, feet first.

Grant merely nodded, unable to form words. He heard footsteps approaching in the hallway outside Evers' office.

Go. Move!

Just as he let go and began his rapid descent through the slide, he heard the door to the office burst open.

Evers' voice matter-of-factly said, "End of the line, eh, boys?"

As Grant's feet landed on terra firma, he heard a gunshot.

Run!

He spotted Hannah hiding behind some bushes not far away. He grabbed her and ran.

It was late afternoon when Lisa exited a cab to step onto the sidewalk in front of the building that housed Daniel's lab. Her next-door neighbor had been kind enough to sit with Daniel at the hospital (he was asleep, or she never would have left his side), while she made a quick trip back to the lab to pick up some of his personal items.

She was still so dazed by the previous day's events that she didn't notice the big black van parked in front of the building. She only snapped out of her reverie when she saw that the front door to the lab was cracked open.

Her heart leapt into her throat. She pushed the door open carefully and looked up the stairs. She could hear loud voices talking and a variety of clanging sounds, like in the kitchen of a big restaurant.

Desperate now at the terrible possibilities of that noise, she ran up the stairs, down the hall, and into the lab. A cacophony of activity met her there, as white-clad men and women were everywhere, examining the lab's equipment, taking the machines apart, putting pieces into plastic bags and cardboard boxes, and carrying them out the door behind her.

There were over a dozen of them there, all in white jumpsuits with the word "FORENSICS" emblazoned across their shoulders.

Lisa ran to the nearest one and grabbed his arm. "What do you people think you're doing? This is delicate equipment! You can't just come in here and do this!"

The short man with a detached expression pushed his black-rimmed glasses up on his nose and tried his best to look down on her. "Are you Mr. Cossick's assistant?"

There was a loud crash in the middle of the room, and she looked up to see two men bickering over who'd dropped a computer server that now lay shattered at their feet.

"*Doctor* Cossick, and yes, I am," she replied, turning back to him with a furious gaze. "Who are *you* supposed to be?"

He lifted his chin slightly. "We're with the LAPD. Your employer was attacked on these premises, ma'am, and we're here with a court order to find out what the attackers were looking for."

She knew exactly whose orders this had come from. She felt as though steam was rushing out of her ears. "That *vile*, no-good, wretched, *spiteful*, corrupt, bottom-dwelling *crook*!!" she screamed in outrage.

Two patrolmen rushed up and grabbed her by each arm, dragging her out of the building. "If Drexel thinks he can get away with this—!" she yelled.

The short man she'd shouted at was unperturbed. "Wait, before you remove her . . ." He turned back to the countertop he had been working at, and held up a small metallic device for her to see.

"Could you tell me what this is for?" he asked.

"*You* . . . sleazy. . . !" Lisa started between clenched teeth. But she was out of the lab before she could finish. The men in blue escorted her down the stairs and back to her car, then stationed themselves on either side of the building's door to ensure she wouldn't come back.

Ten minutes later, she continued to pace on the opposite side of the street. It had taken several minutes of breathing exercises to cool off.

The lab was a total loss.

Daniel would be *so* devastated.

She sat up straight as another thought struck her. She pulled out her phone and hit one of the speed-dial numbers.

"Gordon," she said when Daniel's lawyer answered. "It's Lisa Hazelton. Have you heard what's happened?"

He hadn't. She told him. Then she told him about the lab.

"If they have a court order," he told her, "then there's nothing you can do but stay out of their way."

Lisa sighed, frustrated.

"Do you believe they're genuinely looking for evidence about Daniel's attack?" the lawyer asked.

She glanced back at the building and the two officers standing outside, watching her.

"Not for one minute," she replied.

Half an hour later, Grant and Hannah were speeding back toward downtown. Grant was too lost in thought, rubbing his thumb against his ring, so Hannah was driving, listening to him tell of his encounter with Harlan Evers, while keeping both eyes on the dark road ahead.

After his story had ended and she had allowed him some time to think, she spoke.

"So you're thinkin' the same thing I am, right?"

"Morgan."

"Oh yeah," she nodded. "You *gotta* go to Morgan with this."

"Agreed," he looked away. "But it's late . . . Let's make it tomorrow."

Hannah tossed her hair. "Meet ya there for lunch."

30

Finch Bailey didn't seem to appreciate it when Collin tripped him at the lunch table.

All of the other kids laughed heartily as the larger boy's food went flying and Finch landed in a mound of mashed potatoes. But Finch wasn't laughing.

Just as Collin expected.

When asked later by one of the orphanage workers why he did it, he looked the woman straight in the eye and said, "Just seemed like the thing to do."

Three hours later on the playground, Collin was alone on the swing set, when Finch shoved him from behind in midswing, making Collin dive out of it. As he rose, sand clinging to his face, he snatched a handful of sand and flung it straight into Finch's laughing face.

A caretaker broke in before it went any further but as she led Finch away he turned and mouthed, "Just you wait."

Later that night, Collin was only pretending to be asleep on the bottom of the bunk bed, when he heard footsteps approaching. More than one pair of footsteps.

Hands grabbed all four of his limbs and dragged him out of bed. He struggled against them, but only halfheartedly. Duct tape was placed over his eyes and mouth and the other three or four boys—Collin couldn't tell how many there were, exactly—dragged him roughly out of the building, intentionally banging his head into various solid objects along the way.

Half an hour later, he was lying in the poison oak patch deep in the woods behind the orphanage. The other boys had stripped him to his boxers on the cool spring evening, and used more of the duct tape to strap his feet together and his hands in back.

Then they began hitting. But he only pretended to flinch, to fight back.

Light at first, the impacts grew harder and harder until fists were involved. A hardness coursed through his body with each blow. He willed himself to take it. Soon Collin felt hot, sticky blood running out of his nose. But they stopped long enough to rub ivy leaves across his bare chest, arms, and legs.

It was late the next morning before the frantic orphanage workers found him; he was shivering and wet with the morning dew, with so many dark red rashes covering his body, they'd rushed him to the emergency room.

He'd never bothered to try and free himself or crawl out of the woods because he wanted to see the other boys pay for doing this to him. Almost as much as he yearned for the ordeal to last as long as it possibly could . . .

"NO STOP!!"

Grant bucked straight up in bed, panting, covered in sweat.

He slowly eased himself back down onto his pillow and glanced at his bedside clock. Through the window blinds, he could make out a soft glow as the sun began to greet the horizon. The world was at peace.

But he was not.

He used the bed's sheets to wipe sweat from his forehead as he lay there with his eyes wide open.

Where did that *come from?*

He hadn't thought of that particular episode from his childhood in years.

He decided to leave early for the asylum; he needed advice, and not on anything he'd learned from Harlan Evers . . .

The Thresher was looking straight down at the ground, over twenty-five feet below, when his phone vibrated.

His arms and legs were completely outstretched, bracing his position in the narrow space between two neighboring downtown hotels. The confines of the tight outdoor corridor were far too small to hold a car or truck; instead, it merely allowed for rear entrance to both hotels.

The Thresher carefully released his right hand from the brick wall, shifting his balance to accommodate three limbs, and thumbed open his cell phone.

"Yes?" he whispered.

"Your presence is required."

"Devlin," the Thresher replied in recognition, still whispering. "Been a long time."

"Too long. I've been made aware of your recent movements. You must meet with me, at once."

"If you know what I'm doing, then you know I'm at a critical stage. I've no time for . . . guidance."

"The Secretum disagrees," Devlin replied without emotion.

Below, a door opened and a man carrying a large bag exited.

"Very well," the Thresher said, snapping the phone shut.

He let go of the walls and plummeted to the ground.

Landing without a sound, he rolled to absorb the impact. While on his back in midroll, he kicked the man with the bag.

The man landed sprawled out on all fours a few feet away. He immediately looked up to find the Thresher towering over him from a few feet away, his sword out and pointed right in the man's face. But the blade was turned sideways, and the bag of food hung from it, unspoiled.

"This is the third consecutive Friday morning you've made this delivery," the Thresher said in his soft inflection, holding the sword perfectly motionless.

The young man on the ground was in complete shock, trying to reason out what had just happened. And more importantly, how.

"*Where* are you taking it?" the Thresher asked.

When Lisa walked into Daniel's hospital room bright and early that morning, she was surprised to see him sitting up in his bed. He'd slept the entire previous day, and the rest seemed to have done him well. The swelling around his eyes had gone down, and he could finally see her again.

A nurse was feeding him.

"Lisa!" he nearly shouted, spewing Jell-O everywhere. "There you are!"

"I can't believe you're up!" she exclaimed. "Are you okay?"

"Better now that you're here," he replied weakly.

Her heart did a back flip.

"I went by the office to pick up some things for you, and then I had to call Gordon. May I?" Lisa asked the nurse. The nurse smiled in reply and handed her the tray of food. In a moment, she was gone.

Daniel was rooting around inside his mouth with his tongue. "Huh. I think I'm missing a couple of fillings . . . and the teeth they filled," he said, lost in thought. When she sat next to him, he snapped to attention. "Why'd you meet with Gordon?" he asked evenly. "And why do you have bruises all over you?"

She'd hoped to wait a while before telling him everything, but he seemed much more coherent now and clearly wouldn't accept a postponement to this conversation.

"You weren't the only one that was attacked," she said.

His face registered horror.

"I'm okay. No permanent damage. My car is a thing of the past, but I'm good."

He winced and put an arm over his chest, where the cracked ribs were. "Gordon?" he asked again through the pain.

Lisa sighed. "The lab's been ransacked by the police. A forensics unit pretty much tore the whole thing apart, piece by piece. Gordon said there's nothing we can do—they had a court order, and they've declared the entire premises a crime scene. It's gone, Daniel. I'm sorry."

He looked down, unable to meet her gaze. But instead of despondent and inconsolable, he seemed rather resigned.

"What?" she asked.

Daniel hesitated, then offered something that might have resembled a smile. "Doesn't seem all that bad, compared to being nearly beaten to death."

She winced. Thinking about the attack and how it must have felt was something she couldn't bear to dwell on.

"And the other thing is," he said softly, "this terrible thing meant to harm us might be for the best, all things considered."

"How can you say that?" Lisa nearly came out of her chair.

"I don't believe in coincidences. *Everything* is traceable to cause and effect." He sounded for a moment like his old self.

She threw a quick glance outside the room's door. He nodded.

"Drexel," he concluded. "This was about Drexel trying to get to Borrows. All of it."

"I think so, too," she nodded. "We could probably never prove it, but I think he paid some thugs to attack you, to give him a legal excuse to search our office. He wants Grant's file."

Alarm flashed across his face. "Did you get rid of it?"

"I burned it," she said and then held up a blank CD. "Encrypted, too."

"Good girl," he patted her hand, and leaned back, resting his eyes. He let out a long, painful breath, concerns and troubles fading into pain and exhaustion.

She wished she could simply let him rest, but he needed to know. "Daniel, the police have stationed a cop outside your door at all times. For *protection*."

Daniel looked up at the door sharply. Then he looked back at her, and what was left of his complexion under all of the scratches and blotches turned completely white. "He wouldn't . . ." he whispered.

She turned and looked back out the door again. "I don't think you can stay here."

Daniel started breathing faster, which caused him pain in his chest again. "But I can't even *move!*" he gasped. "The doctor just told me that I'm going to have to relearn how to walk! He said it'll take months of physical therapy. My ankle may even need another surgery."

He looked at her and then back at the door, fear and desperation all over his face. "What are we going to do?"

Butterflies fluttered in her stomach, as everything rested on her shoulders for a change. She wasn't used to being in this position and was in no way convinced she was capable of doing something like this alone.

"We've got no choice. We have to get you out of here."

Grant had just started the Corvette's engine, Julie in the passenger
seat, and begun to back out, when he hit the brakes.

"What?" Julie asked, hurling forward into her seatbelt.

"It's *her*," Grant said, staring into his rear-view.

Julie's head spun around. All she could see was a denim jacket and
simple black T-shirt, standing right behind the car.

He got out of the car; Julie followed suit.

"There's this guy who's in danger and could use your help. In a to-
the-rescue kind of way."

"So?"

"So, that's what people with abilities like yours do, buster," Alex
replied, mildly annoyed. "Or at least, what you *should* be doing."

Grant rolled his eyes. "I don't have time for this . . ."

"Neither does the guy who needs your help. I know you're all consumed with this 'quest for answers,' but don't you think it's about time
you started putting this awesome new ability of yours to good use?"

Grant just stared. He couldn't believe he was getting a lecture on
who to be from this woman.

"There," she said, letting out a long breath. "Any of that get
through? It was, like, my civic duty or whatever."

"A for effort, C for delivery."

"All right, then let me try a different approach," she said, crossing
her arms. "Go see this guy who needs your help . . . and I'll tell you
who was responsible for your Shift."

"You *know* who did this to me?"

"Of course she does," Julie jumped in. On Grant's look of astonishment, she added, "It's obvious, isn't it? She *works* for him."

Grant paused. "Is that true?"

Alex surveyed Julie. "Home run for the rookie. Look, there's not much time. Go do whatever it is you've got to do, but meet me at St. Frances Hospital by sundown. And watch your back."

"That's *my* job," Julie retorted.

When Grant and Julie emerged from the long hallway full of books and into the Common Room, he spotted Morgan and Fletcher sitting in the lounge area, on opposite sides of a chess board. He couldn't hear their conversation, but given how heated Fletcher looked, it wasn't hard to guess.

Grant took his sister by the hand and led her across the floor. Many of the Loci customarily stopped to stare as he entered the room.

"Ah, Grant," Morgan smiled warmly. "Good to see—"

"Wonderful," Fletcher groused. "He's back."

Grant wasted no time. "These are for you." He handed her Julie's college textbooks. "Can we talk in private?"

"Certainly," she replied, rising from her seat. Fletcher was about to protest but Morgan just held up a hand.

Grant followed Morgan through the Common Room. Eyes followed him and the room buzzed.

"Do they have to do that?"

Morgan looked up. The Loci were still standing about the room, watching them as they exited out into the hallway. "They intend to be witnesses."

"Witnesses?"

"To what you are going to do. They mean not to miss it."

The small white room she led him to contained a countertop, cabinets, an examination table, and a couple of tiny, uncomfortable-looking chairs. She sat in one and invited him to sit in the other. As before, she waited for him to speak first.

Grant gathered his thoughts before opening his mouth.

"I need some advice," he began. "I think I'm developing . . . feelings . . . for Hannah."

A hint of a smile played at the corner of Morgan's mouth. "I see," she said in an unsurprised tone of voice.

"Am I nuts to want to pursue something like this now? With everything that's going on?"

Morgan allowed herself one full breath. "Attraction, passion, love . . . these aren't my area of expertise. But if I may be so bold . . . your entire world has fallen apart and rebuilt itself into something unfamiliar, Grant. It's only natural that one of your most fundamental human needs—to be cared for—is going unmet, and that you should attempt to fill that hole. My advice would be to be careful that you genuinely feel for her as you think you do."

Grant considered this, something piquing his curiosity. "Sounds like solid advice. So, uh . . . what makes you think you're not good at this sort of thing?"

"Experience," she replied. "I don't seem cut out for romance myself. My last relationship was . . . well, it was devastating. Goodness, it's been *ages* since I've talked about it."

The hesitancy in her voice made Grant wonder if she always played this role of advice-giver, but rarely had anyone to open up to herself. He felt for her in this position, everyone looking up to her, depending on her. It was a notion he was beginning to identify with.

"What was his name?"

She smiled. "Payton. I met him after the Shift. He was another like us—another Loci. Payton went through the Shift about two years after I did. He was the very first person I met who had undergone the Shift as well. The joy of finally meeting someone else who knows what this feels like! Well, it's overwhelming, isn't it?"

Grant settled back in his chair, listening quietly.

"We fell in love very quickly," Morgan went on. "Perhaps too quickly. It was around the same time that I first discovered the existence of the stone tablet—or rather, the fragments that make up the tablet. Collecting them became my passion, and Payton picked it up quickly as well. He and I spent years flying all over the world—Argentina, Malaysia, Tibet, Zaire, and dozens of other countries—following any leads we got our hands on that could lead us to more of the fragments. We turned up quite a few of them—most of what I have now, what I showed you— came from that trip." She looked away, tears forming in her eyes.

"Something went wrong?" Grant offered.

She nodded. "Payton and I had found evidence of another fragment buried in a cave in France. The French government refused to allow us to dig in the caves—the location is a historical landmark—but we did it anyway. I suppose we dug too deep. There was a cave-in. Payton pushed me clear, but I had to watch as he was buried under a pile of enormous rocks, only inches from where I lay. I tried with all my might to dig him out, but the boulders were too heavy. I tried to find help, but there was no one in the area. So I went back in and found his hand protruding clear of the rubble. It wasn't moving, but I held it until I felt it go cold. And then . . ."

She trailed off and he watched her.

"I *ran*. I just panicked. We had no permission to be there and too many questions would uncover our plans. I loved Payton with all my heart, truly I did. But I'd always led a quiet, uneventful life until the Shift. And I never would have had the nerve to go on these globe-trotting adventures alone. Payton had a vibrant, infectious personality. And when he died and suddenly I was completely alone . . . I didn't know what to do.

"Leaving him there was the hardest and worst thing I've ever done in my life. I couldn't bring myself to go home to London, so I ran away here, to the States. And I entered a deep depression that lasted for years."

Grant could hear the bitterness, the brokenness in her voice, and he realized this was something she'd held inside for a very long time.

"After I reached the States," she said quietly, "I didn't have it in me to continue the search for the tablets myself. The weight of what I'd done bore down on me, and I just wanted to hide. That's when I first began thinking of a place where I and others like me could live in seclusion, safe from the cares of the world."

"Hiding from the world doesn't make it go away," Grant said softly. "I'm beginning to realize that."

She nodded. "I know it as well. Yet I hide anyway. Part of me really *is* afraid to step out into the world, fearful of who else might get hurt or what I might cause. Mostly, I'm just too ashamed to leave this place. The pain that was born in that cave stays with me every moment of every day. My 'miraculous' perfect memory won't let the pain fade. The thunder of the rocks as they fell. Payton's screams. The jagged rock edges my fingers scraped as I tried to dig him out. The dust that burned my eyes. The warmth—and then the cold—of his hand, as the life ebbed . . . I still remember every detail."

"I'm sorry," Grant said. There was nothing else to say.

She wiped the tears from her eyes and smiled. "Thank you for listening."

There was really nothing else for her to say, either.

32

Grant was eating lunch with his sister in the asylum's dining room when Hannah entered the room. She sauntered her way in their direction and helped herself to a seat.

"So . . . I'm not your girlfriend, huh?"

"Huh?" he asked.

"Back at the military base. Evers thought I was your girlfriend, and you were about to tell him I wasn't." She flashed those beautiful teeth before stealing one of his french fries.

He backpedaled. "That's not what I . . . I mean, I'm not *opposed* . . . I just didn't know what to—"

"Relax, darlin'. I just like watchin' you squirm."

Grant didn't laugh, though she was clearly enjoying herself. Instead, he turned to his sister, growing serious. "Could you give us a minute?"

Julie nodded and walked away.

"What's up?" Hannah asked, leaning on top of the table, as if waiting to be filled in on the latest gossip.

"Why are you so determined to help me?" he asked quietly. "I need to know the truth."

Her eyes narrowed. "You saved my life. That ain't reason enough?"

"It *is*, it's just . . ." he grappled for the words. "I have to know why a cat burglar would want to help a total stranger? I mean, say it out loud and doesn't it strike you as strange? Tell me *why*."

"I got no big noble explanation."

He considered this. "Then tell me who you really are. Inside."

Hannah sat back in her chair, uncertainty written across her face. But she seemed to be determined to indulge him. "I'm still tryin' to figure that out. Growing up, I was a brat. Spoiled little rich girl and the apple of my daddy's eye."

She looked away, collecting her thoughts.

She cleared her throat. "Mom passed when I was seven, and I was all he had left, so he showered me with attention and gifts and love. It ruined me, of course, but not a day or an hour goes by when I don't think of him. He was bright and funny. And very brave. He was everything I wanted to be."

"Was?" Grant said.

"He was killed when I was sixteen. Assassinated, in fact. He was a senator, believe it or not. He led the fight on some kind of bill about . . . actually, I can't remember what it was about. It don't matter now. Someone out there didn't like what he had to say," she said, with a far-off look in her eyes.

"So how does a straight-laced politician's daughter turn to a life of crime?"

"Took the scenic route," she offered a wry smile. "And I never said I was straight-laced."

"The scenic route?"

"I went into foster care at sixteen. Ran away a few months later. Fell in love at nineteen. Found out the guy I was in love with was a drug dealer when I saw him get his head blown off by a competing dealer. Went to the police, helped them track down the killer. Testified in court, the whole nine yards. Guy got off, not guilty, 'cause the testimony of a destitute runaway couldn't stack up against his mega-lawyer squad. It was after that, that I started seein' the world in all its splendid shades of gray. If there was no justice in the world, if people you love could get killed right in front of you and no one cared if they got away with it . . . then what did anything matter?"

Grant sat up straighter, engrossed in her story now. Her walls were falling away as Grant watched in fascination. This wasn't easy for her.

"After the trial, I started stealin'. I needed the money but I also wanted to strike back at the world that'd taken everyone away from me. Turns out I was pretty good at it. I'm a little older and wiser now, so I know a lot of the stuff going on in my head that got me here was unjustified. I *know* I shouldn't be doing what I'm doing. But at least now I do it for high-enders; I won't work for criminals. Mostly I get a lot of corporate warfare, that sort of thing. No one gets hurt, and no one suffers. Guess I do it 'cause it's the one thing I'm good for."

"You do it for the rush," Grant clarified.

"I do it for kicks, capitalist rivalry, and the American way."

Grant folded his arms and sat back. "Then why do you help me?" he repeated again.

She sighed, and when she spoke again, her words came out slowly. "I can't put it into words. Maybe I'm seein' something I ain't seen since before my father passed. Maybe I feel the connection of another orphan. We both know nobody should ever feel that kind of alone. Maybe . . ." she hesitated, "I just like you."

Grant felt an urge to reach out and take her hand, but he resisted . . .

"The one thing I can tell you for sure," she concluded, "is that bein' around you makes me want to be *better*."

She sat back now, keeping her gaze fixed on him. "Even Morgan doesn't know all that," she said softly.

Grant was silent for a long time. Hannah waited patiently.

"I, uh . . . I'm not . . ." he fumbled for words when his mouth finally opened. "If you need me as some sort of bridge to your past, to reconnect with your old life, then I'm okay with that. But I don't think you can build a relationship on that. If you want more, then it's time to—"

The sound of a throat clearing came from nearby. Grant turned to see Fletcher peering down on the two of them as if he'd just changed the channel to a soap opera, and couldn't be more disgusted by it.

Hannah, meanwhile, was doing everything in her power to maintain her composure, painting a false grin on her face and blinking hard.

"Morgan wants to see you right away," Fletcher intoned.

"Can it wait?" Grant asked. "We're talking . . ." he explained, grasping at an easy explanation for what he was feeling.

"It's urgent," Fletcher replied, indifferent to Grant's concerns. "Marta wants to meet you."

Morgan massaged her temples as today's migraine—which was actually *yesterday's* migraine refusing to die—slowed her thinking as well as her pace. Grant walked alongside as she led him through the labyrinthine asylum.

"I don't suppose you speak Spanish?" she asked, as they navigated the book-lined halls.

"No," Grant replied, wondering what it must've been like for the patients who once called this place home.

If they hadn't lost their minds before, this place would certainly do it . . .

"No matter," Morgan replied. "I'll translate."

He glanced at her, thoughtful. "How many languages do you speak?"

"Three thousand, eight hundred fifty-seven. But many are dialects."

Grant nearly tripped over his feet.

"What I do is not merely about remembering the facts that I'm exposed to," she reminded him. "I have razor-sharp clarity. I *memorize* every single fact I encounter. Without even having to try."

"So . . . all you'd have to do is read a foreign dictionary once, and you'll become fluent in the entire language?" He began catching on.

"It takes some time to learn syntax and grammar. And idioms, local colloquialisms, and pop culture references are often lost on me, so I don't know how I'd fare if I ever visited any of those countries in person. But I can get by."

Grant dwelled on that a moment. "So what does this Marta do? What's her mental thing?"

"The most peculiar I've ever encountered," Morgan replied. "Think of the most *analytical* person you've ever known. Such a person would be capable of looking at a situation, weighing the possibilities quickly, and determining potential outcomes to various actions they might take."

Grant thought of Evers. "Sure, okay."

"Imagine that kind of analytical mind magnified times ten," Morgan said. "Times *twenty*. Possibly even one hundred."

"So . . . what? She can predict what's going to happen in my future?"

"Not as such," Morgan replied. "She sees . . . potentialities. If she fully grasps the dynamics of a situation—and she always does, very quickly—she can determine all eventual outcomes of that situation. With remarkable accuracy."

Grant absorbed this. "So if meeting her is this important, why didn't you bring me to see her before?"

"It took some . . . convincing . . . for her to agree to meet you."

Morgan approached the lonely door at the far end of one corner of the building. With a gentle knock, she opened it and ushered Grant inside.

"This is Marta," she said.

"Hello," Grant offered, but the elder woman did not react.

"This," Morgan addressed Marta, switching to Spanish, *"is my friend . . ."*

Marta immediately lifted her eyes and focused on Grant. Her pupils contracted at the sight of him, and through her lips suddenly passed the words, *"El Traerador."*

Grant didn't have to speak the language to know what phrase she'd just uttered. He exchanged a glance with Morgan, already frowning at the mention of the Bringer.

"Sí," Morgan replied. "He's come to meet you."

The old woman studied Grant like a dead insect on a microscope slide. She didn't strike him as unkind, yet he was never comfortable with this kind of scrutiny.

"Is she going to talk, or what?" his eyes swiveled to Morgan.

Before she could answer, Marta made what sounded like an off-hand remark to Morgan. Morgan nodded.

"What'd she just say?" Grant asked accusingly.

"She said your impatience will be your downfall."

He scowled.

Marta's tone changed when she began speaking again. She sounded like a storyteller, revealing ancient wisdom with the greatest of passion.

"The winds of change are blowing through these old bones," Morgan translated as Marta seemed to be choosing her words carefully. "And if you have ears to hear, you will know and understand what they are trying to tell you. The very earth feels . . . *different*."

Grant swallowed. "Different how?"

Marta continued before Morgan could relay the question. "Danger surrounds you from all sides. Yet the truth eludes you, though it has been within your grasp from the beginning. Soon you will find it impossible to ignore."

She said something else, which Morgan didn't translate right away.

"Are you certain?" Morgan asked, and Marta repeated her words precisely, the same vocal inflections.

Grant watched.

"She says," Morgan said, facing Grant at last, "that the choices you make will decide the fates of all."

Grant hesitated. "'All' of you here at the asylum?" he clarified.

Morgan conferred with Marta.

"She will only say 'all'," said Morgan.

Marta spoke again.

"Something . . ." Morgan translated slowly, "something *unbelievable* . . . is about to happen."

Outside the asylum, Hannah leaned back against Grant's car. Anyone who saw her there might have assumed she was waiting for Grant to come out.

But instead, she was angrily wiping at her eyes, which were burning red. She gazed upward, searching the afternoon sky. She wiped them again, fighting the overwhelming feeling that was surging up within her.

Finally she stood up, away from the car, and retrieved her phone. She keyed in speed dial.

"I'm out," she said, when the person on the other end answered. "You better think *long and hard* before you threaten me! I did what you wanted. But my part is *over*. I'm out!"

33

"I don't actually know his name . . ." Alex said.

Grant towered over her, angrily staring her down in front of the hospital's main entrance. As agreed, he had met her just as the sun was descending. Her chosen hiding place was behind a grouping of shrubs.

"You said you work for him!" Grant shouted.

"Yeah," Alex replied. "I didn't say the two of us are best pals. I've never even met the guy. Or maybe the gal. I don't really know which. My orders always come by carrier."

Grant sighed, stifling his frustrations once again. His thoughts turned back to Morgan's subtle warning about running headlong into avoidance of how he felt. Once again, he'd been confronted by huge revelations—his father's possible faked death, Morgan's surprising confiding in him, Hannah's admissions, Marta's predictions—and yet here he was, turning to another enormous task.

But what does she expect me to do? Sit around and mope?

And stopping long enough to consider how all of this seemed to center on him, the sheer improbability of it all . . .

It was unbearable.

"So . . . is this boss of yours interested in helping me as much as you are?"

"What makes you think he hasn't already?" she said knowingly. "Be careful who you trust, sweetie, but be *more* careful who you assume your enemy is. Things are never that cut and dried."

"Why is he manipulating all of us? What's he after, in the end?"

"He wants to rig the game, no mistaking that. But as to what the game is exactly . . . you'd have to ask him."

"I don't believe you," he said suspiciously. "You can't tell me you've worked for him—or her—for *this long* and don't know *anything* about him. Is he the good guy or the bad guy?"

She nodded. "All I can give you is his title. I've heard it a few times, though don't ask me how—I'm not supposed to know it. And whatever you do, don't repeat it to anyone."

He waited impatiently as she took a dramatic breath.

"He's called the *Keeper*."

He almost laughed.

The Bringer. And the Keeper.

Doesn't that *sound like a happy combination?*

"Yeah," she replied. "Now I held up my end of the bargain . . ."

"Fine," he said resignedly. "Tell me where to find this person who needs my help so desperately."

"There you go again, always assuming the worst," Alex sighed, hands on hips. "Just because this guy needs your help doesn't mean you're going home empty-handed in this. This guy's in seriously bad condition, but he's in worse danger the longer he stays here. *You're* going to have to find a way to get him out. And he's going to need supplies and equipment to recover—"

"What do you mean, I'm not going home empty-handed?"

"Mosey up to Room 458 and find out."

Lisa stirred when she heard a nurse come in to check Daniel's vitals. It was dusk outside, yet she was surprised to see Daniel awake again so soon. His swelling had gone down considerably in the last few days, and it was nice to see him looking more like his old self again, even *with* all the bandages.

She smiled at him and he offered something resembling a smile in return. But she knew that half-smile better than he realized. His mind was preoccupied.

Lisa waited until the nurse left to speak. "What are you thinking?"

"About how I asked you not to leave me here alone. But it's been days now, and really, if something was going to happen, I think it would have by now. Please go home and get some rest. That chair can't possibly be comfortable."

"What are you talking about?" Lisa replied with a smile. "Me and this chair have bonded. We've been through some experiences together. I'm not going *anywhere*."

He smiled wearily at her. "Lisa, everything you've done for me has been wonderful. I've been through traumatic things before; I've pulled through things—well, maybe not worse than this, but still pretty bad. Now I think it's time to be honest. I'm not escaping from here. What comes, comes."

"Quitter," she replied, in a voice that almost made him smile.

Daniel sighed. "You know . . . even if you *could* get me out of here, where would you even take me? The lab has been destroyed, my home and your apartment probably aren't secure . . ."

"I know a place," she replied. When he eyed her curiously, she said defensively, "I *have* thought this through, you know."

He smiled. "You always have been the brains of the operation."

"I can't believe you finally figured that out!" She laughed out loud.

He laughed as well, but then started gasping when the laughter triggered his cracked ribs. He brought both hands up to brace his chest as he tried to catch his breath. Lisa jumped up and helped, placing his oxygen mask back over his mouth and nose until the pain subsided.

It was a while before he removed the mask and lay back on his inclined bed.

Lisa returned to her chair and shook her head at him. "This Grant Borrows person . . . What makes you so sure that he's worth all this? Worth everything you've been through?"

"I have my reasons," Daniel croaked. When she wouldn't release his gaze, he added, "There are plenty of things about me you still don't know."

She was about to respond when everything went black.

The power went off all over the entire hospital, but the emergency generators immediately kicked in. It wasn't enough electricity to power everything in the building, only the essential systems. The medical equipment Daniel was hooked up to continued unabated, but the only light came from the emergency beams out in the hall.

They heard panicked screams erupt from other rooms on the floor, and nurses running around, trying to keep patients calm and making sure everyone was okay.

Once her eyes had adjusted, Lisa finally saw Daniel again. Terror had returned to his eyes, and she looked away before he saw her notice it. Instead, she took his hand in a reassuring way.

"Must be a storm coming up or something," she tried.

"This is it, isn't it?" Daniel whispered. "They're coming for me."

She tried to show him a reassuring smile, but the screams were closer now. They both turned to look through the open door.

The patrolman outside was already on his feet, and he peeked inside the doorway. "Don't leave this room," he growled. "Lock the door."

Lisa did as commanded and then rejoined Daniel and took his hand again.

"It's okay, it's probably nothing. Maybe a car hit a power line . . ." she was saying. The room was almost pitch dark, the only light now coming from the city lights outside the window.

"Lisa, I ought to tell you something," Daniel said gently.

Her heart pounded madly in her chest, but before he could say anymore, there was a loud crash against the door from the other side. She screamed.

They clutched each other's hands even tighter.

Strange sounds came from outside, and they continued to watch as something else crashed into the door, and then there were grunts and kicks and blows.

A loud pop like a small explosion went off somewhere out there, and there was one last violent crash against the door, before everything went silent. They heard jangling, the sound of keys.

Lisa looked at the man beside her and whispered. "Daniel, I—"

He turned and looked at her. "You've never called me 'Daniel' before."

The door crashed open, and they both gasped.

The policeman slumped to the floor just inside the doorway, his body propped up against it from the outside.

Standing behind him in the doorway was a tall silhouette. A man. He produced an empty gurney and steered it into the room.

"I . . . I'm here to, uh . . . rescue you," the man stated. "Apparently."

"Sorry, *who* are you again?" Lisa asked skeptically as she ran along beside their mysterious savior, dragging Daniel's I.V. stand.

"It's not important," Grant replied, maneuvering Daniel's gurney through the dark corridors and toward an elevator.

"Power's still out," Lisa breathed. "How's an elevator supposed to help?"

"They operate on a back-up grid, in case of emergencies," Grant explained, turning around to drag the gurney onto the elevator car. Daniel looked horrid with both legs outstretched in full casts, his right ankle still sporting the complex metallic contraption. He seemed to be worn out already from all of the excitement, but he startled when Grant pulled him over the doorsill and the gurney bumped.

"Easy!" Lisa screeched. "He's not a sack of potatoes!"

Grant sighed.

"How do you intend to get us out of here?" Daniel whispered.

"No worries," Grant replied. "I've been in tighter spots than this."

"I feel better already," Lisa muttered.

The elevator arrived and Grant allowed the adrenaline to flow, to begin to build up . . .

The lights were coming back up on the bottom floor, where there was a great deal of commotion. It was almost shoulder-to-shoulder as hospital workers kept coming out of their offices to find out what was going on.

"Hannah, are we ready?" Grant whispered into his earpiece.

"*Stand by,*" was the terse reply. She'd been acting funny since their last conversation, but there wasn't time to reflect now.

A moment later, the building's fire alarm went off. Grant wrapped his fingers tightly around the gurney's handle and walked, Lisa working hard to keep up. But instead of heading for the exit, he turned and went deeper into the hospital.

"What are you *doing*?" Lisa cried.

Grant ignored her and kept running. Down a series of winding hallways, he made for a doorway marked "Surgery."

"Get the door," he instructed.

Lisa was exasperated, but she complied, watching Grant with eyes of fire.

He pushed Daniel through, into the abandoned department.

"Third door on the right," Hannah instructed in his earpiece.

"I see it," he answered.

"Who are you talking to?" Lisa exclaimed. Then she noticed the heavy, wide, metal door he was aiming for. It looked like some kind of special exit used only for delivery of organs brought in for emergency transplant procedures. "We'll never get that open!"

"I know," Grant replied, turning inward. He allowed the panic to build and build, until his body convulsed, his brain seized, and he nearly fell to the ground. When he opened his eyes, the metal door was gone, resting on the cement ground outside in two crumpled pieces.

Lisa was gaping at him in shock, but managed to gather her wits as he wheeled Daniel through the open doorway. An ambulance came out of nowhere and screeched to a halt directly in front of them, blocking their path, Hannah at the wheel.

"This thing should have enough supplies to last him a while," she reported quietly. "I'll drop you off, gut it, and ditch it someplace."

Grant and Lisa hitched the gurney into its lowest position and lifted it into the ambulance floor, sliding it inside as though they were paramedics who'd done it all their lives. Once it was secure, and they'd climbed in after, Grant pounded on the front panel and shouted "Go!" to Hannah.

After they were out on the road, Grant climbed up front.

"Are you sure about this?" Hannah asked. "I mean, he's gonna need some heavy-duty medical know-how."

"Let me worry about that, would you?" he snapped.

"Sorry. Just figured you'd want to make sure he gets better."

"Got a lot of people asking me for that these days," Grant muttered loud enough for her to hear it.

A stop light turned red and she was forced to halt the vehicle. "Maybe I shouldn't have come. You're so good at everything, you probably could have handled this just fine without me."

"I probably could!" he shouted louder than he'd intended.

Why am I angry at her? he instantly thought.

Their eyes met—tears in hers and exhaustion in his—and their features softened. An unspoken apology was expressed on her face. Her beautiful face and those round eyes, full of longing . . .

In that moment, Grant knew *exactly* how he felt about her. It was undeniable.

His hand found its way across the space between them and pushed hair out of her eyes, behind one ear, and held its place there, cradling her jaw. She made no move to pull away . . .

"How did you do that thing with the door?" Lisa shouted from the back, after Grant's arm had returned to his seat and a comfortable silence had passed.

"I don't have time to explain," he said, turning around. "My name is—"

"Borrows," Daniel croaked. "You're Grant Borrows, aren't you?"

Grant nodded in shock.

"Then you and I have a great deal to talk about."

34

Thankfully, Grant's keycard operated the service elevator in the Wagner Building or they wouldn't have been able to get Daniel upstairs. Night cloaked their movements and as soon as they had him comfortable and the medical supplies from the ambulance stowed, Hannah left to dump the vehicle.

When she left, Lisa cornered Grant. "You listen to me," she said quietly. "What's happened to Daniel—I mean, *Dr. Cossick* . . . All those broken bones and bruises and internal bleeding? It's because of *you*. He lost everything—"

Grant watched as she stopped to collect herself, pools forming beneath her eyes.

He wondered just how close these two were.

"So I'm telling you *right now*," Lisa said, a fierceness appearing behind her vulnerability. "If I find out that you weren't worth what he's done for you . . . I will make you live to regret it."

Grant blinked, thumbing his ring nervously from underneath. "Um, yeah . . . You got it."

Julie appeared from her bedroom, ignored the visitors and turned straight to Grant.

"What did you do now? And why did you steal an ambulance?" she asked, sleepy.

"How do you know about that?" he asked.

"It's all over the news. Or rather, you are. They've got police sketches of you and everything that they're showing on television.

Saying you were involved in another kidnapping—after *my* abduction—this time of a local research scientist." She saw Daniel for the first time on his gurney near the window and stopped for a long second. "Okay," she said, testy, "explanation. *Now*."

"Well—" Grant replied but Lisa interrupted.

"I tried to get him to take a rest, recover his strength, but he's determined to talk to you. So come on."

Grant and Julie followed Lisa back into the living room. Daniel's head was turned to the window and the shimmering sea of lights that filled the dark as sure as stars filled the sky. He appeared lost in thought at the sight of it all.

As if sensing Grant approach, he let out a shuddering breath.

"I have a question," Daniel said, wringing his hands together again and again, turning his eyes to Grant. "If your entire identity is stripped away from you . . . what remains? What's still there? Who *are* you, really?"

Julie hung back toward the couch, but Grant stood in place. "So you know, then," he said.

"I suspected."

Grant sat on the arm of the couch where Daniel could see him.

"Forgive me," Daniel tentatively began. "This is Lisa. My assistant. Do you prefer Grant or Collin?"

"Grant. My sister, Julie."

"Of course," Daniel nodded nervously. "Please call me Daniel."

Lisa retrieved a clear bag of fluid from a handful of supplies she'd brought from the ambulance—Hannah was due back in an hour or so with more—and hung it from a metallic rod sticking out of the top of Daniel's wheelchair. She plugged the line from the saline I.V. bag into the matching line still sticking out of his forearm.

Daniel nodded a quick thanks to her and then turned his attention back to Grant. Lisa walked to the countertop that separated the kitchen from the living room and leaned back against it. She merely stood there, watching and listening.

"I don't know how to answer your question," Grant said, standing and approaching the gurney. "I'm still trying to figure that out. A few weeks ago, everything was normal. Now, I have a different name, a different face, and a different life. And I can do things that no one should be able to do . . ."

"Yes, I know," Daniel's eyes danced with a twitchy energy that was disproportionate to his damaged body. "And to have come so far in only a handful of days . . ." he echoed thoughtfully. "I, on the other hand, have been waiting for this moment for *much* longer than two weeks."

Daniel swallowed and groaned as he shifted on his makeshift bed. "I have so much I need to tell you, and I hope you'll allow me a bit of patience as I sort all this out. As you can see, it hasn't been an easy road getting here."

"What's happened to you?" asked Grant, unable to hold the question back any longer. "And why were you in danger at the hospital?"

"I had a run-in with a detective named Drexel."

"We've met," Grant grimaced. "*He* did this to you? Why?"

Daniel averted his eyes and dabbed at his forehead again. "I think he was growing desperate. Drexel's one aim of late seems to have been to track you down," he said meekly. "But before you let yourself feel too badly about your part in this, you should probably know that I'm not exactly guiltless, in the grand scheme."

"Meaning?"

"We'll get to that," Daniel said, casting a glance at Lisa. "First, would you mind filling in the blanks for me on what's happened to you? I mean, I know some of it, but I need to piece the details together. All of them."

Grant studied the other man. Daniel already knew what he could do, and he appeared to know the truth about who he used to be. Giving him the remaining particulars posed little risk.

So Grant told him.

He told him about that first day, about his sudden, inexplicable Shift and his encounter with the other man—Collin, the man who'd taken on the identity of his former self. He showed Daniel the ring he wore, and explained what little he understood about his strange new mental ability. He told him about saving Julie from the hit man, Konrad, and their struggle in his old apartment.

Grant continued the story with his adventure at Inveo Technologies and what he found out there about Harlan Evers. He told him about meeting Hannah, and Morgan, and her unusual home and the others who lived there, the Loci. He told him about his encounter at Drexel's home, and what he did to the place. He told him about meeting Harlan Evers at the military base, and the bombshell the old man had dropped on him about his father—before the general was murdered by his own troops.

And lastly, he told Daniel about Alex, and what she claimed her role was in all of this. He ended by mentioning the person Alex said she worked for—the Keeper, the presumed mastermind who had somehow engineered Grant's Shift.

He didn't leave out a single detail that he could recall. It was the first time he had told the entire story to one person, and it was the first time Julie had heard some of the most recent information.

And all the while, Daniel listened with rapt attention, barely moving and hardly blinking at all.

Finally, Grant finished his story and fell silent.

He watched as Daniel processed this new data. It was a while before he attempted to speak.

"That's . . . something," Daniel mumbled. "Under normal circumstances, I would find it all too incredible and coincidental to believe. That is, if I didn't know what I came here to tell you. You see . . . where you see a sequence of random events, random manipulations . . . I see intent at work. I see *purpose*."

Alex was home asleep in her bed when a hand was placed over her mouth to prevent her from screaming.

"My dear little girl . . ."

She froze, her eyes darting about. She knew that voice.

"Don't be afraid," said the man who had forced entry into her home.

Yet she nearly hyperventilated. This was impossible; her home was one hundred percent secure from outside influence.

"I'm not going to kill you. I'm not even going to arrest you," he continued.

Drexel.

"You're much too valuable for that. I have bigger plans."

The Thresher's sword clanged loudly against Devlin's, the regal white-haired man *tsk*-ing and shifting his eyes unfavorably, as his feet danced lightly across the mat.

"I see you still cling to your sword's grip too tightly," the older man frowned, disapprovingly.

The Thresher lunged. "I see you still talk too much during a match."

But Devlin spun away, surprisingly fast for a man of his age, and sliced into the Thresher's left shoulder, leaving a red streak. The Thresher moved like lightning and cut a shallow gash into his mentor's right leg.

They had been at this for hours in a solitary sparring room at a local gym, having told the building's owners that they were merely sparring with rubber-tipped weapons. But they were all too real, and the Thresher had learned long ago not to rush the elder man's speeches. He would make his point when he was ready, and no sooner.

Devlin slashed into the Thresher's arm again, a cut deep enough this time to leave blood on his blade. The old man seemed more put-out by this success than his pupil.

"Is *this* what you consider fast these days?" he spat, taking a closer look at the red streak on his sword.

Which accent was it this time? Australian? Kiwi? The Thresher couldn't tell and had long ago given up trying to guess them all. Devlin had always been shifting between dozens of accents and dialects for as long as the Thresher had known him. It was a way of becoming invisible when the elder gentleman was forced to venture out into public. Yet he kept up the practice daily, whether public or private.

Man of a thousand pretenses, the Thresher thought. It was just one of the many reasons he had come to despise the man.

For his part, the Thresher had no time nor use for deception. He found it pointless.

The Thresher watched him through vicious eyes. "I could take you with ease," he replied, his weapon held low and threatening.

"Yes I know. As do you," Devlin said, lunging sharply to the right. The Thresher dodged the blow with a swift twist to his left and a parry. "Your skills have never been uncertain." The Thresher swung low and Devlin jumped. "You were beaten and taken captive by men with no proficiency of any kind. Because you knew there was no one who could defeat you."

The Thresher stopped. "I've grown overconfident." It was very nearly a question.

But not quite.

"You have no room for exploitable weaknesses. Your task is too critical. You know what is at stake, what now depends on you."

The Thresher swished and disarmed his opponent with a cunning flick. Devlin's sword went flying through the air.

"I do."

"And you know *why* all of this falls to you?" Devlin asked though he certainly knew the answer.

"I know why *you* believe it is my task. And I have agreed to take it on. But I do not share your convictions."

Devlin shook his head. "To know all that you know, and still not worship as the Secretum does. I shall never understand it."

The Thresher met his gaze coldly, uncaring what the other man thought of his beliefs.

Devlin squared his shoulders and placed his hands behind him. Back to business. "You have his location?" he asked calmly.

"I'm close."

"Then return to your duty."

Lisa insisted they stop so Daniel could rest, but the man shrugged her off. He couldn't sleep at this point anyway. It was better to push through. The time to rest would come. Lisa argued, but without success, and finally sulked away.

Daniel asked Grant, "Have you ever heard the term 'psychokinesis' before?"

"Moving things with your mind?" Grant asked.

Daniel nodded. "Right. It's a fringe-science subset of parapsychology. Most 'rational' scientists completely discredit it without bothering to give it any genuine study, even though there are hundreds of documented, proven cases where no other explanation is available to rationalize how an unusual phenomenon occurred. Parapsychology is far more legitimate than it's given credit for.

"In recent years, it's become a central field of study in the science of war. Imagine the balance of power shifting in a fight because all of the enemy's guns have been removed from their hands, or their missiles are triggered to explode in the launch tube. The problem is, in almost every documented case where psychokinesis occurs, it's a random, subconscious act. The by-product of a strong emotion or a violent deed. If it isn't controllable, it's of no use."

"So *this* is what I've been doing? Moving things with my mind?"

"Not exactly," Daniel paused, taking a drink to quench his parched lips. "Your thoughts affect material around you. It's something much stronger than simply forcing your will onto an inanimate object. We found the knife that was embedded in the column in the subway. The results of tests we ran were . . . not at all what I was expecting."

"Keep talking."

"Well, there are pressurized weapons in the world capable of pushing solid metal deep into hardened concrete, but we *know* nothing like that was present in the subway. Which means only a powerful blast of energy or a projected force could have done it. So I was hoping to find a latent energy signature—an after-effect 'fingerprint' of whatever did this to the knife. But instead of showing an energy fingerprint, the readings we got indicated that the knife itself somehow had become energy."

Grant rubbed his forehead, glanced at Julie. "I'm sorry, I'm not following this."

"My theory," said Daniel, "is that somehow, your mind is able to transform its thoughts directly into energy. You didn't move the knife by thinking about it, because I don't think you were in control of what happened that way. When you panicked, your mind released some kind of energy that forced the knife as far away from you as it could go. Your brain produced this blast that was fairly random, but it accomplished its purpose: your life was saved. Now you're learning to control it, aren't you? That's how you got us out of the hospital."

Grant nodded.

"I can help you with this; it's the reason I've been searching for you. If you *do* gain control over it, it's possible that you could even overcome the coinciding headaches you mentioned."

If he was making a sales pitch, Grant was already sold. But something still felt off.

"What's the catch?" Grant said.

"The catch," replied Daniel, looking away, "is that you're going to have to trust me. Despite what I've been involved with."

Grant's eyes narrowed. "Why don't I like the sound of that?"

"For all the right reasons," Daniel said wistfully.

35

"Lisa?" Daniel called. She immediately sprung to attention and ran to him, fearing he was in some sort of pain. When she came near, he said, "I need you to go get something for me."

She looked at him suspiciously. "You want me to leave? *Now?*"

"I need something from the lab."

"There's nothing left at the lab," she said automatically, watching him closely.

"*This* will be," he said, not meeting her gaze. He directed her to move aside the desk in his office if it was still there and pry loose the floor tile directly beneath the left rear leg of the desk. Inside, she would find a box.

"I need that box," he said quietly.

She hesitated.

"I'll be safe here," he said. "Please."

"All right, but I'll be back quick." She turned to go.

"Be careful," he called out. "The police could still be watching the building."

When Lisa came to the door, she stopped short. She turned back to look at Grant, a quizzical expression written across her face.

Grant answered her unspoken question by reaching inside a pocket and pulling out his keys. He tossed them to her, and she caught them in one hand.

"The blue Corvette convertible," he said.

Daniel listened for her to be completely gone before he spoke again.

"Lisa's done most of our fact-finding on you. She's even been here to your apartment, but you weren't at home." His voice trailed off as he became lost in thought again.

Grant said nothing.

"She's a good person," Daniel said, looking back up. "She's treated me like family—closer, like . . ." he swallowed as his eyes moistened. "But she can't know what I'm about to tell you. Not ever. It . . . it would destroy her."

Grant sat up straight, glanced quickly at Julie. Daniel had his attention now.

"Despite what my detractors might tell you," he began, looking back up at Grant, "I *am* a very serious scientist. So please believe me when I say: what I'm about to tell you has taken a long time for me to accept." He took a deep breath and let it out slowly.

"Five years ago, I was working as a research technician at a major lab funded by a megacorporation."

"Let me guess," Grant interjected. "Inveo Technologies?"

"It was a company called Paragenics Group," Daniel replied. "But I understand Inveo has become one of their largest competitors over the years. Anyway, I wasn't working on anything terribly special. There were dozens of us working on the same kinds of things, although we were each allowed to have free rein and try our own methods. I was mapping brain responses to various stimuli.

"I had been there for nine months, happily working at proving various theories I had about the capabilities of the human brain and extra-sensory perception. I was experiencing more success than most of my colleagues, and scuttlebutt said that my work had not gone without notice from the higher-ups, that I would soon surpass my colleagues.

"Then, one day everything at the lab changed. A full staff meeting was called, and we were told that a private investor had purchased controlling interest in the company, and that we might notice a number of unfamiliar faces around the building. We were to think nothing of it."

"Who was the investor?" Grant asked.

"I never found out. But just as they said, soon there were dozens of new workers combing the facility—and not just scientists. Men and women in gray camouflage jumpsuits constantly made the rounds. We

were never told who they were, but we suspected they were some kind
of independent security force. Our building had security already, but
these guys . . . they wore no insignia, no emblem, nothing to identify
them. Nothing changed in regard to our work, though, so after a while,
we just got used to seeing them.

"But slowly, more and more new security measures were put into
place all around our building. None of us knew what it was about, but
you can imagine the rumors. Some of the scientists even resigned in
protest.

"One morning, one of the gray-clad men came to my lab and said I
was to report to a sub-level of the facility only available to those with
the highest level of clearance. He escorted me through a number of
checkpoints and inspections, but it seemed some sort of emergency was
taking place, so they couldn't afford to detain me very long.

"When I reached the secured area, it was a large, white underground hallway, enormous in size, and it ended in the distance with a
heavily secured vault door made of steel. Two security guards stood to
the left and right of the door."

Grant glanced at Julie. This sounded an awful lot like what they'd
found beneath Inveo Technologies.

"My escort handed me off to one of the company's senior staff members—a scientist herself—who met me there in the hall. She made me
sign a nondisclosure form on the spot, and warned me that if I were
ever to tell anyone what I was about to see, they would be within their
rights to bring the full legal weight of the company down upon me.

"To my disappointment, we didn't go through the vaulted door.
Instead, she ushered me into a small side room, where a group of about
half a dozen scientists in lab coats—none of whom I recognized—surrounded a man sitting in a chair in the middle of the room. There was
nothing in the room but the scientists and their subject, who wore a
standard hospital gown." He gestured at his own gown. "My companion
introduced me to the other scientists, and they acknowledged me with
guarded expressions. One or two of them shook my hand.

"They asked me to run some of the specialized tests I'd developed
on the man in the chair. I still have no idea who he was. He had the
most blank expression on his face I had ever seen, and he never moved
or spoke except while I ran the test. I had done these tests dozens of

times before, so even though I was uneasy with such an attentive audience, I did as I was told.

"I ran my tests for hours. I was used to getting maybe one right answer out of every twenty or so, if I was lucky. That was considered a 'good' score, and I'd never gotten anything higher out of the college students and others who volunteered for my tests. So you'll understand that it was one of the most profound moments of my scientific career when I watched this guy *nail* every test I threw at him. He was certifiably gifted; it was the most potent case of genuine ESP I have ever seen. Over the course of the afternoon, I tried every test I knew, and he defeated them all, even though he appeared barely cogent. I believe the scientists would have allowed me to keep going indefinitely, but after a few hours, I simply had nothing else left to try. It was the most thrilling, most astounding thing I'd ever witnessed.

"Finally, the scientists thanked me for my time and told me I could go. I suddenly remembered the nondisclosure agreement and was so disappointed that the vindication for all of my work had finally been discovered, yet I couldn't tell anyone about it. I couldn't imagine any reason they wouldn't want everyone in the world to know about this man and what he could do.

"But just as I was about to leave, the man fell to the floor. I was horrified, afraid that one of my tests had somehow triggered this. But the other scientists did little to help him—it was almost as if they'd been expecting this. I watched as blood oozed from his ears onto the floor.

"He was dead in minutes. Some kind of seizure, they told me. I must've looked panicked, because as soon as they'd determined the man was dead, they all turned to focus their attention on me. The woman who led me into the room grabbed me by the arm and led me back out. As we walked, she assured me that the proper authorities would be contacted and that I had nothing to worry about since I had been conducting perfectly legal, harmless scientific tests.

"I was so stunned, I simply wandered back upstairs to my office. But as the hours passed, the more my suspicions stirred. No ambulance or police cars arrived at the facility that day. No one ever came to question me as a witness. And as far as anyone else in the building proper knew, it was just another typical day at work.

"At quitting time, instead of leaving, I went back downstairs to the underground hallway. I still had my clearance from earlier in the day, and the guards stared at me, but they let me through, probably assuming I had been called back down. I went back to the room where we had conducted the tests, and to my surprise, I could hear from outside all of the scientists from earlier, still in the room. I put my ear to the door and listened.

"I couldn't make out everything they said, but I heard them repeatedly mention something called 'Project Threshold.' From the way they talked about it, succeeding with this project was the focus of whatever they were doing. As these thoughts went through my mind, something hit my head and I blacked out."

Daniel took an awkward pause, his eyes closed tight.

"When I awoke," he continued, "I couldn't move. I remember it was so cold, and so *quiet*. I was lying on my back, and I could turn my head to either side, but beyond that, I was completely immobilized. When my eyes adjusted to the brightness of the room, I found myself in this vast space—to call it a 'room' would be an injustice. It was what was on the other side of that enormous vault door. Lying all around me, filling the entire space were flat, cold, stainless steel tables just like the one I was on, and they were occupied.

"Men and women, all young adults, were lying on every table. And none of them could move, either, even though none of us were strapped down. I came to realize later that some kind of paralytic toxin had been used on us. Do you have any idea how that feels? To be completely unfettered, yet unable to move. It was . . . horrifying."

Daniel closed his eyes again, seeing it in his mind. "Some of the others were awake, some were unconscious. All of them wore hospital gowns like the dead man, and it was then I realized I was wearing one, too."

Grant watched as Daniel paused, closed his eyes, and shook his head.

"I watched as well as I could manage for over three hours as the people on the tables around me were subjected to every stimulus you can imagine. Electroshock, chemicals, gases, even direct neurological surgery. It was grotesque, dehumanizing. I wanted to cry out for help but was afraid to draw attention to myself. I tried to get my body to move, but it wouldn't obey. It was no use.

"The woman who had met me earlier appeared at the head of my table and looked down at me. I could see her upside down if I craned my head back. I asked her what all this was and what they were going to do to me.

"She said that curiosity may have killed the cat, but here, they had much better uses for the curious. The long and short of it is that my suspicions were essentially true. I had become one of the subjects of Project Threshold, which was dedicated to finding individuals with latent mental abilities, and activating those abilities. This was the 'threshold' they were trying to cross and access. What I was proving the existence of upstairs through legitimate testing, these people were trying to *force* into being through any means possible.

"They ran test after test on their subjects' mental outputs; anyone who registered a spike in output they referred to as a 'shimmer.' It was a shorthand code used to indicate a promising subject. But not one of their subjects survived the radical procedures long enough to be considered a success, just like the man I had tested for them earlier. I asked her why they were doing this, but she wouldn't say.

"They hooked me up to an artery line, and another scientist appeared with a syringe containing some kind of ugly, brown liquid. I was more scared than I'd ever been in my life, and all I could think about was that man who had collapsed on the floor, bleeding from his ears. I despised them for what they were doing, but I was . . . I was petrified . . ."

Daniel stopped speaking and suddenly he looked very pale. Tired. Like a feeble, elderly man. Grant wondered how the man lying prone before him could ever have escaped the predicament he described.

"God forgive me . . . I made a deal."

"You *what!*" Grant exclaimed. "How—?"

"I know, I know," Daniel said, dejectedly. "But when you're just lying there, at someone else's mercy, staring death in the face and you're absolutely, unequivocally powerless to stop it . . . the ethical questions just . . . go away. There *are* no options, no alternatives. If you've never been in that situation, you can't know. The human capacity for self-preservation forces all other choices out of the equation."

"*Of course* you had other choices!" Grant thundered. "Listen to you, trying to methodically justify your involvement in this . . . this *conspiracy*! You've actually lived with this long enough to make it into something okay, in your mind, haven't you? How long did it take you to come up with that bit about self-preservation?"

"Easy words when you're sitting in the comfort of home," Daniel replied dolefully. "Remember that if I hadn't made a deal with them, I wouldn't be here now, telling you what I know."

"That doesn't make it right!" Grant spat.

"Don't you think I know that?" Daniel shouted back at him. "Don't you think I lie awake every night, thinking of all those other test subjects, consumed with guilt?" He began coughing, clutching his chest with his good hand.

"Good! You *should* feel guilty!" Grant raged.

"Calm down . . ." Julie said quietly. She grabbed his arm and guided him back to his seat, though he had no memory of having stood. Then she went to the kitchen and got Daniel a glass of water. He received it gratefully.

"To finish my story," Daniel continued doggedly after recovering, "I reminded the Paragenics people of my success rate and managed to convince them that my skills were too valuable to be wasted this way. I suggested that I could help—not with their attempts to create mentally advanced humans, but in finding those who were born with mental gifts. They agreed, and since I had long proven that I work best in solitude, they left me to my own methods. I would function independently, outside of the company. But all of the work I did was for them, and they kept a *very* close eye on my activities.

"They implanted a tracer device into a filling in one of my back teeth. They offered me a strict budget from which to operate, and I was instructed to report back to them weekly on whatever findings I had, or the deal was off. If I missed a week reporting in, if I refused to continue my research, or if I told anyone what they were up to, they would use the tracer to track me down and I would be brought back to the vault. All they required was that I continue my research, attempting to find people with 'potent, enhanced mental skills' like they were looking for. They didn't care what methods I used to do it."

He leaned his head back, spent. "There, that's it . . . That's the secret I've been holding on to for five years, the thing that no one knows. Not even Lisa. I made a deal with the devil to save my skin. I'm a—"

"A *coward*," Grant said bitterly, but without raising his voice this time.

"Yes," Daniel replied. "And now I've got the rest of my life to try to make up for it."

Grant wanted to say more, but he was still angry and didn't trust himself.

When Grant remained silent, Daniel picked up his story. "I created methods of detection that were noninvasive," he said. "If I had to do this, I was determined that no would be hurt because of me. Most of the people I tested never even knew they were being studied. And every day I hoped and prayed that I would never find what I was looking for. But I had to at least *try*, or I was dead."

Daniel shook his head and then offered the tiniest hint of a smile. "When those thugs attacked me and my lab was destroyed . . . a part of me was *relieved*. It meant no more working for Paragenics, no more research. The tracer filling is gone from my tooth; it was knocked loose during the attack. I can finally, legitimately, get out from under their thumb."

Grant was still frowning angrily at Daniel, yet as his temper cooled, he tried to keep telling himself that Daniel had only done what most people would do in the same situation. And the poor guy was certainly broken and defeated enough as it was, without needing anyone else's judgment.

As Grant processed these things, along with Daniel's story, one question rose to the surface.

"You said you made regular reports to them. You called me on the phone over a week ago, so you've known about me and what I can do for at least that long. Did you tell your superiors about me?"

"Of course not!" Daniel looked startled, almost offended.

Grant was unabashedly suspicious.

"Grant, you wouldn't even be sitting here if they knew about you!"

"All right," Grant conceded. But another thought was buzzing in his head—one that had been building for a while as he'd listened to Daniel's tale. "What if I'm one of those people Paragenics experimented on? Or maybe I'm the product of one of their competitors, like Inveo Technologies. Could I be one of their successes?"

Daniel sat up straight, his eyes suddenly brighter.

"That's just the thing," Daniel said, his eyes wider now than Grant had yet seen them. *"That's* what I came here to tell you. Despite the millions of dollars Paragenics poured into its experiments . . . despite everyone that died at their hands . . . they *never* had a success. At least, not one that survived more than a few hours. They even abandoned Project Threshold about a year ago and filled in their underground labs with concrete, to make sure no one would follow their work. The company still exists, and they told me to continue my clandestine research on the off chance that I might succeed. But the 'Threshold' was never crossed. They never succeeded at all.

"Somehow, entirely on your own . . . *you did.*"

36

"Drop it, Fletcher."

"Why won't you tell me what she said?" he replied, watching her with those magnified eyeglasses of his.

"I've told you before, what Marta and I talk about stays between the two of us," Morgan told him, massaging her forehead.

"But something's different this time, I can tell," he whined. "She told you something about Grant, didn't she? Something big. Something you didn't want to hear."

Morgan cut her eyes away from him, mildly irritated. It was then that she noticed how full the Common Room was today. Quite a few visitors staying this week.

Every one of them were Loci, of course.

"I'm not answering your questions, Fletcher."

"You just did."

"Will you leave it alone?" she said, louder. A few others in the room turned and looked.

"Why are you so intent on trusting this guy?" Fletcher said, his volume rising to match hers.

"Why are you so intent on *not* trusting him?" she shouted.

Fletcher frowned and leaned back in his seat. Everyone in the room was watching now. Morgan *never* shouted.

"I'll say it again. His ring may be different than everyone else's," Fletcher said. "But it can't possibly be *that* important."

"And yet," Morgan said, leveling her gaze on him, "it *is*."

"How do you know?" Fletcher challenged.

"Because his coming was predicted over seven *thousand* years ago," she replied, to audible gasps throughout the room. Not one of the Loci knew of the existence of the stone tablet, aside from herself and Grant. "*Believe it*, all of you. In fact, let everyone know," she said, turning to address the entire room. "The magnitude of this cannot be overstated. He is *the Bringer*. And his time is near."

"*You* breached the Threshold, Grant," Daniel said. "This is the reason I've been trying so hard to find you. I couldn't care less about what Paragenics might want with you—I just want to *help* you. Because you've succeeded where no one else *ever* could."

."But I *didn't*!" Grant protested. "At least, I never *chose* to. Everything that's happened to me has been completely outside of my control." .

"Which is the unavoidable point we keep coming back to . . ." Daniel thought aloud, nodding. He looked away, considering this for a few moments, following this thought to its conclusion . . .

And then a dawn of comprehension passed over his face and his mouth opened as he looked up at Grant, locking eyes with him.

"All these years," he said urgently, "I've known *what* Paragenics and their rivals were up to, but I never knew *why*. Why was it so important for them to cross this threshold? *Why* were they willing to risk illegal experimentation with such a high body count? What could *possibly* be so important? And now that I know your story . . . I think I'm finally beginning to understand.

"I assumed," Daniel continued, "that Paragenics was doing what they were doing for military applications. Power. Money. I figured they were trying to create a new breed of soldier—and probably for the highest bidder. But they failed miserably, and their work was abandoned.

"From what you've told me, though, it looks like the results they were after are appearing in hundreds of people—if not more—entirely at random. From a spectator's point-of-view, there's *nothing* connecting all of you to one another, except for these strange rings on your fingers. But what if there *is* something that connects all of you?"

Grant took Julie's hand in his and leaned forward in his chair, desperate to understand. "What, then?"

"The Loci you mention—*all* of their abilities could have strategic defensive or offensive applications, if used correctly. They make you unique—or more *advanced* than your average human. So *if* advanced human beings are popping up all over the world *now*, then the logical conclusion is that there must be a reason for it. I told you I saw a purpose, a design in all of this. What if that purpose isn't one that science can explain?"

"Then what could explain it?" Grant shoved his hand close to Daniel's face. "I mean, look at this thing. There's no way it just landed there on its own."

"If it's not a natural occurrence," Daniel said quietly, "then it must be a *super*natural one."

Grant leaned back, looking at Daniel anew. "I don't believe in the supernatural."

". . . Said the man who was placed inside a new body."

"But you're a scientist! How can you possibly believe in some hocus-pocus explanation for all this?"

"Grant, you have to understand . . ." Daniel said, taking on his best scholarly tone. "Scientists study the order of nature. But one thing science has *never* been able to explain is *why* that order exists. Why are there scientific laws that hold the universe together? Why doesn't everything spiral out of control, into chaos? As much as we try to reason our way around it, some parts of our existence simply can't be explained with formulas or proofs.

"The human brain's complexity, for example. Our ability to be self-aware and have consciousness and reasoning and imagination. The fact that as vast as the solar system is, our planet rests in the one orbit—the one *precise* position around our sun that's capable of supporting life. There are a million examples all around us."

Grant sighed, shaking his head bitterly. "You're sounding less and less like a scientist, Doc. Here I thought you were going to explain to me how all of this is even possible. Instead, you want me to believe that 'fate' magically intervened. Even if that were true, *why*? Why did I have to go through the Shift? Why couldn't I have been given this ring as Collin Boyd?"

"Listen to yourself, Grant," Daniel said urgently. "Don't you see? You're answering your own question. If all this is happening *now*, to *you* . . . then it's happening to you now *for a reason*. A reason outside human understanding," he said with a note of finality.

A reason outside human understanding?

What kind of answer was that?

What possible reason could there be?

Grant froze.

Julie watched him fearfully, not understanding.

A chill crept down Grant's spine as a single thought went off in his head like a flash bomb.

"I'm going to be *needed* . . ." he said, facing Daniel, face stricken with alarm.

Grant looked down, lost in his thoughts. But Daniel studied him intently. Grant followed the line of reasoning through to the same conclusion that the doctor had apparently perceived only moments ago.

Grant's head snapped back up to look Daniel in the eye.

In that instant, he *had it*.

At long last, he *knew*.

All of the questions he had about why this had happened to him. All of his fears. His doubts. His confusion. Everything he had learned about himself, about what he could do. The rings. The stone tablet. The others that had been Shifted.

It all came crashing together in one perfect moment of crystallization.

For the first time in a very long time, *everything* made sense.

"*Something's coming* . . ." he breathed, his eyes enormous.

Daniel nodded gravely. Julie gasped, hand flying up to cover her mouth.

Grant leaned back in his seat, his mind swimming, his heart pounding visibly beneath his shirt.

"Something bigger than *anything* that has ever been," Daniel was saying slowly, with great emphasis. "Something the rest of humanity is not equipped to deal with. I can't even *guess* what shape it might take, or when it will happen, but the logical conclusion here is that you, and possibly the others, are meant to stop it."

Grant sat back in his chair, trying to suppress the feeling of weakness that had overcome him. A cold sweat broke out across his brow and he closed his eyes, trying to get a handle on what all this meant.

He finally understood. Not *how*. But definitely *why*.

Something was coming. Something only he would be able to stop.

It was preposterous!

Who was *he* to save the world? And who would be foolish enough to choose him for it?

He was no one.

And the others? What of them?

As he thought of Morgan and Hannah and all of the others that had been Shifted, an odd sensation encompassed him, as if every part of his body had been hit with a mild electric shock, right down to his marrow.

He opened his eyes to see Daniel gaping at him.

"Grant, what—?" Daniel was saying.

Grant looked down.

His ring was glowing.

It had only glowed one time before—the night it shimmered in the graveyard after Collin had been buried.

But something was different. This wasn't the same as before.

Instead of shimmering evenly, the light was growing.

"Daniel . . ." Grant said in alarm as he watched the light become brighter.

And then the blinding pain returned, jolting him with such intensity that he fell off the sofa. It was worse than ever before. He clutched his head with both hands, as if he could somehow stop the unbearable pain by squeezing his skull.

NO NO NO!!

"Collin!" Julie screamed, kneeling at his side, trying to keep him from convulsing.

The pain spread the brighter the light became. From Grant's head down through every part of his body—chest, arms, hands, legs, feet—it was everywhere. Searing, ripping, shredding through him with an intensity beyond anything he'd ever imagined possible.

He writhed on the floor, screaming, twitching as if his flesh was being wrenched off of his bones.

Morgan had just stood from her chair when a prickling

sensation at the back of her neck told her something was wrong.

All around the Common Room, everything was growing brighter. And the light was still rising.

But it wasn't a natural light; outside it was the dead of night.

Everywhere the Loci sat, stood, talked, played, watched television, read, or slept—throughout the entire facility, all of their rings had begun to glow.

The collective glow grew brighter and brighter until it became impossible to see anything other than white.

Hannah grabbed her keys. She'd dumped the ambulance at LAX, wiped it of prints, and had taken a cab back to her apartment to shower and change. The doctor they rescued probably was asleep which meant she might get Grant to herself.

Before she could open her door, though, a warmth grew at her hand and she watched amazed as the ring on her finger glowed white hot until she melted into it.

Daniel strained to see through the blinding, shimmering light, which continued to grow brighter and brighter, until closing his eyes no longer impeded it.

He tried blocking his eyes with an arm, but still it seemed that he could *feel* the light penetrating every pore of his body. Grant was thrashing about on the floor, and Julie was now screaming as well. Soon, he joined them, until the only sound in the apartment was desperate, anguished wailing.

And then, as unexpectedly as it had began, the light flashed out of existence, as though its power had been cut.

When Daniel opened his eyes, his vision was gone.

"Grant?" he called out repeatedly.

There was no answer, though he could hear Julie weeping.

Several minutes passed before his sight finally returned. When it did, Daniel strained to see the spot where he'd last looked at Grant.

Grant was still lying there on the floor.

But he was unconscious, curled into a fetal ball.

Frozen in a repose of infinite pain.

Julie was cradling him, weeping uncontrollably. Daniel asked no questions of Julie. There were none necessary.

His lips looked blue.

He wasn't moving.

And his chest was still.

All through Morgan's asylum, every person—Morgan, Fletcher, Marta, and the more than fifty other Loci currently in residence or visiting—all of them spontaneously crumpled to the floor, unconscious.

Hannah collapsed by herself next to her apartment door.

All of the others who had experienced the Shift, all around the world—including those who had never been accounted for—all of them, everywhere, slid into oblivion at the precise moment that their rings stopped glowing.

Not a single one of them moved.

Not one of them breathed.

THE KEEPER *knew*.

Knew that Grant had met with Daniel. Knew what the two of them had figured out. Knew who Hannah had been working for, until recently. And that Alex was helping Grant, blatantly against orders, but had just been removed from the playing board.

The Keeper knew exactly what had just happened to all of those who wore the rings, and what it would mean.

Most of all, the Keeper knew of the threat that was coming.

The Keeper smiled at the thought of so much meticulous preparation coming together like a perfectly strategized game of chess.

It was only a matter of time.

History, after all, could not be avoided.

The Bringer was close now.

Very close.

37

A cloud.

No, a mist.

A misty cloud.

That's what it was.

That's what he saw.

That's what he was *inside of*.

It was beautiful, swirling in lovely, soothing hues of purple and pink and blue. It caressed his skin, and he decided he'd never felt a more peaceful sensation.

Some barely conscious part of him knew that nothing like this place existed anywhere in the world. Yet it felt remarkably comforting. Its soothing essence poured through him, saturating him with happiness.

A noise.

He heard something.

Grant looked ahead. A distortion of some kind was visible in the distance. It was an odd mixture of light and darkness, of sound and silence, that seemed to be coming closer. After a moment it resolved into a blurred outline Grant recognized as a person coming toward him.

The figure drew closer, and the sound grew louder.

Soon, he thought he heard words among the sound.

It was a voice.

A person.

Someone spoke. Or was it singing?

Whatever it was, it was drawing nearer in the tranquil, unruffled clouds. Despite his curiosity, and an elusive sense in the pit of his stomach that something wasn't right, Grant couldn't help reveling at the thought of staying here forever.

He only had a mild curiosity about the figure as it drew nearer— near enough for him to make out a humanlike shape. But everything was so peaceful here; there were no concerns, no fears.

"Grant," the voice said.

It came closer now, close enough to reach out and touch, and yet still all he saw was a milky outline.

"Hello, sweetheart," it said, the clouds rippling and shifting colors with every inflection.

He could think of no one who'd ever called him "sweetheart."

"It is an eternity in a moment, given to us," the voice replied.

What's happening to me?

Where did that pain come from?

What is this place? he thought.

"It is the Forging," the shape continued in a remarkably smooth, dignified voice. A hue of yellow formed at the edge of the rippling mist as the shape spoke. "It began the first time the pain took hold of you, but you resist."

It hurts. It's too much. I can't take it.

"I know," it said soothingly. "But this is your portion. Everything has been leading to this moment, and it *must* be done. The others will not last without you."

They wouldn't want me to suffer.

"Suffering is not what this is about," it said sympathetically, the clouds' colors turning to soft pink. "Today is a new step in your journey; it is not the last. You must ask yourself what you are willing to go through, to reach the journey's end. Are you willing to sacrifice? Are you willing to absorb your greatest fear, and make it part of your very being? Are you willing to follow the path that has been set before you?"

No! I don't want this! I don't want any part of it.

"No flesh ever does. That isn't the point." The clouds were growing redder now . . .

I just want to stay here, Grant thought. And then another thought came to mind, something he intuitively knew was true, yet had not explanation for. *I want to stay with you.*

The form began to coalesce into a more distinctive shape. A shape he recognized as female.

"I want that, too, my love. But we are not asked what we want. Only what we are willing to *do*." The clouds reverted to their original blue and purple . . .

But why? *Why must I do this? What is all this about?*

"It's about living."

This is life? *Is this how life is supposed to be? Full of pain and injustice and grief and selfishness? Is this fair? Or right? Or just?*

"One day you will have the answers to every question. Stay true to yourself. *Nothing* is as it seems. Today, you must go back."

Her form took on the properties of skin and hair and clothing, and he saw her face for the first time.

She looked strikingly familiar.

"This is not the path I would have chosen for you, my beautiful boy. But it is what *is*, and there is no other who can traverse it. Go back now. Go back to the ones who need you."

Her face glowed the most beautiful, radiant, white light he had ever seen. It grew brighter and brighter . . .

"Mom!" Grant screamed.

His breathing came too fast; he was going to hyperventilate. But he couldn't slow himself.

Was that really her? Had he just seen his mother?

He looked around. He was in his bedroom. Sitting up in bed. He couldn't remember how he got here.

He felt a staggering soreness all over, as if every muscle in his body had been stretched and pulled and exercised beyond failure. Every movement brought a world of aches.

Before the dream—if it *was* a dream—the last thing he remembered was watching his ring glow brighter than bright. And then the pain, pain beyond imagining that had waged war on his entire system. No wonder he was sore.

But that place . . . that . . . *dreamscape* . . . it was familiar. He had seen it before . . . somewhere . . .

"You're awake!" a voice exclaimed. His sister. *"He's awake!!"* Julie called out, louder.

She ran and threw her arms around him, squeezing him tight. "Are you all right? What happened? How do you feel?"

Grant shook his head, not ready to share his dream yet.

The Forging, she called it . . .

Lisa appeared at the bedroom door. Daniel, too. She was pushing him in a wheelchair.

"Does anything hurt?" Daniel asked, inspecting him like a used car.

"Everything I own hurts," Grant moaned, wincing with each breath, each tilt of his head. Coupled with this was a crushing exhaustion. He barely had the energy to raise a finger.

"You looked like you were . . ." Daniel commented, "I've never seen anything like it."

"I don't—I . . . I can't explain it," Grant whispered, his mind charging full speed ahead though his breathing at last was slowing.

He remembered the pain that had encompassed him and how it felt. It was horrific. And then he had seen the mist and then . . . *her.*

"Did I die?" he whispered, his eyes still closed.

"No!" Julie cried.

Daniel hesitated. Grant couldn't believe the man was in a wheelchair. "I . . . don't know. Your breathing was almost nonexistent. Julie said you were cold to the touch. My best guess: you were in some kind of catatonia."

Grant looked down at his left arm and noticed the line sticking out of it for the first time. He carefully pulled it out, fighting the urge to wince with each new movement.

"We hooked you up to an I.V.," Julie explained, "to make sure you didn't dehydrate."

"I feel okay . . . Aside from the soreness. It's like a truck ran over me . . . and then a tank." He glanced outside his bedroom window, and the midday sun startled him. Plus it finally fully registered that Daniel was in a wheelchair. "Wait—how long was I out?" he asked.

Daniel looked at the watch wrapped around the cast on his broken wrist. "About thirty-six hours now."

Grant just looked at him. "I've been asleep for a day and a half?"

The three of them nodded in unison.

"But it feels like I haven't slept in *days!*"

The only response the others could give was to watch him with concern.

For a day and a half, I've been in a coma. Or . . . something.

What's happening to me?

What is the Forging?

And the woman?

She couldn't have been . . .

Could she?

He looked down at his ring. It had returned to normal. No glowing, no shimmering.

But as Grant settled uncomfortably into this skin again, he realized for the first time that he felt something else, something new that he couldn't explain. It was a very odd sensation.

"Have you talked to Hannah?" he asked. "Or Morgan, or any of the others?"

"No, we haven't heard from anyone," Julie replied.

Thirty-six hours and no word from Hannah or Morgan. Or even Alex.

He looked up again and saw them watching—*scrutinizing*—his every tick and movement.

"I'm going to need a little while to sort this out," Grant said, holding Julie's hands tighter than before. His thoughts were coming faster than he could keep up with—his blackout, his dream, Daniel's revelation about why he had been Shifted, his friends, his father, his mother.

Grant stopped and gazed at Daniel and Lisa. "Thanks for staying to help."

Daniel shook his head, looked down, unable to meet Grant's eyes. "Didn't think it would be a good idea to leave, under the circumstances."

"Thanks," Grant mumbled.

"Hope you don't mind," Lisa offhandedly remarked, "but we helped ourselves to one of your unused apartments. We didn't have anywhere else to go, and this building's got decent security tech . . ."

Grant stopped, midthought. Again. "What do you mean, *my* apartments?"

"This building was anonymously purchased two months ago. It took some digging but we finally found a trail that names you as primary owner," Daniel said. "According to the paperwork, you own the whole thing."

Grant laid back down. "Somebody wake me when the world stops being crazy."

But as soon as he'd closed his eyes, the strange new feeling asserted itself again. It was as though he'd forgotten something, something so significant that it was making him edgy and fretful. And it was becoming more pronounced with each moment that passed.

He sat back up with effort, and gazed out the bright window at the Los Angeles skyline beyond. "Something's wrong."

"I thought we established *that* with our *last* conversation," Daniel retorted.

"Not with . . . the world. It's something else," Grant replied, concentrating. "Something . . . closer, more personal."

"Like what?" Julie asked, watching him closely.

"I don't know, something's just . . . *off*," Grant replied, frustrated. He closed his eyes again. "I feel it."

"Do you feel it yet?" Drexel's voice whispered into her ear. "Has it started taking effect?"

Alex craned her neck to look into his eyes, only inches away from her own. "I really, really wish you were dead," she said drunkenly.

"Mmm," he muttered, backing away from the chair she was tied to. "You wouldn't have lied about that, anyway."

He grabbed another chair and sat directly in front of her. He glanced at his watch, calculating if enough time had yet passed for the truth serum to take effect. Her demeanor had changed in the last few minutes. She looked a little loopy and doe-eyed. But she could simply be trying to throw him off.

"What's your name?" he barked.

"Alex," she replied immediately.

The drug had taken effect.

"Okay, what's your last name?"

"Don't have one," she smiled, and giggled dreamily.

Drexel backhanded her across the face.

"Ow-w-w!" she yelled. "You are a mean, stupid, ugly man. And you're . . . *mean*."

"*Stop* wasting my time, little girl. Tell me everything you know about Grant Borrows."

"Can't," she said.

Drexel was taken aback and nearly struck her again, but stopped himself. She *couldn't* lie or withhold information while under the influence. The drug he'd used was far too powerful, even for someone with conditioning.

"Why not?" he asked.

"He doesn't exist."

"Grant Borrows does not exist?" Drexel repeated.

"*Duh*," she rolled her eyes in an exaggerated, childlike way.

He followed her eyeline to the ceiling far above, where a dimming skylight was letting in the first effects of dusk. The empty warehouse where they sat was musty and dirty and dark, but it suited his purposes. They had been here for hours, days even. The truth serum was his last resort.

He tried a different tactic.

"A military base was raided about a week ago. Sources say they saw Grant Borrows there. *Was* he there?"

"Yep," she replied.

"Why did he go there?"

"To talk to Harlan Evers."

"Who is Harlan Evers?"

"Used to be Frank Boyd's best friend, before he died."

"And who was Frank Boyd?"

"Grant's father," she replied, exasperated, as if it were painfully obvious.

Boyd . . . I know that name.

He took a few minutes to word his next question carefully.

"Does Frank Boyd have any surviving relatives?"

"His kids. Collin and Julie," she said.

Collin Boyd. That was it. *The man who died in the arson in Glendale. The UCLA professor's brother . . . Of course.*

Drexel let out a slow breath as comprehension spread across his face.

Got you now, he smiled.

"Now, my dear," he said, settling into his seat, "we're going to head back to the station and run a background check on Mr. Boyd . . . But first, why don't you tell me everything you know about our good friend Collin."

38

Daniel watched from his wheelchair as Grant paced the living room. It was late at night, and Julie and Lisa had both given up long ago and gone to sleep.

Daniel didn't know Grant very well yet, but he could tell that this was not normal behavior. Despite the dark circles that were now a permanent fixture around his eyes, every step, every gesture, every word screamed agitation.

Grant had decided to try walking around, moving his joints and muscles, which from the way he was walking were incredibly stiff. He'd been at it for hours and had been forced to stop several times, but he seemed determined to push through the pain and exhaustion. Daniel envied him. It'd be weeks before he could pace like that.

"I know something's wrong . . ." Grant said for the umpteenth time. Daniel had heard him say these words so many times now, he'd decided Grant wasn't actually saying it to him. Daniel wished for a way to help, but he was exhausted. A glance at his wristwatch showed "1:57 A.M."

"Why don't we try a mental focusing exercise then?" he suggested, pulling the small electronic device Lisa had retrieved for him the other day from a bag at his side. Grant continued to walk back and forth. "It might help you relax, and it could be a first step toward harnessing your abilities."

"Sure, sure," Grant said, distractedly, plopping down on the sofa. He saw the device.

Daniel noticed his glance and said, "It measures your pyschokinetic output."

"You're going to . . . *clock* my brain power?"

"Something like that. Just ignore it, you won't ever know it's on. Lean back and let your eyes go out of focus," Daniel instructed. Then he began speaking in a soft monotone. "Relax your body, let go of your tension. Ignore the sounds of the world around you. Let everything fade away. Make your mind a blank canvas, with no distractions, no thoughts. No doubts. No worries. Slow your breathing. In . . . and out. In . . . and out. That's good."

He watched as Grant seemed to be following his instructions to the letter, and he suddenly wondered if this might be a bad idea—surely Grant would fall asleep if they kept this up for long. "Very good. Keep your eyes closed, and keep breathing slowly," he said, looking all around, trying to find . . . "Let's see, here we are." He spotted a magazine on the coffee table.

"There's something directly in front of you, Grant, on the table. A magazine. Keep breathing in and out slowly, there you go. Now when I give the word, I want you to open your eyes and focus on that magazine. Don't look at anything else, don't let yourself *see* anything else. Just focus on the magazine, and don't let go of it."

Daniel waited, watching Grant inhale and exhale repeatedly.

"Open your eyes," he instructed.

Grant's eyelids opened leisurely and immediately focused on the magazine atop the table, about four feet away from him.

"Relax, keep breathing slowly, that's good," Daniel was saying. "Focus your attention *only* on the object. Now I want you to picture an imaginary hand, reaching out from your own body and picking up the magazine. Really *see* it in your mind. Use your imagination to stretch out and grab it. Let me know when you have a firm grip on it."

Sweat formed across Grant's forehead as he focused with tremendous intensity on the paper object resting on the table. "I can't . . . I can't see it . . ."

Daniel watched him patiently. "If it helps, reach out with your real hand as far as you can. Use it as a focal point."

Grant extended his arm, which was still a foot and a half shy of touching the magazine. But he found it a little easier to concentrate on holding the paper booklet this way. When at last he felt comfortable with his focus, he whispered, "Okay, think I got it."

Daniel turned to the magazine. "Lift it," he said.

Ever-so-slowly, as Grant's arm inched upward, the magazine did as well. It hung there in midair, suspended by nothing.

Daniel watched in astonishment.

After a second more, Grant let the magazine fall. He seemed dazed. After a moment he asked, "Do you really believe all that stuff you told me the other day, about me and . . . what I'm meant to do?"

"Absolutely!" Daniel answered. "Look at what you just did! Grant, you might as well get used to it: you are a bona fide he—"

"*Don't* say the 'H' word!" Grant bellowed, releasing some of his pent-up energy. "Don't even *think* it! I am *not* . . . one of those, and I never *will* be."

"Yes you are. You're not like *me*," he added. "You're better. Whether you like it or not, you have a responsibility to use this power of yours to help other people."

"I don't *care* about other people!" Grant exploded, the confines of the apartment seeming much too small for him. Daniel thought he almost felt the room shake in time with Grant's tirade. "What have people ever done for me?" Grant fumed. "Walked out on me, that's what! Betrayed me! Manipulated me! I never *wanted* this power, I never *chose* it, and if I could undo it, I *would*!" He thrust a hand out at the magazine and this time it flew apart with a loud *pop*, becoming a fireworks display of confetti. The tiny, shredded pieces fluttered silently to the ground.

Daniel watched the last of the paper bits fall to the table. Silence permeated the air but when he glanced at Grant, the man was far away again.

Farther than ever.

"I see them," Grant whispered. "Oh no . . ." He gasped, and then stood to his feet.

"Who? What's wrong?" Daniel stammered.

"They're not *moving* . . . *That's* what I've been feeling—this strange sensation. I was feeling *them*!" Grant shouted and ran to the front door. "They're still. All of them!"

Then he burst from the door and Daniel was left only with the echo of the man's horror at something Daniel couldn't fathom.

39

What if they're all dead?

The question burrowed its way through Grant's gut like a worm during the impossibly long drive to Morgan's facility. He went far above the speed limit whenever he felt he could get away with it, but had to slow down at the busier intersections. When he finally hit the suburb roads, he floored it.

At last, the cement driveway came into view, and he never slowed as he screeched his tires into a full-on turn onto the long, ruined path. When he came to a stop in front of the asylum, he hopped out of the car and ran to the front steps.

Grant slid the I.D. card Morgan had given him through the reader and was met by a cold stillness when he opened the door. He couldn't claim surprise at what he saw, because he had already *felt* it. But his jaw fell anyway, and the blood drained out of his face.

This can't be real.

Inside, he carefully stepped around the bodies sprawled on the floor. Each one of them looked as if they had been in the middle of something—walking to another room, carrying a tray full of something to eat, writing in a notebook, or looking for a book to read—when they had simply *dropped* to the ground, unconscious.

Grant crept down the long hallway, his eyes lingering on a younger resident sprawled on the ground. A basketball lay nearby.

Just a kid . . . Couldn't be more than seventeen . . .

Tears welled up as he stared at the young man, and for once he was unable to hold them back. A sharp pain began boring into his temples.

Dead . . . They're all dead . . .

A sob suddenly escaped his lips and he couldn't hold it back. It was the only audible sound in the building.

He stumbled over an older man's outstretched arm as he walked past the boy, and then he cried out again.

With great effort, Grant made his way to the Common Room. There he found over two dozen others in similar condition. On the couch. Slumped over the pool table. Lying on the ground.

He found Morgan on the ground near her favorite chair by the fireplace. She was lying chest-down on the ground, her head turned sickeningly to one side.

Tears poured openly down Grant's cheeks and he made no effort to wipe them away. This couldn't be real. He couldn't be seeing what he was seeing . . .

Another headache pain stabbed at his temples, but still he ignored it.

As he glanced around at all of the dead bodies, the enormity of the scene set in. He was the only living person in a building full of dead people.

The room began to spin . . .

He plopped down hard onto the ground, near Morgan, and began weeping openly into his hands. He barely knew most of these people. But somehow, in a way that defied words or reasoning, he just *knew* . . . This was his fault.

His phone chirped in his inside pocket but he let it ring. It stopped after a minute or two but then started again. Aggravated now, he yanked it out and opened it, but couldn't think of anything to say.

"Grant? Hello, are you there?" It was Daniel.

"Yeah," Grant managed to get out. Talking was the last thing he wanted to do. Words were pointless now.

"What happened? Where are you?"

"They're dead," Grant whispered, choking on another sob.

"Are you sure?" Daniel replied. "Have you checked them? We thought *you* were dead at first, too."

Grant felt the headache in his temple again and tried blinking it away. It subsided, and he reached out a hand to feel Morgan's body.

"Morgan's cold. I can't find a pulse."

"Hmm," Daniel said with a clinical tone. "You were cold too, but we eventually found a faint pulse on you. Maybe hers is too faint to detect. What else can you see?"

"Hang on . . ." he mumbled. He stood up on his haunches and carefully rolled Morgan over onto her back. "She's got a nasty bruise on her forehead. She must've hit the corner of the table as she fell."

Daniel's words escaped quickly. "Grant, *dead people don't bruise*."

Grant gasped slightly, a glimmer of hope flickering to life. "Are you sure?" he asked, examining the egg-shaped bruise up-close.

"It's impossible," Daniel said, still talking fast. "When a body dies, blood stops flowing. Without blood flow, a corpse can't develop a new bruise, no matter what you do to it."

Grant's mind spun, and his eyes landed on the ring on her right hand, middle finger.

A ring can be removed after its wearer dies. He remembered her speaking those words to him.

He cradled the phone between his neck and shoulder, and grabbed Morgan's ring and tugged at it. It didn't budge.

His heart skipped a beat and he swallowed. "I think you're right," he said into the phone, his voice growing stronger now. "I think they're still alive!"

Daniel said nothing.

"But how do—what do I *do*?" Grant said.

Daniel's reply was excruciatingly slow in coming. "I've never heard of anything like this before. If they're not dead, then they must be in some kind of catatonia, like you were. If we only knew what it was that woke you up . . ." Daniel said, thinking aloud.

Grant's thoughts shot back to his dream and lingered there.

"You still have no idea what roused you?" Daniel asked when Grant didn't reply.

"Not . . . exactly," he said quietly.

"Well, there's obviously a connection between what happened to you and what happened to them," Daniel began reasoning again. "You're all on parallel paths of some kind . . ."

Grant sat up straight. "What did you say?"

"I said you're all on . . ." he began, but Grant was no longer listening. Something had just triggered in his mind.

How did the woman in his dream say it?

"You must ask yourself what you are willing to endure to reach the journey's end. Are you willing to sacrifice? Are you willing to absorb your greatest fear and make it part of your very being?"

He closed his eyes and remembered the look on her face.

Are you willing? she had said.

I don't want to hurt, he thought. *But I am willing.*

"Grant, are you still there?" Daniel's voice was saying into the phone.

Grant's demeanor had changed, a new resolve now set deep into his bones.

"I'll call you back," he said, and hung up the phone.

He knelt down beside Morgan on the floor, and with a deep, long breath . . . he let go. Let go of his fear, his doubt. His questions and frustrations. His desires and needs. His anger at life for doing this to him.

He released it all.

His heart fluttered, and immediately the pain returned and seized him once more.

But this time, instead of fighting, he disappeared into it.

Its ferocity was beyond imagining, but he didn't struggle. He relaxed and let it overtake him.

Grant managed to force his eyes open as the pain surged through him and he saw that the light had returned. His ring was glowing again, as were all of the others around him, growing and shimmering.

The pain increased again. Scorching and fierce. Every inch of his skin felt as though it was being ripped apart, his bones being crushed into powder. His nerve endings sizzled like cattle prods. His blood raced through his veins like scalding hot oil, burning him from the inside out. And his heart was pumping much too fast . . .

He was sure he would pass out any moment now, and he would welcome it when it came. No one could withstand this kind of pain and remain conscious. It had to be scientifically impossible, as Daniel would probably tell him.

Yet the pain grew larger still, and he remained awake and aware. It became so potent that he could no longer tell one part of his body from another. It melted together and burst outward as though every molecule in his body was being rent and torn from every other.

And for one, brief glimpse of a moment, his senses extended far beyond himself and he touched them . . . *all* the Loci, everywhere.

Then he felt his lungs gasp in a deep breath of air. Slowly—very slowly—he became aware that the pain was subsiding. Feeling returned to his limbs, and his breathing began to slow. His heart decel-erated as well, and his blood no longer burned like acid. It dwindled farther and farther until he felt a tingling sensation all over, and his familiar headache, now a dull echo of a whisper.

Grant opened his eyes and massaged his temples as he looked around the facility. He'd never felt so tired in his life.

The light from the rings was gone.

And silence was no longer the only sound he heard.

Morgan's chest was rising and falling in normal rhythm. The others were breathing as well, and some of them were beginning to stir.

Grant couldn't remember when he'd begun to cry, but his cheeks were soaking wet now, and more tears soon joined them. He could barely move, the after-effects of the pain too crippling.

Yet despite this, he couldn't stop an enormous smile from spreading across his face.

Grant hung up the phone and returned it to his pocket, dwelling on how eager he was to get back home and talk to Hannah, see with his own eyes that she was okay.

As he slowly waddled back into the Common Room, which was now bustling with activity, he drew a number of wide-eyed stares. None of the Loci had any idea what had happened; they knew only that they were alive thanks to him.

Grant made a careful beeline for Morgan, who was watching him from her chair across the room, as Fletcher, per usual, was murmuring in her ear. Meanwhile, another resident—a young girl—was rubbing some kind of ointment on Morgan's forehead with a small cloth.

Grant eased slowly into the chair opposite Morgan, cautious not to overextend his aching muscles.

"Can you tell us what happened?" she asked.

"I think I *understand* what happened, but I don't think I can explain it," he replied, still smiling for no apparent reason. He was beyond tired, yet his body surged with excitement.

"Think about *trying*," Fletcher said, his mouth a thin, tight line.

Morgan turned away from the girl who was nursing her bruise and threw a nasty gaze at Fletcher.

He shivered, despite himself.

Morgan spoke. "I know the rings glowed before we all lost consciousness—all of them. And that's something that's . . . rare, at best."

"But it has happened before?" Grant asked.

"I'm not certain what triggers it, but it always seems to be a precursor to something significant. I've witnessed 'multiple glows' when someone new is given a ring, for example, but I don't believe that to be the only time it happens."

A moment passed in silence.

"I think *I* did it. Whatever happened to you all, I believe I'm responsible for it," Grant said. "But it was something that *had* to happen. I don't know why, I just know it did."

"How do you know?" Morgan said, creasing her brow.

"Because everything's changed," Grant said. "I can feel it."

"Feel what?" Fletcher said.

"*You*," Grant replied. "I have this . . . *sense* of all of you. Not like I can read your minds or feel your feelings. I just have a very strong impression of you. Like I can close my eyes and still see you."

Neither Morgan nor Fletcher spoke as they considered this and studied him. For once, Grant found he didn't mind their stares, nor that of the other Loci. He was still smiling, though he was so drained his eyes were trying to close by themselves.

"So you're saying," Morgan spoke up, "some type of connection has been . . . switched 'on' . . . or forged between you and the rest of us?"

The Forging.

"Yeah," he replied, looking far away. "That's probably a good word for it . . . And none of you experienced the pain that I did?"

Morgan shook her head. "We should be thirsty and starved, but we're fine."

He didn't reply, as she continued watching him.

"What do you think it means?" Grant said at last, ending with a yawn.

She shook her head again, her eyebrows raised. "This is new territory for all of us."

40

Despite his profound fatigue, Grant lay awake most of the night, staring at the ceiling and trying to sort out the Forging. Things were becoming clearer, and he'd made up his mind that it was now time to chase down Evers' clue. He needed to return to his boyhood home. But even with that concluded, other concerns nagged him.

His conflicted feelings for Hannah, for one. They had plans to meet up late afternoon at the asylum.

And then there was the Keeper . . .

Who are you? Grant thought.

Finally well before dawn, he gave up pretending. Sleep would not come. Bleary-eyed and depleted, he roused himself and began preparing for the day, particularly for the inevitable conversation with Julie. How would she handle the idea that their father could still be alive and in hiding somewhere? That during all these years, he'd never bothered to contact them?

How would she feel about returning to their childhood home?

Will she dread it as much as I do?

Then again, she might want *to go . . .*

Grant dressed and left the apartment before his sister was awake.

He descended in the elevator to the parking garage and the door chimed, then it opened.

Some small part of him expected to see Alex. It seemed like time for one of their encounters, but he was greeted only by the silence of the garage.

Grant took a tired step toward his car when there was a flash of movement before his eyes and somehow, he was flying through the air. He crashed into the side of a nearby car and slumped to the ground, rattled. His instincts were telling him to roll, to get to his feet, to look up. But the sleepiness and soreness were too pronounced, his reflexes too sluggish.

Grant struggled to his feet and looked around through bleary eyes. No one. He was all alone in the hollow surroundings of the garage. He shook the cobwebs out of his brain. He may have been tired, but not *that* tired. Whatever just happened—he didn't imagine it.

But he hadn't seen anyone there and couldn't see anyone now.

With a start, he heard a sound from behind and turned to look, yet saw nothing.

But wait, there *was* . . . Something itching at the edge of his awareness. He was too drained to concentrate on it fully, but it was a familiar sensation. He could feel the presence of another.

Grant listened in silence but only heard the sounds of the elevator descending. Finally, he walked toward the car again.

He made it halfway across the garage, when there was another glimpse of movement out of the corner of his eye. Then Grant found himself lying on the ground, a throbbing pain in his stomach, where it seemed he'd been kicked.

"All right!" he shouted. "Who—"

A flash of movement later, and there was a figure standing above him, holding a very long, thin sword that curved slightly along the far end of the blade. It had an unusually long handle, and its tip was only inches from Grant's left eye.

He froze.

Out of his other eye, he made out the shape of the man holding the sword, standing over him. He was shorter than Grant, thin with bulging muscles. He wore a simple black jumpsuit. He was bald.

The man's hands were covered by tight leather gloves, but Grant knew—he could *feel*—a ring hiding under one of those gloves.

"What's wrong with you?" asked the man, his deep-throated British accent neither offering an accusation nor sarcasm; he was genuinely curious. "It should not be this easy." He had a gruff manner and spoke in an all-business tone.

Grant said nothing. The man's sword was so close to his eye, he was afraid to move or provoke him. And Grant's mind was too tired to try anything just now . . .

The man pulled the sword back a few inches. "Up."

Grant complied slowly, and as he rose, so did the sword. When Grant was upright, the man was gone, reappearing at his left side. He brought the sword around and up in a quick slice with one hand. He stopped cold when its tip made contact with the underside of Grant's head, just below his chin. He made a small nick there, enough to bring forth a drop of blood that oozed down Grant's neck.

The attacker held his sword in position with a stillness carved out of stone.

Grant tried to be calm, his chin angled upward to keep from making the incision worse. He held his breath, afraid any movement would project his head downward into the razor-sharp blade.

The man looked him up and down. Finally he shook his head.

"You're a pathetic child," he said, incredulous. "Lost and barely conscious."

The man walked slowly in a semicircle around Grant, ending when they were face to face. Still he held the sword so that its tip never lost contact with Grant's neck.

Grant dared to speak, causing his throat to vibrate against the tip of the sword. "What do you want?" He could barely get the words out, his voice quivering.

"You don't even know who you are," the man decided, disgust evident in his voice.

Finally, he pulled the sword back a few inches—enough for Grant to stand at ease. "I'll not kill a pitiful, untrained fool. Go and rest. Prepare yourself. *Then* we shall begin again."

As far as the other man was concerned, that seemed to be that. He held out the sword, but only in a defensive posture. Grant assumed he was free to go.

He let out a shaky breath and glanced down at the sword again. It was then that he saw there was a row of symbols etched along the length of the blade. The symbols looked familiar.

"What do you want with me?" he said, stalling for time as he stared at the symbols, memorizing them.

The man stood unmoving, the sword still pointed at Grant. "I have no interest in *you*," he replied. "My quarrel is with the *abomination*." His voice full of menace, he made a swift slice through the air, after which Grant felt a stinging pain on the top of his hand. He flinched and withdrew the hand. A bleeding gash extended from Grant's wrist in a straight line down his hand, forming a red line that was unmistakably pointing at his ring.

"I will not show mercy twice," the man replied calmly, straightening himself up and sheathing the sword. "*Go.* I'm allowing you this one chance to ready yourself. *Use it.*"

There was a blur, and Grant was suddenly alone, cradling his bleeding hand in silence.

One heartbeat later, he blacked out.

As the sun was rising, Morgan and Fletcher made their way from room to room throughout the asylum, on his suggestion that they check to make sure everyone "really *did* wake up."

They knocked on doors and carefully peeked inside. Everyone they encountered was perfectly fine—most of them still sleeping soundly.

After a while of this, Fletcher closed another door and continued their private conversation.

"And you don't think there's any chance he did this on purpose?" he asked.

Their feet clicked in unison as they walked down a lonely hallway in the back of the building.

"It's obvious he didn't," Morgan replied, her matter-of-fact tone leaving no room for argument. "He was in tremendous pain."

Fletcher was quiet as they walked along.

"What?" she finally said, noticing his look of frustration.

"If he didn't do it on purpose, then that's even worse!" he cried as they walked.

Morgan stopped, near another door. It was Marta's room.

"How is it worse?" she asked.

"If Grant didn't do . . . whatever he did . . . on purpose," he cried, exasperated, "then that means he has no control over what he's capable of. Who knows what he might do next!"

She turned away from him and knocked on Marta's door. When

there was no reply, she assumed Marta was asleep and opened it.

"Look, I know you trust him, and you probably feel like this was all part of some grand scheme," Fletcher was saying. "But personally, I just feel lucky that we all survived."

"We didn't," she whispered.

He followed her gaze inside the room to the old woman lying on the bed.

Marta's eyes were open, staring at nothing. Her jaw was slack. Her body stiff.

She was dead.

Lisa was lost in thought as she boarded the elevator. She punched in the number for the penthouse, knowing that she could find Daniel there.

He was *always* there.

Lisa and Daniel had become "roommates" in a spare apartment on the floor beneath Grant's place, where she was supposed to be helping him recuperate. But upstairs was where she continuously found him.

She couldn't really blame him for it. Grant's home was certainly where all the action was.

Still, they had that nice, cushy apartment all to themselves . . . and Daniel was only a handful of days out from the attempt on his life. He had a lot of mending to do. She couldn't help wishing, as long as they had to be cooped up in this place, that they might use this time to become better . . . *friends*.

At least, to start with.

It didn't *all* have to be about Grant, did it?

Lisa put her key in the door to Grant's apartment. She half-expected to find Daniel napping in his wheelchair. She'd put a stop to that, it was time to get started with his physical therapy . . .

Instead, she found him at Grant's computer, leaning, squinting into the screen.

"Hey!" she called.

Daniel jumped, and turned off the monitor, knocking the mouse off of the desk in the process.

"Hi," he said distractedly.

"What are you doing?" she asked.

"Just . . . keeping up with the latest science journals," he said, glancing quickly back at the now-dark monitor. "Seeing if there's anything new in parapsychology. Figured it might help the cause."

"Well," she said, "there's plenty of time for research later. Right now, it's time to start working on retraining those muscles of yours."

His shoulders sank. Physical therapy was at the very bottom of his priority list. "All right."

Lisa had him successfully using power bands on his broken arm in under ten minutes. Considering Lisa had no training for this, other than some homework she'd done on the Internet, she felt this was a good beginning. And Grant had offered to help as well . . .

Where was Grant, anyway?

Daniel was beginning to complain that the work was hurting too much when the front door to the apartment burst open.

Grant stood in the doorway. His eyes were drooping, his hair a tangled mess, his clothes rumpled—and his hand was bleeding.

"Grant!" Daniel shouted, losing his concentration on his work and accidentally firing the power band across the room like a slingshot.

"He knew . . ." Grant mumbled, disjointed. "He knew who I am . . ." He staggered inside, ignoring the open door behind him, and threw his keys onto the kitchen counter. He seemed to be having trouble keeping his legs steady.

"What's wrong?" Daniel shouted. "What happened to your hand?"

Grant looked up, noticing them for the first time.

"How did . . . how did he know?" Grant said, barely intelligible.

He collapsed.

41

As he so often did—as he had done nearly every night since the Shift—Grant startled himself awake, screaming.

"Easy!" cried a female voice. It was Julie. She had been sitting across the room, leaning back in a chair, her nose buried in a book, but now she was on her feet and at his side. "Take it easy, honey."

"How long—"

"Ten hours," she replied. "How do you feel?"

"Man, are *you* a snoozer," came a voice from the door. Lisa stood there, hands on her hips.

Grant rose from the bed and walked to the bedroom's picture window, looking out at the late afternoon sun covering the city below.

"Ten hours . . . he'll be coming soon . . ." he mumbled to himself. *What do I do?*

Daniel wheeled himself into the room on his own, complaining about how sadistic Lisa was for refusing to help him get around for "at least two hours," while Grant was sleeping.

Grant walked to Julie's chair, grabbed the book out of it, and flipped to an empty page in the back. He found a pen on his nightstand and made a quick sketch, and then handed the book to Daniel.

"You ever seen symbols like that before?" Grant asked.

"No . . ." Daniel studied it carefully. "Never. They're suggestive of the markings on your ring, though."

"Yeah . . . they really are . . ." Grant said, turning to look out the window again, lost in thought.

"Collin, what's going on?" Julie asked. "How'd you get that gash on your hand?"

Grant glanced down at the bandages they'd applied to the cut. "A man attacked me as I was leaving this morning. I couldn't even touch him. He used this sword . . . And those symbols were on it."

"A *sword*. Really?" Lisa mused.

The others turned to look at her.

"If you want to kill somebody, there are easier ways," she said into their stares. "If he chose a sword over a gun, he must've had a reason for it."

"He's good at it," Grant summed it up. "That's reason enough."

Grant looked back at Daniel. "The way this guy talked, he was . . . formal. He *let* me go because I was too tired to fight. It was like an 'honor' thing. But he's coming back, and he expects me to be 'prepared' when he gets here."

"You have to run," Julie said, as if it was obvious and she couldn't believe she was the only one saying it. "Collin, you have to get out of here, leave town, and don't look back. I'll come with you, we'll go somewhere he can't find us—"

"No," Grant said, stern but resigned. "Running won't help. This guy . . . he's not like Konrad. He's different."

Daniel nodded. "Well," he said, eyes darting back and forth in thought, "I'll help you practice your skills until he shows up. But being prepared also means knowing all you can about your opponent. And the only real clue we have to his identity is the sword."

"That's not the *only* clue we have," Grant said, taking a moment to look each of them in the eye, in turn. "He was wearing a ring. He's one of the Loci."

Daniel whistled. "So that means—"

"He has some sort of mental power, yeah. Thing is . . . he moved fast. Like, *impossibly* fast. I don't see how something like that could be a *mental* power."

"You think maybe he works for this 'Keeper' person Alex told you about?" Julie offered.

"The sword is the key," Daniel repeated. "We need to find out everything we can about it."

"Research girl to the rescue," Lisa chimed in, turning to leave.

"Wait," Grant said. He took the book from Daniel's hands and ripped out the page he'd drawn on. "Could you get a copy of this to Morgan? She might know something about these symbols."

"Okay." She left.

Daniel held up the small device he'd used the day before to test Grant's brainpower. "I can adapt this to alert us if anyone else with mental powers enters the building."

Grant nodded. "Good. That's good."

"You should rest," Julie said, trying to maneuver him back to the bed.

"No, I can't, there's no time—"

"There's *never* time! Morgan was right! You need to slow down. You're running headlong from one thing to the next, when you need to stop and deal with what's happened to you."

Grant fixed her with a stare. "Tell that to the maniac with the sword who wants to run me through."

Daniel watched the two of them in silence for a moment, before gesturing with his good arm toward the living room. "If everything else is settled, we'd better get started."

Three hours later, Grant and Daniel paused for dinner. Daniel was pleased at how quick a study Grant had proven to be. Yet he was his own worst critic as well, never feeling that his efforts were powerful enough to beat this new foe.

They started with simple things—books, matchsticks, CDs, picture frames. Before they'd stopped, Grant was stretching out his arm to "grab" larger, more complex objects. Tables, bookcases, even the sofa.

At the very least, Grant relished that no panicking was required in his efforts, and those mind-blistering headaches vanished as well.

Julie watched the news as the two of them practiced, and was pleased to report that most of the media had pushed him back to brief "still at large" mentions over halfway into the evening broadcasts. At this rate, she suggested, he'd be forgotten by the weekend.

As they sat eating, discussing Grant's progress and theories on who the mysterious man with the sword could be, Grant's phone rang. Morgan's name appeared in the display.

"Hello, Grant. How are you holding up?"

"Morgan, hi. Did Lisa find you okay?"

"Yes, she left here to return to your place some time ago," Morgan replied. She took a deep breath. "We've turned up a few answers about this man with the sword, but there's very little that's definitive."

Grant put the phone on speaker, so Julie and Daniel could hear. "Tell me."

"Well, to start with, I compared the stone tablet with these symbols you sent me—the ones you saw on the sword."

"And?"

"The symbols from the sword are on the tablet as well. If I could translate the rest of the tablet, we may find out more about both of you, but I feel like I'm hitting a brick wall here. You're *positive* this man was one of the Loci?"

"Yeah. I could feel him."

"Hmm. The fact that these particular symbols are on the tablet means that whoever this man is . . . he has a part to play in all of this." She paused, silence lingering in the air. "I heard a story once—I rather thought it was embellished—from one of the private detectives I hired to find the stone tablet fragments. He said he saw a man carrying a sword, dressed in black, who *exterminated* an entire police squadron in Chile. They called him 'the Thresher.'"

"The Thresher . . ."

"Grant, there's something else. Over the years, during my travels and then here at the asylum, I've heard whispers of a group—a *society*—that exists. They are rumored to know everything about our rings: where they come from, how they work, and why they exist. But we have no understanding of their agenda."

"Why didn't you mention this before?"

"Because I had no reason to believe it was true before," replied Morgan.

It was only a second before Grant caught on. "You think Mr. Slice-and-Dice is a member of this secret society? That what—he's acting on their orders to kill me?"

"I don't even know if they exist. But the symbols from the tablet appearing on his sword clearly suggest that there's a much larger plot at work. I wanted you to be aware."

"All right," he said with a sigh.

There was a knock at the door.

"She's back," Daniel said, breathing a sigh of relief.

"What about the name?" Grant asked, walking to the door. "What's a 'thresher'?"

"There's a species of shark called the thresher, of the genus *Alopias*," Morgan said in a schoolteacher tone. "They keep mostly to themselves, though they *are* predators. The thresher has an exceptionally long, thin tail that it uses as a weapon.

He turned the knob to let Lisa in.

Wait, Lisa wouldn't knock, I gave her a key . . .

And suddenly he was standing toe-to-toe with the Thresher.

They both froze.

"You look rested," the bald man said, sizing him up. "Thank you."

The sword appeared in a flash. Grant took a swing at his opponent, but the man vanished. Then when he jerked his head to the left he found the man with the sword standing right beside him.

42

Daniel looked up as he heard a sharp bang from a few feet away. The front door had been blown off its hinges and the Thresher was lying out in the hall.

"Better," said a voice at the door. The Thresher stood there, but none of them had seen him rise from the floor.

At his side stood Grant, breathing fast with a panicked look on his face. Julie crouched behind Daniel's chair and helped him right it.

He's losing control again . . . Daniel thought.

The Thresher made a counterclockwise twist, sword extended. The blade made a deep gash in Grant's left shoulder.

No, not just one gash. There were three of them, like bloody military stripes down Grant's arm.

How is he doing this? Daniel wondered.

Grant gestured toward the coffee table with an outstretched hand and it flew up off of the floor toward his attacker, but the Thresher pivoted in place and sliced it down the middle. He ducked to avoid the two halves, and Daniel used the opportunity to move.

"No!" Julie screamed.

"RUN!" Daniel yelled, crashing his wheelchair into the Thresher from behind, knocking him over.

Grant hesitated only a second. Then he propelled Julie forward with his mind, grabbed her by the hand when she was close enough, and the two of them were gone, out the door and down the hall. They jumped into the elevator just as the doors were closing.

The Thresher was on his feet and spun in the air, sword in hand once again . . . when he stopped, the blade was less than an inch from Daniel's neck.

But he held it there, examining Daniel in his wheelchair for the first time.

He brought the sword up above his head and then swung it down hard against the gasket bolt attached to the chair's left wheel. The wheel immediately fell off of the axle and the chair collapsed.

He turned and stalked out the door after Grant, leaving Daniel helpless and immobilized, all his injuries crying again in agony.

Grant swung into the driver's seat as Julie was already buckling herself into the passenger's side. She flicked the switch that mechanically extended the top until it was up, covering the cab, as Grant brought the engine to life.

"Um," Julie said, her eyes growing as she stared straight ahead, across the parking aisle to the next row, "now would be a good time to go."

Grant followed her gaze just in time to see a man on a high-powered motorcycle racing down the row parallel to them at dangerous speeds. The man on the bike had a sword hanging from his hip.

Grant put the car in reverse and jammed the pedal, swinging out in a right-reverse turn. He threw the Corvette into drive while they were still moving backward, causing the tires' rubber to spin against the pavement. They began moving forward just as the motorcycle turned down their aisle and raced toward them from behind.

The two vehicles remained only a few feet apart as they drove in circles, spiraling down through the parking garage until they came to the street level. Grant was immediately reminded of the snake strangling him in his dreams but there was no time to dwell on it. The electronic gate ahead allowed only residents to enter or exit the garage via a keycard.

Grant floored it, racing toward the gate at fifty miles an hour.

"You *do* see that, right?" a nervous Julie said, leaning back in her seat.

"Down!" Grant yelled.

She ducked and they crashed through the gate and kept going.

Julie turned around to look. "Well, you own the building, so I guess it's okay."

Grant swerved into the left-hand lane, which was unusually empty, and the man on the motorcycle broke out from behind them and came around to the right lane, appearing at the car's passenger side.

"Down!" Grant screamed again.

Her head ducked just as the sword came slashing across the side window, shattering it. Grant swerved right to slam into the motorcycle, which veered away.

Julie sat back up to see them racing ahead of the motorcycle, which was falling behind in the midday traffic.

"Who *is* this guy?" she breathed.

Grant poured on more speed as they entered a busier downtown street, darting dangerously around other cars, trucks, and buses. He glanced into the rearview mirror and saw that the motorcycle was further back now, but keeping pace.

"I thought the rings only give you enhanced *mental* abilities," Julie went on, bracing herself against the side of the car as Grant turned again, ignoring a red light. "Why would extra brainpower let him move super-fast?"

"I don't know!" Grant replied, jerking the steering wheel to the right and narrowly missing the rear fender of a pickup truck that was slowing down to turn. "Maybe he can manipulate time or something."

Julie looked back. "His motorcycle isn't going any faster than the regular variety."

Grant turned left, running a red light and flying through a narrow gap in the oncoming traffic. Julie screamed as the oncoming cars swerved and fishtailed into one another. Straight ahead was the ramp for the 110. The motorcycle quickly appeared and closed the gap between them.

"He's catching up," Julie warned, watching behind again and clutching the door handle with white knuckles.

The Corvette rocketed up the on-ramp and hurtled onto the freeway, finding just enough of a gap between cars to race to an open lane. Grant swerved wildly in and out of the traffic, and immediately the man on the motorcycle shifted lanes to the left to come up beside Grant.

"Hold on!" Grant shouted.

He jerked the car to the right, out onto the shoulder, and slammed the gas. The Corvette growled in appreciation and blasted forward. Soon the other cars on the highway were little more than blurry colors speeding by as the Corvette raced down the edge of the road at well over one hundred miles an hour.

Julie clung to her seat as they edged dangerously close to the cement barrier on her side. "Where did you learn to drive like this?" she shouted.

"I *didn't*! Is he still behind us?" Grant said, not daring to look anywhere but straight ahead.

She turned in her seat. "Yes, but he's further back than before."

"How *far* back?"

"Maybe three hundred feet. And getting further away."

Grant let up on the gas, slightly, and they began to slow.

"What are you doing!" Julie shouted as if he were crazy.

"Make sure your belt is tight," Grant replied, glancing into the rear mirror.

The black motorcycle inched closer and closer, but Grant waited. Waited until he knew the other man would be ready to make his move to try and come up beside them again.

The motorcycle was less than thirty feet behind them now, with nothing between the two vehicles.

"What are you going to do?" Julie cried, watching the motorcycle and shivering with the wild motions of the car.

"Stop turning around!" Grant shouted. "And brace yourself!"

She faced forward, clenching the armrests again.

Grant never took his eyes off of the mirror. The motorcycle drew closer, and Grant watched the handlebars, waiting to see them begin to turn.

They turned.

Grant slammed on the car's brakes with both feet, rising up from his seat, and a violent squeal came from the tire assembly that drowned out all other noise on the busy highway.

The motorcycle had just begun to turn left, and now swung around to slam sideways into the rear of the car. The man in the mask flew forward, landing on top of the car.

When the car finally came to a halt several hundred feet away, smoke was rising from all four tires, and the smell of hot rubber permeated the air. Cars, trucks, and SUVs continued speeding by, mere inches from them.

Grant returned to his seat, out of breath, and Julie was trying to catch hers as well. They both looked up, slowly, at the same time, to see the edge of the other man's head, visible at the very top of the windshield. He looked rattled, but he was alive. His eyes blinked open and he shook his head, trying to clear it. Then he stopped, and his eyes focused on the two of them inside the car.

"Um," Julie said a little louder than usual, "he looks *angry*."

Grant punched the gas pedal again, and in the rear-view, he watched as the man rolled off of the car and continued rolling until he came to a stop on the ground far behind them.

Grant merged back into traffic, and picked up speed. Julie, meanwhile, tore a strip off of her shirt around the bottom.

"Put this around your arm before you bleed to death," she said.

His phone rang in his pocket. He reached inside and tossed it to Julie, while he clumsily worked at tying off the cloth around the three gashes in his arm with one hand and his teeth.

"Hello?" she answered the ringing phone, leaning back in her chair, worn out. She closed her eyes.

"It's Morgan," she said, handing him the phone back. Grant took it, his thoughts still focused on putting as much distance as possible between them and the Thresher.

"Grant, are you all right?" Morgan said. "Daniel just telephoned."

"How is he?"

"Lisa's there with him now. They're okay. Listen, I think you should make for the asylum," Morgan said.

"What?! I'm not leading a dangerous sociopath to your front door!"

"He's one of *us*," she replied. "Perhaps we can find a way to reason with him."

"Forget it," Grant said, his voice leaving no room for argument.

"Very well," Morgan said. "But there's one other thing you should keep in mind: This man is mentioned on the tablet, just as you are. This man is connected to your destiny, Grant. Your friend Daniel told you something was coming, and that whatever it is, you would be all that stands between it and humanity. This Thresher may very well be a precursor to whatever it is. He could even be the *thing* that's coming, himself."

Grant's head began to hurt. "Okay . . . one step at a time. Why don't you take a picture of the tablet and email it to Daniel? It would probably be a good idea to put your heads together—"

"Something's happening!" Morgan suddenly shouted. Grant could hear screaming through the phone, distant, and then a boom that thundered so loud that he pulled the phone away from his ear in pain. Even Julie reacted to the sound.

"Morgan?" Grant yelled into the phone.

No one replied but he could hear breathing. Quick, panting breaths.

Another thundering boom echoed into the phone, followed by crashing of what sounded like glass and plywood.

"Morgan, talk to me!" Grant cried.

"They're here!" Morgan whispered, "Grant, come quickly! Here they come, I have to—"

As the line disconnected, the horror of comprehension hit Grant square in the face. In his mind's eye, he could see all of it.

All of *them*. And what was happening to them.

No . . .

NO!!

43

Morgan huddled quietly with the others she'd grabbed on her way into the underground cave. She pressed an ear to the door.

The hidden basement room, where the tablet fragments were stored, was thankfully still hidden. They were using it as a refuge. But the asylum itself was a different story.

Outside, the world had gone insane.

Some residents were screaming as they ran. A few had refused to run and tried going toe-to-toe with the invaders. Sounds of struggle—grunting, striking, yelling—were soon replaced with silence. Heavy footfalls could be heard all around, along with the crash of windows being destroyed and furniture being overturned.

She forced herself to suppress the urge to open the door and try to gather more inside. They would only be surrendering all of their lives.

Grant . . . we need you.

Come quickly!

She had no idea if Grant could hear her or not—if his newfound "feeling" of them, as he called it, would alert him to their danger.

But she knew he was their only hope.

Morgan had her suspicions about who was behind this raid, but she had no doubts whatsoever about what they were after. They wanted the tablet.

Or rather, *he* did.

Almost in answer to her thoughts, a voice rang out.

"Oh, Morga-a-an! Come out and pla-a-ay!" a squeaky, male voice shouted from some distance away.

"Quiet!" she whispered to the few others that had entered the room with her, and were now cowering at the bottom of the stairs.

She pushed the swiveling door open a hair's breadth, and looked out. The Common Room was clear, aside from a few unconscious residents scattered about. *He* wasn't out there—he was somewhere further away.

The asylum couldn't have been easy to break into, she knew. The few windows there were had bars, and she herself had seen to the installation of a fairly advanced security system. Still, if it was who she thought it was, she knew it was only a matter of time before the secret room would be found.

Her people had probably put up a good struggle, she knew. There were no fighters here, but some of the Loci had more esoteric abilities that could come in handy to keep them hidden or help them elude an attacker. They would be scattered throughout the building, panicked, alone.

The assault had come so fast. Out of nowhere.

Another scream rang out, much closer, and the people inside the hidden room had to stifle screams of their own. Morgan listened closely through the door and thought she heard crying. Whoever it was, they were close.

She risked cracking the door open a little more. Across the Common Room stretched over the double-doorway's threshold, she could see a boy—the seventeen-year-old, Thomas, she thought it was—on his hands and knees. He sniffled, tears in his eyes, but those eyes were angry and bloodshot. Someone from behind put a foot into the small of his back, forcing him facedown onto the ground. Morgan couldn't see who it was; they were on the other side of the door.

She didn't need to see who it was. She already knew.

"Morgan! If you're not standing in front of me in ten seconds, this one gets to eat from a straw for the rest of his life!"

Without hesitating, Morgan opened the door just far enough to squeeze out, closed it, and snuck across the outer wall of the Common Room, so the hidden chamber would remain hidden.

When she was far enough away to consider it safe, she stepped in and leveled a gaze at their attacker.

There he stood. Dirty trench coat in place, too-wide tie lying lop-sided across his ample belly. And he was grinning. As usual.

"What do you want, Drexel?"

"Do you really have to ask?"

Drexel stepped off of the boy's back and grabbed the back of his T-shirt, pulling him up off the ground. He turned the corner and took a few steps into the Common Room, facing Morgan and holding Thomas around the neck, gun pointed at his head.

Morgan matched his steps, backing away carefully, but not too far.

The boy beneath Drexel's arm was squirming but trying not to, as he was leaning back painfully under Drexel's powerful grip, off-balance and unsure how to stay upright. His cheeks were wet.

"How did you find us?" Morgan asked calmly.

"Got me a stool pigeon," he gamely replied, then called behind him. "C'mon in here, Judas!"

A young woman wearing handcuffs in front walked into the room and looked at Drexel like he was the most revolting thing she'd ever seen.

It's that barefoot girl . . .

Alex.

Morgan stared at her in open shock. "You sold us out?"

"Oh yeah, she was only too eager to give up her secrets." Drexel grinned.

The barefoot girl looked at him angrily and opened her mouth to respond, but Drexel reached out and whacked her in the back of the head with the side of his pistol.

"Now, now," he said. "Remember our agreement, little girl. Every word you say equals one bullet I put in one of the freaks here."

Alex clamped her lips shut, refusing to look at Morgan. Instead, she took a seat near Drexel. Her eyes darted back and forth, looking at nothing, as if she was trying to reason her way through something.

"Didn't you know?" Drexel went on, turning back to Morgan. "She spends all of her time watching you people. If you need to find out something about any of you, there's only one person you need to see."

He winked at Alex, then he gestured to Morgan in mock courtesy. "Let's talk. Take a seat, *please*."

She sat on a couch facing him, and he stepped closer, still clutching the boy under his grip.

"Here's the deal," Drexel began. "We both know why I'm here. I'm not going to bother threatening *you*, because we both know you'd sooner let me shoot you in the face than tell me anything about where to find the stone tablet. So I'm going to kill *them*, instead." He nodded at the unconscious people lying around the room. Some were bleeding. All were bruised.

Morgan's mind raced, sifting through the trillions of pieces of information she could call up at will, trying to think of something, anything she could do to stall. Thomas' ability—a highly advanced aptitude for physics—would be of no use in this situation.

"I'm guessing," Drexel continued, "that seeing your precious followers lined up and killed, one by one, would be the strongest possible motivator for you. So we'll start with this one." He looked down at Thomas, whom he had in a powerful vice around the neck. The boy began turning red.

"You wouldn't know how to read it," Morgan said quietly. "You couldn't possibly have any idea—"

"*Don't* try distracting me with that all that extra gray matter of yours," Drexel interjected. "This really couldn't be simpler. Give me what I want, or this one gets a bullet in the head. Three seconds."

Morgan stood from the couch and took a step closer to him. She looked at Thomas struggling to breathe under Drexel's powerful arm. He wouldn't last.

She looked Drexel in the eye. He was awaiting her response.

"Time's up," he said, smiling again. He cocked the safety back and pressed the pistol so hard into Thomas' temple she thought he might break the boy's skin.

So young . . . Thomas had barely begun living.

He had so much yet to experience . . .

Morgan glanced at Thomas and then looked back up at Drexel.

"Shoot him," she said.

Infuriated, Drexel backhanded her across the face with the pistol, and she fell to the floor. But she turned over quickly, resting on her elbows, ignoring the blood oozing from her forehead, and looked at him again.

"I will never help you," Morgan said with icy steel. "You can kill every last one of us—my people know what's at stake. But you will *never* get the tablet!"

A roar of rage escaped Drexel's lips and he threw Thomas to the ground next to her. He leveled the gun on Morgan and pulled the trigger.

Working his horn as heavily as his gas pedal, Grant sped up as he exited the highway and turned onto the surface road where Morgan's facility was located, a few miles outside of just about everything. Neither he nor Julie bothered to speak; their mutual sweat and heart rates were enough to indicate that they were both thinking the exact same thing.

Grant's eyes shifted to the rearview mirror just in time to see something impossible.

The black motorcycle was right behind them again, but the rider wasn't sitting on the seat. He was *standing* on it.

And just as Grant looked up, the man leaped from the seat and flew forward in the air toward them.

There was no time. No time to react, no time to shout a warning, to swerve or duck . . .

The Corvette's fabric top was shredded as the sword slashed vertically down through it.

The sword kept going until it met Grant's right shoulder and pierced his flesh down to the bone.

Grant screamed.

Julie screamed.

He slammed on the brakes, but this time the attacker was ready, bracing himself on his perch atop the car.

Julie wasn't so lucky, her body slamming hard into her seatbelt. The impact and the sudden appearance of the sword were too much of a shock, and she passed out.

Clutching his shoulder, Grant opened the door and let himself spill out onto the empty road. He backed away on his hands and knees.

The attacker jumped from the roof of the car and landed before him on the ground, perfectly balanced. Grant stopped as the sword was pointed at him again. His shoulder ached agonizingly, but he tried to ignore it.

The masked man walked forward until the sword was inches from Grant's face.

"Good chase," he said. "Not good enough."

Grant's hand came up lightning fast and clutched the end of the blade. He focused all his thoughts on the sword. In that split second, the weapon jumped out of the Thresher's hand high into the air and stuck itself in the grassy soil at the edge of the road.

And for that one, brief, glorious second, Grant saw the other man's eyes go wide. Grant didn't know if it was wonder or fear that he saw, and he didn't care. Even if it was only momentary, he'd scored a point.

He didn't waste it. In that same moment, Grant wrapped his legs around the Thresher's, and then straightened them, scissoring the man violently to the ground.

He lunged onto the Thresher, delivering a powerful blow to the head, but his attacker recovered fast and in less than an instant, everything was reversed, and *he* was on top of Grant. It had happened so fast that Grant couldn't stop it.

Punches fell upon Grant's head and stomach, each one coming faster and faster than the one before. Too fast to block. His head turned to the side and he caught sight of a loosely hanging tree limb, on one of the many trees surrounding them aside the lonely road.

As the Thresher continued to strike at him, he focused with all his might on that limb. It broke free and speared through the air, impaling his attacker's arm.

Grant brought both feet up and kicked hard against the man, sending him flying backward.

But he hadn't realized what direction he was facing when he kicked, and he sent the other man sailing toward his sword, still stuck into the ground on the side of the road.

Both men got to their feet at the same time, but the Thresher had his hand around the hilt of his sword before Grant could reach him. By the time Grant was fully standing, he felt a stinging sensation in his stomach and looked down to see a long, straight line of blood stretching across his gut. It wasn't a deep cut, but it stung, and he'd never even seen the swing of the blade.

In the next moment, he was on the ground, his head aching from a strong blow to his jaw.

As the world came into focus around him, he was barely aware of the blade that was once again resting against his throat. Only this time, his attacker stood over him, triumphant.

"I was almost impressed."

He lifted the sword.

"Almost."

44

Gunfire.

Someone was shooting.

Grant's attacker heard it as well, pausing his final strike.

And then, to Grant's great astonishment, the Thresher pulled away, mounted his bike, and roared away. Grant could only lay there in shock, wondering why this man would simply *leave* on the cusp of victory. He was obviously no coward.

"*Collin!*" Julie screamed, exiting the car at last. She bolted to his side and helped him to his feet. Every part of his body ached, his mind bordering on delusion. It was the most brutal attack he'd ever suffered, which, given his history, was saying a lot. The fact that he'd made it out in one piece was as surprising as it was confusing.

Julie practically had to drag him as she gently placed him in the passenger's side of the car. When she was safely in the driver's seat, Grant mumbled through split, bleeding lips, his eyes only half open.

"Where'd he go?"

Julie followed the Thresher's line of exit and it finally hit her. "Wait, isn't the asylum that way?"

Grant would have thought he was out of adrenaline, but somehow it spiked once more.

"GOOO!" he bellowed.

Drexel's bullet only grazed Morgan, though his aim had been true. Something threw him off balance, slamming into him from the side.

On the floor now, Drexel turned to see that Alex was on top of him, kicking and tearing with everything she had. It was a feeble effort; she was unable to cause the big man any pain. He plucked her off of him with one arm and flung her across the room to join Morgan and the boy on the ground.

Morgan was unconscious, bleeding from the graze just above her left ear.

The gun had fallen out of Drexel's hand when Alex pushed him, so he freed the baton that was dangling from the other side of his belt.

"*Big* mistake, girly-girl," he growled, returning to his feet, spinning the stick threateningly in his hands. He advanced on them.

"Not as big as yours," said a quiet, gravelly voice from behind.

Drexel spun but was too late.

The Thresher was on him in a burst of furious motion, the stick flying free of Drexel's hand along with the belt it had been attached to. The gun was nowhere in sight as the Thresher stood atop him, eyes flaring.

"Do you know what your mistake was?" the Thresher said calmly. "It was getting in my way."

"*You*," Drexel breathed, recognizing the other man. Then he laughed. "This is a pretty bold move, don't you think? Crashing a party where you're severely outnumbered?"

"The only person outnumbered here," said Grant's weary voice from the front door, "is *you*, Detective. Your keystone cops ran when they saw *him* coming," Grant nodded toward the Thresher. "I'm getting the feeling that you two have already met."

Drexel threw the Thresher off of him, toward the hallway, and surprised everyone with the fluidity of his massive frame lumbering in the Thresher's direction. The other man was already on his feet, but Drexel crashed into him like a linebacker, plowing him through the double doors.

The Thresher didn't stop to think. He gave in to instinct, springing straight up and driving his fist into the air. It collided with Drexel's chin and knocked him backward onto his rear end.

Drexel had barely hit the ground when he swung his meaty arm into the Thresher's head. Drexel was on top of the other man now, but the Thresher kicked him backward over his head—an astonishing feat

for his lithe frame. Drexel swept the Thresher's feet out from under
him and the bald man landed with a heavy thud. Drexel jumped to his
feet and ran for the front door.

Grant stepped aside, out of his path, but the double doors sprung to
life, crashing together in Drexel's face as he reached them. Then he
was flying through the air, and landed roughly on the cracked cement
at the bottom of the front steps.

Drexel regrouped fast and threw himself onto Grant, pinning him
to the ground. He pressed both hands against Grant's larynx, and
Grant fought the sudden weariness rising within him.

Sleep was a tangible thing that he could reach out and touch . . .
and he *wanted* it . . .

Instead he turned his head to the side and focused on the Thresher,
who was approaching.

But he couldn't focus. The world was too dark.

Drexel spoke.

"You probably think I'm just a dirty cop who dabbles in profiteering,
making shady choices to get ahead. You may even think I'm redeema-
ble. But I want you to know the *truth* about the man who defeated you,
Grant: *I crave the shadow.* The thought of breaking all two hundred
and six bones in your body, one by one, *slowly* . . . before I let you
die . . . It gives me cold chills."

Grant could barely keep his eyes open as the darkness took hold of
him.

But instead of passing out, the pressure on his throat eased up and
he could see again.

Alex stood above the both of them, holding Drexel's gun in both
hands. But she held it steady, unwaveringly trained on him.

The detective twisted to look up. "You wouldn't . . ." he said.

The Thresher appeared over Alex's shoulder and inspected the situation, the fury evident in Alex's eyes. "I rather think she would," he
said simply.

But before Alex got the chance, the Thresher's sword was out again
and Drexel's weight atop Grant was gone. He sat up gingerly and saw
the Thresher holding Drexel at knifepoint. Drexel was seated on the
ground, back up against the driver's side of Grant's car.

Grant gasped angrily for air. Not knowing where the strength within him came from, he stood and wrenched the gun from Alex's hands, joining the Thresher to look down at Drexel in victory. He leveled the gun on Drexel's head.

"Shall I finish it," the Thresher whispered, "or will you?"

The pain and the rage were fueling his movements now, yet Grant's finger hesitated on the trigger. It would be so quick, so easy, to pull that trigger. He didn't even need the gun in his hand. He could just *think* it, and Drexel's head would pop like a grape.

"No, Grant! You *can't!*" Julie shouted, emerging from the other side of the car. "Never give in, never surrender! Remember?"

She rounded the car slowly, watching the fire in Grant's eyes blaze.

Her hand grasped the top of his right wrist, and held to the bracelet there. "Don't forget who you really are," she said softly. "Don't throw away the goodness inside of you—not for *him*."

Grant watched Drexel, saw the fear in his eyes. And suddenly, he stepped back, breathing slower. He turned to Julie with tears in his eyes and embraced her.

"You called me Grant," he whispered in her ear.

She pulled away and smiled.

The Thresher watched all of this dispassionately. "If that's your decision . . ." He brought the sword up and was about to strike . . .

"Payton?" asked a voice from the asylum doorway. A disbelieving voice.

Grant knew that voice.

In the reflection of the blade, he saw her approaching. White hair . . . Middle aged . . .

It was Morgan.

But no, it couldn't be Morgan.

Morgan never goes outside the asylum.

Not for anything.

But there she was, standing on the front steps. She moved slowly forward, daringly stepping within striking distance of the Thresher, but she wasn't looking at his sword.

She was looking into his eyes.

The sword came away from Drexel's neck, and everyone there watched in stunned silence as the blade fell to the ground.

No, that wasn't quite right.

The Thresher had *thrown* it down.

Morgan stared at the man before her, dumbfounded.

"*Payton?*" she cried. "Is it really you?"

"No, love," his soft British accent intoned. "Payton is *dead*."

The blood drained from Morgan's face.

"You left him to die," Payton said. "Remember?"

45

Morgan and Payton stood five feet apart, faces grim, staring at one another. This run-down courtyard, continents away from where they'd last been together seemed hardly the place for a reunion.

Yet here they were.

Morgan looked into Payton's eyes. The eyes she remembered so well. The eyes she could get lost in and feel safer than anyplace else in the world.

But she barely recognized them. Their warmth had been replaced by a steely coldness that chilled her to the bone.

A small crowd began to gather, pouring from the front door. And Alex stood by, watching with tremendous interest. But Morgan and Payton noticed none of this. The world was empty to them, aside from one another.

They heard nothing else, saw nothing else. Refused to blink.

Neither of them spoke. Morgan was still flushed with shock, but Payton faced her calmly, hands clasped behind his back. Birds and crickets chirped in the surrounding trees, but otherwise not a sound was heard.

Grant watched, waiting for someone to speak. Considered speaking himself to break the tension but decided against it.

This man who stood before them—this warrior with a sword who had attacked and nearly killed him, and moved faster than anyone could see—this couldn't *possibly* be the man Morgan had once been in love with.

Could he?

She had certainly never mentioned that he knew how to fight. The way Morgan had described him, he sounded more like a hopeless romantic.

Payton extended his right arm to point at Grant.

"If you lot knew who this man really is," Payton seethed, "you wouldn't be helping him. You would *beg* me to kill him."

Morgan didn't flinch, though a trickle of blood from her head wound dripped onto her shirt. "I *do* know who he is. It's *you* that concerns me. You look like Payton . . ."

Payton took a step closer to her, a mixture of emotions broiling just beneath his surface. "Oh, it's me. No parlor trick. But I am not the man you remember with that flawless memory of yours."

"Certainly not," Morgan stood her ground. "The man I knew was a man of peace. He would *never* have taken another life."

"Nine years is a long time, love."

Morgan tried to keep up a composed appearance, but her breathing had changed, her eyes were shifting around, and her entire body had become tense. "I don't understand. Any of this. What's happened to you?"

"*You* happened. That day in France, when I pushed you out of the way of the cave-in, only to have you leave me for dead while you saved yourself. Everything that happened to both of us after that was a direct result of *your* decision. You could say it was a defining moment."

"You can't possibly think I left you in that cave, knowing you had *any* chance of living. I held your hand until it went cold, I can still remember—"

"Did you have any idea how much I *lived* for you?" he spat, taking a step closer to her. "Did you know that if it had been you buried beneath the earth, I would *still* be there, holding your hand? I would have found a way to get you out. I would have done *something* . . . After I was Shifted, you were the one bright spot in an existence turned upside-down, the one source of hope I had. I would have done *any-thing*—" He broke off, looking away. Then his gaze pierced hers again. "If it had been you, I wouldn't have been able to live. Do you get that? Did you have any clue how *deep* my feelings ran?"

Morgan went pale, then she whispered, "I don't think I did."

"You want to know what's happened to me?" Payton said, his voice rising. He took another step closer until mere inches separated them. "I did what I had to do, to live without you."

She looked down.

"*Forget* the man who loved you," Payton went on, right in her face. "I am not that raving mad, lovesick child who held to the notion that love could make anything better. That man *died* nine years ago. You won't be seeing him again."

A few tears escaped Morgan's eyes as she whispered, still looking down, "Who has taken his place?"

"Someone you don't want to know."

Morgan, Grant could tell, was using every measure at her disposal to keep her composure. He had always known her to be so calm and wise, that even in the short time he'd gotten to know her, he could see that now she was in a turmoil that was unprecedented. She closed her eyes and squeezed out a few more tears while Payton stared her down, daring her to respond.

She took several deep breaths and then forced herself to look at Payton once more.

"What do you want with *him*?" Morgan quietly asked, nodding to Grant.

Payton answered slowly, over-pronouncing his words as if he were speaking to a child. "I want him to die."

"Grant is not your enemy."

Payton blinked for the first time since spotting Morgan. His eyes shifted over to Grant and then back to Morgan. His body weight shifted back a bit, the slightest hint of confusion creeping across his features.

"His name is Grant?" Payton asked suspiciously. "Grant *Borrows*? This man is the great 'savior of the Loci'?"

Morgan nodded, noting his sudden change.

Payton took a full step back and stared at Grant, a dazed sort of doubt overtaking his features. No one spoke. Grant looked back at him in confusion.

"But he wears the *Seal*," Payton said in clench-jawed protest.

Morgan studied him. "The what?"

"This can't be." Payton looked all around, at the ground, at the sky, at everyone present. "Unless . . . unless I have been misdirected."

"Hey, Drexel's gone!" Alex shouted.

Everyone turned to look, and the detective was nowhere to be seen. The woods closed in thickly around the asylum, and he'd slipped off when Morgan appeared. Grant knew he was out there, but they'd never find him now.

Still Morgan was undeterred from her conversation with Payton. "Does that mean you won't harm Grant?" she asked.

Payton turned sharply as he kicked his sword off of the ground, caught the handle, and swished it until the tip was poking Grant in the chest, all in one movement. Julie cried in protest but Grant pulled her behind him with one hand.

"Even if he *is* this man 'Borrows,' he is still wearing *that*," Payton nodded at Grant's ring. "And the time of the Seal is nearly upon us. I have sworn by blood to prevent his coming, and I will fulfill that vow. But this matter of identity must be resolved."

Grant opened his mouth to explain, but he couldn't think of anything. He was too exhausted. And Payton was already walking away anyway, sheathing his sword.

As he mounted his motorcycle, Grant called out, "Hey!"

Payton turned his head.

"Where'd you get that sword?" Grant asked.

Payton roared the bike's engine to life.

"It was constructed centuries ago for a singular purpose," he replied. "To slay the Bringer."

46

"He always had quick reflexes," Morgan explained an hour later to Grant from behind her desk in the Common Room. Fletcher had joined them, and Julie sat beside Grant, applying bandages to his cuts. "I never made the connection until today that his reflexes could *be* his mental gift . . ."

She was silent for so long that even Julie stopped what she was doing—applying a large bandage around Grant's stomach—to look up.

The stillness of the room caught up with her finally, and Morgan snapped out of her reverie.

"I'm sorry," she said. "I can't reconcile the man I knew with the man we just met. And I can't help suspecting that it's all my fault . . ."

Grant allowed her a moment before he spoke again. "I don't understand how extra brain power enables his *body* to move faster."

Alex approached from behind. "Your physical body is regulated by your mental processes," she said. "It's basic physics, sweetie. The neurons that send commands from his brain to the rest of his body move at an accelerated rate—*that's* his mental gift. It's all connected, so his muscles are able to react equally fast. But it only gives him a quick burst of speed. He couldn't maintain it."

"Oh good, it's the turncoat," Fletcher mumbled.

"So, he can't *run* that fast?" Grant asked.

"He could for a few seconds. Enough to get out of sight, disorient his target."

Grant, Julie, and Fletcher were so caught up in her explanation that they never saw Morgan rise from her chair as Alex was talking. The *pop* they heard was their first indication.

Morgan had shoved Alex roughly into a chair and smacked her across the face.

"Do you know how *hard* we've worked to keep this place a secret!" Morgan shouted at Alex, her hands on the chair's armrests, leaning in. "To have found a place where we can live without worrying about being found? Did thoughts like these even cross your mind while in Drexel's custody, or did you ever manage to stop thinking about *yourself*?"

Alex glared at her as everyone watched.

"I didn't tell him about this place. I *did* tell him about you, Grant," she added with a fleeting glance at Julie, "and I would have told him more if he had asked me. I couldn't stop myself."

Grant studied her. "What, he used some kind of truth agent on you?"

She nodded.

Morgan was taken aback by this, and returned to her chair, sullen and dismayed. "I'm sorry."

"Wait a second," Julie broke in. "Just thought of something . . . Payton called your ring a Seal. *The* Seal. He said its 'time' was almost here."

Morgan turned to Julie, picking up on her train of thought. "And Marta told me that Grant would find out the truth soon. Then there is the prophecy on the stone tablet."

Grant finally caught on. "Whatever's happening to me—the Shift, the powers, the Forging, all of it—it's unfolding according to some kind of *timetable*."

"You know," Fletcher griped. "I had this figured out *weeks* ago, but does anyone ever listen to me?"

"So, the question then becomes . . ." Morgan began.

"What happens at the end of the timetable? And who made it to begin with?" Grant finished, throwing a quick glance at Alex. "We should talk to Marta about this."

"Oh, she's dead," Fletcher announced without import. "Marta never regained consciousness when the rest of us did after the recent . . . *incident*."

Grant gaped at Morgan. "But you told me *everyone* woke up after the Forging!"

"Marta was *very* old," Morgan said just as Fletcher was about to speak again. "She had a weak heart. We don't know if it was this 'Forging,' as you call it, that ended her life or not."

Grant digested this slowly. *Another one . . . Another one gone because of me . . .*

"Can we return to the matter of Drexel for a moment?" Morgan asked, partly because she meant it and partly to distract Grant from unpleasant feelings. "If Alex here didn't reveal our location to him, then who did?"

Everyone looked at Alex. She shrugged. "I *woulda* told him, while I was drugged, if I'd known. I've never been here before today. But he never asked me."

"Which means he likely knew already," Morgan reasoned. She turned. "Fletcher? Any intuition as to who our traitor is?"

He never hesitated. His eyes moved to Grant, staring for a long moment but as Grant was about to protest he looked past him and pointed: "Her."

They all turned, but Morgan said it before they could see who Fletcher was looking at.

"*Hannah*," she gasped.

Hannah had just run into the Common Room, slinging her blond locks over one shoulder and reacting in horror to the destruction and injuries she saw.

Grant stood, his features hardening. "Hello, beautiful."

Hannah froze at Grant's tone of voice. She gazed around, taking in the dozens of eyeballs all pointing in her direction. Something about the coldness of this greeting . . .

"Some-body's bust-ed," Alex sing-songed.

"How could you sell me out?" Grant asked, his face an unnerving, even calm.

Hannah's eyes went wide, her face flushed. "I didn't . . ." she blurted.

"How could you sell them out!" he shouted, pointing at the Loci.

Hannah stared at him blankly. "I, I didn't think—" she stammered.

"No, you've been doing a *lot* of thinking," Grant seethed. He was fighting to keep his voice calm, not to shout again. As he spoke something new clicked. "All this time you've been spying on me, reporting back to Drexel about my actions. That's how he's been able to keep such close tabs on me. And you gave him the asylum. All of this misery and bloodshed is on *your* hands."

"No! I never meant—" Hannah started, tears forming in her eyes.

"But you *did*!" Grant bellowed. Small objects all around the room jumped in place as he shouted. "When you make someone trust you while lying to them, that's something you *mean* to do!" Grant's thoughts lingered on the conversation they'd had in the dinner hall of this very building, only days before.

The pool table upended itself and crashed against a wall.

"Grant, calm yourself," Morgan said.

Hannah spoke, her voice barely above a whisper. "My feelings for you—"

"When you sell out everyone who trusts you," Grant said coldly, "then no matter what the reason . . . it's premeditated. It's calculated." He took a dangerous step toward her. "It's *personal*."

Hannah glanced around at the anger in every face surrounding her, even from faces she didn't recognize.

A single tear appeared.

And then she moved.

"You're going to just let her *leave*?" Alex asked, not believing her eyes.

"She's not going *anywhere*," Grant said in a determined voice, still watching Hannah where she stood.

"You might want to tell *her* that!" Alex said, eyes wide.

"Stop her!" Morgan shouted urgently.

Grant looked at Morgan quizzically, startled. Then he looked back at the Common Room door where Hannah had stood, and saw that it was closed. Hannah was nowhere in sight.

One second after his feet were in motion, he realized what she'd done—used her misdirection ability on him to escape.

Alex was hot on his heels as he opened the door, but he turned and put a hand out.

"I've got this. Stay with the others."

"But if you're alone, she can use her mojo to slip away from you," Alex protested.

Grant walked out the door. "She won't get the chance."

"Grant, wait!" Alex called.

He turned around in the hallway, angry now. Alex was looking all around.

"Where's your sister?" she said.

He looked.

Julie was gone.

Hannah was in a hard run, rounding the back of her car, when Julie crashed into her from behind, dragging her to the ground.

Julie had Hannah by the throat before Hannah figured out what was happening, and Hannah reflexively launched a defensive punch into Julie's face. Julie's head whipped around with the blow, but she didn't let go, a wildfire blazing in her eyes. Her whole body was shaking with anger.

"He *trusted* you!" she cried, hot tears forming, but she refused to let them fall. "He *cared* about you!"

Unable to deflect Julie's fury but not wanting to harm her, Hannah brought one knee up to her chin and kicked outward with her foot straight into Julie's chest. Julie flew backward, landing on her back a few feet behind Hannah's sleek black sports car.

Hannah jumped to her feet and got in the car.

She looked behind her and couldn't see Julie anywhere.

She's gone to get Grant. Go!

She put her key in the ignition.

Grant burst through the front door just as Hannah was starting her car.

"Stop!" he screamed, beating a path down the front steps.

Hannah put the car into reverse and hit the gas, as Grant came running toward her, waving his arms.

The back of the car lurched violently, and Hannah slammed on the brakes.

Grant stopped and knelt by the passenger's side of the car. Hannah stopped the car, a sickening weakness settling in her stomach. She got out of the car and ran to the other side just in time to see Grant pulling Julie from beneath it.

Grant gently tugged on Julie's legs until he had her all the way out from under the car. She was lying in repose, frozen in the same position Hannah had last seen her in after kicking herself free. Except that her chest bore a black tire mark across it, and dirt and soot were all over her clothes.

Hannah took a step forward to see if Julie was breathing, but Grant gathered his sister up into his arms and turned sharply away from her.

Hannah couldn't seem to get her mouth to close. The inside of it went dry, and all of the moisture in her body now seemed to be spilling from her eyes.

"Grant, I . . ."

He turned slowly to face her, looking at her as if she were a thing. A thing he no longer recognized.

Stumbling backward, she found herself back in the car. A few moments later, she was racing down the drive and out onto the black roadway, her mind filled with images of Julie's unconscious body and the hatred in Grant's eyes.

That look on his face . . .

It was all she could see.

47

"She's still comatose?" Daniel asked.

"Yeah," Grant said, rubbing his forehead. He held the phone with one hand, and stroked Julie's hand with another, as she slept. "She has some injuries to her vital organs. There was . . . internal bleeding."

"What's the prognosis?" asked Daniel's maddeningly clinical voice on the other end of the phone.

"She got out of her second surgery a little while ago," said Grant. He sounded weak, as if all of the strength had left his body. "All they can do now is keep her comfortable, and—" he huffed—"and hope she pulls out of it."

A breathy sob escaped Grant's lips, and Daniel remained silent, allowing him the moment.

Forty-eight hours had passed since Grant's confrontation with Payton and Drexel. Grant had not yet left Julie's side except during her surgeries, when he paced relentlessly in the waiting room. He wore a hooded sweatshirt, trying desperately to keep the nurses from seeing his face; the news still showed his photo every so often.

He had dozed occasionally since planting himself by her bed, but he would jerk himself awake after a few minutes.

Sometime during the last two days it had finally dawned on him that he needed to talk to someone. There were too many emotions and thoughts stomping through his mind, and he couldn't take it much more.

He was doing a good job of holding things in check when he was around the others. Morgan believed so strongly in him; whether he agreed with her or not, he couldn't bring himself to divulge to her the true depths of his doubts. Daniel might one day become a trusted friend, but it was much too early to bare his soul to the scientist yet. Alex he still felt like he barely knew, despite what had just happened. Julie had been taken from him.

And Hannah . . . Hannah had done the taking.

But she was gone now.

He barely cared where she was. And he didn't trust himself or what he might do to her if he ran into her right now.

Alex had arrived an hour ago to sit with him. It was early morning—though Grant had long since lost track of the time—and this was at least the third time she had visited in two days.

Daniel was giving Grant a wide berth. They kept in touch over the phone every few hours, and Grant had given him enough details for the doctor to piece together what had happened with Hannah. And Drexel.

"Grant, do you really think it was wise to let Drexel escape? I mean . . . I understand your desire to maintain Morgan's cover at the asylum, and we *don't* have any evidence to prosecute him, but—"

"No one *let* Drexel go."

"Right, but still, shouldn't we be looking—"

"Can we . . . another time?" Grant choked. "I can't . . ."

Alex grabbed the phone out of Grant's hand.

"It's all good, Doc," she said. "Go count some molecules or something."

She hung up.

Alex dropped the phone into Grant's jacket pocket as he reached out and took Julie's limp hand in both of his. He squeezed it, wishing that the warmth and life of his body could enter hers as he gazed imploringly into her lifeless face.

"Wake up," he pleaded.

He could only weep. His throat constricted with the effort, and once more he thought of the vision of the snake, wrapping itself about his neck and squeezing . . .

"Please come back," he whispered. "I can't do this alone."

Dozing in and out of sleep for hours, Grant's thoughts wandered . . .
Julie.

Her Parkinson's, which he'd discovered because it was in her medical records.

Marta.

The Forging.

The ring he wore . . . Why did Payton call it "the Seal"?

Payton . . .

Morgan . . .

The Loci and their unique talents . . .

The stone tablet . . .

Alex . . .

Her boss, the Keeper . . .

Hannah . . .

Daniel . . .

Drexel . . .

Harlan Evers . . .

His life before the Shift . . .

And his life now.

All the way back to that first day, stepping off the bus and seeing himself . . .

It couldn't be random, Grant was sure of it. There was something at work here, a plan—but he couldn't see it.

And according to Morgan, it was on some kind of schedule. *Tick, tick, tick . . . .*

Despite his best efforts, no matter where his thoughts began, they always circled back and ended on Hannah. Thoughts of her betrayal choked him. Why would she do this? It made no sense.

But it was done. Irreversible.

And if I need any reminders of that, all I have to do is sit by this bed.

Grant thought of Payton and Morgan and wondered if he might ever become as bitter a man as Payton was. No, he and Hannah had never gotten far enough along to have fallen in love.

Yeah, keep telling yourself that.

you can do this.

Daniel finished typing the words and looked at his watch. "6:04 P.M.," it read.

He nervously tapped his fingers on the keyboard, waiting. This was taking too long.

Come on. Say something.

```
i can't, i'm sorry
```

think it over
please

```
sorry
```

no don't leave

```
[user logged off]
```

who was in the kitchen, but the sentiment was there all the same.

He had taken to using the desk chair as a makeshift wheelchair, since his had been destroyed by Payton. But Lisa had acquired a pair of crutches and was threatening to make him start using them any minute . . .

The sun was setting as Grant entered the apartment for the first time in three days. Daniel quickly logged off the chat room and switched off the monitor before Grant or Lisa noticed. Grant had made no effort to acknowledge his houseguests, and Daniel could see how red his eyes were and the lifeless sagging of his movements.

"Grant?" prompted Daniel gently.

"Huh?" Grant replied, barely coherent.

"How is she?" Lisa asked.

"Um . . ." he searched the floor as if trying to find the words. "No change. Did you get the uh . . . the picture of the tablet from Morgan?"

"Yeah, yeah," Daniel replied. "I spent a few hours hunched over it, but didn't seem to be getting anywhere so I was taking a break . . ."

Grant offered a barely perceptible nod. He changed jackets and retrieved some cash from the jar in the kitchen where they kept extra.

"Where are you going?" Lisa asked.

"Oh, I uh . . ." he mumbled, "I have to go home."

Lisa and Daniel looked at one another.

"Home?"

"My old home," he explained. "Where my dad and my sister lived."

"Right, of course, to find your father's safe," Daniel nodded. "Are you sure that can't wait, though? You need some rest."

Grant suddenly came to life. "No, what I need are some *answers*!"

"Grant, you're exhausted," Lisa said. "And scared."

"Don't tell me what I am!" he shot at her. "I've had it with all these secrets and games. I want to know what my parents have to do with any of this. I want to know who this Keeper person is that's playing chess with my life. I want to know why Hannah betrayed me. I want to know what this lousy thing *is*"—he held out his ring—"and why it *won't come off*! And I want to know *now*!"

A beeping sound startled all three of them in the silence that followed.

"It's the detector!" Daniel whispered, wild-eyed. "There's a shimmer in the building!"

"Can you tell where?" Grant asked.

Daniel grabbed his small device and studied it. "It's close."

"You two get in the bedroom—"

Before Grant could finish issuing orders, there was a knock at the door.

48

Grant put a finger over his lips, and walked to the door. He looked through the peephole.

"It's *him*, get down!" he whispered to Daniel and Lisa, looking frantically around for something he could use as a weapon. He spotted a broom leaning against the far corner in the kitchen.

Knock, knock.

Grant reached his arm toward the faraway broom. It twitched in place before finally leaping into the air and flying toward him. Daniel's detector immediately started beeping again, as Grant grabbed the broom out of the air and held it like a bat.

Blowing out a big breath, he placed one hand on the doorknob.

He opened it.

Payton stood on the other side, perfectly composed, hands clasped together in front.

Grant swung the broom hard and fast, a home run in the making. There was a blur of movement and then Payton was standing perfectly still again, in the same calm pose as before.

Half of the wooden broomstick lay on the floor at their feet; the other half was still in Grant's hands. Payton had drawn his weapon, sliced the broom, and sheathed the sword, all faster than any of them could see.

"If I wanted you dead, you would be," Payton said offhandedly. "Time is running out. And there are some things you should know."

"What could you have to say that I would want to hear?"

"My story," Payton replied.

"Not interested," Grant said.

"It's connected to your own."

Grant looked Payton up and down, but the other man's body language was impossible to read. This could easily have been a ruse; on the other hand, if Payton had wanted to attack, nothing Grant could muster would be likely to stop him.

And he hadn't attacked.

Grant glanced at Lisa and Daniel; Lisa was cowering on the floor behind the kitchen counter, while Daniel remained at the computer. Daniel shot him a "whatever you think" shrug, but Lisa looked as if she would kill the lot of them if Grant let Payton in.

"Very well." Grant stepped aside and Payton entered.

Lisa threw Grant a nasty look as she helped Daniel slide precariously to the living room in the desk chair. Grant kept a close eye on Payton, who took a seat opposite the sofa. Soon they were all settled in the living room, but Lisa was on the edge of her seat beside Daniel, seemingly ready to pounce should the intruder make a move toward him.

Payton broke the silence first. "I regret that it was necessary to damage your chair."

"Oh hey"—Daniel's expression soured—"if you *have* to destroy a guy's wheelchair, then, you know, I guess you just have to."

"Maybe you should say what you came here to say," Grant recommended.

"I came to give you this," Payton said, pulling a folded piece of paper out of his pocket. But instead of handing it to Grant, he extended it to Daniel.

Daniel took it. "What is it?" he asked, unfolding it.

"A key," replied Payton.

Daniel examined the paper, which was filled with symbols and alphanumeric letters.

"It's not a complete translation, but it's close." Payton said.

"This is the language from the stone tablet?" Daniel exclaimed.

Payton nodded, while Daniel immediately looked to Lisa. She answered his unspoken question by retrieving a printed copy of the stone tablet photo that Morgan had sent him.

"I'm sure Morgan has explained to you our history," Payton began, "and how it ended."

Grant nodded.

"That was nine years ago. After the cave-in in France, I was rescued and resuscitated. But it was not by luck or chance that my life was spared. The three men who found me had come looking for the same thing that Morgan and I were searching for—a fragment from the stone tablet.

"These men—they were kind to me, but eccentric, to say the least. They revived me, took me to the local hospital, but they never inquired about my identity or told me who *they* were. Not at first. They visited me several times in the hospital, and when I got out, they offered me a job. I had no intention of seeking out Morgan, so I took the job.

"Eventually, they told me that they knew of the significance of the ring on my finger. They explained to me that the rings are the keys to our mental powers, and they helped me figure out what my power was. One day I asked how they knew so much about me and about the rings. And on that day, they finally told me that they were members of a highly secretive order called the Secretum of Six."

He paused, leaned forward. "Words cannot adequately convey the power and authority this organization has at its disposal. They are like nothing else on this planet. So influential are they, so skilled in the arts of deception and camouflage, that even the world's governments know nothing of their existence. They are a small number of individuals who reside all over the world, though when they gather, it is at a central location. I've heard the word 'substation' more than once. They and those who preceded them have been watching and waiting for *millennia* for the coming of the rings and their wearers."

"Why? What are the rings? Where do they come from? Do you know?"

Payton shook his head. "The men of the Secretum call them the Rings of Dominion. The origin of the rings is the deepest of mysteries, but what I was taught is that sometime, somewhere, the Rings of Dominion were once worn and used by another group of people. The men who rescued me believed that the rings had been plucked out of some long-forgotten chapter of history and deposited here in the present. And now someone has put them to use again, using their mind-enhancing effects to create—"

"Heroes," Grant reluctantly said, leaning back in his chair. He let out a slow breath.

Payton nodded. "Perhaps. Perhaps not. You and *your* ring they have searched and waited for with the greatest consternation."

A secret order. Morgan mentioned a secret group that knew about the rings . . . said that Payton himself could be a member.

"Why?" Grant asked.

"Your ring is very, very special. It makes you similar to the rest of us, but *not* the same."

"Not the same how, exactly?"

"I don't know," Payton said. "But they called it the Seal of Dominion."

"Did you join this 'Secretum'?"

"I wasn't allowed. Ring-wearers may not join. As I carried out the work they assigned me, I picked up bits and pieces such as this. Eventually, I caught enough to understand why they were so interested in the stone tablet."

"Why?"

"They believed it foretold the time and circumstances surrounding the Bringer's coming. Everything they did was assigned a sense of urgency because of this looming event. Now that you're here, plans, devices, and strategies prepared centuries ago have been set into motion."

"And your sword? I've never seen anything like it. Where did it come from?"

"It was given to me by the men of the Secretum. One year to the day after I began working for them, they told me that they had been studying the ancient texts and had found a passage that referred to one ring-wearer who would die and be reborn, and then fulfill a specific role concerning the Seal and the one who wears it."

"You're supposed to kill me," Grant said.

Payton nodded. "It was all part of the prophecy. It is my destiny. It's the reason I'm here, and the reason I died and was revived. This I have been taught. They gave me the sword on that day. It's an ancient weapon, specifically fashioned to kill the Bringer—the wearer of the Seal.

"They sent me to study, to train, to learn every method of dispensing death known to man. But my assigned duty was a righteous one; they weren't creating a murderer. They wanted a *warrior*. They taught me about the Bringer's abilities and what you would be able to do. They taught me to strike quick, never to stop, to be relentless. Every day for over six years, it was drilled into my head that the wearer of the Seal *must* die, and that *I* would be the one to kill him."

"Then why *didn't* you?"

Payton broke eye contact for the first time and looked down. "I'm not certain. I am bound by a vow of honor and blood to end your life. And regardless of this prophecy business, I must fulfill that oath. But meeting you has caused me to question my purpose."

"Why would this Secretum want me dead?"

Payton shook his head. "It's not *you* they fear. It has never been about you. It's the Seal. They fear it mortally. Something about the Seal of Dominion is vastly different from all the other rings. Two years ago, they told me my training was complete and sent me out into the world to prove myself worthy. During my travels, I have spoken to others around the world who have experienced the Shift, and in recent weeks, I began hearing your name. Word is spreading about you. Those like us, those who know the truth about the rings, believe that you are here to save the world."

"You think maybe these men from the Secretum weren't being truthful with you? That they tricked you into coming after me? Is that why you're telling me all of this?"

"Doubt was planted, yes. This is the reason I have let you live. I've tried to reach the Secretum to confirm my suspicions, but they no longer answer me. It's possible they know that I have refused to fulfill my mission and have disavowed my actions."

Grant sat back in his chair, digesting this tale.

"*Grant!*" Daniel shouted.

"You figured out what the tablet says?"

Daniel looked up from his chair at the desk, his eyes wide with fear.

"Part of it. I've found what appears to be a key bit of the text."

Grant swallowed, listening closely.

"First of all, please keep in mind that the tablet is ancient. So some of these passages simply don't appear to have a direct English translation—"

"I'm with you, Doc. Just give me whatever you can."

"The tablet is called the 'Dominion Stone,' and in essence, it was created to tell of—rough translation here—a 'miracle-man' who would one day come, called the Bringer."

"I know this already," Grant replied impatiently. "This 'miracle-man' . . . What is he here for? What does he *do*?"

"Wait, there's something else. The tablet speaks of another figure of importance. By my best guess, this second person is the 'overseer of destruction.'"

"The Keeper," Grant said, though there was no need.

"*Or* . . . it could be the Thresher," Lisa offered. "The second person is not mentioned by name."

"How is he mentioned?"

"If I'm reading this correctly . . ." Daniel explained, "it says that on a day of reckoning, these two will clash to 'set the course of the future.'"

So there it was. It would be a fight.

"Um," Daniel spoke slowly, reluctantly, "it *also* says something to the effect of . . . 'no act of man can prevent the torment that day will herald.'"

49

Daniel gingerly sat up in bed, the darkness of night obscuring his vision. He rubbed at his eyes.

His "borrowed" hospital bed creaked slightly in its spot in the living room. He froze in place, listening for any evidence that his movement had been detected.

The apartment he shared with Lisa was dead silent; the only audible sound was her gentle breathing coming from the bedroom. The small condo had suited them well as a safe house during his recovery, but they couldn't stay here forever.

So now's as good a time as any, he decided.

Ever so carefully, Daniel strained in silence and threw his legs slowly over the side of the bed. His legs still wore the casts; it had only been a few weeks, but he was beyond ready for them to be removed. Constantly itching and unbearably hot, they often kept him awake at night. Still his broken ribs seemed to be mending nicely, and his wrist no longer caused him pain when he used it.

His hands reached out in the darkness and laid hold of the crutches. The rubber tips on the ends softened the noise as he hefted his weight up onto them and stood. Daniel froze again to listen, making sure Lisa hadn't heard him.

When he was satisfied that his movements were still unnoticed, he wobbled carefully to the front door, fumbled with the lock while trying to hold the crutches still with rigid elbows, and finally, cautiously, wrangled the door open.

Still Lisa remained peacefully unaware.

She would kill *me if she caught me trying this . . .*

On the other hand, she might just applaud me for learning how to use these blasted crutches.

He hobbled awkwardly out into the hall, careful to shut the door quietly behind him. Once out of the apartment, less stealth was required, and he took the elevator down to the ground floor. He shuffled out and looked around the lobby, only to realize that he'd never seen it before. They'd entered via the parking garage on the third floor when Grant had brought him here.

The lobby was larger than he expected, with a checkerboard pattern of large marble tiles on the floor, an ornate chandelier hanging from the ceiling, and a large collection of stainless steel mailboxes beside the stairwell door on his right. A set of glass double doors lay straight ahead, leading outside.

His crutches and teetering steps echoed loudly in the empty lobby until he got his hands on the front door. Double-checking that his keys were still in his front pocket, he pushed the release mechanism to open the main entrance and step out into fresh air for the first time in weeks.

He wasn't dressed for the night's unexpectedly cool temperature, but he tried to ignore it. He turned left onto a small concrete sidewalk that led to a set of electricity meters and panels attached to the front of the building and hidden by a row of tall bushes.

A young man sat on a skateboard there behind the brush, watching Daniel approach while shifting his eyes in all directions.

"You came," Daniel said with some effort, relieved.

"Yeah, and I was on time, too," the young man replied, sizing him up.

"Sorry," Daniel said, coming closer and lowering his voice. The kid couldn't have been more than fourteen. "I, uh, never caught your real name."

"Will," the boy said, looking around again. "Still don't know why we had to do this in person."

"Just needed to make sure," Daniel said, lowering his voice to a whisper now. "You understand what I'm asking you to do?"

The boy nodded in nervous, fast movements, but kept his expression even and cool.

"It's won't be easy," Daniel said. "And it will probably be painful."

"Just sign me up, man. I get it."

"Do you really?" Daniel said, edging closer. "I want you to be sure about that. You won't be the same after this is over."

Will looked Daniel in the eye. "I *told* you already. Just say when and where."

Daniel nodded slowly, sizing the kid up. *Okay, then.*

"Stay in contact with Sarah and the others," Daniel said, readjusting himself on his crutches. "Be reachable, and be ready to move. It'll happen fast."

Will nodded then hopped up onto his skateboard and rolled past Daniel and down the sidewalk.

Daniel watched him go in silence, sighing long and hard at his young friend and the innocence he had just thrown away.

Morning came, and Grant got up early to visit Julie before his big road trip to the old house.

Under different circumstances, it might have pained him to see his car in the condition he found it—the damage Payton had caused prevented him from putting the top up or using the windows. The passenger-side glass was entirely gone.

But then, today was not a normal day.

If such a thing existed anymore.

He needed to fill Morgan and the others in on all that Payton had told him last night, but he didn't want to put off this trip home any longer. It was a six-hour drive in normal traffic. Time to get it over with.

Grant revved the engine and spiraled downward to the exit. As he turned the final corner, a familiar tingle crossed the back of his neck . . .

A tingle that told him he was about to see someone he didn't want to see.

He drove up to the exit—which still sported a broken barrier from when he had crashed through it ahead of Payton—and suddenly he slammed on the brakes.

Hannah stood right in front of the car, blocking his way with her hands on the hood. The first day he'd met her at Inveo, she'd been so in-control. So strong. Confident. Now she looked like a teenager who'd run away from home. Her blond hair was matted down as if it hadn't been washed in days, her makeup had worn off long ago, and her clothes were filthy.

"Move or I'll move you," he shouted from the car. "I mean it."

"I need to talk to you," she said in a sad voice, "but I don't know what to say."

"Let me guess. You have information to share with me? Everyone I meet seems to have just the right information at just the right time."

Hannah looked down and shook her head. She slowly walked around to stand beside his car door. "I've only got one piece of information to offer you, big boy, and that's *why*."

"You know," he said, the car shaking slightly, "if I concentrated hard enough, I really think I could grind your bones into powder." He raised an arm in her direction.

"I don't believe you'd do that," she said softly, but took a step back all the same.

He looked into her eyes. "You've given me *so* many reasons to. Don't give me another."

She looked away, unable to maintain eye contact with him. "You won't let me explain myself?"

"Explain it to my sister," he growled, turning back to the steering wheel. The car shook violently.

Grant was about to drive off, but Hannah stepped closer, close enough to touch him. "Drexel tried to kill me," she said.

He paused, but wouldn't look at her.

"He blamed me for everything that happened. He was furious. I managed to get away, but he's still out there, and I think he's going to try and finish the job."

Grant's eyes swiveled to meet hers. "Come near me again, and he won't have to."

A squeal of tires and a cloud of blackened smoke punctuated his exit.

50

DANGER, the sign read in red block letters. *This structure is declared unsafe . . .*

He sighed. The grass and brush were severely overgrown to the point that it was difficult to see much of the house beyond. What he could see appeared to be suffering from heavy termite damage.

Condemned. They condemned my childhood home.

Grant made his way across the yard—feeling as though he needed a jungle knife to cut through the foliage—and approached the front door. Yellow tape was stretched across it twice, forming a large "X".

Grant took a step back, glanced over his shoulder to ensure no one was watching, and raised his arm. Focusing on the door, he shoved his hand forward, and the door was swallowed by the gloomy shadows of the house's interior.

He whipped out a flashlight and entered. The stench of rotted wood was overpowering. The interior of the house looked nothing like the vague images he retained of the few years he lived here as a child. The carpet was ragged and barely clinging to the floor. Many of the walls had holes that went all the way through. The kitchen was inaccessible, the wooden framework and ceiling over the room having buckled and collapsed inward.

He was almost glad Julie wasn't there to see it.

Making his way into the master bedroom, he found the attic door in the ceiling where he remembered it and pulled down on the small piece of cord that still dangled from it. A ladder that seemed sturdy enough, though it creaked with every careful step he took, folded down from the door.

In the musty, moth-infested attic, he had no real idea of where to begin looking for his father's safe.

Where do you hide something in a big, hollow, empty space?

At the far end of the room, his eyes landed on a small canoe, mounted from the ceiling via a set of rope pulleys.

In plain sight, maybe?

In early afternoon, Morgan walked out of the hidden basement and stopped in place.

Across the Common Room one of her residents—the teenage boy, Thomas, who had been held at gunpoint by Drexel—was in one corner, waving a sword through the air. A crowd was gathered around him, watching with interest.

"Better, but there's more power in your wrist than you realize," a familiar voice was saying. "Less elbow, more wrist. No, don't lead with your shoulder."

Morgan marched straight into the gathering.

"What are you *doing*!" she shouted. "We have no use for such things here." She snatched the sword out of Thomas' hand and tossed the sword at Payton's feet.

"You'd prefer a blanket to cower under? Your little fort here has already been invaded once. Drexel knows where you are. You really think he won't try again? If the others choose to fight, you won't be able to stand in the way."

"You have no authority in this place," she said with a forced calm, staring him down, unblinking.

"I knew you were a control freak, love," Payton replied, polishing the sword between folds of his shirt, "but I had no idea you considered yourself so lofty. If these people really are your 'friends,' then you owe them the right to choose their own fate."

"Get out," she said.

No one moved.

She turned to the others. "Not him! The rest of you! OUT!"

Everyone filed out except Payton and Morgan, who never took their eyes off of one another.

When the room was empty and the door closed, Morgan spoke again. "Let's get one thing straight. You said you've changed over the last nine years. Well, guess what? You're not the only one. So you've faced danger. So you've been brought back from the edge of death. So you've learned how to poke at things with a big piece of steel. You think that makes you special?

"You have *no idea* what most of these people have been through before they came here. I do. I know them. I know their stories, their fears, what makes them laugh, what makes them hurt. Because that's what I do. I take care of them." She stepped closer until she was inches from his face. "Don't you *ever* come in here and tell these people how to live their lives!"

Payton stared at her for a long moment, unperturbed. She was almost red in the face now. He still appeared unmoved.

"You're right, you *have* changed," he said slowly, not breaking eye contact.

Morgan let out a breath. She looked as though she wanted to slug him, but she merely clenched her fists.

"But not nearly enough."

If it was possible, her face became even redder.

"Your 'friends' were just telling me," he went on, "about how much they respect you. How they look up to you and rely on you. They seem to see you as some noble figure who's always collected and in control. That *persona* you project—it's so practiced and measured. But I see the truth below."

He walked around her as she stood unmoving. "You're holding it in," he said. "You keep it buried all neat and tidy, and you'd be mortified if they ever saw the *real* you. But it's making its way to the surface now. After all these years."

Her features remained red and angry, but took on the slightest hint of uncertainty.

"Feed that rage, love," Payton said, deadly serious. "You're going to need it. We all are."

He turned and began walking away, but Morgan remained rooted to her spot, breathing hard and fast.

"I won't become an animal. Violence solves nothing," Morgan said quietly.

He cast a glance over his shoulder. "You'd be surprised how many things it will solve."

The pulleys holding the canoe in place were rusted and didn't want to turn. Grant finally gave up and made it break loose with his mind. The old wooden boat shattered on the floor.

In the remains of what used to be the front section of the canoe lay a small, hard plastic, store-bought safe on its side, no more than a foot wide and tall. Grant hoisted it from the debris, found a secure place to sit and opened it.

He didn't toy with guessing the safe's combination. He merely focused his thoughts on the small front door and *lifted* it from its hinges. Inside were five Army file folders marked "Classified." Each had its own label. The first four, in turn, were "Frank Boyd," "Cynthia Boyd," "Julie Boyd," and "Collin Boyd."

His entire family.

Why would the Army keep top secret files on my family?

He flipped to the last file.

"The Secretum of Six."

Grant's heart fluttered. His father had known about the Secretum?

He began by opening his father's file. The first paper was an official commendation on his service record, signed by "Gen. Harlan Bernard Evers." Grant scanned the page. One paragraph jumped out at him:

> Frank is the finest officer to ever serve under my
> command, representing the best of what the United
> States Army has to offer. He has earned my full
> confidence and absolute trust. Major Boyd has
> become the leading intelligence gatherer in our
> entire department. His experience has proven
> vital to unraveling the mysteries of the Secretum.

So. Payton was wrong. The U.S. government *did* know of the Secretum, after all.

But what did Evers mean by "his experience"?

The next page was a photocopy of a large black-and-white photograph of his parents. Smiling both, his mother was sitting at a desk which his father was leaning over from the opposite side. It looked like the photographer had caught them in a candid moment, but they both turned to look into the lens and smile before the shutter was triggered.

Grant saw the indentations of handwriting through the paper; he turned it over to read what it said.

A scribbled note read, "Frank and Cynthia. X marks the spot."

X?

He flipped the page again and examined it closer. He gasped when he spotted it: a tiny "x" had been marked on the photo with a black pen; just above it, a miniature tattoo was visible on his father's left wrist. And . . . *There!* His mother had one too, in the same spot.

The tattoos looked remarkably like one of the symbols found on Grant's ring.

"Mom and Dad . . ." he breathed, unbelieving. "They knew all about the Secretum."

Grant leaned back, putting an arm behind him for support.

It couldn't be true.

He discarded the other folders for now and skipped to the one with "Collin Boyd" written on it.

The first document he came upon inside was a birth certificate.

A birth certificate for . . .

He shuddered.

The certificate was for "Grant Borrows."

There's a real Grant Borrows? I thought that name was just made up and given to me!

But this paper he held was no copy. It was an original; he could see the pen's indentations, though it bore no notary watermark.

He thumbed through the remainder of his file, the contents of which included photos from his early childhood, the results of his father's test on his mental acuity, and little else. No other birth certificate was enclosed.

Grant couldn't figure out what this meant. Why would his father have a birth certificate with "Grant Borrows" on it?

His thoughts started coming faster and faster, reeling back to past conversations, remembering things he had been told.

"So you're me, now," he heard his own voice saying to Collin that first day. *"Does that mean I'm you?"*

"It doesn't work that way," Collin had replied. *"I'm just a volunteer.*

I'm no one important. You're different."

Then the moment between moments where the hazy outline of his mother had spoken to him.

"Stay true to yourself. Nothing is as it seems," she said in that silky, dreamy voice.

And Harlan Evers had said before his death, *"If you go and find your father's files, you're going to learn things that will be hard to accept. Things about your parents* and *about yourself . . . Once this corner is turned, once you know this truth, there will be no going back."*

Finally, he thought of Morgan, quoting something that the old woman Marta had told her . . .

"She said you've always *been* who *you are now."*

And the truth dawned on him.

He didn't know how it was true, but he could feel in his bones that it was.

This couldn't be.

It just couldn't.

It was madness.

Grant could only shake his head.

"I wasn't changed *into* this person," he whispered. "Grant Borrows is the real name I was given at birth . . ."

51

"Bike won't start," Payton said to someone from the front hall. "Been knacked since I crashed it into Grant's car."

Terrific, Morgan thought from the Common Room. *He's stuck here. With us.*

A tremendous commotion came from the hall, where numerous residents seemed to be gathering near the front door. "Oh, lovely," came Payton's voice above the din.

Morgan followed his voice to find the front door open. Payton stood at the front of them, looking out over the threshold. Fletcher was next to him.

"What's going on?" she asked, forcing her way through the men and women who were already elbow-to-elbow, looking outside the door.

"You have a visitor," Payton said, not turning around. "The snitch."

Morgan's eyes drew into narrow slits when she finally made it to the front door.

Hannah stood just outside the door, leaning against the door post. She looked as if she barely had the energy to stand. She was filthy, her eyes were bloodshot, and—covered in sweat but not out of breath—she was probably running a fever.

Morgan had never seen the southern belle like this before.

"What do you want, Hannah?" asked Morgan.

"To warn you," Hannah said wearily, struggling to get the words out.

"About what?" Morgan replied, unimpressed.

"I'm not . . ." Hannah mumbled, trying to remain upright, "I . . . I don't *know*, exactly! Somethin's going to . . . I don't know *what*, but I overheard . . ."

"She's lying," Fletcher started to say, but broke off when Hannah's eyes rolled up into her head. She began to collapse . . .

In a flash, Payton had dropped his sword and she was resting in his arms. He was already holding her long before the sword ever hit the ground.

"Brilliant," he said, frowning, as he gazed down with disdain at Hannah, unconscious in his arms. He turned to face Morgan. "What am I supposed to do with *this*?"

"You'll think of something," Morgan replied. "But don't kill her. Well . . . wouldn't be the end of the world, but *try* not to kill her."

The Corvette pointed south, Grant sped toward L.A. on 395, letting the car almost drive itself. Traffic was light and so Grant's distracted thoughts didn't matter much. He was breathing fast, his blood pressure rising.

This . . . none of this . . .

His parents, members of the Secretum? The identity he'd known his entire life, a fabrication?

It *couldn't* be true.

He'd always assumed that those two words—*grant* and *borrow*— were someone's idea of a joke, given his current situation.

But no.

Rooting through some papers on the passenger seat, he found military discharge papers dated roughly one month before Julie's birthday. Grant began piecing it together . . .

Julie has no idea that the name she uses is not her real name, either, because she's never been told differently. Once we were living at the orphanage, all of our official documents had our assumed names on them, so no one had reason to believe they weren't real.

He turned to the file marked "The Secretum of Six" and opened it. This was the thickest file of all, full of handwritten notes, memos, and official Army documents.

One page was labeled "Official Enlistment Request Form." It had never been fully completed, but the names "Frank Boyd" and "Cynthia

Boyd" were scribbled hastily on top, followed by a brief, handwritten paragraph below:

> *The operatives listed above seek application to U.S. Army officer status. As former operatives for the Secretum of Six, their insider knowledge could help us decipher the mysterious organization's identity and intentions once and for all. Subjects created pseudonyms for themselves (listed above) to facilitate their escape from the Secretum, and have argued that their true names should be kept to prevent the Secretum from hearing of their defection. Subjects' extreme compliance with strenuous hours of debriefing indicate a willingness to submit to and work with U.S. authority. Applicants are highly recommended for fast-track approval.*

That was it, then. His parents had been operatives for the Secretum but fled and joined the U.S. military. In exchange for giving the government every piece of information they knew about the Secretum, the Army made them officers.

There never *was* a Collin Boyd. It was only a pseudonym used to protect him from being found by the Secretum. He had perhaps three hours left before he reached the asylum and he knew one thought would dog him that whole time.

My whole life has been one lie built upon another . . .

And what if his father had never left? What if he was a double-agent? Grant couldn't bend his mind around the reasons the man would disappear. It made no sense.

Nothing made sense anymore.

Another hour and a half in the car only cleared up a few points. He had managed to read through a few more of correspondence and the pieces began slipping together. Grant's father must have learned of the Secretum's plans for the Bringer, joined Army Intelligence after defecting, earned their trust—no doubt along with plenty of enemies within the secret order—and spent his time researching the Bringer and how he would be identified.

What a cruel twist of fate that it turned out to be his own son.

Or was it really a twist? Daniel was always saying that there are no coincidences . . .

Grant turned back to the "Secretum of Six" file and rifled through it some more.

A detailed report written by his father stated:

> The Secretum of Six is an ancient religious order, dating back several millennia. Shrouded in the utmost secrecy, their beliefs are built upon a stone tablet they call the Dominion Stone. There are conflicting theories on where the Stone came from, but the Secretum claims it is the oldest existing object on earth. The predominant theory is that it was a marker, placed upon some kind of enclave built to protect the Rings of Dominion—a seal meant to lock the away the Rings until the time was right.
>
> It contains a prophecy, regarding an important figure who leverages an event that has not yet come to pass. We have been unable to determine what this future event is, but we know that all of the Secretum's activities are centered around it. Approximately six hundred years ago, enemies of the Secretum found a way to break the Stone into smaller fragments, and scattered the pieces around the globe. The Secretum seems to have been largely unaffected by losing it, as their scholars had studied and deciphered the writing on it several thousand years ago. Having the Dominion Stone back now would be merely an act of devotion.

A hand-written memo also in the file said,

> The Secretum has money and resources that are vast, capable of wielding unimaginable levels of influence. Several major corporations report to them, including Paragenics Group.

And Inveo Technologies, Grant guessed.

Secrets and lies. Speeding toward L.A., Grant felt his pulse hammer in his palms as he gripped the steering wheel. He knew answers to his questions were closeer than ever, but like a mirage shimmering in the mid-day sun on the highway, still of reach. Somebody, soon, would need to answer to him.

When Hannah finally awakened, Payton, joined by the uninvited Fletcher, began trying to pull more information from her. Even Payton's sword, however, failed to uncover little more than what she'd already offered.

"Something big is in the works," Payton said slowly, never taking his eyes off Hannah. "You don't know what it is, but you 'overheard' mention of it. That sum it up?"

Hannah nodded, and took another sip out of the glass she held with both hands. She looked like a caged animal, hoping to be rescued.

"Then tell me *who* you heard it from," Payton said slowly.

She looked down.

"Listen, young lady—" Fletcher began sternly, then stopped, as if realizing something. "It's obvious who she heard it from. Matthew Drexel."

"Drexel . . ." Payton uttered, a deadly gleam settling into his eyes. "I need to borrow a car."

"All right," Fletcher replied, suddenly curious. "Your motorcycle won't start at all?"

"No," Payton said absently. "It was making an odd sound."

Fletcher looked far away, the gears in his mind spinning rapidly. "What *kind* of sound?"

"Clacking of a loose screw, maybe."

Fletcher paused, then his eyes swiveled to Payton's. "Could you wait here just one moment?" He walked at a brisk pace out of the Common Room and toward the front door.

Morgan stood, alarmed by Fletcher's sudden exit.

"How much does he know about motorcycles?" Payton asked.

"Nothing I'm aware of," Morgan replied.

Fletcher ran back in at a dead sprint and pulled down on an old fire alarm attached to the wall.

"Everybody *out of the building*! Go out the back! Quickly!" he yelled. For a moment, no one moved. They merely stared at him, startled. "RUN!" he bellowed at the top of his lungs. "*NOW!!*"

In the Corvette, Grant abruptly gulped in a full breath of air and slammed back into his seat, as if he'd been punched in the stomach. All thoughts of his investigation were gone, replaced by an image that had intruded upon his mind. His eyes squeezed shut so tight, for a long second, the Corvette blasting ahead regardless.

When he opened his eyes again, he was pasty white, clammy, and an unchecked panic radiated from every pore of his body.

They were dying.

52

Lisa was growing increasingly tense.

Not only tense. She was angry at herself.

Bitter, even.

Daniel had stopped acting normal *days* ago, keeping secrets and telling half-truths. And he was always on that computer.

Something was up.

She'd tried to watch him closely but it'd led nowhere and finally she'd gone to her room, planning to keep tabs on him as best as she could. Maybe if she were out of sight, he might give up a clue. But nothing happened. And her eyes grew heavy.

She didn't know what woke her up that night, until she heard the whisper of the apartment door close.

Her heart racing in her chest, she dashed out into the living room—noticing the empty computer chair along the way—and looked one-eyed through the peephole in the front door.

Just in the far periphery of her sight, she saw Daniel hobbling onto the elevator.

She had to follow.

Heading into the hall and taking the second elevator, she pushed the button for the ground floor, assuming Daniel, in his condition, wouldn't be heading to the garage.

The elevator door opened onto an empty lobby. Through the glass front windows, she saw plenty of pedestrians and vehicles; the city was illuminated by multitudes of streetlamps and a flood of evening traffic.

But no Daniel. Yet he'd have to have headed outside.

She pushed through the lobby doors and stepped onto the sidewalk. The noise of the city rushed at her. It had been so quiet of late. One sound in particular caught her ear. A crash as if a trash can had been tipped over. It had come from the alley to the side of the building. She crept to the building's corner and peeked around.

Standing there on his crutches, about forty feet away, was Daniel, speaking forcefully to two very large, very . . . *capable*-looking men, who wore dark leather jackets and skull caps. Most startling of all was that Daniel appeared to be in no danger. Quite the contrary. The men were listening intently to what he was telling them . . . then staring intently at the thick bundles of money he'd placed in each of their hands.

What was going on?

Was he no better than Hannah? Was he something far worse?

No, that was nuts.

Lisa ducked behind a bush just as she spotted the three of them headed her way. She watched as the two bigger men turned and walked away from the building, while Daniel painstakingly hobbled his way back inside.

Devastated, she dragged herself inside and up the stairs to Grant's apartment instead of her own.

But Grant was still gone, and Daniel hadn't returned, either, apparently going back to their apartment one floor down. The apartment was empty.

The computer.

Daniel spent an awful lot of time on Grant's computer.

She crossed the room and sat down at the desk, flicked on the PC's monitor, and began digging through hidden system files for a keystroke log.

53

Payton's first thought when he began to come around was that something was burning in the oven.

And it might've been him.

He drunkenly thought back . . .

He had been talking to Fletcher, who panicked about something or other, and then . . .

And then came the blast so loud he'd thought the world itself might have exploded.

Payton finally opened his eyes to find himself surrounded by flames. The asylum was *roaring*, consumed in fire and heat. Horrified screams came from all directions. Unmoving bodies lay about, and smoke was pouring everywhere, running into his eyes and making it hard to breathe.

So much fire . . . It couldn't have spread this fast . . . Where did it come from?

He was vaguely aware that his head was thundering in pain. And something wet was running down his right arm. A *lot* of something wet.

But there was no time for that now . . .

"Morgan!" he shouted when he spotted her through the haze. She seemed to be having trouble waking up, jerking lazily there on the floor, up against the wall. Something had *blown* her clear across the room . . .

She had several nasty cuts and her shoulder didn't look quite right . . .

Payton quickly regained his bearings and stood to see what was happening.

Fletcher was helping people up, appearing to have taken only a few scratches from the blast . . .

Hannah was rising from the floor by the couch, looking all around, tears pouring from her eyes . . .

His eyes met hers from across the room. There was no gloating in her face. Only despair. She had known something was coming. And he wouldn't listen.

She turned and began helping others get up . . .

But some of them could not be roused.

In the distance, entire sections of the building collapsed, causing deafening rumbles.

How did this happen? It was too fast, much too fast . . .

Reflection would have to wait. Payton joined in the escape efforts as the building's girders groaned and creaked above him. The building wouldn't—*couldn't*—remain upright for very long. The survivors gathered and Hannah and Fletcher began leading them out of the Common Room, toward the facility's back door.

Payton got close enough to see that Morgan's shoulder was indeed out of its socket, as he'd suspected, but she appeared to be ignoring the pain.

If she even felt any.

She merely watched her people and her surroundings, all burning.

The asylum would be a total loss in a matter of minutes.

Morgan couldn't look away from her dream dying, no matter where she turned. He grabbed her by the arm and steered her after the others.

Several hallways were completely blocked off, and they were forced to find new routes more than once.

And as they ran, they encountered more residents. Burning and bleeding.

Crying.

Grieving.

Some of them were on fire even now, motionless on the ground.

But there was no time . . . no time to stop and help . . . no time to think . . .

They soon had gathered the remaining survivors into a pack, all racing toward a rear entrance, the front hallway having caved in from the blast that had undoubtedly come from something rigged to Payton's motorcycle.

Morgan stopped in the rear hallway to check another body on the ground, which was wrapped hideously around a free-standing pillar in the middle of the corridor. Whoever it was, they weren't moving.

Payton carried two survivors—one over each shoulder—but stopped next to her as the ceiling groaned again.

"She won't hold together long!" he yelled over the roar of the flames and the collapsing building. With that, he was gone, faster than she could see.

Others passed by as Morgan continued to check for signs of life.

Hannah hobbled by, half-walking, half-dragging another limping resident.

From high above them, a great, terrible crack reverberated, so loud it drowned out all else.

The post Morgan knelt by began to fracture and crumble . . .

"*MORGAN!*" Hannah shrieked.

Before Morgan could react, she felt herself being shoved, as a violent crash shook the foundations of the entire building.

She looked up to see that the entire pillar had come down. It had brought much of the ceiling and this part of the building down with it, but she was clear and unscathed. Wiping debris off her body, she sat up and gasped in horror.

Trapped under the largest remaining section of the pillar was Hannah.

Unmoving.

Grant drove his scratched, dented blue Corvette faster than he'd ever dared before, blazing a lightning trail down the evening highway. Traffic was building, the closer he got to L.A., but he zoomed around everyone in sight.

Flashing red-and-blue lights appeared in his rearview mirror, but he ignored them, seeing only what was in his mind's eye.

Seeing it *all*.

Grant flinched as various sections of the asylum collapsed. A few times, he felt the unique light in his soul dim as another ring-wearer fell. And another.

He could *feel* them. Falling. Fading away.

He was already too late, he was at least another hour away . . .

I wasn't there . . .

When they needed me, I wasn't there!

"Hannah!" Morgan yelled over the burning building and the ongoing crashes around them.

"Morgan," Hannah tried to shout, but it came out quietly. She was completely pinned under the cement pylon, unable to move even her arms. "Get out of here, go . . ."

"Payton! Fletcher! *SOMEBODY!!*" Morgan screamed. Her useless shoulder was no good, but she propped the other one up against the pillar and threw her entire body weight against it.

The pillar never budged, and the fire, which had spread up into the ceiling, leaped hungrily down onto the pillar.

"It's all right," Hannah said, smiling, as the fire crept toward her like lava rolling down a hillside.

Choking on the billowing smoke, Morgan reached out and took Hannah's hand.

Her pulse was fading . . .

"It's as it should be," Hannah said softly, trying to keep her eyes open. "I deserve this. You don't."

Morgan cried.

She could do nothing else.

Tears rained openly down Morgan's face as Hannah closed her eyes.

Whoever this woman had been, whatever she was responsible for . . . Morgan was alive because she had taken her place.

The building shook again, and Morgan knew she should be running away as fast as her feet could carry her.

But she clutched Hannah's hand even tighter.

Daniel made his way carefully upstairs to Grant's apartment as darkness fell over the city. Lisa had never come down for supper. He'd been on the phone for the last hour, making final preparations, so it hardly bothered him. But it was odd of her to disappear for so long.

He placed his key in the lock and swung the door open. Lisa sat at the computer, across the room.

"There you are," he said, hobbling inside, "Where have you been all—?"

"You want to tell to me what this is?" she said quietly.

He looked at her—*really* looked at her—for the first time. She had been reading something on the screen . . . A very familiar-looking screen . . .

She was calm as she looked upon him, but he could tell that she was serious.

Dead serious.

"You want to *explain* to me why you're making secret plans with people you meet in *chat rooms*? Or why you're holding clandestine meetings in dark alleys? Why money has changed hands between you and a couple of rhino-sized thugs?"

He closed his eyes and looked down. His shoulders sagged. "Look, I know how it—"

Lisa jumped up from her chair and traversed the room in a few quick paces. She crossed her arms, facing him with a grim, resolute face.

"Skip the excuses and explain, right now," she said. "Lie to me, and I'll break your crutches."

"*Payton!*" Morgan screamed again.

In a flash he was outside the building's exit, just down the hall—what remained of it—looking in.

"We need—help here!" she shouted back, coughing through the smoke.

He was about to spring into action when a figure casually walked out from a side hall to stand between them, facing Payton. The darkened figure was illuminated only by the dancing light of the flames that continued to grow. He wore a hat and overcoat.

Payton could make out none of the man's features; his mouth and nose were covered by a handkerchief.

"What's wrong?" the man said, and Payton could hear a smile in his voice. His eyes glimmered with a madness that was fitting of the chaos and destruction that surrounded him. "I should think a man like you would appreciate a little violence and mayhem."

"You did this?" Payton asked, carefully placing his hand on the hilt of his sword.

"Fun for a girl and a boy," the man replied, smiling again.

"What do you want?" Payton asked. "Who are you?"

"Who am I? What a strange question," the man sounded genuinely perplexed. "Especially at a time like this. Look around you. Don't you think your priorities are a little misplaced?"

The man threw off his trench coat to reveal a black jumpsuit covered in pockets. Guns and knives of all makes and sizes were tucked into those pockets, and his arms dangled loosely at his sides, ready to make use of his weapons.

Payton didn't respond to his question.

"Oh, very well," the man replied patiently, removing his hat and untying the handkerchief around his face. He threw them both aside.

Payton didn't recognize the man, but he had to fight the urge to look away in revulsion. The man's scalp was covered in hideous red scabs, and the skin on his face was disfigured—portions of it had melted.

"My name is Konrad," he said, whipping out pistols from hip holsters on each side. "As for what I *want*, well . . . Let's just say I've developed a fondness for the smell of burning flesh."

54

"Konrad," Payton repeated the man's name, while sharply drawing his sword. "The mercenary."

His first instinct had been to draw the sword using a burst of speed and jump quickly into action. But he could still hear Devlin's warnings about tipping your hand too early in a fight.

When you have the tactical advantage, maintain it for as long as possible.

Besides, he needed time to size the other man up.

"I know you," Payton said. "The Secretum sent you to attack Grant the day he underwent the Shift. Did you know you were there merely to test his instincts? The Secretum *knew* you had no hope of success. It is written in prophecy that *I* will be the one to kill him."

Konrad eyed him angrily. "You can keep your signs and portents. I couldn't care less. Borrows is *mine*, and if you want another shot at him, it'll be over my dead body."

As you wish.

Payton weighed his options. He could strike quickly now and end it, but his eyes drifted to Morgan. She knelt on the ground, not far behind Konrad, holding the hand of the traitor, Hannah. He couldn't see from where he stood if Hannah was alive or dead. Behind them all, a handful of survivors had gathered in the hallway, needing to escape the flames that continued to spread, but were now unable to reach this exit—the only remaining way out—because Konrad was blocking it.

And if what he had heard about this Konrad was true, the mercenary was resourceful and not to be underestimated. Even if he was mad from his injuries, he'd still survived them, and probably through sheer will.

"What does destroying this building get you?" Payton said, taking one step into the burning building. The sound of the rushing flames was so deafening he had to shout to be heard. The heavy thickness of the billowing, gray smoke seeped into his eyes and lungs. His throat protested the noxious fumes, but he forced himself not to cough. Not now.

"A blissful night's sleep," Konrad replied, leveling both pistols on Payton's position and releasing the safeties. He grinned a disgusting smile through his deformed, misshapen lips.

Payton didn't like the idea of fighting Konrad here, amidst this out-of-control hurricane of heat, smoke, and flames. Which no doubt had been Konrad's plan from the beginning. He had nothing to lose here—it wasn't like his burned body could get much worse. Payton, on the other hand, was surrounded by collateral damage waiting to happen.

This was a no-win situation.

After the last few days, Payton had no idea where his allegiances lay anymore, but he wasn't in the habit of allowing brutal death to come to the innocent.

The guilty, however, he executed without hesitation.

And no small amount of satisfaction.

"Don't suppose you'd care to tell me who hired you for *this* job?" Payton took another step forward, sword at the ready. Only six or seven paces now separated them. He had to time this just right . . .

"Doesn't matter now, you won't live long enough to meet him," Konrad replied, as if it were obvious. "In case you haven't caught on yet, you are not the adversary I was hoping to fight today." Konrad took a step forward as well.

"Well then," Payton whispered. "Keep hope alive."

He sprung.

A split-second later, he was rounding Konrad, but the mercenary raised the pistol in his right hand and pointed it at Payton's head, just as Payton grabbed Konrad in a headlock. The sword, still in Payton's other hand, instantly came around to slice into Konrad's throat.

Konrad fired.

But instead of a bullet, Payton felt some kind of liquid drenching his face and stinging his eyes.

A water gun?

He flinched, and pulled away, blinking hard.

That's not water . . .

"Thing is," he heard Konrad's voice say, "I know you, too, Mister *Thresher*. Read the full dossier. And I know exactly how to put the brakes on your hustle and bustle. Start with the eyes, and work your way down."

Payton could hear him smiling again.

But he could no longer see him, blinded by the gasoline Konrad had sprayed in his face. He wiped off as much as he could with his free hand, but the stench was overpowering, it had soaked into his hair and shirt . . .

And heat advanced on him from every direction. He staggered backward, grasping about with his free hand, unable to get his bearings. He was certain the flames swirling around him would lick his face any moment, igniting the gas.

"Look out!" Morgan screamed, just as a shot was fired.

At first, Payton stood still, believing that Konrad had missed.

Then he felt a searing pain in his left side, just above his waist.

Payton fell backward, onto his rear end. His strength seemed to be running out of his body along with the oozing blood.

He was dazed, his internal alarms allowing too much time to pass before his pain receptors triggered the growing heat on his right side. He choked, pulling backward quickly.

The wall is on fire . . .

All the walls are on fire, he realized.

What remained of the building would collapse soon, they were out of time, he couldn't see anything, and Konrad had killed him . . .

The exit finally appeared in sight, but Grant's focus remained elsewhere.

He watched.

He saw the column collapse, saw Hannah push Morgan out of the way.

Saw a shadowy figure appear out of the flames like some twisted, gnarled demon straight from Hell. But he couldn't see who it was.

It was then that he snapped back to reality and first noticed the flashing lights in his rear-view.

But instead of panicking, Grant barely gave the police a passing thought, focusing momentarily on the squad car's four wheels as he watched them in the mirror.

He closed his eyes for a single instant . . .

And the tires gave an ear-splitting *pop*, bursting into shreds of rubber. The police car dropped and began spitting sparks from all four wheel assemblies, digging grooves into the asphalt.

It was forced to stop.

Grant turned off onto the old service road that led to the asylum, still miles away.

No no no!!

I'll never make it in time . . .

"Payton!" Morgan screamed from somewhere behind him.

Payton's instincts kicked in as he felt a slight shift in the air to his left.

He brought his sword up super-fast, which was jarred by a heavy *clang*. He was an experienced enough fighter to recognize the weight and sound of the sound that impacted his blade—Konrad was using some kind of knife.

"I can't express to you how disappointing this is," Konrad's voice said from his left. The knife drew back and Payton forced himself to his feet, his free hand clutching his wounded side, from which blood continued to pour.

"First, Grant doesn't have the courtesy to show, and I can't *tell* you how much I was looking forward to seeing him again," Konrad continued, his voice circling Payton now, as Payton spun in place, struggling to keep up. "But the prospect of fighting the legendary swordmaster seemed like the next best thing. You *do* know you're a legend, don't you?"

Payton didn't respond, dizzy from trying to audibly keep track of Konrad's position.

Again he heard the whisper of Konrad moving, from behind this time. The mercenary thrust again with his knife, but Payton spun and blocked the blow. Without his vision, though, he wasn't able to match Konrad's movements perfectly. Konrad slashed at Payton's outstretched arm, cutting deep into his forearm.

"Grant bested me on his very first day. He was sloppy—not to mention ridiculously lucky—but he got the job done," Konrad went on, still circling Payton's position. Sometimes his voice was close, sometimes it was further away. "And yet here *you* are, trained to be unbeatable and I've crippled you with a child's toy."

Payton staggered left, felt flames all-too-close, and jerked back quickly.

Too quickly.

Sweat streamed off his forehead as he lurched backward, and Konrad kicked his feet out from under him. Payton went down onto his back, coughing and hacking through the smoke.

"So much for the great warrior," Konrad muttered from above him.

Payton's strength was all but gone as he heard the real gun's safety click into place.

"No!" Morgan screamed.

"Don't worry, sweetheart," Konrad said. "You're up next."

Payton was certain that somewhere nearby, he could hear whispering. It sounded like Hannah's voice, what was she doing . . .

His eyes had cleared just enough to make out Konrad's dark, blurry outline above him through the smoke and noise, and the outstretched arm that held the gun trained on him.

Payton could barely make out what looked like Morgan's shape, standing to Konrad's right with a piece of concrete from the fallen pillar . . . *He should be able to see her, why hasn't he noticed her standing right there . . .*

Hannah.

An unholy roar escaped Morgan's lips, and she slammed the concrete block as hard as she could into Konrad's head.

Konrad howled and stumbled forward. But he was on his feet again surprisingly fast, enraged and somehow oblivious to all pain. He punched Morgan sharp and hard in the face, and she flew back onto the ground. Konrad never stopped to see if she stayed down; instead, his momentum carried him back to stand above Payton again, and

Payton could now see red blood oozing out of a gash on the side of the mercenary's head.

"That's the thing about pain," Konrad said, grinning through his grotesque, blood-stained face. "Endure enough of it, and it doesn't even slow you down anymore."

Something inside Payton snapped. "Endure this."

Clenching the sword, he swung with abandon, arcing out sideways from where he lay, strong and fast.

Konrad howled like a rabid animal as his lower legs were separated from his feet at the ankles in one stunning stroke. The gun in his hand went off as he toppled down, but the shot was wide.

Payton had just enough strength left to prop himself on one arm beside Konrad and knock the gun out of his hand. Konrad was lost to the pain, screaming at the top of his lungs, unaware Payton was even there.

Through the thick smoke, Payton's eyes met with Morgan's, who had also propped herself up from where Konrad had sent her smashing to the floor. They both coughed violently through the smoke, but never wavered in their gaze.

And despite the years and circumstances that separated them, he could still read her like an open book. He knew she was thinking about how, even if only for a moment, she'd become the enraged animal she swore she'd never be. The sad resolve in her eyes told him that she didn't care anymore.

She knew exactly what was left for Payton to do now.

And she wasn't going to protest.

Payton flipped the sword around in his hand to hold it outstretched over Konrad's prostrate neck, and then swung it down sharply with every last bit of rage and strength he had left.

The adrenaline faded, loss of blood asserted itself, and he was lost in a sea of black.

55

The Corvette screeched to a halt at the end of the driveway, but he couldn't move.

Nothing remained.

Where the building once stood, was now blackened brick, burning doors and window frames, and orange fire burning out of control, pouring black smoke high into the sky. What remained of the building's walls were no more than fragments sticking up like shards of broken glass. A fifty-foot crater in the front yard was all that was left of Payton's motorcycle, and the entire front of the building had blown in from the blast, effectively destroying any chance of exit that way.

He knew many of the residents were still alive—he could feel it—just as he knew some of them were buried inside, unable to escape on their own. Some of them he only had faint impressions of. They were fading fast.

Grant exploded out of his car, running to find the few whose life he still felt, heading directly around to the back of the building.

There he found a congregated group of twenty or so survivors, all huddled together, crying, holding each other, choking and coughing on the flames and smoke. Tears smudged the soot on their faces in long streaks, and most of them never even noticed his arrival. They couldn't take their eyes off of the asylum.

Their refuge from a cruel world. Destroyed.

"MORGAN!" Grant screamed, rounding to the rear exit in a full sprint.

"In here!" he heard a faint cry.

He could see nothing through the smoke and flames, which were impossibly thick now. But he entered anyway.

How do I put this out?

Grant couldn't create water; he could only manipulate existing objects. Which gave him no advantage in this situation.

"Grant, quick!"

Morgan's voice.

"Where are you?" he yelled. He stumbled in the smoke, so thick it blocked out light, even the flickering of the flames.

"Here!" Morgan cried again, her voice closer this time.

He turned right and went forward several paces to find Morgan kneeling on the floor next to Hannah, who was still buried under the broken pillar.

"She's not breathing!" Morgan screamed hysterically, her face soaked with tears and sweat and soot.

"Back up, get back!" he yelled.

Morgan stood and took several steps backward.

Grant reached out with both hands, focusing his mind as hard as he could on the heavy pillar trapping Hannah.

But it wouldn't budge. It was too heavy . . .

"Come on . . ." he mumbled. "*Come on!*"

He forced himself to relax, going through the exercises Daniel had taught him. He closed his eyes and envisioned himself reaching out with two giant hands and picking up the column.

He opened his eyes to see the column floating a few feet over Hannah's body.

"*Get her!*" he roared.

Morgan flew in quickly and began hefting the younger woman out.

"I can't hold it!" he screamed.

Nearby, another part of the building came tumbling down in an unrestrained display of destructive power. A sharp blast of wind struck them both, and Grant stumbled off-balance for a moment.

He lost control of the pillar just as Morgan pulled Hannah to safety.

More screams penetrated the smoke and heat, from all directions.

"*Help me!*"

"Please!"

"Somebody!"

Grant turned to Morgan and pointed to the exit. "Get her out of here!"

"Payton—he's over there," Morgan bellowed, pointing. With that, she hoisted Hannah up over her shoulders in a manner Grant wouldn't have thought the older woman capable of, and swiftly made her way to the exit.

Grant turned to the direction she'd pointed and found Payton on the ground, bleeding badly from a wound in his side and another on his shoulder. A deep cut into his arm seemed to have stopped bleeding, but from the looks of it, he had already lost a great deal of blood.

Still, he had a faint pulse, so Grant followed Morgan's lead by heaving the big man over his shoulders and staggering through the smoke and flames.

Outside, he dropped Payton to the ground, where some of the others attended to him, including, Grant noticed, the boy Thomas.

Morgan knelt over Hannah, performing CPR. She turned and vomited up an ugly mess of black soot from somewhere deep inside her, but never stopped pumping up and down on Hannah's chest.

There was no time to get the rest of them out, they would die before he could reach them, the fire had spread to the whole building, going back in would be suicide . . .

The earth shook as another section of the building gave way and they all turned to look. A great gush of wind swept into Grant's face once again, and the feeling triggered an idea . . .

It had taken all the focus he had to levitate the pillar; this was a whole other level.

Still, it was the only idea he had, and there was no alternative.

"Morgan, get the others out of here!" he screamed.

She pulled up from breathing into Hannah's mouth to face him. "Where?! There's nowhere to—"

"Just take them out to the street or something!" he yelled, turning to the gathered crowd. "All of you! Get as far away from the building as you can!"

The group jumped into action as he tore off a section of his button-up shirt and tied it around his mouth. He ran recklessly back into the raging furnace. Fire leapt up to meet him as he jumped through what remained of the exit, but he ducked around it as best he could.

His shirt caught fire and he dropped to the ground and rolled. But he bumped into a wall, and there was no room left to roll. He stood and tore the shirt off, leaving only a white T-shirt underneath.

The screams continued, along with the cries for help.

He closed his eyes, envisioning each of them where they were. He estimated there had to be at least a dozen of them. Some were trapped under rubble. Others were free but blocked off by the collapsed building or flames on all sides. A few wouldn't live more than a few minutes. And none of them were accessible from his location.

"Everyone that can hear my voice!" he thundered. *"Get down on the floor as low as you can! But don't hold onto anything! Just lie still!"*

He gave them a moment to comply, watching those he could see in his mind's eye.

Grant made his way farther, deeper into the building. Eyes watering, lungs burning for oxygen, he knew he only had a matter of seconds.

When he could go no farther, when he felt his mind going hazy with lack of air, he stopped, let his arms hang at his sides, and looked around.

He was in the Common Room.

It'll have to do . . .

He closed his eyes and let out a breath. He needed more this time than he was able to safely control through concentration . . .

He needed the fear.

He thought of the building he was in and those that were about to lose their lives. Because he hadn't been there to help them. He thought of Hannah, almost certainly dead outside on the ground. And Payton, and Morgan . . . And he thought of how he might never get to speak to his sister again, hear her voice, feel her embrace . . .

The panic came, shooting through him in a savage wave of terror, and he bore down hard, opening his arms wide and flexing every muscle in his body . . .

A gargantuan rumble shook the foundations of the building, and suddenly every wall and the parts of the roof that still stood—all of which were engulfed in a sea of red-hot inferno—every piece of the building ripped free of its moorings and *flung* itself skyward, a cataclysm that tore the air.

For just a blink, Grant hesitated. Then he let panic stab his heart once again, unable to hold back a tremendous scream of emotional detonation. The pieces of the building still flying upward into the air, still in flames, exploded outward with a shockwave that toppled Grant to his knees.

Morgan and the others screamed, running to avoid the larger pieces of debris now falling from the sky like firebombs.

He'd done his best, but portions of the building flew everywhere, outward, into the surrounding woods, the street, the driveway. One barely missed Grant's car. They rained down in fire, but Grant had no strength left to run. He only hoped none would find him.

When the echoing blast faded, Grant opened his eyes again. The fire had vanished along with the building, and the smoke was beginning to dissipate as well, much of it swept away by the force of the blast.

He made a slow three-hundred-sixty degree turn, taking in every direction. He could see several survivors making their way carefully toward him, shell-shocked but alive. A few others he could feel alive but unable to move, flung aside by the clearing rubble or simply unconscious.

It was only when he stood that he saw the many charred bodies lying on the ground, cast about randomly like black feathers blown in the wind.

Some of them were burned beyond recognition.

A few he recognized, their faces frozen in horror, but hearts no longer beating.

So many he had failed. Failed them all.

Lisa sat back in her seat on the couch, and attempted to digest the story Daniel had just told her.

"You . . ." she sputtered, "Seriously?"

He nodded, watching her carefully.

"This . . ." she said, "I mean . . . It can't be *legal*."

"No," he replied, then added softly, "And, I could use your help."

Hands planted on hips, time seemed to stop as she glared daggers into him where he sat. "Have you *lost your mind?!*"

Daniel gave no answer.

"You. Want. My. Help?"

"No. I need your help," he said.

"I'm not your research assistant anymore!" she snarled, but besides the fire in her eyes, there was something else. Curiosity, perhaps. "What would I have to do?"

"I'll need a ride the night we do it, and I need a few supplies . . ."

Daniel could practically feel steam cascading off of her.

"How far are you willing to go with this?" Lisa asked, still looming above him.

He looked into her eyes with a hardened edge. "As far as it takes."

She said nothing for a long moment, then nodded. "I'll come. But I'm only coming to keep an eye on you."

56

Hours upon hours passed. The sun rose and set and rose again.

And Grant never stopped.

Never stopped lifting, moving, sifting through the wreckage. He left nothing unturned, refusing all help, sleep, or food.

More than once, Morgan or one of the others tried to get him to stop, slow down, take a break.

But Grant wouldn't hear them.

The police, fire department, and ambulances eventually arrived, but even they could not deter Grant or hold him back, as the medics quietly treated the wounded and the firemen doused the flames that had spread to the forest.

Even with all of the activity taking place, there was very little sound to be heard. A reverential hush consumed the entire property, save Grant's relentless searching. None of the survivors spoke; they merely watched. Everyone seemed immobilized by the fire, the death, and what Grant had done. And what he was still doing now.

Occasionally, he would emerge from the building carrying another body. He deposited them all at the edge of the blast crater, where Morgan waited to covertly remove the rings from their dead fingers. He had no idea if she planned to dispose of them or hide them, but either way he knew they'd be out of the picture in her hands.

The EMTs took it from there.

Grant, meanwhile, went back in. Every time.

Morgan was breathing oxygen through a mask hours later when she suddenly sprang up from her seat at the back of an ambulance and tore off the mask.

Before anyone could stop her, she ran past the medics and police and into the smoldering ruins. She passed Grant, who was still working like mad, using his powers to sift through what remained of the wrecked building.

Morgan never stopped running, winding her way through the building, searching for something . . .

"It's gone!" she shouted after a few minutes.

"What?" Grant turned in her direction.

She reappeared in front of him, defeated. "The stone tablet! It's gone!"

Grant glared at her sideways, returning to his work. "Who *cares*, Morgan! You've got the whole thing memorized, anyway! People are *dead* here—"

"Grant," she said softly, placing a hand on his arm. He stopped.

"It's the *reason* they're dead," she said.

He turned sharply to stare into her eyes. Eyes that were weighed down by immeasurable sorrow.

"The Keeper . . . he took it," Grant breathed heavily. "That's what this was about—he just wanted the Dominion Stone . . ."

She walked away, leaving him to his work.

Whoever you are . . . I'll kill you for this.

On and on Grant went, covered in grime and despair.

He never stopped once, angrily defying exhaustion its prize.

After almost thirty hours, many of the survivors had finally dispersed—some taken to the hospital by the medics, others gone off in search of homeless shelters or other places they might stay.

The sun was setting on the second night after the fire as Morgan and the few others who still remained watched Grant emerge from the wreckage like a specter for the last time.

It was done. He'd saved all that he could save and recovered what was left of those he couldn't.

Dirty, exhausted, and covered in grime, a dangerous expression darkened his features like a heavy storm cloud ready to strike.

All told, nineteen bodies had been recovered from the wreckage.
Nineteen.

Nineteen lights extinguished in his soul.

Grant was too spent to shed any tears for them. That might come
later. For now, the devastation around him had crept into his heart and
left no room for anything else. There were no words. No emotions. No
energy.

Grant walked slowly past Morgan and the others, as well as the
two ambulances that remained. Two EMTs came over and grabbed him
by the arms, meaning to finally drag him back to their equipment and
treat his smoke inhalation, but he angrily jerked loose and kept walking.

Morgan ran around in front of him, blocking his path. He noticed
for the first time that her arm and shoulder had been set in a sling.
Her hair and skin were dark and muddy, blood encrusted on her hands
and fingers. Her eyes were impossibly puffy, yet more tears poured out
now as she locked gazes with Grant.

But he never stopped walking or even slowed down. He simply
stepped around her. She reached out with her good arm and placed her
hand on his shoulder from behind. He paused only a moment before
dropping his head and shaking it slightly.

"Please don't," he whispered.

He kept walking until he reached his car.

Slowly the engine came to life and the car limped its way down the
lonely drive until it was out of sight.

No one spoke to Grant for the next forty-eight hours. They tried,
but he was unresponsive. He had returned to the apartment, walked
past Daniel and Lisa—who hushed instantly when he entered—without comment, and collapsed on his bed.

There he slept fitfully, stirring awake often. Hours upon hours, he
drifted in and out of asleep and awake states and all the subtle hues in
between.

Dreams came in spurts—violent, terrifying visions of roaring flames
and horrified screams. He awoke repeatedly with the putrid taste of
burning death in his mouth.

He went to the bathroom and washed his teeth several times,

trying to get rid of the taste of the heat and the smoke and the burning bodies. But it wouldn't leave.

All the while, every one of the Loci continued about their business—most of them in hiding or in the hospital, recovering from injuries—and all of them aware that the time of the prophecy was drawing ever closer.

Even Grant was aware of the passage of time and what it meant, but he was too drained, too emotionally decimated to do anything about it.

He wouldn't answer his phone, and he locked himself in his bedroom.

And without him, the others had no idea what to do.

Grant's first visitor since the tragedy came in the early evening, four days after the fire.

A gentle knock at the door barely captured his attention as he sat in the kitchen alone eating a bowl of cereal, staring into space.

He glanced at the door and kept eating.

Another knock. Louder this time.

"Go away, Morgan!" he said.

The door nearly caved in at the next knock. He stood up from his stool so fast he pushed it over and ran to the door.

Throwing it open wide, he shouted, "I said, *go away!*"

It wasn't Morgan.

"Hi," said the visitor.

It was Hannah.

Why hadn't he felt her arrival? He looked down; her ring was still on. But then, he'd stopped trying to feel her.

"You were hurt," he blurted. She looked better than she had the last few times he'd seen her. Shaken and battered, but not crushed.

"Cracked ribs," she said, placing a steadying hand across her torso, "and plenty o' scrapes and bruises. It's pretty hard to catch my breath. But thanks to you and Morgan, no permanent—"

"What do you want?"

She met his eyes, briefly. "Somethin' I can never have."

For a reason he couldn't define, Grant suddenly couldn't bring himself to look at her. He examined her shoes instead.

"Then . . . we have something in common," he said.

Hannah entered timidly, walking carefully around him, but refused to sit. She stood a few yards away, and she kept glancing at him nervously, but she was unable to keep her eyes upon him for very long.

Grant closed the door behind her and crossed his arms over his chest. He never offered her a chair.

Minutes passed in silence.

"Everyone kept telling me to slow down, to take time, think . . . *feel* . . ." Grant said quietly. "They finally got their wish. It feels like . . . I think I'm still on that street corner, standing at the bus stop. Watching myself walk down the street. I think maybe . . . I never left that spot."

Hannah looked down, unable to hold his eye.

"I know what you did for Morgan."

"It doesn't change anything," she stated the obvious.

He frowned, "No, it doesn't."

"I want to explain. I want to justify what I've done. But there ain't no happy ending to get to. Drexel hired me to spy on you, to find out everything I could. I never meant you any harm, personally. Do you remember that day we met, crawling through those air ducts at Inveo? I warned you then you shouldn't trust me."

Grant's thoughts and emotions were a million miles away.

"But you did. And instead of ditching you, like I should have—I felt something. Before I knew how or why . . . I found that I cared about you, deeply. I still do."

"Hannah," he interrupted, his voice a dry monotone, "I know what you came here for, so just say it and get it over with."

It wasn't an accusation. He was merely tired. He had no use for accusations now.

"I . . . didn't come to apologize," she replied.

He looked up at her for the first time.

"If I did, would it matter? What would it change?" she said, sadness filling her voice.

"I don't know," he replied. "Probably nothing."

"I did what I did, and there ain't an excuse big enough to undo it. . . . I'd probably be crying *now* if I was capable of any more tears, but after *everything*, and then the last few days . . . I feel like coffee beans that've been spilled all over the floor . . . Or no—which nursery rhyme was it? The one who couldn't be put together again?"

"Humpty Dumpty," he replied quietly.

"That's me," she said, nodding hopelessly. "Humpty Dumpty. No matter what I do, what I've done will always be there . . . A long, ugly list of demerits on my permanent record. And I can't ever reverse it."

Grant's demeanor suddenly changed, and he looked up, outside his window. His gaze was far away. "No," he said quietly. "You can't."

Despite her claim of being all out, tears spilled from her eyes.

"And maybe you're not supposed to," he said, emotion rising in his voice.

She got lost in his eyes, alone and confused.

"It's something my sister was trying to tell me . . . I didn't understand it *then*, but . . ." he said, shaking his head, then he took a single step closer to her. "We can't ever go back to the way things were after mistakes are made. There are always consequences . . ."

She examined his coffee table in great detail, afraid to look at him.

"But maybe it's not about what *you* do next," he continued, swallowing. "Maybe it's not up to *you* to fix what's broken."

More tears leaked out of her eyes, and she almost turned her body fully away from him now.

Something opened in Grant's heart—it had been stopped up by despair and grief—but now he found that his own eyes were moistening.

This was stupid. He had every reason to hate this woman.

It wasn't rational. It wasn't what any sane person would do.

But what Hannah needed right now was the very thing that Grant was craving more than life itself. And he hadn't realized it until now, seeing her in this state.

Since he couldn't give it to himself, he did the only thing he could do.

He offered it to Hannah.

He crossed the distance between them and grabbed her by the shoulders, forcing her to look into his face. And he embraced her.

Hannah was overcome. He could see the shock in her face. The question. She knew what she *deserved* and it wasn't this . . .

Her body went limp, breaking into sobs so violent that she shook uncontrollably, and she wasn't holding herself up by her own power . . .

No, Grant was doing that.

He was holding her tight. And he was shaking and sobbing as well.

"I'm sorry!" she wailed, head buried in his chest. "*Please*, Grant—I'm *so* sorry! I'm sorry I'm sorry I'm sorry . . ." She continued to blurt it out between heaving breaths until she had no more strength or words or breath.

When she finally stopped, he whispered in her ear.

"It's okay. It's all going to be okay now."

57

Very late that night and into the early morning hours, Matthew Drexel attended a scheduled rendezvous, made the drop, and then checked his watch as he struggled to get into the backseat of his car.

"Let's go," he growled at his driver. He was running late.

He rubbed his aching back as the driver took him to his next destination. He was still suffering from his run-in with Grant and Payton over a week ago, and he'd taken to using a cane to get around.

He knew the address of the meeting was among some warehouses on the outskirts of the city, so when his driver raised his eyebrows at the neighborhood, Drexel growled for him to keep his eyes on the road. This lead and the money it might offer were too good not to check out. Besides, he'd been in places far worse than this.

A dozen minutes later, his car pulled up next to a sagging old building and Drexel got out.

He was overcome by the desire not to stay in this place one minute longer than necessary. The building left him feeling . . . unsettled. But he couldn't put his finger on why.

Drexel approached the door and rapped his knuckles on it five times, as instructed.

The door opened to reveal a dark interior.

"Enter," a voice commanded.

"What is this?" Drexel said, put off by the lack of visibility inside the building.

He received no answer, and was about to turn around when something crashed into his head from behind. He lurched and wobbled, and fell to his knees, seeing stars.

"What the—!" he yelled.

Immediately two sets of hands were lifting him from under his arms and dragging him forward into the pitch-black interior.

They reached the center of the room, and the two who held him threw him forward, onto the ground. His eyes could see very little, but the room seemed like an abandoned warehouse with a shorter ceiling. Empty. He couldn't see far past the shadows before his face.

The shadows moved again and a fist landed square in his nose. He yelped and tried crawling away, but another set of hands grabbed his feet and dragged him back. And then what had to be no less than three men—*strong* men, to be able to take a big guy like him down—were everywhere at once, all over him, punching, kicking, bashing. A tooth was knocked loose. His legs screamed in agony as they were kicked again and again. Fists landed across his chest and stomach.

Minutes passed and then suddenly they stopped.

Then without a word, the three shadowy figures walked away, leaving him lying there.

A bright spotlight from somewhere above switched on and bathed him in light.

He spit blood out of his mouth to the side and squinted, peering out into the darkness.

"How does it feel?" a voice called out of the dark.

"Who are you!" Drexel demanded. "What is this?"

A figure approached out of the darkness, bearing down on him where he still lay on the floor.

But the figure wasn't walking. He was rolling in a wheelchair.

He came into view and Drexel recognized him.

"I want to tell you a story, Mr. Drexel," said Daniel, rolling his new wheelchair just out of Drexel's reach. A pistol rested in his lap.

"Cossick," Drexel said, piecing it together. "Do you have any idea what I'm going to—"

"It's a good story, full of blood, violence, and adult content. Right up your alley," Daniel said, cold and unwavering. "So *shut up* and listen."

Daniel's eyes pierced furiously into Drexel, but Drexel stubbornly held his gaze.

"Once upon a time," Daniel began, "there was a boy named Daniel. He was a happy little toddler until one day when he crawled up to an electrical outlet and stuck his finger inside. Afterward, the doctor told his parents that he was lucky to be alive. He took his first steps a few days later."

Drexel eyed the crippled man warily. He had no idea what this game was, but he didn't like where it was going.

"Daniel grew up and went to college. One morning on the way to class, his car was slammed into by an eighteen-wheeler. The car was smashed beyond repair, and the truck took heavy damage as well. But Daniel walked away from that accident with only a few cuts and scrapes. The police deemed it a fluke, 'one-in-a-million' they called it."

Daniel watched the man on the ground with contempt, everything inside him wanting to *spit* on this waste of human flesh.

"Three weeks ago, Daniel came down the stairs of this very building from his lab on the second floor and walked outside, where three thugs beat him within an inch of his life. It happened right out there—outside the very door you walked through just a few minutes ago."

A young brunette Drexel recognized as Cossick's assistant appeared from behind the wheelchair and raised up the footrests in front. Daniel very slowly and gingerly placed his legs—still in their casts—down onto the cold concrete floor. The brunette braced the chair from the back as he pulled himself up by his arms. Then she produced crutches.

Carefully, he took a few baby steps forward to face Drexel at arm's length, leaning heavily on his crutches. The brunette stayed behind the chair, watching him with a motherly concern that made Drexel want to wretch.

"You can knock me down as many times as you want. But I promise you, I will always—*always*—get back up."

"If you're going to kill me, just do it already so I don't have to listen to any—"

He stopped. And blinked.

They weren't alone in this enormous room. Over a dozen figures emerged from the shadows, forming a circle that surrounded him.

"Listen, we can just—"

"It's not a good feeling, is it?" Daniel asked, leisurely waving the gun about. "To be all alone. In the dark. Outnumbered. These are my new friends, by the way," he gestured wide to the circle. "All of *them* have stories, too. I bet you don't even remember Sarah here," he said, and a young woman stepped into the light. Daniel was right; Drexel didn't recognize her.

"But I'm sure you remember her mother, Joanna," Daniel said. "She was raped to death by a thug who broke into her home and stole a big-screen TV, a computer, and a few hundred dollars. The culprit was a 'friend' of yours, so you had Sarah's father framed for the crime."

Drexel wanted to back away from them all, but there was nowhere to go. They were everywhere.

"Or how about young Will," Daniel continued as a young boy slid into view atop a skateboard. "His older brother was one of your fellow officers. Yeah, I'm sure you remember him. He tried to take you down a few years ago, but he and his wife both died in a freak car accident. An *accident!*" Daniel repeated, underscoring his thoughts on that word.

"We could go on like this for hours. You've ruined so many lives . . . but you always got away with it. Those connections with the higher-ups pay off, don't they? When you get results."

"I just do what I'm told, that's all I've ever done."

"Nobody in the Los Angeles police—"

Drexel stopped him with a sour laugh. "The force?" He shook his head, watching Daniel's growing awareness. "Doctor, you need to think a little bigger."

Daniel was stunned. "All this time," Daniel said, aghast, "even before you met Grant or me . . ."

"We *all* answer to someone," Drexel said, a smile teasing the corners of his lips. "What? You're shocked and appalled that I was able to keep my true loyalties a secret?"

Drexel let out a single chuckle.

"You work for the Keeper."

"We *all* work for the Keeper, little man. Since minute one with you and your friends, we've been feeding into his plans. You're working for him *right now*, doing his dirty work, tying up a loose end that he won't have to contend with."

"Loose end. . . ?" Daniel said. He looked at Drexel differently. "What have you done?"

"Don't you read the newspapers?" Drexel grinned. "Your friends were involved and everything . . ."

"You were behind the arson at the asylum," Daniel gasped. He swallowed, realizing something else. "You hired Konrad! *You took the Dominion Stone!*"

"At *any* cost," he said. "Though the higher the better, I always find."

"Where is it?" Daniel asked. Drexel had turned his back to him. He could hear the hatred in Daniel's voice. That was good. He had him upset, thinking poorly.

"You're the Ph.D. Where do you *think?"*

"The Keeper," Daniel whispered.

He has the tablet.

Drexel suddenly moved, retrieving a gun from an ankle holster. This punk was in over his head. He spun quickly to face Daniel . . .

And Daniel shot him between the eyes.

Everyone froze as Drexel's body snapped backward and slammed into the ground.

Lisa's mouth was hanging open, but she couldn't move. It was almost as if by not moving, she could undo what had just happened.

Daniel still pointed the gun at Drexel's body, an inhuman expression on his face.

Lisa walked slowly forward for a closer look at Drexel's massive body, sprawled out on the floor. Blood poured slowly from the hole in his forehead. His eyes were still open. But he wasn't breathing.

"He's dead . . ." she despaired, turning to Daniel in disbelief. "You killed him!"

Daniel was locked in an emotion somewhere between shock, sickness, and satisfaction.

He'd really done it.

And he'd *meant* it.

Daniel brought his good hand up to cover his mouth as he searched an empty spot on the floor ahead. He didn't know whether to laugh or cry.

He felt like doing both.

58

Grant found a new vigor and sense of urgency the next morning, after sleeping deeply for the first time in weeks.

His first action was to track down Morgan and invite her and as many of the Loci as they could find to come to his apartment. Then he checked in with his sister at the hospital; she was showing increased brain activity, indicating deep dreams. The doctors said she could wake anytime. On his way back to the apartment, around mid-morning, he stopped at Daniel and Lisa's to ask them to come to the meeting as well. Lisa came to the door having just been roused from her bed by the doorbell. Apparently, she and Daniel had had some kind of very long night.

By early afternoon he was welcoming Hannah into his apartment for the meeting.

"Am I early?" she said, at his door.

"Not too bad," he smiled. "Morgan and the others should be here soon. I've offered to let as many of them stay here in the Wagner Building as we have space for. We need to talk things through and figure out where to go from here."

"You mean us?" she asked, alarmed.

"No, the *group*. As in, what's our next step. With the prophecy and everything."

"Oh. Right," she let out a breath and turned a pinkish shade of red. "Well, look at that, I made us both uncomfortable. Way to go, me." She laughed nervously.

He smiled, but said nothing.

"How's Payton?" she asked.

"Too stubborn to die, I believe is the way Morgan described it. He should be all right. He's coming to the meeting, in fact, against doctor's orders."

"*I* wouldn't want to be the one who tried to keep him away," she smiled.

They stared at each other for an awkward moment.

"Grant?" she asked, taking a seat next to him on the couch. "I was wondering something . . . about whether something *else* besides just me could ever be put back together . . ."

She didn't have to say any more; he knew exactly where she was going.

"I honestly don't know," he said. "Forgiveness is one thing, but with everything that's happening, I don't know if it's a good idea for us to . . ." He couldn't bring himself to say the rest.

"I understand," she nodded, looking away. "It's a shame, though. We never even had a first kiss."

He blushed.

"But you're right," she concluded, nervously standing up. "It's way too soon, *not* a good idea. I don't know what I was thinking . . ." she let out a nervous breath.

She walked away, but Grant followed, reaching to grab hold of her arm.

"I know *exactly* what you were thinking," he said, pulling her close. "Because it's all I can think about, too."

The world and all its sights and sounds and concerns and logic and reason faded to nothing, and it was simply *happening*.

Grant's heart pounded so loudly that blood rushed past his ears, but all he cared about was her lips on his and . . .

Before he got the smallest taste of her, the apartment door slammed shut.

They jumped apart, and twisted to face the door.

Alex stood there, her clothes hanging in tatters. She was breathing hard, unable to catch her breath.

She had a nasty black eye, she bled from a swollen lip, bruises covered what could be seen of her arms, and she stumbled toward them, limping, about to collapse.

"It's happening!" she gasped. "The end of everything . . ."

Grant caught her and lowered her to the ground.

She closed her eyes, but before unconsciousness swallowed her, she whispered:

"It's happening *now*."

One by one, Grant welcomed his friends into his apartment. Most he knew by name, a few he didn't.

Hannah and Alex were still there, of course, Hannah watching over Alex, who was resting uncomfortably on the couch. Hannah spent a while cleaning Alex's scrapes and bruises. They exchanged pained looks from time to time, and Alex winced frequently.

But neither spoke.

Half an hour later, Daniel and Lisa arrived. Daniel hobbled to Grant's bedroom, where the two men had a private discussion. Lisa sat uncomfortably in the living room watching the other two women, barely aware they were there.

Morgan and Fletcher arrived next, trailed by a small group of Loci. Morgan was still haggard and unrested, and her shoulder remained in the sling, but she'd cleaned herself up. When Grant emerged from his room—no longer smiling—her eyes were trained on him with intense interest. Daniel followed slowly. Fletcher was fidgety, his eyes darting about as he took in every detail of Grant's home.

Grant suddenly looked far away. Someone had just registered on his radar, entering the building. He'd been watching, waiting.

A few other Loci straggled in before Payton entered the room. He strode in scowling, as if nothing were wrong, though everyone else tensed sharply at the sight of him. The evidence of his recent fight was obvious: a long bandage could be seen sticking out from his sleeve, and though he tried to hide it, his good arm hugged his abdomen firmly where Konrad had shot him. There was a slight stagger to his gait.

Lisa turned angrily to Grant. "What's 'Sir Hacks-a-lot' doing here!"

The twenty or so present had gathered in a large circle in Grant's living room, but now many of them were on their feet.

"Payton is here at my invitation," Grant offered. "Everyone please relax. Like it or not, he's a part of this. And whatever's going on concerns us *all*."

"Here, I'll play nice," Payton said, as he unbuckled his sword from his belt and tossed it sideways to Fletcher who, disgusted, dropped it onto the coffee table with a loud clatter.

Grant waited until they were silent and watching him. When he had their attention, he began.

"Here's where we're at. Someone out there calling himself the 'Keeper' is using us. The rings were given to us intentionally, to turn us into something else. Something . . . superior."

"Someone's trying to make us into heroes," Fletcher said. It wasn't a question.

"Yeah," Grant replied, surprised. He had been planning to ease into that part of the conversation.

Fletcher nodded. "I suspected as much."

"Heroes," Morgan repeated slowly, straining to find a more comfortable position for her shoulder. "That's what this is all about? The Shift? The rings?"

"They're called the Rings of Dominion," Grant began. From there, he told them the highlights of Payton's story, about the Rings, the Secretum, and his ring, the Seal of Dominion. He revealed his trip to his childhood home, the truth of his identity, and his parents' membership in the Secretum. He finished by sharing the prophecy from the Dominion Stone that Daniel had translated.

No one spoke and significant glances were scarce as everyone present tried to accept the enormity of what had just been set out before them. Even Grant, who had spent some time with these facts already, found himself once again pondering it all.

Mostly, everyone stared at the coffee table in the center of the circle.

"I understand it's a lot to digest, but time is running out . . ." Grant said.

Morgan nodded, not looking up. "I get it, I'm just . . ."

Grant watched her face, which was showing a mixture of alarm and disbelief.

"This isn't what you were expecting," Grant offered.

Morgan looked up. "It's what I expected for *you*. I've known you were meant for something like this since the moment I met you.

But . . . you have to understand, Grant . . . the rest of us . . ."

"I know you're afraid," Grant said, "So am I."

"Fear is pointless," Fletcher announced. "My reservations about Grant notwithstanding, even I can no longer deny what's plainly before us. Everything that's happened to him—to *all* of us—it's been preordained. We've been cast in certain roles. We may have no choice but to perform them."

"No," Morgan was saying, shaking her head, breathing faster. "We'll find someplace new, a safe refuge where we can—"

"*Morgan*," Grant said forcefully, and everyone in the circle looked up sharply. "Lines are being drawn. Sides are being taken. Hiding, trying to keep the world at bay—it's not an option anymore.

"I know we've all been through some . . . painful experiences of late," he went on. "But there's a fight coming, and I think it's fair to say we all feel the weight of it, growing heavier. Dr. Cossick has new information to share with the group. But first, Alex has some news." He turned to her. "Maybe you should start by explaining what's happened to you."

"The Keeper happened to me. This," she glanced down at herself, "is my reprimand. I was a fool to think it could be kept from him."

"How did you escape?" Payton asked.

"He let me go on the condition that I would come straight here and tell you that the end has arrived. Whatever's coming that you all have to stop—it's coming now."

No one spoke.

"Once again," Fletcher piped up, breaking the silence, "it falls to me to point out the obvious. She's admitted that she is employed by the enemy. What proof do we have that she's a genuine double agent? Does *anyone* here really know anything about her at all?" he said, facing her.

Alex sighed, her face tilting down to examine her bare feet.

"Hate to admit it, Alex," Grant said, "but he's right. You told me that everyone has their own agenda, but you've never told me what yours is. I think we have to know."

She let out a very long breath and looked back up.

"Everything I told you about me was the truth. The Keeper really *did* hire me to keep tabs on you all. But that wasn't . . . the *whole* truth. It *is* my job to watch you, to keep up with your activities and report back on your progress," she said, stopping to take a sip. "What I didn't tell you . . . is that it was also my job to *select* each of you in the first place."

Murmurs filled the room as dark glances were exchanged.

"I was given a list to work from," she continued, "and assigned to seek out these people who were good candidates for the Shift."

"What criteria were used for creating this list?" Morgan asked.

"I don't know. But I *do* know that the information from my reports was the deciding factor on which of you were selected for the experiment. I'm sorry," she said, sad but resolute.

"Did you select me?" Grant asked.

"No," she replied. "You're special. You always have been. From what I gather, you were *always* earmarked for the experiments, but you were saved for last."

"So we're just 'experiments' to you? Trial runs so that *he* could be perfected?" Payton muttered bitterly, angling his head toward Grant. He locked cruel eyes on Alex. "I wonder what kind of person it takes to uproot and erase another's life?"

Alex's head unexpectedly turned to Payton in a flash. "I may have cleared you for the experiments, but the person you became after that was *your* doing. *Not* mine. And I *had* no choice in any of this; it was either take the job or take a nice long nap six feet under."

"I think it's safe to say," Grant spoke up, looking at everyone in the room individually, "that everyone in this room has regrets of some kind. We've all done things we'd like to take back." His eyes lingered on Daniel for a moment, before he turned back to Alex again. "But this is the moment of truth, Alex. And we need all of it."

She faced Morgan.

"You were the only one I never got to watch. Because, as you've always assumed, you were the first one to ever go through the Shift. And that's the truth. You *were* the first."

Alex looked down at her toes again and swallowed.

"I was the second."

"What?" Grant voiced what the entire room was thinking. "*You* were Shifted? But you're not wearing a ring."

"The Keeper was still in the early stages of his work back then. I had no idea then who he was or that he even existed, of course, I was just confused and afraid like all of you, but . . . there was an accident. I was just learning how to control my mental ability, and I was trying to help this guy. Unfortunately, he got some bad news and took it out on me; heated words were exchanged, and he . . . slapped me. And in a moment of anger, I used my mental power to . . . *damage* him."

"Damage him how?" Morgan asked.

"He's lived the last ten years of his life in a straitjacket, where he will probably remain until the day he dies. He would gladly hurt himself if he could. He's tried many times, over the years, or so I've heard. I was . . . absolutely horrified by what I'd done, and even more frightened because I couldn't *undo* it. I was just devastated. I never knew myself capable of such rage. And I was only a teenager . . .

"The Keeper found me, brought me to some kind of facility, and explained that I was his first failed experiment. I begged him to remove my ring, to take the power back. I told him I'd do anything he wanted if he would just take it away. I thought he was going to kill me, but he agreed. He used drugs to stop my heart long enough to pry the ring off my finger. And with that, my power was gone. But I was still living inside this new life that I didn't know or want. Like each of you, I couldn't go back to who I was before."

No one said anything as they all tried to absorb her tale.

"Being powerless to do anything about any of this . . . being forced to work for him all these years . . . I . . . It made me so . . . That's the reason I made contact with you, Grant, the day you were Shifted. It's been fourteen years, and I had nearly given up hope. But I knew you were different from all the others, and I thought you might be my last hope of escaping him."

"Who is he?" Grant asked.

"Grant, I've never seen him . . ."

"You just said you bargained with him to get your ring off."

"It was done by intermediaries, scientists, people who spoke for him and worked *with* him at this facility where they took me. I never even knew where I was, they blindfolded—"

"*What is his* name?" Grant shouted.

Alex flinched at his outburst before she collected herself.

"I would have told you already if I knew. I'm beginning to think he doesn't even *have* a real name."

Alex sat back in her seat, apparently finished.

Grant sighed. "All right. Thank you for telling the truth. Better late than never. Your turn, Doc," he said, but didn't stop watching Alex.

"The Keeper has the Dominion Stone," Daniel announced, generating a new swell of murmurs around the circle.

"So it's safe to assume that he knows everything we know," Grant said.

"It's safer to assume he knows *a whole lot more* than we know," said Fletcher.

"How did you come by this information, Doctor?" Morgan inquired.

"Matthew Drexel told me," he replied.

"You've *seen* him?" Morgan asked in a quiet voice. "Was it *him*—?"

Daniel nodded. "He hired Konrad to burn your building to the ground," he said, which drew another round of surprised expressions and mumbling. "But Drexel himself was acting under orders. He was working for the Keeper all along."

Grant fought the urge to curse.

Another manipulation.

This had to stop.

Now.

"Where is Drexel currently?" Payton snarled. It was plain to see that he was thinking exactly as Grant was.

"He's, um—"

"A dead issue," Lisa blurted out, lifeless eyes staring ahead into nothing.

"And we know for certain that Drexel was working for the Secretum? There's evidence of this?" Morgan asked.

"Oh, come on, Morgan," Grant said forcefully, before Daniel could answer. He rose from his chair with an exasperated expression. "Look at how Alex has been used for so long. He reeled Hannah in because she could get close to us. *You've* been a pawn in this thing for over a decade, with the tablet and Drexel and everything that happened at the asylum. Daniel nearly lost his *life* a few weeks ago. Payton was saved and trained at the hands of the Secretum. And then there's everything that's happened to me . . .

"Does *anyone* in this room seriously believe that they haven't been manipulated by the Keeper in one way or another? Everything that's

happened to all of us points straight back to *him*. And personally . . .
I'm sick of it."

Grant was pacing now, holding their full attention.

"I've just had enough, haven't you?" he asked them all. "Everything
we're talking about comes back to this one issue: The Keeper has
ruined all of our lives. He's killed innocent people. He's Shifted us, and
given us bizarre abilities that none of us asked for. To what end, I can't
imagine. He's manipulated our entire lives, pulled and prodded us,
changed everything about who we are . . ."

He stopped pacing.

"And I don't know about you, but I'd like to show him the *depth* of
his mistake."

Payton's eyes lit up, but everyone else looked at one another timidly.

"So it's like this. We can either sit back and wait for whatever's
going to happen . . . or we can *end* the manipulations and stop all this
before it happens. Right now."

"But how can it be stopped?" Hannah spoke up for the first time. "If
it's predestined to be, then isn't it inevitable, no matter what we do?"

Grant was pensive, lost in thought.

No one spoke as his mind filled with thoughts at a frenetic pace,
weighing options and making very fast decisions.

"What are you thinking, Grant?" asked Morgan.

His shoulders dropped. "I'm thinking I'm tired of running defense.
I'm tired of just *taking* whatever is dished out at me. I'm thinking it's
time we *end this*."

"How?" Morgan asked.

"Look around this room, all of you. In this one location, we have
over a dozen individuals who can do things that no one else in the
world can do. Haven't *any* of you wondered what might happen if we
pooled those gifts and used them in a single, concerted effort?"

From their reactions, most of them hadn't.

"I know," he continued, "this is not what any of you want. But I
refuse to believe that fate reigns supreme. I believe we might just be
able to pull off the impossible."

Glances were exchanged once again, though many of them were
filled with fear. Others, with a hardened resolve.

"I'm in," Payton said, his arms folded across his chest. "But the Keeper could be any Joe Bloggs on the street. How are we supposed to find him?"

"We don't have to. I think I've finally figured it out," Grant replied, turning his gaze to Hannah. "I just remembered. It was a secret place . . . underground."

Hannah nodded back to him, thinking the same thing.

"We're going to need detailed plans of that facility," Grant said, still gazing at Hannah.

"You'll have them," she replied, her features confident and set.

"Once we have those plans, Morgan, I want you to memorize every square inch of them. Put your head together with Fletcher and Daniel to formulate a strategy for getting us in."

Morgan nodded apprehensively, immediately catching on.

"Payton, you and I will be on point. Hannah, we'll need you to cover us with misdirection."

"I've got plenty of tricks left up my sleeve," she replied, smiling grimly.

Grant nodded. "It's not going to be as easy this time . . . Surely they've beefed up security since we were there."

When no one said anything for a few moments, Grant took the lead. "Let's get to work, then. Everyone without an assignment, you know your talents. Make yourselves useful. We go at sundown tomorrow."

59

"Lisa, you in position?" Daniel's voice echoed in her ear. He sounded nervous and it was nice that his concern was for her.

"Have I mentioned how much I hate this plan?" she whispered back in a helpless voice through her earpiece.

"Only in every way possible," Daniel replied. *"Just be careful."*

Lisa peered out through the windshield of the van, noting with growing fear that dusk was nearly over.

Which meant it was time.

She glanced at her watch. Almost seven o'clock.

The comm link was silent as she said nothing, running over the plan once again in her mind.

All the while, her eyes twitched to and fro across the landscape before her, her thoughts racing back to the events of two nights ago, when the man she loved had taken another's life in cold blood.

Well, that wasn't exactly right. Drexel had been about to fire at *him* . . .

Still, Daniel could have shot him in the arm or something.

But he didn't. *He* chose *exactly where to—*

"The others are ready," Morgan reported to both of them, also on the communications system.

"Let's get this over with," Lisa sighed.

"Fletcher, get ready for my signal," said Daniel.

Fletcher put his hands on the wheel of his van, which was identical to the one Lisa drove.

"I'm ready whenever," he said in a bored voice.

Grant held Hannah by both hands. They'd been interrupted before he could show her that he'd forgiven her and things had only gotten busier since then. Payton waited behind them, ready to spring into action. There'd been little point, despite the man's injuries, in trying to convince the swordsman to sit this out.

This was endgame.

"Hannah, we need you in place," Morgan said.

"You know what to do," Grant said to Hannah, mustering confidence. He'd surrendered to his feelings before and those he'd loved had disappeared or gotten hurt.

"I always know what to do when I'm with you," Hannah replied. Still confident, still calm.

He watched her—watched every square inch of her—with longing.

But there was nothing else to say. The silence between them said it all.

"It's time," Payton said from behind, still looking away.

Grant let go of her and turned to join Payton.

"Be careful," Hannah called out.

"You too," he spun his head.

But she was already gone.

"Please be careful," he whispered.

Did they have any chance of succeeding at this?

Was it crazy, what they were about to attempt?

No. The Keeper has to be stopped. No more manipulating.

He closed his eyes, remembering the sight of that enormous, round metal door underground . . .

"We're standing by," Grant heard Payton say into his comm link.

Grant's eyes were out of focus, staring into nothing. Payton glanced at him.

"Are you sure you're ready for this?" Payton whispered, covering his microphone.

Grant nodded vacantly.

"You *know* not everyone will survive," Payton said.

"Yeah," Grant replied, his voice already dead.

"Alex, are you in place?" they heard Daniel's voice say into their ears.

"Almost," Alex replied.

Grant snapped back to reality with something that had been tugging at the back of his mind since yesterday.

"Hey Alex?" Grant said. "You never said what your special ability was. When you had a ring of your own."

"I was empathic," she replied, whispering. *"I could feel other people's emotions. I could even zero-in on someone feeling a specific emotion and find them in a crowd."*

"But how would that drive a person insane?"

"I could implant *emotions, too.* Force *others to feel what I wanted them to feel."*

Grant didn't reply.

"This is harder than I thought," she said softly. Grant realized she was talking about the task at hand.

"Come on, Alex, it's time to go," said Daniel.

"Working on it. . . ." she replied.

"Can you do this, girl, or do you require help?" Payton grunted.

Grant frowned.

"I said I've got it," Alex replied. *"Call me 'girl' again and I'll choke you in your sleep."*

"Lisa, you're up," Daniel said.

In reply, Lisa punched the gas pedal, and her van roared to life. She ignored her instincts, which were telling her to slow down, and instead increased her speed, aiming straight at the barred gate ahead.

"On my mark . . ." Morgan said.

The gate drew closer, and she could see men pacing on either side of it in the distance.

"I think it's now!" Lisa cried, fingering a switch attached to a device in the empty seat beside her.

"Not yet," Morgan replied calmly, sounding distracted. She was no doubt keeping track of several things in her head—the speed of the van, the distance of the gate—in order to time this just right.

Lisa chose to trust her, but her heart was pounding so hard she thought she might pass out.

She was barreling forward at more than sixty miles an hour, and the gate was so close that she could read *Inveo Technologies—Security* written across the white metal arm in red.

"Now!" Morgan said.

Lisa flicked the switch and opened her door at the same time. The small device began to beep.

Five seconds . . . Not nearly enough time, what were they thinking!

She caught a fleeting glimpse of the guards ahead spotting the van for the first time as it devoured pavement on its way to meet them . . .

And then she was hurling herself out of the van and rolling on the grass beside the driveway. There was no time to stop, she picked herself up and ran for cover behind a brick wall on one side of the gate.

But before she reached it, an explosion ripped through the air behind her and toppled her.

Flames, smoke, and noise engulfed her. But she was in. Just as planned.

Fletcher floored the gas pedal on his van, racing toward another gate on the opposite side of the massive Inveo campus.

At Morgan's command, he bailed too, and a second explosion went off.

Grant and Payton scaled a tree right outside the Inveo property to a branch high among its limbs and watched the action on the ground inside. Right on cue, the two explosions went off one after the other. Guards poured from the various buildings and ran for the first gate when the second blast caught them by surprise.

Grant had to admit, his experience at Inveo two months ago had obviously made an impression. Their security force was at least three times the size it was when he was last here, and the black-clad men appeared much more efficient and better trained.

A few of the guards barked orders, and then several broke off from the main group and got into security cars, driving to the second gate. Others made for the two remaining gates, as a preemptive measure.

But the garage facility that he and Payton watched with interest was still occupied. Only now the guards they could see inside stood at attention, their weapons held at the ready. The security force was prepared for this. They wouldn't allow all of their men to be distracted so easily.

As expected, Grant thought.

But there was no time to lose. Police and firemen would be along soon.

"Alex, your turn," Daniel said.

Pandemonium reigned inside the Inveo complex.

The second shift was hard at work when the alarms started blaring and the warehouses and business towers were ordered to evacuate immediately.

Workers filed quickly out of the buildings, directed by guards telling them where to go and repeatedly shouting, "Please remain calm!"

"Coast is clear, Alex," Morgan whispered.

Alex took a deep breath and emerged from her hiding place by the garage bunker.

She steadied herself as she walked lazily in front of the large garage doors, all three of which were raised and open. Men stirred about inside, many gripping formidable weapons in their hands.

There was a moment's stunned silence as the men spotted her.

Alex wore nothing but a terrycloth robe. Her hair was sopping wet, and she was uncharacteristically wearing makeup—Hannah, who had cooked up this part of the plan, seemed to relish giving her a "much needed makeover." Hannah herself had desired this job, but she was needed elsewhere.

Alex peered at the nearest guard over dark sunglasses with a bored expression. An unlit cigarette dangled between two fingers, and her other hand rested in a side pocket.

"This area is restricted, ma'am," the stunned guard said, still taking her in, scrapes, bruises, Band-Aids, and all.

She noticed his look and glanced down at herself. *"Dreadful* golfing accident. I'd rather not dwell," she said, offering her best impression of Hannah's sultry accent and turning to look back at the chaos running rampant all around them.

"You're not allowed to be here," the guard said, nearly tripping over his own feet.

"Then perhaps you could be a *sweet thing*," Alex replied, massaging her neck with one hand, "and direct me to the executive jacuzzi. I could really use some . . . *downtime*."

"Umm . . ." the man stared at her bug-eyed, as several other guards gathered round, all of them sizing her up and down, many with smiles.

"All this excitement is making me *ever* so tense, boys," she said, smirking. The sunglasses had slid down to the tip of her nose now and she looked over them, even batting her eyes once.

"I'll take you there," one of the other guards said, grinning.

"Thanks, handsome," she said. She walked to him and lit her cigarette. "Hold this for a second, would you?"

She slid her sunglasses back up.

The guard held the fake cigarette in his hand just as it went off.

The entire group of guards shouted in pain and staggered backward, blinded by the brilliant light of a flash bomb.

Alex flung the robe aside to reveal a tank top and rolled-up jeans underneath. She pulled a small canister the size of a tube of lipstick from her pocket and sprayed it into the faces of the hunched-over guards. The gas worked quickly and soon each fell unconscious.

Pocketing the canister, Alex fingered her earpiece with her free hand.

"Grant, time to ring the bell," she said, unable to suppress a smile.

60

Hannah watched from her position as Grant and Payton jumped over the fence from their high perch in the tree. A nearby guard was turning in their direction but Hannah held her gaze on him until Grant and Payton were clear, ensuring he saw nothing but empty ground.

Hannah turned a full circle, keeping an eye on every direction. Three hundred yards away stood a guard tower from which a bright search light swept back and forth across the grounds. She could barely make out the tiny outline of the guard who stood behind the light, scanning for intruders.

You are going to be a problem, she thought.

She heard a female guard approaching her own position but deflected the woman as soon as she came into view. The guard walked close enough to touch Hannah yet never saw her.

"Hannah," Grant whispered.

She turned. At the corner of one of the taller buildings, a few hundred feet away, she spotted Grant and Payton crouching. Grant was watching her. A group of guards drove past them in a security car, and they ducked down as low as they could get. A separate guard paced across the front of the building, blocking their next move. As the patrol car passed them by, she sent an image into the marching guard's mind. Spotting a flickering flashlight at the other side of the building, he started and then ran toward the imaginary light.

Away from Grant and Payton.

They had their opening and bolted for the garage.

Then she spotted the search beam again from high above, and it was getting closer.

She turned back to the guard tower and focused her mind on the tiny speck of a guard she could see there.

It was a stretch at this distance, but Hannah sent a terrifying image into his brain, high atop the watchtower. Soon the searchlight's sweep ended. The guard disappeared, no doubt descending to the ground so he could escape the tornado he saw chewing up the property.

When he was far away from the tower, Hannah turned her attention back to Grant and Payton.

But they were gone, out of sight. She didn't see them at the garage bunker in the distance, either.

She bolted toward the last place she'd seen them . . .

Grant and Payton ran side-by-side for the garage without a word.

A pair of golf carts containing security guards stopped before them, blocking their path.

"Halt!" one of men shouted.

In a flash, the guard who had spoken was down, Payton standing over him with his sword pointed at the other men.

The security men split into two groups, some of them rounding on Payton, the others approaching Grant.

Grant gestured at one of the golf carts and it began driving by itself. It ran down one of the men who approached him.

Grant and Payton were now left with three opponents each.

Payton made easy work of his first, slicing and stabbing in non-lethal ways per an earlier appeal from Grant.

Grant knocked the first guard off his feet as the other two approached . . . A nightstick hanging from one of their belts caught Grant's attention and it flew free, whipping up to smack the guard in the nose.

Payton faced off with one of his two remaining guards, who was doing a surprisingly good job of blocking Payton's sword with his nightstick. Payton never saw the other guard whip around with a furious kick. The sword was knocked out of his hand and flew several yards away.

Blows to the head and the chest stunned him but he recovered quickly, tackling the two guards to the ground at the same time and laying atop them.

"Grant!" he shouted.

Grant was sparring hand-to-hand with his last guard as he saw Payton on the ground out of the corner of his eye. Grant threw a brutal back-handed punch to his attacker's face, disorienting him. Then he turned and searched the ground. He spotted the sword and it instantly leapt into the air and twirled end over end until it landed perfectly in Payton's outstretched hand. Payton had never bothered to look up.

Instead he smiled at the two men beneath him as the sword fell into his hand from above.

Grant was kicked hard in the back and went down. He spun as the guard pulled a Taser out of his belt.

Grant had just caught sight of the gun as the guard pulled the trigger.

Grant gasped, sweating heavily as the Taser's two metal darts shot toward him . . .

And then they stopped, frozen in mid-air, as his eyes were trained on them.

The guard tried to retract the darts, but there was a burst of movement and the wires connecting the darts to his Taser were sliced in two. The darts dropped to the ground.

"Cute toy," glowered Payton, who was suddenly standing in front of the guard. He knocked the man out with an open-handed thrust to the jaw.

"Thanks," Grant gasped, still trying to catch his breath.

"Save it," Payton said, pulling him to his feet. "This is taking too long."

They both ran once more for the garage bunker, which was close. Grant caught sight of other Loci at various points in the distance and heard Morgan instructing them on where to go, what to do . . .

Hannah ran in behind them as they approached the garage.

"I don't want you here for this," Grant shouted at Hannah. "It's too dangerous!"

She didn't acknowledge him, just kept walking, and he didn't have time to argue.

Grant led the way to the back corner of the building where he and

Hannah had emerged from after their last visit.

"Security cameras above on both sides," Morgan said in their ears.

The cameras on the ceiling flew from the walls at Grant's command and crashed to the ground with sparks.

It suddenly struck him that the stairwell in the floor may not even be there anymore. *It was only a backdoor entrance of some kind, they could have filled it in or covered it over.*

But no, there it was.

They descended the stairs quickly without speaking, Grant uprooting more of the cameras before they were caught on tape.

The trio arrived at the command room, and Grant and Payton made quick work of the three guards remaining there. Then they joined Hannah outside in the hall and ran to the small door opposite the stairwell.

Grant's heart jumped into his throat. He hadn't been nervous or anxious until this moment, but it just hit him out of nowhere.

This is really it . . .

They opened the door.

Waiting for them there was the massive, three-story-high round metal vault door, set into a small alcove that offered just enough room to swing the massive door open. He had forgotten about the dull humming that filled the room.

The control panel beside the door flickered, beckoning him. He pulled out the small electronic device that Daniel had given him and attached it to the panel.

"We're set, Doc," Grant said, fingering his earpiece.

"Stand by," Daniel replied into his ear.

Daniel set to work on overriding the door's controls remotely.

Minutes passed and glances were exchanged. Hannah repeatedly checked her watch.

"The police should be here by now," Payton grumbled.

"Daniel! What's the holdup?" Grant cried impatiently.

"I can't crack it!" Daniel said. "It's one of the most complex algorithms I've ever seen. This thing is unbelievable . . . It'd take *weeks* just to crank this thing through my laptop and get a real handle on it."

"Plan B, then," Payton said, eying Grant.

"Get back," Grant ordered.

The three of them backed out into the hallway, but Grant stood at the threshold, his eyes on the door.

He let out a deep breath and settled his shoulders.

"Calming breaths, Grant," Daniel's voice said in his ear. *"You can do this."*

"Then shut up and let me," Grant mumbled.

He breathed in and out, very slowly.

He envisioned the door opening in his mind.

Or rather, he *tried* to.

But it wouldn't budge.

Even in his thoughts, it was too heavy.

He bore down, straining hard, but it wouldn't move.

"I can't," he winced, bearing down. "It's too much, I can't get it . . ."

His eyes popped open. Someone's hand had grasped his.

Hannah stood there, smiling calmly.

"You're the Bringer," she said. "You can do *anything*."

He held her hand tight as he closed his eyes again and concentrated once more on the massive metal door.

Sweat poured from Grant's brow, and finally a loud crack was heard as the seal was broken.

It groaned noisily as it slowly swiveled open to the left.

Grant blinked when he saw what was before him.

The vast open space of the underground facility he expected to see . . .

. . . was instead nothing more than a sheer wall of dirt and stone.

Nothing but a cross section of earth.

"What. . . ?" Hannah said beside him. "I don't get it."

"The Keeper lured you here, probably to test your abilities," Daniel mumbled.

Grant closed his eyes, and his face began turning red. "It's another setup," he said softly. *"He* planted it here for me to find. It was just another manipulation!"

"Grant . . ." Hannah began.

"Another manipulation!" he roared, and the door that towered above them slammed itself shut with a deafening *boom*.

"Move!" he barked, marching out into the hall.

He no longer cared about the security cameras or the guards or anything else.

This was too much.

They heard footsteps racing down the stairs, but Grant merely walked away from them, down to the other end of the hall. Then he turned and faced the stairs, hands at his sides.

Waiting.

Payton and Hannah hurried to get behind him, positioning themselves for the fight ahead.

Over a dozen armed men spilled out of the stairwell and into the hallway, aiming rifles and Tasers and other weapons at them, screaming, "Hands up!" and "Down on the ground!"

Grant's hands balled into fists at his side, he let out a primordial scream. Every one of the guards whipped violently backward away from him, crashing into the far wall, and then collapsing into heaps on the floor.

Grant started walking again, making for the stairs.

"Grant—!" Hannah called.

But he never acknowledged her. She and Payton were forced to run to keep up with him.

At the top of the stairs, he emerged into the large garage full of vehicles and unconscious guards.

Grant stepped to the middle of the room and froze there.

His face was completely red now, and his breathing was hard and thick. He closed his eyes.

Hannah had never seen such a venomous look on his face.

It was almost a . . . *bloodlust*. The thought came to her with a chill.

"Don't do this, Grant!" she cried.

"I strongly suggest," he breathed in a voice of homicidal calm, "you both run."

Payton grabbed her by the arm and pulled her toward the exit. "Come on!"

She screamed "Grant!" again as Payton wrenched her away.

Payton and Hannah had just cleared the building when the vehicles inside came to life and crashed through all four walls of the building, driving off in every direction. A pair of sedans moving their way forced the two of them to roll aside.

Cars, vans, and golf carts drove and drove until they crashed into whatever was in their path. Sometimes it was buildings. Sometimes it was trees or the outer fence. A few ran over security guards and kept going.

"Grant, stop!" Hannah screamed, rising to her feet.

But he wasn't finished.

An ear-splitting crack followed next, as if a fissure had opened up in the earth.

She and Payton were knocked backward to the ground once more by what could only be described as a visible *wave* of energy, rippling outward from the building, tearing through everything in its path. The garage was reduced to rubble instantly, and the wave moved outward in a widening circle. From the rumble beneath them, Hannah surmised that it had probably caved in the underground facility as well.

The wave lost energy as it expanded outward. The blast had enough power to tear down a few smaller buildings nearby, exploding them outward with the wave of the blast. Bricks and wood and cement made a terrible dissonance of sounds, coming from all directions. But the larger buildings in the distance merely trembled, without falling.

When the energy faded, Hannah and Payton looked up to see Grant sunk down to his knees, sobbing into his hands at the center of where the garage had stood.

Just as they reached him, his phone rang.

Grant angrily pulled it out and saw a text message waiting from an unknown source.

It read:

```
                    you're finally
                         ready
```

61

Weary and defeated, the group returned to the Wagner Building, dispersing silently, once inside, for empty apartments scattered throughout. Hannah and Alex helped Grant get back to his place. He was too tired and distraught to be trusted to make the trip alone.

They tried to steer him directly to his bed, but he went to the couch instead.

His body was worn, but his mind was alive, burning, swimming with thoughts.

It was a diversion, a manipulation, from him . . .

To get me "ready" . . .

Ready for what?

If we only knew what the prophecy means . . . If only I knew what's coming . . . Or who the Keeper really is . . .

Hannah and Alex left him alone to stew. They conferred quietly, gazing out the big picture window at the city's dark night below. But all three of them—and probably all of the others, wherever they were—were thinking exactly the same thing.

Whatever was destined to happen, whatever was "coming," it had to be soon.

And they couldn't stop it.

Grant jumped as his phone rang.

Again.

He saw that it was the same unidentified number that had sent him the text message. He answered it.

"Who is this?" he said, and Hannah and Alex turned to watch.

"Someone you know," a male voice answered.

"The Keeper?" Grant said, his breath catching in his throat. He was afraid to know the answer.

"Of course."

Tears formed around Grant's eyes.

That voice . . .

He knew that voice. Even now, he could remember the exact sound of it.

He would never forget it.

"Dad?"

"Son," came the calm reply.

"But . . . how are you even alive?"

"It's time for you to come find out," the voice replied.

"No, you tell me how any of this is possible," Grant said, eager to keep the conversation going. He glanced at his watch. "Everything, the rings, the Shift, what I can do . . ."

"Very well," the Keeper replied. "But after I have explained, you will come down to meet me. At once." It was neither a request nor a question. It was a prediction.

Come down to meet me . . .

Payton said something about a "substation" . . .

Of course! How could I be so stupid!

"Before the existence of the earth," the Keeper said, in a tone that indicated he was reciting a story he knew by memory, "a vast war was waged throughout the universe. It was war on a scale unparalleled throughout recorded history. The essence of evil dawned in the hearts of those who once knew only good. And they made a choice.

"They gave themselves over to that evil. Rebellion was sparked throughout the cosmos, and all that was pure was forever tainted by betrayal. The leader of this rebellion was caught, tried, and confined here, to the earth.

"Some believe that a man named Ezekiel recorded this leader's trial in a vague account:

'You were the seal of perfection,
Full of wisdom and perfect in beauty . . .

Every precious stone was your covering:
The sardius, topaz, and diamond,
Beryl, onyx, and jasper,
Sapphire, turquoise, and emerald with gold . . .'"

Grant's heart filled with dread. But he had little time to consider it as the Keeper continued . . .

"'You were the anointed cherub . . .
I established you . . .
You walked back and forth in the midst of fiery stones.
You were perfect in your ways from the day you were created,
Till iniquity was found in you . . .
You became filled with violence within . . .
Therefore I cast you as a profane thing
Out of the mountain of God.'"

The Keeper paused his soliloquy. "Is it becoming clear to you?"

Grant's blood was ice cold. "I, I'm not . . . I don't know . . ." was all he could manage, even though it was *painfully* clear.

"The leader of this rebellion—the one Ezekiel wrote about," the Keeper continued, "was the most beautiful of his kind. He was adorned with handsome garments and precious stones. But his pride was his undoing, and so he and all who followed him were cast down from the higher realm, and he and his servants were given *dominion* over all the earth. But all of his vestiges, raiment, and adornments were stripped from him. It is the *last* of these adornments—his most powerful insignia—that now rests upon your finger."

Grant couldn't breathe.

Couldn't think.

Couldn't believe.

"Dad . . . Are you telling me . . ." he gasped, "that this thing—this ring that *won't come off*—was worn by. . . ?"

"It was the seal placed upon him to signify his dominion and power. The Seal of Dominion."

Grant's stomach lurched.

"The rings worn by the others were salvaged from similar vestiges stripped of his followers," the Keeper ended his story. "Similar in make, yet wholly different in purpose."

"Why are you doing this?" Grant cried. "Why use these rings to turn us into some kind of . . . heroes?" Grant blurted out.

"My boy," the Keeper said, disappointed and reproachful, "don't be so *obtuse*. Have you heard nothing I've said? The Seal of Dominion is the highest emblem of absolute evil. Besides, what use would someone like *me* have for *heroes*?"

"What are you saying?" Grant asked, his voice low.

"Ask yourself how often you've been angry, confused, and frustrated since this began. How many times have you lost your temper? Why is your first instinct when threatened to snuff out your enemy's life sharp and efficient? You think this is a side-effect of your confusion? I gave you the instincts of a killer. A well-trained one. I gave you a body capable of using those instincts. And the Seal is feeding you the *will* to use them.

"Ask yourself why every one of you that underwent the Shift was one of society's outcasts. The lonely, the forgotten, the orphans. The ones no one would ever miss."

The world around Grant blurred and spun, and he didn't want to hear anymore. He thought he was going to throw up, but he couldn't stop listening.

"*Now* ask yourself why a man as powerful as me would seek to create heroes. Oh, my boy. *Soldiers*, yes. But heroes? Not even *close*."

Grant couldn't hold back the tears now. This was beyond anything he could've expected . . .

"But why me?" Grant shouted.

"I fashioned you to be the Bringer. And you *must* play your role, and face what is to come. There is no one else who can."

"And if I don't want to?" Grant asked, even though he didn't want to know the answer.

"I've already proven that I will go to any lengths to ensure that you're ready for what's coming. But the time for talk is over. Your destiny has come, and it's waiting for you. And I will do whatever it takes to ensure that you seize it."

"You're insane . . ." Grant sobbed. "You can't do this . . ."

"I can do *anything*, or haven't you learned that by now?" the Keeper replied malevolently.

"How could anyone be this—"

"Spare me the pontificating. Your mother served her purpose, and when the time came, she had the good grace to let go. Now it's your girlfriend's turn to do the same."

Time ran like molasses. Grant's face contorted in horror as the phone fell from his hands. Hannah turned to him, worried, from where she stood in front of the large picture window. He heard the shot ring out from far away.

And instinctually, he panicked.

A silver platter resting on a nearby shelf launched itself spinning into the air, passing between Hannah and the window . . .

But it was too late by a fraction of a second . . . The window shattered, and she fell.

"*NOOO!!!*" Grant screamed, running for her.

With Alex's help, he dragged her from the view of the window and whoever was out there shooting. Her eyes were closed . . .

No! No! No! No! No!

"Hannah!" he cried, brushing her hair back. "Wake up! Stay with me!"

Alex was contorted with shock and sorrow as she gazed back and forth between Grant and Hannah.

Hannah stirred as Grant cradled her in his arms, inspecting the wound. The bullet had struck her shoulder, but it looked like a clean hole, it wasn't that bad . . .

She's going to make it, she's okay . . .

He was looking into her eyes, smiling in relief when he realized *she* wasn't taking her eyes off of *him*.

And blood was everywhere, all over him, on Alex, the carpet . . .

Words she'd spoken once flashed through his mind.

"I have to be on a line-of-sight with whoever I'm doing it to for it to work . . . and I can only do it to one person at a time."

Grant looked at Alex. Her features were stricken.

Grief-stricken.

But still Grant saw only the flesh wound on Hannah's shoulder, as she gazed on him without blinking.

"It's all right, big boy, I'm going to be fine . . ." she whispered.

Pain swelled within him but he choked back the tears until he felt like his throat might explode.

But he held her tighter, rocking her slowly. Only his whimpers could be heard.

Hannah's pulse faded as Grant kissed her forehead, pushing her hair out of her face . . .

She fought to keep her eyes open, her voice fading. "Don't . . ." she said groggily. "Don't let them take . . . your soul . . ." she said, struggling to speak.

"Hannah—!"

She stopped breathing.

Her eyes fell closed.

And then Grant was finally able to see the truth. The wound wasn't in her shoulder.

It had torn open her neck.

She had bled to death in his arms in a matter of seconds.

Grant stopped breathing, too.

He couldn't take his eyes off her, couldn't blink, no words would come. Inside him, her light dimmed, dimmed, and then, with a sigh, vanished.

Grant pulled her tight with his eyes closed and rocked her back and forth, holding nothing back in his grief.

"Grant," Alex said quietly.

He didn't hear her, he only continued rocking and crying.

"Grant, she's gone."

She's really gone, he thought.

No!

I never got to tell her . . .

He let go of Hannah and looked up at Alex, his heart flattened in despair. Still he said nothing as he cried, his soul dark and empty without her.

Alex watched as Grant turned loose of Hannah's lifeless body. But he was no longer rocking back and forth. He was trembling. And as he did, a deep, powerful rumble shook the building to its foundations.

Perfect time for an earthquake, she thought at first. *Typical L.A.*

At least it *felt* like an earthquake.

But then she saw Grant's face. His skin had turned red, his eyes were open, looking all around through a haze of water, his cheeks were soaked, and veins appeared on his forehead as he trembled harder and harder in a blinding fury.

Grief and rage burned in his eyes. The building was shaking violently now, and Alex found that she couldn't get up off the ground, even as she watched Grant rise to his feet.

Everything in the apartment rattled as the tremors grew worse. Small objects took on a life of their own and flung themselves across the room. Furniture and appliances uprooted themselves, falling over. Dishes and picture frames whizzed by in all directions and shattered against the walls.

Alex put her arms up to protect herself from flying papers, books, plates, picture frames, and other objects swirling about the room in a wild hurricane of power.

She could barely see Grant anymore as he walked unharmed through the heart of the storm toward the apartment door.

The door threw itself open, crashing into the wall beside it, and Grant stalked onward.

"Grant!" Alex shouted above the din.

He spun around in a violent blaze, and the apartment seemed to turn with him. *"He killed her!"* he roared, his voice booming like a clap of thunder.

Alex saw madness in him, and she realized in horror that she was looking into the face of a stranger . . .

What was that?

Something in his eyes . . . .

No, now there was nothing.

"He is not going to get away with it!"

"Grant, *no!*" she screamed, grappling for words and trying not to hug the carpet as the terror around them built to an impossible crescendo. They held each other's gaze, but she couldn't mask her terror at what she was witnessing.

What would Julie say to him right now?

"Grant, if you do this . . ." she shouted, finding her voice, "you will lose *everything* in you that's *good!*"

His face was hard as granite as his next words came out through clenched teeth.

"I wasn't *made* to be good."

He turned and walked out, leaving her to stare in stunned silence at the spot where he'd been.

The door slammed itself shut behind him.

The deadbolt and chain locked themselves.

62

Los Angeles quaked.

Rippling waves shuddered the city to its core, and the upheaval grew ever worse. Bricks fell free from buildings, awnings crashed to sidewalks, ceilings caved in, and light posts and power lines were uprooted.

Electricity went out and night engulfed the city for miles.

Cars screeched and crashed into one another. Fire hydrants were shaken loose and overturned, water gushing high into the air. Pedestrians spilled out of businesses, residences, and other buildings in droves. Mothers and fathers picked up their children and tried to get as far away from the stampedes of the rioting city as possible. But they didn't know where to run.

And then everything changed.

It began with a single scream.

Then another. Others followed, lifting their gazes to the night sky, and the panicked cries spread like an outward-growing ripple in a pond. One after another after another joined in the chorus as all eyes turned upward.

The moon and stars were gone.

Fierce, pitch-black clouds billowed and churned uncontrollably through the sky as if a thousand volcanoes were erupting.

Bright orange hues danced behind the clouds and around their edges. The heavens themselves were sparking into a scorching holocaust of heat and flame behind the swelling storm.

All light was gone, darkness swallowing the city whole, broken only by hair-trigger flashes of angry orange light from above.

Terror struck every heart, and everyone inexplicably knew that *something*—something that would change the world forever—was coming.

It was coming now.

On the bottom floor of the Wagner Building, the elevator doors ripped apart and Grant emerged, trembling and cloaked in malice. His cyclone of rage surrounded him, whipping up dirt and dust and anything else in its path, and stretching wide enough to blow out the windows on the ground floor.

Outside, the world had gone mad.

But Grant had no interest in what was outside the building.

Hannah's blood still dripped from his clothes, the coppery smell flooding his nostrils and fueling his turmoil.

His thoughts returned again and again to the words of the Keeper . . .

After I have explained, you will come down to meet me . . .

He knew what it meant.

The Keeper was very near, and had been all along.

Grant turned before reaching the front door and entered the emergency stairwell. He descended to the basement, retracing his steps from the day he was first Shifted to the small mechanical room where he'd hid from Konrad.

The spartan room was exactly as he remembered it: musty, dim, and filled only with a pulsing hum, as if you could hear the building's heartbeat. The narrow, emergency "fire escape" door that led to the subway was to his right in the back.

But the furnace was symmetrical in design, and a similar space was open amid the pipes on the left side of the room. But there was no door there.

At the room's threshold, Grant's eyes went dark as they settled on the furnace.

The massive heating device *ripped* itself free from its moorings and exploded out into the hall. Grant himself was unscathed and unmoved.

The subway door gave way from the blast, and a hole appeared in the opposite wall.

The hole was roughly the size of a man, and Grant went through, stalking down the dark corridor beyond.

Sweat poured off of him, his breathing fast and hard. He came upon a small set of double doors that slid apart as he approached. A stark, stainless steel elevator car waited on the other side.

He entered.

Grant never bothered with the buttons on the panel. He merely thought *down*.

And down he went.

Like a falling bomb.

Waiting to explode on impact.

Alex made it to her feet as the miniature storm in Grant's apartment subsided.

Hannah's broken body held her attention, outstretched as she was on the floor. The girl was already pale, the blood having drained from her neck wound. Alex blinked back the tears and tried to think straight, tried to decide what she should do next.

Morgan. I should find Morgan.

A light from the broken picture window flashed in the corner of her eye.

Another tremor unbalanced her stance, but this one felt different.

It wasn't localized around the building—she could see the entire city shaking outside, high-rises swaying back and forth ever-so-slightly.

Peering down at the streets far below, she gasped at the massive swell of the crowd. Every person in the entire city seemed to be fleeing in all directions, running for their lives.

She looked up.

It was a sight no human had ever before laid eyes on. The sky roiled and crashed like waves at sea in a turbulent storm. Clouds darker than any black she had ever seen collided, swirled, stirred, sparked, and detonated.

Fire was devouring the night sky, and it was spreading . . .

Spreading *downward*.

It was *here*.

But Grant had gone mad.

And Hannah was dead.

A wild notion rushed through her thoughts, from out of nowhere. She decided it was the best idea she'd ever had.

Payton needed to see it for himself.

Using the stairs, which buckled wildly beneath him, he made a treacherous journey to the bottom floor of the Wagner Building where, like many of the other Loci, he had taken up residence in the last few days.

He met Morgan halfway down, flanked by Fletcher. Daniel and Lisa were already in the lobby on the ground floor when the three of them staggered out of the stairwell. Not escaping their notice was the door that led to the stairs, which had been ripped off of its hinges, but they had no time to consider it.

Payton coolly met the eyes of the others—all of which were filled with fear—and then gazed again through the empty window frames.

No words were exchanged.

As a group, they filed through the front door and took in the full scope of the event before them.

They'd no sooner regrouped outside than a monstrous tendril of flame leaped out of the sky and bored into the earth. All five of them were knocked off their feet as an office complex two blocks down was hit by the massive fire bomb; glass, steel, and everything within the building sparked to flame as if it had been superheated in a single moment.

They rose to their feet again and watched an enormous plume of smoke rise from where the office building had stood. They doubted anyone had been inside at this hour of the night, but it was still a fearsome sight.

Payton's hand was instinctively on his sword. "We must do something before this gets worse," he cried urgently.

Morgan turned to him, resigned. "What would you suggest?"

Payton had no answer.

Lisa's face was more stricken and terrified than Daniel had ever seen it. He placed a hand on her shoulder, and she side-stepped into his grasp, until his entire arm was holding her.

"What is it?" Lisa whispered.

"Something bigger than anything that has ever been," Daniel replied quietly, repeating words he had once spoken to Grant.

"Alex was right," Morgan spoke up.

They all turned to her.

"It's the end of everything," she said.

Grant's fists were clenched tight as the elevator door slid open after a long ride to the bottom.

"Mr. Borrows. Right on time," a voice to his right said. It sounded busy, occupied, impatient.

Grant stepped out and found a short, balding man holding a clipboard and watching him through round, wire-rimmed glasses. He wore a scientist's white lab coat and a detached expression.

"If you'll just come with me, he's eager to get underway . . ." the little man said, turning to walk away.

Grant barely gave the man a fleeting glance.

Instead, his eyes swiveled all about, taking in the sight before him, just as the bald man was suddenly jerked away to the side, crashing into a distant wall.

Grant was inside an immense hollow that looked as if the dirt and rock underground had been scooped away. It was like being within an enormous crater that was upside down. The vast, circular space was over half a mile in diameter.

Directly in its center stood a gleaming silver cube of solid steel, offset by metal girders thatched across its surface. It rose over ten stories above him, not quite touching the top of the hollow. A set of double doors lay straight ahead. The whole area smelled unnaturally clean, like a hospital.

A contingent of guards in black jumpsuits guarded the entrance. They already had weapons trained on him as he approached. But Grant was moving unstoppably forward, a force of nature. The guards were knocked hard to the ground on either side, as if the Red Sea had parted before him.

The double doors before him were labeled in big letters:

SUBSTATION LAMBDA-ALPHA

The doors never opened.

Grant glanced at them, and both doors exploded outward in a tremendous blast. He deflected them with an instinctive thought, and the two doors parted, falling to either side of him.

All the while, he never stopped moving forward.

He never slowed down.

Alex ran out into the ground floor lobby, scanning everything for Grant's trail.

She caught sight of the stairwell door lying broken on the ground. She looked inside and pieced it together.

He hadn't gone out into the city.

He'd gone under it.

She raced down to the destroyed mechanical room, surveying the damage, grim evidence of Grant's outrage. A thin path led through the devastation, across the floor to the far wall.

Which meant there was no time to waste. Into the opening in the wall and to the waiting stainless steel elevator she ran . . .

Inside the tall underground structure, black-clad militia men advanced on Grant in droves as he continued his slow, steady progress through the building. Unarmed scientists in lab coats ran screaming from his presence.

Everyone who came within sight of him was lifted up off their feet and blown aside.

Walls, doors, windows, lights, even the floor tiles were all caught in the hurricane of Grant's approach, and he showed no signs of tiring.

Blood in his eyes and death in his heart, he moved steadily toward the heart of the building through a tall, wide main corridor made from the same pristine steel as the outside.

But he was oblivious to it all, the image of Hannah's bloodstained body consuming his vision.

He was equally oblivious to the shimmering glow coming from the ring on his finger. Brighter and brighter it glimmered, its radiance outshining the building's own lighting.

Still he continued on, destroying, uprooting, tearing apart.

Searching.

Where.

Are.

You?

Alex jogged out of the underground elevator and took in the unconscious bodies and destruction in the gigantic cavern.

She had to find him . . .

She had to *stop* him . . .

There was no one else left, she couldn't let him do this, not *now*, when he was so badly needed outside . . .

But she knew she was going to be too late.

"*Grant!*" she bellowed.

Alex was answered by distant shrieks from within the tall subterranean structure ahead.

She followed the screams.

Down the main corridor, all was dark save a glimmering, hazy light in the distance.

"*Show yourself!*" a thundering voice boomed.

It was Grant.

63

The small storm surged around Grant, whipping up a frenzy of wind, debris, and demolition.

The coals of hatred had taken hold of him and he was stoking them with every ounce of energy he had.

"*Come out!!*" he raged, adrenaline surging through every vein in his body.

"Stop him!" someone shouted from behind. He heard a large collection of footsteps approaching . . .

He lashed out with a swift, spinning backhand. He was too far away for the blow to connect, but three guards flew backward anyway, their heads cracking hard against the cold, steel walls. Weapons were unholstered, but a blink from Grant later, the guns were floating high in the air above the militiamen.

"I am getting very"—Grant said with a dangerous calm—"*impatient.*"

On his last word, a surge of energy released from him in a wave, and everything around him—the guards included—flew backward and crashed in a ferocious display.

"You have truly exceeded all my hopes," said a calm voice.

A very familiar voice.

The same voice he'd spoken to on the phone in his apartment.

Before Hannah had been . . .

Hannah . . .

Grant turned to see who stood before him.

A figure was there, cloaked in shadow, just over ten feet away. But it was clearly a man, wearing some kind of business suit.

"And now you are ready to face your destiny," the man said again, taking a step forward.

"Grant, *don't!*" someone shrieked from behind.

Grant turned to see Alex running to catch him.

"The world's gone mad, they need you—!" she was shouting.

Grant spun back around to face the man.

The light from Grant's ring poured upon his face and at long last, Grant saw—

All of the breath escaped from his body and he felt weak and sick. The fury around him stopped cold.

Alex skidded to a stop next to him, facing the other man, but Grant ignored her.

"No . . ." he whispered, shaking his head in disbelief.

Dressed in a crisp navy suit, the Keeper was an older gentleman. His hands were clasped in front of him, a pristine gold watch at his wrist, barely concealing a tattoo, like the ones Grant's parents had displayed in the old photograph he'd found. A neatly trimmed salt-and-pepper mustache adorned his upper lip. He was stiff and emotionless, studying Grant's every breath and gesture.

And he was utterly calm and unaffected by the chaos and destruction Grant had wrought.

"Grant. . . ?" Alex asked loudly, turning toward him but keeping her eyes trained on the Keeper.

Grant was frozen, absolutely unmoving. He stared at the other man with a mixed expression of rejection, shock, and betrayal.

Grant took in unsteady gulps of air and stared sorrowfully into the face of this man who had destroyed his life. The pieces were falling into place in his mind, one by one. The snake in his mind had begun winding around and around again, and now he knew its identity.

"You said he didn't have a real name, Alex," Grant said, anger rising. "You were wrong."

She looked at Grant. "What is it?"

"Maximilian," Grant replied.

He never took his eyes off the Keeper as he extended his left arm out in front of her.

The old bracelet on Grant's wrist peeked out from under his shirt sleeve. A sloppily-scrawled inscription was engraved by hand into the metal surface of the old shell casing. It read:

Max B. 1943

Grant's arm fell to his side as he looked into the other man's eyes.

"He's my grandfather," Grant said.

Alex's jaw dropped, and she glanced back and forth between them. They plainly recognized each other, but they were also seeing each other for the first time in decades.

It was true, then.

Grant started breathing fast again.

"Where is my father?" he asked, barely able to find his voice.

"Long dead," the Keeper replied calmly.

"*You* killed him," Grant spat, the whirlwind around him surging. "Didn't you?"

"No," the Keeper replied without deceit. "The coward took his own life. To keep you from *me*."

"What?"

"When he found out what I believed about you—what I believed you would *become*—your father had your mental acuity tested to see if it was true. Or even possible. The results were precisely as I told him they would be. With your mother dead, he knew that alone, he would never be able to keep you from me forever. But he also knew that with him dead and gone, I couldn't take custody of you and your sister without exposing the Secretum. So he killed himself and cut me off. You and your sister were declared wards of the state. You know the rest."

Grant looked down, staggering backward a few uneasy steps. The fury around him built once more, objects and debris again swirling about the corridor . . .

"You're the reason . . ." he said, "that they're gone. The reason they're dead. The reason I had to grow up in that awful place . . ."

"Your father believed he was shielding you by taking his own life," the Keeper said, still perfectly calm. "The fool had no idea how far I was willing to go to ensure that you met your destiny. Outside of my influence, you grew up and chose for yourself a life of solitude—a life you were never meant to have. Steps had to be taken to correct this."

Grant shook his head through a cascade of tears, eyes locked on his grandfather. The insanity of it all . . . that someone could presume to predetermine the entire course of his life and manipulate it to that end . . .

"I'm going to kill you now," Grant said, barely audible among the cacophony. He balled his fists and bore down, closing his eyes.

The Keeper did not react. He merely watched in silence.

The ground trembled as Grant prepared to let out another primordial surge of energy . . .

But something struck his head from behind, and the havoc around him ended as everything faded to black.

"I think he's coming around, sir."

Grant tried to blink.

But something was covering his eyes.

He couldn't move.

And he was dizzy.

Very dizzy.

"Sorry about all this," said the Keeper, his voice oddly swirling all around Grant.

That's when Grant realized that he was strapped in a standing position to something upright that was *spinning* in place.

And the Keeper was his grandfather.

His grandfather! His father's father . . .

How was it possible?

All he remembered of this old man was a handful of visits as a young boy and old pictures he had seen once of his grandparents together. He'd never even heard from the old man after his parents died, and assumed him to be dead as well.

"What's going on? Why am I . . . going in circles?" Grant stammered.

"I know it's uncomfortable. It won't last any longer than necessary, I assure you," the old man said. "But you could destroy this entire structure with a single thought, if you laid eyes on it. Which is the precise reason for the blindfold. Your friend Hannah told you her abilities only worked on line-of-sight. She was partially right. *Awareness* is the real key. You could destroy an object behind you right now if you knew where it was."

Grant didn't reply, absorbing this.

His grandfather pressed on. "It's the same for all of you. Morgan can only remember facts that she's directly exposed to. Payton can only enact his super-burst of speed against opponents that he can *see*. Likewise, if you're disoriented, your powers are useless."

"I could still let out a blast of energy in all directions," Grant said, his jaw rigid, his teeth grinding.

"Of course you could," the Keeper replied. "But if you did, Alex would no doubt suffer the consequences as well."

"What did you do with her?" Grant asked in as much of a menacing tone as he could muster.

"She's here. She's fine. For the moment."

Alex watched.

Strapped to a stationary table of her own in the structure's colossal inner chamber, she watched as across the room, the table holding Grant slowly spun.

She couldn't move, couldn't speak. Tape covered her mouth.

Three armed guards surrounded her, watching her every move.

Which seemed like overkill.

After all, what could she do in this position?

Let's hope they're thinking that, too . . . she mused.

Meanwhile, she kept her eyes trained on Grant.

Waiting for an opportunity, an opening, to put her plan into motion . . .

"What is all this about?" Grant cried. "What have you done to me? *What do you want?*"

"I want to stack the deck in your favor. Rig the game so you win. I want *the Bringer*," the Keeper replied, as if it were obvious. "Events are unfolding very quickly, so time is short. But I'll try to explain as best I can. Let me begin at the beginning . . .

"As I told you on the phone, the Rings of Dominion—as well as the Dominion Stone itself—were hidden for millennia. Buried and sealed in a place shrouded in utmost secrecy, they were entombed. Sealed beneath the earth by the Secretum of Six. The Dominion Stone covered their hiding place."

"What *is* the Stone?" Grant asked as he continued to quietly spin.

"A marker, pointing to both the past and the future. They say it cannot be destroyed. But somehow, it was broken centuries ago by the enemies of the Secretum. Wars were fought for centuries for possession of the Stone and the rings—most especially *your* ring, the Seal of Dominion. Legend has it that the Seal was sought by dictators and rulers the world over, including the likes of Napoleon, Hitler, and Alexander. But thanks to the efforts of the Secretum, the Seal has been kept safe throughout history, and no one was permitted to wear it. Until *you*."

"Was it the ring that caused the Shift?" Grant asked.

"No," the Keeper replied. "*I* caused the Shift. You see—or well, I suppose you don't at the moment, but if you could—I'm wearing a ring myself, a ring almost as special as yours. Not gold in color but silver, with a blue stone. And the talent it gives me is the transfer of consciousness from one living being to another."

"How can you be one of the Loci if I can't feel you?"

"There has always been a Keeper to lead the Secretum, and the Keeper has worn the ring I now wear since the Secretum was formed. They say that it was stolen—*taken*—from the opposite number of he who once owned *your* ring. The one this ring was taken from—'He alone knows the soul of man,'" the Keeper quoted knowingly. "And as the Secretum came to realize, if you can *see* a thing, then you can *change* it."

"Why do all this?" Grant said, trying not to shout. His rage was resurfacing in the form of impatience. "Why bother Shifting us, if it's not necessary for using the rings?"

"Now you're disappointing me," the Keeper said edgily. "There is only *one* practical application of this: *anonymity*. Think of it, Grant. You are the most powerful being on the planet, yet for all intents and purposes, *you do not exist*. Untrackable. Untraceable. A member of society, yet completely unknown by it. You're the perfect soldier. You can do *anything* by simply thinking it, and no one need ever know who you are."

Tears formed behind Grant's eyes once again, soaking into the cloth over his eyes.

"This body I'm wearing, these people you put us inside of . . . who were they before?"

"Husks. Vessels," the Keeper said with a hint of disgust. "Yours was a soldier who worked in covert ops, which is why you're able to fight so well. His instincts remain in you. But they were volunteers, all of them. For them, it was the highest calling."

"You've killed so many. You're responsible for *everything* that's happened to me, aren't you?"

"Of course."

"But why send Konrad and Drexel to try and kill me? How does that help you?"

"All part of the process. The apartment, the money, the car—it all came from me. Resources you needed to fulfill your role. If you hadn't been through everything you've gone through, if you hadn't learned, adapted, and grown with each new experience . . . if you hadn't *survived*, then you wouldn't have been worthy of your destiny. But I never doubted it."

Grant was reminded of something Daniel had told him the day they met.

"Where you see random occurrences, I see a purpose," Daniel had said.

Alex tensed.

Whatever else may have been happening here, this man was starting to get through to Grant. She could see it. She could practically feel the wheels turning in Grant's head.

And there was no time . . .

High above them, reality itself was rending at the seams, falling apart. Plunging the world into ruin.

Come on, Grant . . . make a move!

"So now you know the truth about how you were made. Above us is the *why*," the Keeper said simply. "Aboveground, the surface is crumbling. A cataclysm like nothing the earth has ever seen is taking place."

"You're just going to turn me loose to go fight it?" Grant asked incredulously, his temperature still rising.

"It's not quite that simple," the Keeper replied. "Destiny has come calling. But it's still up to you to answer."

Grant frowned.

"You must pass the final test. *Prove* to me that you are prepared to take this all the way. Right now, I have three armed men with semi-automatic weapons ready to fill Alex's body with holes—"

"Leave her alone!" Grant screamed.

"That choice is yours to make. They will obey *your* command. If you tell them to, they'll fire, and you'll be released to go perform your function. If you order her life spared, then countless others will lose their lives to the threat above. Prove to me that you're willing to pay any price to get the job done, and this will end."

Grant was trembling.

"I don't care if you *are* my grandfather, you're either very brave or very foolish to be making me angry," he said quietly.

"I have nothing to fear from you," the Keeper replied matter-of-factly. "You're powerless until *I* let you go. You can't even save Alex in your current state."

Grant gave a calm, easy laugh and his body relaxed.

On his finger he felt the warm glow of his ring begin to rise.

"I don't *have* to save her," Grant said. His blindfolded head slowly turned to point straight at Alex's location across the room, and stayed fixed on her position as he continued to rotate. "I can *feel* her."

The tape ripped itself off of Alex's mouth, and he heard her shout, though it seemed more in delight than pain.

"*Terror*," Alex said to the guards surrounding her, and Grant heard the men howl in fright and dropping to the floor.

Grant continued to whirl in place but he felt Alex next to him. And her ring.

"We removed your ring," the Keeper growled. "How could you possibly?"

"How quick the mighty forget," she said, rising from the table. " 'A ring can only be removed after its wearer dies,' " she recited.

"Hannah . . . *her* ring . . ." he whispered. He backed away.

"You may not have to *fear* your grandson, bubbles," she said, nodding at Grant. "But if you remember what *I* can do with one of these things"— she held up her ring—"then you should *fear me!*"

At the word *fear*, Grant heard the man topple, screaming and begging.

"By the way," Alex said, her voice closer now. "*I quit.*"

Grant heard her scuffling about him and then the sound of gears clicking into place. At once, his spinning slowed, then a few seconds later, stopped entirely. Alex pulled the cover from Grant's eyes and he forced himself to stand, despite his dizziness.

He looked up for the first time at the vast chamber they were in. Overflowing with scientific equipment and gear, as well as computer stations and huge monitors, the room was monstrous in size, stretching several stories high. Balconies overlooked their position from above. The Dominion Stone rested on an easel nearby, a bright spotlight illuminating it from overhead.

Grant approached his grandfather, who was still cowering on the floor, shivering.

Grant, too, was shaking. But not in fear.

Alex grabbed him by the arm. "We've got to go—"

They were knocked off of their feet by an explosion.

Alex lost her concentration and the Keeper sprang to his feet, fingering a remote device of some kind in his hand.

"That's more like it," he said, eyeing Grant. "I've been waiting for you to exert yourself."

A contingent of over fifty soldiers—all wearing gray jumpsuits with no insignia—entered the chamber, surrounding them on every side.

"Grant," Alex said, grabbing his arm again, "knock these guys out and let's just get out of here."

But Grant wouldn't budge, his eyes locked on his grandfather.

"Grant, forget him! Don't listen to anything he says!" she exclaimed.

"You really think I would *let* you escape?" the Keeper replied. "You think I wouldn't be *prepared?*"

His finger was still on the remote, even though the bomb it triggered had already gone off . . .

"Consider that first blast just a warm-up. His big brother is next, more than enough force to level this entire cavern and bring the building on the surface crashing down as well."

"You're willing to kill yourself over this? *Why?*" Grant asked between hard breaths.

"When I called you on the telephone earlier, I sealed my fate by defying the Secretum. I am no longer one of them; their purposes for you are not *mine. I* want to unleash your full potential. That's all I've ever wanted. The Secretum wants you under its thumb. They believed I was working toward that goal, but I wanted what was best for my blood and kin. To do that, your defenses had to be removed one-by-one through a carefully calculated game. I'm sorry for the pain the process has caused you, but it was the only way."

"And the Loci?" Grant panted. "Why did you do this to them?"

"Package deal. They're your army. Created to suit your specific needs, as the Bringer. The Forging has bonded you to them forever."

Grant looked around, into the eyes of the soldiers surrounding them. He was sure he could take all of them with a single thought, but didn't think he could stop his grandfather from pressing that trigger at the same time.

The Keeper rolled his eyes again, watching Grant. "My boy, if you had any *inkling* of what you were doing at all, you could have called the others here to help you by simply *thinking* it."

Grant met his grandfather's eyes with an even, triumphant glare.

"He did," a voice called from high above.

It was Payton.

The Keeper turned sharply to look up. His eyes danced at the sight of dozens of ring wearers encircling them on the balconies above.

All of their fingers were glowing.

64

"Payton," the Keeper said in recognition. "I had such high hopes for the Thresher."

"Anyone else *bored*?" Payton called out.

With that, he leapt over the edge of the balcony and landed neatly on the ground floor. If he ached from his recent battle with Konrad, he didn't show it. Sword in hand, he was off, slicing into guards on all sides in blurry swells of movement.

Grant used the distraction to force the bomb trigger out of his grandfather's hand and it sailed across the room.

The others above them followed Payton's lead, some jumping down as he did, others finding safer routes. All were met by the gray-clad guards, fists flying, guns blazing.

The guards outnumbered the Loci, but the battle was woefully one-sided. Payton zipped about, stabbing and parrying, taking down two or three at a time . . . Alex forced fear or embarrassment or misery into the hearts of everyone she looked upon . . . Morgan and Fletcher had put their heads together earlier and planted booby traps in connecting corridors, and now triggered them as some of the guards tried to flee . . . Even Daniel and Lisa were in the fight. They had stolen Taser guns from the Inveo plant the previous night and now used them on any nearby target.

Grant and his grandfather squared off in a solitary corner of the room. They began circling opposite one another, mirroring each other's moves.

Neither took his eyes off the other.

"What are you not telling me?" Grant bit out his words. "What is this *really* about? What's the big thing up top that 'only I can stop'?"

The Keeper's eyes flashed, briefly.

The building was rumbling again, keeping time with Grant's anger.

"It's you, isn't it?" Grant spat. "*You're* doing it. I kill you, and it all stops."

He wasn't asking.

The Keeper edged closer to Grant and then froze in place.

"No, my boy," he replied. "It's *you*."

Grant froze, his mouth gaped open.

"The darkness," the Keeper said, "the storm raging in the skies above . . . it's the pain you feel. Your hatred for me. Your grief over Hannah. Your *blind rage!*"

Grant's head began shaking from side to side.

The Seal glowed, brighter and brighter . . .

"No . . ." he whispered weakly.

"What did you *think* this was about!" his grandfather roared, his countenance suddenly altering its cool exterior to reveal a venomous contempt. "You miserable little fool . . . it was *always* about *YOU!!*"

A mighty rumble shook the ground beneath them . . .

His ring glowed brighter . . .

But Grant was too stunned to move. His eyes were hazed over, lost, unfocused, looking far away at nothing.

This isn't happening . . .

It can't be true . . .

"The Bringer is a *force of destruction*," the Keeper shouted. "The power of the atom . . . the energy of the sun . . . Crumbs on the table compared to what you're capable of. There is only one universal truth in this life: you are either *in* control, or you are *under* it. I've seen to it that *you* will take control of your own destiny and sweep through this world like nothing that has ever been. *You* will seize it and make it your own. *That* is your destiny, boy! It's the reason I saw to it that you were born. You will *take* dominion over this earth. Whether you want it or not!"

"But why?!" Grant cried. "*Why* did it have to be me?"

"History marches, son," the Keeper said, and he began side-stepping again, "and this is your moment in it. There is *nothing left* but for you to play the role that history has written for you—the Secretum has seen to that. It simply *is* what is."

"No," Grant tried to cry out with all that was in him, but only a whisper came to the surface. He was too lost, unmoving, staring straight ahead—almost catatonic.

He tried to focus his emotions, tried to concentrate on being calm, tried to quiet the storms within and without.

But all he could think of was Hannah and Julie and his father and his life that had been stolen and the innocent people above who were dying now and the blood that still soaked his clothes down to his skin.

"If only you could rein in those out-of-control emotions . . ." the Keeper taunted, circling him. "But you *can't*, can you? You've been pushed too far. You've lost *everything*! You've slipped over the edge and now you're falling. Farther and farther you go—do you feel it? There is *nothing* but grief and hate and pain. There's no one left for you to love."

A war raged inside Grant. As hard as he wanted to contain his emotions, all he could do was *feed* them. It was too much. The Keeper was right; he *had* gone over the edge and there was no coming back now.

Maybe he *should* just let go, it would feel so *good* . . .

The ring was glowing so brightly now, and it felt *right* . . .

"I have given you the ultimate power, my boy," the Keeper's voice intoned evenly. "You can change the world itself with a *thought*. You're in control. And I can only imagine what you must want to do to me at *this very moment* . . ."

Give in, Grant, he thought desperately.

Just give in.

Every blood vessel, every pore, every hair follicle on his body was screaming it.

Destroy him!

It will be so easy . . .

Grant was losing himself, he could feel it, and he didn't care . . .

Let the world turn to ash.

Nothing matters anymore, anyway.

"Do it!" the Keeper screamed maniacally. "Destroy this place! Take control and *bring the whirlwind!!*"

Grant bore down with all that was within him and beat it back.

"*No!*" he screamed and backhanded his grandfather so hard the old man flew across the room.

His knees buckled and he collapsed onto them.

Grant balled his fists and closed his eyes, straining to rein it in.

"Foolish child," the Keeper was saying. "Reluctance has *always* been your downfall. *Must* you take time to *think* about everything? That was your mother's fatal flaw as well, you know."

Time seemed to stop, and the struggle within Grant paused as he turned to the old man.

"My mother died giving birth to me. She died during labor."

A smile played at the edges of the Keeper's lips and he nodded. "*During* labor."

He got up off the floor and stepped closer to Grant.

"But not *from* labor," he said.

A titanic blast of energy exploded from Grant, shattering half the building.

The earth shook violently.

"*You murdered her!!*" Grant screamed.

The Seal shone so brightly now that the Keeper had to put a hand up to block it from his eyes, barely able to see through the glare.

But Grant could see the old man shrug indifferently as he struggled to remain upright. "She spit out the boy I needed," his grandfather said. "Her purpose was concluded. And she intended to keep you from me. I had no option."

The earth's rumbling grew stronger as Grant's face turned beet red.

Blood, hate, adrenaline, and rage surged through his entire being.

"I'll never forget the *sound* she let out," the Keeper shouted over the din, "as I put my gun into her chest and pulled the trigger. It was ear-splitting, like nothing I've ever heard! You gave your very first cry at that same moment, Grant. It was the sound of birth *and* death. And it changed the world."

Grant's fingernails dug grooves into his scalp, he wanted to yank out his hair by the fistful, this was just too much, he couldn't hold it in anymore, he was going to explode and deliver the world into the same madness that now consumed him . . .

"Come on, Grant," the Keeper said cloyingly. "*Become* the Bringer."

The building began to shake free of its foundations, crumbling all around. The great steel panels fell hard. Mortar, Sheetrock, and concrete crashing to the ground and shattering on impact.

It was a disaster zone.

"Everybody out!" Payton shouted.

"The Dominion Stone!" Morgan yelled, moving toward it.

"Leave it, there's no time!" Payton replied.

Alex stopped her efforts and turned to where she'd last seen Grant circling his grandfather. He was collapsed on the floor, head buried in his hands, and sobbing so loud she could hear it over the noise and destruction. The Keeper stood over him, speaking into his ear. And his ring was glowing brighter than the sun.

"*Grant!*" she screamed.

He didn't move.

The building was coming down, there was no time left.

She was barely aware of Payton grabbing her by the arm and pulling her toward the exit.

"No! Something's wrong—we have to help him!" she cried.

But it was no use, everyone was running, stampeding from the building. No one even heard her protests.

Only Grant and his grandfather remained inside as the outer walls of the building crashed down in a terrible cacophony. The destruction was working its way in, and Grant felt powerless to stop it.

This was who he was.

He was the Bringer.

Death and destruction were his reality, his purpose.

"No, Grant, you *know* who you are," a female voice said.

He looked up.

The room was gone, replaced by familiar swirling clouds of purple and pink. But he remained on the ground, and he could still feel the building quaking around him.

His mother approached and knelt before him.

"This is not your hour, Grant."

Yes, it is! he thought to her.

"No, baby," she said, watching him with utmost compassion. "Not this day."

His tears followed him to this place, even though he'd once thought that tears couldn't exist here.

Wherever "here" was.

They soaked his face, and he didn't care. *I want it to end!* he cried. *I can't keep going anymore! It's too much. He took you away from me, and I just want it to end!*

"I know," she said, smiling but sad. "One day you and I will get back the time that was stolen from us."

He sobbed.

"But not yet. Do you remember what I said to you?" she asked gently.

You said I had to be willing to sacrifice to reach the journey's end.

She nodded soothingly. *"Are you?"*

NO! he protested. *I can't go any farther!! NO MORE!!*

"You must," another voice said.

Grant looked up and gasped.

A second person stood before him amidst the clouds.

It was Julie.

Julie . . . are you dead?

"No. Don't you recognize this place? It's our safe house, where you and I meet in our dreams."

His sister was unlike he had ever seen her before.

She was radiant. Gone was the evidence of her illness, her injuries. She was still, at peace. She glowed with more than mere light. Her smile beamed down upon him, and he could *feel* it caressing his skin.

I don't have anything left! he cried. *I can't do this anymore, Julie, I can't!*

"That's a lie," Julie replied without accusation. "This flesh," she said, "is telling you to give up. It's telling you to let go. But *you are more.*"

I can't . . . This isn't . . . I . . .

"You promised me," she said gently.

He looked up at her.

"Never give up or give in," she said. "No surrendering to despair. I held up my end. And I want my brother there with me when I open my eyes."

But I'm not even me *anymore!* he exploded. *I don't know* who *I am!*

Julie took his hands and placed them over her heart.

"Listen to me," she said.

The clouds began to flash and fade, the underground complex peeking through. The rumbles and quakes grew worse still, and the entire building shuddered, ready to fall.

"*Listen*," she said again, and he focused on her calm, glowing face. "The face changes," she said slowly, with great seriousness. "The body breaks. And blood runs cold."

He looked up into her face, tears streaming out of him.

She leaned in closer to him and smiled, holding his eyes in gentle contact.

"But *who you are* . . ." she said, placing a hand over his chest, "is *indestructible*."

A gust of air escaped his lips as his chest collapsed, and he cried in tremendous heaves.

Julie squeezed his hand. Grant cried out and threw himself around her shoulders, holding her tight.

And he felt the warmth of her heart flowing through him.

The tears came down but they were different than before. Now they were strengthening him.

After a long squeeze, he let her go, and Julie backed up to stand beside his mother.

They both watched him, beaming with warm smiles.

Swimming in the warm feelings they flooded him with, Grant squared his shoulders.

He placed one hand on the cloudy ground beneath him.

And very slowly, he extended his legs.

The moment he was on his feet again, reality returned and he was inside the crumbling underground structure.

The ring on his finger—the Seal of Dominion—was glowing too brightly to look at. Its shimmering light filled up the entire chamber.

Still the Keeper stood there watching him, oblivious to the danger.

Grant took a deep breath and let it out slowly.

Peacefully.

He turned to face his grandfather.

And the earthquake immediately stopped.

Grant knew without seeing that the violence raging in the skies above, outside, had vanished also.

The Seal stopped glowing, as if someone had simply unplugged it.

But the underground structure was too far gone, and it continued its imminent collapse.

The Keeper's eyes grew big, disbelief written across his face. "What are you *doing*? Your hour is at hand! The prophecy—"

Grant didn't react. He only looked at the old man in pity.

"The Secretum wants to twist you and use you for their own purposes! But I made you master of your own fate! Will you so easily throw away the control I've given you?"

Grant spoke softly. "In all this time, has it never occurred to you that perhaps none of *us* are the ones in control?"

He turned away from him and walked to where the Dominion Stone stood on its easel. The spotlight that had shown upon it had long since fallen there in the dying building. But the tablet itself stood upright, stubbornly clinging to its easel.

He pushed the whole thing over.

"What are you *doing*?" the Keeper screamed.

"Making my choice," Grant replied simply.

The Keeper stared at Grant, thunderstruck yet making no move to stop him or even flee. "The Secretum is forever, boy! Even if I fall, another will take my place!"

Grant walked calmly away, though he could hear his grandfather's voice screaming, fading in the distance . . .

"You really think you can *resist* the Seal of Dominion?! Your destiny is written in stone! You may keep it at bay for a time, but the Seal is chaos, and it cannot be restrained!"

The structure finally collapsed and came to a rest behind Grant, his grandfather's echoes dying away, as he found his way back to the elevator.

Great billows of smoke chased him up the elevator shaft. He was forced to exit through the subway, as more quakes on the surface had collapsed much of the Wagner Building.

Ascending the subway stairs, he was greeted by blue skies and the light of a bright, beautiful, cloudless morning.

Cresting the top of the stairs and out onto the sidewalk, he found the others there waiting for him. But they weren't looking at him.

An enormous crowd had gathered, watching them. Quizzical expressions colored the spectators' faces. Every age, every race, every working class, every walk of life was represented among those who looked at the long line of men and women who had emerged from the collapsing building they stood before.

Grant, Alex, Morgan, Payton, Fletcher, Daniel, Lisa, and over a dozen others stood side-by-side in a row, stunned at the sight of the sea of people before them.

The world had just changed in plain view of everyone there. It would never be the same again.

No one spoke, as both sides of this strange spectacle looked at the other in consternation.

Grant's group certainly appeared the most bizarre, especially Grant himself. He was covered in soot and grime and blood, his clothes were torn, his hair was mussed, he looked as though he had drowned in sweat and tears.

He glanced down at the abominable object that rested on his finger and would never come off. His thoughts turned to his mother and his father. And to his sister, whom he knew would be awake soon.

And he thought of Hannah, as he looked back into the eyes of every person there. They seemed more interested in him than any of the others.

It was as if they were waiting. Watching, to see what he would do next.

From the corner of his eye he saw Alex surveying the crowd in front of them. She seemed like she expected it somehow. After a second, she turned to him, looked him in the face and, with a frown said, "You're not gonna *cry* again, are ya?"

Despite himself, despite everything, Grant grinned wide.

Then he laughed.

Out loud.

So hard his shoulders shook.

"Help me!"

Grant's head snapped up, scanning the crowd. The others did the same.

"Fear of falling," Alex said, squinting, looking about. "I feel it . . . over there!" She pointed past the crowd.

The entire crowd turned to look as Grant and the rest did, and saw a woman dangling from a metal fire escape ledge, three stories off the ground, just one block away.

Grant felt Alex's hand on his shoulder just then, but he didn't look at her.

There was no need.

No need for any more words.

He was tired, emotionally spent, every muscle in his body ached.

He had absolutely *nothing* left.

"Somebody please!" the woman screamed in the distance.

Grant set his jaw firmly in place.

Every person present watched and waited.

Waited for someone who would save the day.

"I can't reach!" the woman cried.

Grant let out a steadying breath.

He stepped forward.

"Hold on," he called out. "I'm coming."

Substation Omega Prime
The Secretum of Six
Ruling Council Inner Chamber

Far away and buried deep beneath the earth's surface, the ruling body of the Secretum of Six scanned the latest report. Glances were exchanged, notes written on paper.

"Substation L.A. is lost," one of them said, "as is the Dominion Stone."

"The Stone no longer matters," Devlin replied at the head of the table. Today his accent of choice was a hard, German inflection. "Its absence serves our end goal. Everything is falling precisely into place, as we've always known it would."

"Maximilian Borrows is dead," offered another.

"Also irrelevant," a woman spoke up. "Another will be chosen. What matters is that we have what we have awaited for so long. The Bringer has come."

Devlin smiled and intoned in his booming deep voice, "The prophecy of Dominion is fulfilled. The one we have prepared for and awaited for thousands of years walks among us. Everything is unfolding as we know it must. And do not forget, we still have a great advantage."

"What advantage?" the woman asked.

"The wheels turn all around him," Devlin replied. "Yet the Bringer does not see . . . does not *know* . . . what he will *bring*."

ACKNOWLEDGMENTS

Thanks to . . .

- My entire family for putting up with my insane work schedule. Special thanks to my wonderful, long-suffering wife Karen for enduring the "must write now" absences of your newlywed husband. We're in this together, babe. Now and forever.

- Ted Dekker for your friendship and all the great career advice.

- My friends Todd, Tina, John, Laura, Dylan, Mary P., Steve, and Mary S. for all the prayers and encouragement. Thanks for not letting me give up.

- All of the teachers, professors, and writing professionals who have, over the years, offered instruction and support.

- My editor David Long and his magic pencil.

- My brother Ross and his family, for always showing excitement and wanting to help.

- Mom, for demonstrating faith, expressing love, and always letting me chase my dreams.

- And my Father above, for proving to me time and again that everything is under your perfect control. You are so good to me.

Don't Miss the Sequel to
Relentless

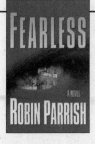

After the events of *Relentless*, the world has changed. Hundreds of super-beings walk among Earth's inhabitants, an unexplained series of natural disasters have shaken the populace to its core, and fear fills the heart of every human being. But there is hope—the man known as Grant Borrows. After an extraordinary discovery in London, Grant realizes that the world's only hope may come from unraveling the truth about himself once and for all. But what he comes face-to-face with leaves even this most powerful of men shaken with fear....

Fearless by Robin Parrish

If You Liked *Relentless,*
Try These Reads

WHAT DOES IT MEAN WHEN YOU DIE THREE TIMES?
Jude Allman has died—and come back to life—three times. Frustrated and frightened by a life in the public eye and a past he doesn't understand, he retreats into hiding. At the same time, children are mysteriously disappearing around his adopted hometown of Red Lodge, Montana, and the key to solving these missing-children crimes may lie within the mysteries of Jude's deaths. Now he has to face his past to save his own life—and the lives of those he loves.

Waking Lazarus by T.L. Hines

ARE THE DEAD REALLY DEAD?
When Candace MacHugh hears her dead father's voice whispering to her from the shadows, she joins a giant organization that shares the secrets of the dead with our world. But she soon finds it's a shadowy conspiracy hiding something much more sinister. Is her father really dead? Is she really communicating with departed spirits? Why? If she can't find the answers in time, thousands of people—herself included–will go up in flames.

The Dead Whisper On by T.L. Hines

JASON BOYER JUST GOT AN INHERITANCE TO DIE FOR
Jason Boyer knew his father's corrupt business empire would pass to different hands—which suited him fine. But when an accident claims his father's life, everyone is stunned by the unveiling of a revised will. As Jason tries to handle the business more honestly than his father, he soon finds that standing for what's right may bring murderous consequences.

The Heir by Paul Robertson

MIND-BLOWING SUPERNATURAL SUSPENSE
As Abby's awe-inspiring vision launches her on a quest through distant lands and ancient history, Dylan is hired by an ancient foe to silence her. As these two lives collide, each learns how to wage war in a realm they never knew existed… Spanning continents and centuries, *The Watchers* is a riveting blend of action, spiritual warfare, and redemption.

The Watchers by Mark Andrew Olsen